WHEN HUMANS BECOME MIGRANTS

When Humans Become Migrants

Study of the European Court of Human Rights with an Inter-American Counterpoint

MARIE-BÉNÉDICTE DEMBOUR

OXFORD
UNIVERSITY PRESS

OXFORD
UNIVERSITY PRESS

Great Clarendon Street, Oxford, OX2 6DP,
United Kingdom

Oxford University Press is a department of the University of Oxford.
It furthers the University's objective of excellence in research, scholarship,
and education by publishing worldwide. Oxford is a registered trade mark of
Oxford University Press in the UK and in certain other countries

First Edition published in 2015

Published in the United States of America by Oxford University Press
198 Madison Avenue, New York, NY 10016, United States of America

British Library Cataloguing in Publication Data
Dataa vailable

Library of Congress Control Number: 2015932305

ISBN 978–0–19–966783–3
ISBN 978–0–19–966784–0 (pbk.)

To Bob
You have followed the journey of this book and its author like no other.

To Ellis
You too have enlightened my life.

In Aziz's memory
Fresh from Tangiers, you arrived at Bruxelles-Midi as an étudiant boursier, without a word of French. No local address in your pocket, but a smile that opened doors. This smile would broaden into a laugh which still resonates in our ears, lightening our hearts.

To those who shape the law
May your sense of humanity always guide you.

To all migrants of the world
For whatever reasons, we have decided to leave and make our lives elsewhere. Despite all that we bring, offer and contribute, we often encounter rejection or abuse. But against the distrust, pain and injustice we experience, we also come across those who welcome us as the fellow humans we are, and this is most heartening.
Human rights have no borders.

Acknowledgements

My first debt is to the generations of students, both undergraduates and post-graduates who, over the last two decades, have helped me develop my thoughts on migration and human rights. I am thankful to the Leverhulme Trust for awarding me a Major Research Fellowship (2009–2012). Without these debates with my students and the luxury of this research period, this book would not even have started to take shape.

Once the project was formulated, I enlisted the help of dozens of people, some I had never met, others I have known for many years.

At Strasbourg, I conversed with judges, members of the Registry and other employees of the Court and the Council of Europe. My gratitude goes to the many individuals who agreed to meet and talk to me. I am especially indebted to Françoise Tulkens, former Vice-President of the Court, who wholeheartedly supported this project from its infancy to its very end. The help I received from her former personal assistant, Sylvie Ruffenach, has been extremely precious too. The Archives Service of the Court never failed to respond to my requests promptly and diligently. Being able to rely on the Court's librarian and her staff was invaluable.

In my two trips to Costa Rica in 2010 and 2012, I experienced first-hand Latin American hospitality and generosity at the Inter-American Court. The Registrar, Pablo Saavedra, introduced me to the Court. Despite the marathon of the judicial sessions, the judges endeavoured to find a window in their unremitting schedule to talk to me. Attorneys and interns patiently explained the work of the Court. Library and other staff went out of their way to answer my questions and make me feel welcome. My subsequent email queries always got answered. Oscar Parra was particularly generous in sharing his knowledge and insights.

My first visit at the Inter-American Court coincided with the hearing of the *Vélez Loor* case. This made it possible for me to talk directly to Jésus Vélez Loor about the case which bears his name. Conversations with Jan Schneider, who was visiting the Court for his doctoral research, were illuminating. Being in San José enabled me to contact and draw on the experience of staff at the Inter-American Commission on Human Rights and legal representatives, especially the Director of the Center for Justice and International Law (CEJIL). I met a variety of experts in different settings, including at the 2012 summer course organised by the Institute of Human Rights. A phone conversation with the assistant of the Rapporteurship on the Rights of Migrants at the Inter-American Commission was most valuable.

I have called upon the expertise of a host of experts and colleagues during the five years I have worked on this book. Special thanks are due to Diego Acosta, Bridget Anderson, Ed Bates, Upendra Baxi, Isidore Bonabom, Mary Bosworth, Eva Brems, Laurence Burgorgue-Larsen, Antonio Cançado Trindade (Judge), Galina Cornelisse, Catherine Costello, Daniela DeBono, Alexis Deswaef, Andrew

Drzemczewski, Nadine El-Enany, Marjorie Farquharson, Ali Huseyinoglu, Mark Jordan, Tobias Kelly, Elisabeth Lambert-Abdelgawad, Anthony Lester (Lord), Peter Leuprecht, Marie Martin, Jeremy McBride, Susanne Melde, Catherine Meredith, Sally Engle Merry, Nuala Mole, Claire Rodier, Séverine Rudloff, Prakash Shah, Ramnik Shah, Dallal Stevens, Véronique van der Plancke, Adam Weiss, Tristan Wibault, Louis Wolcher, Helena Wray, Thanos Zartaloudis, as well as the mentor from my youth, Jacques Vanderlinden, as dependable as ever.

I was privileged to have the opportunity to present the book project at various stages of its development, at the Centre for the Study of Justice and Violence and the Sussex Centre for Migration Research at the University of Sussex, the Oxford Human Rights Hub at the University of Oxford, and the Migration and Diversity Centre at the Vrije Universiteit of Amsterdam. Critical comments from participants and discussants, including from Christina Oelgemöller, Bas Schotel, and Nanda Oudejans, were most enlightening. The feedback I received after delivering the keynote speech at the Conference 'A Sea of Troubles? Problematising Migration Law' of the Migration Law Network at Birkbeck College in March 2014 was invigorating.

Drafts chapters have benefited from the generous feedback of friends, colleagues, and experts. Dana Baldinger, Helen Dancer, Franz Ebert, Emily Haslam, Rosemary McKechnie, Kate Nash, Jan Schneider, and Alexandra Timmer read one or more chapters. Stefanie Grant, Lourdes Peroni, Neil Stammers, and Françoise Tulkens ended up commenting on most of the book in draft form. My partner, Bob Morton, was summoned to read every single chapter, often more than once, which he did with good grace. All the comments I received were invaluable, the encouragement precious, the assistance priceless.

In June 2012, Thomas Spijkerboer and his Faculty generously invited me to visit the Migration Law Research Program of the Vrije Universiteit of Amsterdam during the following year. The book's draft manuscript became the basis for the *Capita Selecta* course he led in spring 2013. Not only did this most extraordinary offer enable me to continue working solidly on the book for three months, but the detailed and insightful feedback on seven draft chapters led me to reconfigure central arguments. Thanks are due to the students who were on the course, Daan Bes, Anne de Hingh, Irmela Kodzaga, Banafsheh Moghaddasi, Bibi van Alphen, and Claudia van den Berg, as well as, of course, Thomas himself and the colleagues who joined some of the classes. Being based in the Migration Law Centre meant I benefited from the expertise of a number of researchers, including Hemmes Battjes, Pieter Boeles, Karen de Vries, and Lieneke Slingenberg. Evelien Brouwer and Karen Geertsema commented on a draft of Chapter 12. Juan Amaya Castro came up with the title of the book. Sarah van Walsum had followed the project from its early days and continued to dispense her wisdom throughout my visit. It seems hardly conceivable that her cherished, generous and inspirational voice is now confined to our memories, leaving bereft the Migration Law as a Family Matter group, from whose meetings I have also greatly benefited.

During my time at the University of Sussex, I enjoyed the friendship and intellectual sharpness of many colleagues, especially those at the Centre for the

Study of Justice and Violence, the Sussex Law School, and the Sussex Centre for Migration Research. I would particularly like to acknowledge Anastasia Christou, Elizabeth Craig, Zdenek Kavan, Tarik Kochi, Anna Stavrianakis, and, closest to my soul, Jane Cowan. In 2013, I moved to the University of Brighton. Aidan Berry, Dean of the Brighton Business School, and my new colleagues immediately welcomed and trusted me, making me feel like I had always been there. Most importantly, they gave me time to finish the manuscript.

Three research assistants contributed to the preparation of the manuscript in the months directly preceding its submission to the Press. Tom Harris undertook the thankless job of bringing consistency to my references. Zach Woodham brought me up to date with various aspects of the Strasbourg case law. Thomas Southerden checked the text, both for its English and the intelligibility of its arguments. Lourdes Peroni took on the task of writing the chapter on the latest Inter-American case law.

Except for Chapter 14, the ideas expressed in this book are mine. Any error or weakness is my responsibility.

The manuscript was submitted to Oxford University Press on 18 June 2014. It has been a privilege to benefit from Merel Alstein's professionalism and dedication at Oxford University Press and to be able to trust that her team would deal effectively with any problem which might arise.

Last but not least, my deepest gratitude goes to the friends and family members who have sustained me, laughed with me and, in the last two years of the preparation of the manuscript, allowed me to work more than we would all have wished. I hope the book will prove worthy of your patience and care.

Contents—Summary

III. PROSPECTS

Contents

II. CONSOLIDATION

Stylistic Note

Female migrants are often overlooked in policy circles and in the academic literature. I did not wish to reinforce this tendency by systematically using the masculine pronoun and possessive when referring to a generic applicant. At the same time, using the feminine form throughout the book appeared strange, as the majority of Strasbourg migrant applicants are male. The compromise upon which I have settled is to use the feminine in odd-numbered chapters and the masculine in even-numbered chapters. I have tended to extend this practice in respect to other nouns as well.

List of Tables

Table of Cases

EUROPEAN COMMISSION OF HUMAN RIGHTS

EUROPEAN COURT OF HUMAN RIGHTS

COMMITTEE OF MINISTERS OF THE COUNCIL OF EUROPE

INTER-AMERICAN COURT OF HUMAN RIGHTS

List of Abbreviations

ABC	*Abdulaziz, Cabales and Balkandali v. United Kingdom*
ACHR	American Convention on Human Rights
AIRE Centre	Advice on Individual Rights in Europe (London-based NGO)
ANAFE	Association Nationale d'Assistance aux Frontières pour les Etrangers (French NGO)
BPP	British Protected Person
CEJIL	Centre for Justice and International Law (American-based NGO)
CIA	Central Intelligence Agency (US)
CIMADE	Comité Inter Mouvements Auprés des Évacués (French NGO)
CUKC	Citizen of the United Kingdom and Commonwealth
DRC	Democratic Republic of the Congo
ECHR	European Convention on Human Rights
EComHR	European Commission of Human Rights
ECtHR	European Court of Human Rights
ECRE	European Council on Refugees and Exiles
EEA	European Economic Area
ETA	*Euskadi Ta Askatasuna* (Basque Fatherland and Liberty)
EU	European Union
EURODAC	European Dactyloscopy
GC	Grand Chamber (of the European Court of Human Rights)
HUDOC	Human Rights Documentation (the database of the ECtHR)
IAComHR	Inter-American Commission on Human Rights
IACtHR	Inter-American Court of Human Rights
IRA	Irish Republican Army
IVF	In-Vitro Fertilisation
LGBTQ	Lesbian, Gay, Bisexual, Transgendered, Queer
LIBE Committee	Committee on Civil Liberties, Justice and Home Affairs (European Parliament)
MERCOSUR	*Mercado Común del Sur* (Southern Cone Common Market)
MP	Member of Parliament (UK)
MSS	*M.S.S. v. Belgium and Greece*
MUDHA	*Movimiento de Mujeres Dominínico-Haitianas* (Dominican-Haitian Women's Movement; Dominican-based NGO)
NGO	Non-Governmental Organisation
OAS	Organization of American States
OFSTED	Office for Standards in Education (UK governmental office)
PACE	Parliamentary Assembly of the Council of Europe
PC	European Court of Human Rights sitting in plenary formation
PCom	European Commission of Human Rights sitting in plenary formation
UDHR	Universal Declaration of Human Rights
UK	United Kingdom
UN	United Nations

UN GA	UN General Assembly
UNHCR	United Nations High Commissioner for Refugees
UNICEF	United Nations Children's Fund
US	United States
USSR	Union of Socialist Soviet Republics

1

Introduction

Migrants are human beings too. As this is incontrovertible, if one believes in human rights it means that migrants have human rights, just like any other human being who has not migrated. From this perspective, things are simple: a migrant is a human being and as such, in a society which professes its faith in human rights, is an individual endowed with human rights which must be respected. This is the theory. In practice, things are more complicated. Migrants are routinely treated in a way which arguably negates their human dignity or appears discriminatory. This suggests that migrants' human rights are often violated. One might thus expect human rights courts to be quick to reach verdicts of violation in cases brought by migrants. This book demonstrates that it has always been and continues to be extremely difficult—indeed too difficult—for migrants to have violations of their human rights recognised and denounced by the European Court of Human Rights (hereafter, the European Court, the Strasbourg Court, or the Court). Such a message flies in the face of the way the Strasbourg Court is portrayed by politicians and the media, especially in the UK. The distorted image which is projected about Strasbourg makes it important to set the record straight. In addition, the book shows that another regional human rights court, the Inter-American Court of Human Rights (in practice, very much a Latin American court), seems far more inclined to push for the recognition of migrants' rights. This provides food for thought on a number of fronts.

I. The Strasbourg Reversal or Putting the Migrant First

The European Convention on Human Rights (hereafter, 'the European Convention' or 'the Convention') was adopted in 1950 in order to defend citizens—not any human being—against arbitrariness by the state. The hope was that the revolutionary mechanism put in place, with complaints by mere individuals allowed for the first time in history to be adjudicated by an international court, would make it possible to avoid another European descent into anything resembling Nazism or fascism, while it would at the same time provide a bulwark against an extension of communism into Western Europe.[1] As Chapter 2 explains,

[1] Italy and France were conceived to be at particular risk in this respect: Mikael Rask Madsen, *La genèse de l'Europe des droits de l'homme: Enjeux juridiques et stratégies d'Etat (France, Grande-Bretagne et pays scandinaves, 1945–1970)* (Strasbourg: Presses Universitaires de Strasbourg, 2010) 113.

migrants were hardly a consideration in the newly created human rights scheme. The Convention was not meant to sustain their claims.

The European Court understood this very well. The European Commission of Human Rights (hereafter, 'the European Commission' or 'the Commission'), the institution which was set up in order to filter the cases brought by individuals which would be allowed to proceed before the Court, also took the message on board.[2]

Ever since the Convention came into force in 1957, migrants' applications have routinely been found to be without what lawyers call 'merit'. Even more commonly, they have been declared 'inadmissible' at an early stage of the proceedings (meaning that the substantive complaints raised by the applicant are not examined). In such a context, it arguably took an inordinately long time before migrants started to be successful in the complaints they were lodging at Strasbourg regarding their situation as 'aliens'—to use the ugly legal term which denotes non-nationals in the English language. In this respect, 'the sleeping beauty' which the Convention system was in the first two decades of its existence, awakened particularly late.[3]

This is so even though migrants and their legal representatives had been amongst the first to understand and to try to use the potential of the Convention. They came knocking on the Strasbourg doors as soon as the Convention came into force. This translated into an early and rather abundant case law by the Commission regarding applications by individuals who were, for example, seeking family reunification or objecting to their expulsion. The Commission endorsed a number of 'friendly settlements' between migrants and respondent states, leading to these cases being 'struck out' of its list (i.e. closed without adjudication of the merits) after the state had proposed a solution to the dispute which was formally accepted and thus presumably found to be satisfactory by the applicant. Despite these settlements, it remains fair to say that the majority of migrants came up against a brick wall at Strasbourg. As a result the Court first pronounced on a 'migrant case'[4] only in 1985, at a time when it had already developed an important case law in other areas.[5]

[2] The now defunct European Commission of Human Rights was an institution of the Council of Europe based at Strasbourg. It is not to be confused with the European Commission, which was originally set up as an institution of the European Coal and Steel Community (CECA), European Economic Community (EEC and later EC), and the European Atomic Energy Community (Euratom); it is now an institution of the European Union which has its seat in Brussels. Similarly, the Strasbourg Court is not to be confused with the Luxembourg-based Court of Justice of the European Union (formerly, European Court of Justice).

[3] See Chapter 7. For a view diametrically opposed to the perspective argued in this book, see: Marc Bossuyt, *Strasbourg et les demandeurs d'asile: Des juges sur un terrain glissant* (Brussels: Bruylant, 2010).

[4] Given my interest in the way in which the two courts approach the person who is the migrant, this book refers to 'migrant cases' rather than using the more objective-sounding expression 'migration cases'.

[5] See Chapter 4. Few studies of the European Convention are written in a way which traces the development of the case law in a historical manner. For an interesting exception, see: Ed Bates, *The Evolution of the European Convention on Human Rights: From its Inception to the Creation of a Permanent Court of Human Rights* (Oxford: Oxford University Press, 2010). More conventional studies of the Convention include: D.J. Harris, M. O'Boyle, E.P. Bates, and C.M. Buckley, *Law of the European Convention on Human Rights* (Oxford: Oxford University Press, 2009);

The first judgment of the Court in a migrant case, *Abdulaziz, Cabales and Balkandali v. the United Kingdom*[6] (hereafter referred to more simply as *ABC*), was a major disappointment for those who had been fighting the case on the side of the migrants. It established two principles which run counter to a logic which would have been propitious to an expansive interpretation of migrants' rights. One is that a state party to the European Convention is normally under no obligation to admit on its territory the family members of someone who is living on its territory, even if she is legally settled. The motivation given for this principle was that the Convention had never intended to entitle spouses to choose the country where family life would be conducted. According to the Court, as long as this life can be conducted elsewhere, non-admission does not breach Article 8 ECHR (which provides for the right to respect for family—as well as private—life).

Such a formulation admittedly leaves open the possibility of exceptional circumstances when non-admission would violate Article 8. However, to this day, the European Court of Human Rights has reached verdicts of violation in only a handful of family reunification cases, as we shall see in Chapter 4. The exceptionality of these verdicts confirms the legitimacy under European Convention law of the general principle that immigrants need not be admitted. Given that family reunification has been the most common route for legal immigration into Europe for close to half a century, the lack of any firm entitlement to reunification on European soil inevitably means that human rights law as interpreted at Strasbourg has little to offer 'the normal migrant',[7] i.e. the migrant who does not happen to have a specific ground for international protection, and her family. This 'deficiency' is something which has escaped the attention of most commentators, who take for granted the existence of the principle of non-entitlement to admission and thus praise the European Convention system for the few tools it extends to migrants, without drawing attention to the principles which considerably restrict its potential reach.

The second principle identified by the Court in the *ABC* judgment is even broader. Pertaining to the whole of the migrant case law, it consists in the acknowledgement of a state prerogative to control the entry and residence of aliens (hereafter, state control prerogative or state control principle). The Court presents this principle as 'well established in international law'. Bas Schotel has convincingly argued that it actually lacks legal foundation. His study is crucial, showing as it does that the Court is *legally* wrong to rely on the principle.[8] The

Robin C.A. White and Clare Ovey, *Jacobs, White and Ovey: The European Convention on Human Rights* (Oxford: Oxford University Press, 5th ed., 2010); Alastair Mowbray, *Cases, Materials and Commentary on the European Convention on Human Rights* (Oxford: Oxford University Press, 3rd ed., 2012); Philip Leach, *Taking a Case to the European Court of Human Rights* (Oxford: Oxford University Press, 3rd ed., 2011); Karen Reid, *A Practitioner's Guide to the European Convention on Human Rights* (London: Sweet & Maxwell, 4th ed., 2012).

[6] *Abdulaziz, Cabales and Balkandali v. United Kingdom*, appls 9214/80, 9473/81, 9474/81, GC Judgment (ECtHR), 28 May 1985.

[7] I borrow this expression from: Bas Schotel, *On the Right of Exclusion: Law, Ethics and Immigration Policy* (Abingdon: Routledge, 2012).

[8] Schotel.

present book adds to this critique by pointing out that the way in which this principle has become a cornerstone of much of the Strasbourg case law which deals with immigration, is also problematic from a human rights perspective.

In *ABC*, the state control principle was merely mentioned by the Court as one element amongst others which had to be taken into consideration. Subsequently, however, it has often become the starting point of the Court's reasoning on the merits of a substantive complaint which is related to a migrant issue. The place of choice attributed to the principle gives the impression that the Court conceives of the rights guaranteed in the Convention as exceptions which temper the general principle of state sovereignty regarding migration control, rather than the Court conceiving the state control prerogative as tempering human rights norms which would themselves be the foundational principle. A central argument of this book is that this is a problematic logical inversion from a human rights perspective.

Which 'human rights perspective' are we talking about, however? As the author of a four-school human rights model, I am very much aware that there is more than one way to understand human rights.[9] In this model I proposed that human rights are typically approached in four different ways: (a) in a 'natural' perspective, whereby human rights are conceived as given entitlements due to every human being *qua* human being; (b) in a 'deliberative' perspective, whereby human rights are conceived as arising from political agreements which establish principles of good governance which society agrees to follow; (c) in a 'protest' perspective, whereby human rights are conceived as a response against human suffering which may give rise to legal guarantees—but with the attended risk that these legal provisions then become used by the powerful for their own benefit rather than the benefit of the exploited; and (d) in a 'double talk' perspective, whereby the hypocrisy with which those in power resort to the discourse of human rights is denounced. The first two schools can be said to belong to the liberal tradition; the last two propound a wide project of social emancipation which purports to go beyond liberal tenets.

Applying this framework to the position described above as the state control principle, this book speaks of a 'Strasbourg reversal' in order to stress the incongruous nature of a human rights reasoning which starts with a prerogative which neither serves to affirm human rights nor is inscribed in the text which the adjudicating court's task is to interpret and apply. The natural school of human rights would surely expect a human rights court to start its reasoning with the relevant human rights entitlement; the deliberative school, with the relevant agreed legal standard. The protest school would presumably regard the starting point of state control prerogative as sidestepping the interests of the relatively powerless migrants, while the double-talk school would view this prerogative as

[9] Marie-Bénédicte Dembour, 'What Are Human Rights? Four Schools of Thought' (2010) *Human Rights Quarterly* 32, 1–20; *Who Believes in Human Rights? Reflections on the European Convention* (Cambridge: Cambridge University Press, 2006) Chapter 8.

confirmation that those who profess to support human rights are not really interested in applying them.

The typical choice made by the European Court to start its reasoning in migrant cases with the principle that states have the prerogative to exclude migrants is thus bizarre, even if it has become such a staple of the Strasbourg case law that we tend to accept it as normal. When the Court examines criminal justice cases, it does not start its reasoning by saying that the state has the power to punish those who have offended; it starts with Article 6 ECHR, which provides fair trial guarantees. One suspects that starting the reasoning in criminal cases with the power to punish rather than with Article 6 would shift the default position of the Court further towards the state and away from the claimant. The question arises: why does the Court not similarly start its reasoning in migrant cases with the relevant provision of the Convention (e.g. Article 8 ECHR in family reunification cases)?[10] This is a big question whose answer only superficially lies with the Court, for it really implicates the whole way in which Europe approaches migrants.

The Strasbourg reversal has for effect to consider the migrant applicant first of all as an 'alien' who is subject to the control of the state, rather than just as a human being. As Hannah Arendt observed back in the 1950s, human beings *qua* human beings all too easily fall outside the human rights net when they are outside a specific institutional framework of state protection.[11] As previously mentioned, the European Convention was not adopted with migrants in mind. As we shall see, it took an intervention by the Italian government to ensure that non-citizens falling within the jurisdiction of a member state were nonetheless specifically included in the Convention's ambit.[12] Migrants were clearly not conceived as among the Convention's most natural beneficiaries. This is so much so that throughout the 1990s commentators wrote as if migrants had been very lucky to be able to rely on the Convention provisions at all. Migrants were said to have achieved this 'indirectly' (in French, *par ricochet*).[13] From a perspective where all human beings are entitled to human rights, this is a puzzling way of putting things, although it must be granted that this may actually start to make

[10] The response that this is because migrant rights are not directly granted by the Convention does not hold. For example, the right to a clean and quiet environment is not specifically laid out in the Convention, but when discussing it, the Court starts its reasoning with the most relevant article of the Convention, namely Article 8. See e.g. *Hatton v. the United Kingdom*, appl. 36022/97, Judgment (ECtHR), para 96. I am grateful to Thomas Spijkerboer for suggesting these comparisons.
The cavalier way with which the Strasbourg Court treats migrant cases is also illustrated by its readiness to neglect in these cases guarantees upon which it normally insists. The obvious example in this regard is the Court's interpretation of Article 5(1)(f), about immigration detention, which has done away with the 'necessity test' which is applied in other detention cases. See Chapter 11.

[11] Hannah Arendt, *The Origins of Totalitarianism* (London: Allen and Unwin, 1968).

[12] See Chapter 2.

[13] Frédéric Sudre, 'Le renouveau jurisprudentiel de la protection des étrangers par l'article 3 de la Convention européenne des droits de l'Homme', in Hugues Fulchiron (ed.) *Les étrangers et la Convention européenne des droits de l'homme et des libertés fondamentales* (Paris: E.J.A., 1999) 61–82 at 63. A participant to the discussions of this colloquium provided an even stronger image by suggesting that the migrants had entered the Convention system '*par effraction*' (forced illegal entry): François Burrachot, in Fulchiron (ed.) 380.

sense from a perspective which conceives of human rights as principles of good governance agreed by states—given that the signatories never had any intention of relinquishing their assumed sovereign right to control migrants when they signed the Convention. We shall come back to this point, which drives our attention to the perpetual tension between state sovereignty and individual rights.[14]

II. Human First: The *Pro-Homine* Bias of the Inter-American Court

The situation appears rather different at the Inter-American Court of Human Rights (hereafter, the Inter-American Court or the Court)[15] which was set up as an institution of the Organization of American States (OAS) in 1979 and is based in San José, Costa Rica. Like many European human rights lawyers, I knew little about this Court before embarking on this study. My resolve to get better acquainted with its work came after reading its advisory opinion on the rights of migrant workers in preparation for a class on the legal aspects of migration.[16] I remember sharing with the students the next day my excitement at having discovered a judicial text which was expressing all that I would have wished a human rights court to state—but which I had grown accustomed to not hearing from the Strasbourg Court. As will be detailed in Chapter 8, the opinion unequivocally affirmed the rights of migrant workers from within a reasoning which rested on the principle that all human beings are equal. Most startlingly, the Inter-American Court declared this principle to be *jus cogens*, thus including it in the bedrock of international law from which states cannot derogate, irrespective of their lack of formal consent to it. Such judicial boldness immediately raised my admiration and curiosity. When I sought research funding in order to write this book, my application mentioned an exploratory visit to the Inter-American Court, suggesting that this might allow me to make some comparative observations. At this early stage, my research proposal was nonetheless squarely focused on the European Court. A three-week visit to San José persuaded me that the

[14] See e.g. Robert McCorquodale with Richard Fairbrother, 'Globalization and Human Rights' (1999) *Human Rights Quarterly* 21, 735–766; Brian Opeskin, 'Managing International Migration in Australia: Human Rights and the "Last Major Redoubt of Unfettered National Sovereignty"' (2012) *International Migration Review* 46, 551–585. At the same time, it would hardly be possible to deny migrants human rights. For a brief but highly enlightening history of the way in which migrants came to be incorporated into the human rights UN regime, see Stefanie Grant, 'The Recognition of Migrants' Rights within the UN Human Rights System: The First 60 Years', in Marie-Bénédicte Dembour and Tobias Kelly (eds), *Are Human Rights for Migrants: Critical Reflections on the Status of Irregular Migrants in Europe and the United States* (Abingdon: Routledge, 2011) 25–47.

[15] This book thus uses the expression 'the Court' to refer either to the European Court of Human Rights or to the Inter-American Court of Human Rights, with the introductory paragraphs or sentences making clear in every section of the text which is which.

[16] *Juridical Condition and Rights of the Undocumented Migrants*, Advisory Opinion OC-18/03 (IACtHR), 17 Sept. 2003.

contrast the Inter-American Court offered to the Strasbourg Court deserved more than the occasional footnote.

For a seasoned observer of the European Convention system, one of the most striking features of the Inter-American case law must be its resolutely *pro-homine* orientation.[17] The label '*pro-homine*' (meaning pro-human being in Latin) is used by the Inter-American Court itself to describe its own approach, which can be summarised as characterised by a bias towards the human being. Such a bias makes complete sense within the history of this court, which would have been left without raison d'être had it not been for the fierce determination of its judges to find every possible way through which they could manage to offer redress to the victims of human rights violations who were appearing before it in its early years. This was especially the case in respect of its 'contentious jurisdiction' (where one party brings a case in order to resolve an actual dispute against a state, rather than requesting an abstract interpretation of the law under its so-called 'advisory jurisdiction'). The contentious case law emerged from the most serious human rights violations committed during the brutal dictatorships which engulfed Latin America in the 1970s. The facts of these cases were invariably in dispute, with the victim's side making allegations (e.g. of forced disappearance, torture and massacres) which the defendant state then contested. Normal legal practice imposes on the party who brings a complaint before a judge to prove the veracity and pertinence of her complaint. A strict adherence to this principle would have killed the possibility for the Inter-American Court to reach verdicts of violation. As the victims' allegations corresponded to practices described in reports authored by reliable sources, the Court decided to shift the burden of proof onto the defendant states, in turn enabling it to reach verdicts of violation as regard to facts which the victims had not proven 'beyond reasonable doubt'. This was obviously a crucial step which was then accompanied by other moves through which the Inter-American Court relentlessly pushed the development of human rights standards in a way which sought to recognise, repair, and prevent the repetition of the suffering of the victims. A more conventional—lawyers might call it 'prudent'—interpretation of human rights law would have rendered the Inter-American Court unable to meet the challenges of the experience it had to confront. The *pro-homine* impulse, once established in its case law, was to benefit subsequent alleged victims, including the few migrants who have appeared before the Inter-American Court.[18]

[17] Ludovic Hennebel, *La Convention américaine des droits de l'homme: Mécanismes de protection et étendue des droits et libertés* (Bruxelles: Bruylant, 2007) 41–42; Laurence Burgorgue-Larsen, Les méthodes d'interprétation de la Cour interaméricaine des droits de l'homme: Justice in context' (2014) *Revue trimestrielle des droits de l'homme* 97, 23–71 at 25.

[18] For authoritative commentaries on the Inter-American Court in English, see Laurence Burgorgue-Larsen and Amaya Úbeda de Torres, *The Inter-American Court of Human Rights: Case Law and Commentary* (Oxford: Oxford University Press, 2011); Jo M. Pasqualucci, *The Practice and Procedure of the Inter-American Court of Human Rights* (Cambrige: Cambridge University Press, 2nd ed., 2012).

III. The Contrasting Bias of the Two Courts

As I see it, in the Inter-American system the migrant is first of all conceived as a human being in need of protection; in the European system, by contrast, the migrant is first of all conceived as an alien subject to the control of the sovereign state. The bias of the Inter-American system is thus towards the applicant, that of the European system towards the state. The contrast in these respective biases is pervasive. It manifests itself not only in regard to the substantive interpretation of the human rights standards which the two courts apply in migrant cases but also in regard to the procedural decisions which they take as judicial proceedings unfold before them.

Speaking of a bias may seem incongruous. In a system which values the rule of law, the point of judicial proceedings is ordinarily understood to be to offer a determination which originates from an impartial and independent body. An adjudication which does not suffer from any bias is certainly the ideal, which the practice must strive to approximate—and does approximate in recognisably greater or lesser degrees. However, perfect neutrality can never be achieved.[19] Biases keep introducing themselves (or keep being identified when they were not previously recognised). The biases of the judicial exercise should not be ignored. If they happen to reflect the underlying political or moral values which society wants to promote, they should be endorsed as conscious, explicit choices. If they do not, they must be presumed to have a negative impact, and attempts should be made to redress them.

That the biases identified above surfaced at all should not come as a surprise. A case before a human rights court typically involves an individual applicant/alleged victim and a respondent/defendant state. If a third party such as a court favours one of these two parties, it seems logical that this will automatically be to the disadvantage of the other party. This is arguably exactly what happens before the European and Inter-American Courts. Putting it crudely, the former overall favours the state, making it difficult for the migrant applicant to win, while the opposite happens before the Inter-American Court. Of course, this is not to deny that both courts strive, and presumably regard themselves as being successful, at properly balancing the interests of the two parties who appear before them. However, one of the conclusions of this book is that it is not clear how the interests and concerns of migrant individuals on the one hand and of states on the other could possibly be balanced without a bias for either one or the other being expressed (not necessarily explicitly): achieving a neutral position is an elusive goal when the individual and state interests at stake are constructed so differently from each other.

The overall contrast between the two courts does not mean that the state always ends up having the upper hand before the European Court and the alleged victim always wins before the Inter-American Court. Nonetheless the odds are stacked

[19] Jacques Derrida, *Force de loi: Le 'Fondement mystique de l'autorité'* (Paris: Galilée, 1994).

in favour of the state in the European system and in favour of the victim in the Inter-American system (at least once her case reaches the Inter-American Court, which happens only very rarely, as we shall stress).[20]

IV. Explaining the Contrast

The figure of the state as guardian or villain

This book argues that the European and Inter-American Courts display an overall bias towards, respectively, the state and the (alleged) victim. It further argues that the cause for these contrasting orientations cannot be attributed to purely legal factors, given that the two courts apply broadly similar human rights standards. The idea that their difference in approach is due to the terms of the conventions of which they are the guardians does not hold: Strasbourg judges themselves observe in their dissenting opinions to verdicts of non-violation that the European Court *could* act in a more pro-migrant manner. If the law does not provide the key for understanding the respective biases displayed by the two examined courts, this must be because the underlying causes for their contrasting approaches originate from outside the law. While it is beyond this book to investigate these causes, some potential explanations nonetheless come to mind. One of these relates to the political context into which the courts were born and the relationship which they have developed with the figure of the state to which they address their judgments.

This factor has already been alluded to earlier in the chapter. If the Inter-American Court had not pushed the human rights logic in favour of the victim, it would have put itself out of a job, so to speak. The first contentious case it decided upon was *Velásquez Rodriguez v. Honduras*.[21] The case concerned a 35-year-old university student who had been kidnapped in 1981, in broad daylight, by heavily armed men wearing civilian clothes, never to reappear to his family. The Court accepted evidence to the effect that, in Honduras in the early 1980s, between 100 and 150 persons had been forcibly disappeared—kidnapped, detained, interrogated, tortured and sometimes murdered and buried in clandestine cemeteries—as part of a government practice aimed at eliminating students, labour leaders, and other people whom the authorities considered dangerous to state security. Having found this practice to be established, the Court shifted the burden of proof onto the defendant state to explain what had happened to Mr Velásquez Rodriguez. Honduras being unable to do so, the Court found a breach of the provisions of the American Convention on the right to life, personal liberty and humane treatment.[22] This ruling, adopted in 1988, started a wave of judgments

20 For a pioneering comparative analysis between the two Courts, see Marie Rota, 'L'interprétation des Conventions américaine et européenne des droits de l'homme. Analyse comparée des deux Cours de protection des droits de l'homme', 2013 PhD thesis, University of Caen-Basse-Normandie.

21 *Velásquez-Rodríguez v. Honduras*, Merits, Judgment (IACtHR), 29 July 1988.

22 For further interpretative tours de force accomplished by the Inter-American Court in this judgment, see Claudio Grossman, 'The *Velásquez-Rodriguez Case: The Development of the Inter-American System*', International Law Stories (Place: Foundation Press, 2007) 77–113.

which reflected the violent internal armed conflicts and state terror which had marred the South American continent from the 1970s. Initially the cases brought before the Court (by the Inter-American Commission on Human Rights, as victims cannot do this independently) concerned the violation, with extreme violence, of the rights to life, liberty and integrity. This case law was soon expanded to include an examination of the institutional legacy of an authoritarian past, leading to the identification by the Inter-American Court of principles regarding, for example, the right to justice, the right to truth, the democratic constitutional order, and the separation of powers.

The Inter-American case law is now diversifying. For example, the *Artavia Murillo et al. ('In Vitro Fertilization') v. Costa Rica* case, decided in 2013, concerned the legislative deprivation of access to IVF treatment for infertile couples on controversial religious grounds.[23] To begin with, however, the sheer physical brutality of the contested facts of the cases that were brought in the Inter-American system meant that the Court had to confront states. The Inter-American Court had to help petitioners put their case across, otherwise there would have been no point to its existence. These circumstances impacted on the way the Court treated not just evidentiary matters, but also other aspects of the proceedings, such as measures of protection for victims and witnesses, admissibility criteria, and the power to order reparative measures,[24] not to mention a progressive interpretation of the norms contained in the American Convention and human rights law more generally. All this created a certain way of thinking and of doing things which, by being *pro-homine*, was inevitably comparatively less supportive of the state.

The history of the Strasbourg case law has gone in the opposite direction. Until the 1990s the European system had a reputation for dealing with issues of 'fine tuning'. States party to the European Convention were seen to consist of democracies which, overall, were functioning well. Occasional and relatively benign, rather than systematic and deeply serious, violations of human rights formed the staple of the Strasbourg Court's early work. The issues the Court had to deal with were thus conceived to require a delicate, almost subjective, assessment, rather than lending themselves to obvious, clear-cut conclusions. Differences of views were possible over the outcome.[25] This changed with the accession of Russia and other states with a history of strong political repression.[26] Nonetheless, in its formative years, the European Court did not feel the need to go strongly against the

[23] *Artavia Murillo et al. ('In Vitro Fertilization') v. Costa Rica*, Preliminary Objections, Merits, Reparations and Costs, Judgment (IACtHR), 28 Nov. 2012.

[24] Elisabeth Lambert-Abdelgawad and Kathia Martin-Chenut (eds), *Réparer les violations graves et massives des droits de l'homme: la Cour interaméricaine, pionnière et modèle?* (Paris: SLC, 2010).

[25] This may contribute to explaining the preponderant position which the doctrine of the margin of appreciation has come to assume in the European system—at the same time, one should not forget that the doctrine emerged as a way to countenance state interests in colonial repression: A. W. Brian Simpson, *Human Rights and the End of Empire: Britain and the Genesis of the European Convention* (Oxford: Oxford University Press, 2001) Chapter 18.

[26] Although Turkey was an original signatory of the Convention which had entered into force in its respect in 1954, it only accepted the jurisdiction of the Court and the right of individual petition in 1987 and 1990, respectively.

state. Indeed, there is a widespread consensus that it would have been counterproductive, perhaps even suicidal, for the Strasbourg Court to take a hard stance against states, as it might have incited them to abandon the Convention system altogether.[27]

An oversimplification could therefore have it that the state originally appeared as an overall benevolent force which could be left to its own devices in the European system, but as a 'villain' that needed to be reined in at all costs in the Inter-American system. A second oversimplification could follow from this, according to which European states would have been paradoxically less open than their Latin American counterparts at receiving guidance from the international human rights court set up in their region.

Many states which had participated in the drafting of the European Convention after World War II had done so not so much to help themselves but to assist others. For example, the UK, France, and the Netherlands were each very proud of their domestic constitutional arrangements and did not feel they themselves needed a Convention. These states imagined that they were developing human rights standards 'for export', i.e. for the benefit of states with lesser democratic credentials than they themselves enjoyed.[28] They therefore did not expect to be found in breach of the Convention they had just created (although, to be on the safe side, France delayed accepting the jurisdiction of the Court until it had lost most of its colonies).[29] Verdicts of violation by the Strasbourg Court in respect of these states were received as unwelcome interferences with their sovereignty. European states resented the mingling of an international court with what they regarded to be their internal affairs. One might say that the more the Strasbourg Court affirmed its authority, the more the states emphasised the Court's subsidiary role, with this process having recently culminated in the signature of Protocol no. 15, which explicitly inscribes the principle of subsidiarity in the Convention's Preamble.[30]

On the Inter-American side, pro-democracy governments have been known to welcome the legitimacy that the Inter-American Court lends to their intended reforms. For example, the Peruvian government elected in 2000 hastily reinstated its recognition of the Court's contentious jurisdiction, which had been withdrawn by President Fujimori following adverse Inter-American judgments and the expectation that Peru would yet again be condemned in the *Ivcher Bronstein v.*

[27] Madsen *La genèse* 120; Bates *The Evolution* 428; Anthony Lester, 'The European Court of Human Rights after 50 Years', in Jonas Christoffersen and Mikael Rask Madsen (eds) *The European Court of Human Rights between Law and Politics* (Oxford: Oxford University Press, 2011) 98–115 at 100.

[28] Madsen *La genèse* 50 and 113; Barbara Oomen, 'The Rights for Others: The Contested Homecoming of Human Rights in the Netherlands' (2013) *Netherlands Quarterly of Human Rights* 31, 41–73.

[29] See Chapter 3.

[30] For a critique of this development, see: Françoise Tulkens, La Cour européenne des droits de l'homme et la déclaration de Brighton. Oublier la réforme et penser l'avenir' (2013) *Cahiers de droit européen* 2012/2, 305–343 at 330–332. For a different view, see: Kantstantsin Dzehtsiarou, 'Much Ado About Nothing', post dated 17 April 2013 on the ECHR blog maintained by Antoine Buyse, available at: http://echrblog.blogspot.co.uk/2013/04/ngo-reaction-to-draft-protocol-15-and.html, accessed 9 May 2014.

Peru case.[31] This example also indicates, however, that states parties to the American Convention do not always welcome rulings by the Inter-American Court.[32]

Laurence Burgorgue-Larsen and Amaya Úbeda de Torres tellingly open their treatise on the Inter-American Court by noting that '[OAS] States are pathologically reluctant to recognize a truly *effective* court protection of human rights'.[33] The former President of the Inter-American Court, Sergio García Ramírez, concurs with their assessment that '[v]ery few elements, virtually none in fact, could predict the subsistence or success of a system that evoked the Pan-American dream, which had never before been fulfilled and which seemed to belong to the field of magical realism rather than juridical realism'.[34] Another former President, Thomas Buergenthal, has explained:

> In 1978, when the American Convention on Human Rights entered into force, much of Central America and South America was ruled by dictatorships of either the right or the left. Of the eleven States whose ratifications had brought the Convention into force, fewer than one-half had democratically elected governments at the time. The remainder ratified for a variety of political reasons, including the pressure brought to bear by the Carter administration and the fact that some of these States were convinced that ratification posed no serious risks to them because the system established by the Convention would never be implemented.[35]

It is important to stress that things could have turned out differently in each system. It is only with the benefit of hindsight that everything appears fitting and logical. The 'pro-victim' attitude of the Inter-American Court was audacious rather than inevitable. Likewise, it would be wrong retrospectively to regard the more deferential orientation of the Strasbourg Court as having been predictable right from the start. Nonetheless, once these orientations began to establish themselves, they were more likely to become enduring features of the respective systems, although not without attracting contestation both from within these institutions and from outside.

The sociological make up of the two institutions

It is difficult to explain why the history of the two courts unfolded as it did. There may be some purchase in the idea that the state tends to be regarded as a protector of the public interest by the European Court and as a likely abuser of

[31] *Ivcher-Bronstein v. Peru*, Merits, Reparations and Costs, Judgment (IACtHR), 6 Feb. 2001, the merits of which are briefly reviewed in Chapter 5, refused to give effect to the Convention's denunciation by the Fujimori government.

[32] The other denunciations have been by Barbados and Trinidad and Tobago and, most recently, Venezuela.

[33] Burgorgue-Larsen and Úbeda de Torres *The Inter-American Court* 7, emphasis in the original.

[34] Sergio García Ramírez, 'Foreword: The Inter-American Human Rights Jurisdiction: A Long Journey', in Burgorgue-Larsen and Úbeda de Torres *The Inter-American Court* xvii–xxviii at xx.

[35] Thomas Buergenthal, 'Foreword', in Jo M. Pasqualucci, *The Practice and Procedure of the Inter-American Court of Human Rights* (Cambridge: Cambridge University Press, 2nd ed. 2013) xv–xvi at xv.

human rights by the Inter-American Court. This, however, is not the whole story, the more so since this argument oversimplifies the reality. Another contributory factor to the contrast in the development of the courts must lie in their sociological make up. Indeed, anyone who visits the seats of the two courts cannot but immediately be struck by the enormous difference in their material conditions and institutional outlook.

For over 20 years, the European Court has occupied a purpose-built, modernist building designed by the award-winning architect Richard Rogers (at a time when the demise of the European Commission had not yet been envisaged, hence the two aisles of the building).[36] The private villa the Costa Rican government donated to the OAS remains, after important transformations, the seat of the Inter-American Court. In August 2012, the total number of people the Inter-American Court employed was 61. This number included the seven judges, the Registrar and Deputy Registrar, the Registry's attorneys and their assistants and teams' secretaries, the clerical staff, accountants, receptionists, librarians, drivers, guards, and cleaners.[37] In the same period, the European Court counted 47 judges and 652 members of staff working for the Registry.[38] When I was visiting the Inter-American Court, the only people who seemed older than me were the judges; the majority of attorneys were in their thirties and interns were often younger. I was told that the Inter-American Court suffered from a high turnover of staff, with most of the Registry's attorneys leaving after four or five years. By contrast, many people I interviewed at the European Court were in their fifties and above, and seemed to have enjoyed a long career at the Strasbourg Registry.

The Inter-American Court projects the image of a small, young, vibrant institution. Until recently the judges of the Inter-American Court received no monetary compensation for the time they devoted to their judicial role (except for their expenses), ensuring that only individuals fully committed to the human rights cause would come forward to assume this role. The Court could not function without the work and dedication of the attorneys it employs and the interns it hosts, who bring an enthusiasm and idealism which generate audacious ideas, the logic of which I am told they are encouraged to pursue to the full. The shoestring budget on which the Court is forced to operate, always on the verge of not being able to balance its books, is deplorable. One might surmise, however, that it has generated a broad and generous interpretation of human rights. As already hinted in this chapter, the Inter-American Court renders only a few rulings a year. Its current infrastructure certainly would not allow it to increase this limited output substantially. On a positive note, the Court almost invariably pushes the boundaries of human rights law when it deals with the one or two dozen contentious cases

[36] On the symbolic significance of the created design, see: Lord Rogers of Riverside, 'The Design of the *Palais des Droits de l'Homme*', in Paul Mahoney, Franz Matscher, Herbert Petzold, and Luzius Wildhaber (eds) *Protecting Human Rights: The European Perspective. Studies in Memory of Rolv Ryssdal* (Cologne: Heymanns Verlag, 2000) 1213–1214.

[37] Arturo Herrera, personal communication on 3 September 2012.

[38] Number at 1 September 2012, personal communication of the Strasbourg Registry, 4 October 2013.

lodged annually by the Inter-American Commission, with effects which can then reverberate throughout the whole region.[39]

By contrast, the European Court is a well-established and settled institution which has—inevitably—gone through a process of bureaucratisation. It produces 100 judgments on the merits every month and declares close to 100 times as many cases inadmissible.[40] Much of its attention seems to focus on getting through as many files as swiftly as possible in order to reduce a backlog which peaked at over 160,000 cases in 2011. These efforts have paid off: the backlog stood at just below 100,000 at the end of 2013.[41] In the words of a lawyer who has regularly appeared before the Court to represent applicants: '[i]t is a factory system, dominated by the Registry, attempting to achieve high productivity in delivering mass production of mainly negative decisions'.[42] Compared to the Inter-American Court, the European Court appears heavy and bureaucratic, thus less propitious for ambitious interpretations which would be more destabilising of state interests.

A word of caution is nonetheless again necessary: while establishing a correlation between institutional outlook and judicial output may be justified, it does not explain everything. It is worth observing that even when the Strasbourg system was in its infancy and thus less bureaucratic, it was already reluctant to develop a *pro-homine* approach in the field of migration, as this book will show. The contrast between the two courts highlighted in this book cannot be attributed to a single cause and nor can it be understood to have taken place in an automatic way.

The different outlooks of migration in Europe and Latin America

The tentative political and sociological explanations provided in this chapter in order to account for the pro-state and pro-victim approaches of the European and Inter-American Courts' orientations are general rather than specific to the migrant case law. It seems reasonable to hypothesise that the different ways in which the social phenomenon of migration presents itself in the European and Latin American continents is another factor which could usefully be taken into consideration when attempting to explain the contrast in the approaches of the two Courts noted in this book.

[39] There are regrettable exceptions, including, e.g., *Cabrera García and Montiel Flores v. Mexico*, Preliminary Exceptions, Merits, Reparation and Costs, Judgment (IACtHR), 26 Nov. 2010.

[40] In 2013, the European Court adopted 916 judgments (a low number compared to previous years). In the same period, close to 90,000 applications were declared inadmissible: 80,500 applications by single judges (the new type of judicial formation introducted by Protocol no. 14); 4,900 by three-judge committees (a formation which in the past also used to do the job now performed by single judges); and 4,200 by chambers (this latter number includes decisions of both inadmissibility and striking out): European Court of Human Rights '2013 Annual Report' http://www.echr.coe.int/Documents/Annual_report_2013_ENG.pdf, accessed 19 May 2014, p. 61.

[41] '2013 Annual Report', pp. 9 and 61.

[42] Lester, 'The European Court' 109. See the same article for remarks on judges' salaries and the Court's overall budget (which, in 2010, was less than one-fifth of that of the European Court of Justice): Lester 107, note 43.

Both the European and the Latin American continents are extremely diverse, and it is dangerous to attempt generalisations on their respective migration patterns. With circumspection, two elements can nonetheless be offered. The first is that throughout the history of the European Convention, European states—at least those that count politically—have thought of themselves as 'receiving countries' (with Italy a notable exception until recently). In the last 30 years, Latin American countries have primarily thought of themselves as 'sending' countries (with the United States the most important destination), with the realisation coming relatively late that some (e.g. Argentina, Brazil, Chile, Ecuador) are also 'receiving' countries.[43] As a result, one can expect the Inter-American Court to encounter far less resistance than the European Court when it produces rulings favourable to migrant rights. Indeed states parties to the American Convention have on a number of occasions explicitly asked the Court to go in this direction, as we shall see in Chapters 9 and 14. The second point is that the figure of the immigrant is often (not always) perceived by Europeans to be more threatening than is the case in Latin America. With the important exception of legislation adopted by military dictatorships in the 1970s and 1980s,[44] the Latin American attitude towards migrants might be described as relatively relaxed. This can be explained by a number of factors: a broadly similar background between locals and migrants of South American origin; relatively small economic differentials, weakening the risk of the host population developing the fear of being submerged by have-nots in search of a better life; and the absence of an elaborate state social security system, lessening the perception that newcomers would unjustly benefit from a system which was built prior to their arrival. An additional possible factor might be the relative culture of informality existing in Latin America, which may have made it possible for migrants to live without too many problems in a legally irregular situation (i.e. without their stay being formally authorised as legal terms require). One should note, however, that it is precisely in order to tackle the problem of irregularity that activists in a number of countries started to push—in a number of instances successfully—for a domestic legislative framework which recognises the right to migrate and grant rights to migrants, irrespective of their legal status, and that Mercosur, the Latin American Southern Cone Market which can be regarded as a kind of pendant to the European Union, decided to transform the migration regime for South Americans.[45]

[43] On migration patterns in Latin America, see: Jorge Durand and Douglas S. Massey, 'New World Orders: Continuities and Changes in Latin American Migration' (2010) *The Annals of the American Academy of Political and Social Science* 630, 20–52; SICREMI, 'International Migration in the Americas: Second Report of the Continuous Reporting System on International Migration in the Americas (SICREMI)' (2012), http://www.oecd.org/els/mig/G48952_WB_SICREMI_2012_ENGLISH_REPORT_LR.pdf, accessed 10 May 2014.

[44] Some of these remain in force at the time of writing. For details, see: Feline Freier and Diego Acosta Arcarazo, 'Beyond Smoke and Mirrors? Discursive Gaps in the Liberalisation of South American Immigration Laws', manuscript dated 2013.

[45] Ana Margheritis, 'Piecemeal Regional Integration in the Post-Neoliberal Era: Negotiating Migration Policies within Mercosur' (2012) *Review of International Political Economy* 20, 541–575.

The result is a perceived chasm, at least at discourse level, between 'Fortress' Europe and 'open-doors' inclined Latin America.[46] This does not make the migrant situation in Latin America idyllic, however. The fate of migrants in Latin America can be extremely hard as the Inter-American case law reviewed in this book demonstrates. The racism against indigenous and black and coloured people is an entrenched feature throughout the continent which can affect the situation of migrants.[47] Despite this, one can assume that the continents' respective history and experiences make Latin America more likely than Europe to regard at least some migrant figures in a sympathetic light and to accept the need to bestow them rights, at least in some circumstances.[48] This is another factor which may have to be kept in mind when trying to understand the reasons for the differences in the judicial approaches of the European and Inter-American Courts highlighted in this book.

V. The Oranges and Apples of Human Rights Law

The political, institutional, and social contexts in which the European and Inter-American Courts work are vastly different. Not surprisingly, the cases upon which they adjudicate are never directly comparable either. Given this, the exercise attempted in this book is not a one-to-one comparison between the results which the two courts would have reached in cases which could be considered to be directly comparable in their actual facts and political and social context. Rather, what the book does is to use the Inter-American Court's migrant case law strategically, as a counterpoint to the Strasbourg migrant case law, in order to further the book's principal aim, which is to provide a critical assessment of the Strasbourg case law.

Putting it differently, studying the choices made by the Inter-American Court becomes an opportunity to show that the European Court does not share the reflexes which come 'naturally' to the Inter-American Court, thus highlighting in yet another way the state bias of the Strasbourg system. This is done to demonstrate that it would not have been *legally* impossible for the Strasbourg Court to develop an approach which was resolutely more pro-migrant than it has done, if such had been the will of the majority of Strasbourg judges.

The book tries to make sense of the way in which the case law has unfolded, especially in the Strasbourg system. It does so with the awareness that the two systems

[46] Diego Acosta Arcarazo and Andrew Geddes, 'Transnational Diffusion or Different Models?' Regional Approaches to Migration Governance in the European Union and Mercosur' (2014) *European Journal of Migration and Law* 16, 19–44.

[47] Ariel E. Dulitzky, 'A Region in Denial: Racial Discrimination and Racism in Latin America', in Anani Dzidzienyo and Suzanne Oboler (eds) *Neither Enemies nor Friends: Latinos, Blacks and Afro-Latinos* (New York: Palgrave Macmillan, 2005) 39–59.

[48] Paradoxes and contradictions in approaches to migration in Latin America nonetheless came out clearly from the papers presented at the conference 'A Liberal Tide: Towards a Paradigm Shift in Latin American Migration and Asylum Policy-Making', held at the University of London on 18 March 2013 and promoted at http://rli.sas.ac.uk/aliberaltide/, accessed 10 May 2014.

which have produced the reviewed case law are exactly that: *systems*. This means that the respective bodies of jurisprudence should not be conceived as a sum of discrete elements, as if each of these could be transferable in isolation and could be expected to produce after transposition the same effect as it did in its original setting.

In other words, it may be useful to approach the European and Inter-American Courts metaphorically as two differing fruits of human rights law. One should not be expected to have the ability to become the other. It is nonetheless enlightening to decipher their respective qualities and features, and to compare them, in the same way as one might wish to compare the vitamin content, texture, and flavour of different species of fruit. Having said this, it would also be a mistake to approach each system as a fixed entity rather than a continually developing process which has the capacity to be both internally imaginative and to borrow elements which have emerged elsewhere.

VI. One European Court or Several?

Lawyers typically talk about a 'court' in the singular, as if it was always the same institution which was deciding the cases that come before it. Of course, in one sense, this is correct. In another sense, however, this is a gross misrepresentation.

In the European system, every state party to the Convention is entitled to have one judge at the European Court.[49] Today the Strasbourg Court counts 47 judges (with the exact arrangements for the election of the 48th judge who will be sitting for the European Union, the last party to have acceded the system, still to be finalised at time of writing). Originally there were ten judges. In 1998, Protocol no. 11 came into force in response to the problems caused by an ever increasing caseload and backlog. To accelerate the time it would take to process a Strasbourg application from beginning to end, Protocol no. 11 transformed the Strasbourg Court into a permanent institution and abolished the Commission, thus stopping cases from having to be examined by two separate Convention organs. The number of state parties—and thus judges—more than doubled in the 1990s, following the collapse of communist regimes in Eastern Europe. Past and present judges have all arrived at Strasbourg with vastly different experiences and career trajectories. It seems sensible to assume that they rarely share the same opinion on how the legal issues which come before the Court should be tackled.

In other words, the Court does not reproduce itself from one case to the next, in an automatic way. This is the more so since it operates in an extremely complex and constantly evolving institutional setting. Exercising direct or indirect influences upon it are its Registry, the other institutions of the Council of Europe, the states parties to the Convention, the national courts to which the Court

[49] In the Inter-American system, the seven judges can no longer sit in cases directed against their own country.

implicitly addresses its judgments, organisations emerging from civil society,[50] and, of course, the overall political and social climate of the time. In such an intricate context, it is perhaps something of a miracle that it is not a cacophony that comes out of the Court, but a case law which is overall coherent and which follows established principles, the broad lines of which are ascertainable.

As I started the research for this book in earnest, I was privileged to meet the jurisconsult of the Court, Vincent Berger, in October 2009. The jurisconsult post emerged in the late 1990s, as it was thought that it could prove useful to have a mechanism limiting the risk of having the newly created different sections of the Court developing lines of jurisprudence in contradiction with each other.[51] Indeed, when Protocol no. 11 came into force, the judges of the Court were organised into four Sections (a number since then increased to five). The great majority of Strasbourg judgments are produced by Chambers which are made up of seven judges who are drawn from one of the Sections of the Court. The comparatively rare judgments of the Grand Chamber, composed of 17 judges, including Presidents and Vice-Presidents of Sections, yield more authority. There are two routes leading to a Grand Chamber judgment. The first dates from the old Court and was confirmed by Protocol no. 11; it consists of the relinquishment of a case by the Chamber to which the case was originally assigned. The second route, introduced by Protocol no. 11, consists of the 'appeal' against a Chamber judgment by one of the parties. (This appeal, called 'referral', must be approved by a panel of five judges.[52]) The main function of the jurisconsult, assisted by his team, is to examine the rulings planned by the various Sections, so as to alert the judges, if appropriate, that they are heading in different directions, thus giving them the opportunity to revise their rulings if they so wish, prior to adoption, in order to maintain the coherence of the Strasbourg jurisprudence.

In our meeting in autumn 2009, the jurisconsult told me that the principles governing the Strasbourg case law relating to migrant issues were well established, clear, and relatively simple to follow. He explained that the core principles had not changed over the years. The Grand Chamber's judgment adopted by the 'old' Court in *ABC* still held. In the months which had preceded our interview, Berger elaborated, the Court had seen quite a few cases concerning immigration detention, especially in Lampedusa, Malta, and the Canary Islands, but many of these cases had been struck out because the applicants were at some stage released from detention and had then vanished, ceasing to give instructions to their legal representative. He added that the Grand Chamber's verdict of non-violation in *Saadi v. the United Kingdom*,[53] about a short spell in detention, for the purpose

[50] For a useful conceptualisation of civil society, see Emily Haslam. 'Subjects and Objects: International Criminal Law and the Institutionalization of Civil Society' (2011) *The International Journal of Transitional Justice* 5, 221–240.

[51] An ad hoc solution originally designed to keep the former Registrar of the Court in post, the jurisconsult function is not mentioned in the Rules of the Court, let alone the Convention: Vincent Berger, personal communication.

[52] See further Chapter 5.

[53] *Saadi v. the United Kingdom*, appl. 13229/03, GC Judgment (ECtHR), 29 Jan. 2008.

of facilitating the determination of an asylum claim, in appropriate conditions, meant that subsequent applications raising the same point were now summarily declared inadmissible by committees of three judges, for these committees (replaced, since the entry into force of Protocol no. 14, by single-judge formations) must follow the precedents set by the Grand Chamber. Berger explained that failed asylum seekers were regularly requesting provisional measures prohibiting the state from having them expelled. When such a request was successful, the measure granted by the Court was binding since the adoption by the Grand Chamber of the *Mamatkulov and Askarov v. Turkey* judgment of 2005.[54] Berger mentioned during the same interview that there were issues with Greece, which just did not process asylum claims; in relation to this, he informed me that a very significant case was forthcoming about 'Dublin'.[55] We discussed other areas of the case law, such as the expulsion of long-term migrants who have committed a crime and of people who are ill.

At one stage, the jurisconsult observed that there had not yet been any 'mutiny' from sections of the Court. The notes I took during our meeting do not record the tone with which this was said. It might have been a perfectly neutral observation which simply indicated that it can never be guaranteed that the Court will always speak with one voice. If so, the statement is more difficult to maintain five years on.

Significantly, Berger expressed scepticism about the wisdom of writing a monograph exclusively focusing on the migrant case law. He did not think I would find sufficient material for a whole book. His warning was, of course, related to his view that the Strasbourg case law on migration was coherent and amounted to a few well-established and clear principles. Of course, our interview took place in 2009 and since then the migrant case law has developed at a fast and unanticipated pace. Even if it had not, I would still have found more material than I could possibly tackle in one book. Admittedly this is because of my unusual approach: I am interested as much in the European Court's undercurrents which go in a different direction than that followed by the Strasbourg mainstream, as in the coherent case law that Berger was describing.

VII. Documenting the Strasbourg Undercurrents and Neglected Mainstream

Inevitably, the bias of the European Court towards the state translates into an attitude which is less sympathetic to the applicant than it could be. This bias has not gone without generating controversies, including within the Court

[54] *Mamatkulov and Askarov v. Turkey*, appls 46827/99, 46951/99, GC Judgment (ECtHR), 4 Feb. 2005.

[55] This was obviously *M.S.S. v. Belgium and Greece*, appl. 30696/09, GC Judgment (ECtHR), 21 Jan. 2011, discussed in detail in Chapter 12.

itself. The existence of acerbic internal debates sometimes transpires in dissenting opinions, which as a result are given particular attention in this book. Judges who belong to a bench which has ruled on the merits of a particular case always have the opportunity to explain why they disagree with the judgment adopted by the majority. (By contrast, no separate opinion can be expressed regarding Chamber decisions as to admissibility; these decisions—which are not called judgments—are simply recorded as having been adopted 'by unanimity' or 'by majority', without further detail being provided. They are not open to a referral before the Grand Chamber.) Dissenting opinions not only show that the Strasbourg organs do not speak with one voice; they also indicate that it would have been possible, from a legal perspective, for the organ to follow a path which would have led to the opposite result than the one actually reached.

Oscillations in the case law, which goes in one direction and then another, sometimes in a seemingly repetitive pendulum, also testify to deep controversies which animate the Strasbourg Court. For example, it appeared for a few years in the early 1990s that a new jurisprudential principle was being established towards finding the deportation, following criminal conviction, of a 'quasi-national' to her country of nationality (but not socialisation), normally contrary to the Convention. The case law seemed to be heading towards giving the paramount hand to the right of the migrant to be able to remain in the country where she had spent most and sometimes all or virtually all her life, thus relegating the principle that the state had the power to exclude aliens to a second position. Such a resolution of the tension between the human right/state poles did not hold, however. A first verdict of non-violation followed the string of verdicts of violations which had been adopted in the previous years, leading one of the dissenting judges to predict in 1996 that the case law concerning the deportation of convicted criminals would become a 'lottery'.[56] This book demonstrates that Judge Martens' characterisation remains apposite to a large extent today, not only in this specific area[57] but also in other areas of migrant case law.[58]

If something akin to a lottery is at play in much of the Strasbourg migrant case law, this lottery is nonetheless stacked in favour of the state. Thousands of migrants have brought applications to Strasbourg since the 1950s. These applications have given rise to an appreciable number of judgments which have developed European human rights law norms and brought judicial redress to the applicants who lodged them. Those familiar with the Strasbourg case law will for example immediately cite, in a non-exhaustive list, *Berrehab v. the Netherlands*,[59] *Gaygusuz v. Austria*[60] and *Chahal v. the United Kingdom*,[61] or, more recently,

[56] Dissenting opinion of Judge Martens in *Boughanemi v. France*, appl. 22070/93, Judgment (ECtHR), 24 Apr. 1996.

[57] See Chapter 6 for the Article 8 return cases.

[58] See especially Chapters 7, 12, and 13.

[59] *Berrehab v. the Netherlands*, appl. 10730/84, Judgment (ECtHR), 21 June 1988.

[60] *Gaygusuz v. Austria*, appl. 17371/90, Judgment (ECtHR), 16 Sept. 1996.

[61] *Chahal v. the United Kingdom*, appl. 22414/93, GC Judgment (ECtHR), 15 Nov. 1996.

Saadi v. Italy,[62] *M.S.S. v. Belgium and Greece*, and *Hirsi Jamaa v. Italy*.[63] This book gives due credit to these and other judgments in the same vein which seem resolutely to affirm migrants' rights. However it also documents how these positive rulings are dwarfed by the far more numerous Strasbourg rulings, which have done nothing to develop the human rights of migrants. The fact is, the great majority of migrant applicants today lose at Strasbourg, just as they did 20, 30, and even 50 years ago.

Prior to the coming into force of Protocol no. 11, individuals had to lodge their complaints before the Commission. If the Commission declared a case admissible, it adopted a report on its merits, which was not legally binding. As the filtering Strasbourg organ, the Commission was then free to bring the case to the Court within three months of the adoption of its report. (The respondent state could also do this—as well as the applicant after Protocol no. 9 came into force.) More often than not, however, the Commission declared applications inadmissible. This is still the fate of most applications today: only a small fraction of cases are declared admissible by the 'new' Court. Decisions of inadmissibility have the effect of closing avenues for the development of the Strasbourg jurisprudence which would generally favour applicants. Like dissenting opinions, although they are generally neglected in legal commentaries, they are of paramount importance to this study.

Without them, it would barely be possible to document the fact that migrants' rights have not been recognised by the European Court as much as they could—or perhaps, should—have been. This thesis, central to this book, is in direct opposition to the many Convention commentaries which praise the Strasbourg achievements.[64] Such praise, however, is too often based on a truncated examination of the outputs of the Convention system. Borrowing the conclusion of Mathias Möschel in his review of the Strasbourg Court's racial discrimination case law which is widely celebrated for promoting the rights of the Roma minority '[i]t is as if one focused on the three wins of one's preferred soccer team and simply ignored the roughly 40 losses or ties'.[65]

[62] *Saadi v. Italy*, appl. 37201/06, GC Judgment (ECtHR), 28 Feb. 2008.

[63] *Hirsi Jamaa v. Italy*, appl. 27765/09, GC Judgment (ECtHR), 29 Feb. 2012.

[64] Compared to the mid-1990s when I first started to study the ECHR system, scholarship critical of the Strasbourg case law is now more frequent. It nonetheless remains relatively rare. Lawyers' reticence to highlight weaknesses in the case law may be linked to their determination to keep a positive outlook, especially in a context where the European Court is their last chance of a judicial victory. For example, after Article 6 was found inapplicable to immigration cases, no one highlighted the impact of this ruling. Efforts were devolved instead at attempting to develop the case law on Article 13, which was seen as offering potentially similar guarantees to Article 6 (which is true up to a point). Apart from the fact that I regard my task as an academic to say how things are, however unpleasant, I also doubt the value of leaving the Strasbourg Court off the hook. I believe there is a risk of losing the opportunity to respond to rightwing attacks which argue that the Court is too generous in bestowing rights if one does not highlight the timidity of its pronouncements. The Court is an essential institution, with a crucial role in Europe and beyond. Hopefully this book can help it navigate its immense task in appropriate ways.

[65] Mathias Möschel, 'Is the European Court of Human Rights' Case Law on Anti-Roma Violence "Beyond Reasonable Doubt"' (2012) *Human Rights Law Review* 12, 479–507 at 497.

VIII. A Dissecting Method of Analysis

My disappointment with the European Court's decisions which set back the fight for the rights of migrants provided the original impetus of this study. I was angry, for example, at judgments such as *ABC, Vilvarajah and Others v. the United Kingdom*,[66] *Maaouia v. France*,[67] and *Saadi v. the United Kingdom*,[68] amongst others. *ABC* has already been introduced. *Vilvarajah* condoned the return of failed asylum seekers and other migrants to civil war; adopted in 1991, it stood as the law for 20 years. *Maaouia* was one of the first rulings of the 'new' Court sitting as a Grand Chamber; it rejected the idea that fair trial guarantees might apply to immigration issues, a principle still applied today. *Saadi v. the United Kingdom* (not to be confused with *Saadi v. Italy*)—a Grand Chamber's judgment of 2008—accepted the principle that immigration detention did not need to be a 'last resort' to be lawful under the Convention.[69]

As I was researching the Strasbourg case law, it became apparent that these prominent rulings were only the tip of the iceberg. Numerous, largely unknown decisions had been adopted over the years, which formed a coherent case law made up of principles which reinforced each other and led, admittedly with exceptions, to the rejection, through inadmissibility decisions and verdicts of non-violation, of most of the complaints which migrants brought to Strasbourg. I became interested in tracing the development of this case law. I found it crucial to identify not only the mainstream but also the undercurrents of the case law.

My training as an anthropologist helped. This is a training which teaches one to be alert to contradictions, ambivalence, and ambiguities. It would have led me to wonder where Strasbourg pronouncements and principles come from, what supports them, and to what extent those pronouncements and principles reflect 'practice' (including the practice of the Strasbourg Court itself). I was eager to approach every decision as a piece of anthropological mini-fieldwork: a conversation between different voices (some of them submerged), framed in a fairly formal way, producing many expected results, but at the same time developing with unanticipated twists. I read every last word of every decision quoted in this book. One could say that I was dissecting[70] the case law, in order to try both to trace shifts in the development of the case law and to understand the conditions which made a particular pronouncement 'thinkable'.

[66] *Vilvarajah and Others v. the United Kingdom*, appls 13163/87, 13164/87, 13165/87, 13447/87, 13448/87, Judgment (ECtHR), 30 Oct. 1991.

[67] *Maaouia v. France*, appl. 39652/98, GC Judgment (ECtHR), 5 Oct. 2000.

[68] *Saadi v. the United Kingdom*, appl. 13229/03, GC judgment (ECtHR), 29 Jan. 2008.

[69] *Saadi*, para 70.

[70] '*Décorticage*' is actually the word which instinctively comes to mind to describe my method. Its most appropriate translation in English seems to be 'dissection'. However, '*décorticage*' better conveys the idea of having to peel through tricky material in order to get to what really interests you (or is the core of the matter), such as getting to and cleaning the bits you will eat after you have cracked a nut.

IX. The Book's Historical Structure, European Focus, and Inter-American Counterpoint

The book's structure reflects the history of the case law. For the sake of convenience, Part I is entitled 'Foundations' (even though foundational moments are themselves obviously based on what came before them). Its first chapter (Chapter 2) documents the way in which the European Convention was elaborated in order to protect primarily citizens, while the American Convention always addressed the plight of migrants such as the refugee in search of asylum and the foreigner born without a nationality. The following 12 chapters examine relevant rulings by these two courts. Due to its sheer abundance, this is done in a selective manner in respect of the Strasbourg case law. By contrast, the directly relevant case law of the Inter-American Court, which is numerically limited, makes it possible to undertake a comprehensive review. The tremendous influence of the Inter-American Commission on Human Rights upon the Inter-American Court is unfortunately not considered in this study.[71]

Chapter 3 focuses on the famous *East African Asians* case which never came before the European Court but nonetheless saw the European Commission adopting an important, confidential report on its merits in 1973. The case dealt with the legislation hastily passed by the British government in 1968 in order to deprive Asian holders of British passports, then being expelled from East Africa, of their right of abode. The Commission concluded that the legislation arose from race motivations such that the UK had acted in a manner which contravened Article 3 ECHR which prohibits inhuman or degrading treatment. Chapter 3 notes the difficulty which the drafters of the Convention met in seeking to proclaim human rights in a context which remained colonial and discusses the links between (post-)colonialism, immigration patterns, and the limits of human rights. The first judgment of the European Court in a migrant case, the *ABC* case decided in 1985, is the subject of the next chapter. Chapter 4 traces the way in which earlier cases on family reunification were dismissed by the Commission, identifies the human rights reversal which characterises the majority of the Strasbourg migrant case law, and reviews the current state of affairs in the family reunification area. Part I closes with a chapter which reviews the first ruling of the Inter-American Court on a migrant issue. This ruling, adopted under the advisory (rather than contentious) jurisdiction of the Inter-American Court in 1984, concerned conditions of access to nationality through naturalisation in Costa Rica. As the main aim of the book is to examine the approach of the Strasbourg Court, Chapter 5 takes the opportunity to discuss the Costa Rican case in order to review how the Strasbourg Court has approached cases which bring out nationality issues.

[71] The important role played by the Commission surfaces from the way in which OAS recently undertook a process 'to strengthen' (read: weaken) it. See 'Reflections on Strengthening the Inter-American Human Rights System' published by the Due Process of Law Foundation in the magazine *Aportes DPLf* in 2012, available at http://www.dplf.org/uploads/1338572412.pdf, accessed 10 May 2014.

It also sketches important differences in the composition of the European and Inter-American Courts.

Part II of the book is entitled 'Consolidation'. It could be summarised by saying that the fruits of the early rulings of the European and Inter-American Courts in the *ABC* and the Costa Rican naturalisation cases reviewed in Part I became fully apparent. This part is made up of five chapters, yet again organised in the chronological order of the central ruling upon which each chapter focuses. Chapter 6 discusses the *Berrehab v. the Netherlands*[72] judgment of 1988 but also numerous rulings which followed in *Berrehab*'s wake regarding the expulsion, generally after criminal conviction, of a long-settled migrant. In this case law, the main question for the European Court is whether the expulsion has actually been or would be (if it were to be implemented) in violation of Article 8 ECHR. The Court is shown to be prevaricating on this question and unable to come up with firm principles, thus illustrating particularly clearly how various currents and undercurrents are present within it. In 1989, the Strasbourg Court adopted its judgment in *Soering v. the United Kingdom*.[73] An extradition case, *Soering* is traditionally presented as having made it possible for failed asylum seekers and other migrants to contest their forced return on Article 3 ECHR grounds. Chapter 7 presents this history in a different light. It questions why *Soering*, rather than *Vilvarajah v. the United Kingdom* which had been previously lodged by a number of failed asylum seekers from Sri Lanka,[74] became the leading case in Article 3 return cases. It also identifies the regrettable seeds—from a human rights perspective—which the *Cruz Varas v. Sweden*[75] judgment, of the same period, planted, with effects discernible to this day. Chapter 8 revisits *Gaygusuz v. Austria*,[76] a 1996 Chamber judgment. It demonstrates that at the time of its processing the 'old' Court had not thought the case important. *Gaygusuz* has nonetheless become celebrated for having entrenched the principle of equality between legally settled migrants and nationals in the field of social security. The reasons for this are revealed to be not as straightforward as generally assumed.

As was done in Chapter 4, each of the three 'European' chapters included in Part II open with early cases of the Commission and close with recent case law by the 'new' Court. Throughout the discussion, close attention is paid to both inadmissibility decisions and dissenting opinions. This way of proceeding is rare amongst lawyers. These methods, however, serve to highlight both the enduring and the controversial character of the principles followed at Strasbourg.

The use of Inter-American material as a counterpoint to Strasbourg rulings comes as an additional method which is used in this book in order to refine the critique of the Strasbourg case law. As such, the last two chapters of Part II take as their immediate focus pronouncements by the Inter-American Court. Chapter 9

[72] *Berrehab v. the Netherlands*, appl. 10730/84, Judgment (ECtHR), 21 June 1988.

[73] *Soering v. the United Kingdom*, appl. 14038/88, PC Judgment (ECtHR), 7 July 1989.

[74] *Vilvarajah and Others v. the United Kingdom*, appls 13163/87, 13164/87, 13165/87, 13447/87, 13448/87, Judgment (ECtHR), 30 Oct. 1991.

[75] *Cruz Varas v. Sweden*, appl. 15576/89, PC Judgment (ECtHR), 20 Mar. 1991.

[76] *Gaygusuz v. Austria*, appl. 17371/90, Judgment (ECtHR), 16 Sept. 1996.

reviews advisory opinion no. 16 on consular assistance, dating from 1999, and advisory opinion no. 18 on the rights of migrant workers, adopted four years later.[77] Chapter 10 reviews the judgment of 2005 in the contentious case of *Yean and Bosico v. the Dominican Republic*,[78] which turned around the refusal by the authorities of the defendant state to register the birth of the victims, thus denying them automatic access to nationality as well as other rights. As in Chapter 5, these 'Inter-American' chapters are approached as an opportunity to demonstrate the comparatively more restrictive approach of the European Court towards migrants' rights. Chapter 9 does this through the examination of substantive norms; Chapter 10, through a discussion of procedural mechanisms, including the conclusion of friendly settlements, the ordering of reparation measures, and the supervision of the execution of judgments.

Part III is entitled 'Prospects'. It is organised along the same lines as the previous parts. Chapter 11 discusses the *Vélez Loor v. Panama*[79] judgment of 2010, in which the Inter-American Court identified a number of stringent guarantees required for the use of immigration detention, which it moreover only allows as a last resort. This is in stark normative contrast to the interpretation given by the European Court as to what states can do in this respect under European Convention law. Chapter 12 continues the story of the post-*Soering* case law which had been started in Chapter 7. It provides a critical appraisal of the remarkable *M.S.S. v. Belgium and Greece*[80] judgment of 2011, which did not hesitate to bring into question in a most decisive way a central piece of the Common European Asylum System put in place by the European Union. *M.S.S.* is selected for review because it is one of the furthest reaching judgments of the Strasbourg 'new' Court in the migration field. Any shortcoming that its examination reveals can therefore be assumed to exist only in starker form in case law which is not immediately as promising for the development of migrants' rights. Chapter 13 was originally conceived as an examination of whether the failures of the anti-discrimination Strasbourg case law highlighted in Chapter 8 might have been remedied through an application of Article 3 ECHR which would accept to deem the treatment of migrants by European states 'inhuman' or 'degrading'. It ended up as a fierce critique of the residence permit refusals Strasbourg case law. Chapter 14 returns to the Inter-American Court where the migration case law has exponentially expanded in the recent past and shows that, so far, the San José Court holds to its chosen course.

Chapter 15 is the concluding chapter for both Part III and the whole book. Amongst other reflections, it considers whether a convergence between the two

[77] *The Right to Information on Consular Assistance in the Framework of the Guarantees of the due Process of Law*, Advisory Opinion OC-16/99 (IACtHR), 1 Oct. 1999; *Juridical Condition and Rights of the Undocumented Migrants*, Advisory Opinion OC-18/03 (IACtHR), 17 Sept. 2003.

[78] *The Girls Yean and Bosico v. the Dominican Republic*, Preliminary Objections, Merits, Reparations and Costs, Judgment (IACtHR), 8 Sept. 2005.

[79] *Vélez Loor v. Panama*, Preliminary Objections, Merits, Reparations and Costs, Judgment (IACtHR), 23 Nov. 2010.

[80] *M.S.S. v. Belgium and Greece*, appl. 30696/09, GC Judgment (ECtHR), 21 Jan. 2011.

courts is likely to take place in the near future. On the one hand, in a general political context in Europe which continues to be hostile to migrants, it is difficult to believe that the emergence of *M.S.S.* and other judgments resolutely favourable to migrants' rights can be taken to signal a determined shift in the Strasbourg mainstream. On the other hand, one would hope that the principles of the *pro-homine* approach are sufficiently well established in the Inter-American case law to prevent the Inter-American Court from suddenly veering towards a position which would be strikingly less protective of migrants' rights. Recent defiance shown by states party to the American Convention towards the Inter-American system has nonetheless led Laurence Burgorgue-Larsen to wonder whether the Court's evolutive jurisprudence will be able to continue at the same rhythm and with the same audacity as in the past.[81] If there were a convergence, one fears that it might not be cause for celebration.

X. The Scope of This Study

The Strasbourg and San José Courts

This book's main aim is to critique the migrant case law of the European Court of Human Rights. Of course, the Strasbourg Court is not the only court which provides supranational rulings on migration matters in Europe. The Luxembourg-based Court of Justice of the European Union, previously called and still informally known as the European Court of Justice, does so too, on the basis of the more market-orientated European Union law. Interestingly, Luxembourg rulings often have something to offer migrants, arguably more so than Strasbourg pronouncements. No doubt many a reader would have been interested in finding in this book a comparison between the case law and reasoning of the two European courts. After much hesitation, such a comparison has been left out because it would have required far more than a short summary of a few key cases of the Luxembourg Court to be persuasive. It therefore had to be considered beyond the scope of this book.[82] The same conclusion was reached regarding the quasi-judicial bodies instituted by United Nations human rights treaties, as well as the European Committee of Social Rights. Although the case law of these multiple bodies is more sparse, their internal logic, limitations, and inconsistencies could not have been understood without further developments.[83]

[81] Burgorgue-Larsen 'Les méthodes' 58.

[82] But see Cathryn Costello, *The Human Rights of Migrants in European Law* (Oxford: Oxford University Press, forthcoming).

[83] This comes out very clearly from Dana Baldinger's nicely executed comparative study on the level of scrutiny which various European and international mechanisms apply to domestic asylum procedures: Baldinger, *Rigorous Scrutiny versus Marginal Review: Standards on Judicial Scrutiny and Evidence in International and European Asylum Law* (2013 doctoral dissertation submitted to Radboud University Nijmegen and printed by Wolf Legal Publishers).

For the same reason, this book neither seeks to tackle the relationship between the European Court of Human Rights and domestic courts nor to explore the effects of Strasbourg judgments in the domestic sphere of states party to the European Convention. Even proceedings which do not deliver a final victory to the individual applicant may positively affect the internal order. For example, no violation of Article 3 ECHR was found by the Strasbourg Court in *Vilvarajah and Others v. the United Kingdom*[84] but the expectation by the British government that it would lose the case nonetheless spurred it on to introduce for the first time a right of appeal in the UK against a determination by the administrative authorities that an asylum claim was to be rejected.[85] Similarly, the Strasbourg rulings which are presented in this book as not forceful enough on points of principle often have had a beneficial effect on the domestic setting because the national authorities receive them as a warning that their way of proceeding has not been found utterly satisfactory by the European Court. The undoubtedly complex interplay between the domestic and the Strasbourg spheres is not the object of this book.

Immigration issues

As has repeatedly been mentioned, this book is concerned with the 'migrant case law' of the European and Inter-American Courts of Human Rights. Etymologically, a migrant is any person who migrates, that is, according to the dictionary of my student days, any person who passes from one place to another, who moves from one place of abode to another, who leaves one's country to settle in another.[86] This covers many persons: the visiting student, the professional globetrotter, the asylum seeker, the 'illegal' and others who are all subject to many distinct and overlapping legal regimes. Moreover, even when a migrant is settled and has become legally incorporated in the host society through the acquisition of the nationality of her new state of residence, she or her children do not necessarily cease to be regarded socially as 'migrants' (including by themselves). A comprehensive study of the migrant case law could have led to exploring an abundance of issues, related to immigration status, cultural identity, and social integration. This book has a more restricted focus.

It is the fate of the most unprivileged migrant, the 'underdog', which I really wanted to examine. However, the case law related to her could not have been understood without also studying the case law of migrants who are in a socially more privileged position. For example, *Vilvarajah and Others*, about the forced removal to Sri Lanka of young Tamil men whose asylum applications were rejected by the British government,[87] cannot be understood outside the context

[84] *Vilvarajah* judgment, para 116.

[85] For the influence of the ECHR on immigration issues in the UK, see: Nicholas Blake and Raza Husain, *Immigration, Asylum and Human Rights* (Oxford: Oxford University Press, 2003); Gina Clayton, *Textbook on Immigration and Asylum Law* (Oxford: Oxford University Press, 5th ed., 2012).

[86] *The Shorter Oxford English Dictionary on Historical Principles* (Oxford: Oxford University Press, 1973) 1322.

[87] *Vilvarajah* judgment, para 11.

of the leading case of *Soering v. the United Kingdom*, in which the applicant was the son of a German diplomat accused of having murdered the parents of his American girlfriend in the United States.[88] As an extradition case, moreover lodged by a European citizen, *Soering* should not have been of prime interest to this research project. However, its foundational status for all subsequent Article 3 ECHR return cases makes it pivotal to this study.

The aim was not to set the boundaries of this study in a technical, legal manner. However, the research developed in such a way that this book has ended up focusing almost exclusively on matters of immigration, by which I mean the permissibility or not of living in another country. Having taken the decision of organising the book in chronological order, I examined a limited number of cases which were to form the core of the book. My aim was then to place each of these cases in a context which could illuminate the default position and controversial character of the developing case law. The result is an immigration focus. This is not to deny that other matters are just as important to migrants' lives, but to acknowledge that they have become peripheral to this book. Accordingly the book, for example, hardly touches upon racism,[89] the construction of identity, or the respect of different cultural practices. It also says nothing about Islam and the difficulty which the European Court has in relating to people who are Muslims.[90] This is not that these issues were not of deep interest to me. Rather, it is that I never got there, so to speak. Allowing the unprivileged migrant to 'be here' is already such a big issue in the European jurisprudence that the question of her treatment once admitted often ends up being relegated to another day by the Court itself.[91]

No intersectional analysis

As noted, migrants do not constitute one simple category. There are many different ways of being a migrant, and one migrant is not the same as another. Above, I said I was particularly interested in examining how the 'underdog' was treated. This vocabulary has class connotations. However, the difficulties associated with the lack of privilege come in many forms. Feminist theorists have demonstrated how one form of oppression tends to intersect with other forms. Being young, old, female or disabled, having a sexual identity which is not mainstream or possessing a nationality that arouses suspicion with the immigration authorities, are all

[88] *Soering* judgment, para 13.

[89] But see: Marie-Bénédicte Dembour, 'Postcolonial Denial: Why the European Court of Human Rights Finds it so Difficult to Acknowledge Racism', in Kamari Clarke and Mark Goodale (eds) *Mirrors of Justice: Law and Power in the Post-Cold War Era* (New York: Cambridge University Press, 2010) 45–66.

[90] But see e.g. Peter G. Danchin 'Islam and the Secular *Nomos* of the European Court of Human Rights' (2011) *Michigan Journal of International Law* 32, 663–747; Carolyn Evans, 'The "Islamic Scarf" in the European Court of Human Rights' (2006) *Melbourne Journal of International Law* 7, 52–73; Eva Brems and Laurens Lavrysen, 'Procedural Justice in Human Rights Adjudication: The European Court of Human Rights' (2013) *Human Rights Quarterly* 35, 176–200 at 187–188.

[91] An example of this could be *Al-Nashif v. Bulgaria*, appl. 50936/99, Judgment (ECtHR), 20 June 2002.

factors which can directly affect how one is being treated in any particular situation. An intersectional analysis of both the circumstances of the cases examined in this book and the response they generated either from the European or the Inter-American Court would be extremely apposite but is not attempted in this book.[92]

XI. The Open Borders Intuition

This book takes issue with the way in which the European Court tends to side with the state rather than with the applicant in migrant cases. A reasoning by the Strasbourg Court which would be more sympathetic to the applicant's position would result in the state having to justify under the European Convention law, more than it does at present, its refusal to admit people, its denial of legal residence status to individuals factually present on its territory, as well as its differential treatment of non-nationals compared to nationals in a number of spheres including, for example, legal access to the labour market. Admittedly, once the necessity of a justification is recognised in relation to a case which from a migrant's perspective would be crying out for one, it should be easier to win the argument that justification is also required in respect of a case which initially does not appear to demand it as strongly. A domino effect towards justification could thus eventually result in having all cases of migrant exclusion by the state appear suspicious. The recommendations contained in this book often would lend themselves to open up such a domino effect if they were adopted. Inevitably, then, this book can be said to advocate a position which veers towards an open borders philosophy.

This philosophy is opposed to the practice of controlling borders which is itself a recent phenomenon in the history of humanity. The control of borders could only be established after the spread of literacy, the creation of population records, and the employment and training of immigration officers by the state, amongst other factors. Historians agree that the attempt by the state at controlling its borders emerged in earnest in the late nineteenth century and that World War I provided an additional impetus for the development of this practice.[93] The second half of the twentieth century saw states multiplying efforts in this direction as they faced major geopolitical transformations, such as decolonisation as well as human movement on an unprecedented scale following the expansion of air travel. About 20 years ago, as border controls were presented as the last bastion of state sovereignty in an increasingly global world, 'managing' migration became the order of the day.

[92] For an excellent article which indirectly sheds light on the promises of such an approach, see Fulvia Staiano, 'Good Mothers, Bad Mothers: Transnational Mothering in the European Court of Human Rights' Case Law' (2103) *European Journal of Migration and Law* 15, 155–182.

[93] John Torpey, *The Invention of the Passport: Surveillance, Citizenship and the State* (Cambridge: Cambridge University Press, 2000).

Constant technological advances and political developments offer states the promise that they will be able to check the status of any individual, not only at their physical borders, but also within the space included in their territory as well as extraterritorially.[94] In practice the state aim of control is never fully realised; so-called 'illegals' keep surfacing.[95] This reality has not deterred states from continuing to pursue their unattainable objective. On the contrary, increasingly more resources are devoted to it. The resulting apparatus is now extremely sophisticated and multilayered. As for the legal and administrative regime, or rather regimes, they never cease to be revised and are of a nightmarish complexity, which even expert lawyers find difficult to master.

Some of us can more or less escape this world, being in the fortunate position of not having to think about border controls beyond the inconveniences of having to go through immigration queues at airports and of applying for occasional visas when travelling abroad. However, the migrant management regime wrecks the lives of others. Through it, human beings are routinely separated from their loved ones, barred the means of realising their life projects, induced to travel in dangerous conditions which can prove fatal, left to languish in immigration detention centres, or driven to lose their pride and sense of identity. The reasons why the migrant management regime condemns part of humanity to such a miserable fate have to do with power, lack of privilege, race, class, religion, and the other divisive factors which assail humanity.

The sense of deep injustice which emanates from migration management as well as the awareness of the acute suffering which it creates for fellow human beings has spurred into being a grass-roots movement for 'open borders'.[96] This movement is not centrally organised, but made of a multitude of local and transnational initiatives. It is brought together by the slogan 'no one is illegal', which itself arises out of the conviction that there is no legitimacy in the official view according to which some people can be refused the recognition that they have the right to be *here*, i.e. to exist where they are or want to be. Underlying the advocacy of the movement for the abolition of the visa regime is a firm commitment to the equality of all human beings.

One day, immigration control may well retrospectively appear to have been one of the greatest abominations of our time. The regime rests upon the attribution of

[94] For a critique of these developments in refugee law, see: Thomas Gammeltoft-Hansen, *Access to Asylum: International Refugee Law and the Globalization of Migration Control* (Cambridge: Cambridge University Press, 2012); Maarten den Heijer, *Europe and Extraterritorial Asylum* (Oxford: Hart, 2013).

[95] Catherine Dauvergne, *Making People Illegal: What Globalization Means for Migration and Law* (Cambridge: Cambridge University Press, 2008).

[96] The voice of this movement was articulated in the pioneering text of: Teresa Hayter, *Open Borders: The Case Against Immigration Controls* (London: Pluto, 1st ed., 2000). See also: Philip Cole, *Philosophies of Exclusion: Liberal Political Theory and Immigration* (Edinburgh: Edinburgh University Press, 2000); Joseph H. Carens, *The Ethics of Immigration* (Oxford: Oxford University Press, 2013); Bridget Anderson, Nandita Sharma, and Cynthia Wright (eds), 'No Borders as Practical Politics' (2009) Special issue of *Refuge* 26(2); Antoine Pécoud and Paul de Guchteneire (eds), *Migration Without Borders: Essays on the Free Movement of People* (UNESCO and Berghahn, 2007).

different nationalities to different people.[97] The problem is that some nationalities have the effect of opening all kinds of physical and metaphorical doors to those who have the good fortune, through the 'birthday lottery',[98] of happening to possess them, while the possession of other nationalities closes these doors, almost automatically, although this is never how the official story puts it. Classifying human beings according to nationalities (to which should also be added 'statelessness') is not a 'natural' phenomenon. It is an entirely social construction which perpetuates inequality on a grand scale and on an ethically spurious basis. As such, immigration control may come to be seen to be on par with the institutions of slavery and the incapacity of women, which were considered to make complete sense and were legally endorsed and organised before they became outlawed. Comparing racial and/or sexual discrimination to difference on grounds of nationality may appear disproportionate to some. It makes sense, however, once the measure of the extreme suffering induced by the migration management order is appreciated.

Having said this, expecting the European Court to reject the border control regime is unrealistic at present. We live in an era where the state is expected to privilege its citizens. Admittedly this principle is not absolute. For example, the European imagination has successfully refused to remain enclosed within it in order to construct the European Union. Still, few would argue that EU law has entirely displaced the Westphalian logic of a polity organised around the figure of sovereign nation-states. In the current political and social context, it would be folly for the European Court suddenly to advocate an open-border philosophy.

However, it should be within the remit of the Strasbourg Court to highlight circumstances where human rights can be understood to require the migrant to be treated with greater humanity—and the state with greater suspicion. The Court can do so little by little, in regard to specific issues which come before it in particular cases. For it to take such steps, one at a time, could do much to fetter the state prerogative of border controls, bringing us closer to the ideal of human equality which is at the root of the human rights concept.

XII. Migrants First, Who Next?

The ethical case for working towards more open borders should be sufficient to move us—and the European Court—into protesting the painful and entirely state-made consequences of the border control logic. But, if not, selfish motivation can also put us on this path.

The great poem 'First They Came', attributed to Pastor Martin Niemöller, was written as an indictment of the intellectual elite of Germany's failure to speak out

97 Pieter Boeles, Maarten den Heijer, Gertie Lodder, and Kees Wouters, *European Migration Law* (Antwerp: Intersentia, 2009) 33.

98 Ayelet Shachar, *The Birthday Lottery: Citizenship and Global Inequality* (Cambridge, Mass.: Harvard University Press, 2009).

against the creeping spread of Nazi persecution of minority groups. Throughout the 1940s, it was regularly re-written, with different groups, including socialists, Jews, incurables, and trade unionists, being added to the list of those subjected to oppression with the quiescence of the intellectual class, so that when 'Then they came for me... there was no one left to speak for me'. Tellingly, Niemöller's poem has recently started to be re-written with the opening line 'First they came for the immigrants'.[99]

Once the state gets away with treating vulnerable migrants in a harsh way, it is legitimate to fear that it will start meting out the same treatment to other people on the margins of our society. Today, it is the migrants from poor and war-torn countries who have come to be presented as the scourge of our societies. If we were to believe what both politicians and the media say about them, immigrants are undeserving, unworthy, filthy, criminal, not to mention perennial abusers of the social security system. However, as neo-liberal policies continue to dominate the political agendas of wealthy democracies, their bite is no longer restricted to the figure of the migrant.[100] We have remained inactive to our peril in the face of the inhumanity with which migrants are treated. It is high time to wake up.

[99] I have come across two examples of this in July 2013 in the UK. The first instance is in the Free Movement blog reviewing how the use of closed materials (i.e. secret proceedings) which was 'piloted' in immigration cases was being introduced in civil proceedings: http://www.freemovement.org.uk/2013/07/01/ellsberg-kissinger-and-the-questionable-value-of-secret-material/, accessed 10 September 2013. The second objects to proposals to get migrants to pay for NHS services: http://www.opendemocracy.net/ournhs/greg-dropkin-karen-reissman/healthcare-in-britain-first-they-came-for-immigrants, accessed 10 September 2013.

[100] Bridget Anderson, *Us and Them: The Dangerous Politics of Immigration Control* (Oxford: Oxford University Press, 2013).

PART I

FOUNDATIONS

INTRODUCTION

This book argues that the European and Inter-American Courts of Human Rights display the tendency of first approaching the migrant either as an alien subject to the control of the state or as a human endowed with inalienable rights. Part I examines four foundational moments in which a crystallisation of these contrasting approaches can be said to have occurred.

Chapter 2 looks at the founding texts of the European and American Conventions. It traces the drafting history of a little discussed provision, Article 16 ECHR, which restricts the rights of migrants, and compares it (by juxtaposition) to Article 22 ACHR, which expands the rights of migrants by specifically guaranteeing due process in expulsion procedures, asylum, and the prohibition of returning migrants to a country where their lives or personal freedom would be endangered. Chapter 2 thus shows that the conventional texts contain the seeds of the fundamental difference between the two systems highlighted in this book. It nonetheless intimates that it is the differences in the conceptions which have engendered these texts—rather than the texts themselves—which have encouraged the development of different attitudes towards the migrant in the two courts.

Chapters 3 and 4 focus on the foundational moments which are represented by two famous early migrant cases of the European system. Involving nationality rules and immigration exclusion in a post-colonial context, the *East African Asians* case saw the European Commission of Human Rights take in the early 1970s an extremely promising ruling,[1] though one which not only remained unconfirmed by the European Court of Human Rights, but which also did not bear in practice the fruits of its apparent interpretative promises. This is reviewed in Chapter 3. *Abdulaziz, Cabales and Balkandali v. the United Kingdom*[2] is the central case reviewed in Chapter 4. It had been brought by 'immigration widows' who were

[1] *East African Asians v. United Kingdom*, appls 4403/70-4419/70, 4422/70, 4423/70, 4434/70, 4443/70, 4476/70-4478/70, 4486/70, 4501/70, 4526/70–4530/70 (joined), Report (EComHR), 14 Dec. 1973.

[2] *Abdulaziz, Cabales and Balkandali v. United Kingdom*, appls 9214/80, 9473/81, 9474/81, GC Judgment (ECtHR), 28 May 1985.

prevented by immigration rules from being joined by their husbands. When the Plenary Court gave judgment on it in 1985, this was the first time the European Court ever ruled upon a migrant case. With the first judgment by this Court dating back to 1961,[3] this can only be described as a late happening, with the delay due to migrants knocking on the doors of Strasbourg in the early days finding that these were virtually closed to them (due to the conceptual mindset highlighted in Chapter 2). Chapter 4 starts to document this reality by reviewing cases which preceded the *ABC* litigation. As mentioned in Chapter 1, the case paved the way for a logical inversion in human rights reasoning which would prove detrimental to the development of the protection of migrants rights at Strasbourg. This of course is alluded to in Chapter 4. However, it is only in Parts II and III that the full impact of the *ABC* decision can be appreciated.

Closing Part I, Chapter 5 turns to the Inter-American Court and presents the first ruling of this Court on a migrant-related issue, namely, naturalisation.[4] The chapter shows how the Inter-American Court was already perceptive to the needs of migrants in the mid-1980s, putting it on a very different course from the one adopted by the European Court.

[3] *Lawless v. Ireland*, appl. 332/57, PC Judgment (ECtHR), 1 July 1961.

[4] Proposed Amendments to the Naturalization Provision of the Constitution of Costa Rica, Advisory Opinion OC-4/84 (IACtHR), 19 Jan. 1984.

2

The Alien in the Social Imagination of the Founding Texts

The first section of the European Convention lists the rights and freedoms which it guarantees. It ends with a provision which rarely receives attention, Article 16 ECHR.[1] Until I embarked on the research of this book, I myself had never really seen it. It reads: 'Nothing in Articles 10, 11 and 14 shall be regarded as preventing the High Contracting Parties from imposing restrictions on the political activities of aliens'. In other words, Article 16 entitles states to restrict the political activities of non-nationals without infringing the provisions of the European Convention which guarantee freedom of expression (Article 10), freedom of association (Article 11), and the prohibition of discrimination (Article 14).

Giving states such leeway can only be based on the idea that 'the alien' is a human being who does not and should not have the same rights as a citizen. From today's perspective, this is odd. Perhaps not surprisingly, then, calls for the abolition of Article 16 have been expressed since the late 1970s.[2] However, and irrespective of the fact that Article 16 has never been relied upon by the European Court of Human Rights to restrict the rights of aliens, the question arises as to why 'the alien clause', as I call it, made sense in 1950. Other international human rights instruments, including the Universal Declaration of Human Rights (UDHR) and the American Convention on Human Rights (ACHR) do not have an equivalent provision. Why did the European Convention go down this route?

This chapter tries to answer this question. In short, the response it gives is that the imposition of restrictions on aliens' activities seems to have been the price to pay for having the protection of the European Convention extended to 'everyone' falling under the jurisdiction of a member state, as proclaimed in Article 1 ECHR.

[1] Karen Reid, *A Practitioner's Guide to the European Convention on Human Rights* (London: Sweet & Maxwell, 2004), does not discuss Article 16 at all. For brief discussions, see D.J. Harris, M. O'Boyle, E.P. Bates, and C.M. Buckley, *Harris, O'Boyle and Warbrick: Law of the European Convention on Human Rights* (Oxford: Oxford University Press, 5th ed., 2010) (Oxford: Oxford University Press, 2009) 647–654; Philip Leach, *Taking a Case to the European Court of Human Rights* (Oxford: Oxford University Press, 2005) 167–168.

[2] Parliamentary Assembly of the Council of Europe (PACE) Recommendation no. 799 (1977), discussed on 17 September 1976 and 25 January 1977. See also PACE Recommendation 1500 (2001) Participation of immigrants and foreign residents in political life in the Council of Europe member states and PACE Recommendation 1940 (2008) State of Democracy in Europe. Measures to improve the democratic participation of migrants, point 4.3.

The faculty for the state to impose such restrictions merely reflected domestic practices which had been put in place in a number of European states since the late nineteenth century. These practices in turn emerged because the alien was socially imagined, either as a figure with potentially subversive political affiliations or as a temporary guest worker with no reason to be involved in the political affairs of his host-state. The result is that, as the debates about the kind of European Convention which should be instituted proceeded in the Council of Europe from 1949 to 1950, the alien clause did not appear to be an oxymoron to the human rights logic. Instead, it seemed to consist in an entirely natural provision. This is confirmed by the fact that the alien clause was hardly debated during the *travaux préparatoires* of the Convention, every participant to these implicitly taking its necessity for granted.

However, it is doubtful that the alien clause was ever needed. In fact, the European Convention provided multiple avenues for restricting the rights of migrants. The clause's redundancy may be confirmed by the fact that the European Court of Human Rights has only referred to it once in the whole of its immense case law.[3] Other regional and international human rights instruments have not opted to have such a clause. One exception is the (Latin) American Declaration of the Rights and Duties of Man of 1948, which has such a clause, though one phrased in terms far less favourable to the state than Article 16 ECHR.

Strikingly both the American Declaration and the legally binding American Convention which followed it in 1969 offer specific safeguards to the alien. Both instruments include provisions on asylum and nationality, with the American Convention additionally assorting expulsion with guarantees. The Universal Declaration also covers this. By contrast, such protective intent is absent from the European Convention, which contains only two references to the alien: Article 16 and Article 5(1)(f), with the latter providing for immigration detention and thus also curtailing rather than expanding the rights of migrants.

It is beyond the scope of this book to seek to identify the origins of these different orientations, which are obviously linked to the respective social and political histories of the two continents. One element which can nonetheless be put forward is that the European Convention was the result of a determination to protect *citizens* against the arbitrariness of the state. Another is that the American Declaration and Convention seem to have partaken in a centuries-long Latin American tradition of seeking to preserve the dignity of human beings against oppression within a framework which goes beyond the nation-state.

The chapters which constitute this book are not short. In order to enable the reader quickly to identify the sections of particular interest to him, I shall explain how every chapter is organised at the end of its introduction. Accordingly, Chapter 2 starts with a review of the history of the elaboration of the European Convention (outside of the context of the alien clause), followed by a section which stresses that the overall aim had been to create a mechanism

[3] *Piermont v. France*, appls 15773/89, 15774/89, Judgment (ECtHR), 27 Apr. 1995.

of international complaint for individuals to use against their own state, thus explaining the Convention's implicit focus on citizens. This general history is followed by a number of sections which reconstitute, from the published *travaux préparatoires* of the Convention, the history of the drafting of the alien clause. It is first shown that the idea of restricting the rights of aliens emerged in response to an Italian amendment which had suggested expanding the personal scope of the Convention, no doubt because Italy as a 'sending country' was concerned about the treatment of its nationals abroad, including during World War II. The Italian suggestion was readily accepted, but on the understanding that the state would be permitted to limit the political activities of aliens. This idea proved uncontroversial, which is not surprising given that such restrictions replicated domestic procedures then in place in a number of European states. When the alien clause was shrunk at a later stage of the *travaux*, this deflation was no more debated than its appearance or inflation had been, probably because states were aware that the Convention would provide mechanisms making it possible to restrict the rights of aliens outside the alien clause. To summarise, the alien clause hardly attracted any debate; once it was stated, it was accepted as a given. The chapter then turns to other instruments, especially (Latin) American ones. It starts with a brief examination of the Universal Declaration of Human Rights which, far from restricting aliens' rights, provided them with special 'international' rights. This innovation is traced to a Latin American influence. The way the American Declaration ensured that migrants would receive protection is noted, as well as the way in which the subsequent, and this time binding, American Convention accentuated this trend. A contrast is then drawn with the European Convention, which opted to offer migrants no special protection. The chapter ends by noting the long-term significance of Article 16 ECHR, despite its virtually nil application. It points to a possibly enduring European attitude of closure and discrimination towards the migrant, at odds with the apparently more open attitude, which seems to pervade the Inter-American system of human rights protection.

I. The Drafting of the ECHR: A History of Political Compromises

In 1945, Europe needed to be reborn from its ashes. There was an acute determination in Western Europe to see institutions set up which would make it impossible for another Hitler to rise by abusing domestic democratic institutions. The fear that a communist regime might take hold in France or Italy also galvanised energies. A 'European Movement' emerged which saw 1,000 politicians and intellectuals gathering in The Hague in May 1948 for a meeting of Congress. In its final resolutions, the Hague Congress advocated the creation of an economic and political European union which would guarantee security, economic independence and social progress; the establishment of a consultative assembly elected by national parliaments; the drafting of a European charter of human rights; and the creation of a court which would be able to enforce its decisions.[4] The movement's International Juridical Section set to prepare texts for a supra-national court immediately after the Congress had ended. The resulting drafts envisaged the creation of a court with the power to interfere in the internal affairs of sovereign states. These drafts were communicated to the Council of Europe as soon as this body was created—from the political will of basically the same people who had participated in the Hague Congress.[5]

To summarise a history which has been recounted in greater detail by others,[6] the Statute of the Council of Europe was signed on 5 May 1949 by ten states.[7] It came into force the following August,[8] after seven ratifications. Two main institutions were established: the Committee of Ministers and the Consultative Assembly. As the representative of state governments, the Committee of Ministers was clearly the lead institution. At its first meeting, it was the established view that the development of international human rights law should be left to the United Nations, where the Universal Declaration of Human Rights had been adopted on 10 December 1948 and where more precise instruments were due to be elaborated. (In the event, the onset of the Cold War delayed the adoption of the International Covenant on Civil and Political Rights and the International Covenant on Economic, Social and Cultural Rights by almost two decades.) The Committee of Ministers of the Council of Europe was determined not to include any item related to human rights on the agenda of the first meeting of the Assembly,[9] which it was its responsibility to draw. The Assembly rebelled, protesting that the Council of Europe had been created precisely to maintain and further realise human rights in Europe; it argued that human rights had to be a core item on its agenda.[10] The Committee of Ministers relented.[11]

The ball was thus returned to the Assembly's court when it held its first session from 10 August to 8 September 1949. The French law professor Pierre-Henri

[4] Bill Bowring, 'The Russian Federation, Protocol No.14 (and 14bis), and the Battle for the Soul of the ECHR' (2010) *Goettingen Journal of International Law* 2, 589–617 at 593.

[5] A.W. Brian Simpson, *Human Rights and the End of Empire: Britain and the Genesis of the European Convention* (Oxford: Oxford University Press, 2001) 649–662.

[6] Ed Bates, *The Evolution of the European Convention on Human Rights: From its Inception to the Creation of a Permanent Court of Human Rights* (Oxford: Oxford University Press, 2010) Chapter 4. For a discussion which places the negotiations in the context of the time, see Simpson *Human Rights*.

[7] The signatories were the five parties to the Brussels Treaty of 17 March 1948, namely, France, the UK, Belgium, the Netherlands, and Luxembourg, as well as Denmark, Ireland, Italy, Norway, and Sweden. In May 1949, Iceland, Greece, and Turkey were admitted as members of the Council of Europe: Emmanuel Decaux, 'Les Etats parties et leurs engagements', in Louis-Edmond Pettiti et al. (eds) *La Convention européenne des droits de l'homme: Commentaire article par article* (Paris: Economica, 1999) 3–25 at 7.

[8] The exact date is 3 August 1949.

[9] The vote was as follows: seven states were against including this point, four were for including it, and one abstained: Council of Europe, *Collected Edition of the 'Travaux Préparatoires' of the European Convention on Human Rights* (The Hague: Martinus Nijhoff, 1979) Vol. I, 12. My references are to the original recording of the discussions. For a concise history, see Decaux 'Les Etats parties'. For a comprehensive and magisterial account from a British perspective, see Simpson *Human Rights*.

[10] *Travaux préparatoires* I, 19.

[11] Simpson *Human Rights* 667.

Teitgen, who had been the chair of the Juridical Section of the European Movement, presented the tone of the session, speaking with the credentials of having been part of the resistance, escaping from the Gestapo and joining the de Gaulle government in London.[12] Teitgen's opening speech to the Assembly on 19 August 're-affirmed' the fact that 'every man... has certain [inalienable] rights'.[13] (The *travaux préparatoires*, in their English version, speak of 'indefensible rights', which is obviously an error of translation attributable to the limited resources which the Council of Europe would have had at its disposal at its inception.[14]) These rights, Teitgen continued, were endangered by the state's 'permanent temptation' to abuse its powers; totalitarian doctrines and practices which had 'poisoned certain sections of public opinion'; as well as economic and social conditions which had led some people 'to renounce their freedom in exchange for a little more bread' instead of insisting that social justice and freedom be made inseparable.[15] Teitgen stressed the urgency of the task facing the Council of Europe. His recommendation was that 'seven, eight or ten fundamental freedoms that are essential for a democratic way of life' were guaranteed.[16] He conceded that the resulting charter would not be perfect, but argued that quick action was better than striving for a comprehensive and general definition of all the rights which should be conferred on Europeans, as this would take years to achieve, by which time disaster might have struck. Teitgen reinforced the idea that one should be 'content with the minimum which we can achieve in a very short period'.[17]

Teitgen became the rapporteur of the Committee on Legal and Administrative Questions of the Consultative Assembly; the British Sir David Maxwell-Fyfe, who had been rapporteur of the European Movement's Juridical Section, was elected its chairman.[18] On 5 September, the Legal Committee presented what came to be known as the Teitgen Report to the Assembly. The report proposed that ten of the rights proclaimed in the Universal Declaration be collectively guaranteed through the establishment of a European Court of Justice and a European Commission for Human Rights. It left these rights undefined, simply referring to the corresponding provisions found in the Universal Declaration. After discussion, the Assembly adopted Teitgen's report on 8 September and forwarded it to the Committee of Ministers in its 38th Recommendation.[19]

The Committee of Ministers rejected this recommendation. It found both the lack of definition of the guaranteed rights and the idea of a strong mechanism of enforcement unacceptable. The way forward, it decided in its second session, two

[12] *Travaux préparatoires* I, 48; Simpson *Human Rights* 656–657. For a short biography of Pierre-Henri Teitgen, a centre-right political figure, see: Mikael Rask Madsen, *La genèse de l'Europe des droits de l'homme. Enjeux juridiques et stratégies d'état (France, Grande-Bretagne et pays scandinaves, 1945-1970)* (Strasbourg: Presses Universitaires de Strasbourg, 2010) 114–115.

[13] *Travaux préparatoires* I, 38–39.

[14] The French original is 'droits imprescriptibles': *Travaux préparatoires* I, 38–39.

[15] *Travaux préparatoires* I, 40–43.

[16] Simpson *Human Rights* 658.

[17] Simpson 44.

[18] Simpson xxvi.

[19] The vote was as follows: 64 for, 1 against, and 24 abstentions. For a summary of the Convention proposed in the Teitgen Report, Simpson 675–680; for the debate it attracted in the Assembly, Simpson 680–682.

months after having received the recommendation, was to convene a committee of governmental experts which would examine anew the question of a human rights charter. Understanding this move as a way to shelve the project forever, the Assembly expressed its disappointment, but to no avail.[20] Twelve governments each sent a delegate to participate in the sessions of the Committee of Experts.[21]

This Committee met on two occasions: for one week in February 1950 and for another week the following month. Its first meeting was devoted to examining the Assembly's project;[22] and its second meeting was to review a proposal which had been submitted by the British government in the form of an *aide-mémoire* consisting of 15 articles.[23] From the start, the UK's representative at the Committee of Ministers had made it clear that the British government did not think that the Assembly's project constituted an adequate basis on which to draft a convention. His government thus presented an alternative project on 18 February 1950.

At the end of its examination of the two proposals, the Committee of Experts was unable to recommend whether the rights to be protected should merely be enumerated (as the Assembly had suggested) or defined in detail (as the British were proposing). The Committee also felt that the question of whether a court should be established was political in nature; it was not in favour of a body constituted of experts like itself to decide. Its final report to the Committee of Ministers contained a number of alternative texts,[24] with what came to be known as Alternative A mostly (but not wholly) corresponding to the Assembly's proposal, and Alternative B corresponding to the British proposal.

On receiving the report from the Committee of Experts, the Committee of Ministers decided that the way to proceed was now to convene a Conference of Senior Officials with instructions from their governments, so that the Conference would be able to vote and to take the political decisions which the Committee of Experts had been unable to take. The Conference of Senior Officials met for ten days in June 1950, at the end of which it presented the Committee of Ministers with one single text reflecting the (shifting) majority of views expressed on each issue. By then, it was clear that the jurisdiction of the Court to be established would have to be optional for each state party to the Convention. The question of whether individuals would be able to bring complaints against states alleging violations of the Convention remained undecided. This was to be resolved by the ministers themselves.[25]

At this stage, the project returned to the Assembly. Its Legal Committee examined it for two days in June 1950 and the Assembly proposed a series of amendments. These were mostly rejected by the Committee of Ministers, which adopted on 7 August what the Assembly regarded as a watered-down project, mostly based on Alternative B and thus highly influenced by the initial British proposal. Two

[20] Decaux 'Les Etats parties' 11.

[21] Belgium, Denmark, France, Greece, Ireland, Italy, Luxembourg, Norway, the Netherlands, the UK, Sweden, and Turkey sent an expert. For their names, see: *Travaux préparatoires* III, 250–253.

[22] On this meeting, see: Simpson *Human Rights* 690–695.

[23] Simpson 695.

[24] *Travaux préparatoires* I, xxvi.

[25] *Travaux préparatoires* I, xxvi.

weeks later, the Assembly, resigned to the fact that a more ambitious text would not see the day, followed suit and also adopted this project. It proposed some amendments (including in respect of the 'colonial clause' examined in detail in Chapter 3 of this book). The Committee of Ministers accepted only trivial changes to the text agreed in early August. As a political gesture, it nonetheless conceded to the Assembly the task of drawing up the Preamble. It also endorsed the idea of negotiating a Protocol over the rights of property and the right to education, the phraseology of which had proved impossible to agree. The European Convention on Human Rights and Fundamental Freedoms was formally signed by a dozen government ministers on 4 November 1950 in Rome.[26] It is commonly known as the European Convention on Human Rights.

II. The Citizen-Centred Focus of the Post-1945 Human Rights Regime

Never before had individuals been permitted to access a mechanism whereby they could complain before an international institution about the treatment states meted out. Andrew Moravcsik has asked what led a number of European states to agree to devise a system of human rights protection the outcome of which was 'to constrain [their] domestic sovereignty in . . . an unprecedentedly invasive . . . manner.'[27] How had the great powers managed to sway smaller states into accepting a limitation to their national sovereignty? Was the human rights idea now so morally persuasive that states wanted to see it embodied in law? Moravczik concludes that the empirical evidence supports neither the first (realist) nor the second (idealist) hypothesis. His study of the negotiations which took place over 1949 and 1950 demonstrates that the member states were divided: Austria, France, Germany, and Italy supported the creation of a court with mandatory jurisdiction and wanted clear, well-defined, justiciable rights; Denmark, the Netherlands, Sweden, and especially the UK were sceptical of these plans; and the remaining states were undecided.[28] The deadlock was avoided by making optional first the jurisdiction of the court and then the right of individual petition.[29]

Moravcsik's analysis stresses that it was the governments of newly established democracies which actively propounded reciprocally binding human rights obligations, which were by contrast consistently opposed by established democracies.[30] His argument is that the European Convention resulted from 'an instrumental calculation' on the part of the (re)-emerging democracies, intent on consolidating their nascent or re-emerging democratic institutions and locking themselves

[26] Belgium, Denmark, France, Iceland, Ireland, Italy, Luxembourg, the Netherlands, Norway, Turkey, the UK, and West Germany. For constitutional reasons, Greece and Sweden could not sign at that time but did so shortly afterwards. Simpson *Human Rights* 753.

[27] Andrew Moravcsik, 'The Origins of Human Rights Regimes: Democratic Delegation in Postwar Europe' (2000) *International Organization* 54(2), 217–252 at 219.

[28] Moravcsik 231, note 47. [29] Moravcsik 242. [30] Moravcsik 225.

into democratic governance against future opponents.[31] His conclusion is that the Convention arose from these states' self-interest; it had nothing to do with 'a conversion to moral altruism'.[32]

For our present purposes, this analysis indicates that the European Convention came into being in order to ensure liberty 'for us', citizens of states which had gone astray during World War II (and which it was feared might go astray again if communism took hold).[33] Up to this point, a state's treatment of its own citizens had been considered its own business and no one else's under international law.[34] The emerging human rights regime eroded the sacrosanct principle of state sovereignty. This is true not only of the European Convention, but also of the Universal Declaration, as is well encapsulated by the reply which René Cassin, the French delegate to the United Nations' Human Rights Commission which was then working on elaborating the Universal Declaration, gave his USSR counterpart:

> The right of interference is here... Why? Because we do not want a repetition of what happened in 1933, where Germany began to massacre its own nationals, and everybody... bowed, saying 'Thou art sovereign and master in thine own house'.[35]

Although aliens were not necessarily excluded from the nascent human rights scheme, they were not its primary consideration. Citizens were.

III. Broadening the Personal Scope of the European Convention: An Italian Initiative

The draft European Convention prepared by Teitgen proposed in its Article 2 that the member states were to undertake to ensure to 'all persons residing within their territories' ten rights considered essential for democracy.[36] During the Committee of Experts' first meeting in February 1950, the Italian delegate expressed some dissatisfaction with this phrasing and proposed to substitute the words 'living in' for 'residing within'.[37] The response his proposal attracted makes clear that his aim was 'to widen as far as possible the categories of persons who are to benefit by the guarantee contained in the Convention'.[38]

For the Italian government to have called for the broadening of the personal scope of the Convention makes sense. Italy was then the European 'sending

[31] Moravcsik 248–249. [32] Moravcsik 248.

[33] As Ed Bates' account makes clear, the Convention was therefore best conceived as a safety net for when things were going wrong rather than a project to aim higher than what had been achieved so far: Bates, 'The Birth of the European Convention on Human Rights—and the European Court of Human Rights', in Jonas Christoffersen and Mikael Rask Madsen (eds) *The European Court of Human Rights between Law and Politics* (Oxford: Oxford University Press, 2011) 17–42 at 41; Bates *The Evolution* 372.

[34] Mary Ann Glendon, *A World Made New: Eleanor Roosevelt and the Universal Declaration of Human Rights* (New York: Random House, 2002) xvi, 9, 60, and 235. Glendon refers to the Universal Declaration of Human Rights but her point applies also to the European Convention.

[35] Cited in Glendon at 60. [36] *Travaux préparatoires* II, 276.

[37] *Travaux préparatoires* III, 200. [38] *Travaux préparatoires* III, 200.

country' par excellence. Having started to keep official statistics in 1876, in the ensuing century some 26 million Italians left the country.[39] Although many returned, this record gives Italy 'the dubious honour of having registered a larger number of emigrants than any other country' in the relevant period.[40] The majority (13.5 million) went to other European countries.[41] In particular, the French census included 250,000 Italians in 1881 and 800,000 in 1931, making them by far the largest foreign community in France in the inter-war period.[42]

Now, up to the nineteenth century, the distinction between the national and the alien had been mostly irrelevant.[43] It did not matter socially, and it was not an important issue for either the legislator or the administration. As the historian Frank Caestecker explains, 'State administration was not very dense, political rights were for the happy few, and social rights were scarce'.[44] In such a context, there was 'no need for a clear delineation [between nationals and non-nationals] as the majority of the population had no direct relationship with the central state whatsoever'.[45] This began to change in the late nineteenth century and early twentieth century. Many European countries started to adopt nationality legislation, to affirm their alien policy, to feel threatened by political exiles, and to turn away 'undesirable' aliens. World War I accentuated this trend. By the time the inter-war period came, the 'subversive alien' had become a figure of paramount concern.[46]

In Belgium, for example:

> [At] every Council of Ministers meeting, a number of subversive aliens who had acquired residency status were ordered expelled. Legislative action to enlarge the amount of leeway the authorities had in dealing with these undesirable political actors was strongly urged and in the field of nationality law this even made it possible to revoke the Belgian nationality of subversive Belgians of foreign origin.[47]

A 'radical alien policy' was developed which 'introduced overtly discriminatory rules directed against aliens residing in the country and implied a roll-back of their civil and social status. [Immigrants] became a category with an inferior legal status, and due to changes in nationality legislation, it became more difficult for them to escape this condition.'[48]

[39] Rudolph J. Vucoli, 'The Italian Diaspora, 1876–1976', in Robin Cohen (ed.) *The Cambridge Survey of World Migration* (Cambridge: Cambridge University Press, 1995) 114–122 at 114.

[40] Vucoli 114.

[41] 5.5 million went to the United States and 5 million to Latin America: Vucoli 114.

[42] Gérard Noiriel, 'Italians and Poles in France, 1880–1945', in Cohen *Cambridge Survey* 142–147 at 142.

[43] Mary Dewhurst Lewis, *The Boundaries of the Republic: Migrant Rights and the Limits of Universalism in France, 1918–1940* (Stanford: Stanford University Press, 2007) 155.

[44] Frank Caestecker, *Alien Policy in Belgium, 1840–1940: The Creation of Guest Workers, Refugees and Illegal Aliens* (Oxford: Berghahn, 2000) 17. Caestecker is speaking here of Belgium, but his account can be extended to Belgium's neighbours. Note, however, that the consolidation of the concept of the national already started to happen in the nineteenth century in Germany: Caestecker 260–271.

[45] Caestecker 17.

[46] Caestecker 261.

[47] Caestecker 261; see also 268.

[48] Caestecker 269.

Although written in respect of Belgium, these words capture the general trend of what was happening in continental Western Europe.[49] Numerically significant guest-worker schemes had been developed in France, Germany, Belgium, and the Netherlands in the inter-war period. The stay of—mostly male and single—guest workers was supposed to be temporary, lasting no longer than the time for which their labour was needed. These men were not supposed to have an existence beyond work.[50] Their presence was justified exclusively by reference to their labour; granting them rights in the political sphere would have been considered an oxymoron. This was the more so given the fear of anarchism and communism. It appeared logical not to grant immigrants the same rights as nationals.

In France, for example, political rights were strictly and exclusively reserved for French citizens.[51] This principle targeted the right to vote and/or to be elected not only for governmental and administrative posts, but also in the corporate and cooperative world. Residents of hostels for immigrants could not form associations to defend their interests, in contrast to 'co-tenants'—a status inaccessible to supposedly transient migrants.[52] Only French citizens could lead trade unions. Foreign publications were subject to a regulatory regime, which ensured that they could easily be prohibited from circulation in the country, under penal sanction.[53] Non-nationals were also prevented from accessing the professions in fields such as law, medicine, midwifery, architecture, and accountancy.[54] This type of regime was not exclusive to France.[55]

[49] Caestecker 257–287.

[50] The model was entrenched. In the late 1970s, the great sociologist Abdelmalek Sayad, who has done so much to document and to analyse the phenomenon of immigration in France (by then predominantly from Algeria), made immigrants' reduction to their labour by government and society the central theme of his studies, highlighting both the dehumanising and depoliticising effects of such a policy and worldview. See Sayad, *L'immigration ou les paradoxes de l'altérité* (Brussels: De Boeck-Wesmael, 1991).

[51] Serge Slama, 'Droits et libertés des étrangers: Les paradoxes d'une évolution récente' (2009) *Pouvoirs* no. 130, text with notes 5 and 6; Richard Plender, 'Introductory Report' in Council of Europe (ed.) *Human Rights of Aliens in Europe: Proceedings of the Colloquy on '"Human Rights in Europe'* (Dordrecht: Martinus Nijhoff, 1985) 33–63 at 50; Jacques Maily, untitled, in Slama 171–174 at 174. For a rich and complex account of the guest worker regime in France, see: Lewis *Boundaries*.

[52] Sayad *L'immigration* 88.

[53] Slama *Droits et libertés des étrangers* text with notes 6 to 13.

[54] Slama text with note 24.

[55] See e.g. Ergun Özsunay, 'The Participation of the Alien in Public Affairs (Political and Associative Life)', in Council of Europe (ed.) *Human Rights of Aliens* 197–254. In Germany, the difference in treatment is embedded in the constitution. The Constitution of Weimar of 1919 listed a number of rights that 'all Germans' had. See its Articles 109 (equality in front of the law), 111 (freedom to move and settle down), 112 (emigration), 118 (freedom of expression including in print and images), 123 (assembly), 124 (clubs and societies), and 126 (petitions and grievances to Parliament). There remain a number of fundamental rights reserved to Germans in the current German Constitution: freedom of assembly (Article 8), freedom of association (Article 9), freedom of movement (Article 11), occupational freedom (Article 12), and the right to citizenship and prohibition of extradition (Article 16). This can be said to be in line with the ECHR and international law. An English translation of these two constitutions is available respectively at: http://www.zum.de/psm/weimar/weimar_vve.php and http://www.gesetze-im-internet.de/englisch_gg/index.html, accessed 19 May 2014.

With so many Italians emigrating, the Italian government undertook a number of initiatives designed to protect its nationals abroad, for example by striving to negotiate and to check the working and living conditions of guest workers.[56] This did not have much effect, even if it may occasionally have provided a buffer.[57] For example, when Belgium expelled the foreign members of the Belgian Communist Party in 1929, Italians were spared.[58] Still, Italy was in no position to insist in 1950 that its nationals be treated in host countries on an equal footing with home nationals.[59] As the terms of the Convention were being debated at the Council of Europe, Italy would have been acutely aware of the benefit there would be to spell out that the protection bestowed by the Convention was not to be restricted to citizens of member states. This, then, is part of the context in which to explain the emergence of the Italian amendment to broaden the scope of the European Convention. Another important element of this context must be the policy of internment of 'enemy aliens' which had been pursued in World War I and again in World War II.

IV. The Memory of the Internment of 'Enemy Aliens'

When Italy entered the war in June 1940, Italians found themselves incarcerated in a number of countries which were fighting on the side of the Allies. For example, following immediate instructions to the British police to detain 'all male Italians aged 16–70 with less than 20 years' residence in Britain as well as those Italians, male or female, on MI5's suspect list', about 4,000 Italians were interned in the UK—alongside 22,000 Germans and Austrians.[60] Their conditions of detention were deplorable, with the worst camp described as 'a rat-infested disused factory with a broken glass roof' equipped with 18 water taps to supply 2,000 internees and 60 buckets for toilets.[61]

The arguments for internment quickly started to look 'more like military panic than military strategy'.[62] The idea that all 'enemy aliens' were potentially dangerous was contradicted by the fact that most internees were refugees from the Nazi regime. A second argument, according to which it was worth interning thousands of innocent people if it meant catching some enemy agents, however few, soon appeared untenable in view of the appalling conditions endured by many internees. On 2 July 1940, the *Arandora Star*—a ship carrying 1,500 deportees from the UK to Canada as part of a policy designed at dissipating

[56] Caestecker *Alien Policy* 63.

[57] For an understanding of how alien policies provide ample discretion and constant opportunities for discriminating between aliens, see: Lewis *Boundaries*.

[58] Lewis 115.

[59] The very principle which, not much later, would be at the core of the market-orientated European Communities.

[60] Neil Stammers, *Civil Liberties in Britain during the 2nd World War: A Political Study* (London: Croom Helm, 1983) 39.

[61] Stammers 43. [62] Stammers 41.

the perceived danger of having too many aliens staying in the country—was sunk in the Atlantic. Responses to questions raised in Parliament revealed that many deportees on the ship had in fact opposed the Nazis and Italian fascists.[63] In the following weeks and months it became easier for internees to apply for release on the grounds that the policy on internment had been mistakenly applied to them. Nearly 60 per cent of the summer's 27,000 internees were nonetheless still in detention in February 1941.[64] In November 1941, 3,695 enemy aliens remained interned in Britain, with another 5,000 interned in the Dominions.[65]

A number of Italians and Germans were also interned in the Belgian Congo. Pierre Ryckmans, the colony's Governor General, had responded to de Gaulle's call from London in June 1940 and thus followed the instructions coming from the Belgian government in exile (rather than those from the government in place in occupied Belgium). A relatively relaxed policy of internment of 'enemy aliens' ensued.[66] This policy was also pursued elsewhere, including in respect of Japanese nationals in the United States and Canada.[67] The internment of 'enemy aliens' is not regarded as the Allies' finest moment during the war, but it shows how discriminating against aliens could appear as an entirely legitimate course of action, at least initially.

V. The Appearance of the Alien Clause in European Debates

Why it took an Italian representative to suggest broadening the reach of the Convention now makes sense. In turn, it is the Italian amendment which provoked an alien clause to emerge. It is worth examining in detail the exact phrasings which were proposed for this clause, as shown in Table 2.1.

Initially there had been no thought of including such a clause in the European Convention. The Assembly's original project was to 'borrow' some rights considered essential for democracy from the Universal Declaration and to have them enforced by a European court; there was nothing resembling Article 16 ECHR in the Universal Declaration and the Assembly's project did not include any proposition foreshadowing it. Likewise the British had not thought of inserting an alien clause in the 15-article project it submitted to the Committee of Ministers. The idea clearly surfaced in reaction to the Italian amendment.

63 Stammers 46–47. 64 Stammers 55. 65 Stammers 56.

66 Jacques Vanderlinden, *Pierre Ryckmans 1891–1959. Coloniser dans l'honneur* (Brussels: De Boeck-Wesmael, 1994) 425–426.

67 On the US, see e.g. Mae M. Ngai, *Impossible Subjects: Illegal Aliens and the Making of Modern America* (Princeton: Princeton University Press, 2004) Chapter 5; Wendy Ng, *Japanese American Internment during World War II: A History and Reference Guide* (Westport: Greenwood Press, 2002). On Canada, see: Michael Marmen, 'Mémoire: L'application de la Loi sur les mesures de guerre, en 1914 et 1939, et ses répercussions sociales et juridiques au Canada', manuscript dated 16 March 2007, University of Moncton.

Table 2.1 The Drafting History of the Alien Clause in the ECHR

Body	Date of meeting	Alien clause
Committee of Ministers (First Session)	9 August 1949	N/A (draft agenda of Assembly)
Consultative Assembly (First Session)	10 August–8 September 1949	The clause is not considered.
Committee of Ministers (Second Session)	5 November 1949	N/A (decides to convene a committee of experts)
Committee of Experts (First meeting)	2–8 February 1950	The clause appears after an Italian amendment broadening the protection of the Convention to all those 'living in' member states
Committee of Experts (Second meeting)	6–10 March 1950	The clause appears in Alternative A ('Each State shall be competent to establish the particular rules...') and Alternative B ('Nothing in Articles 11 and 12 shall be regarded as...')
Committee of Ministers (Third Session)	30 March–1 April 1950	N/A (decides to convene a Conference of Senior Officials)
Committee of Ministers (Fourth Session)	3 June 1950	N/A (decides that the Consultative Assembly's Committee on Legal and Administrative Questions will be able to discuss resolutions passed by the Conference of Senior Officials)
Conference of Senior Officials	8–17 June 1950	The clause is not discussed (though reference to discrimination provision is added in final report)
Consultative Assembly's Committee on Legal and Administrative Questions meeting	23–24 June 1950	The clause is not discussed
Committee of Ministers (Fifth Session)	3–9 August 1950	The text of the Convention, including Article 16, is agreed on 7 August
Consultative Assembly (Second Session)	7–28 August 1950	Article 16 is not discussed as the report of the Committee of Ministers is debated on 24–25 August
Committee of Ministers	3–4 November 1950	Final amendments brought to the text of the Convention on 3 November do not concern Article 16. The Convention is signed the next day in the Barberini Palace, Rome

A Sub-Committee of the Committee of Experts was charged to examine the amendments, including that submitted by Italy on 4 February 1950. The next day, it reported as follows:

> Since [the aim of the Italian amendment] is to widen as far as possible the categories of persons who are to benefit by the guarantee contained in the Convention, and since the words 'living in' might give rise to a certain ambiguity, the Sub-Committee proposes that the Committee should adopt the text contained in the draft Covenant of the United Nations Commission: that is, to replace the words 'residing within' by 'within its jurisdiction'.[68]
>
> It is realized that since certain of the rights enumerated under Article 2 cannot be guaranteed to aliens without any restrictions, particularly the rights contained in paragraphs 6 [freedom of opinion and cxpression], 7 [freedom of assembly], 8 [freedom of association] and 9 [freedom to unite in trade unions], a reference to these restrictions should be inserted in the text of [the general and limitation provisions of what was then, in that draft] Articles 5 and 6.[69]

This new proposition by the Sub-Committee replicated the domestic curtailment of the political rights of aliens in a number of countries and must have appeared entirely convincing to the Committee of Experts, as it did not comment on it.

On 15 February 1950, the Committee of Experts submitted to the Committee of Ministers an intermediary report with a Convention text drafted on the basis of the Assembly's project (Alternative A). In this version, the alien clause was broader than the formulation put on the table ten days earlier. Without any explanation being provided, it read:

> Each State shall be competent to establish the particular rules applicable within its territory for the ensurement [*sic*] and exercise of the rights enumerated in Article 2, paragraphs 3 [prohibiting arbitrary detention and providing for a fair trial], 6, 7, 8 and 9 by persons who are not its nationals, subject to the [general principles of law recognised by civilised nations].[70]

The possibility for states to restrict the rights of aliens was thus extended to two areas: detention and fair trial. Presumably these additions were spurred on the one hand by the memories of having interned enemy aliens during the two world wars and by the realisation that the long peace-time practice of detaining foreigners administratively for short periods and without recourse to due process, for

[68] This proposition was accepted, with Article 1 ECHR providing in its final version: 'The High Contracting Parties shall secure to everyone within their jurisdiction the rights and freedoms defined in Section 1 of this Convention'. This phrasing has lent itself to a much broader interpretation than could ever have been imagined by the fathers of the Convention. The question of the conventional responsibility of member states for acts conducted during military operations abroad has notably been hotly debated in the last decade.

[69] *Travaux préparatoires* III, 200.

[70] *Travaux préparatoires* III, 238. In this particular draft, this provision was numbered Article 7 c). It is worth noting for the benefit of any reader who is interested in examining the various drafts closely that the reference to 'Article 3, paragraph 2' recorded in the formulation proposed on 7 February must be a typographical mistake: *Travaux préparatoires* III, 224. Article 2 had become Article 3 in the text of 7 February. Its paragraph 2 then referred to the prohibition of slavery. Surely it was paragraph 3, related to detention and fair trial, which should have been mentioned.

example in view of their expulsion, might otherwise be under threat. On the positive side, the final words of the new proposal were obviously designed to rein in the potential arbitrariness with which states might use the alien clause.[71]

At the end of its February meeting, the Committee of Experts commented that the aim of the alien clause was 'to make provision for the fact that, in accordance with a universally admitted practice, the exercise of the fundamental rights by foreigners (non-nationals) may be subject to certain restrictions not applicable to nationals'.[72] This is an implicit reference to the national legislative framework reviewed above which restricted the political activities of aliens and condoned their summary detention and expulsion. Such practices may not have been very old, but they were already entrenched and taken for granted.

VI. A Largely Redundant Alien Clause Open to Reduction

The Committee of Experts met in March 1950 to discuss the British Convention project. During this meeting, the Swedish expert proposed a text for the alien cause which clearly inspired the eventual Article 16 ECHR. His proposal read:

> Nothing in Articles 11 [freedom of expression] and 12 [freedom of assembly] shall be regarded as preventing any State party to this convention from imposing such restrictions as may be necessary to prohibit persons who are not nationals of that State from engaging in political activities.[73]

Compared to the version presented on 15 February, the Swedish text abandoned the idea of allowing restrictions in the areas of freedom of association and freedom to unite in trade unions, arbitrary detention, and guarantees of fair trial. Again no explanation for the new phrasing is recorded. In the report at the end of this meeting, the Committee simply records that the alien clause 'required no comment'.[74]

The shrinking of the clause to just two areas may at first sight appear puzzling. On further analysis, it is not. The removal of the reference to rights of association and participation in trade unions is easily comprehensible. Not only does it relate to two rights which were not explicitly foreseen in the Convention but also these rights would in any event have been understood to be subsumed under the rights to freedoms of expression and assembly which remained open to restriction in the Swedish version.

[71] This in itself was an innovation: until the rise of the human rights regime, the treatment of an alien by a state was considered an international rather than a domestic matter in the sense that the alien had no right whatsoever against his host state; instead, any wrong he suffered was conceived to be a wrong against his state of nationality, with the latter free to choose to act upon this grievance. See Richard B. Lillich, *The Human Rights of Aliens in Contemporary International Law* (Manchester: Manchester University Press, 1984) 1–2 and Chapter 1.

[72] *Travaux préparatoires* III, 266. [73] *Travaux préparatoires* III, 308.

[74] 'Preparatory work on Article 16 of the European Convention on Human Rights', information document prepared by the Registry of the European Court of Human Rights dated 25 May 1967 and now accessible on the website of the Court's library at http://echr.coe.int/Documents/Library_TravPrep_Table_ENG.pdf, accessed 18 June 2014, p. 7.

The removal of the reference to detention is more intriguing. Admittedly, for the Convention to have allowed '*arbitrary* detention' to take place might have been thought to defeat the very purpose of establishing a human rights regime. However, this difficulty could easily have been avoided by a slight change of vocabulary, namely, referring to '*administrative* detention'. In all likelihood dropping the reference to detention seemed unproblematic because mentioning it in the alien clause appeared redundant. On the one hand, regarding the internment of enemy aliens in times of war, a state would still be able to reinstate such a policy without violating the Convention by making a derogation, as provided by what became Article 15 ECHR. On the other hand, regarding peace time, the provision which would eventually become Article 5(1)(f) was being prepared, making the reference to detention in the alien clause redundant.[75]

The third removal—concerning fair trial—can be explained in a similar way. What became Article 6 ECHR provides for fair trial guarantees only in respect of the determination of civil rights and obligations and criminal charges, to the exclusion of the adjudication of administrative matters, including immigration issues. In other words, there was no need for fair-trial guarantees to be mentioned in Article 16 for states to be able not to grant fair trial guarantees in immigration matters.[76]

VII. The Discriminatory Alien Clause Enters the European Convention Uncontested

States are largely empowered to restrict the rights of aliens under the Convention without requiring them to resort to Article 16 for this to be possible. Given this, what is surprising is that an alien clause was thought to be necessary at all. The second paragraphs of Articles 10 and 11 (plus, of course, Article 15) give states ample scope to restrict the political activities of aliens as they deem fit. However, no one thought to argue against the clause's inclusion in the European Convention during the *travaux préparatoires*.

Indeed, after the Swedish intervention, there is only one additional reference to the alien clause in the whole of the *travaux*. This occurred as the Luxembourg delegate took position during the Conference of Senior Officials in June 1950 on the highly controversial questions of the establishment of an international court and its possible competence to examine petitions originating from individuals. He declared himself in favour of the right of individual petition provided the proposal for an alien clause found its way into the Convention.[77] After this, the *travaux*

[75] This will become clear in Chapter 11.

[76] On this, see Chapter 7 which discusses the leading case of *Maaouia v. France*, appl. 39652/98, GC Judgment (ECtHR), 5 Oct. 2000.

[77] The minutes of the sitting of 10 June 1950 of the Conference of Senior Officials report that: 'Mr. Majerus (Luxembourg) declares himself in favour of [the right of individual petition to the European Commission of Human Rights]. He, however, gives his approval to it, provided that Article 7, para. 3 of the draft [which will become Article 16], which makes a distinction between nationals and aliens, is to be maintained'. The text in French is more elegant and must have been the

préparatoires do not mention the clause again. Even the most progressive elements of the Consultative Assembly failed to comment upon the clause which, in its final adopted version, provides that restrictions to the political activities of aliens are not considered to be an infringement of the freedom of expression (Article 10), freedom of association (Article 11), and the guarantee of non-discrimination (Article 14).

The late addition of a reference to Article 14 is interesting as it indicates that it was understood that the alien clause could be seen to discriminate against aliens. As we shall discuss in more detail in Chapter 8, liberal thought has forever been hovering between the perceived need to treat nationals and non-nationals differently, in order to be seen to protect the polity envisaged as a somewhat closed group, and the ethical call to treat every human equally. The elaboration of the alien clause can be seen as the European Convention's initial attempt to resolve this inescapable tension within liberalism.

That the clause was adopted without any contestation whatsoever suggests that its inclusion was considered essential as soon as it was mentioned. This perspective is supported by the way in which the Registry of the European Court of Human Rights introduced the *travaux préparatoires* related to Article 16 ECHR, in its 1967 collation related to each provision of the Convention.[78] To quote the Registry:

> The Consultative Assembly appears to have *overlooked the problem* that can be raised by the political activity of aliens, on the territory of Contracting States. Recommendation no 38 of 8th September 1949, in particular, does not contain any provision foreshadowing Article 16. This is also true of the texts by which the Assembly was largely influenced in its early proceedings, namely the Universal Declaration of Human Rights of 10th December 1948 and the drafts of the European Movement (May 1948, February 1949 and July 1949).[79]

The Registry thus presented the inscription of the possibility for states to restrict aliens' political rights in the ECHR as a welcome step which responded to a necessity. In its view, the failure by other international human rights instruments to have done so could only have been the result of a regrettable oversight. One can question, however, whether the inclusion of the alien clause in the European Convention demonstrated foresight. On the basis of both subsequent European experience (including the lack of case law on Article 16) and the operation of other systems, the alien clause rather seems to have merely expressed prejudice against the figure of the migrant.

original: 'M. Majerus (Luxembourg) se déclare en faveur du droit individual. Toutefois, il y donne son adhésion sous réserve du maintien de l'article 7 para 3 du projet qui porte une distinction entre les nationaux et les étrangers'.

[78] The resulting text is available on the website of the European Court of Human Rights. See http://echr.coe.int/Pages/home.aspx?p=library/collections#n13699176741940206875943, accessed 8 January 2014.

[79] *Travaux préparatoires* information document prepared by the Registry, CDH (67) 4, 1, emphasis added. This document was originally confidential, but it is now available on the European

VIII. The Entry of Special Migrant Rights in the Universal Declaration

The Registry of the European Court did not hesitate to suggest that the Universal Declaration of Human Rights had failed to restrict the rights of aliens by oversight. This seems unlikely, however. By the time the Universal Declaration was proclaimed by the General Assembly of the United Nations in December 1948, there already existed a model for such a clause in a human rights international document. This was in the American Declaration of the Rights and Duties of Man, also known as the Bogota Declaration, which had been adopted in April 1948 by the Organization of American States (OAS). The Declaration's final clause, Article XXXVIII, reads: 'It is the duty of every person to refrain from taking part in political activities that, according to law, are reserved exclusively to the citizens of the state in which they are an alien'. This antecedent has admittedly less impact on migrant rights than Article 16 ECHR. Its very existence nonetheless makes it difficult to rule out that the possibility of having an alien clause never crossed the mind of the drafters of the Universal Declaration. It appears more reasonable to speculate that those who would have been aware of Article XXXVIII ADHR found the inclusion of a parallel clause in the Universal Declaration either unnecessary or inappropriate.

This scenario seems even more persuasive in the light of the fact that the Universal Declaration positively opted for guaranteeing a set of rights which were of direct benefit to migrants.[80] Article 13 UDHR provides that 'Everyone has the right to leave any country, including his own, and to return to his country'; Article 14 that 'Everyone has the right to seek and to enjoy in other countries asylum from persecution'; and Article 15 that 'Everyone has the right to a nationality' and that 'No one shall be arbitrarily deprived of his nationality nor denied the right to change his nationality'.

Johannes Morsink has painstakingly traced the 'internal' drafting history of the provisions of the Universal Declaration.[81] He observes that these three rights were exceptional in that they had not found their inspiration in member states' existing domestic constitutions—which were left out because their implementation involved more than one nation.[82] Morsink calls them 'special international rights'. For the purpose of this book, I shall call them 'special migrant rights', even though this is not entirely satisfactory: the inspiration for these rights were rooted in the circumstances around the victims of the Holocaust who perished after having been stripped of their nationality

Court's website: http://www.echr.coe.int/LibraryDocs/Travaux/ECHRTravaux-ART16-CDH(67)4-BIL1338903.pdf, accessed 8 January 2014.

80 Johannes Morsink, *The Universal Declaration of Human Rights: Origins, Drafting and Intent* (Philadelphia: University of Pennsylvania Press, 1999) 76 and 80.

81 Morsink xiii.

82 Morsink 72.

and then denied the right to asylum.[83] In the majority of cases, these victims were not migrants.

Mary Ann Glendon is the other authority on the drafting of the Universal Declaration.[84] Her focus has been more on the political and global dimensions of this history. Like Morsink, Glendon draws attention to the innovatory character of this set of rights.[85] She is right in doing this. Her presentation nonetheless obscures the fact that the lesser known American Declaration had brought this type of provision on the international legal scene prior to the Universal Declaration. Indeed it is probably thanks to Latin American pressure that they were included in the Universal Declaration.

IX. Migrants' Rights: A Latin American Innovation?

Accounts of the history of human rights emerging from the North tend to overlook the fact that Latin America has long been an important contributor to human rights thinking. They often focus on the US and French declarations of the eighteenth century and then on the United Nations.[86] In order to counteract the bias which approaches Latin American affirmations of human rights as 'inferior copies of grand, rich European ideas',[87] Paolo Carozza has highlighted four key moments which demonstrate the crucial role Latin America has played in the history of human rights. This section suggests that the introduction of 'special migrant rights' could well have been part of the story told by Carozza.

The first moment Carozza identifies in his chequered history goes back to the sixteenth century when Bartolomé de Las Casas defended the *equality* of all human beings and put the notion of rights on a *universal* plane in order to oppose the brutality of the Spanish conquest of the New World.[88] Surprisingly, even though Latin America is commonly understood to comprise the predominantly Spanish- and Portuguese-speaking areas of continental America south of the United States together with the Spanish-speaking Caribbean and Haiti.[89] Carozza does not mention the Haitian Revolution of 1791 which has received extensive attention in recent scholarship.[90] The second moment he highlights involves a jump to the early nineteenth century, when Latin American constitutional republics exhibited, following Simón Bolívar's leadership, concerns for equality and fraternity, the positive role of law, and the duties that are correlative to individual rights.[91] The third moment is constituted by the Mexican Constitution

[83] Morsink 76 and 80. [84] Glendon *A World*. [85] Glendon 182.

[86] See e.g. Ed Bates, 'History', in Daniel Moeckli, Sangeeta Shah and Sandesh Sivakumaran (eds) *International Human Rights Law* (Oxford: Oxford University Press, 2010) 17–38.

[87] Paolo G. Carozza, 'From Conquest to Constitutions: Retrieving a Latin American Tradition of the Idea of Human Rights' (2003) *Human Rights Quarterly* 25, 281–313 at 283.

[88] Carozza 293, emphases in the original.

[89] *The Cambridge History of Latin America VI*, Part 2 (Cambridge: Cambridge University Press, 2008) viii.

[90] See e.g. David Patrick Geggus, *Haitian Revolutionary Studies* (Bloomington: Indiana University Press, 2002); Laurent Dubois, *Avengers of the New World: The Story of the Haitian Revolution* (Cambridge: The Belknapp Press, 2004).

[91] Carozza 'From Conquest' 300.

of 1917 which incorporated extensive social and economic guarantees and became a model for virtually every Latin American constitution thereafter.[92] The fourth is the Latin American involvement in the genesis of the Universal Declaration in the mid-twentieth century, which is well documented in Morsink and Glendon's works (upon which Carozza relies heavily in this section of his account).

Even if they failed in their goal of getting a human rights bill incorporated in the Charter of the United Nations, Latin American countries managed to have seven references to human rights included in this document.[93] 'The Latin American connection'[94] is also credited for having ensured that a prominent place be given to social and economic rights in the Universal Declaration. It is not clear that these rights would have been included had it not been for this connection,[95] which in practice took the form of an excellent working and social relationship between John P. Humphrey and Hernán Santa Cruz.[96] Humphrey was the first Director of the Secretariat's Division on Human Rights at the United Nations and the author of the first drafts of the Universal Declaration, with his texts becoming the basis for the subsequent works of the Human Rights Commission.[97] Santa Cruz was the Chilean delegate to the Human Rights Commission. He informally acted as the spokesman for the collective views of the Latin American nations and was 'the most vocal and consistent advocate of the [Universal] Declaration's social and economic rights'.[98] Humphrey and Santa Cruz's friendship was undoubtedly instrumental in producing the 'nearly perfect' match between the American and the Universal Declarations' social and economic provisions.[99]

The same can probably be said of the 'special migrant rights' which found their way into the Universal Declaration. Morsink's account of the drafting process of the provision on freedom of movement which became Article 13 UDHR records that Humphrey's initial provision closely followed the text submitted by Chile on behalf of the Inter-American Juridical Committee.[100] Morsink mentions that the nationality provision, which became Article 15 UDHR, was also moulded on a Chilean proposal.[101] While he does not specify the exact inspiration which drove Humphrey's initial draft of the provision on asylum, which eventually gave rise to Article 14, it is nonetheless clear from his account that the Latin American bloc was overall in support of a broad provision on asylum.[102]

Articles 13–15 of the Universal Declaration bear a striking resemblance to three provisions of the American Declaration—which was very much a Latin American Declaration as neither Canada nor the US participated in its elaboration.[103] Article VIII of the American Declaration concerns the right to residence and free

[92] Carozza 304.

[93] Morsink, *The Universal Declaration* 2 and 130–131; Carozza 'From Conquest' 284.

[94] The expression is from Morsink *The Universal Declaration* e.g. 130.

[95] Morsink 133. [96] Morsink 131. [97] Morsink 5.

[98] Carozza 'From Conquest' 286. [99] Morsink *The Universal Declaration* 132.

[100] Morsink 73. A separate article included the right to move between states: Morsink 73.

[101] Morsink 80. [102] Morsink 79.

[103] The American Declaration was adopted as part of the Final Act of the Ninth International Conference of American States held at Bogota from 30 March to 2 May 1948, which also established the OAS. For institutional histories, see Inter-American Institute of International Legal

movement and announces Article 13 UDHR (even though the former extends only to nationals). Article XIX ADHR starts: 'Every person has the right to the nationality to which he is entitled by law'; Article 15 UDHR mirrors this. Article XXVII ADHR reads: 'Every person has the right, in case of pursuit not resulting from ordinary crimes, to seek and receive asylum in foreign territory, in accordance with the laws of each country and with international agreements'. It appears to have acted as the model for Article 14 UDHR, however much the provision was curtailed as it was debated in the United Nations—not only because, along with the right to movement and nationality, it constituted a 'most neuralgic issue for the Eastern bloc',[104] but also because Western Europeans, especially the UK, were uneasy about having a provision on asylum included.[105]

The American Declaration could not have inspired the initial stages of the drafting of the Universal Declaration, which was adopted a mere seven months later. Nonetheless the Latin American connection can probably be said to have been a determinant in getting migrant rights included in the Universal Declaration. These rights fit the description of the Latin American take on human rights as 'strongly universalist in its orientation [and] founded on the equal dignity of all members of the family'.[106] The reason why Latin Americans were so intent on having migrant rights recognised in human rights instruments may be related to their own history as a continent of immigrants, for whom migration is very much part of everyday life and exile a common experience,[107] giving a particular reverberation to the immediate prompt of the horrendous events which had taken place in Europe in the immediately preceding years.

Studies, *The Inter-American System: Its Development and Strengthening* (New York: Oceana, 1966) Introduction; Cecilia Medina Quiroga, *The Battle of Human Rights: Gross, Systematic Violations and the Inter-American System* (Dordrecht: Martinus Nijhoff, 1988) Chapter 3; Thomas Buergenthal and Dinah Shelton, *Protecting Human Rights in the Americas: Cases and Materials* (Kohl: Engel, 1995) Section 2 of Chapter 1. Canada became a member of the OAS in 1990, after having held observer status for some 18 years: Scott Davidson, *The Inter-American Court of Human Rights* (Aldershot: Dartmouth, 1992) 8, note 6. The United States became an OAS member at its foundation in 1948.

[104] Glendon *A World* 92 and 96. This conclusion is also born out by Morsink's detailed account of the drafting of the three provisions: Morsink *The Universal Declaration* 72–88.

[105] In November 1948, shortly before the Declaration was proclaimed, the British delegate observed in the General Assembly's third committee that 'a right to be "granted" asylum would conflict with the immigration laws of nearly every country'. And so it is that from an original text which spoke of the right 'to be granted' asylum, Article 14 UDHR eventually referred to the right to 'enjoy' asylum: Glendon *A World* 153. Also, it should be noted that Humphrey had originally proposed having an additional provision ensuring that expulsion be conducted with assorted procedural guarantees. This project was quickly abandoned in the face of strong opposition from the UK, the United States, and Australia with René Cassin dropping it from his second rewrite: Morsink *The Universal Declaration* 80.

[106] Carozza 'From Conquest' 311.

[107] Thomas W. Merrick, 'The Population of Latin America', in Leslie Bethell (ed.) *The Cambridge History of Latin America* (Cambridge: Cambridge University Press, 1995) Vol. 6, Part I, 3–61 at 44; Cohen, 'Part Seven: [Introduction to] Latin and Central American Migration', in *Cambridge Survey* 203–204 at 204.

X. Migrant Rights are Expanded in the (Latin) American Convention

Lawyers know very well that declarations are just that: declarations which are, as such, legally non-binding. Admittedly, this status can change. The Inter-American Court has, for example, elevated the status of the American Declaration to a binding document for OAS members—to the loud and persistent objection of the United States—[108] and some provisions of the Universal Declaration are widely accepted to have become part of customary international law. Still, declarations are easier to adopt than legally binding conventions. Thus, one can say that the test of the Latin American will towards migrant rights arose when there was talk of including these provisions in an instrument which was intended to be legally binding from the start. The American Convention on Human Rights was adopted by the OAS in 1969. Far from reneging on the rights bestowed on migrants in the Bogota Declaration, the American Convention expanded them.

The last paragraphs of Article 22 ACHR are particularly striking for our purposes:

> 6. An alien lawfully in the territory of a State Party to this Convention may be expelled from it only pursuant to a decision reached in accordance with law.
> 7. Every person has the right to seek and be granted asylum in a foreign territory, in accordance with the legislation of the state and international conventions, in the event he is being pursued for political offenses or related common crimes.
> 8. In no case may an alien be deported or returned to a country, regardless of whether or not it is his country of origin, if in that country his right to life or personal freedom is in danger of being violated because of his race, nationality, religion, social status, or political opinions.
> 9. The collective expulsion of aliens is prohibited.

Article 20 ACHR, which concerns nationality, is also highly relevant. Its second paragraph reads: 'Every person has the right to the nationality of the state in whose territory he was born if he does not have the right to any other nationality'. Last but not least, a parallel to the alien clause of the American Declaration is nowhere to be found in the American Convention.

The *travaux préparatoires* of the American Convention have not been published in as detailed a manner as has been done for the European Convention, making it impossible to attempt to trace the history of the drafting of the quoted provisions without in-depth research which is beyond the scope of this book. Whatever objections may have been raised during the drafting process against Article 20 or 22, it is immediately apparent that the final text of the American Convention demonstrates a

[108] Ludovic Hennebel, *La Convention Américaine des Droits de l'Homme: Mécanismes de Protection et Etendue des Droits et Libertés* (Brussels: Bruylant, 2007) 24–30. Under the presidency of Jimmy Carter, the US signed the American Convention, but has never ratified it.

concern for the position of the alien, which translates into rights that are most valuable to him.[109] The American Convention's catalogue of rights has been described as 'more advanced and enlightened' than that in the European Convention.[110] The manner in which it includes migrant rights is one of the elements that supports this conclusion.

XI. Europe Chooses not to Protect the Alien in the ECHR

Had the political will been available, the European Convention of 1950 could have taken the American and Universal Declarations of 1948 as models and bestowed the alien rights addressing his specific situation. That it failed to do so is an omission which happened by design.

We have seen earlier in this chapter that the Consultative Assembly of the Council of Europe wanted to adopt an enforceable Convention quickly, without quibbling over the substance of the protected rights. Hersch Lauterpacht, the Polish-born and Cambridge-based author of the first book in English on the legal protection of human rights,[111] was not impressed by the Convention project which the Consultative Assembly submitted to the Committee of Ministers in September 1949. One of his criticisms was that it left unaddressed issues of nationality and statelessness, asylum, and freedom of movement.[112] In his magisterial analysis of the genesis of the Convention, the legal historian Brian Simpson observes that '[t]here is no evidence that any attention was paid to these criticisms'.[113]

Soon after Mr Teitgen's impassioned opening speech of 19 August 1949, the problem of displaced persons was brought to the attention of the Consultative Assembly.[114] The Belgian Delegate, Etienne de la Vallée-Poussin, expounded:

> We know that, at the present time, some 600,000 to 700,000 European displaced persons, still in receipt of temporary assistance from the United States, are deprived almost entirely of their freedom and their rights.
>
> Can we possibly, in this Assembly, discuss merely in the abstract, the protection of human rights, while giving no more than a passing glance at the misery spread before our eyes?[115]

Special attention was drawn by de la Vallée-Poussin to the 60,000 'hard core' amongst the displaced—the old, ill, amputees, and mothers of large families with no husbands and no means of support of any kind, whom no state would choose to host as they would necessarily become a burden.[116] He proposed that the

[109] For antecedents, see the Conventions which emanated from the OAS on (respectively) Diplomatic Asylum (29 December 1954), http://www.refworld.org/docid/3ae6b3823c.html, accessed 10 January 2014; Political Asylum (26 December 1933) http://www.refworld.org/docid/4f3d180a2.html, accessed 10 January 2014; and Territorial Asylum (29 December1954) http://www.refworld.org/docid/3ae6b36614.html, accessed 10 January 2014.

[110] Buergenthal and Shelton *Protecting* 42.

[111] Hersch Lauterpacht, *An International Bill of the Rights of Man* (New York: Columbia University Press, 1945).

[112] Simpson *Human Rights* 690.

[113] Simpson 690.

[114] Travaux préparatoires I, 96.

[115] *Travaux préparatoires* I, 98.

[116] *Travaux préparatoires* I, 98.

Secretariat of the Council of Europe research methods to deal with this problem.[117] As Chair of the Committee of Experts who met in February and March 1950, however, de la Vallée-Poussin did not highlight the potential relevance of this issue.

If anyone had pushed for it, a right to asylum would assuredly have proved controversial, as it had been in the United Nations. But there is no indication that anyone did. Refugees, guest workers and other foreigners were left outside the parameters of protection devised by the Council of Europe. Their exclusion seems to have rested upon a consensual understanding.

Occasionally, the explicit intention of excluding the rights of the foreigner from the ambit of the Convention surfaces in the *travaux préparatoires*. For example, the delegate to the Committee of Experts from Luxembourg, who declared that he was open to accepting the right of individual petition if the alien clause made it into the European Convention, expressed his alarm at the Assembly's proposal to proclaim 'freedom from arbitrary arrest, detention, *exile and other measures*'.[118] To quote him:

> the text might give rise to uncertainties. [T]he expression 'and other measures' after the word 'exile' [might give the impression that it embraces] expulsion measures which certain States take by administrative action against undesirable aliens. Since these measures are taken by administrative and not legal action, they might be interpreted as meaning that they are arbitrary measures... It is therefore suggested that it should be indicated that the word 'exile' refers only to the victims of an expulsion measure taken by the State of which they are nationals.[119]

The Luxembourg expert was not alone in holding this view, even if he may have been the only one to have expressed it during the formal meetings on the elaboration of the Convention. Simpson reports that the British came to the table of negotiations holding that 'aliens could be expelled by administrative action, and that settled the matter'.[120] And so any reference to exile or to protecting aliens against arbitrary expulsion was dropped. Any provision towards recognising that refugees might have some rights was silently left out too.

Within the Council of Europe no one wanted to raise the view which had prevailed two years earlier at the OAS and the United Nations according to which the right to leave a country and be granted asylum elsewhere could be anything other than a question of human rights.[121] Barely a decade had passed since potential Holocaust victims had been required to obtain a visa before being permitted entry to the UK.[122] In May 1947, Operation Keelhaul saw the last Russian prisoners of war being forcefully returned to Stalin's regime to meet an early death.[123] Asylum

[117] *Travaux préparatoires* I, 100.

[118] Travaux préparatoires III, 192, emphasis in the original.

[119] *Travaux préparatoires* III, 192. This view was expressed on 4 February 1950.

[120] Simpson *Human Rights* 391; see also 688.

[121] For the United Nations, see: Morsinck *The Universal Declaration* 332.

[122] Louise London, *Whitehall and the Jews 1933–1948: British Immigration and the Holocaust* (Cambridge: Cambridge University Press, 2000).

[123] Julius Epstein, *Operation Keelhaul: The Story of Forced Repatriation from 1944 to the Present* (Old Greenwich, Conn.: Devin-Adair, 1973).

obviously touched too sensitive a European nerve to be positively discussed as the Convention was debated.

Admittedly, Protocol no. 4 to the European Convention, signed in 1963, is more generous towards aliens. Its Article 2 concerns freedom of movement, including the freedom 'to leave any country, including his own'; Article 3, the prohibition for a state to expel its own nationals or to deny them the right to enter its territory; and Article 4, the prohibition of the collective expulsion of aliens. At the time of writing, it has been ratified by 43 member states—excluding the UK which signed it in 1963 but never ratified. Article 1 of Protocol no. 7, signed on 22 November 1984 and ratified by 43 member states—again, excluding the UK—provides for procedural guarantees in the case of expulsion.

XII. The Significance of Article 16 ECHR Today

A close reading of the history of the elaboration of the European Convention on Human Rights indicates that its drafters were more interested in curtailing than in protecting the rights of aliens/migrants. Objecting that such a conclusion gives the almost forgotten Article 16 an undue importance would not be appropriate.

Admittedly, as noted earlier, Article 16 has hardly ever been applied since the entry into force of the Convention. The European Court of Human Rights has discussed it only once in its huge case law. This was in *Piermont v. France*, decided in 1995, as the respondent state vainly tried to rely on it to justify its interference with the freedom of expression of the applicant—a German Minister of the European Parliament who had publicly spoken in French Polynesia against the French government policy of, amongst other things, using the region for nuclear tests.[124]

I am told, however, that Article 16 occasionally surfaces in the deliberations of the Court which sometimes brings it in its deliberations *proprio motu* (without being prompted to do so by one of the parties to the case). There will of course always be cases which could lend themselves to an application of Article 16. One example could have been *Karakurt v. Austria* which was decided in 1999.[125] The case concerned the annulment of the applicant's election to a works council in Austria on account of his Turkish nationality. The Chamber to which the case was assigned ruled it inadmissible on the grounds that a works council was not an 'association' in the sense of Article 11—thus without invoking Article 16. Another example where Article 16 could perhaps have been applied is *Dritsas v. Italy* which was decided in 2011. It had been lodged by some 50 Greek nationals who had been intending to demonstrate at the G8 summit of Genoa of 2001 and who claimed that they had been brutally prevented from entering Italy.[126] It was declared inadmissible without Article 16 appearing in the reasoning of the decision.

124 *Piermont v. France* judgment.
125 *Karakurt v. Austria*, appl. 32441/96, Decision (ECtHR), 14 Sept. 1999.
126 *Dritsas v. Italy*, appl. 2344/02, Decision (ECtHR), 1 Feb. 2011.

The way these and other cases are disposed of show that the Convention opens various avenues outside Article 16 for states to restrict the political activities of migrants. One is to say that the provisions of the Convention are inapplicable. Another is to apply the second paragraph of a provision such as Article 10 or 11, which permits restrictions to the guaranteed right in order to protect interests such as national security, health, morals, or the rights of others. A third avenue could see a state resorting to making a derogation under Article 15.[127] This suggests that, far from other instruments missing an important element by not having an alien clause (as the Registry intimated in 1967), no such clause was necessary in the European Convention. That the drafters did not think twice about including it once the idea of an alien clause had surfaced is in itself highly significant about the way the alien was then socially and politically imagined in Europe.

XIII. Conclusion

This chapter has shown that the European Convention sought to restrict the rights of migrants while the (Latin) American instruments were ready to grant them rights which specifically addressed their situation as non-nationals.

Even though Article 16 ECHR is never invoked—one single exception hardly counts in the sea of case law produced by the European system—the provision cannot be disregarded as an accident of history. The fact that no one has ever had to suffer directly from its application does not change the fact that the clause embodied a way of approaching human rights law which was not favourable to the alien/migrant.[128] Article 16 must be treated as a significant manifestation of the thinking which presided at the elaboration of the Convention. Going further, it is likely to be an expression of general European reflexes. If so, these reflexes would also be found within the benches of the European Court of Human Rights. The idea that the alien can be discriminated against by contrast to citizens might then still be a premise which remains at the heart of the way in which the European Court of Human Rights approaches migrant cases today. By contrast, one can assume that the protective impulse at the heart of the American instruments puts the Inter-American system in good stead to protect migrants.

[127] This has never been attempted in respect of Articles 10 and 11. By contrast, it is worth noting that the UK sought to derogate from Article 5 in order to justify the detention of foreigners suspected of terrorism whom it could not deport to their country of origin because their return might put them at risk of ill treatment contrary to Article 3 ECHR in their home country. Both the House of Lords and the European Court of Human Rights found that, if the intention was to fight terrorism—as asserted by the British government—in order to fall within the ambit of Article 15, it made no sense to detain suspected terrorists who happened to be aliens, while leaving British suspected terrorists in liberty: *A and Others v. the United Kingdom*, appl. 3455/05, GC Judgment (ECtHR), 19 Feb. 2009.

[128] Conor Gearty has suggested that social democracy is good for everyone: any good manner learnt between citizens will benefit the other: Gearty, 'Doing What Comes Naturally? Asylum, Human Rights and the Duties of Humanity', Asylum Aid 20th Anniversary Lecture, 2 Nov. 2010, http://www.asylumaid.org.uk/wp-content/uploads/2013/02/Conor.pdf, accessed 8 January 2014. I doubt such an optimistic view is borne out in practice.

The rest of this book will demonstrate that—notable exceptions notwithstanding—the default position of the European Court of Human Rights is to consider the migrant first as an alien; by contrast, the Inter-American Court of Human Rights adopts an approach which stresses the equality of all humans and considers the migrant first of all as a human. It would be wrong to attribute the differences between these two bodies of case law to the texts of the European and American Conventions. Although the founding legal text is a conventional starting point for legal doctrine, there is no real start as the start is always nourished by what came before. What I am trying to say is that neither Article 16 ECHR nor Article 22 ACHR appeared out of nowhere. Instead, they were the fruit of a much longer history than a review of their formal, institutional elaboration could suggest. And precisely because they emerged from an established tradition, they also signalled the way the two systems would evolve.

3

Rejecting the Legacy of Empire: Postcolonial Dereliction

(*East African Asians* Case)

This chapter examines the first migrant case to have achieved notoriety in European human rights law. Numerous other migrant cases had come to Strasbourg beforehand, but they had been dismissed or had led to friendly settlements which were not widely publicised.[1] This case was different. It concerned a piece of British legislation which had been passed in 1968 in order to withdraw automatic right of entry into the UK from British passport holders of Asian origin who were settled in East Africa. This had been adopted as members of the East African Asian community felt pushed to move to Britain following 'Africanisation' programmes pursued by the newly independent Kenyan and Ugandan governments, which made the life of Asians in this part of the world increasingly difficult. In an era where yearly net migration was not counted in six figures, the 13,000 East African Asian arrivals in the first two months of 1968 frightened the British government which rushed through the Commonwealth Immigrants Act 1968 in February of that year. Two months later, Enoch Powell would make his 'Rivers of Blood' speech.

From 1970 to 1973, over 200 East African Asians complained to the European Commission of Human Rights about the way in which the UK was seeking to turn them away from its shores.[2] Deprived of a passport which would still give them the right to enter the UK, they were often initially detained on arrival. Many were then removed. Not being a national of any other country, they would be refused entry and residence in the country to which they had been sent back, and would reappear at a British port. In this event, they risked being detained and removed again. Eventually, after this scenario had been repeated two or three times, they would be granted admission. The Commission declared admissible thirty-one applications in the autumn of 1970.[3] Its report on their merits followed

[1] Examples of such early applications are provided in Chapters 4, 6, and 7.

[2] The Commission had received 243 applications from East African Asians by the end of 1973: personal communication of the Archives of the European Court of Human Rights, 15 October 2013.

[3] The Commission took a first decision on 26 applications on 10 October 1970: *'East African Asians' I, Samji Maji Lalji Patel and Others v. the United Kingdom*, appl. 4403/70 and twenty-four others, Decision (EComHR), 10 Oct. 1970. A second decision on six applications followed on 18

in 1973.[4] In a nutshell, the Commission found that discrimination based on race constitutes 'a special form of affront to human dignity which, in aggravating circumstances, can amount to degrading treatment in breach of Art. 3 [ECHR]'.[5] The shortest of all the provisions of the European Convention, Article 3 reads: 'No one shall be subjected to torture or to inhuman or degrading treatment or punishment'. The Commission expressed the opinion that it had been violated by the UK in the *East African Asians* case. This was the first time the Commission was issuing a report in an individual case involving the UK.

The Commission's opinion remained officially confidential for over 20 years.[6] It nonetheless opened an extremely important door in human rights law. This explains why the case is still commonly cited today. Acting 'boldly',[7] the Commission had handled the case with 'audacity' and 'courage', to use a number of terms which are found in legal commentaries in order to indicate approval (more rarely, disapproval) of innovative judicial interpretations.[8] Having said this, the case was not a panacea. On a practical level, its impact was not as strong as one might have wished and, even on its own terms, the reasoning demonstrated regrettable limitations, setting the subsequent Strasbourg migrant case law on a restricted path.

The case did not succeed in simply opening the doors of the UK to East African Asian holders of British passports. The contrary would have been surprising given that there would have been very little appetite for such a straightforward result. For one, the case was not brought before the European Court of Human Rights, something which came as a relief to Anthony Lester who was representing two of the applicants.[9] For good reason, Lester found it unlikely that the Court would

December 1970. I received the full text of these decisions from the Court's Archives in a document paginated 92–131. I refer to this document hereafter in abbreviated form as '*East African Asians* decision'.

4 *East African Asians v. the United Kingdom*, appl. 4403/70 and thirty others, Report (EComHR), 14 Dec. 1973. The 127-page report was communicated to me by the Archives of the European Court of Human Rights, and it is with this text which I have worked (rather than the summary available on HUDOC).

5 *East African Asians* report, para 207. This finding is cited in various commentaries, including: Karen Reid, *A Practitioner's Guide to the European Convention on Human Rights* (London: Sweet & Maxwell, 2004) 265–266. See also e.g. D.J. Harris, M. O'Boyle, E.P. Bates, and C.M. Buckley, *Harris, O'Boyle and Warbrick: Law of the European Convention on Human Rights* (Oxford: Oxford University Press, 2009) 101.

6 By contrast, the admissibility decision was published. The report's public disclosure in 1994 followed a parliamentary intervention by Lord Lester: Lord Lester of Herne Hill, QC, 'Thirty Years On: The *East African Asians* Case Revisited' (2002) *Public Law* 52–72 at 56.

7 For such a characterisation, see e.g. Prakash Shah, *Refugees, Race and the Legal Concept of Asylum in Britain* (London: Cavendish, 2000) 95 note 60.

8 This vocabulary is typical of commentators who applaud 'activism' and deplore 'self-restraint', and thus lament judicial 'timidity'. Commentators of the opposite political persuasion typically denounce judicial activism and encourage courts to display more restraint. On these labels, see further Chapter 9, 304.

9 Anthony Lester, 'East African Asians versus the United Kingdom: The Inside Story', lecture delivered on 23 October 2003 and available at <http://www.odysseustrust.org/lectures/221_east_african_asians-sharma.pdf>, accessed 7 January 2014, at p. 6. Lester represented a married couple at the origin of one application.

have gone as far as the Commission in its findings.[10] In accordance with the terms of the European Convention prior to Protocol no. 11, the case was forwarded instead to the Committee of Ministers, a political body which was not interested in pillorying the UK and did not confirm the finding of violation.[11] East African Asians who continued to try to come to the UK in the 1970s thus remained subject to immigration control and to abject procedures. Only in 2002 did the British Nationality, Immigration and Asylum Act rectify this 'unsatisfactory situation' out of a 'moral obligation' to deal with 'unfinished business'.[12] As for the European Court of Human Rights, it was slow to confirm the Commission's stance in subsequent rulings. Amongst the thousands and thousands of judgments that its case law contains, only one is a verdict of violation of Article 3 because of the racist and therefore degrading nature of governmental action.[13] Even the general Strasbourg case law on racial discrimination (under Article 14 ECHR) developed slowly and can be said to have remained seriously underdeveloped to this day.[14]

What came to be called 'the' *East African Asians* case—in a formulation which neglects the dozens of similar applications which were declared inadmissible or struck out[15]—is remembered for the Commission's progressive interpretation of the Convention. Reading its report with today's eyes, however, and allowing a somewhat anachronistic perspective, one regrets that the Commission did not highlight that many applicants were minors in need of particular protection due to their young age. With the benefit of hindsight, it is also disturbing to observe that the detention of applicants in prisons hosting convicted criminals was reported by the Commission without attracting any comment. In the context of this book, the most pertinent criticism of all relates to the fact that no one seemed to worry at the time, or to recall today, that six of the more than 30 original applications were dismissed by the Commission as groundless simply because they originated from individuals who held the status of British protected persons (BPPs).

[10] The Commission had a reputation of being more progressive than the Court, due to its generally more liberal findings. See e.g. Frédéric Sudre, *Droit international et européen des droits de l'homme* (Paris: Presses Universitaires de France, 2001) 449–450.

[11] Andrew Drzemczewski, 'A "Non-Decision" of the Committee of Ministers under Article 32(1) of the European Convention on Human Rights: The East African Asians Cases' (1978) *Modern Law Review* 41, 337–342. See also more generally on this mechanism: Andrew Drzemczewski, 'Decision on the Merits: By the Committee of Ministers', in J. Macdonald, F. Matscher, and H. Petzold (eds) *The European System for the Protection of Human Rights* (London: Kluwer Law International, 1993) 733–754.

[12] Ramnik Shah, 'A Wrong Righted: Full Status for Britain's "Other" Citizens' (2003) *Immigration, Asylum and Nationality Law* 17, 19–24 at 19.

[13] *Cyprus v. Turkey*, appl. 25781/94, GC Judgment (ECtHR), 10 May 2001, para 310.

[14] Marie-Bénédicte Dembour, 'Postcolonial Denial: Why the European Court of Human Rights Finds it so Difficult to Acknowledge Racism', in Kamari Clarke and Mark Goodale (eds) *Mirrors of Justice: Law and Power in the Post-Cold War Era* (New York: Cambridge University Press, 2010) 45–66; Mathias Möschel, 'Is the European Court of Human Rights' Case Law on Anti-Roma Violence Beyond Reasonable Doubt' (2012) *Human Rights Law Review* 12, 479–507; Ruth Rubio-Marín and Mathias Möschel, 'Genocide or Nothing: Racial Violence and Evolving Equality Law under the European Convention on Human Rights'.

[15] Out of 243 applications lodged by East African Asians with the Commission, 31 were declared admissible, 38 inadmissible, and 174 were struck out. This happened in the course of eight years, up to 9 October 1978: personal communication of the Court's Archives, 15 October 2013.

The difference in status between BPPs and citizens of the UK and Colonies (CUKCs) was an accident of history. Holding one or the other status made no difference whatsoever in the daily life of a British colonial subject.[16] The Commission chose to ignore the reality of the communalities in the situation of the applicants and the fact that BPPs were British passport holders too. It reasoned instead in formal legal terms and found a violation of Article 3 in respect of twenty-five applications because the Commonwealth Immigrants Act 1968 reneged on Britain's own prior legislation, namely, the Commonwealth Immigrants Act 1962, which expressly gave a right of entry to CUKCs (but not BPPs). It did not try to examine whether the legislation was granting nationality in a fair way, let alone whether a former colonial power had some moral—and thus human and legal rights—duties towards her former colonial subjects. Obviously, for the Commission to declare a piece of legislation contrary to the Convention at a time when it was not even clear that it had the power to do so was a big step. In a critical perspective attuned to migrants' rights, however, the *East African Asians* case can be described as a series of missed opportunities.

Migration patterns to Europe in the decades following independence very much followed colonial connections with, for example, Nigerians seeking to go to the UK, Algerians to France, and Zairians/Congolese to Belgium. Whether at state level, at Strasbourg, or within the public conscience, there was no sense in Europe that something was owed to these new migrants because of the colonial past. In times of refugee-producing crises, such as the East African exodus which unfolded in the 1970s, the entrenched European reluctance to think in terms of postcolonial responsibilities was particularly problematic. It therefore seems apposite to talk of postcolonial dereliction.

The dereliction did not arise from nowhere, but from the leftovers of ideology which saw nothing wrong in colonising other people, described as primitives, and thinking that the economic and political benefits which were drawn from this were rewards for the 'burdens of empire'. Within the Strasbourg context, this ideology is evident in the way the drafters of the European Convention envisaged dealing with 'the problem' of the colonial situation, a situation which was anticipated to continue for a long time as the exact phrasing of the Convention was being debated. The response to this dilemma came in the form of Article 63 (now Article 56) ECHR, often referred to as the Convention's 'colonial clause'. This provision proves, if proof were needed, that the proclamation of human rights to all human beings is inevitably difficult to reconcile with a colonial logic of governance. The intense debates which the clause attracted during the *travaux préparatoires*, reviewed in this chapter, testify to this inherent difficulty.

Today, the colonial clause is mostly regarded as a historical curiosity, a provision which never acquired much significance due to the waves of decolonisation which followed World War II. This view obscures the foundations upon which

[16] P. Ghai and J.P.W.B. McAuslan, *Public Law and Political Change in Kenya. A Study of the Legal Framework of Government from Colonial Times to the Present* (Nairobi, London, and New York: Oxford University Press, 1970) Chapter 1.

the European human rights regime was built. Admittedly, in 1949 and 1950 it was accepted that colonial subjects could not be excluded from the theoretical ambit of the Convention. However, this did not prevent colonial powers from instigating strategies aimed at avoiding the inclusion of colonial subjects in the Convention's practical ambit. One postcolonial extension of this logic is the fierce and successful resistance to any claim that states should admit on their territory ex-colonial subjects-turned migrants. This is indeed one way to read the *East African Asians* case. The fact that this analysis is unusual[17] does not make it any less crucial.

Chapter 3 opens with the drafting history of the Convention's colonial clause and an examination of the different strategies that the various colonial powers of the time deployed in order to avoid the Convention's potentially biting teeth in their colonies. Special attention is devoted to the British position, given that a number of migrant cases directed against the UK laid the ground for the development of the Strasbourg migrant case law. The chapter then turns to the *East African Asians* case. First, the colonial position of this population is briefly discussed. This is followed by a review of the British domestic laws concerning citizenship and a history of the passing of the Commonwealth Immigrants Act 1968. The position of the European Commission is then examined, including one dissenting view which was clearly in favour of the British government and thus highlights, by contrast, the tremendous achievement of the Commission's majority opinion. The chapter then explores what could be called the postcolonial legacy of the case. One section explains how BPPs' applications were dismissed as groundless. The next one notes how East African Asians continued to be subject to immigration controls after the Commission adopted its confidential report. The final section observes how, in times of crises which produce refugee movements, the common tendency by states which can afford to do so is to erect gates against the entry of these people. The *East African Asians* case is an early example of the way in which European human rights law does not find this inherently disturbing, even in a very clear postcolonial context.

I. The Colonial Clause: At the Heart of the European Convention

Proclaiming human rights on the basis of the equality of all human beings is not easily reconcilable with colonial governance. The resulting contradiction had to be navigated as human rights instruments were being elaborated in the wake

[17] However, for arguments attuned to those developed in this chapter, see David Farrier, *Postcolonial Asylum: Seeking Sanctuary Before the Law* (Liverpool: Liverpool University Press, 2011); Ian Law and Graham Huggan, *Racism Postcolonialism Europe* (Liverpool: Liverpool University Press, 2009); Olivier Le Cour Grandmaison, 'Colonisés-immigrés et "périls migratoires": Origines et permanence du racisme et d'une xénophobie d'Etat (1924–2007)' (2008) *Cultures et Conflits* 69, 19–32; Pascal Blanchard and Nicolas Bancel, *De l'indigène à l'immigré* (Evreux: Gallimard, 1998).

of World War II, at a time when over 263 million people lived in dependencies of one kind or another.[18] Despite this obstacle, the drafting of the Universal Declaration of Human Rights was managed at record speed, just before the Cold War set in.[19] The situation was trickier in Europe where the intention was to create an instrument with teeth. As a result, the question of the geographical application of the European Convention arose with acuity right from the moment its creation was envisaged. It was not easily resolved. Opinions within the Council of Europe were highly divided as to how to approach the question of the application of the Convention to the colonies. In marked contrast to the alien clause,[20] the colonial clause thus ended up being debated at every stage of the *travaux préparatoires*, up to the very last moment[21].

The Consultative Assembly had originally proposed to have a Convention which applied more or less wholesale in the colonies. Recommendation no. 38, through which the Assembly communicated its initial project to the Committee of Ministers in September 1949, provided for a wide territorial application of the Convention. In the Teitgen Report, the provisions concerning elections and the right to political criticism and opposition were the only ones which were specifically reserved for the metropolitan territory.[22] The view expressed by some members of the Assembly that the Convention should provide rights only 'to all persons residing within the metropolitan territory of a member State',[23] was dismissed by the other parliamentarians as 'fail[ing] to appreciate exactly the difficulties which [this arrangement] might raise'.[24]

Belgium, at the time an important colonial power with possessions in central Africa,[25] considered it politically unfeasible to devise a Convention which would not apply in the colonies. What it advocated was a watered-down application of the Convention in the colonies. In February 1950, the Belgian delegate suggested to the Committee of Experts that the European Convention be applied 'within the overseas territories, in conformity with local needs and the standards

[18] Brian Simpson, *Human Rights and the End of Empire: Britain and the Genesis of the European Convention* (Oxford: Oxford University Press, 2001) 276.

[19] Simpson 522. By contrast, reaching agreement upon the ensuing binding Covenants took almost two decades, with one difficulty being the recognition of a right to self determination: Mary Ann Glendon, *A World Made New: Eleanor Roosevelt and the Universal Declaration of Human Rights* (New York: Random House, 2002).

[20] See Chapter 2.

[21] A reminder that Chapter 2 includes a review of the different states of the *travaux préparatoires* which led to the European Convention.

[22] 'Preparatory work on Article 63 of the European Convention on Human Rights', information document prepared by the Registry of the European Court of Human Rights dated 2 March 1978 and now accessible on the website of the Court's library at <http://echr.coe.int/Documents/Library_TravPrep_Table_ENG.pdf>, accessed 6 January 2014, p. 6.

[23] This had been Teitgen's original idea: 'Preparatory work' p. 4.

[24] 'Preparatory work' p. 5.

[25] The diplomatic skills of Léopold II, King of the Belgians, had persuaded European powers to recognise his stake in the Congo at the Berlin Conference of 1885. Nonetheless, Belgium formally became a colonial power only in 1908, following the king's relinquishment of the territory after the 'red-rubber' abuse triggered international condemnation. After World War I, Belgium was entrusted with the administration of Ruanda-Urundi.

of civilization of the native population, which may not yet have been able to reach the conditions necessary for the practice of democratic freedom'.[26] This formulation was typical of the paternalism which characterised Belgian colonialism and considered 'natives' as children in need of education.[27] France quietly supported the Belgian position, which could be reconciled with its constitutional proclamation of a union between the French and the people of the French overseas territories 'based on equality of rights and duties without distinction of race or religion'.[28] The Committee of Experts adopted the Belgian proposal without specifically referring to the colonial situation through a reformulation which laid down that the rights guaranteed in the Convention 'shall be applied in overseas territories in the light of local exigencies'[29] (except for the provisions related to elections and political criticism which were not considered to be applicable at all in the colonies).

This approach was unacceptable to the British. The UK had repeatedly explained at the United Nations that the autonomy which its dependent territories constitutionally enjoyed prevented it from being party to any international instrument which would automatically apply in these territories.[30] The argument was repeated at the Council of Europe:[31] the UK would have no option but to oppose any European Convention which did not have a 'Colonial Application Article' of the kind which had become customary to include when it was party to international treaties.[32] The British added that each of the territories for whose international relations they were responsible would nonetheless be encouraged to join the Convention system. In consideration of this position, the Committee of Experts devised a clause which kept the Belgian idea but added that the 'Convention shall only apply to territories of the High Contracting Parties ... when the consent of the appropriate authorities has been obtained'. The text immediately continued: '[These Parties] shall, if necessary take steps to obtain this consent'.[33]

The Committee of Experts thus ended up sending the Committee of Ministers various proposals for a 'colonial clause'—as it was always referred to, much to the chagrin of the British who kept observing that they did not entertain a colonial relationship with all their dependent territories (as the example of the Isle of Man demonstrates).[34] The Conference of the Senior Officials of June 1950 saw the British representative propose a clause which made the extension of the Convention to territories for which a member state had international responsibility dependent upon an expressed notification by this member state.[35] This mirrored a

[26] 'Preparatory work' p. 9. The Belgian expert was de la Vallée-Poussin, whom we have encountered in the previous chapter. This was said on 6 February 1950.

[27] Marie-Bénédicte Dembour, *Recalling the Belgian Congo: Conversations and Introspection* (Oxford: Berghahn, 2000) 48.

[28] Simpson *Human Rights* 285.

[29] 'Preparatory work' p. 10.

[30] 'Preparatory work' p. 10; Christopher Lush, 'The Territorial Application of the European Convention on Human Rights: Recent Case Law' (1993) *International and Comparative Law Quarterly* 42, 897–906 at 901.

[31] 'Preparatory work' p. 9.

[32] 'Preparatory work' p. 9.

[33] 'Preparatory work' p. 11.

[34] Lush 'The Territorial Application' 901.

[35] 'Preparatory work' p. 14.

proposal the UK had tabled at the United Nations regarding the binding Covenant which was being negotiated following the adoption of the Universal Declaration (and which would eventually become not one but two covenants). This became known as Alternative A (even though it was British backed). Alternative B, proposed by the Swedish delegation, provided that efforts would have to be made for obtaining consent that the Convention would extend to colonies.[36] The firmness of the British opposition to Alternative B persuaded some delegates, including the Swedish, to support Alternative A.[37] Other delegates remained in favour of Alternative B, including the Italian delegate who, perhaps having in mind the many Italians who had established themselves as traders in African colonies,[38] said that 'the benefits of [the] Convention should extend as far as possible to all the inhabitants of overseas territories'.[39]

The Convention project briefly returned to the Legal Committee of the Consultative Assembly at the end of June. This Committee expressed its preference for the 'more liberal' Alternative B.[40] This, however, was a non-starter for the UK, and when the project came back before the Committee of Ministers, it was not clear how the stalemate would be broken.[41] A Sub-Committee was formed to examine the question, but it too failed to reach any agreement. It ended up putting three alternatives on the table.[42] At this stage, the British suggested an amalgamation of two of these through a colonial clause which provided *both* for subjecting any extension beyond the metropolitan territory to a specific declaration *and* for an application of the Convention with due regard to local requirements.[43] This satisfied everyone, and the proposal was adopted unanimously.

However, this was not the end of the matter. The Conference of Senior Officials had agreed to make the jurisdiction of the Court optional,[44] but had not yet managed to resolve the question of whether individuals should be able to petition Strasbourg or not,[45] and by early July 1950, there remained two states opposed to the right of individual petition: the UK and Greece. At this stage, some figures in the British government were beginning to feel that their position was untenable. In the words of one: 'It is really inconceivable that, if the French and Italian Governments for example are prepared to accept the system, we should say that... we find it too dangerous'.[46] As the ministers met in Strasbourg on 3 August, the British were still hoping to manage to get the right of individual petition deleted from the Convention on the grounds that 'a flood of petitions sponsored by Communist agitators' should otherwise be feared.[47] But this view failed to persuade all governments. In particular, the Irish representative stated that 'the Irish Government is not prepared to agree on any further whittling

[36] 'Preparatory work' p. 14.
[37] 'Preparatory work' p. 16.
[38] Chapter 2 has already alluded to the relatively strong Italian presence in the Congo as part of its discussion of the internment of 'enemy aliens'.
[39] 'Preparatory work' p. 16.
[40] 'Preparatory work' p. 18.
[41] 'Preparatory work' p. 20.
[42] 'Preparatory work' p. 21.
[43] 'Preparatory work' p. 22.
[44] Simpson *Human Rights* 719.
[45] Simpson 723.
[46] Pierson Dixon to the Colonial Office, FO 371/88753/US17311/54, quoted in Simpson 724.
[47] Instructions from Bevin quoted in Simpson 731.

down' of the proposed Convention as this would render the project 'of little or no value and cause grave disappointment'.[48] Alongside Ireland, France and Italy insisted that they too were not ready to sign a Convention which did not offer a right of individual petition. With the UK holding the exact opposite position, Sweden offered a compromise: to include the right but to make its acceptance optional.[49]

This solution was accepted on 7 August.[50] Having been endorsed for the Convention in general, it was then also specifically applied to the colonial clause,[51] as a result of which its final phrasing came to read:

1. Any State may at the time of its ratification or at any time thereafter declare by notification addressed to the Secretary General of the Council of Europe that the present Convention shall, subject to paragraph 4 of this Article, extend to all or any of the territories for whose international relations it is responsible.
2. [Provides for a one-month delay before this declaration comes into force].
3. The provisions of this Convention shall be applied in such territories with due regard, however, to local requirements.
4. Any State which has made a declaration in accordance with paragraph 1 of this article may at any time thereafter declare on behalf of one or more of the territories to which the declaration relates that it accepts the competence of the Court to receive applications from individuals, non-governmental organisations or groups of individuals as provided by Article 46 [now 34] of the Convention.

This phrasing was stronger than any colonial clause proposed previously during the *travaux préparatoires*. The double idea of requiring a specific declaration and of accommodating local requirements was kept, with the fourth paragraph providing yet another safeguard, from a colonial power's perspective, of making the right of individual petition in the non-metropolitan territories dependent upon a specific declaration to this effect by the colonial state.

This result was not to the pleasure of the Consultative Assembly which examined the Convention project one last time in early August 1950. The colonial clause now included in the Convention was very different from what its 38th recommendation had proposed, and the new phrasing appeared utterly objectionable to many parliamentarians. Some felt their only option was now to oppose the insertion of *any* colonial clause.[52] Their arguments were twofold: first, that the clause would constitute a field day for proponents of communism who would use it to denounce the hypocrisy of liberal philosophy—and the more illiberal the colonial clause was, the more damaging this would be;[53] second, that the clause ran against the universal ideal which animated the whole human rights project.[54] An impassioned speech by the French Member of Parliament Léopold Senghor, who was later to become the President of Senegal and is remembered as

[48] Quoted in Simpson 732. [49] Simpson 733. [50] Simpson 735.
[51] Simpson 376. [52] 'Preparatory work' pp. 25–27.
[53] This was the argument of a Danish representative (Mr Lannung).
[54] This was the argument of a French representative (Mr Silvandre).

the father of *négritude*, eloquently pleaded that the colonial clause had no place in the Convention.[55] Sir David Maxwell-Fyfe replied that Senghor's points were well conceived and would be given full consideration but that meanwhile the draft Convention needed to be put into operation in all the states represented in the Assembly, which Senghor's amendment would make impossible.[56] This was to no avail. Senghor's amendment for the suppression of the colonial clause was carried on 25 August by 46 votes against 37 in the Consultative Assembly.[57]

The impact of this result on the Committee of Ministers was nil: the Convention was signed in November with the colonial clause drafted by the ministers in early August included as Article 63. This provision remains intact today, albeit renumbered Article 56 ECHR. It had never been meant to apply to colonial territories exclusively. Nonetheless, the colonial conundrum had been its driving force. The British had had their way, and so had the other colonial powers.

II. An Array of Strategies for Keeping the Convention out of the Colonies

The Convention needed nine ratifications to come into force, which was achieved in September 1953. Although the ratifying states were then legally bound by the Convention and expected under international law to respect it, the ratification did not in itself mean that they opened themselves up to the risk of having to respond to a case brought against them at the newly established European Court of Human Rights. Neither the jurisdiction of the Court nor the right of individual petition, as it came to be known, was automatic. Individuals could bring a complaint before the Commission (not the Court) only if a state made a declaration recognising this faculty under what was then Article 25 ECHR. The Commission then issued a non-legally binding report on whether the merits of the case disclosed a violation of the Convention. After this, cases could be lodged before the Court either by the Commission (the usual scenario) or by a member state (a rare occurrence in practice) only if the defendant state had made a declaration under Article 46 ECHR, which 'could be made unconditionally or on condition of reciprocity on the part of several or certain other High Contracting Parties or for a specified period'.[58] As we have seen, additional declarations were necessary for the Convention on the one hand and the right of individual petition on the other to apply in regard to a member state's dependent territory.

All this means that there were many different ways through which a member state could navigate the Strasbourg system of enforcement until Protocol no. 11 came into force in 1998 and abolished the optional clauses originally provided by Articles 25 and 46. In order to keep the Convention out of the reach of its colonial

[55] 'Preparatory work' pp. 31–33. [56] 'Preparatory work' p. 33.

[57] Council of Europe, *Collected Edition of the 'Travaux Préparatoires' of the European Convention on Human Rights* (The Hague: Martinus Nijhoff, 1979) Vol. V, 192.

[58] Original Article 46 ECHR.

subjects, a colonial power could refrain from signing or ratifying the Convention altogether, refrain from accepting the jurisdiction of the Court under Article 46 and/or the right of individual petition under Article 25, or abstain from making a declaration under Article 63 either (1) or (4). Five European states remained colonial powers in 1950: Belgium, Denmark, France, the Netherlands, and the UK. Each approached the question of the application of the Convention in their colonies in a different way.

Table 3.1 bears out this diversity. It provides the dates on which member states accepted the ECHR system of supervision, as manifested by their signature and ratification of the Convention as well as by their first declarations under both Articles 25 and 46, up to the time all original signatory states to the ECHR had made such declarations (i.e. up to January 1990).[59] States are listed in chronological order of their first declaration under Article 46. The order following the other criteria would be slightly different, as Table 3.1 also indicates. However, whichever of the last two criteria is used, Denmark is the first colonial power to have accepted the ECHR system of supervision, Belgium the second, the Netherlands the third, the UK the fourth, and France the fifth. This is the order in which this section will review the strategies deployed by the colonial powers.

Denmark comes first because it did not face any problem. It ratified the Convention in April 1953 and, on the same day, made a declaration under Article 63 in order to extend the application of the Convention to its colony, Greenland. This was not a politically sensitive move as Greenland was due to become part of its main territory a mere two months later (this is why Denmark appears in a light shade in Table 3.1).

Belgium ratified the Convention in 1955, thus, as the twelfth member state to do this, relatively late. At the time, no one was anticipating that the independence of the Congo would come, precipitously, a mere five years later. Despite the then expectation that it would remain a colonial power for decades to come, within three weeks of its ratification of the Convention, Belgium accepted the right of individual petition and the jurisdiction of the Court. This may seem astonishing. What Belgium refrained from doing, however, was to extend the application of the Convention to the Congo and to Ruanda-Urundi through an Article 63 declaration. The strategy paid off. When three Belgian nationals complained in 1961 that they had been excluded from participating in the elections held in Belgium and in Congo and that they had lost their estates in the debacle of the Congolese independence which could and should have been both predicted and prevented by the Belgian government, the Commission declared their application inadmissible. The applicants' argument that the Belgian Congo had formed an integral part of the national territory was to no avail. The Commission found that it was contrary

[59] Following the demise of the USSR, there would be many accessions in the following decade. The development of the 'new Europe' through its Eastern Enlargement is unfortunately not studied in this book, even though it clearly had an impact upon national and European migration policy, and thus upon migrants' experiences and, one can in turn assume, upon the development of the Strasbourg migrant case law.

Table 3.1 State Acceptance of the ECHR Supervision Mechanism (up to January 1990)[1]

Contracting state	Signature of ECHR		Ratification		Entry into force of ECHR	Date of first declaration under Art. 25		Date of first declaration under Art. 46	
Ireland	1	*Barberini*	5	*25.02.53*	*03.09.53*	2	25.02.53	1	Idem
Denmark	1	*Barberini*	7	*13.04.53*	*03.09.53*	3	13.04.53	2	Idem
Germany	1	*Barberini*	4	*05.12.52*	*03.09.53*	4	05.07.55	3	Idem
Belgium	1	*Barberini*	12	*14.06.55*	*Idem*	5	05.07.55	4	Idem
Luxembourg	1	*Barberini*	9	*03.09.53*	*Idem*	8	28.04.58	5	Idem
Iceland	1	*Barberini*	8	*29.06.53*	*03.09.53*	7	29.03.55	6	03.09.58
Austria	15	*13.12.57*	14	*03.09.58*	*Idem*	9	03.09.58	7	Idem
Netherlands	1	*Barberini*	11	*31.08.54*	*Idem*	10	28.06.60	8	31.08.54
Norway	1	*Barberini*	2	*15.01.52*	*03.09.53*	6	10.12.55	9	30.06.64
United Kingdom	1	*Barberini*	1	*08.03.51*	*03.09.53*	11	14.01.66	10	Idem
Sweden	1*	*28.11.50**	3	*04.02.52*	*03.09.53*	1	04.02.52	11	13.05.66
Italy	1	*Barberini*	13	*26.10.55*	*Idem*	12	01.08.73	12	Idem
Switzerland	17	*21.12.72*	17	*28.11.74*	*Idem*	13	Idem	13	Idem
Portugal	18	*22.09.76*	18	*09.11.78*	*Idem*	14	Idem	14	Idem
Spain	19	*24.11.77*	19	*04.10.79*	*Idem*	15	01.07.81	15	Idem
France	1	*Barberini*	16	*03.05.74*	*Idem*	16	02.10.81	16	03.05.74
Liechtenstein	20	*23.11.78*	19	*08.09.82*	*Idem*	17	Idem	17	Idem
Greece	1*	*28.11.50**	6	*28.03.53*	*03.09.53***	18	20.11.85	18	30.01.79
Cyprus	16	*16.12.61*	15	*06.10.62*	*Idem*	20	01.01.89	19	24.01.80
San Marino	21	*16.11.87*	21	*22.03.89*	*Idem*	21	Idem	20	Idem
Turkey	1	*Barberini*	10	*18.05.54*	*Idem*	19	28.01.87	21	22.01.90

[1] Table 3.1 was collated by using the following source: Emmanuel Decaux, Pierre-Henri Imbert, and Louis-Edmond Pettiti (eds), *La Convention européenne des droits de l'homme: Commentaire Article par Article* (Paris: Economica, 1999) 1159–1160.

* Sweden and Greece had participated in the elaboration of the European Convention, but were prevented from signing the text on 4 November 1950 for constitutional reasons.

** Greece denounced the European Convention on 12 December 1969 (which came into effect on 13 June 1970) and re-ratified it on 28 November 1974.

Barberini = signing the Convention in Palazzo Barberini in Rome on 4 November 1950.

Shaded areas = colonial powers at the time of the signing of the European Convention.

Idem = see date appearing immediately on the left.

both to the official view of the competent Belgian authorities and to the natural and customary understanding of the words contained in Article 63.[60]

Like other states which had participated in the elaboration of the Convention, the Netherlands felt strongly that human rights were 'for export'.[61] The view of the Dutch government was that its good record meant that it had little to fear from the European Court of Human Rights. The Dutch accordingly accepted the jurisdiction of the Court in 1954, on the same day as they ratified the Convention. In December 1955, it made a declaration under Article 63 in respect of Surinam and the Dutch Antilles. However, it would not risk hastily accepting the right of individual petition. It made a declaration under Article 25 only in 1960, and then let another four years pass before extending it to Surinam through an Article 63(4) declaration.[62]

The British situation is discussed at length in the next section. Suffice it to say for the moment that the UK took the jump of fully accepting the supervision system put in place by the Convention in 1966, under a Labour government intent on showing its European credentials, and at a time when the British Empire had been reduced to a minuscule portion of what it had been at its height. Soon afterwards the government was dragged to Strasbourg to defend the *East African Asians* case.

If the Dutch and British delayed their commitment to the ECHR system because of their colonial position, this is nothing compared to what the French did. France had been one of the signatories of the Convention at the Palazzo Barberini in November 1950. At the Conference of Senior Officials, its delegate had insisted that it would not be able to accept a Convention which did not include a right of individual petition. But when the opportunity came, France was in no hurry to make a declaration under Article 25. It did not ratify the Convention until 1974, at which time it also accepted the jurisdiction of the Court. From then it took another seven years and the presidency of the socialist François Mitterrand for it eventually to accept the right of individual petition. It was 1981. There is no doubt that this delay was due to the sensitivity of its colonial position.

III. The British Response to the Potentially 'Biting Teeth' of the Convention

At first, neither the Universal Declaration nor the European Convention had appeared to be politically crucial projects to the states, colonial or otherwise,

[60] *X and Others v. Belgium*, appl. 1065/61, Decision (EComHR), 30 May 1961.

[61] Barbara Oomen, *Rights for Others: The Slow Home-Coming of Human Rights in the Netherlands* (London: Routledge, 2014); 'The Rights for Others: The Contested Homecoming of Human Rights in the Netherlands' (2013) *Netherlands Quarterly of Human Rights* 31, 41–73 at 44–45.

[62] Ed Bates, *The Evolution of the European Convention on Human Rights: From its Inception to the Creation of a Permanent Court of Human Rights* (Oxford: Oxford University Press, 2010) 111 note 15. To my knowledge, the literature on the history of the ECHR emanating from Dutch scholars fails to discuss this point, demonstrating how the significance of the colonial take of the European Convention is now ignored.

participating in the elaboration of these documents. Reflecting this relatively low status, the projects had been developed through the efforts of officials who were not top-ranking. When the exercise drew to its close and governments examined the results, they were sometimes taken aback as it dawned on them that the system about to be put in place had the potential to develop in ways which were not judged desirable. This realisation was particularly 'painful'[63] to the British government. Its history throws some light on the resistance traditionally displayed by some sections of the British government towards the Strasbourg system, which continues to this day. It is also worth reviewing it here given that the Strasbourg migrant case law involving the UK often constituted an occasion for the Strasbourg institutions to establish major lines of jurisprudence.[64]

On 25 July 1950, a memorandum written by a British Minister of State who had helped the European Convention project to take shape made clear for the first time to the British Cabinet the level of progress which was being achieved at Strasbourg. 'There was an immediate storm'.[65] In a context where the British Empire remained intact outside the Indian sub-continent, the Colonial Secretary, James Griffiths, immediately objected:[66]

> The introduction of such a system of appeal to an international authority is likely to cause considerable misunderstanding and political unsettlement in many Colonial territories. The bulk of the people in most Colonies are still politically immature and the essence of good government among such people is respect for one single undivided authority…The right of petition to an international body would obscure this principle…[The resulting] confusion would undoubtedly be exploited by extremist politicians in the Colonies…Loyalty would be shaken: administration would be made more difficult and agitation more easy.[67]

From a slightly different perspective, the Chancellor of the Exchequer, Sir Stafford Cripps, found it 'intolerable that the code of common law and statute law which had been built up in this country over many years should be made subject to review by an international court administering no defined system of law'.[68] Lord Chancellor Jowitt was incensed too. How was it possible that the Convention project could have proceeded so far without having been submitted for the consideration of ministers, they all wondered. The response to this question was that it had been the Foreign Office which had been in charge of conducting the negotiations, and it happened to be headed by the ailing Ernest Bevin, whose diminishing

[63] Anthony Lester, 'Fundamental Rights: The United Kingdom Isolated?' (1984) *Public Law* Spring 47–72 at 49. For the full details of this story, see Simpson *Human Rights*. For more streamlined accounts, see: Geoffrey Marston, 'The United Kingdom's Part in the Preparation of the European Convention on Human Rights, 1950' (1993) *International and Comparative Law Quarterly* 42, 796–826; Bates *The Evolution*.

[64] This is true of the present chapter, but also Chapters 4 and 7 and, to a lesser extent, Chapters 6 and 8.

[65] Lester 'Fundamental Rights' 50.

[66] Marston 'The United Kingdom's Part' 825.

[67] C.P. (50) 189, dated 28 July 1950, CAB 129/41 34611: quoted in Lester 'Fundamental Rights' 50.

[68] As summarised by Lester 'Fundamental Rights' 50–51.

state of health had not allowed him to follow the developments taking place at Strasbourg as closely as would have been desirable.[69]

The Cabinet was so uncomfortable with the draft Convention that it wanted the project to be altogether remitted for further consideration. But it was already the end of July 1950. Bevin observed that the UK could not withdraw from the project at this late stage without sending the politically unfeasible message that it did not want human rights.[70] With the assent of Prime Minister Attlee, he proposed approaching the task of formally agreeing the final text of the ECHR as a damage limitation exercise. To be more specific he would look at making the right of individual petition optional and at reinforcing the colonial clause.

Even after these demands were granted by the Committee of Ministers at Strasbourg in August 1950, the reluctance of the Lord Chancellor did not abate. Jowitt recognised that the government would have to accept the Convention, but he looked at this as an 'unqualified misfortune'. He argued:

> It completely passes the wit of man to guess what results would be arrived at by a tribunal composed of elected persons who need not even be lawyers, drawn from various European States possessing completely different systems of law, and whose deliberations take place behind closed doors... Any student of our legal institutions... must recoil from this document with a feeling of horror.... I cannot view with equanimity [an] appeal to a secret court, composed of persons with no legal training, possessing the unfettered right to expound the meaning of 17 Articles which may mean anything, or—as I hope—nothing.[71]

Despite the Cabinet's misgivings, the UK was the first state to ratify the Convention, on 8 March 1951. This was after the Convention had been laid for 21 days on the table of both Houses of Parliament, as should happen before the ratification of any treaty.[72] There was no parliamentary debate, which can only have been appropriate if the Convention was not considered to be an important treaty.[73] In the absence of any debate, no Member of Parliament objected to the ratification.[74] Although the Convention was ratified, '[t]here was, of course, no acceptance of the right of petition or of the Court's jurisdiction'.[75]

Two and a half years later, on 23 October 1953, the Convention was extended to 42 overseas territories for whose international relations the UK was responsible. As we have seen, British officials had said and repeated throughout the *travaux préparatoires* that the UK was not in a constitutional position to sign any convention which would automatically be applicable in its colonies until the dependent

[69] Lester 'Fundamental Rights' 51. [70] Lester 53.

[71] Paper dated 13 October 1950, CAB 130/64 xc/A034022, quoted in Lester 'Fundamental Rights' 52–53. These strong words have led Brian Simpson to reflect on the strangeness that 'a person with such an uncritical understanding of the British legal system, and with such parochial opinions, should nevertheless have risen to so high an office': Simpson *Human Rights* 743. Declarations by the British government since Simpson's book was published at the start of the millennium may put Jowitt's paper in a different light, as pointing to the deep roots of British euroscepticism and the diversity of views which has always coexisted within the British government.

[72] Lester 'Fundamental Rights' 54; Anthony Lester, 'Taking Human Rights Seriously', (1994–1995) *King's College Law Journal* 5, 1–15 at 2.

[73] Lester 'Taking Human Rights Seriously' 2. [74] Lester 2.

[75] Lester 'Fundamental Rights' 54.

territories had each accepted to be bound by it. In line with this argument, it had requested, from an early date, every British territory to state whether it wanted to have the Convention applied in its respect.

Isidore Bonabom has examined how the process unfolded in the Gold Coast (now Ghana).[76] Bonabom has uncovered a confidential memo which was sent as early as 1949 by the Colonial Office to Gold Coast's Governor Charles Arden-Clarke to ask about the possible extension of the Convention to this territory.[77] By 1951, the prevailing view in the Colonial Office was that the Convention had been drafted with sufficient 'provisos and careful phrasing' to make its extension entirely acceptable.[78] It was regarded as 'obviously desirable that as many as possible, preferably all, territories should have this convention extended to them'.[79] The extension was regarded as having the potential of neutralising criticisms of British colonial practices at home and at the United Nations, as well as appeasing the colonial intelligentsia minority which was making demands for fairer governance in the colonies.[80] Colonial Secretary Griffiths now thought it 'essential that the Colonial Governments should [be] encouraged to adhere to the Convention'.[81]

In the event, the Convention was extended to 97 million people residing in territories as diverse as Cyprus, Jamaica, Kenya, Nigeria, and Tanganyika, amongst others.[82] The only British territories to which the Convention was not extended were Hong Kong, Southern Rhodesia, and the oil protectorates of the Arabian Gulf.[83] Not surprisingly, the declaration under Article 63, paragraph 1 was not accompanied by a further declaration under Article 63, paragraph 4. The hope was that refraining from opting into the full mechanism of supervision would ensure that British practices, especially in the colonies, would escape Strasbourg scrutiny. This strategy was not entirely successful.

Inter-state applications before the Commission were possible right from the start in the Convention system. In the spring of 1956, Greece, an original Convention signatory, lodged a series of complaints against the UK in respect of the then British colony of Cyprus. Referring to the grievances related to the 'deportations in detention' of Archbishop Makarios and others to the Seychelles, a Foreign Office official minuted: 'It seems an almost intolerable position if, by subscribing to the Council of Europe's Convention, we have in fact deprived ourselves of the possibility of removing a person from a colonial territory and detained him in another colony'.[84] To the relief of the British government, in its report of 26 September 1958 on 'the First Greek case', the Commission decided that

[76] Isidore Bonabom, 'The Development of a Truth Regime on the "Human": Human Rights in the Gold Coast (1945–1957)', PhD thesis, University of Sussex, 2012.

[77] CO 936/67/3, cited in Bonabom 110.

[78] CO 936/157, cited in Bonabom 110.

[79] CO 936/156, cited in Bonabom 110.

[80] Bonabom 111. Simpson *Human Rights* 825; see also Kirsten Sellars, 'Human Rights and the Colonies: Deceit, Deception and Discovery' (2004) *The Round Table* 93, 709–724.

[81] CO 936/157, cited in Bonabom 'The Development' 111.

[82] 1 YB 12–14, cited in Bates *The Evolution* 111 note 14; Simpson *Human Rights* 827–830.

[83] Karel Vasak, *La Convention européenne des droits de l'homme* (Paris: Pichon et Durand-Auzias, 1964) 255–256; Simpson *Human Rights* 829.

[84] Simpson 914.

the deportations had not breached the Convention. Although there were three powerfully argued dissenting opinions, as well as two abstentions, in the view of a majority of six commissioners, the Convention had deliberately not wanted to forbid member states from exiling their own citizens.[85] It is unlikely that anyone would have wanted to bring the case before the Court, but as the UK had not yet recognised the jurisdiction of the Court, the question did not even arise. A second application by Greece concerned allegations of torture. This put the British government in a potentially difficult spot. The Commission, however, was not intent on pursuing the case. In early 1957, as a political settlement over the status of the island was reached, the Commission was relieved to be in a position to follow the wishes expressed by both the Greek and the British states to have the Strasbourg proceedings in 'the Second Greek case' terminated.[86]

One decade later, on 14 January 1966, the UK made declarations accepting for the first time the jurisdiction of the Court under Article 46 and the right of individual petition under Article 25, for a period of five years. Compared to many of the other original Convention signatories, this was late, as Table 3.1 demonstrates. The delay was due to Britain's continuing position as a colonial power up to this time. It would have been embarrassing for the UK to recognise the jurisdiction of the Court and to grant the right of individual petition at home but not overseas.[87] The British government thus waited until January 1966 when its empire had dwindled for making declarations under Articles 25 and 46 of the Convention. When the right of individual petition was extended via Article 63(4) to 21 British territories 20 months later, this affected fewer than 3.5 million people.[88] By then, geopolitical considerations had shifted considerably since the early 1950s. The British empire was fast becoming a thing of the past and the Labour government under Harold Wilson was intent on entering the European Economic Community. After de Gaulle's veto of 1963, it was therefore important for the UK to show itself to be 'Euro-friendly'.[89]

As with the Convention's ratification in 1951, Parliament was not consulted about all these declarations.[90] Nor even was the Cabinet: the momentous decision of extending the right of individual position was adopted by ministers in mere interdepartmental correspondence.[91] This was following guidance by a legal advisor to the Foreign Office who commented:

> The approach of the Commission...has in my experience been reasonable. I do not see why we should expect less of the Court, which is composed of even more eminent men than the Commission.[92]

This assessment may be controversial to some. My own view is that it was neither misinformed nor mistaken in its assumption of favourable treatment for the

[85] A conclusion the leading legal historian Brian Simpson has qualified as bizarre: Simpson 1014. However, see Chapter 2 for material potentially supporting the view that governments had meant to allow exile under the Convention.

[86] Simpson 1051.

[87] Bates *The Evolution* 179.

[88] Bates 187 note 87. Hong Kong remained excluded.

[89] Bates 187.

[90] Lester 'Taking Human Rights Seriously' 3.

[91] Lester 3.

[92] Quoted in Bates *The Evolution* 187.

British government at Strasbourg, however much the latter would subsequently decry at regular intervals—and never as strongly as today—Strasbourg decisions going against it.

IV. The Asian Presence in East Africa

Wanting to proclaim universal human rights at the same time as not wanting to have them extended to colonial subjects was a dilemma for four states that had participated in the elaboration of the European Convention. They initially resolved it through a colonial clause which, taking the form of Article 63 ECHR, even managed to avoid any literal reference to colonialism. Once the Convention came into force, the UK and France refrained—the former until 1966, the latter until 1981—from making it possible for the system of European human rights protection to be biting in their respect, largely in fear of the consequences a full acceptance of the system would mean for their colonial governance. With the exception of the 'Greek cases', there is no Strasbourg case law which directly relates to a colonial situation. By contrast, a lot of case law deals with postcolonial ramifications. In fact, given the development of post-World War II patterns of migration along ex-colonial lines, much of the migrant case law can be said to fall in this category. This, in particular, is true of the *East African Asians* case, which is best approached through an understanding of the position that Asians came to occupy in East Africa during the British colonial period.

In its report on the case, the European Commission correctly recalls that there is a 2,000-year history of links across the Indian Ocean between the Indian sub-continent and East Africa.[93] Only in the nineteenth century, however, did Indians start to settle on the East African coast, as they were involved in the ivory and slave trade.[94] After the abolishment of slavery, they were sent to work on sugar plantations.[95] Their move from the coast to the interior happened slightly later, following the European 'scramble for Africa' in the last quarter of the nineteenth century.[96] J. S. Mangat explains,

> The officially sponsored participation of the Indians in the process of 'opening up' of the interior led to an increasing flow of Indian immigrants—skilled and semi-skilled employees, businessmen, and traders—into the East African territories. With these immigrants came also some of the institutions of British India—including the rupee currency which

[93] *East African Asians* report, para 7.

[94] Michael Twaddle, 'The Settlement of South Asians in East Africa', in Robin Cohen (ed.) *Cambridge Survey of World Migration* (Cambridge: Cambridge University Press, 1995) 74–76 at 74; Mahmood Mamdani, *Politics and Class Formation in Uganda* (London: Monthly Review Press, 1976) 66.

[95] Daniel D.C. Don Nanjira, *The Status of Aliens in East Africa. Asians and Europeans in Tanzania, Uganda and Kenya* (New York: Praeger, 1976) 4. 'Thus official slavery was replaced by its disguised form': Mamdani *Politics and Class* 68.

[96] J.S. Mangat, *A History of the Asians in East Africa c. 1886 to 1945* (Oxford: Clarendon Press, 1969) 63.

became the standard currency all over East Africa, and Indian laws—as well as British Indian methods of administration. These had the combined result of greatly strengthening the Indian presence in the territories. In fact, at the turn of the century, suggestions were not lacking that British East Africa had become a virtual 'appendage' of British India and was governed as one of its provinces.[97]

The construction of railways in the closing years of the century also famously brought indentured labour from India to East Africa.[98]

The Indian presence in East Africa was a response to the difficulties the European powers encountered in economically developing on their terms the territories they were occupying. An official report to the British Colonial Office complained in 1904 that 'every possible means were tried to induce the natives to labour, but without avail; even under the pressure of famine in 1898–1899, nothing would persuade them to work continuously or systematically'.[99] Labour was thus brought in from the Indian sub-continent. In *The Rise of Our East African Empire*, originally published in 1893, Lord Lugard had already observed: 'From the overcrowded provinces of India ... we could draw labourers, both artisans and coolies, while they might also afford a recruiting ground for soldiers and police'.[100]

As this quote suggests, not all Indians in East Africa had originally been 'coolies' or, later, *dukawallahs* (small traders). There were also many clerks and artisans amongst them.[101] And as the twentieth century progressed, the Indians became a distinct if internally diverse class. They enjoyed their own, comparatively well-funded school system. The British encouraged their occupation of a middle position within the two-tier system they had created. Their position, however, came to be increasingly resented by the Africans (as well as by the Indians themselves who wanted to be treated as equals to the whites). After World War II, the economic boom in East Africa quickened the pace of Asian settlement in the region. In that period, studies suggest that between 80 and 90 per cent of commercial trade and a fair slice of industrial investment may have gone through Asian hands.[102] Many if not all Asian families rose above the poverty line.[103] This prosperity encouraged the development of a stereotype amongst Africans that the Asians were economically exploitative. It also fed into the charge that Asians kept themselves socially apart.[104]

Uganda achieved independence on 9 October 1962; Kenya on 12 December 1963. In anticipation of these events, a £50 million land purchase fund was set up to buy European farms in these countries at generous 1959 prices. A scheme was also set up for European civil servants to retire prematurely or to receive compensation. Nothing comparable was set up for Asian traders and civil

[97] Mangat 63. [98] Mangat 67.

[99] Quoted in Mamdani *Politics and Class* 67.

[100] Quoted in Mangat *A History* 68.

[101] Michael Twaddle, 'Was the Expulsion Inevitable?', in Michael Twaddle (ed.) *Expulsion of a Minority: Essays on Ugandan Asians* (London: Athlone Press, 1975) 1–14 at 2.

[102] Shah *Refugees* 78. Ann Dummett and Andrew Nicol, *Subjects, Citizens, Aliens and Others: Nationality and Immigration Law* (London: Weidenfeld and Nicolson, 1990) 198.

[103] At least in Uganda: Twaddle 'Was the Expulsion' 6. [104] Twaddle 6.

servants.[105] Likewise, the citizenship issue was resolved differently for the two groups. The new states agreed that citizenship would be automatically granted to those individuals who had been born in the country, provided their parents had also been born there. Under the British Nationality Act 1964, which introduced the so-called 'grandfather' rule, European settlers were entitled to resume their British nationality if they had come to renounce it in order to acquire the nationality of another Commonwealth country. Asians who did not automatically become citizens of the new African states because they did not have a parent born there could apply for the new African citizenship for two years from the date of independence. Alternatively, they could remain British.

Few Asians availed themselves of the possibility of becoming citizens of the new African states. Wanting to keep their options open and to see from where the wind was blowing, they prevaricated. It is not exactly clear how many people this concerns as figures of the Asian population residing in East Africa at the time of independence are not readily available. Hugh Tinker gives the following estimates for 1969: Kenya, 182,000; Tanzania, 105,000; and Uganda, 76,000.[106] Compared to other parts of the world such as Malaysia, Mauritius, and Guyana, the Indian population in East Africa was not large, whether in absolute numbers or by percentage of population.[107] However, resentment against Asians in East Africa had built considerably. It was moreover capitalised on by the new African authorities which wanted to be seen to be keen to redistribute economic resources and political power away from the Asians to the Africans.

The new African states latched onto the Asian population's reluctance to embrace the new citizenship. They said this indicated a lack of loyalty. Kenya, the country with the largest Indian population in the region, started a programme of 'Africanisation'. Its Immigration Act 1967 provided that 'the presence in Kenya of any person who is not a citizen of Kenya shall, unless otherwise authorized under this Act, be unlawful, unless that person is in possession of a valid entry permit or a valid pass'.[108] The Trade Licensing Act 1967 provided: 'After the appointed day, no person who is not a citizen of Kenya shall conduct a business in any place which is not a general business area; or in any specified goods, unless his license specifically authorises him to do so'.[109] In addition, African civil servants were appointed to replace Asian ones.[110] Uganda and Tanzania followed the Kenyan example.

In Uganda, the Trade (Licensing) Act 1969, adopted under President Obote, was adopted in order to facilitate, so it was said, the Ugandanisation of wholesale and retail trade. It was shortly followed by the Immigration Act 1969, which nullified all existing immigration permits and introduced a new system of

105 Shah *Refugees* 79.

106 It is likely that these figures relate to Indians only and thus exclude Pakistanis and Bangladeshis.

107 Hugh Tinker, 'Indians Abroad: Emigration, Restriction, and Rejection', in Twaddle *Expulsion* 15–29 at 15.

108 *East African Asians* report, para 30.

109 *East African Asians* report, para 30.

110 Dummett and Nicol *Subjects* 199.

documentation for all non-citizens resident in Uganda.[111] Then, in January 1972, President Idi Amin, who had come into power through a coup d'état, warned that British Asians would have to go. He officially announced the policy in August, when he said Asians were to go by mid-November. A fortnight later, it became clear that all Asians, not just those with a British passport, might be targeted.[112] It is estimated that there were about 28,000 British Asians in Uganda at this time.[113]

The expulsion was obviously the result of a combination of factors, including but not limited to Amin's notorious lunacy. It has been suggested that the UK's determination to block the exit of British Asians to Britain itself played a role by exacerbating tensions and pushing Amin towards extremism and expulsion.[114] A few years before, the British government had indeed attempted to block any exit route to Britain by having Parliament adopt, in three days and two nights, the Commonwealth Immigrants Act 1968. Such speed in adopting legislation in the UK was unprecedented and has not been seen since. This piece of legislation is the one which gave rise to the *East African Asians* case at Strasbourg. It is best understood in the context of the development of British citizenship law.

V. British Citizenship and the Right of Entry up to the Commonwealth Immigrants Act 1968

In the early twentieth century, A.V. Dicey, one of the most respected English constitutionalists, proclaimed that any 'British subject, whatever be the place of his birth, or the race he belongs to,... has, with the rarest possible exceptions, the same right to settle and trade in England which is possessed by a natural born Englishman'.[115] This claim to legal equality was hiding distinctions based on colonial status and race. For example, the Merchant Shipping Act 1906 had introduced a language test for those signing onto British ships, which made it possible to discriminate against non-white sailors.[116] The theory was nonetheless that all British subjects enjoyed both right of entry and freedom of movement on British soil. In practice, such theoretical freedom of movement was not exercised. It only became seen as problematic as international travel became more commonplace.

On a different plane, a legal difficulty arose as old Commonwealth countries which were now independent, such as Canada, were beginning to adopt their own nationality laws. The British Nationality Act 1948 was adopted as a response to this new situation. It retained the principle of a right of entry for all British subjects. At a time when the Commonwealth was continuing to be thought of as of major strategic importance, the 1948 Act provided for a number of different categories of British subjects, including a new status of 'citizenship of the UK

[111] James S. Read, 'Some Legal Aspects of the Expulsion' in Twaddle *Expulsion* 193–209 at 199.

[112] Shah *Refugees* 84.

[113] Read 'Some Legal Aspects' 208.

[114] Shah *Refugees* 80; Lester 'Thirty Years On' 54.

[115] Quoted in Shah 70.

[116] Shah 70.

and colonies' and that of citizenship of an independent Commonwealth country. People in these two categories were free from immigration control.

The Commonwealth Immigrants Act 1962 changed this. As we shall see in more detail in Chapter 4, the aim of this piece of legislation was precisely to subject to immigration control citizens who either had not been born in the UK or had not had their passports issued in the UK—in plain terms, colonial British subjects. Colonial British subjects held passports issued by the colonial authorities; in law their passports were deemed not to have been issued in the UK. Colonial British subjects could therefore be refused admission to Britain or be admitted for a restricted period or subject to conditions as to employment.

After independence, British Asians living in Kenya and Uganda were no longer colonial subjects. If they chose to retain their British citizenship rather than to become Kenyan or Ugandan nationals, even though the passports had not been issued on actual UK soil, in law they were deemed to have been issued in the UK (as they were issued by a diplomatic representative who represented the British government directly). Under the 1962 Act, British Asians living in Kenya and Uganda after independence thus remained free from immigration control.[117]

The aim of the Commonwealth Immigrants Act 1968 was to counteract this and to subject British Asians living in Kenya and Uganda to immigration control. This was achieved by adding a clause in the existing legislation providing for the exemption of British subjects from immigration control. Now to be exempt, one had to be British and either have a parent or grandparent born in the UK, or be registered as a citizen in a country which, at the time of this registration, was mentioned in section 1(3) of the 1948 Act. This section listed the Commonwealth countries which were already independent in 1948. Of course, Kenya, Uganda, and Tanzania were not on this list. Without using explicit racial terms, the effect of the 1968 Act was thus to subject British Asians from East Africa to immigration control.

VI. Cabinet Papers Reveal the History of the Passing of the Commonwealth Immigrants Act 1968

The loss of their automatic right of entry to the UK was exactly what British Asians had feared would happen. Indeed this fear had contributed to swelling the numbers who had chosen to resettle in the UK from 1965 onwards. In turn, the rising numbers of British Asian arrivals—6,150 in 1965; 13,600 in 1967; and 13,600 in January and February 1968[118]—frightened the British government, thus prompting it to act, despite its awareness that the measures it proposed were in breach of the international obligations the UK had just undertaken under the nascent European human rights law regime. This story of the British government's dilemma has been told by Anthony Lester who wrote a detailed account of the passing of the Commonwealth Immigrants Act 1968

[117] *East African Asians* report, para 23.

[118] Lester 'Thirty Years On' 54.

after the Cabinet papers related to it entered the public domain, 30 years later.[119] The following description closely mirrors his account—and all the quotations are from his article.

In July 1965, the Home Secretary alerted the Cabinet that a potentially large number of East African Asian UK citizens might want to enter Britain. The Minister of State for Commonwealth Relations opposed any thought that they could be deprived of their citizenship, as this would be seen by Commonwealth countries as 'a purely racial move'. The Minister of State for Foreign Affairs concurred: denying UK citizens entry to the country of which they were nationals would be contrary to the Universal Declaration of Human Rights, the Fourth Protocol of the European Convention on Human Rights, as well as to customary international law. There was nothing to do but to keep the subject under review.[120]

A Cabinet Committee meeting on 2 March 1966 recorded much the same: no action was to be taken at present to deprive 'coloured' UK citizens in independent Commonwealth countries of their right of entry, but officials should keep a close watch on the rate of immigration and be ready to bring a statement if necessary. 'Meanwhile, it was important to avoid any publicity about coloured United Kingdom citizens' rights'.[121]

By September 1967, memoranda no longer referred to 'coloured' UK citizens. They used instead the phrase 'citizens of the United Kingdom and Colonies who do not belong to the United Kingdom'. On 17 October 1967, the Home Secretary, Roy Jenkins MP, stated that there were 'some strong arguments for legislating' but that 'the objections were formidable'. Many of the people affected had based their lives on the knowledge—or at least the expectation—that their UK citizenship conferred on them certain rights, including a right of entry into the UK. Accusations that British action was manifestly unjust would be very difficult to counter.[122]

When James Callaghan MP became Home Secretary in late November 1967, he felt the time had come to legislate and made a proposal to this effect on 8 February 1968. His mind was made up. He thought the legislation needed to be adopted quickly so that its purpose would not be defeated by giving time for Asians to come to the UK before it came into force. On 12 February, Callaghan circulated a memorandum to the Cabinet saying that a Bill was needed as a matter of urgency. Spinning it, he claimed that it would contribute to developing a 'multi-racial society free of strife [by] striking the right balance between the number of Commonwealth citizens we can allow in and our ability to ensure them, once here, a fair deal not only in tangible matters like jobs, housing and other social services but, more intangibly, against racial prejudice'. The imminent Race Relations Bill would also help to show the fair balance which was strived for.[123]

[119] Lester 54. [120] Lester 60–61. [121] Lester 61–62.
[122] Lester 62–63. [123] Lester 64–66.

In the Commonwealth Immigration Committee meeting of 13 February, the Minister of State for Commonwealth Affairs yet again objected that 'legislation of the sort proposed would in effect discriminate against the Asians from East Africa because of their colour. This would contradict all we had previously said on the subject'. The Attorney-General noted that Callaghan's proposal 'did not spell out the difficulties which legislation of the kind proposed would entail for us in the context of a number of international instruments dealing with human rights and racial discrimination'. Nonetheless, the majority of the Committee considered that legislation was needed in order to prevent 'a large influx from the Asian Community in East Africa to this country'.[124]

A brief memorandum of 14 February by the Attorney-General was now putting forward possible legal arguments in defence of the proposed legislation. The first was that the legislation was based on criteria of territorial connection with the UK which had nothing to do with race, colour, national, or ethnic origin. A second argument was that the UK had signed, but not ratified, the Fourth Protocol to the European Convention. According to the Home Secretary, under the new legislation, 'Asians in East Africa and others similarly placed will be treated exactly as all other Commonwealth citizens'. The Home Secretary declared: 'I believe that this equality of treatment and our policy of a fair deal all round, as evidenced by the forthcoming Race Relations Bill, should be sufficient to show that we are not dishonouring any of the international obligations…'. The Secretary of State for Commonwealth Affairs recorded his dissent once more. He remarked that people would be made stateless in practice, if not in law. He also observed: 'The proposal leaves us open to the charge of breaking faith with many Kenyan Asians who, because of their actions by past British Governments for their own purposes, now find themselves possessing citizenship of the United Kingdom and Colonies. There is a moral issue of fundamental importance here.' In the Cabinet meeting of 15 February, the Attorney-General confirmed that, if the proposed legislation were passed, 'Our position in relation to relevant international agreements and declarations would be difficult but not impossible'.[125]

The Cabinet met again on 22 February 1968. The minutes record that: 'Although the moral and legal objections to [the legislation], and the problems it would raise for us internationally and administratively, were recognized, these were thought to be outweighed by the consequences for the social services, in terms of additional expenditure, and for our race relations policy, if the flow of immigrants from Kenya was allowed to continue unchecked'. The Bill was presented and read the first time in the House of Commons the next day. It was debated in the Commons on 27 and 28 February, and in the House of Lords on 29 February. Powerful critics from all parties denounced both its discriminatory nature and the breach of faith or pledge it involved.[126] Interestingly, its defects from an international law perspective were not commented upon.

124 Lester 65. 125 Lester 67–69. 126 Lester 70–71.

VII. The European Commission: A Racially Motivated and thus Degrading Piece of Legislation

From 10 February 1970, the European Commission of Human Rights started to receive applications from East African Asians.[127] On 10 October 1970, the Commission gave its decision as to the admissibility of 25 of these applications. All these applicants had had problems with their entry into the UK. Twenty-two of them had attempted to enter the UK from Kenya. They stated in their applications to Strasbourg that they were in detention in England and expected to be expelled from that country soon, but that Kenya would not allow them back in.[128] By the time the Commission took its admissibility decision, they had been released from detention and admitted to the UK for at least three months.[129] The remaining three applicants had come from Uganda.[130]

The applicants in these 25 applications were almost all young, single men,[131] a fact which was not commented upon by the Commission. Only four were above 25 years old.[132] Eleven were teenagers, with the youngest two aged 15.[133] There were just two women, and they too were young: 18 and 22.[134] According to Ramnik Shah, a lawyer based in Nairobi at the time, the applicants' profile reflects the fact that young Asian men in Kenya were the first to suffer the full consequences of the 'Africanisation' programme. By contrast, older members of the Asian community with an established trade were in a less uncomfortable position. They could find ways—possibly through the payment of bribes—to access the permits they were now required to possess. In addition, many families were thinking that their best strategy was to send their young men, who could then be joined in due course by other family members if this became appropriate or necessary.[135]

I have not traced the history of the mobilisation of British civil society which produced the stream of 243 East African Asian applications to Strasbourg between 1970 and 1973. What is clear is that the involvement of the young but already maverick Anthony Lester in just one of these applications influenced the whole of the Strasbourg proceedings. Lester—now Lord Lester of Herne Hill—has become one of the most distinguished human rights advocates in the UK. To the imaginative lawyer that he was, human rights must have appeared to be a potentially promising lens with which to approach issues related to the colonial past and migration

[127] *East African Asians* report, Appendix I 'History of Proceedings' 111.

[128] *East African Asians* decision, 92.

[129] *East African Asians* decision, 92

[130] *East African Asians* decision, 92–93.

[131] This comes from reading the facts of the cases: *East African Asians* decision, 93–100.

[132] 26: appl. 4416/70; 35: appl. 4405/70; mid-forties: appls 4434/70 and 4486/70.

[133] Appls 4409/70 and 4417/70.

[134] Appls 4423/70 and 4476/70.

[135] Ramnik Shah, personal communication, 15 October 2013. A member of the affected community, Shah was a close partisan and astute observer who took an active role in Nairobi in trying to diffuse the crisis and alleviate its consequences for Asians. In a letter entitled 'This "Diabolical Piece of Chicanery"', published by the *East African Standard* on 26 February 1968, Shah predicted that there would be Strasbourg proceedings which would see the Commission finding the UK in violation of the Convention, but without any binding sequels.

governance, offering a real alternative to the logic of state sovereignty. It was a challenge, however. As he explained to me during a phone conversation, in this case he was facing the problem that none of the Convention provisions seemed to fit the situation encountered by his clients.[136] The case seemed to turn around discrimination, suggesting to plead a violation of Article 14 ECHR. This provision, however, does not guarantee a 'freestanding' right. It reads: 'The enjoyment of the rights and freedoms *set forth in this Convention* shall be secured without discrimination on any ground such as sex, race, colour, language, religion, political or other opinion, national or social origin, association with a national minority, property, birth or other status'.[137] As the highlighted words demonstrate, Article 14 requires a link to be made with another provision of the Convention. This was problematic for the East African Asian applicants as no such link directly suggested itself. Any connection which would have been presented by the applicants' legal representatives might have appeared artificial. Prompted by Yale Law Professor Charles Black, Lester was persuaded 'to argue boldly that racial discrimination is inherently degrading in terms of Article 3, without the need to rely upon Article 14'. Lester then got Black to come to Strasbourg so that they could argue the point together in front of the Commission during the hearing on admissibility which took place over three days in early October 1970.[138]

They were obviously persuasive. In its decision as to admissibility of 10 October 1970, the Commission declared to be 'of the opinion that, quite apart from any consideration of Article 14, discrimination based on race could, in certain circumstances, of itself amount to degrading treatment within the meaning of Art. 3 of the Convention'.[139] Its decision continued by stating that 'it is generally recognised that a special importance should be attached to discrimination based on race, and that publicly to single out a group of persons for differential treatment on the basis of race might, in certain circumstances, constitute a special form of affront to human dignity;... therefore, differential treatment of a group of persons on the basis of race might be capable of constituting degrading treatment where differential treatment on some other ground, such as language, would raise no such question'.[140]

The Commission's report on the merits followed three years later. It reproduced the quoted statements with hardly any alteration.[141] Then applying these to the facts, the Commission found it established that the 1968 Act had racial motives.[142] At a time when the Cabinet's papers were unavailable, this was done on the sole basis of the parliamentarian debate reproduced in *Hansard* (the Parliament's official report of its proceedings). The Commission also recalled the difficult situation which the Asians were facing in East Africa.[143] This led it to conclude, by

[136] Mr and Mrs Dhunna, appl. 4423/70.

[137] Emphasis added.

[138] *East African Asians* decision, 125. Lester has recalled the friendly atmosphere in which these early proceedings took place: Anthony Lester, 'The European Court of Human Rights after 50 Years', in Jonas Christoffersen and Mikael Rask Madsen (eds) *The European Court of Human Rights Between Law and Politics* (Oxford: Oxford University Press, 2011) 98–115 at 102.

[139] *East African Asians* decision, 117.

[140] *East African Asians* decision, 117.

[141] *East African Asians* report, paras 196 and 207. The words 'such as language' were omitted from the final version.

[142] *East African Asians* report, para 199.

[143] *East African Asians* report, para 206.

majority,[144] that a violation of Article 3 had occurred in 25 cases. It obviously deemed irrelevant the fact that the applicants had by this stage been admitted indefinitely to the UK.[145]

VIII. One Commissioner's View: The British Government was Entitled to Pass the Legislation

In order to measure the extent of this victory, it is important to observe that the opposite argument could have won. One commissioner, Felix Welter, was thoroughly persuaded by the defence of the British government. To quote him,[146]

> The respondent Government has explained convincingly that following the grant of independence to Kenya and Uganda and the policy of 'Africanisation' adopted in those countries, the number of United Kingdom citizens of Asian origin who wanted to leave Africa to settle in the United Kingdom rose substantially to a point where it was no longer possible to absorb all who might wish to enter. In these circumstances... it became necessary to introduce immigration control to cover persons who, although they were citizens of the United Kingdom and Colonies, had no real link with Great Britain. The 1968 Act was directed at the same time to avoiding over-population and to assuring racial harmony. In order to achieve this double purpose it placed restrictions on the immigration of Asian citizens coming from Africa. These restrictions were, and remain, strict. They have never amounted to an absolute prohibition.[147]

The last assertion was true. A system of vouchers was in place which allowed the people fortunate enough to be granted one of them to come to the UK. The vouchers were limited in number, however. The total annual allocation of 'special vouchers'[148] for UK passport holders from East Africa who were heads of households had increased from 1,500 in 1968 to 3,000 in 1971,[149] which was completely insufficient to cater for the needs of the East African Asian population. The queue for one of these vouchers was such that it would take decades before some passport holders would be able to get them. The Commission did not discuss this, focusing instead on the issue of principle: the withdrawal of the pre-existing right of entry.

[144] The majority was six to three. However, two further members of the Commission—absent at the time of the vote—were expressly reported to have agreed with the majority: *East African Asians* report, para 209. The President of the Commission and British member, J.E.S. Fawcett, did not find a breach of Article 3. Instead he found a breach of Article 5, both on its own and in combination with Article 14, arguing that 'Article 5 establishes the principle... that personal status shall not be so changed by law in any of its elements as to make the life or position of the individual insecure': *East African Asians* report, para 239.

[145] *East African Asians* report, para 1.

[146] For his argument related to Protocol no. 4, see: dissenting opinion of Mr F. Welter in *East African Asians* report, para 258.

[147] *East African Asians* report, para 261.

[148] This was in contrast to the employment vouchers then used by the UK in its general immigration policy.

[149] *East African Asians* report, para 47. This number was increased again, to 3,500 in 1972 and to 5,000 in 1974: Drzemczewski 'A "Non-Decision"' 340 including note 6. Canada, the United States,

Welter, by contrast, was drawn towards the supposed practicalities of the situation. For him, the racial tensions mentioned by the government were real, for 'foreigners mix very little with the native population', given their 'natural tendency to settle in closely-knit groups', immigrants 'run the risk of constituting "foreign bodies" and [of being] a source of conflict', so that 'a chance event [might easily] degenerate into acts of violence'. The fears of the respondent government were thus in his view 'in no sense imaginary'. 'Responsible for public peace and order, the Government adopted measures which certainly took account of considerations involving race but which could not, in [Welter's] view, be said to amount to discrimination based on the colour or race of the people affected'.[150]

Welter recognised that the applicants had 'certainly been exposed to cruel sufferings, sufferings which were partly inflicted by the British authorities'. These, however, 'were the inevitable result of the putting into effect of the control measures devised by the 1968 Act. Their primary cause should [have been] sought in the harsh decisions taken in the countries where the applicants had lived for so many years—decisions for which the respondent Government [could] not be held responsible in the light of the Convention'.[151]

It is interesting that the last argument seemed to have had no weight on the other members of the Commission. This is despite the fact that a similar logic long prevented a finding at Strasbourg that the forced return by a European state to a country where the expelled individual would be at risk of being subjected to torture or inhuman treatment or punishment would be in violation of the Convention at Strasbourg. This jurisprudence did not start to change until the 1990s, as Chapter 7 reviews.[152] It is therefore worth stressing that the argument according to which it should not have been the UK which was blamed for the suffering of the applicants was not found persuasive by the Commission in the *East African Asians* case. Cause or consequence, in its rather short reasoning,[153] the Commission chose to focus on the withdrawal by the UK of a right (the right of entry) which the government had itself, of its own free will, granted the individuals who were now suddenly being deprived of it.

IX. Postcolonial Dereliction: BPPs Lose their Case

The Commission's focus on the withdrawal of the applicants' pre-existing right of entry may have helped to rebut some of the arguments advanced by the British government, as suggested in the previous section. But it also prevented a wider

Australia, and New Zealand also took some East African Asians: Ramnik Shah, 'The Nationality Factor in the Migration of Gujaratis to East Africa and Beyond', in Sharmina Mawani and Anjoom Mukadam (eds) *Gujarati Communities Across the Globe: Memory, Identity and Continuity* (Stoke on Trent: Trentham Books, 2012) 10. On the gender implications of the 'household head' criterion, see: Jacqueline Bhabha and Sue Shutter, *Women's Movement: Women under Immigration, Nationality and Refugee Law* (Chester: Trentham Books, 1994) 113–117.

150 *East African Asians* report, para 262.

151 *East African Asians* report, para 263.

152 The case which signalled this jurisprudential change is *Soering v. the United Kingdom*, appl. 14038/88, PC Judgment (ECtHR), 7 Jul. 1989.

153 *East African Asians* report, paras 179–215.

pro-applicant case to be made, as this section will show. While the *East African Asians* case is remembered for the way in which the Commission stood up to the British government and linked racism to degrading treatment, this should not obscure the fact that the Commission's reasoning also displayed shortcomings which, in a critical perspective, are highly significant. The Commission said nothing, for example, about the applicants' detention or 'shuttlecocking' (being sent to and fro between countries).[154] And most importantly for the subject of this book and the postcolonial perspective adopted in this chapter, the Commission washed its hands of the fate of BPPs.

In its report of 14 December 1973, the Commission considered 31 applications. Twenty-five of these had been lodged by citizens of the UK and its Colonies; the remaining six, by BPPs. This distinction in the legal status of the applicants had arisen from an accident of history. Due to the evolving relationship, from 1895 onwards, between the Imperial British East Africa Company, the Sultan of Zanzibar, and the British government, a strip of land running for ten miles along the Kenyan coast had received the title of 'Protectorate', while the interior had become a 'Colony'.[155] Over the ensuing decades, the UK held on to this vocabulary, for political reasons which had nothing to do with internal governance and all to do with international relations.[156] For those who lived in Kenya prior to independence, being a colonial subject or a protected person entailed no practical consequence whatsoever. The distinction in legal status between these two categories was entirely formal.

This distinction, however, made or broke the case of the applicants before the Commission because of the formality of the reasoning which this institution adopted. Its premise rested on the fact that 'according to English law, British protected persons, although not aliens, are not British subjects'.[157] BPPs had been subject to immigration control under the Commonwealth Immigrants Act 1962. This was taken to mean that the Commonwealth Immigrants Act 1968 had not changed their position as regards entry to the UK.[158] The Commission's unanimous

[154] The expression appeared in Ramnik Shah's letter published in the *East African Standard* on 26 February 1968. It is also used by the Commission.

[155] Ghai and McAuslan, *Public Law*, Chapter 1 entitled 'The Legal Origins of Colonial Power in Kenya'.

[156] '[B]y the turn of the [twentieth] century the protectorate authorities had acquired almost as full powers within the protectorate as they would have had if the whole area had been annexed as a colony, and whatever powers were lacking were soon obtained. The British Government appreciated this fact, and not only in relation to East Africa. In 1902 there was a discussion in the Foreign Office as to the desirability of annexing African protectorates. It was pointed out that though jurisdictional problems had existed and caused difficulties in the past, they were now tending to diminish and alterations in English law could virtually remove those that remained. On the other hand, there were political advantages in retaining protectorates. One could withdraw from them more easily, and conversely annexation might cause jealousies and objections from other powers. The Government thought it would be as well to avoid the possibility of friction, and maintain protectorate status': Ghai and McAuslan 33–34.

[157] *East African Asians* report, para 213.

[158] *East African Asians* report, para 213. In fact, CUKCs were also subject to immigration control under the Commonwealth Immigrants Act 1962, and the 1968 Act affected CUKCs and BPPs equally. Furthermore, once the 1968 Act was passed, the Quota Voucher scheme set up in its wake specifically included BPPs within its remit, thus putting them on a par with CUKCs. This was

conclusion was that, as regard BPPs, the 1968 Act could not be regarded as discriminatory and even less degrading in the sense of Article 3 of the Convention.[159]

Part of the applicants' case had been that, during the negotiations leading to the independence of Kenya and Uganda, the UK had effectively promised the Asians living there that they would be able to remain British, which had been received by this population as an important safeguard against any future difficulty.[160] East African Asians felt that the 1968 Act had reneged on the British government's pledge. They were not alone in thinking this: much of the unease which had been expressed in Parliament about the Act concerned the breaking of this implied pledge. The Commission, however, refused to enter these waters. It categorically stated that it '[did] not find it established that the United Kingdom gave an *express* understanding, by way of a *formal* pledge, that its citizens of Asian descent in East Africa would always be free to come to Britain'.[161]

Had a pledge, however informal, been at the centre of its reasoning, the Commission would have found it more difficult to dismiss the case of the BPPs. But the Commission carefully stayed away from questioning anything which might suggest that as a former colonial power, Britain had responsibilities towards her former colonial subjects. Any argument suggesting that postcolonial subjects would have had a moral claim to be welcomed in their former metropole was bound to have fallen on deaf ears. This does not mean that it had no ethical purchase. However, it could not have been explicitly aired during the Strasbourg proceedings.

In its report, the Commission observed that the question before it was not whether racial discrimination in immigration control constituted as such degrading treatment.[162] It circumscribed this question as being whether the Commonwealth Immigrants Act 1968 was contrary to Article 3 of the Convention.[163] The question was then examined in rather narrow and formal terms, as already noted. The adopted reasoning allowed the Commission to take domestic nationality law as a given, without questioning its foundations. In the following years and decades, the Commission would always stick to this approach, never starting to ask whether or not there was any sense in which the granting, or lack of, citizenship in national law was legitimate.[164]

achieved through a new nomenclature of 'United Kingdom Passport Holders' (UKPHs), a category which included BPPs and British Subjects without citizenship as well as CUKCs. It is finally worth noting that upon the commencement of the British Nationality Act 1948, BPPs could enter the 'mother' country without any let or hindrance—their passports were not even stamped on arrival. I am thankful to Ramnik Shah for drawing my attention to all these facts. See further: Shah, 'Britain and Kenya: Some Immigration and Nationality Issues' (1992) *Immigration and Nationality Law in Practice* 6, 35–39. It has not been checked whether these facts were put to the Commission.

159 *East African Asians* report, para 214.

160 Shah 'The Nationality Factor' 1–12 at 7–8.

161 *East African Asians* report, para 203, emphases added.

162 *East African Asians* report, para 196.

163 *East African Asians* report, para 196.

164 Recent cases have occasionally forced the Strasbourg Court to start approaching this question, but without much appetite. See Chapter 5, Section VI.

In the instant case, the 1968 Act proved problematic, only because the UK had traditionally adopted a wide definition of citizenship.[165] Had it always defined citizenship narrowly and labelled the East African Asians as aliens, it is unlikely that any applicant would have managed to persuade the Commission that the sudden immigration controls to which they were subjected were contrary to Article 3.

X. The East African Asians Story Continued: More Immigration Controls

As it was, 25 applications were successful before the Commission. What impact the Strasbourg proceedings may have had on the fate of East African Asians, beyond the applicants, is difficult to assess. In 1972, East African Asians were expelled from Uganda. The British government publicly said and repeated that it had a moral and legal duty to accept them for settlement.[166] As is well known, once in Britain, they were sent to camps and enjoined not to settle in some areas—a prescription they tended to ignore in order to enjoy the support of family and community networks. But even before this, they encountered serious difficulties in obtaining the vouchers they required to be able to enter the UK. The ignominies they faced are described in some detail in a short book which was published in 1975, entitled *Slamming the Door*.[167] The authors of this book were hoping that their readers would find the story they told, on the basis of carefully collected and collated testimonies, disturbing.[168] Judging from my experience, they were successful in this aim. They explained that in practice—though not in theory—no one was eligible for a voucher until they were actually unemployed,[169] so that Asians were forced to remain in East Africa on low salaries.[170] Documents which had not been required would suddenly be deemed necessary, even if these were impossible to produce; documents previously accepted were rejected.[171] People were told at the last minute that they could go, making it impossible for them to organise their departure.[172] Some did not receive their voucher until their children had reached the age of majority, barring them for coming as a family, which they thought was done purposely by the authorities.[173] The list of obstacles put to the departure of British Asians from East Africa seems to have been endless.[174]

[165] As the British government saw and observed in its submissions to the Commission: *East African Asians* report, para 114.

[166] Robert Moore and Tina Wallace, *Slamming the Door: The Administration of Immigration Control* (London: Martin Robertson, 1975) 29.

[167] Moore and Wallace.

[168] Moore and Wallace, Foreword.

[169] Moore and Wallace 30.

[170] Moore and Wallace 32.

[171] Moore and Wallace 36.

[172] Moore and Wallace 34.

[173] Moore and Wallace 43.

[174] It should be noted that East African Asians are now commonly seen as a success story of entrepreneurship and good integration in Britain. See e.g. Vaughan Robinson, 'Marching into the Middle Classes? The Long-term Resettlement of East African Asians in the UK' (1993) *Journal of Refugee Studies* 6, 230–248.

XI. Closure of the Gates in Time of Crisis: A Paradox of Human Rights Law

Time and again, obstacles are erected as increasing numbers of human beings decide to flee a situation which they feel is becoming increasingly desperate. In the late 1930s, 'all the democratic countries where Jews sought refuge [from Germany and Austria] found ways of manipulating immigration procedures to exclude them'.[175] The result was that, to take just one example which has been meticulously detailed by historian Louise London, 'escape to Britain was an exception for the lucky few; exclusion was the fate of the majority'.[176] When Europe confronted its worst refugee crisis since World War II during the Yugoslav wars of the 1990s,[177] governments responded again by hastily requesting visas from those who were fleeing. One exception was Germany, whose citizens felt a duty to help refugees.[178] Today, it is the Afghans, Syrians and other victims of conflicts and poor governance who find themselves at the receiving end of exclusionary measures. No doubt the same reflex of rejection awaits the 'hordes of people' who, sooner or later, will move due to unbearable environmental pressure. It might be reasonable to assume that one function of the law would be to provide a safety net for these human beings who are in a particularly precarious situation. It seems the opposite is true. The equation which seems to hold in practice is that the more acute the crisis, the greater the obstacles. The *East African Asians* case has nothing to offer to counteract this tendency. Neither the European Commission as it was examining the case nor the European Court in its subsequent case law has shown any readiness to insist that de facto refugees must be treated first as human beings with human needs which must be catered for, before being categorised as foreigners with barely any legal entitlements.

XII. Conclusion

The Commission's finding in the *East African Asians* case was a clear moral victory for those who had fought on the side of the applicants. Declaring the Commonwealth Immigrants Act 1968 to be racially motivated and to constitute, as such, a degrading treatment contrary to Article 3 of the European Convention

[175] Louise London, *Whitehall and the Jews 1933–1948: British Immigration Policy and the Holocaust* (Cambridge: Cambridge University Press, 2000) 5.

[176] London 12. London estimates at over 500,000 the number of files in the archives of the main Jewish organisation which dealt with refugees at the time; about 80,000 Jewish refugees were admitted in the UK.

[177] Henry Kamm, 'Yugoslav Refugee Crisis Europe's Worst Since 40's', *The New York Times*, 24 July 1992, available at <http://www.nytimes.com/1992/07/24/world/yugoslav-refugee-crisis-europe-s-worst-since-40-s.html>, accessed 8 January 2013.

[178] BBC News, 'World: Europe Refugees arrive in Germany', 9 April 1999, available at <http://news.bbc.co.uk/1/hi/world/europe/314948.stm>, accessed 8 January 2013.

was a doctrinal achievement of potentially considerable import, which continues to be cited today. However, the case cannot be said to have produced a resounding legal victory. First, the confidential report of the Commission did not spur the British government into repealing the legislation; British Asians continued to experience difficulties in entering and living in the UK throughout the 1970s. Second, the doctrinal development of linking racism to degrading treatment failed to be embraced by the Strasbourg institutions in subsequent cases (with the sole exception of *Cyprus v. Turkey*). Third, the Commission's report did not denounce in any way the all-too-familiar phenomenon whereby a state closes its doors even more tightly as more and more individuals face increasing difficulties in their place of residence and seek refuge elsewhere—even when this state contributes to the unbearable character of the situation developing in the country of residence. Fourth, the case took nationality laws as a natural fact of life rather than a social construct in need of careful scrutiny under a human rights lens. Fifth, and most importantly, it left postcolonial responsibility outside the human rights equation.

This chapter has shown how crucial a context the colonial situation was in the development of the Strasbourg system of human rights protection. Neither Belgium, France, the Netherlands, nor the UK would have been persuaded to become party to a convention which did not offer them the possibility of averting that its guarantees extend to the colonial subjects under their jurisdiction. This was achieved through Article 63 and/or Articles 25 and 46 ECHR. Once colonialism had ended, the same exclusionary philosophy would guide the way postcolonial situations would be approached by the Strasbourg institutions, as in the *East African Asian* case.

Dealing with postcolonial British passport holders suddenly denied a right of entry to the UK which they had formally enjoyed, this case certainly fits the classification of postcolonial. The odds were stacked against the applicants: postcolonial responsibility had never been part of the human rights language. Saying the same thing the other way around, postcolonial dereliction has always been entirely acceptable in the human rights framework. So-called BPPs lost outright; those with the status of citizens of the UK and its Colonies half won—or half lost.

Given that most migration routes across the world followed former colonial links throughout the second half of the twentieth century, the institutional resistance to finding anything wrong with a colonial power abandoning or turning away from its former colonial subjects is of central importance when thinking about the human rights of migrants. Barring the exceptional circumstances of the British legislation of 1968, the Commission would not have brought within the ambit of human rights law the treatment by a former colony of its former colonial subjects.

The reader will have noticed that the first case against the UK to reach Strasbourg was a colonial case—the *Greece* case—and the first case lodged by an individual upon which the Commission adopted a report on the merits, which happened again to be against the UK, was a postcolonial one—the *East African Asians* case. This colonial/postcolonial trope should not be regarded as purely coincidental. The first individual case against the UK which the Commission declared admissible (without proceeding to adopt a report on the merits) is again a postcolonial case, as we shall see in Chapter 4. In this case, the applicant, represented by none other than Anthony Lester, was a Pakistani mill worker in the Midlands whose son had been refused admission to the UK. Lester must have considered human rights to constitute a most promising lens through which to approach issues related to the colonial past and/or migration (two issues which at the time would have appeared to be largely conflated). Under domestic law, a postcolonial case could conveniently be dismissed as 'no longer our State's responsibility'; the non-admission of former colonial subjects as 'falling within our sovereign discretion' logic. Lester must have hoped that human rights law could offer a real alternative to the state law logic. He was right, but only to a certain point, as this chapter has demonstrated.

Colonialism now appears like a bygone era, the colonial roots of the European Convention forgotten. In contrast to this perspective, this book argues that we must remember that ECHR rights were not meant for colonial subjects. There exists a long-established legacy of ignoring colonial connections and leaving postcolonial patterns outside human rights law. Indeed this pattern pertains to the whole of the migrant Strasbourg case law. In opposition to it, this book urges keeping in sight the way in which the European Convention embodies in its very text the contradictions between the proclamation of universal aspirations and realpolitik interests of political subjugation, enabling some human beings to move whilst wishing and indeed ordering others to stay put.

4

Dislocating Families: The Strasbourg Reversal

(Abdulaziz, Cabales and Balkandali)

At the heart of this chapter is the very first judgment which the European Court of Human Rights rendered in a migrant case. The case's full name is *Abdulaziz, Cabales and Balkandali v. United Kingdom*,[1] but it is shortened here to *ABC*, as was done informally in the 1980s.[2] The applicants were three 'immigration widows'; women who were living in the UK without their husbands because immigration rules prevented the latter from joining them. The Court, sitting in its plenary formation, rendered its judgment in the case in 1985. This was comparatively late: by then the Court had already been active for over 25 years.[3] *ABC*, its 74th judgment, came out when a number of important general human rights doctrines were already developed. This new judgment asserted the principle, which it claimed was 'well established in international law', that states have a right to control the entry and residence of aliens. Such a premise was inevitably unfavourable to migrants' rights. Adopted unanimously by a Plenary Court, *ABC* remains a leading case today, to which the Court continues to refer on a regular basis.

ABC was not the first complaint lodged at Strasbourg regarding the refusal by the state to admit the applicant's family members—far from it. The very first individual application against the UK which the Commission had declared admissible already concerned family reunification. It was brought by a Yorkshire mill-worker originally from Pakistan whose teenage son had been refused entry into the UK. The Commission declared the case, called *Alam and Khan*, admissible in 1967.[4] It did not proceed to write a report on its merits, however, for the parties reached a friendly settlement. Having failed to produce any binding interpretation of the Convention, the case fell into oblivion (except for the occasional reference in Anthony Lester's—the applicants' representative—writings).[5]

[1] *Abdulaziz, Cabales and Balkandali*, appls 9214/80, 9473/81, 9474/81, PC Judgment (ECtHR), 28 May 1985.

[2] Jacqueline Bhabha and Sue Shutter, *Women's Movement: Women under Immigration, Nationality and Refugee Law* (Stoke-on-Trent: Trentham Books, 1994) 73. This case should not be confused with the officially named *A, B and C v. Ireland*, appl. 25579/05, GC Judgment, 16 Dec. 2010.

[3] *Lawless v. Ireland*, appl. 332/57, Judgment (ECtHR), 1 July 1961.

[4] *Alam and Khan v. United Kingdom*, appl. 2991/66, PCom Report (EComHR), 17 Dec. 1968.

[5] See e.g. Anthony Lester, 'Fundamental Rights: The United Kingdom Isolated?' (1984) *Public Law* Spring, 47–72 at 65.

A second application, similar to *Alam and Khan*, had been lodged on the same day, also by Lester. The Commission declared it inadmissible because it concerned the entry into the UK of the father (rather than the underage son) of a migrant worker.[6]

This chapter reviews in detail these two applications, which were put forward at a time when the Strasbourg slate was blank, so to speak. In this pioneering period, the parties could have felt free to advance any argument which appeared reasonable to them. Likewise, members of the Commission and judges were able to phrase their reasoning outside the constraints arising from previous pronouncements.[7] A close reading of these early decisions can thus be extremely instructive, making it possible to trace the origins of staple principles of European human rights law, including some which had not initially appeared obvious.

Having said this, such a study reveals that the Commission *always* endorsed the state's prerogative to exclude aliens. This approach constitutes an application of the principle of state sovereignty and does not encourage a wide interpretation of migrants' rights. In time, the Court, as expected, followed the Commission,[8] and thus confirmed the relative closure of the European Convention system to the predicament of migrants. *ABC*, its first judgment in a migrant case, ruled that it would have been up to the applicant women to go and live with their husbands in their country of nationality/residence if they wanted to pursue family life with them; the UK had not infringed their Convention right to private and family life (although the government had been wrong in making it more difficult for migrant women than migrant men to be joined by their spouses). This set the Strasbourg case law on a course from which it has rarely diverted. To this day, with some rather heavily circumscribed exceptions, European human rights law does not prohibit states from disallowing family reunion.

This position has become so normalised that it is perhaps important to clarify its implications. It means that European Convention law has nothing to say about the way in which state immigration laws force many families to live in a condition of dislocation by preventing family reunion and leaving the family 'dismembered' (as members are kept in different locations). It also pushes for a relocation of the whole family in a place which the family would not have considered primarily suitable, were it not for the restrictions they experienced under immigration laws (another form of dislocation). As this chapter demonstrates, European human rights law is by and large impervious to the pain suffered by these families.

Sociologically speaking, it is fitting for the first leading case of the migrant Strasbourg case law to have concerned family reunion. This reflects the fact that family reunion came to replace labour recruitment as the major source of migration into Western Europe after the economic expansion of the immediate

[6] *H.S. v. United Kingdom*, appl. 2992/66, Decision (EComHR), 15 July 1967, document D 20.224 communicated to the author by the Court's Archives Service.

[7] This is in stark contrast to today's 'tyranny of the precedent', lamented by some judges who regret the cut-and-paste technique applied by the Registry in its preparation of draft judgments.

[8] As noted in Chapter 3, (60 n. 3) the Commission had the reputation of being less progressive than the Court.

post-World War II came to a halt. Between 1945 and 1973, foreign labour was actively recruited in all the highly industrialised countries of Western Europe (as well as North America and Australasia). Workers from less developed countries were sought at one stage or another to work in the fast-developing industries of the following countries: the UK, Belgium, France, Switzerland, the Netherlands, Germany, Luxembourg, and Sweden. Labour demand also fuelled spontaneous migration to Britain, France, and the Netherlands from former colonies. All this came to an end with the 'oil crisis' of 1973–1974, at the latest. Then, family reunion became the main legal route for migrants from 'the South' to enter Western Europe, with the transition occurring slightly earlier in the UK.[9]

This chapter starts by placing *Alam and Khan* and its sister application in this historical context. It continues with a review of the pioneering arguments which had been submitted by Lester and the British government in these cases. It explains that it soon became clear that the Convention was going to be interpreted in a way which would not contemplate the idea that migrants might have a right to choose their country of residence. The chapter then turns to the *ABC* case. The change in British immigration policy which spurred the case is first noted. This is followed by a detailed review of the ruling, including the facts of the three test cases which the Commission selected for examination; the Court's confirmation of the absence of a right to family reunion in the Convention; its verdict that the UK had violated the prohibition of discrimination on grounds of sex; and finally, its opposite finding regarding race. The implications of this unanimous judgment by the Plenary Court are then teased out. The fact that the Court seems to share states' fear of immigration is noted before shifting the attention to the supposedly, but neither historically nor theoretically, 'well-established' principle of international law, according to which states can exclude most aliens without justification, which occupies a central place in the case law. This leads to the identification of a conceptual reversal which mars the Strasbourg migrant case law.

The discussion proceeds from there by noting that applicants denied family reunion are occasionally successful at Strasbourg—often due to the poignancy of their personal circumstances, such as in *Tuquabo-Tekle and Others v. the Netherlands*, and/or the constitution of the bench which examines their case. Moving on towards jurisprudential prospects, it is intimated that the rarity of verdicts of violation in family reunion cases seems to make it unlikely that the Court might come to decide that the increasingly restrictive immigration policies pursued by European states infringe the Convention. The chapter ends by observing that the Court's resistance to defending even the conventional (from a European mainstream perspective) family lives of migrants means that it is not in a good position to defend migrants' more unconventional family patterns, with disastrous consequences if the recognition of a variety of cultural mores is considered to be at the core of the human rights project.

[9] Stephen Castles and Mark J. Miller, *The Age of Migration: International Population Movements in the Modern World* (New York: Palgrave Macmillan, 2009) 96–101 and 108.

I. From Labour to Family Migration

From the late 1950s, migration from the New Commonwealth, understood to comprise former or remaining British colonies in the Caribbean, the Indian sub-continent, and Africa, was increasingly considered problematic in Britain. By contrast, immigration to the UK from the Old Commonwealth (Canada and Australia) did not attract the same response. Half a million people of New Commonwealth origin had settled in the UK by 1961, over 50 per cent more than a decade previously. The fear that immigrants would keep coming and coming led the UK to pass the Commonwealth Immigrants Act 1962, which for the first time subjected those with a British passport issued by a colonial authority to immigration control. Coupled with the stagnation then experienced by the British economy (which happened earlier than in the other European countries), this virtually brought labour immigration to the UK to an end.[10]

In this new phase, the British government initially continued to celebrate family as a cherished value, and there was no question of limiting the rights of entry of the wives and children of those permitted entry to the UK under the 1962 Act. Wrongly assuming that primary migrants were in virtually all cases male, this piece of legislation facilitated family reunion to wives but also to women living in a 'permanent association' with a man, either out of respect for 'local custom' or in order to avoid having the 'risks' of having large numbers of unaccompanied males in the country.[11]

Possibly inspired by fear of further immigration restrictions, family immigration increased rapidly after the passing of the 1962 Act. In turn, the rising number of dependants became a source of anxiety and debate, fuelling new restrictive measures. Monthly immigration statistics (including on countries of origin) started to be kept in 1965. Helena Wray notes that, 'From this period there were fewer statements of unequivocal support in favour of family reunion and fewer sentimental paeans to the immigrant contribution to health and other public services'.[12] This, therefore, is the context in which to understand the family reunion applications against the UK lodged at Strasbourg in 1966.

II. Joined Applications but Distinct Fates: *Alam and Khan*'s Friendly Settlement v. *H.S.*'s Inadmissibility

Two applications were lodged with the European Commission against the UK on 20 December 1966: applications nos 2991/66 and 2992/66. They bore striking similarities, and the Commission joined them. As already mentioned, one was

[10] Castles and Miller *Age of Migration* 102.

[11] These 'risks' were considered to include the spreading of venereal diseases. See Helena Wray, *Regulating Marriage Migration into the UK: A Stranger in the Home* (Farnham: Ashgate, 2011) 41–44.

[12] Wray *Regulating* 68–71.

lodged by a citizen of Pakistan, Mr Alam, whose 13-year-old son Khan had been denied entry into the UK; the other by a British national of Indian origin, a Mr H.S., whose widowed father had also been denied entry. The two main applicants had come to the UK for the first time in 1957, one aged 40, the other 23.[13] Both applicants were illiterate and worked in Yorkshire, one as a mill worker and the other as a textile worker. They were both defended by Anthony Lester.[14]

By his first marriage, Mr Alam[15] had three children, the eldest of whom was with him in England. After the death of his brother, Mr Alam had married his brother's widow. By his second marriage, he had another three children. He returned to Pakistan in November 1963 and flew back to England in June 1965, accompanied by the two sons, aged 13 and 10, from his second marriage. The boys' details appeared in his passport. What happened next is recounted in the admissibility decision of the Commission in the following words:

> The Applicant was permitted to enter the country, but his two sons were refused entry and were repatriated to Pakistan on the same day. The Applicant states that the immigration officials said that MK and K were not his sons. He states that when he was questioned about his family he had only disclosed the names of one of his two wives because he was 'afraid that if [he] revealed the fact that he was twice married [he] might be exposed to criminal prosecution'.
>
> The Applicant then made renewed efforts to secure the admission of his son MK, through an Immigration Consultant and through the Pakistan High Commission in London. As a result, MK again travelled to England by air, arriving at London Airport at 6.0 a.m. on 10th July, 1966. The Applicant was there to meet him.
>
> The Applicant states that he was again questioned through an interpreter about his family history, at intervals throughout that day. He did not fully understand the interpreter. He states that he was not 'allowed any representation', although his eldest son by his first marriage was present and could have interpreted for him.
>
> The Applicant was informed by officials that his son MK would be sent back to Pakistan. He asked the officials to delay repatriation while he tried to have the decision changed. The Applicant then on the following day consulted a solicitor. On the next day he tried, through the Pakistan High Commission, to obtain telegraphic confirmation that MK was in fact his son. It appears that he was allowed 24 hours by the immigration authorities to establish the relationship. On 13th July, 1966, at noon, in the Applicant's absence, MK was repatriated.
>
> It appears that the Applicant was only permitted to see his son MK briefly on two occasions at London Airport.

[13] This account is based on Document D 20.224, consisting of the 'Decision of the Commission as to the Admissibility' of these two cases. The Archives Service of the European Court of Human Rights kindly communicated me this document after I requested the permission to consult the files of these two cases—a request which was denied due to the confidential character of the Commission's files.

[14] The official documents say that the applicants were represented by Messrs Theodore Goddard and Co. In practice, the defence seems to have been assured by Anthony Lester. As the legal representative of two of the applicants in the *East African Asians* case, Lester was already mentioned in Chapter 3.

[15] The decision of admissibility of 15 July 1967 refers to Mr Alam as 'MA'. However, the report of the Sub-Commission of 17 December 1968 names him.

The second application pointed to a very similar story: difficulties of interpretation at the airport, misunderstandings in questions and answers (such that the applicant had e.g. been understood to say that his mother was still alive while he was at that point talking about an aunt with whom he had lived as a child), frantic efforts on the part of the applicant to try to obtain assistance from the Indian High Commissioner in London and provide proof of his relationship with his father, and the permission to see his father only twice and briefly during what can only be described as the latter's detention at the airport.

The two applications argued that the British authorities had violated three articles of the European Convention: Article 6 guaranteeing fair trial, Article 8 guaranteeing family life, and Article 13 requiring that a domestic remedy before a national authority be in place in case of a violation of the Convention. Along with Articles 3 and 14, already cited in Chapter 3, these are the provisions most often referred to in this book, and it is worth citing them.

The first sentence of Article 6 reads: 'In the determination of his civil rights and obligations or of any criminal charge against him, everyone is entitled to a fair and public hearing within a reasonable time by an independent and impartial tribunal established by law'.[16] Consisting of two paragraphs, Article 8 states: '(1) Everyone has the right to respect for his private and family life, his home and his correspondence. (2) There shall be no interference by a public authority with the exercise of this right except such as is in accordance with the law and is necessary in a democratic society in the interests of national security, public safety or the economic well-being of the country, for the prevention of disorder or crime, for the protection of health or morals, or for the protection of the rights and freedoms of others'. The phrasing of Article 13 is testimony to the revolution which the Convention's willingness to bring authorities to task represented in 1950. It states: 'Everyone whose rights and freedoms as set forth in the Convention are violated shall have an effective remedy before a national authority notwithstanding that the violation has been committed by persons acting in an official capacity'.

Going back to the two applications, the Commission ruled on the one concerning the father's refused entry that, having regard to the adult status of the applicant and the long period during which he and his father had been living apart, no family life had been established within the meaning of Article 8. It thus held the part of the *H.S.* application regarding Article 8 manifestly ill-founded. As a result there was no 'civil right' in dispute within the meaning of Article 6 either. The complaint under Article 13 fell too.

Application 2991/66, concerning the son's refused entry, was deemed to be different. The Commission accepted that in this case the complaint under Article 8

[16] Subsequent provisions need not be reproduced here given that the Strasbourg institutions have found that Article 6 is not applicable in immigration proceedings. See *Maaouia v. France*, appl. 39652/98, GC Judgment (ECtHR), 5 Oct. 2000, discussed later in this chapter and especially in Chapter 7, Section IX (223–4). The full text of the Convention is widely available, including on the Court's website: <http://www.echr.coe.int/Documents/Convention_ENG.pdf>, accessed 18 June 2014.

raised 'issues of law and fact whose determination should depend upon an examination of the merits of the case'. Significantly in view of subsequent case law, the Commission also held that 'the determination of a right to respect for family life under Article 8 may well be considered as the determination of a civil right within the meaning of Article 6' so that the complaint under Article 6 could not be declared manifestly ill-founded. By contrast, the Commission thought that Article 13 did not raise any issue worthy of separate examination.

By decision of 15 July 1967, the Commission held the father's case inadmissible but the son's case admissible. The latter application then followed the normal course at the time, which was for a Sub-Commission to be set up which placed itself 'at the disposal of the parties concerned with a view to securing a friendly settlement of the matter on the basis of respect for Human Rights as defined in [the] Convention'. Indeed, a friendly settlement was reached in the case (so that the Commission never adopted a report stating whether it thought a violation of the Convention had occurred in the case). The settlement, recorded on 17 December 1968, provided that the UK would grant Mr Alam's son an entry certificate and pay his air fare from Karachi to London. This was offered ex gratia, the government maintaining that the issues raised by the applicant were devoid of any merit.

Through the friendly settlement, Mr Alam and his son got what they wanted. The law, however, was not settled: neither the Commission nor the Court had pronounced on what the Convention did and did not require. In the light of subsequent case law, it is nonetheless clear that the argument presented by the government at the admissibility stage would prove persuasive in the long run and thus be incorporated into European human rights law. Moreover, a clear lesson had already emerged from the Commission's decision of inadmissibility in *H.S.*: the parent–child relationship would normally fall outside the protection of Article 8 ECHR when family reunion was sought between adults. Aside from the fact that this arguably goes against the concept of the family prevailing even in the West,[17] it certainly did not bode well, in migrant cases, in respect of any concept of family that did not fall squarely within the Western model of the nuclear family.

III. What Does the Human Right to Family Entail? The Migrants' Response

The first complaint which had been put forward by the applicants in *Alam and Khan* and *H.S.* concerned Article 6. It will not be reviewed in detail here

[17] As suggested by the fact that European Community/Union law has always allowed workers to be joined by their parents in their movements if it could be shown that the elder relatives were dependent on that worker. See Article 10 of Regulation (EEC) No. 1612/68 of the Council of 15 October 1968 on Freedom of Movement for Workers within the Community; now replaced by Articles 2 and 3 of Directive 2004/38/EC of the European Parliament and of the Council of 29 April 2004 on the right of citizens of the Union and their family members to move and reside freely within the territory of the Member States.

except to say that Lester started with it, presumably because he thought that it was either the most logical or the most winnable allegation of a violation of the Convention. Since the Grand Chamber's judgment of 2001 in *Maaouia v. France*, only a very daring lawyer would think of invoking Article 6 in an immigration case (see more on this in Chapter 7). However, in the 1960s, there was no reason to think that this complaint would necessarily fail. Lester argued that the *summary* refusal of having a son (*Alam and Khan*) or father (*H.S.*) join their relative in a state party to the Convention contravened Article 6 which lays down the guarantees which must be met for a trial to be fair. According to him, the son was entitled to enter the UK under the domestic legislation in force, and so was the father under the instructions issued to the immigration authorities. The main problem could therefore be conceptualised as procedural rather than substantive.[18] Rather than finding the complaint manifestly ill-founded (as would be likely today), the Commission declared it admissible.

Lester's second claim was that Article 8 had been violated.[19] It is worth quoting his submission at length in order to enable the reader to decide whether the arguments advanced by Lester held:

> The notion of freedom to choose the family place of residence is inherent in the principle of respect for family life under Article 8, paragraph (1) and is limited only in so far as is permitted under Article 8, paragraph (2)....
>
> A State which ratifies the Convention agrees to restrict the free exercise of its rights under general international law so as to conform to the obligations imposed on it by the Convention. Such a State must, therefore, exercise its right to control immigration into its territory in a manner which does not violate Article 8....
>
> Having admitted the Applicants to permanent residence there was an obligation on the part of the United Kingdom Government to permit the members of their families to join them subject to the exceptions set out in Article 8, paragraph (2)....
>
> The definition of family is a question of fact in each case but it must include a young son and an aged widowed father.
>
> ...

[18] Lester claimed that the way admission had been refused was deficient under Article 6 because: the proceedings through which this had happened had not been public; the applicants had not been permitted to be legally represented; they had not had the opportunity to explain apparent inconsistencies in their statements; the immigration officers' decisions had not been explained; his clients had neither been given sufficient time or facilities to obtain evidence nor been put in a position to communicate with the authorities in their language; and they could not resort to an independent and impartial tribunal. This had occurred in respect of a civil right, namely, the right not to be separated from one's family.

[19] Lester did not try to argue that Article 3 of the Convention had been violated. In line with this, the applications do not recall anything about the way the 13-year-old son and the 'aged' father had experienced their detention, interrogation, and removal. They are likely to have felt anxious and helpless, the more so in an environment where, presumably, their language was not spoken. In all likelihood, Lester thought that a claim for inhuman and degrading treatment would not appear to have been sufficiently severe to engage Article 3. In this, he would have been right. The high threshold set for Article 3 to be deemed applicable is discussed in Chapter 7.

> Even after the Commonwealth Immigration Act 1962, a child under 16 is entitled as of right to enter in order to join his father who is settled permanently... in the United Kingdom and, by virtue of the general instructions issued to the immigration authorities under the Act, a widowed father over sixty would also be entitled to join his son settled in the United Kingdom....
>
> The Applicants were entitled to have their close relatives, in one case the father and in the other case the son, to live with them at the place chosen by the family.... [20]

This reasoning may appear incongruous today. Convention lawyers will know that the Convention has not been interpreted in the way suggested by Lester and even the non-expert may be aware that the prevailing view is that the admission of 'aliens' is a prerogative of the state—hardly ever a right. However, this need not have been a given of European human rights law.

There were three strands in Lester's submission which had the potential of becoming foundational in Convention law. The first is that judicial reasoning in response to alleged violations of the Convention should take as their starting point the provision which is the subject of the dispute and the right it provides. It might be thought that such a proposition was obvious. However, the Strasbourg case law is replete with rulings in which Article 8 ECHR is not the starting point of the reasoning adopted by the Commission and the Court in migrant cases. The significance of this point cannot be overstated and will be discussed in detail later in this chapter. The second strand laid by Lester was the suggestion that when state actions are questioned in a way which is not frivolous, the state must show that its actions are in accordance with the rights provided in the Convention. This proposition is defended in this book as central to the rule of law. However, with rare exceptions,[21] the Strasbourg institutions take the view that the state has no obligation towards an 'alien' who is not on its territory, with the consequence that the state is not required to demonstrate how it respects Convention rights in relation to him (as it is held to have no responsibility towards him). The third strand would have rested on the observation that respecting a human being entails considering this person not only as an isolated individual but also as a social being, for whom the family is typically an important grouping. Admittedly this last proposition was always bound to encounter resistance, as it goes against the individualism which pervades the liberal legal rights tradition. It did not take root: the person protected by the Convention is generally conceived as an isolated individual.[22]

[20] *Alam and Khan* report, pp. 8–9.

[21] See e.g. *Tuquabo-Teke and Others v. the Netherlands*, appl. 60665/00, Judgment (ECtHR), 1 Dec. 2005, reviewed below, Section XIII of the current chapter.

[22] A certain feminist critique might add that this individual tends to be male, white, and middle class. See generally V. Spike Peterson, 'Whose Rights? A Critique of the "Givens" in Human Rights Discourse' (1990) *Alternatives* 15, 303–344; Dianne Otto (ed.) *Gender Issues and Human Rights* (London: Elgar, 2013). See also Marie-Bénédicte Dembour, *Who Believes in Human Rights: Reflections on the European Convention* (Cambridge: Cambridge University Press, 2006), Chapter 7.

IV. The Government's Reply: The State's Right of Exclusion

The government had replied to Lester's submission with an argument which started from a completely different standpoint:

> At international level the United Kingdom has the undoubted right to exclude all persons who are not citizens of the United Kingdom and Colonies, whether aliens or Commonwealth citizens. If the member States by entering into the Convention intended to limit this right they would have done so in clear terms but the whole Convention contains no reference to the question of immigration. It is impossible to read into Article 8 a right for immigrants to enter regardless of the laws of the State concerned.
>
> If the Applicant's contention amounts to saying that once one member of the family has been accepted he has the right to be joined by all his possibly numerous relatives, such contention is untenable. What Article 8 really means is that within the jurisdiction of each country families must not be forced to separate. To construe the Article as abrogating in a large measure immigration laws which all countries have in one form or other is absurd.
>
> The Applicants came to the United Kingdom in 1957 leaving their families behind them. In so doing they were clearly prepared to accept the disruption of their family life at any rate for the time being. The admission into the country concerned of a member or alleged member of the original immigrant's family in order to remedy such a situation is not a matter covered by Article 8, paragraph (1) of the Convention. The separation has been caused by the Applicants and not by the immigration laws.
>
> The immigration laws are necessary inter alia in the interests of the economic well-being of the country and therefore not in conflict with Article 8.[23]

To some readers, each of these propositions will appear sensible and their combination a tight and entirely logical argument. Indeed, it is this argument which became the Commission's mainstream way of understanding (the lack of) entitlements to family reunion under the European Convention. The Court then overall followed suit when it finally started to receive migrant cases from the mid-1980s onwards.

With the benefit of hindsight, the government's argument of 1967 must nonetheless be said to have gone too far in two respects. First, it wrongly suggested that state sovereignty entails *complete* discretion for the state to grant or refuse access to its territory to any alien. It has now long been recognised that there are cases where the presence of an alien must be allowed to take place—for example, when a forced return entails the risk of torture in the country of origin. Second, whenever family life is established,[24] the refusal to let a family member join their kin is considered to raise an issue under Article 8, a point the government did not grant in its original submission. This, however, does not prevent the refusal to be

[23] Alam and Khan report, pp. 7–8.

[24] Establishing family life is a factual question. The Court says that it depends upon the reality of close personal ties. The one exception concerns the parent–child relationship which is normally accepted to fall, as such, within the ambit of 'family life': Nuala Mole, *Asylum and the European Convention on Human Rights* (Strasbourg: Council of Europe Publishing, 2010) 96.

justifiable under paragraph 2 of Article 8, as the government intimated at the end of the quoted passage.

Apart from these two points, the reasoning presented by the government in *Alam and Khan* became the staple interpretation of Article 8 by the Commission and the Court. The following assumptions can be said to form part of Convention law (though not without great discomfort from some judges, who sometimes manage to bring in a different logic in the case law):

- The point of departure of any reasoning on family reunion and other immigration issues is the principle that States are entitled to exclude aliens.
- The Convention purposely refrained from giving migrants rights, so that migrants' rights emerge in the Convention indirectly (in French, *par ricochet*).
- State immigration laws are acceptable.
- Family separation arises out of the migrant applicants' own actions (with possible exceptions in rare circumstances).
- It is understandable and acceptable for the government's allegiance to be first and foremost to the country of which it is in charge.
- The defendant state does not have to explain in detail how it understands its duty to act in its country's best interests as regard its policy and practice on the admission/rejection of aliens.

In this scheme, neither long-lasting colonial links nor active labour recruitment programmes of the post-World War II are thought to have any influence over the situation of family dislocation in which migrants find themselves; this dislocation is conceptualised as having emerged independently from any governmental action. As a result, neither the national authorities nor the Strasbourg Court take the position that the state has any obligation to migrants seeking family reunion: it is the migrants who have provoked the family separation of which they complain. *They* are responsible for the situation which has arisen from their own actions, decisions, and choices, adopted of their own free will. *They* are also the ones on which the onus falls for sorting it out. If family relationships are so important to them, *they* can return to their country of origin. Family dislocation has nothing to do with the government—nor, then, with human rights.

V. From a Blank Slate to No Right to Choose One's Country of Residence

Back in the 1960s, that these assumptions would become Convention law was not yet clear. The UK obviously thought that there was a risk it would lose *Alam and Khan*, or it would not have invited Mr Alam's son back, so as to reach the friendly settlement. This was at a time when the jurisprudential slate was blank and everything was seemingly possible.

With no previous case law to go by, it would have been difficult to predict which, of Lester's or the UK's arguments, had the most chance of succeeding after the Commission had declared *Alam and Khan* admissible. If anything, the fact that the Commission had not been persuaded simply to declare the case inadmissible could have appeared slightly ominous for the government. The stakes were high: everyone would have been aware that once the Commission, and then, in due course, the Court started to follow a particular reasoning, there was no turning back to a blank slate. The construction of a distinct jurisprudential avenue would have begun. From then on, reverting to and following an alternative reasoning would be difficult, if not impossible.

The starting point of the arguments the parties submitted in *Alam and Khan* was utterly different: the right to family life under the Convention for the applicant, the right of the state to exclude migrants for the government. Accommodating both these logics within the same reasoning hardly appears feasible. Moreover, each of them seems likely to produce a different result: one respectively favourable to the migrant on the one hand and to the state on the other—even if it is possible to imagine some cases where an identical outcome is reached whichever logic is followed. Inevitably, in time, the Strasbourg institutions would have to choose one reasoning over the other.

To begin with, there was nothing in the law which would have told the members of the Commission and the judges which reasoning was superior or preferable. Their initial instinct in this respect must have come from their moral or political intuition rather than imposing itself on them as legally necessary. With the passing of time, however, this would change.

What happened is that in the years following *Alam and Khan*, the Commission made it repeatedly clear that migrants did not have any right to choose their country of residence.[25] The Court endorsed this view in 1985 in the *ABC* judgment. The principle is now taken for granted in European human rights law.

VI. The (Non-)Admission of Foreign Husbands: British Policy in the 1960s and 1970s

Before discussing *ABC*, it may be useful to briefly introduce its social and policy background.

Throughout the 1960s, the British government had defended family reunion in the name of 'common humanity' and also in order to prevent 'social problems in the community'. However, following the disclosure in Parliament that 1,676 male Commonwealth citizens had been admitted for marriage in 1968, the Home Secretary announced in January 1969 restrictions on the admission of

[25] See e.g. *X. and Y. v. Federal Republic of Germany*, appl. 7816/77, PCom Decision (EComHR), 19 May 1977; *X. v. UK*, appl. 9088/80, PCom Decision (EComHR), 6 Mar. 1982; *X., Y. and Z. v. UK*, appl. 9285/81, PCom Decision (EComHR), 6 July 1982; *S. and S. v. UK*, appl. 10375/83, PC Decision (EComHR), 10 Dec. 1984.

husbands and fiancés. In a parallel move, the British government made obtaining entry certificates prior to departure effectively compulsory for all dependants of Commonwealth entrants. Up to 1969, Commonwealth entrants would most often have their claim to have a right of entry checked at their port of arrival. This had obvious disadvantages: prospective migrants might find that they were refused entry after having sold their home or giving up their job; evidential problems arose and long admission queues formed at ports of arrival; harrowing situations could develop, especially when vulnerable persons were detained and then returned. The government therefore had no difficulty in justifying the entry certificate requirement by reference to the well-being of prospective migrants. As Helena Wray notes, however, 'there were also less noble motives'.[26]

Amongst these was the government's fear that migrants from the New Commonwealth were marrying women who were settled in the UK as a means of entering and working in the UK outside the Employment Voucher scheme. Intent to curtail such male 'secondary' immigration, the government decided that a male spouse would normally not be able to join his foreign wife who was settled in the UK. In such cases, immigration would only be allowed if the marriage presented 'special features', for example because the wife could not be expected to relocate. The assumptions which underpinned the new measures were racist and culturally mistaken. They took for granted that a white woman would find it more difficult to relocate than a woman from an 'ethnic minority' background, whose culture was essentialised.[27] They also assumed that a man from the New Commonwealth would only be enticed to join his wife in the UK by the prospect of entering the British labour market. The idea that, even in an arranged marriage, the husband would want to respect the wishes of his wife to continue living in a place where she was comfortable did not cross the mind of the policy makers, despite evidence presented to them to this effect.[28]

In the early 1970s, it was more or less possible for white British men to bring in their foreign spouse. No one else could. Women of New Commonwealth origin were those who encountered the greatest difficulty. Some white women, however, also suffered from the rules. Under pressure from women in this situation, the ban on husbands' admission was lifted in 1974. The number of Commonwealth husbands and fiancés arriving in the UK immediately rose: from around 500 in 1974 to around 1,800 in 1976. As Wray notes, this was 'hardly an inundation'. (These figures can be read alongside the current official aim of the British government—impossible to achieve in practice—to keep annual net immigration under 100,000.) The fear of the floodgates being opened nonetheless sparked a debate in Parliament and led to the introduction in March 1977 of the concept of 'primary purpose' in the Immigration Rules.[29]

At first, 'primary purpose' was conceived as a way to prevent settlement through marriages of convenience. However, following the election of Margaret Thatcher as Prime Minister, it was refined in November 1979, so that 'primary purpose' was

[26] Wray *Regulating* 74–77. [27] Wray *Regulating* 75. [28] Wray *Regulating* 75.
[29] Wray *Regulating* 80–83 and 88.

now distinguished from the intention of the spouses to live together. Even when it was clear that the marriage was genuine, husbands were expected to demonstrate that their main motive for getting married was *not* to live in the UK if they were to be admitted. It was virtually impossible for couples reliably and objectively to prove that their main motive was altogether different. Scores of husbands were refused admission after the measure came into force.[30]

Some Members of Parliament had been rather explicit in explaining the real aim of the adoption of the new measure. The crudest amongst them was possibly Tony Marlow, who had declared in Parliament that brown and black families 'can go home and rejoin their families in their country of origin'.[31] Opponents argued that this was a highly illiberal measure, which would not even succeed in reducing immigration numbers in any significant way. This was to no avail. The warnings by the Home Affairs Select Committee that the proposals breached the European Convention were likewise ignored.[32] In fact, the European Court of Human Rights' eventual ruling on the matter, in May 1985, was far less damning of the Government's policy than NGOs, such as the Joint Council for the Welfare of Immigrants, would have wished.

VII. Three Test Cases

Many women who were separated from their husbands by the 1980 Immigration Rules lodged applications with the European Commission of Human Rights.[33] The reason why all the husbands had been refused admission was because neither the applicants nor the applicants' parents had been born in the UK. Had these women been men, their spouses would have been less likely to be refused admission. The Commission chose three test cases for consideration.[34]

The first applicant, Mrs Abdulaziz, was of Indian origin and was born in Malawi in 1948. She said she had become stateless following Malawi's independence. The British government initially contended that she was a citizen of Malawi. It was not disputed that she had arrived in the UK in 1977 to join her parents and four siblings who had preceded her a little earlier. In May 1979, she was given indefinite leave to remain and thus obtained the right to reside permanently in the UK. In December 1979, she married Mr Abdulaziz, a citizen of Portugal of Indian origin born in India in 1951. She had met him the preceding autumn, days after he was admitted to the UK for six months as a visitor. Her application for leave to remain for her husband was refused in July 1980 on the ground that neither she nor her parents were born in the UK. Her husband remained in the UK, thus overstaying his visa. A son was born to the couple in

[30] Bhabha and Shutter *Women's Movement* 78.

[31] H.C. Hansard, 14 November 1979, col. 1344, quoted in Wray *Regulating* 94.

[32] Wray *Regulating* 93.

[33] Bhabha and Sutter *Women's Movement* 72.

[34] Appls 9214/80, 9473/81 and 9474/81.

October 1982. Mr Abdulaziz worked as a chef in a restaurant; Mrs Abdulaziz was not in employment.[35]

The second applicant, Mrs Cabales, was a citizen of the Philippines and of Asian origin. She was the oldest of the three applicants (and was thus expected to remain childless even if her husband joined her in the UK). In 1967 when she was in her late twenties, she came to the UK, trained as a nurse, and started to work in mental hospitals, which she still did at the time of the Court's judgment. A decade later, she met her husband during a holiday in the Philippines, where her parents had remained. The couple married in the Philippines in 1980. By then, Mrs Cabales had gained the right to remain permanently in the UK for nearly a decade. When her husband applied for an entry certificate to join her in the UK, he was refused on the grounds that his wife was not a citizen of the UK and Colonies who was born in the UK or had a parent who was born there.[36] By the time the case came before the European Court of Human Rights, Mrs Cabales had lost her Philippine citizenship following her acquisition by naturalisation of British citizenship in April 1984. Three months later, the British government questioned the validity of her 1980 marriage, solemnised through a ceremony without legal licence (such a marriage would have been legally recognised in the Philippines after the couple had lived together as husband and wife for five years). Following this and under the new Immigration Rules of 1983, Mr Cabales applied for, and was granted, a visa entitling him to enter the UK for three months for the purposes of marriage. Mr and Mrs Cabales were formally married in the UK in January 1985. Mr Cabales was granted leave to remain as a husband for the next 12 months, on the expiry of which he was eligible to apply for indefinite leave.[37]

The third applicant, Mrs Balkandali, was born in Egypt in the late 1940s. She came to the UK aged 25, studied there, and started to work as a journalist. Her parents remained in Egypt. In 1978, she married a British citizen by birth, Mr Corbett, and became a citizen of the UK and Colonies by registration. However, the marriage did not last. It was dissolved in 1980, by which time the applicant had already met Mr Balkandali, a citizen from Turkey who had entered the UK as a student in January 1979. A son (also a British citizen by birth) was born in the UK in April 1980. The couple married the following January. In March 1981, Mr Balkandali applied for a variation of his leave to allow him to remain in the UK with his wife. This was refused two months later on the ground that neither his wife nor one of her parents were a citizen of the UK and Colonies born in the UK. Representations to the Minister of State through the applicant's Member of Parliament and the Joint Council for the Welfare of Migrants led, after the new Immigration Rules came into force in 1983, to Mr Balkandali being granted a further period of leave to remain. In September 1984, Mr Balkandali was working in the catering business and was planning to open a restaurant; his wife was working two days a week in a crèche.[38]

[35] *Abdulaziz, Cabales and Balkandalis,* appls 9214/80, 9473/81, 9474/81, PCom Report (EComHR), 12 May 1983, paras 35–42; PC Judgment (ECtHR), 28 May 1985, paras 39–43.

[36] *ABC* report, paras 43–47.

[37] *ABC* judgment, paras 44–49.

[38] *ABC* report, paras 48–53; *ABC* judgment, paras 50–54.

The applicants at Strasbourg were the women. (Today their children might also be put forward as applicants.) They submitted that immigration control fell within the scope of Article 8 of the Convention, that their separation from their husbands was caused by the government's action, and that the interference with their family lives by the government could not be justified under paragraph 2 of Article 8 because it was not responding, in a proportionate manner, to some pressing social need.[39] They further submitted that there had been a violation of Article 14 coupled with Article 8 in that they had suffered discrimination both on grounds of race (of the first and second applicants) or birth (of the third applicant) and on grounds of sex (of all three applicants). They also relied on Article 3 (prohibiting inhuman and degrading treatment) given the second applicant's enforced separation from her husband and the anxiety due to the uncertainty of their situation suffered by the first and third applicants. They finally invoked a violation of Article 13 (effective domestic remedy).

The Commission adopted its (non-binding) report as to whether violations of the Convention had occurred on 12 May 1983. The Court, sitting in its plenary formation, delivered its judgment in the case two years later on 28 May 1985 (at a time when the UK had revised its Immigration Rules slightly in 1983). Broadly speaking, the two institutions were in agreement: Article 8 applied, but it had not been violated; there had been a violation of Article 14 taken together with Article 8 on grounds of sex as well as a violation of Article 13; there had been no discrimination on grounds of race (a finding disputed by three members of the Commission); and the claim under Article 3 was dismissed.[40] In opposition to the Commission's findings, the Court rejected the discrimination claim on grounds of birth.

VIII. No Right to Family Reunion: *ABC* sets the Tone for Strasbourg Migrant Case Law

In a repeat of previous submissions, including those in *Alam and Khan* and the *East African Asians* case, the government argued that the applications fell outside the scope of the Convention altogether, given that 'no Article of the Convention applies to immigration control, apart perhaps from the Fourth Protocol'.[41] A victory for the government on this point would have been catastrophic for the defence of migrants' rights. The Commission rejected the government's reasoning:

> The right of a foreigner to enter or remain in the territory of a High Contracting Party is not guaranteed, as such, by the Convention. However, in adhering to the Convention, the Contracting Parties agreed to restrict the free exercise of their powers . . . to the extent and within the limits of the obligations which they assumed under this treaty.[42]

[39] *ABC* report, paras 61 and 62.

[40] The claim under Article 3 did not require examination according to the Commission; it did not hold according to the Court.

[41] *ABC* report, para 83; *ABC* judgment, para 59.

[42] *ABC* report, para 94.

The Court followed the Commission.[43] This crucial finding made it clear that migrants were not without rights under the Convention. Migrants' rights were recognised in an indirect way—French scholars used to say, '*par ricochet*'. This was a victory for migrants' rights, but a limited one. In practice, it would often lead to migrants' rights being saved only in extreme situations. An even worse scenario—where migrants were left without rights altogether—was nonetheless avoided.

Having ascertained that the application fell within the ambit of Article 8, the Court went on to examine whether Article 8, taken alone, had been violated.[44] For the Court, it was obvious that 'family life' must include the relationship that arises from a lawful and genuine marriage.[45] The Court did not entertain the idea that the issue at stake was essentially a negative obligation for the state to do nothing and just let their husband enter the territory. Instead, the question was framed as to whether the government had any positive obligation under Article 8 to admit onto its territory relatives of settled immigrants.

The Court did not think that such a positive obligation arose.[46] Borrowing from previous judgments, it reasoned as follows:

> The Court recalls that, although the essential object of Article 8 is to protect the individual against arbitrary interference by the public authorities, there may in addition be positive obligations inherent in an affective 'respect' for family life. However, especially as far as these positive obligations are concerned, the notion of 'respect' is not clear-cut: having regard to the diversity of the practices followed and the situations obtaining in the Contracting States, the notion's requirements will vary considerably from case to case. Accordingly, this is an area in which the Contracting Parties enjoy a wide margin of appreciation in determining the steps to be taken to ensure compliance with the Convention with due regard to the needs and resources of the community and of individuals. In particular, in the area now under consideration, the extent of a State's obligation to admit to its territory relatives of settled migrants will vary according to the particular circumstances of the persons involved. Moreover, the Court cannot ignore that the present case is concerned not only with family life but also with immigration and that, as a matter of well-established international law and subject to its treaty obligations, a State has the right to control the entry of non-nationals into its territory.[47]

[43] *ABC* judgment, para 60.

[44] By contrast, the Commission examined Article 8 only taken in conjunction with Article 14.

[45] *ABC* judgment, para 62. Whether there is a lawful and genuine marriage can be a thorny issue, as the case of Mrs Cabales shows. Not surprisingly given its general closure to migrant issues and the Court's frequent reliance on the principle of the margin of appreciation in issues relating to marriage law (see e.g. *Schalk and Kopf v. Austria*, appl. 30141/04, Judgment (ECtHR), 24 Jun 2010), the recognition of marriages (or other family arrangements such as child adoption) not directly following a immediately recognisable Western legal format has hardly generated any case law. This is regrettable.

[46] Four judges, however, thought that the state did have obligations in this area under Article 8, but that the interferences with the right to family life of the applicants were justified under paragraph 2 of Article 8: Concurring opinion of Judge Thór Vilhjálmsson and Concurring opinion of Judge Bernhardt, with which Judge Pettiti and Judge Gersing agreed.

[47] *ABC* judgment, para 67, references to previous case law omitted.

As has already been noted, the last words here are crucial, and we shall come back to them below. The Court continued its reasoning by stating that '[t]he duty imposed by Article 8 cannot be considered as extending to a *general* obligation on the part of a Contracting State to respect the choice by married couples of the country of their matrimonial residence and to accept the non-national spouses for settlement in that country'.[48] This was a repetition of what the Commission had said in a number of decisions.

The Court then turned to applying Article 8 in *this* particular case. It found that the applicants had not shown there were obstacles to establishing life in their own or their husbands' home countries; moreover, they should have known at the time of their marriage that, under the rules then in force, their husbands were unlikely to be admitted to remain, settle or enter the UK. Article 8, taken alone, had not been breached.[49] This presaged future decisions: in subsequent case law Article 8 was interpreted by the Court as imposing very few duties on states regarding migrants' rights to family reunion.

Having decided that there was no violation of Article 8 taken alone, would the Court accept that there was a violation of Article 14 taken together with Article 8? The government denied that the 1980 Immigration Rules were racially motivated. It conceded that the Rules might have affected until then more women of Asian and Commonwealth origin than women who happened to be white, but it argued that this did not change the fact that the Rules were objective and were applied regardless of race and colour.[50] Nine members of the Commission accepted this argument. In the words of the Commission's report, for states to 'give preferential treatment to their own citizens or nationals from countries with whom they have the closest links, excluding other foreigners, cannot be considered to be racial discrimination'.[51] Three members of the Commission dissented. They noted that the massive immigration to the UK over the last 30 years had been from the Caribbean and Indian sub-continent and that the Rules were acknowledged to bear adversely on persons originating from these places. The three dissenters did not think that this main effect was accidental, as parliamentary history showed that the purpose of the Rules was to minimise the number of 'coloured immigrants'. In their view, the Rules were 'indirectly racist', so that there had been a violation of Article 14 taken in conjunction with Article 8.

The Court did not pay much attention to this opinion, and followed the majority of the Commission. It accepted the government's argument that 'the main and essential purpose of the 1980 Rules was to curtail "primary immigration" in order to protect the labour market'. Unanimously, the Plenary Court stated that the Rules were 'grounded not on objections regarding the origin of non-nationals wanting to enter the country but on the need to stem the flow of immigrants at the relevant time', which was acceptable.[52] There had been no discrimination on

[48] *ABC* judgment, para 68, emphasis added.

[49] *ABC* judgment, para 69. Four judges thought that the government had interfered with the family life of the applicants, but that this interference was justified under paragraph 2 of Article 8.

[50] *ABC* report, para 110. [51] *ABC* report, para 113. [52] *ABC* judgment, para 85.

ground of race. This finding also indicated the direction of subsequent case law: it would take decades before the European Court of Human Rights would eventually find a state guilty of racial discrimination (in a context altogether different from immigration).[53]

Of the three *ABC* applicants, Mrs Balkandali was the only one who was a UK citizen. She said she had been treated differently from other UK female citizens solely because neither she nor her parents had been born on UK territory.[54] She claimed she had been discriminated against on grounds of birth (rather than race).[55] The government responded that the difference of treatment she had experienced had been justified 'in view of the hardship that would be caused to women with close ties with the United Kingdom being compelled to live in a country with which they have no personal connection'.[56] This argument did not persuade the Commission, which considered that 'in granting a person citizenship, a State accepts that the individual has established close ties with its territory'. (This is of course consistent with its decision in the *East African Asians* case, reviewed in Chapter 3.) The Commission found that Mrs Balkandali had been discriminated against on grounds of birth in contravention of Article 14 taken in conjunction with Article 8. The Court, however, disagreed. It accepted that 'there are in general persuasive social reasons for giving special treatment to those whose link with a country stems from birth within it'.[57] The Court's finding that there had been no discrimination on the grounds of birth[58] is in line with its longstanding reluctance to entertain a postcolonial critique, as noted in Chapter 3. It is also related to its refusal to examine the compatibility of nationality laws with the Convention, as we shall see in Chapter 5.

IX. Sexual Discrimination under Scrutiny, but without Producing Rights

Where the applicants' reasoning was found persuasive by both the Commission and the Court was in respect of the claim that they had suffered discrimination on grounds of their sex. The government had conceded that the 1980 Immigration Rules entailed a difference of treatment on these grounds, in that it was easier for the spouse of a foreign man than that of a foreign woman to be admitted to the country, but it had argued that this policy followed 'the aim of limiting "primary immigration" ', which was in turn 'justified by the need to protect the domestic labour market at a time of high unemployment' as well as by the aim of advancing

[53] Namely, related to the treatment of Roma people in Eastern Europe: *Nachova and Others v. Bulgaria*, appls 43577/98 and 43579/98, Judgment (ECtHR), 16 Feb. 2004; GC Judgment (ECtHR), 6 July 2005.

[54] *ABC* report, para 117.

[55] A somewhat similar argument surfaced recently in *Biao v. Denmark*, appl. 38590/10, Judgment (ECtHR), 25 Mar. 2014, to no avail, as discussed later in this chapter, Section XV.

[56] *ABC* report, para 117.

[57] *ABC* judgment, para 88.

[58] *ABC* judgment, para 89.

'public tranquillity'. Before the Court, the government claimed that the 1980 Rules led to an annual reduction of 5,700 husbands being admitted in the UK[59] (it had estimated this figure at 2,000 before the Commission). The Court rejected this claim. For the Court, the reduction, whatever its level, might have been due to the contemporaneous increase in unemployment in the UK.[60]

The Court also implicitly accepted the applicants' argument that the government's reasoning ignored the modern role of women, many of whom were likely to be working.[61] While the government's aims were legitimate, the means to achieve them were not. The all-male Court declared 'the advancement of the equality of the sexes... a major goal in the member States of the Council of Europe', so that 'very weighty reasons would have to be advanced before a difference of treatment on the ground of sex could be regarded as compatible with the Convention'.[62] Such reasons had not been presented by the government. As to achieving public tranquillity, it was not at all clear how the difference of treatment to which husbands and wives were subjected could contribute to this aim.[63] In short, there was discrimination on grounds of sex which violated Article 14 taken in conjunction with Article 8.

However, rather than opening up possibilities for family reunion, the *ABC* litigation resulted in the admission of *all* foreign spouses being made difficult. The British government chose to eliminate the discrimination identified by the Court by applying their rules on foreign spouses equally to both male and female migrants. Needless to say, this had not been the aim sought by either the applicants or their supporters. There was little to celebrate in the judgment from the perspective of migrants' rights. The worst—the total denial of rights to migrants—had been avoided. However, by the end of the *ABC* litigation, migrants had fewer rights than they had when the case had been lodged.

X. The Court Shares the States' Fear of Immigration

On the positive side, the Court had been willing to scrutinise the motivations advanced by the government in its attempt to justify sex discrimination. The same cannot be said of racial discrimination, where the explanations offered by the state were accepted by the Court at face value. Furthermore, the *ABC* judgment reproduced the fear of uncontrolled immigration articulated by the state. Added to this, the finding of sex discrimination did not give rise to any compensation.

59 *ABC* judgment, para 75.
60 *ABC* judgment, para 80.
61 *ABC* judgment, para 75.
62 *ABC* judgment, para 78. The 'very weighty reasons' pronouncement was to be repeated by the Court in *Gaygusuz v. Austria*, appl. 17371/90, Judgment (ECtHR), 16 Sept. 1996, in respect of discriminatory treatment of legally settled foreigners as compared to nationals in the field of social security. However, in *Gaygusuz*, the Court refrained from declaring equality between nationals and foreigners to be 'a major goal'. See Chapter 8.
63 *ABC* judgment, paras 79 and 80.

The early part of the *ABC* judgment devoted to 'the facts' contains a section devoted to the 'History and background' of domestic law and practice. It includes the following paragraph:

> A *rapid rise* in the influx of immigrants, especially in 1960 and 1961, and the consequent *danger* of the rate of immigration *exceeding* the country's capacity to absorb them led to a radical change in the situation [whereby all Commonwealth citizens had freedom to enter the United Kingdom for work and permanent residence, without any restriction]. The Commonwealth Immigrants Act 1962, and then the Commonwealth Immigrants Act 1968, restricted the right of entry of, and imposed immigration controls on, certain classes of Commonwealth citizens...[64]

The Court is likely to have borrowed this phrasing from the government's submissions. The question arises as to why the quoted passage made it into the judgment. In the *East African Asians* case, the Commission had found the 1968 Act in violation of Article 3 because of its racial motivations.[65] Not only does the Court not allude to this but it seems explicitly to endorse the assumption that immigration is potentially 'dangerous'. It accepts that a country has a limited capacity of 'absorption' of immigrants and that the government should take measures to stem immigration. The Court presents these assertions as 'facts' without distancing itself from them in any way or relying on additional evidence, even though the numbers involved in the situation under review were relatively low. (The highest figure given by the British government being 5,700).

In addition, the Court refused the applicants' claim for monetary compensation. In making this finding, the Court said it had regard to the factors upon which the government relied on this point.[66] These were that the applicants had not proved the adverse effects of the violations of the Convention they alleged on the development of family ties and on the making of long-term plans. The government added that, were the Court to disagree on this point, a finding that the Convention had been violated would of itself constitute sufficient just satisfaction because:

> [A]t the time of their marriage, the couples concerned knew that they were not entitled to live together in the United Kingdom; in fact, [the first and second applicants] had not been prevented from doing so; and since they could have lived in Portugal or Turkey, family ties and long-term plans had not been adversely affected. Similar pleas were advanced concerning [the third applicant].[67]

Following the government, the Court considered that 'in the circumstances of these cases its findings of violation of themselves constitute sufficient just satisfaction'.

The *ABC* case established that migrants have no right under the Convention to choose where to conduct their family life. This is not far removed from the statement by the Member of Parliament who had said that brown and black families

[64] *ABC* judgment, para 12, emphases added. [65] See Chapter 3.
[66] *ABC* judgment, para 96. [67] *ABC* judgment, para 95.

'can go home and rejoin their families in the country of origin'.[68] Jacqueline Bhabha and Sue Shutter commented optimistically after the *ABC* case that perhaps the wording and operation of the 1980 Immigration Rules had been too subtle for the Court to see that they were discriminatory on grounds of race.[69] Thirty years on, the Court has revealed itself to be weak at confronting this type of discrimination.[70] This is disturbing. Seen from this perspective, racism might have to be considered the elephant in the room of the Court's migrant case law.

If so, what contributes to this elephant escaping virtually everyone's notice is arguably the focus on the right of the state to control the entry and residence of aliens. This principle deserves attention.

XI. A Well-Established Principle of International Law

The principle according to which the state enjoys an almost unfettered power to control the entry and residence of aliens dominates the Strasbourg migrant case law. As noted, it was introduced in the *ABC* judgment at the end of a long paragraph in which it was claimed that 'as a matter of well-established international law and subject to its treaty obligations, a State has the right to control the entry of non-nationals into its territory'.[71] The principle does not seem to be in any danger of being ignored; the Court commonly starts its reasoning with it in migrant cases.[72] When referring to it, the Court invariably asserts it is 'well established'. Both on historical and legal grounds, this adjective appears inappropriate.

The principle is in fact recent—unsurprisingly, as recent as state control over migration. In the nineteenth century, there was no recognised right for the state to curtail immigration. Indeed, it would have hindered colonial enterprise. This is well encapsulated by the complaint a planter based in Mauritius made to the territory's Colonial Secretary about new regulations, saying: 'no example does exist, to my knowledge, in any civilised country, in modern times at least, of the creation by legislative acts of obstacles to the augmentation of the labour and industry of a community'.[73] Citing a number of examples, Radhika Mongia concludes that it was considered 'an exceptional, and largely indefensible, exercise

[68] Quoted earlier, 109. [69] Bhabha and Shutter *Women's Movement* 77.

[70] Marie-Bénédicte Dembour, 'Postcolonial Denial: Why the European Court of Human Rights Finds it so Difficult to Acknowledge Racism', in Kamari Clarke and Mark Goodale (eds) *Mirrors of Justice: Law and Power in the Post-Cold War Era* (New York: Cambridge University Press, 2010) 45–66; Marie-Bénédicte Dembour, 'In the Name of the Rule of Law: The European Court of Human Rights' Silencing of Racism', in Gurminder K. Bhambra and Robbie Shilliams (eds) *Silencing Human Rights: Critical Engagements with a Contested Project* (Basingstoke: Palgrave Macmillan, 2009) 184–202; abridged and revised as 'Still Silencing the Racism Suffered by Migrants...The Limits of Current Developments under Article 14 ECHR' (2009) *European Journal of Migration and Law* 11, special issue on 'The European Court of Human Rights and Immigration: Limits and Possibilities', 221–234.

[71] *ABC* judgment, para 67.

[72] See e.g. *Üner v. the Netherlands*, appl. 46410/99, GC Judgment (ECtHR), 18 Oct. 2006.

[73] Quoted in: Radhika V. Mongia, 'Historicizing State Sovereignty: Inequality and the Form of Equivalence' (2007) *Comparative Studies in Society and History* 49, 384–411 at 399.

of sovereign power', well into the nineteenth century, 'for the state or sovereign authority to hinder the free movement of persons, traveling for "peaceful and lawful reasons"'.[74] The book *Foundations of International Migration Law* similarly opens by explaining that 'the great writers of international law of the eighteenth and nineteenth centuries...took a liberal attitude to the movement of people across borders for trade, commerce and other purposes', with few exceptions.[75] Swiss diplomat and legal scholar Emmerich de Vattel was one such exception. Through selectively invoking him, the US Supreme Court proclaimed in 1889, in the *Chinese Exclusion* case, the principle of state immigration control 'an accepted maxim of international law'.[76] This idea immediately took hold, notably informing the Strasbourg migrant case law. In fact, it sat on shaky historical grounds.

The principle is also highly problematic from a legal theory perspective. Bas Schotel has persuasively argued that states are wrong to believe that they can deny 'normal' migrants admission to a country without justifying this exclusion. Schotel observes that in a rule-of-law perspective state powers are not conceived as unlimited; they are purpose constrained. There is no good reason why this precept would not apply in the immigration field. This is to say that authorities must explain the relevant facts and reasons which justify any decision on their part to deny admission. Schotel's thesis leads him to argue that the admission logic must be reversed; for exclusion to be legitimate, '[t]he authorities must [first have shown] that the exclusion is necessary to obtain the objectives of the immigration policy and that exclusion was the only and the least burdensome measure available'.[77]

XII. Putting State Sovereignty before Human Rights: The Strasbourg Reversal

Applying Schotel's insight to Strasbourg cases would produce a very different body of case law from the current strain of jurisprudence. The starting point of the *ABC* case would be that applicants have a right to see their family life respected under paragraph 1 of Article 8, subject to legitimate curtailments under paragraph 2 of the same article. State interferences with this right would be considered justified only if they were provided by law, pursued a legitimate aim, and were demonstrably 'necessary in a democratic society'—to quote Article 8 ECHR. In this scheme the onus would fall on the state to show that these conditions are met.

[74] Mongia 'Historicizing' 400, referring to: Richard Plender, *International Migration Law* (Leiden: Stijhoff, 1972) 38–50.

[75] Brian Opeskin, Richard Perruchoud, and Jillyanne Redpath-Cross, 'Conceptualising International Migration Law', in Opeskin, Perruchoud, and Redpath-Cross (eds), *Foundations of International Migration Law* (Cambridge: Cambridge University Press, 2012) 1.

[76] Opeskin et al. 'Conceptualising' 2.

[77] Bas Schotel, *On the Right of Exclusion: Law, Ethics and Immigration Policy* (Abingdon: Routledge, 2012) 1.

From a human rights perspective, it would be normal to consider the human being before anything else. In the Strasbourg case law, however, it is the right of the state which is typically (although not always) considered first. This inevitably relegates Convention rights to the status of exceptions which (most often) merely serve to limit the principle of state sovereignty, the latter being the default position.[78] The result is that the Strasbourg case law has largely been allowed to develop in a way which puts state sovereignty (or interests) before human rights. Such a reversal cannot but undermine the human rights cause.[79] The first abiding principle should be the requirement that human rights are respected; state sovereignty should be a secondary consideration.

XIII. Who are the Successful Applicants? The Exceptional *Tuquabo-Tekle v. the Netherlands*

The central place which the 'well-established principle' of state exclusion occupies in the Strasbourg case law means that it was always going to be difficult for the Court to reach the conclusion that state exclusion was in violation of the Convention. Verdicts of violation have nonetheless occasionally happened. These outcomes have typically been reached when the bench included some judges attuned to the rights of migrants—with the national judge often holding a pivotal role—and/or when the applicant(s)' individual circumstances were particularly stark.

The first example of a refusal of admission on family grounds being found to breach Article 8 was a case directed against the Netherlands, a country which has acquired the reputation of being at the forefront of the most restrictive family reunion policies in Europe.[80] *Sen v. the Netherlands* was decided in 2001 by a bench which contained the progressive Wilhelmina Thomassen as the national judge.[81] In this case, the Court ruled that the refusal to let a Turkish child join her parents and two younger siblings, who were all lawful and permanent residents in the Netherlands, violated the Convention. The Court justified this unusual conclusion by reference to the facts of the case. In particular two younger siblings were born and bred in the Netherlands and it said that they could not be

[78] Some readers may object that the Court grants states the power to exclude 'subject to their obligations under the Convention'. It is true that if the Convention were clearly given the upper hand in the reasoning, the exclusion power would best be seen as an exception to the Convention rights. However this is not the case. For an illustration of a reasoning where the human rights are given the upper hand and the state power to exclude is considered to have to be encompassed within these rights, see the rulings of the Inter-American Court, as reviewed in Chapter 9.

[79] The negative effect of this reversal is clear in many different areas, including the deportations of migrants from the country where they have constructed all or most of their life, as explained in Chapter 6.

[80] For the historical and policy context of the Dutch family migration policies, see: Sarah van Walsum, *The Family and the Nation: Dutch Family Migration Policies in the Context of Changing Family Norms* (Newcastle upon Tyne: Cambridge Scholars Publishing, 2008).

[81] *Sen v. the Netherlands*, appl. 31465/96, Judgment (ECtHR), 21 Dec. 2001, in French only.

expected to go and live in Turkey.[82] The Court reached a similar verdict in 2005 in *Tuquabo-Tekle and Others v. the Netherlands*.[83] This case, which is discussed below, illustrates how extreme the circumstances of the applicant may have to be before a complaint regarding denial of family reunion is upheld. Further occasional verdicts of violation have also arisen from time to time, but they are few and far between. One example is *Nolan and K. v. Russia* dating from 2009. In this case, the refusal by the respondent state to re-admit to its territory a US citizen on account of his religious activities was found to violate Article 8. The first applicant had thought he was leaving Russia only for a short trip abroad. He had left the second applicant, his ten-month-old son—of whom he was the sole custodial parent—with his nanny. It would be a further ten months before father and son were reunited.[84]

In *Tuquabo-Tekle*, the government presented the story of the applicants in the following way (as recounted in the Court's judgment):

> Mrs Tuquabo-Tekle had left Mehret behind in the care of her grandmother and uncle of her own free will. Meanwhile, Mrs Tuquabo-Tekle had started a new family in the Netherlands with Mr Tuquabo and had had two children. Mehret had never been part of that family. It has also not been shown that Mrs Tuquabo-Tekle was involved in Mehret's upbringing in the moral sense of that she exercised any authority over her, the family ties between mother and daughter consisting primarily of financial support.... [Despite having held a residence permit since 1993] Mrs Tuquabo-Tekle had not taken any steps to bring Mehret [to the Netherlands] until 1997.[85]

What this account does not say is that the family was from Eritrea, from where Mehret's mother fled in 1989 as the country was in the grip of a civil war and she had lost her husband. One of her sons, whom she had left in Ethiopia, managed to join her in Norway in 1991 after she was granted a residence permit on humanitarian grounds, but it had not been possible to procure the departure of her other two children who had remained in Eritrea. In 1992, Mrs Tuquabo-Tekle married Mr Tuquabo, a refugee living in the Netherlands. Two children were born to the couple. The applicants said that their intention had always been to get Mehret, born in 1981, to the Netherlands.[86] Mrs Tuquabo-Tekle and Mr Tuquabo mistakenly believed that this would not be possible until they could show suitable housing. Accordingly, they bought a house in what they described as a less reputable area of Amsterdam in order to comply with this legal requirement (which, it turned out, did not apply to them because of Mr Tuquabo's refugee status).[87] This done, in 1997 they filed a request for a provisional residence visit for Mehret to join them in the Netherlands. The authorities denied this request on the grounds

[82] In *Sen*, the Court did not mention the 'well-established principle' of state exclusion discussed in the previous section.

[83] In *Tuquabo-Tekle*, the 'well-established principle' of state exclusion was mentioned as part of a number of factors to take into consideration: *Tuquabo-Tekle*, para 43.

[84] *Nolan and K. v. Russia*, appl. 2512/04, Judgment (ECtHR), 12 Feb. 2009.

[85] *Tuquabo-Tekle* judgment, paras 38 and 39.

[86] *Tuquabo-Tekle*, paras 8 to 11.

[87] *Tuquabo-Tekle*, para 35.

that 'the close family ties between Mrs Tuquabo-Tekle and her daughter were considered to have ceased to exist and such ties had never existed between Mr Tuquabo and his stepdaughter'.[88]

The Court found 'questionable' the government's assertion that Mrs Tuquabo-Tekle had left Mehret behind 'of her own free will', given that she had 'fled Eritrea in the course of a civil war to seek asylum abroad following the death of her husband'. The Court also noted that two children had been born from her new marriage in the Netherlands, which had been the decisive factor in its judgment in *Sen*.[89] Moreover, contrary to what had been found in other cases, Mehret's relatively advanced age did not make her less dependent on her mother. This was because her grandmother had taken her out of school after she had reached what was considered a marriageable age in Eritrea.[90] Because of all this, the Court found that 'the respondent State ha[d] failed to strike a fair balance between the applicants' interests on the one hand and its own interest in controlling immigration on the other'.[91] There was accordingly a violation of Article 8 of the Convention.

Tuquabo-Tekle is not a casuistic decision, from which no general lesson can be drawn, except that there will be circumstances where the denial of family reunion will amount to a violation of the Convention. The Court specifically rejected the idea that, in the absence of very specific and cumulative circumstances, the state would have been under a positive obligation to allow Mehret to reside in the Netherlands.[92] It repeated the *ABC* finding according to which 'Article 8 cannot be considered to impose on a State a general obligation to respect the choice by married couples of the country of their matrimonial residence and to authorise family reunion in its territory'.[93]

Eva Hilbrink has noted that the focus of the Strasbourg Court in family reunion cases is 'mainly on the circumstances on the side of the individual'. This, Hilbrink remarks, is 'strictly logical', given that the Court feels its task is to examine whether the individual interest outweighs the interest of the contracting party and that, in this balancing exercise, the Court treats the interest of the state 'as an abstract, non-variable factor', unaffected, for example, by an existing economic situation of either growth or unemployment, thus leaving the individual interest as the only variable capable of being assessed.[94] This, in turn, explains why 'a case won by the individual does not necessarily force the State concerned to change its policy'. The exceptional poignancy of the individual's circumstances may lead the Court to decide that a state has failed to strike the balance fairly in a particular case, without this decision affecting the policy per se.[95] In cases such as *Sen*,

[88] *Tuquabo-Tekle*, para 12.
[89] *Tuquabo-Tekle*, para 47.
[90] *Tuquabo-Tekle*, para 50.
[91] *Tuquabo-Tekle*, para 52.
[92] *Tuquabo-Tekle*, para 50.
[93] *Tuquabo-Tekle*, para 43.
[94] The Court already said this much at paragraph 67 of the *ABC* judgment when it declared, '[I]n the area under consideration, the extent of a State's obligation to admit to its territory relatives of settled immigrants will vary according to the particular circumstances of the persons involved'.
[95] Eva Hilbrink, 'The proportionality principle; two European perspectives. How serving the community interest may end up to be in the individual's best interest' <http://dare.ubvu.vu.nl/bitstream/1871/15826/5/proportionality%20ECJ%20v%20ECtHR.pdf>, accessed 26 April 2011.

Tuquabo-Tekle, and *Nolan*, strictly speaking, it is indeed the individual application of the policy in one particularly poignant case which is found wanting under European human rights law, not the policy itself.

Sarah van Walsum has observed that the Dutch admission refusals to children of migrant mothers residing in the Netherlands has often been motivated by the fact that the administrative and/or judicial Dutch authorities doubted that any effective bond subsisted between the mother and her children. Migrant mothers were effectively punished for having left their children behind. These women were viewed as having failed to be 'good mothers' attending to the needs of their children on a daily and all-encompassing basis, even when it was clear that the women were financially contributing to the upbringing of their children. Ironically, in Dutch society, such a model of the good parent was fast becoming outdated: Dutch citizens were gaining rights *vis-à-vis* biological children with whom they had little contact, sometimes thanks to the European Court of Human Rights which was willing to adopt, and force upon the contracting states, a dynamic and diverse view of family life which did not rely upon living under the same roof. The discrepancy in the level of protection of the family the Court afforded to citizens and migrants did not go unnoticed. As suggested by van Walsum, discomfort at this glaring discrepancy may have contributed to the Court's conclusion that the Convention had been violated in *Sen*, which in turn contributed to *Tuquabo-Tekle*.[96]

XIV. Family Reunification: Why not a Right under the European Convention?

In all likelihood, over the decades, many applications to Strasbourg will have concerned family reunion. No one talks about them. They are untraceable, having been destroyed 12 months after having been rejected as manifestly unfounded by 'committees of threes' or, recently, single-judge formations. No doubt they hide intense emotional suffering. In line with its status as a 'non-right', family reunion fails to receive express mention in several major commentaries on the European Convention.[97] The handful of cases where applicants have been successful serve to confirm the general rule, which is that the state is normally not under an obligation to admit aliens.[98] Clearly, in our global society not everyone is affected in the

[96] Sarah van Walsum, 'Against All Odds: How Single and Divorced Migrant Mothers Were Eventually Able to Claim their Right to Respect for Family Life' (2009) *European Journal of Migration and Law* 11, 295–311.

[97] One example is: Karen Reid, *A Practitioner's Guide to the European Convention on Human Rights* (London: Sweet & Maxwell, 2nd ed., 2004). Philip Leach devotes five lines to *Sen* in *Taking a Case to the European Court of Human Rights* (Oxford: Oxford University Press, 2005) at 305. See also: D.J. Harris, M.O' Boyle, E.P. Bates, and C.M. Buckley, *Law of the European Convention on Human Rights* (Oxford: Oxford University Press, 2009) 395–396.

[98] This situation is in stark contrast to that pertaining to European Union law, where the idea has always been put forward that rights of free movement should be extended to workers' family members if the aim was to have workers moving within what was originally called the 'Common Market'. This may contribute to explaining the rather positive outcome of a case such as *Chakroun*

same way by the logic and intensification of border controls. Some on our planet have the privilege of being able to let their sentimental and emotional life develop largely outside the constraints of state immigration policies. Wherever they fall in love or have located a most suitable life partner, they can be nearly certain that one way or another they will be able either to make a life there or to find a place where a joint life is possible. Others cannot make this assumption.

As states make admission increasingly more difficult including, for example, through language and integration tests or minimum-income requirements, it remains to be seen whether the Strasbourg Court will find itself able to declare these conditions contrary to Article 8. Case law is expected on this point. First to be tested is likely to be the situation in the Netherlands, as the country which, in 2005, set the trend in Europe of subjecting the admission of non-nationals for family reunification purposes to new conditions.[99]

The Dutch rules require a language and integration test to be taken by persons aged between 18 and 65 who: (a) wish to settle permanently in the Netherlands; (b) require authorisation to enter the country on a temporary basis; and (c) are obliged (under previous legislation dating back to 1998) to participate in a civic integration programme after arrival in the Netherlands.[100] Citizens from member states of the EU and EEA, Surinam, Australia, Canada, the United States, Switzerland, New Zealand, Iceland, Japan, and North Korea do not need authorisation to enter the country for a temporary stay and are thus exempt from this test. Also exempted are: migrants with a work permit, the self-employed and highly educated migrants; migrants granted long-term residence status under EC Directive 2003/109; the family members of a refugee (except if the family link derives from a marriage concluded after the refugee was granted his/her residence permit); and migrants unable to pass the test due to a mental or physical disability (but not illiteracy).[101]

(Case C-578/08), which related to the refusal to admit the Moroccan wife of a Moroccan national born in 1944 who had lived in the Netherlands since 1970 and had a permanent resident permit. At the time of the Luxembourg judgment, the couple had been married for 37 years. I shall leave to others to assess whether the Luxembourg Court is more promising to migrants than the Strasbourg Court—which, if so, would have the ironic result of demonstrating that the economic logic of working towards a common market works at least sometimes better for human beings than the human rights promise of attempting to respect the dignity of every human being.

[99] Tineke Strik, Anita Böker, Maaike Luiten, and Ricky van Oers, 'The INTEC Project: Synthesis Report. Integration and Naturalisation tests: the new way to European Citizenship. A Comparative study in nine Member States on the national policies concerning integration and naturalisation tests and their effects on integration', Centre for Migration Law, Radboud University Nijmegen, the Netherlands (December 2010) 11. The UK is not far behind. A minimum income requirement of £18,600 has been introduced for an applicant to be eligible to bring their spouse into the UK, with additional increases per non-UK citizen child. The legality of this requirement and its compliance with Article 8 is being tested through the domestic courts in the case of *MM & Ors v. Secretary of State for the Home Department*. The first decision in this case, *MM & Ors v. Secretary of State for the Home Department* [2013] EWHC 1900 (Admin), ruled that while a financial threshold is a legitimate tool of immigration control, the level at which the government had set it was 'unjustified and disproportionate'. This decision was appealed by the government, and a hearing at the UK's appellate court was held in March 2014. The judgment of the Appeal Court remained awaited at the time of going to press.

[100] Strik et al. 'The INTEC Project' 18.

[101] Strik et al. 18.

Entering the Netherlands for family reunification is increasingly costly. In December 2010, expenses were estimated at €1,440 if the migrant passed the language and integration test the first time.[102] The test is difficult to pass, not only because the language requirement is set at a relatively high level but because it is not easy to access Dutch language teaching in every part of the world.[103] One refused applicant from Eritrea objected that he first had to learn English in order to learn Dutch from the available educational material. The Dutch judge who reviewed his case found that the requirement was proportionate given that his wife could go and join him in Eritrea or Sudan if this was what the couple wanted.[104] An additional difficulty for the applicants is that the result of the test is valid for only 12 months. After this period, they must retake and pass it again to be admitted.

According to Tineke Strik, non-Western spouses were the clear target of the new policy, at a time when the integration process was thought to have been 'held back by the fact that a large number of second generation migrants opts for a marital partner from the country of origin'.[105] Two governmental advisory bodies warned before the legislation was adopted that the test would contravene Article 8 ECHR if it de facto prevented a large group of migrants from living with their spouse.[106] After the legislation was passed, Human Rights Watch issued a report which concluded that the policy disproportionately affected residents of Turkish and Moroccan origin in the Netherlands who wanted to live with their spouse and children, and was as such incompatible with Article 14 of the European Convention as well as other international human rights instruments. From within the Council of Europe, the European Commission against Racism and Intolerance and the Commissioner for Human Rights were also critical. In March 2010, the Committee on the Elimination of Racial Discrimination found that the exemption granted in the legislation led to discrimination on the basis of nationality, particularly between 'Western' and 'non-Western' state nationals.[107] Despite these criticisms the Dutch government has recently added a written test to the language test initially introduced in order to further reduce the number of lowly-educated applicants.[108]

The Dutch government has successfully defended its policy before its national courts by arguing that the exemption is not discriminatory because it protects its economic relations with the countries whose nationals are exempted. Whether this argument will persuade the European Court of Human Rights when it is called to examine the Dutch policy, as one expects it will be, remains to be seen. On the one hand, past Strasbourg case law suggests that the Court would not readily adopt a principled stance against the Dutch policy. On the other hand, the many voices which have already been heard against the policy, including from international quasi-judicial bodies, as well as developments generally more favourable to migrants in the Court of Justice of the European Union, may lead the

[102] Strik et al. 12.
[103] Strik et al. 40.
[104] Strik et al. 12.
[105] Strik et al. 21.
[106] Strik et al. 22.
[107] Strik et al. 23–23.
[108] Strik et al. 44.

Strasbourg Court to decide that it is time for it to adopt a stance which is more clearly in defence of the human rights of migrants.

XV. Back to *ABC*: *Biao v. Denmark*

The judgment of 25 March 2014 in *Biao v. Denmark*[109] does not augur well on this front, however. The first applicant in this case was a Danish national by naturalisation, the second applicant his wife, a Ghanaian national. They complained that the refusal to grant the second applicant a residence permit based on family reunion breached both Article 8 taken alone and Article 14 taken in conjunction with Article 8. Their request for family reunion had been refused because they had been unable to demonstrate, as Danish legislation required, that their 'aggregate ties' to Denmark were stronger than those they had with Ghana.[110] People who had held Danish citizenship for 28 years could bring their family to Denmark without having to demonstrate a stronger attachment to Denmark (even if they had never lived there; for example, having been born of a Danish parent abroad). The first applicant in *Biao* had become Danish at the age of 31; he would therefore have needed to wait until the age of 59 before having the opportunity of being joined by his spouse to Denmark without having to demonstrate that his aggregate ties there were stronger than any he had in Ghana. The seven judges constituting the Chamber unanimously dismissed the Article 8 complaint.

Regarding the Article 14 complaint, the Court specifically drew [etc]. The Court specifically drew a parallel with the situation of Mrs Balkandali in *ABC*. Relying on this judgment, the Court found that distinguishing between different groups of nationals, some of whom can be presumed to successfully integrate into Danish society, is acceptable.[111] The three minority judges were incensed.[112] They wrote a virulent dissenting opinion. Amongst other arguments, they noted the danger of seeing differential treatment on the basis of national internal classification morphing into what they called 'ethnic racism'.[113] They further criticised the Court for having effectively misquoted its own case law.[114] The details of this misrepresentation are too long to explain here. Suffice it to say that the dissenting judges observed that the partial representation of the case law made it possible for the Court to ignore the effect that the impugned legislation has on a whole 'class of citizens who are treated with suspicion on the ground of their alleged lack of strong ties due to their national origin, regardless of whether they are longstanding residents [or] have no other citizenship'.[115] The dissenters also railed against the creation of a fiction which allowed the Court to examine the applicants' situation by reference to the date of the communication of the residence permit refusal decision (at which time the consequences of the absence of family reunion remained relatively benign), leading the Court to

[109] *Biao v. Denmark*, appl. 38590/10, Judgment (ECtHR), 25 Mar. 2014.
[110] *Biao*, para 13. [111] *Biao*, paras 97–99.
[112] Joint dissenting opinion of Judges Sajó, Vučinić and Kūris in *Biao*.
[113] Sajó et al. para 13. [114] Sajó et al. para 19. [115] Sajó et al. para 19.

ignore the ongoing and long-lasting character of the situation complained of by the applicants.[116] On the positive side, *Biao* has been accepted for referral to the Grand Chamber.[117] This will hopefully result in a different approach being taken to the case than that which was adopted by the majority at chamber level.

XVI. Definite Losers: The Family Patterns Prevalent in Non-Western Societies

It is not an exaggeration to say that there is no right to family reunion under the European Convention. If this is true for family members who are incontrovertibly spouses or minor children of European residents (whether aliens or citizens), then it is even more true for those whose family link is not incontrovertibly established, either because it is not documented in the acceptable Western legal format or because it is outside the model of the family dominant in the West. This is a concern.[118] Judge Kovler has spoken in favour of recognising, for example, the important family ties linking grandparents and children in some societies.[119] His, however, is a singularly lonely voice at Strasbourg. The European Court has been called upon to open up the recognition of adoption by homosexuals and marriage by transsexuals and has slowly started to do so.[120] By contrast, the recognition of family arrangements not following an immediately recognisable European pattern, however diverse, has hardly generated any case law.[121] This is not surprising given the general closure of the Strasbourg Court to migrant issues. It is nonetheless a striking failure of European human rights law.[122]

[116] Sajó et al. paras 26–30.

[117] Grand Chamber Panel's decision of 8 September 2014.

[118] As Prakash Shah's research on customary marriage and adoption indirectly demonstrates: Shah, 'Inconvenient Marriages, or What Happens When Ethnic Minorities Marry Trans-Jurisdictionally' (2010) *Utrecht Law Review* 6, 17–32; 'Transnational Hindu Law Adoptions: Recognition and Treatment in Britain' (2009) *International Journal of Law in Context* 5, 107–130. See also: Eva Brems, 'Human Rights as a Framework for Negotiating/Protecting Cultural Differences: An Exploration of the Case-Law of the European Court of Human Rights', in Marie-Claire Foblets, Jean-François Gaudreault-DesBiens, and Alison Dundes Renteln (eds) *Cultural Diversity and the Law: State Responses from Around the World* (Brussels: Bruylant, 2010) 663–715 at 696–701; Katayoun Alidadi and Marie-Claire Foblets, 'Framing Multicultural Challenges in Freedom of Religion Terms: Limitations of Minimal Human Rights for Managing Religious Diversity in Europe' (2012) *Netherlands Quarterly of Human Rights* 30, 388–416 at 409.

[119] *Sisojeva and Others v. Latvia*, appl. 60654/00, GC Judgment (ECtHR), 15 Jan. 2007.

[120] See e.g. Marie-Bénédicte Dembour, 'Why Should Biological Sex Be Decisive? Transsexualism Before the European Court of Human Rights', in Shirley Ardener and Alison Shaw (eds), *Changing Sex and Bending Gender* (Oxford: Berghahn, 2005) 39-59.

[121] In *Muños Dias v. Spain*, appl. 4915/07, Judgment (ECtHR), 8 Dec. 2009, the Strasbourg Court found the non-recognition of a Roma marriage for the purpose of a surviving spouse's pension in violation of the Convention. In *Serife Yigit v. Turkey*, appl. 3976/05, GC Judgment (ECtHR), 2 Nov. 2010, the Court reached the opposite conclusion in a case concerning an Islamic marriage. See also on *kafala*, the closest Islamic equivalent to adoption, *Harroudj v. France*, appl. 43631/09, Judgment(ECtHR), 4 Oct. 12.

[122] Brems 'Human Rights as a Framework' 712–715; Kristin Henrard, 'A Patchwork of "Successful and "Missed" Synergies in the Jurisprudence of the ECHR', in Kristin Henrard and

This is all the more striking since the Strasbourg Court has always endorsed—in its non-migrant case law—the proposition that the notion of the family is flexible and a question of fact. This has famously enabled the Court to develop a case law on the family strand of Article 8 which stands out for its particular capacity to take into account social and technical developments. To quote from the *Law of the European Convention of Human Rights*, '[f]amily life is now understood as extending beyond formal relationships and the family based on marriage and in some circumstances it can include potential or planned relationships, as well as those whose ties are more social than biological in nature'.[123] This characteristic, however, can hardly be said to apply to the migrant case law, an area where family life is typically approached by the Court in a limited rather than expansive way.[124]

XVII. Conclusion

With the benefit of hindsight, it is difficult to imagine today that the European Court of Human Rights would ever have insisted that a government which gives migrant workers permanent residence because it needs their labour would then be under the obligation to permit the members of their families to join them. This argument (which has incidentally made it at least partially into European Union law) did not always sound unreasonable, however. Otherwise, Lester would not have taken *Alam and Khan* to Strasbourg; the Commission would not have found the same case admissible; and the British government would not have sought to avoid a judicial pronouncement on its merits through a friendly settlement.

Nevertheless, it became rapidly apparent that the Strasbourg system was disposed to be more attuned to a state discourse of sovereignty than to migrants' human rights arguments. With hindsight, this position should have come as no surprise. It was in line with the premises on which the European system of human rights protection had been built by the drafters of the Convention. To recall, although the system did not exclude migrants from the ambit of the Convention, it did not wish to consider their predicament and specifically grant them rights, as explained in Chapter 2. Neither did it wish to marshal any sense of postcolonial responsibility, as Chapter 3 has documented.

So it was that the unanimous *ABC* judgment rendered by the Plenary Court in 1985 made reference to a 'well-established' principle in international law according to which states enjoy the power to exclude aliens. This principle was destined to assume a central place throughout the whole of the Strasbourg migrant case law. This is so much so that one can talk of a human rights reversal. In a human rights reasoning one would expect human rights to come first, so that

Robert Dunbar (eds) *Synergies in Minority Protection: European and International Law Perspectives* (Cambridge: Cambridge University Press, 2008) 314–364.

123 Harris et al. *Law of the ECHR* 371–372.

124 Lourdes Peroni, 'Challenging Culturally Dominant Conceptions in Human Rights Law: The Cases of Property and Family' (2010) *Human Rights and International Legal Discourse* 4, 241–264.

what is checked is that states are exercising their functions in a way which respects these rights. Instead, the fact that the Strasbourg reversal has in effect given the state power to exclude aliens is generally considered as the master principle in the Strasbourg migrant case law; inevitably, then, human rights appear merely as exceptions which, if they are persuasive enough, manage to curtail the state not quite completely unfettered power to act as it wishes. The default position is nonetheless state sovereignty. To put this in a different way, the reversal means that instead of human rights law serving to scrutinise state behaviour as its function should be, it is the behaviour of the individual which comes under scrutiny.

In the *ABC* case, the consideration which the Court paid to this principle had effectively dashed any hope of seeing the suffering of 'immigration widows' brought to an end. The Court's position was clear: Article 8 ECHR does not entail a right to family reunion; couples are free to pursue their family life outside the contracting state if they so wish. This last proposition is nonetheless problematic on at least three counts. First, the Court does not seriously examine this assumption but just takes it for granted that relocation is a real possibility. Second, the Court refuses to see that migrants' life decisions are not purely individual actions but actions posited under economic and/or political pressure to which states are no stranger. Third, the Court ignores the fact that immigration controls are not exercised in the same way towards all human beings: the intention is to exclude some people while giving others the freedom to travel.

Had the Court been so inclined, it could have drawn out the implications of the inequality of this phenomenon and scrutinised admission refusals. This would have chimed well with a postcolonial critique of imperialism which reminds us that we prefer not to recall that the colonial powers of yesteryear were happily relying on the idea that circulation in the world should be free.[125] It would also have recognised that the transformation of the world from which European states have benefited and significantly engineered may, or even should, give rise to special responsibilities on their part towards people originating from the regions they colonised in the past or are occupying or waging wars in today.

However, such a morally ambitious agenda was not pursued at Strasbourg. On the contrary, the range of options open to lawyers thinking of taking migrant cases to Strasbourg is arguably extremely limited, as the *ABC* judgment of 1985 started to make clear. Some points which would have appeared reasonable before the Commission are simply no longer arguable. This is not to deny that new arguments will continue to emerge which favour the migrant applicant.[126] This is also not to imply that the Court is a unified body which always speaks with one voice and invariably moves in the same direction. It is nonetheless necessary

[125] With exceptions which did not affect them. Colonial subjects in the Congo for example needed a so-called 'transfer passport' ('*passeport de mutation*') to be able to go and live outside their natal region.

[126] One example is the reliance on the relatively new concept of 'the best interests of the child', borrowed from the UN Convention on the Rights of the Child, which indirectly figures in the *Nolan* judgment: *Nolan* judgment, para 88. Other examples will be provided in subsequent chapters.

to recognise that precedents which have cut off interpretative routes in the past establish a legacy which have long-lasting implications for future developments.

In particular, following on from as authoritative a judgment as *ABC*, it should come as no surprise that few applicants have managed to convince the Court in the last three decades that, in their individual circumstances, the refusal to admit a family member constituted an infringement of their right to family life under Article 8. As for a finding of violation in regard to the actual state policy (rather than its application), in the field of family reunion it has yet to happen.

This book will continue to demonstrate that the Strasbourg case law overall follows a state logic. By contrast, the Inter-American Court prides itself in adopting what it itself calls a *pro-homine* (pro human being) reasoning. The next chapter, which reviews the first migrant case the Inter-American Court has dealt with, starts introducing this approach.

5

Not-so-Threatening Foreigners: Nationality as a Core Human Rights Issue

(Advisory Opinion 4/84)

The first ruling of the Inter-American Court of Human Rights concerning migrants related to Costa Rican naturalisation provisions. Adopted in 1984, it consisted of an advisory opinion: instead of the Court deciding on a complaint *against* a state party to the American Convention on Human Rights (ACHR) in the context of its contentious jurisdiction, the Court *interpreted* the Convention outside the context of an actual dispute, under its so-called advisory jurisdiction. In this case, the request for interpretation emerged from the government of Costa Rica, which was looking to give some work to the Inter-American Court. The Court had been established in 1979 in San José, the Costa Rican capital city, but the lack of referral of contentious cases by the Inter-American Commission on Human Rights risked condemning it to irrelevance, which Costa Rica did not want. Its request concerned its plans to tighten the naturalisation conditions inscribed in its national constitution, following the perception that 'threatening others' (to borrow the apposite title of a book on Costa Rica)[1] were flowing into the country from neighbouring Nicaragua. The question Costa Rica asked the Court to answer was whether its constitutional proposals were in conformity with the American Convention, including Article 20 on the right of nationality, which has already been discussed in Chapter 2.

The resulting advisory opinion—the fourth in the history of the Inter-American Court, delivered in 1984, hence its numbering 4/84—contained important observations on the right to nationality as it affects migrants.[2] The length at which the Court commented upon naturalisation conditions is in itself remarkable, given that nationality is generally conceived as a domain in which the sovereignty of the

[1] Carlos Sandoval-García, *Threatening Others: Nicaraguans and the Formation of National Identities in Costa Rica* (Athens: Ohio University Press, 2004).

[2] *Proposed Amendments to the Naturalization Provision of the Constitution of Costa Rica*, Advisory opinion OC-4/84 (IACtHR), 19 Jan. 1984. This is referred to later as AO 4/84.

state can exercise powers without barely any constraint. Features in the reasoning of the Inter-American Court which are also worth noting include:

- The way the Court dispenses with a close analysis of legal provisions.
- Its readiness to comment upon situations which are not specific to the instant case.
- Its broad reasoning.
- The borrowing of the expression 'doctrine of the margin of appreciation' from the European Court of Human Rights but in a way which keeps expressing limits to the sovereignty of the state.
- The placing of human rights at the starting point of its reasoning—thus reversing, so to speak, the Strasbourg approach discussed in the previous chapter.
- The expansive interpretation of human rights law beyond the array of issues which were directly put before the Court by Costa Rica.
- The strong concern with equality, which the Court brings in the opinion out of its own motion.

Whether one approves or disapproves of these features, what emerges from Advisory opinion 4/84 is that the Inter-American Court had never any intention of merely following in the steps of its 'big sister' institution and to replicate the way the European Court of Human Rights (ECHR) thinks about and approaches cases. In this early ruling the Inter-American Court shows itself speaking with a distinct voice of its own. This is a voice which is propitious to a potentially broad interpretation of migrant rights, as state powers in the field of naturalisation are recognised, but are nonetheless viewed as significantly limited by human rights norms.

This chapter starts by reviewing the context which gave rise to Advisory opinion 4/84, with a first section recalling the Inter-American institutional set up and a second elucidating the domestic situation which led Costa Rica to tighten its hitherto generous naturalisation conditions. The chapter continues with a close analysis of Advisory opinion 4/84. This allows characteristic features of the Inter-American Court's reasoning to be identified. Two judges appended a separate opinion to the main advisory opinion; these are also reviewed in detail as they demonstrate further the appetite which existed on the bench of the Inter-American Court for a broad and progressive interpretation of human rights law. This is followed by a section which stresses the reluctance of the Strasbourg Court to venture into nationality issues, a contrast which is all the more striking since the Inter-American system has continued to affirm, subsequently to Advisory opinion 4/84, its conviction that nationality issues are at the heart of human rights law. A final section offers some observations on the composition of the two courts, given that, whatever the respective founding texts say and whatever perspective the overall social and political contexts of the two continents may seem to favour, the reaching of a particular judicial outcome ultimately depends upon the actual judges who are in the position to make the decision.

I. A Slow Start for the Inter-American Court of Human Rights

The Inter-American Court of Human Rights owes its existence to the ACHR, which was adopted by the OAS in 1969 and came into force in 1978, after 11 state ratifications. By that time, the Inter-American Commission on Human Rights had long been in place. This is because the Commission was originally established in 1959 as an OAS 'autonomous entity' following a resolution by the OAS Ministers of Foreign Affairs and then, following the amendment of the OAS Charter in 1967, as one of the OAS organs. Under the Charter, the Commission's principal function is 'to promote the observance and protection of human rights'. It has always accomplished a lot as a Charter institution, including carrying out on-site visits and writing country reports.[3] It was only in 1979 that the Commission acquired the additional and separate function of being an organ of the American Convention on Human Rights. In this role, the Commission receives and examines complaints lodged by individuals and other legal persons under the Convention. After expressing a (non-legally binding) opinion on whether or not the respondent state has breached its obligations under the Convention, the Commission can (and, indeed, now *must* if certain conditions are fulfilled) bring contentious cases before the Inter-American Court.[4] It is the sole institution empowered to do this—with the exception of state parties to the Convention which are generally not inclined to do so.[5]

Although the Court was established in 1979, the Commission did not refer a case to it until seven years later. After this watershed, cases continued to arrive to the Court in a trickle. By 1995, the Commission had still referred no more than ten cases to the Court. The question arose as to why: was it because, as much of Latin America was in the grip of dictatorships at the time, the Commission had no time available for fulfilling its function under the Convention, absorbed as it was by the work it was accomplishing under the Charter of documenting and denouncing large-scale violations of human rights? Or was the Commission snubbing the Court which it did not trust?[6] Whatever the response, it was feared by the Court's proponents that the absence of referrals from the Commission might condemn the Court to irrelevance. This was something which Costa Rica was determined not to let happen.

[3] Jo M. Pasqualucci, *The Practice and Procedure of the Inter-American Court of Human Rights* (Cambridge: Cambridge University Press, 2nd ed., 2013) 84.

[4] Rules of Procedure of the Inter-American Commission on Human Rights, Article 45; see further Laurence Burgorgue-Larsen and Amaya Úbeda de Torres, *The Inter-American Court of Human Rights: Case Law and Commentary* (Oxford: Oxford University Press, 2011) 36 ff.

[5] As of 5 April 2014, only ten states had accepted the Commission's competence to receive inter-state complaints and only two inter-state complaints had ever been filed.

[6] Tom Farer, 'The Rise of the Inter-American Human Rights Regime: No Longer a Unicorn, Not Yet an Ox' (1997) *Human Rights Quarterly* 19, 510–546 at 543–544.

Costa Rica is a country with the reputation of being committed to human rights, fulfilling a human rights promotional role 'vastly disproportionate to its size, wealth and power'. The entry devoted to it in the *Encyclopedia of Human Rights* edited by International Relations scholar David Forsythe reports its presence in 'virtually every major human rights initiative and institution'.[7] Alison Brysk, the entry's author, notes its participation in all major UN human rights initiatives. Costa Rica frequently had someone sitting in the Human Rights Commission and the Human Rights Sub-Commission for the Prevention of Discrimination and Protection of Minorities, and even occupied leading roles in these now defunct institutions. It has been involved in campaigns towards the expansion of the human rights regime and in getting the UN General Assembly to pass human rights resolutions. More importantly for our purposes, it has been a key player in the development of the Inter-American system. For example, when the OAS Assembly failed to adopt a budget for the Court in its first year of existence, it offered financial assistance. It also provided the villa where the Court is still based today.[8]

It is thus in keeping with the proactive human rights role for which it became renowned that Costa Rica stepped in and took advantage of the Inter-American Court's unusually broadly phrased advisory jurisdiction[9] to bring the Court its first case in 1982. The case related to the killing of a prisoner by a member of the Costa Rican Civil Guard. Costa Rica asked the Court to say whether the killing amounted to a violation of the Convention, arguing that such an authoritative and speedy ruling would facilitate a quick settlement of the case. The Inter-American Court declared the request inadmissible on the ground that for it to issue an opinion would bypass the procedure before the Commission and thus impair the function assigned by the Convention to the Commission.[10] Undeterred, the government of Costa Rica continued to ask the Court to interpret the Convention on another two occasions, when issues of fact were not at stake. Requesting the Court to assess its proposed constitutional provisions regarding naturalisation under the Convention was one of these.[11] Before reviewing the opinion issued by the Court, it is useful briefly to highlight the national context of the case.

[7] Alison Brysk, 'Costa Rica', in David P. Forsythe (ed.) *Encyclopedia of Human Rights Vol. 1* (Oxford: Oxford University Press, 2009) 416–420 at 416 and 417.

[8] Thomas Buergenthal, 'Remembering the Early Years of the Inter-American Court of Human Rights', Centre for Human Rights and Global Justice Working Paper no. 1 (2005) *NYU School of Law*, 6.

[9] Pasqualucci, *Practice and Procedure* 39. There is no pendent to the advisory jurisdiction of the Inter-American Court in the Strasbourg system, although domestic judges will be able to ask questions of interpretation to the European Court following the entry into force of Protocol no. 16. See further Kanstantsin Dzehtsiarou and Noreen O'Meara, 'Advisory Jurisdiction and the European Court of Human Rights: A Magic Bullet for Dialogue and Docket-Control?' (2014) *Legal Studies* 34, 444–468.

[10] *Matter of Viviana Gallardo et al.* (Costa Rica), Decision (IACtHR), 13 Nov. 1981.

[11] The other case concerned a law then in force in Costa Rica which in effect restricted the practice of journalism to graduates of the University of Costa Rica: *Compulsory Membership in an*

II. Foreigners Perceived as Threatening: '*Nicas*' in Costa Rica

Costa Rica is renowned for its exceptionalism in Central and indeed Latin America. While its neighbours have suffered repeated coups d'état, civil wars, and dictatorships, this 'small, poor country from a troubled region'[12] was able to maintain political stability, to achieve relative economic prosperity (20 per cent of its population nonetheless lives under the poverty line), and to become a beacon of human rights promotion. How did it manage this feat? Brysk locates the answer in its 'inconvenient location for colonization, sparse indigenous population, and lack of mineral or plantation wealth, producing light colonial settlement and the development of agricultural production by independent smallholders rather than large labor-exploitative plantations'. She also mentions the way labour rights, universal social services, and basic civil liberties were introduced early in the twentieth century in an effort to modernise the country. Later, diplomats positioned it as the region's 'island of peace',[13] a label made persuasive by the absence of military forces since they were abolished in 1948 and an unusually open civil society.

This does not mean that Costa Rica is altogether without problems. Brysk herself mentions that 'immigrants...face some discrimination'.[14] From the perspective of these immigrants, this can only be an understatement. In *Threatening Others: Nicaraguans and the Formation of National Identities in Costa Rica*, the sociologist Carlos Sandoval-García argues that the country's national identity was founded and continues to be built upon 'representations of Costa Ricans as a "white" middle-class population, in sharp contrast with the violent, dark-skinned deprived Nicaraguan other'.[15] In everyday Costa Rican speech, '*ticos*' is used to refer to Costa Rican citizens, while immigrants from Nicaragua are referred to as '*nicas*', which has become a term of denigration.[16] With their different way of speaking Spanish, their assumed negative character and their association with the Nicaraguan state with which Costa Rica has a long-standing border dispute, *nicas* are in the Costa Rican social imaginary what *ticos* are not.

A stable electoral democracy and an enduring peace are the defining elements of which the country, with a current population of about 4.5 million,[17] is proud. The discrimination suffered by *nicas*, who come from the second-poorest country in Latin America after Haiti, is another defining element, but one which, although pervasive and very much for all to see, is not commonly confronted. In his book, Sandoval-García quotes a young boy who asks his father whether he has Nicaraguan blood. On his father's positive reply, the boy interjects: 'So how can

Association Prescribed by Law for the Practice of Journalism, Advisory opinion OC-5/85 (IACtHR), 13 Nov. 1985.

[12] Brysk 'Costa Rica' 416. [13] Brysk 416. [14] Brysk 416.

[15] Sandoval-García *Threatening Others* xxii.

[16] Even though Nicaraguans themselves use the term (there is a TV station called 'Telenica' and a bus company called 'Transnica' in Nicaragua).

[17] Costa Rica Demographics Profile 2013, <http://www.indexmundi.com/costa_rica/demographics_profile.html>, accessed 24 May 2014.

I get rid of it?'[18] The poignant feelings embodied in this exchange, collected in the late 1990s, is the product of a long history between the two countries whereby 'Nicaragua as a state and Nicaraguans as citizens became undesired others in Costa Rican imagery'.[19]

In the early twentieth century, US interventions in Nicaragua and the civil war produced massive death and displacement (20 per cent of the population died, according to some estimates).[20] Nicaraguans in Costa Rica became criminalised in the late 1950s after Nicaragua, under the dictatorship of Anastasio Somoza García, tried to invade Costa Rica.[21] While Costa Rica's President Rodrigo Carazo (1978–1982) initially lent public support to the Nicaraguan war of liberation against Somoza, this changed with the mounting US intervention against the Nicaraguan Sandinista government, represented as a communist threat, and with the developing economic crisis in Costa Rica. It is not clear exactly how many Nicaraguans fled the ensuing civil war in Nicaragua and moved to Costa Rica, but by 1989 the United Nations High Commissioner for Refugees had recorded 23,750 fleeing a country whose population numbered a little over 3 million.[22]

By all accounts, the early 1980s were a period of heightened fear of, and prejudice against, *nicas* in Costa Rica.[23] This, then, is the context which led Costa Rica to want to change its constitutional provisions regarding naturalisation, which became the object of Advisory opinion 4/84 of the Inter-American Court.

III. Advisory Opinion 4/84: Human Rights First

On 9 August 1983, the government of Costa Rica sought an advisory opinion from the Inter-American Court on whether its proposed amendments to the Constitution regarding naturalisation were compatible with the American Convention on Human Rights. Under the Costa Rican Constitution then in force, nationals of other countries of Central America could become Costa Ricans after one year of residence in Costa Rica; native-born Spaniards and Ibero-Americans after two years; and other foreigners after five years. In 1983, the Costa Rican Legislative Assembly proposed raising the minimum length of residence required to five years for native-born nationals of the other countries of Central America, Spaniards, and Ibero-Americans, and to seven years for all other foreigners. The previous condition of providing evidence of good conduct remained. In addition,

18 Sandoval-García *Threatening Others* 128.

19 Sandoval-García xxii.

20 Sandoval-García 94–95.

21 Sandoval-García 96.

22 United Nations High Commissioner for Refugees, 'Situation of Nicaraguan refugees in Costa Rica', 1 March 1989, <http://www.refworld.org/docid/3ae6aaf673.html>, accessed 10 March 2014.

23 Discrimination continues to be rife, as transpires from: Carlos Sandoval-García, 'Public Social Science at Work: Contesting Hostility Towards Nicaraguan Migrants in Costa Rica', in Thanh-Dam Truong, Des Gasper, and Jeff Handmaker (eds) *Migration, Gender and Social Justice: Perspectives on Human Insecurity* (2014) <http://link.springer.com/chapter/10.1007%2F978-3-642-28012-2_20#page-1>, accessed 31 January 2014.

applicants for naturalisation would have to show that they had a known occupation or means of livelihood and that they could speak, write, and read the Spanish language. They would also have to submit to an examination on the history of the country and its values. Naturalisation would be extended to a foreign woman who by marriage to a Costa Rican lost her nationality or who indicated her desire to become a Costa Rican, although this would happen only two years after the marriage. The Costa Rican government asked the Inter-American Court whether these proposals respected Article 20 of the American Convention on the right to nationality and Article 17 on the equality of spouses.[24]

The Court rendered its advisory opinion on 19 January 1984. On issues of jurisdiction, it decided, for reasons which need not detain us here, that the case was admissible. Regarding the substantive issues, the Court added one question to those raised by the Costa Rican government, namely, whether the proposed provisions were compatible with Article 24 of the American Convention, guaranteeing equality before the law.

The first issue the advisory opinion considers is the compatibility of the proposed provisions with the right to nationality established by Article 20 ACHR. The Court's discussion starts as follows, with the opening sentence deserving special attention:

> It is generally accepted today that nationality is an inherent right of all human beings.... Thus, despite the fact that it is traditionally accepted that the conferral and regulation of nationality are matters for each state to decide, contemporary developments indicate that international law does impose certain limits on the broad powers enjoyed by states in that area.
>
> The classic doctrinal position, which viewed nationality as an attribute granted by the state to its subjects, has gradually evolved to the point that nationality is today perceived as involving the jurisdiction of the state as well as human rights issues....
>
> The right of every human being to a nationality has been recognized as such by international law.[25]

The opening sentence can be said to reverse the Strasbourg reversal identified in Chapter 4 and to put the human rights perspective back on its feet. Instead of human rights being conceived as an exception which qualify the principle of state sovereignty, the Inter-American Court begins its reasoning by affirming the human right to nationality. From a human rights perspective this order of reasoning must be applauded. However, the Court's presentation is not without its own difficulties.

The Court's affirmation that nationality is a human right is far from uncontroversial. On a legal plane, declaring the right to nationality to be 'generally accepted today' as a human right is simply unconvincing. The American Convention is the sole instrument of international law which grants a right to the nationality of a *specific* state.[26] Normally, when international law concerns itself

[24] AO 4/84, para 7. [25] AO 4/84, paras 32–34.

[26] Lisa Pilgram, 'International Law and European Nationality Laws', published under the auspices of the EUDO Citizenship Observatory and dated March 2011 <http://eudo-citizenship.eu/docs/Pilgram.pdf>, accessed 24 January 2014, p. 4.

with nationality, if it does so at all, it is merely to exhort states to avoid statelessness and to prohibit the arbitrary deprivation of nationality. An incidental but sure sign that the human right to nationality is not firmly established is that its gradual recognition was celebrated by the doctrine, even after Advisory opinion 4/84 was rendered.[27] Far from the Court just interpreting a pre-existing norm of international law which is widely recognised and settled, what happens in the advisory opinion is that the Court works at *developing* international human rights law.

The opening sentence serves the function of casting a wide protective net around vulnerable individuals, including stateless persons. With the benefit of hindsight, it can be seen to constitute an early embodiment of the *pro-homine* approach, by which the Court puts the human being at the very centre of its reasoning and for which it would become renowned.[28]

Its propensity for such an approach leads the Court to start its reasoning with pronouncements on human rights rather than with recalling state powers. The powers enjoyed by states in the immigration field are recognised but they are mentioned only as a second step in the Court's reasoning. Also, they are not presented as forming a 'well-established' principle of international law. Rather, the Court identifies a 'gradual evolution' in the classic doctrinal position regarding the way nationality is conferred and regulated. This position, which refrains from envisaging state powers in this area as an intangible principle, facilitates the development of an approach which accepts and perhaps even demands that nationality laws be examined for their compatibility with human rights principles.

Not only the paragraph already quoted but also the next-but-one paragraph recognise the latitude states enjoy in deciding the conditions individuals will need to fulfil in order to be granted their nationality. To quote:

> As long as [nationality rules] do not conflict with superior norms, it is the state conferring nationality which is best able to judge what conditions to impose to ensure that an effective link exists between the applicant for naturalization and the systems of values and interests of the society with which he seeks to fully associate himself.[29]

Further in its reasoning, the Court accepts the fact that changing these conditions and making them more restrictive is not in itself problematic:

> [S]ince a state's perceived needs do not remain static, it is quite natural that the conditions for naturalization might be liberalized or restricted with the changed circumstances.[30]

Nevertheless, after these introductory remarks, the Court finds a way of commenting critically about the Costa Rican proposals. Although it says it will not

[27] See e.g. Johannes M.M. Chan, 'The Right to a Nationality as a Human Right: The Current Trend Towards Recognition' (1991) *Human Rights Law Journal* 1–14; Gerard-René de Groot, 'Towards a European Nationality Law' (2004) *Electronic Journal of Comparative Law* 8(3).

[28] Ludovic Hennebel, *La Convention américaine des droits de l'homme. Mécanismes de protection et étendue des droits et libertés* (Brussels: Bruylant, 2007) 42.

[29] AO 4/84, para 36.

[30] AO 4/84, para 36.

rule upon them, it obliquely admonishes Costa Rica for having given way to what could be called its darker sides:

> The Court will consequently not address certain issues that were raised during the public hearing... Here one might note [the doubts which have been expressed] regarding the following questions: whether the spirit underlying the proposed amendments as a whole reflects, in a general way, a negative nationalistic reaction prompted by specific circumstances relating to the problem of refugees, particularly Central American refugees, who seek the protection of Costa Rica in their flight from the convulsion engulfing other countries in the region; whether that spirit reveals a tendency or retrogression from the traditional humanitarianism of Costa Rica; whether the proposed amendment, in eliminating the privileged naturalization status enjoyed by Central Americans under the current Constitution of Costa Rica, is indicative of a position rejecting the unity and solidarity that has historically characterized the peoples of Central America who achieved independence as a single nation.[31]

The Court concludes its discussion about the compatibility of the Costa Rican proposals with the right to nationality by conceding that the proposals do not affect the right guaranteed by Article 20 ACHR since they 'do not purport to withdraw [Costa Rican] nationality from any citizen currently holding it, nor to deny the right to change that nationality'.[32] While the Court expresses some reservations about the two-year waiting period imposed on a foreigner who becomes Costa Rican upon marriage, it nonetheless concludes: 'the proposals do not in any formal sense contravene Article 20 of the Convention'.[33]

Of its own motion, the Court then decides to examine the proposed provisions, which distinguish between native-born nationals of Central American countries and other foreigners, in regard to Article 24 of the American Convention guaranteeing equal protection. This in itself is extremely interesting, as it shows the Court willing to take a proactive role in the way it responds to the request put to it and it also signals its attachment to equality as a founding value of human rights. The reasoning of the Court on this point is noteworthy for the philosophical and principled way in which it proceeds:

> The notion of equality springs directly from the oneness of the human family and is linked to the essential dignity of the individual. That principle cannot be reconciled with the notion that a given group has the right to privileged treatment because of its perceived superiority. It is equally irreconcilable with that notion to characterize a group as inferior and treat it with hostility or otherwise subject it to discrimination in the enjoyment of rights which are accorded to others not so classified. It is impermissible to subject human beings to differences in treatment that are inconsistent with their unique and congenerous [*sic*] character.[34]

One could say that the Court is less interested in a 'legally legal' construction as in trying to understand and spell out the implications of the *idea* of the equality of human beings.[35]

[31] AO 4/84, para 40. [32] AO 4/84, para 42. [33] AO 4/84, para 42.
[34] AO 4/84, para 55.
[35] For a penetrating (but in my view ultimately unpersuasive) critique of this approach, see: James L. Cavallero and Stephanie Erin Brewer, 'Reevaluating Regional Human Rights Litigation in the

Either in a strategic move designed to lend legitimacy to its ruling by borrowing from a more established and thus authoritative institution or because of its cosmopolitan outlook, the Inter-American Court then refers to the European Court of Human Rights and cites the *Belgian Linguistic* case of 1968, in particular its statement that 'a difference in treatment is only discriminatory when it "has no objective and reasonable justification"'.[36] However, having cited this authority, the Inter-American Court rephrases the idea in more general terms. It states, 'no discrimination exists if it does not lead to situations which are contrary to justice, to reason or to the nature of things'.[37] In the instant case, the Inter-American Court does not think that it would 'be inconsistent with the nature and purpose of the grant of nationality to expedite the naturalization procedures for those who, viewed objectively, share much closer historical, cultural and spiritual bonds with the people of Costa Rica'.[38] In conclusion, the Court does not find that the constitutional proposals, if adopted, would violate Article 24 of the American Convention.[39]

Instead of stopping its reasoning there, the Court adds an aside, made up of three sentences which together reinforce the message already implicitly present earlier in the advisory opinion, according to which the Court considers it within its remit to scrutinise naturalisation provisions in respect of their impact on human rights. To quote:

> In reaching this conclusion, the Court is fully mindful of the margin of appreciation, which is reserved to states when it comes to the establishment of requirements for the acquisition of nationality and the determination whether they have been complied with. But the Court's conclusion should not be viewed as approval of the practice which prevails in some areas to limit to an exaggerated and unjustified degree the political rights of naturalized individuals. Most of these situations involve cases not now before the Court that do, however, constitute clear instances of discrimination on the basis of origin or place of birth, unjustly creating two distinct hierarchies of nationals in one single country.[40]

The reference to the 'margin of appreciation' in the first sentence of this passage is clearly borrowed from the European Court. However, the Inter-American Court only follows the European Court superficially (and would refer to this doctrine again only twice in its subsequent case law).[41] In Advisory opinion 4/84, the margin which the Inter-American Court concedes to states is very limited indeed. The second sentence suggests that the Inter-American Court considers that states exceed the margin they enjoy in the nationality field when they curtail in an 'exaggerated' manner the political rights of naturalised individuals. In the third

Twenty-First Century: The Case of the Inter-American Court' (2008) *The American Journal of International Law* 102, 768–827.

[36] AO 4/84, para 56. [37] AO 4/84, para 57. [38] AO 4/84, para 60.

[39] AO 4/84, para 61. [40] AO 4/84, para 62.

[41] Marie Rota, 'L'interprétation des Conventions américaine et européenne des droits de l'homme. Analyse comparée des deux Cours de protection des droits de l'homme', 2013 PhD thesis, University of Caen-Basse-Normandie, at 259. However, Burgorgue-Larsen does not rule out that a change of direction in judicial interpretation might allow the margin of interpretation to enter San José jurisprudence in the future: Laurence Burgorgue-Larsen, Les méthodes d'interprétation de la Cour interaméricaine des droits de l'homme: Justice in context' (2014) *Revue trimestrielle des droits de l'homme* 97, 23–71 at 66.

sentence, the Court indicates that it is aware of provisions which in its view discriminate unjustly between different nationals. Irrespective of the wisdom or otherwise of alluding to facts which are not directly pertinent to the case at hand, this shows the Court's readiness, almost keenness, to envisage and identify nationality provisions and practices which fall foul of human rights principles, and thus human rights law—two concepts which it seems not to wish to distinguish.

The Court then continues by expressing an opinion about the Costa Rican proposal to condition naturalisation to a Spanish test and an examination of the country's history and values:

> These conditions can be deemed, prima facie, to fall within the margin of appreciation reserved to the state as far as concerns the enactment and assessment of the requirements designed to ensure the existence of real and effective links upon which to base the acquisition of the new nationality. So viewed, [the conditions] cannot be said to be unreasonable and unjustified... The Court feels compelled to emphasize, however, that in practice, and given the broad discretion with which tests such as those mandated by the draft amendment tend to be administered, there exists the risk that these requirements will become the vehicle for subjective and arbitrary judgments as well as instruments for the effectuation of discriminatory policies which, although not directly apparent on the face of the law, could well be the consequence of its application.[42]

With this passage, the Court seems to warn Costa Rica that, if its formal proposals do not contravene human rights law, their actual application may do so.

In conclusion, the only problem which the Inter-American Court identifies with the Costa Rican provisions relates to gender equality.[43] This finding was expected—so much so that the breach of Article 17(4) ACHR that it entailed had already been corrected through an amendment submitted to the Costa Rican Parliament by the time the advisory opinion was delivered.

This outcome may remind the reader of the judgment of the European Court of Human Rights in *Abdulaziz, Cabales and Balkandali*.[44] If so, any sense of déjà vu is arguably misplaced, as will shortly be discussed.

IV. The Features of the Inter-American Approach So Far: Recapitulation

Before proceeding, it is useful to recapitulate the characteristics of the Inter-American Court's approach, as they emerge from Advisory opinion 4/84. This can be done as follows:

- Human rights comes first.
- State sovereignty is recognised but comes second in the reasoning, and is moreover decisively restricted by human rights provisos which loom large.

[42] AO 4/84, para 63. [43] AO 4/84, para 67.

[44] *Abdulaziz, Cabales and Balkandali*, appls 9214/80, 9473/81, 9474/81, PC Judgment (ECtHR), 28 May 1985, discussed in Chapter 4.

- The Inter-American Court borrows from the European Court, but does so in a superficial way.
- Its overall aim is to develop international human rights law.
- General statements are posited which are bound to appear controversial in the absence of a coherent and completely settled body of international human rights law.
- The Court uses the case at hand to go beyond the confines of the interpretation which had been requested by the lodging party.
- Equality is a major concern, which the Court brings in of its own motion.
- The reasoning is not 'lawyerly legal' but broad and philosophical.
- A *pro-homine* bias is already perceptible.[45]

V. Pushing the Equality Agenda Further: The Separate Opinions of Judge Piza Escalante and Judge Buergenthal

For two of the six judges sitting on the bench which adopted it, Advisory opinion 4/84 was not going far enough. Each for their own reasons, they found the Costa Rican proposals discriminatory on grounds other than gender. Reviewing their separate opinions allows us to measure how far they would have wanted to push the equality agenda.[46]

Judge Piza Escalante, who had presided from the inception of the Court in 1979 to 1981, wrote a separate opinion, which at 14 pages, was almost as long as the Court's own opinion. He started by spelling out his favoured method of interpretation, by recalling his

> old inclination to have the Court, in performing... especially its advisory duties, gradually abandon the traditional reluctance of all Courts of Justice to state principles, doctrines, and criteria of interpretation that are not those indispensable for resolving each specific case it considers, and plunging forward on the pretext of such consideration, to establish its more far-reaching mission of creating jurisprudence with the audacity, breadth, intensity and flexibility that are possible without any restriction other than the impassable limits of its competence—and a little beyond that, if possible![47]

The former President of the Court considers human rights to be 'progressive and expansive'. In his view, attention must be paid to their 'potential for growth',

[45] Although too much should not be made of this as it may be the work of the translator, it is also intriguing that the word 'state' is written with a lower case throughout this early advisory opinion, as quotations in Section III of this chapter illustrate.

[46] Until recently the great majority of separate opinions expressed by judges of the Inter-American Court regretted what they saw as a lack of audacity by their colleagues: Burgorgue-Larsen 'Les méthodes' 61–62.

[47] Judge Piza Escalante's separate vote, AO 4/84 (IACtHR), para. 1.

outside the restriction of the literal text in which they are inscribed.[48] In line with this idea, he believes that states, having agreed 'to develop human rights progressively', should not be permitted to reduce the ways in which they have already implemented human rights, however accidentally rather than purposefully.[49] In other words, states should not necessarily be allowed to take away what they have previously granted of their own free will.[50] Despite this, Judge Piza Escalante can 'think of no valid reason . . . to object to, from the standpoint of human rights, the general conditions and periods proposed for domicile or residence' before naturalisation can be considered. He nevertheless allows himself to express the view that 'the residence periods in the present Costa Rican Constitution [of one year for Central American nationals] sound more reasonable than those proposed'.[51]

While Judge Piza Escalante thus reluctantly accepts that he cannot legally object to Costa Rican proposals regarding a longer period of residence, he feels that the language requirement which is also proposed does not pass the human rights test. Spanish, he notes, is not spoken throughout Costa Rica: there are small and isolated Indian communities as well as a large English-speaking community of Jamaican origin.[52] In his view, even so, 'it does not appear unreasonable . . . to require persons desiring to acquire Costa Rican nationality to know the official language well enough to communicate in it, without which language it would be little less than impossible . . . to integrate themselves fully into the nation'.[53] The problem for him lies with the imposition of a writing test which 'has little or nothing to do with integration into the national community', which he sees as the very purpose of naturalisation. The atmosphere in which the proposed provisions were devised, Judge Piza Escalante argues, indicates that the language text will be implemented so as 'to reduce the granting of nationality to [educated] persons'. This is in his view unjustifiable. He perceives the same discriminatory and objectionable intent in the history test, reminiscent of US practices which used to serve to exclude 'southern negroes' from the vote.[54]

Judge Buergenthal was the second dissenter in Advisory opinion 4/84. He did not think that the Costa Rican constitutional proposals respected Article 24 of the American Convention on the right to equal protection. His particular issue was with the fact that naturalised nationals of Central America, Spaniards, and Ibero-Americans were treated less favourably than nationals by birth from the same regions. The proposals were for these citizens by naturalisation to be required to have resided in Costa Rica for at least seven years (instead of five years for nationals by birth) before being eligible to apply for Costa Rican naturalisation.

[48] Piza Escalante in AO 4/84, para 3.
[49] Piza Escalante in AO 4/84, para 5.
[50] Piza Escalante in AO 4/84, para 31.
[51] Piza Escalante in AO 4/84, para 17.
[52] And slave origin, which Judge Piza Escalante did not mention.
[53] Piza Escalante in AO 4/84, paras 23 and 24.
[54] Piza Escalante in AO 4/84, paras 25 and 26. See also paras 27–36 on why Judge Piza Escalante finds the proposed provisions relating to naturalisation through marriage discriminatory.

Judge Buergenthal could not see what legitimate governmental end might be accomplished by making them wait this extra two years, the more so since the individuals concerned would already have had to fulfil conditions for naturalisation in a Spanish-speaking country and since they were to be subjected to a language and history test in Costa Rica in any event.

Judge Buergenthal's biography predisposed him to be sensitive to the plight of the naturalised migrant. Born to Jewish parents in 1934, he was taken to Auschwitz from the Jewish ghetto of Kielce in Poland during World War II, survived, and migrated to the United States in 1951.[55] Such a trajectory would have exposed him personally to the pain and injustice of being implicitly or explicitly considered a second-class citizen, including after 'naturalisation'. His own take on the case thus makes sense. The more intriguing question then becomes: why did not the other five judges then sitting on the bench of the Inter-American Court follow him?

The more one thinks about the proposed distinction between naturalised and born nationals of Spanish-speaking countries, the more difficult it is to see what practical function the distinction is supposed to achieve. Its function appears entirely symbolic: that of distinguishing between various kinds of foreigners, so as to hammer home the point that some people are assumed to be closer to 'us' (in this case, Costa Ricans) than others. Should such a distinction be acceptable under human rights law, which supposedly enshrines the equality of all human beings? Presumably, despite its *pro-homine* and non-statist perspective, the Inter-American Court did not want to be seen to examine too closely every detail of decisions taken in a domain traditionally conceived of as being at the heart of national sovereignty. Thus, with the exception of Judge Buergenthal, the Inter-American Court was persuaded to let the proposals be. Perhaps this was on the expectation that the measure was symbolic and as such unlikely to bear significant adverse practical consequences for anyone. If so, Judge Buergenthal might nonetheless have gained one concession from his colleagues, namely, that remarks about the 'exaggerated' restrictions to which naturalised citizens are too often subjected in their political activities be included in the advisory opinion, despite not being wholly germane to the case (as reviewed previously).

Together, Judges Piza Escalante and Buergenthal voted against the Court's majority on three points. Their separate opinions testify to the strongly progressive character of the wind which was blowing at the Inter-American Court in its early days. They also act as a reminder that the Inter-American Court could have given an even broader interpretation of the requirements of human rights law than the one it offered in its advisory opinion. This, of course, is always the case. Human rights law does not operate as an on-off switch, despite what apparently clear-cut verdicts of violation or non-violation might suggest. Human rights law is an interpretative process in which a particular perspective can always be taken further.

[55] Thomas Buergenthal, *A Lucky Child: A Memoir of Surviving Auschwitz as a Young Boy* (London: Profile Books, 2010).

VI. Underdeveloped Strasbourg Case Law: The Case of the Slovenian 'Erased'

These dissenting opinions do not take away the fact that Advisory opinion 4/84 shows that the Inter-American Court was more than willing to consider that questions of access to nationality are integral to human rights law. The same cannot be said of the European Court which took 50 years before starting to discuss nationality as a human rights issue.

The ultimate explanation for this contrast does not lie with the founding treaties. Admittedly the European Convention has no equivalent to Article 20 ACHR. Moreover, its whole structure, including of course Article 16, seems to legitimise keeping non-nationals 'outside' the polity, as explained in Chapter 2. However, once in force and implemented, any legal text acquires a life of its own, which develops outside and even against the imagination of its drafters. For example, the European Convention system has chosen to affirm the rights of children born out of wedlock, even though there would have been no appetite for this in 1950. Had there been such a will, it would have been possible for the European Court also to find ways to develop rights to give access to nationality—through recourse to Article 8 on private and family life or Article 3 prohibiting inhuman and degrading treatment.

The applicants invited the Court to do precisely this in the case of the 'Erased'. They had been citizens of the Republic of Yugoslavia in Slovenia, prior to its break up. After the Slovenian declaration of independence in 1991, their names—along that of 18,000 others—were erased the following year from the Register of Permanent Residents. This was because they had failed to become Slovenian through registration within the six-month limit provided in the law. In turn, this was for a variety of reasons, including the inability to provide the documentation required due to the outbreak of war in their country of origin, a failure to understand the material published on the subject, or a belief that because they had been born in Slovenia they would acquire its citizenship automatically.[56] Many individuals became stateless as a result. The Strasbourg case concerned, amongst other matters: loss of citizenship and resident status; denial of housing; denial of access to free medical service; deportation, barring re-entry into the country and family separation; lack of protection against work without pay; and deprivation of pension rights. The Court conceded that 'an arbitrary denial of citizenship might in certain circumstances raise an issue under Article 8 of the Convention because of the impact of such a denial on the private life of the individual'.[57] It ruled, however, that because the Convention had entered into force in respect of Slovenia only in June 1994, the complaint regarding citizenship and

[56] *Milan Makuc and Others v. Slovenia*, appl. 26828/06, Decision (ECtHR), 31 May 2007, para 10.

[57] *Makuc*, para 160. See also *Kurić and Others v. Slovenia*, appl. 26828/06, GC Judgment (ECtHR), 13 July 2010, para 353.

residence status was not compatible with the Convention *ratione temporis*.[58] The applicants had also complained under Article 3 that 'they had been subjected to deliberate discriminatory and illegal treatment which had seriously undermined their human dignity and confined them to a life on the margins'.[59] This too was declared inadmissible. Although the Court said it was 'well aware of the anguish and in security the applicants must have undergone during several years of uncertainty over their resident/citizenship status in Slovenia, it consider[ed] that the facts of the case [did] not meet the threshold required to attract the protection of Article 3'.[60]

Other complaints were found admissible. In July 2010, a Chamber found a violation of Article 8 because of the continual denial of access to a residence permit, contrary to a number of decisions by the Constitutional Court,[61] a situation which therefore also entailed a violation of Article 13 (about effective domestic remedies).[62] On referral from the respondent state, the Grand Chamber confirmed these findings in June 2012. In addition it found a violation of Article 14, prohibiting discrimination. Whilst the Chamber had found that this complaint (previously declared admissible) had given rise to 'no separate issue' under Article 14, the Grand Chamber ruled that, given the importance of the issues at stake, Article 14 should be considered. It went on to rule that the claimants had been discriminated against on the grounds of their national origin, when compared to other foreign citizens (the so-called 'real' aliens) who continued to live in Slovenia on the basis of temporary or permanent residence permits.[63]

The Grand Chamber decided it could not reopen the citizenship complaint which had been declared inadmissible by the Chamber.[64] There is no indication that it did this with regret. For the European Court, nationality laws fall within the discretionary sovereign domain of the state. As a result, it normally thinks it is beyond its jurisdiction to scrutinise them for their compatibility with the European Convention.

The one exception to this trend is a case concerning Malta. The Court found a violation of Article 14 taken together with Article 8 in October 2011 in this case which involved a discrimination between children born in and outside of marriage: the law made it possible for a child born to a foreign mother and a Maltese father to become Maltese only if the parents were married—while a non-married Maltese woman could pass on her nationality to her child.[65] This verdict cannot

[58] *Makuc*, para 165. In *Yean and Bosico v. the Dominican Republic*, the Inter-American Court, facing a similar situation, found this to be a continuous situation rather than an instantaneous act. See Chapter 10.

[59] *Makuc*, para 198.

[60] *Makuc*, para 200.

[61] *Kurić and Others v. Slovenia*, appl. 26828/06, Judgment (ECtHR), 13 July 2010, paras 348–376.

[62] *Kurić* judgment, para 383.

[63] *Kurić* GC, para 394.

[64] *Kurić* GC, para 231.

[65] *Genovese v. Malta*, appl. 53124/09, Judgment (ECtHR), 11 Oct. 2011, in English only. The preceding year, Malta had been found in violation of Article 8 for having refused to register a marriage between someone who had become Maltese by naturalisation (through a marriage subsequently annulled) with a national of his original country (Russia): *Dadouch v. Malta*, appl. 38816/07, Judgment (ECtHR), 20 July. 2010, in English only (with a Russian translation).

be said to invalidate the conclusion that nationality laws generally fall outside the radar of the European Court. This conclusion can be supported by numerous examples. Four are offered here.[66]

Chapter 4 noted that there is a question mark as to whether the Strasbourg Court would wish to examine, and declare contrary to the Convention, policies introduced by the Netherlands or other European states in order to subject the admission of migrants for family reunification purposes to the successful passing of language and integration tests and/or minimal income levels.[67] For the Court to consider such conditions problematic when what is at stake is not mere admission but the actual granting of nationality would be an even greater, and thus arguably more unlikely, step. It certainly has not happened so far, even though one can easily imagine that cases concerning such conditions would have been lodged with the Court, had the Strasbourg case law signalled to potential applicants that the Court was open to review these kinds of policies. This is the first example.

The second example is related to the next chapter. Foreigners who have served time in jail after criminal conviction have commonly become subject to deportation orders, at least in some countries such as the UK. This has given rise to a huge case law at Strasbourg where the Court is called on to examine whether the individual circumstances of the applicant prevent deportation because of the strength of their family ties to the host country. Nationals can never be deported. Thus, if these ex-prisoners were nationals, the very idea of deporting them could not arise. Despite this, the Strasbourg Court has never commented upon, let alone questioned, the human rights quality of the nationality law of the deporting state. The force of the argument according to which nationality law is a matter of national sovereignty seems such that no one, not even applicants' legal representatives, would wish to challenge the way long-settled migrants can be maintained in a status which classifies them as 'foreigners'—for an arguably inordinate period of time.

The third example derives from the second, and this is that the Strasbourg Court does not seem inclined to comment about situations where, a second nationality having been granted, it is then rescinded. At least this is what a judgment such as *Daoudi v. France*, from 2009, suggests.[68] Mr Daoudi had arrived in France in 1979 aged five. The section of the judgment which lays down the facts of the case reports that he had been naturalised French in 2001.[69]

[66] *Biao v. Denmark*, appl. 38590/10, Judgment (ECtHR), 25 Mar. 2014; discussed in Chapter 4, is another example. See also *Zeïbek v. Greece*, appl. 46368/06, Judgment (ECtHR), 9 July. 2009, in French only; discussed in Chapter 8, Section XV. It may be worth noting that the cases brought by 'permanently resident non-citizens' who, being of Russian origin and having lived for long periods in Latvia and became stateless following the break up of the Soviet Union, have not directly implicated nationality laws. The Latvian case law concerning residence permits is discussed in Chapter 13. See also *Andrejeva v. Latvia*, appl. 55707/00, GC Judgment, 18 Feb. 2009 (concerning retirement pensions and briefly mentioned in Chapter 8, Section XIC).

[67] As discussed in Section XIV of Chapter 4, on the face of Advisory opinion 4/84, the prospect of similar policies being declared by the Inter-American Court compatible with human rights law would appear limited.

[68] *Daoudi v. France*, appl. 19576/08, Judgment (ECtHR), 3 Dec. 2009, in French only.

[69] *Daoudi*, para 13.

Following his alleged involvement with Islamic groups close to Al-Qaida, the French government wanted to deport him to Algeria. The Court found that such an expulsion would risk exposing him to inhuman and degrading treatment and would therefore be in breach of Article 3 ECHR, if implemented. The Court failed to mention, however, the applicant's loss of French nationality. This loss must have happened as otherwise it is difficult to comprehend how Mr Daoudi would ever have been thought deportable. At a time when revocations of nationality, typically for alleged security reasons related to the 'War on Terror', are becoming an increasing and controversial state practice,[70] it is astonishing that the Court refrained from even mentioning Mr Daoudi's loss of French nationality.

Less concrete, but equally telling, our fourth example is that the term 'statelessness' yielded a mere six results—including the two judgments on the Slovenian 'Erased'—in a HUDOC search conducted on 28 January 2014. It is difficult to comprehend how there can be so little case law on such an important issue. De facto statelessness, described by the Equal Rights Trust as a 'human rights blind spot', has become a major problem in Europe which affects thousands and thousands of people.[71] The least one can say is that the European Court is not attuned to problems of (lack of) nationality.[72]

It is hardly persuasive to attribute the underdeveloped character of the Strasbourg case law on these four issues to the text of the European Convention. The Court could have found the means of developing its case law on these issues if it had wanted to—as the verdict of violation it eventually reached on a nationality issue in *Genovese v. Malta* indicates.

VII. The Prominence of Nationality Issues in Inter-American Case Law

The situation is different in the Inter-American system, where Advisory opinion 4/84 was followed by other rulings concerning nationality.

On 6 February 2001, the Inter-American Court issued its judgment on the merits of the contentious case of *Ivcher Bronstein v. Peru*.[73] Mr Ivcher Bronstein had renounced his original Israeli nationality and had become Peruvian in 1984. Thirteen years later, the Peruvian state annulled the naturalisation it had granted him through

[70] See e.g., for the UK, Celia Rooney, 'Stateless Terrorists: Citizenship in an Age of Risk' (2014), <http://bordercriminologies.law.ox.ac.uk/citizenship-in-an-age-of-risk>, accessed 12 February 2014; <http://www.thebureauinvestigates.com/2013/05/16/home-secretary-strips-two-more-people-of-british-citizenship/>, accessed 30 January 2014; *The Guardian*, 30 January 2014.

[71] The Equal Rights Trust, *Unravelling Anomaly: Detention, Discrimination and the Protection Needs of Stateless Persons* (London: The Equal Rights Trust, 2010) 22.

[72] Anna V. Dolidze, 'Lampedusa and Beyond: Recognition, Implementation and Justiciability of Stateless Persons' Rights under International Law' (2011) *Interdisciplinary Journal of Human Rights Law* 6, 1. See Chapter 13.

[73] *Ivcher-Bronstein v. Peru*, Merits, Reparations and Costs, Judgment (IACtHR), 6 Feb. 2001.

a 'directorial resolution', the form of which was not legally recognisable. This was clearly in order to silence investigative journalism: Peruvian law provided that one needed to be Peruvian to own companies with licences for TV channels in Peru; Mr Bronstein owned a channel which had shown programmes denouncing acts of torture and specific acts of corruption. At the time the Inter-American Court examined the case, Peru had unilaterally withdrawn from the Inter-American system of human rights protection. It refrained from submitting any defence and did not attend the proceedings. The Inter-American Court nonetheless ruled that this did not affect its jurisdiction. It found numerous violations of the Convention, including regarding Article 20 ACHR.

Admittedly, one could say that *Ivcher Bronstein* had more to do with political repression than with nationality issues. *Yean and Bosico v. the Dominican Republic* followed a few years later.[74] Analysed in Chapter 10, it is concerned with the refusal by the state to grant nationality to children born on its territory whom it considers of foreign origin. The most recent advisory opinion on the rights of migrant children also contains a number of pronouncements related to nationality.[75] This is to say that the Inter-American case law, quantitatively scant compared to the Strasbourg case law, is nonetheless resolutely bringing nationality issues to the fore of human rights concerns.

VIII. Who are the Judges?

Like any other legal text, human rights conventions are open to many interpretations. Which of these prevails in any one case depends not only on the law (though this obviously has a crucial bearing) but also on the personalities, sensibilities, and experiences of those who are vested with the authority to interpret them. The personal and social trajectory of individual judges is hardly ever the object of academic research.[76] Without attempting to fill this gap, this section nonetheless offers a few brief notes on the composition of the European and Inter-American Courts of Human Rights.

In the European system, every state party to the Convention is expected to send a judge (as well as, in the past, a Commission member) to Strasbourg. In the American system, the intention has never been to have all states parties (originally 11, currently 25) represented. The Inter-American Court and Commission count seven members, a number which may have been borrowed from the European system where, except for a short decade,[77] Chambers have consisted of seven judges.

[74] *The Girls Yean and Bosico v. Dominican Republic*, Preliminary Objections, Merits, Reparations and Costs, Judgment (IACtHR), 8 Sept. 2005.

[75] *Rights and Guarantees of Children in the Context of Migration and/or in Need of International Protection*, Advisory Opinion OC-21/14 (IACtHR), 19 Aug. 2014, paras 94, 218 and 280.

[76] Nonetheless, see Daniel Terris, Cesare Romano, and Leigh Swigart, *The International Judge: An Introduction to the Men and Women Who Decide the World's Cases* (Oxford: Oxford University Press, 2006).

[77] Under Protocol no. 8, which came into force on 1 January 1990, a Chamber consisted of nine judges.

In the 'old' days of the European system, the President of the Court and the 'national judge', i.e. the judge elected in respect of the respondent state, were part of the bench *ex officio*, with the other judges chosen by lot from the whole pool of judges available. When Protocol no. 11 established the 'new', permanent, European Court in 1998 (at the same time signalling the demise of the European Commission of Human Rights), the Court was divided into Sections. It is from these Sections of about ten judges that Chambers are now drawn. At the time of writing, there are 47 judges and five Sections, constituted in order to ensure some geographical and gender balance. Cases are normally allocated to the Section where the national judge sits.[78] In the early days of the European system, a Chamber could relinquish its jurisdiction to the Plenary Court. Today, a Chamber can relinquish its jurisdiction to the Grand Chamber, which is composed of 17 judges: the President and the two Vice-Presidents of the Court, the other three Presidents of Sections, as well as an additional 11 judges drawn by lot. The Grand Chamber also rules on appeals of Chamber judgments whose referral has been declared admissible by a panel of five judges.

An additional sign of the nation-centred character of the European system is the details of the rule, common to both systems, according to which each state party to the Convention must (in the European system) or can (in the American system) nominate three candidates. The European Convention provides that at least two of these candidates should be nationals of the proposing state, while the Inter-American Convention presents it the other way around and provides that if a state party proposes three candidates (which it does not have to do), at least one of those candidates should be a national of another state party to the OAS. Moreover, in the Inter-American system, the reference is indeed to the OAS rather than to the American Convention. (This explains how Judge Buergenthal, a US citizen, could become judge of the Inter-American Court.[79]) However, having a judge who is not the national of a state party to the Council of Europe is possible in the European system.[80]

The national judge plays a crucial role in the European system. This is under the rationale that she is cognizant of, and thus better able to understand, the legislation and practice of her country.[81] Not only is she part of the bench deciding a case against 'her' state, but she not uncommonly acts as *rapporteur* in Chamber cases,[82] thus being the member responsible for preparing the documents, including the summary of the case, upon which the Chamber normally bases its decisions. In Grand Chamber cases, the national judge is part of the drafting committee and speaks immediately after the judge *rapporteur*. Such an involvement is arguably regrettable. One should nevertheless note the quiet 'denationalisation' revolution

[78] This is not possible when a respondent state attracts a large number of applications.

[79] Determined to turn the Court into a successful institution, Costa Rica had approached him: Buergenthal 'Remembering' 4–5, note 2.

[80] The Canadian Ronald St John MacDonald used to be the judge for Liechtenstein.

[81] The feminine form is used here as per the convention announced at the start of this book.

[82] Françoise Tulkens, 'Brèves réflexions sur le juge national', in Patrick Titiun (ed.) *La conscience des droits: Mélanges en l'honneur de Jean-Paul Costa* (Paris: Dalloz-Sirey, 2011) 649–656 at 655.

which Protocol no. 14 has achieved by providing that the 'single judge', whose task it is to summarily dismiss applications, can never be the national judge.[83] In the Inter-American system, a defendant state which was not 'represented' amongst the serving judges used to be able to nominate an ad-hoc judge (without this judge, however, being given any special role within the procedure). This option has now been eliminated: in the current Inter-American system, a judge can *never* sit on a case which involves his state.[84]

Both systems sketch the qualifications required for becoming judges in the broadest terms. Judges must be persons of 'high moral character' (European Convention), or of 'the highest moral authority' (American Convention), and they must possess the qualifications required 'for appointment to high judicial office' (European Convention), 'for the exercise of the highest judicial functions' (American Convention). Such phrasing must be seen as the legacy of the agreement reached in the League of Nations when the first World Court was established: states held such diverse views in 1920 as to whom they thought could serve as an international judge that devising specific criteria for their appointment proved impossible.[85]

From the early twentieth century, it was understood and accepted that nominations to supranational judicial office would have to be left to the wishes of the nominating states. Combining judicial and political roles—as long as they are staggered in time—is not regarded as problematic, perhaps especially so in the Inter-American system.[86] Since Protocol no. 11, the European system specifically prohibits the exercise of activities incompatible with a judge's office.[87] Neither the European nor the American systems require their judges to have prior judicial experience. In fact, in its first formation, the Inter-American Court did not count one single judge with this kind of experience—possibly explaining its appetite for a broad, rather than 'legally legal', reasoning. The European Convention states that 'jurisconsults of recognized competence' can be appointed. The American Convention is slightly more specific by stating that this competence must be 'in the field of human rights'.

The European system has encountered serious problems with state nominations. The unsuitability of some nominations has been so glaring that a real sense of crisis developed, with the President of the Court, Jean-Paul Costa, writing to the Committee of Ministers of the Council of Europe in 2010 to warn: 'The system will fail if judges do not have the necessary experience and authority'.[88] The

[83] Françoise Tulkens, 'La Cour européenne des droits de l'homme et la déclaration de Brighton. Oublier la réforme et penser l'avenir' (2013) *Cahiers de droit européen* 2012/2, 305–343 at 312.

[84] It seems inappropriate to use the feminine here as there is currently *no* female judge at the Inter-American Court.

[85] Guillaume Sacriste and Antoine Vauchez, 'The Force of International Law: Lawyers' Diplomacy on the International Scene in the 1920s' (2007) *Law and Social Inquiry* 32, 83–107.

[86] This flexibility proved beneficial when, following his tenure as judge at the Inter-American Court, Carlos Roberto Reina became the President of Honduras, and the reparations which the Court had ordered in the first contentious cases it had decided suddenly got paid.

[87] Article 21.3 of the European Convention.

[88] Quoted in Laurence Burgorgue-Larsen, 'Between Idealism and Realism: A few Comparative Reflections and Proposals on the Appointment Process of the Inter-American Commission and

crisis by then had been already more than a decade in the making.[89] The efforts on the part of (some quarters within) the other institutions of the Council of Europe to create mechanisms to remedy excessively politicised nominations have yet to produce their full effects, as their success depends on the political goodwill on the part of all the actors involved.[90]

The Parliamentary Assembly of the Council of Europe, made up of members of national parliaments, is the body which votes on the three-candidate lists submitted by any state whose judge is due for renewal. Many believe that it is too lax with accepting unsuitable lists. There have been examples of lists returned to the state, resubmitted without any change, and then voted upon.[91] The concerns relate to lack of competence, but also to the fact that some lists contain no women, contrary to the Assembly's recommendations.[92] Unfortunately, after Malta presented an all-male candidate list which the Assembly rejected, the European Court expressed the advisory opinion that having a woman amongst the three candidates was not an absolute requirement.[93] The last election of the Belgian judge proceeded out of a list which contained no women. This was deemed acceptable, which is difficult to comprehend.[94] Leaving aside problematic state nominations, the Assembly's choices within the three-candidate lists submitted by states, have not always been the most inspired.[95]

It is also an election which closes the Inter-American process of judicial nomination. In the Inter-American system, states parties to the American Convention vote the judges in at a session of the OAS General Assembly. When a seat becomes vacant, any individual interested in filling the vacancy must persuade their government (more rarely, another government) to put them forward. This becomes a very political process as it is well known that a process of vote trading takes place, whereby the state concerned tries to secures votes for its candidate at the

Court of Human Rights Members', Working Paper no. 1 on 'The Future of the Inter-American Human Rights System', dated May 2014, University of Notre Dame, p. 16, note 65.

[89] Until his untimely death, Jean-François Flauss had relentlessly documented the problems affecting elections at the Strasbourg Court through a series of articles published in *Revue trimestrielle des droits de l'homme* and cited in Burgorgue-Larsen 3, n. 13.

[90] For details, see Burgorgue-Larsen.

[91] N.P. Engel, 'More Transparency and Governmental Loyalty for Maintaining Professional Quality in the Election of Judges to the European Court of Human Rights' (2012) *Human Rights Law Journal* 32, 448–455.

[92] PACE Resolution 1366 (2004), as amended by Resolution 1426 (2005), although this has subsequently been weakened by Resolution 1627 (2008), para 4.

[93] *On certain legal questions concerning the lists of candidates submitted with a view to the election of judges*, Advisory opinion (ECtHR), 12 Feb. 2008.

[94] The previous Belgian judge was Judge Tulkens (1998 2012). At the time of her appointment, it was an open secret that she had been the Belgian government's least-favoured candidate. She had been included in order to respect the recommendation of having at least one candidate of each sex in the three-candidate list. For the 2012 election, Belgium ranked fourth a female candidate who was promising to continue in Judge Tulkens's remarkable steps. In terms of Belgian linguistics politics, this candidate, being Flemish, would have been suitable to succeed the French-speaking Tulkens. The Assembly accepted the Belgian list.

[95] Ben Emmerson had such a high profile as a human rights lawyer that he had been widely predicted to succeed Judge Bratza. Although he made it into the three-candidate list presented by the UK, the Assembly failed to elect him in 2012.

Court from other governments in exchange for returning the favour of voting for allied candidates in different OAS, UN, or other international bodies. This is not ideal.[96] Moreover, the lack of any requirement regarding gender balance has proved extremely damaging. There have been only four women judges in the history of the Inter-American Court, and it has returned to being an all-male court in 2013.

It is difficult to make any generalisation about the type of persons who fill the benches of the two courts. One can nonetheless venture to say that *raison d'état* is well represented at the European Court.[97] This refers to the fact that the Strasbourg Court counts many judges who originate from administrative courts in their own country (e.g. the former President of the Court, Jean-Paul Costa, who was at the French *Conseil d'Etat* before arriving in Strasbourg), or who used to appear before the Court as a state representative (e.g. Nicolas Bratza, from the UK, who succeeded Judge Costa at the presidency of the Court), or who are academics drawn from the international law field, where the traditional view is that international law is and must remain based on state consent. By contrast, the Inter-American Court has had a more pronounced tendency to attract lawyers with a personal commitment to the human rights cause.

This could be linked to the origins of the Court. As Judge Buergenthal reminisced:

> In the Americas [at the time of my election in 1979], the Cold War permitted the military regimes and civilian dictators to torture and disappear anyone whom they labeled [*sic*] as subversives. Often, too, the mere public discussion of human rights could land a person in jail or worse.[98]

Four of the Inter-American Court's initial judges, including Buergenthal and Piza Escalante, had experienced jail terms for political reasons.[99] Judge Cançado Trindade, its President from 1999 to 2004, takes pride in having supported accountability for massive human rights violations. His successor at the presidency of the Court, Judge Cecilia Medina, lived her childhood in exile from Chile in the Netherlands.[100] Another former President of the Court, Pedro Nikken, went on to serve as the President of the International Commission of Jurists, one of the most highly regarded global human rights organisations, from 2011 to 2012.

One should not be too quick, however, to associate the European Court with *raison d'état* and the Inter-American Court with human rights activism. On the

[96] For recommendations on the selection of Inter-American judges which would not involve amendments to the Convention, see Burgorgue-Larsen 'Between Idealism and Realism'. For an earlier call to involve civil society in the nominating process: Judith Schönsteiner 'Alternative Appointment Procedures for the Commissioners and Judges in the Inter-American System of Human Rights' (2007) *Revista IIDH* 46, 195–215.

[97] Erik Voeten, 'Politics, Judicial Behaviour and Institutional Design', in Jonas Christoffersen and Mikael Rask Madsen (eds) *The European Court of Human Rights between Law and Politics* (Oxford: Oxford University Press, 2011) 61–76 at 66, quoting Judge Tulkens.

[98] Buergenthal 'Remembering' 4.

[99] Pasqualucci *The Practice and Procedure* 31.

[100] See her portrait in Terris et al. *The International Judge*.

one hand, there has always been a diversity of profiles at Strasbourg (with Judge Tulkens, a former Vice-President, a prominent figure of the 'undercurrent'). On the other hand, even though the Inter-American system is generally open to civil society's influence,[101] figures with a traditional international law orientation have started to appear at San José.[102]

IX. Conclusion

This chapter has focused on the earliest ruling by the Inter-American Court on an issue which concerns migrants. Advisory opinion 4/84 found that for the Costa Rican Constitution to be revised in such a way that nationals of 'close' countries would no longer be eligible to become naturalised after having resided in Costa Rica for one year would not infringe human rights.

In many ways, any other outcome would have been untenable. What is remarkable, then, is not so much this outcome as the way in which the Inter-American Court accepted being drawn into examining the legitimacy of naturalisation conditions under human rights law at all. By adopting a reasoning which was outside the letter of Article 20 ACHR, the Inter-American Court showed itself, both in Advisory opinion 4/84 and in subsequent case law, ready to embrace matters related to nationality as being at the heart of human rights law. No doubt, this is because it perceives the way a state chooses to attribute or withhold nationality as pregnant with implications for the recognition of the person as well as for equality. Indeed, whilst the attribution of nationality is a matter which those of us who have the privilege of being granted a politically 'useful' nationality from birth need never worry about, nationality issues often ruin the lives of those who either happen to possess the nationality of the 'wrong' state or who legally or on a de facto basis have no nationality at all.

The fact that the European Convention elected not to include any provision on nationality has made it possible for the Strasbourg Court, even in extreme circumstances such as those experienced by the 'erased' in Slovenia, to refuse to be drawn into issuing rulings directly concerning citizenship law. No doubt this is because the Strasbourg Court considers nationality to constitute a matter of near-absolute state sovereignty upon which it cannot encroach, bar absolutely exceptional circumstances. This attitude, however, denotes a conspicuous, if largely unnoticed, closure of the European system to what could, or arguably should, be considered a vital area of human rights law.

Advisory opinion 4/84 offers a counterpoint to the Strasbourg perspective. It reveals a court willing to put human rights, including the human rights of

[101] Mónica Pinto, 'NGOs and the Inter-American Court of Human Rights', in Tullio Treves et al. (eds) *Civil Society, International Courts and Compliance Bodies* (Cambridge: Cambridge University Press, 2005) 47–56.

[102] As seems demonstrated by the separate opinions of Judge Vio Grossi and, to a lesser extent, Judge Pérez Pérez, who both took office in 2010: Burgorgue-Larsen 'Les méthodes' 37 and 61–66.

migrants, at the start of its reasoning (turning around the Strasbourg reversal, so to speak). The Inter-American Court accepts that states enjoy a wide latitude in deciding to whom to grant their nationality, but it nonetheless insists that this latitude must be exercised within the confines of human rights. There is no sense—as there is in the European Convention system—that states can do more or less whatever they wish in terms of immigration and nationality, as long as they do not glaringly violate human rights norms.

The reasons for the ultimately radical difference in the approaches of the two human rights courts are complex. As intimated in the introductory chapter, they are linked to the history of their respective continents, which in turn informs local social and political conceptions. The influence of the personal orientation the judges bring to the benches must also be an important, albeit under-researched, factor, as highlighted in the last section of this chapter.

PART II

CONSOLIDATION

Part I has demonstrated that the European Convention system was established without incontrovertibly intending to extend the human rights protection it offers to foreigners and/or migrants. In contrast, the Inter-American system was never imagined to be conceivable without this protection. These early trends, Part II argues, entrenched themselves in the following decades. The European side of this argument goes against the grain of received history. However, this is what a close and comprehensive reading of the Strasbourg case law indicates.

Chapters 6, 7, and 8 focus on, respectively, *Berrehab v. the Netherlands*,[1] *Soering v. the United Kingdom*,[2] and *Gaygusuz v. Austria*.[3] These three judgments are rightly taken to have been instrumental in opening up the rights of migrants in decisive areas. *Berrehab* established the possibility—and indeed the duty—to weigh the family and/or private rights of prospective deportees under Article 8 ECHR against the state's interest in deporting the migrant (often following his criminal conviction). *Soering* confirmed that the prohibition of torture and inhuman or degrading treatment contained in Article 3 ECHR is absolute and that it applies even when the risk of such treatment would originate, following extradition or deportation, in a third country. *Gaygusuz* clarified the need under Article 14 ECHR to treat nationals and non-nationals equally in the sphere of social security.

These judgments date from, respectively, 1988, 1989, and 1996. Each marks the start of an important jurisprudence. Furthermore, an attentive reading reveals that the Court never refers at any point to the 'well-established' principle of international law according to which states have a right to control the entry and residence of aliens—identified in Part I of this book as signalling a regrettable reversal in human rights reasoning.[4] We shall see that subsequent rulings do not always avoid this pitfall. Indeed a long-term perspective which considers both subsequent verdicts of non-violation and previous rulings by the Commission

[1] *Berrehab v. the Netherlands*, appl. 10730/84, Judgment (ECtHR), 21 June 1988.

[2] *Soering v. the United Kingdom*, appl. 14038/88, GC Judgment (ECtHR), 17 July 1989.

[3] *Gaygusuz v. Austria*, appl. 17371/90, Judgment (ECtHR), 16 Sept. 1996.

[4] To recall, this supposedly well-established principle was first mentioned by the Court in: *Abdulaziz, Cabales and Balkandali v. the United Kingdom*, appls 9214/80, 9473/81, 9474/81, PC Judgment (ECtHR), 28 May 1985, simply referred to in this book as *ABC*.

reveals that, although *Berrehab, Soering*, and *Gaygusuz* at first sight appear to be turning points in the Court's jurisprudence, they have had a lesser impact than one might have thought.

The story told in Chapters 6 to 8 disrupts the received image of the Strasbourg Court as an institution at the vanguard of human rights protection in Europe. It is nonetheless in line with a fierce critique which emanated in the early 1980s from leading personalities of the Council of Europe itself. Peter Leuprecht, the then Council of Europe's Director of Human Rights, was so appalled by the record in the area of migrants' rights that he took the opportunity on the 30th anniversary of the entry into force of the ECHR to organise a high-profile event which put the issue on the agenda. He found an ally in the Portuguese government for this initiative and then secured the blessing of the Steering Committee of Human Rights and the Committee of Ministers. The result was a colloquy entitled 'Human Rights of Aliens in Europe' which took place in Funchal, Madeira (the Funchal Colloquy), in October 1983,[5] with the aim of highlighting and hopefully remedying the failure of the European system of human rights to embrace migrants.

Speeches by the President of the Republic of Portugal (as host), the President of the Parliamentary Assembly of the Council of Europe, a judge representing the President of the European Court of Human Rights, the President of the European Commission of Human Rights, and the Secretary-General of the Council of Europe, amongst other figures, opened the Funchal Colloquy. Over 200 politicians, civil servants, judges, lawyers, representatives of NGOs, journalists, and even some 'aliens' attended.[6] The tone of the proceedings is well represented by the words of the then Secretary General, Franz Karasek:

> It is often complacently pointed out that the European philosopy [*sic*] of human rights is a universal one, insofar as it seeks to protect everyone, regardless of nationality. In the next three days, we shall ultimately have to ask ourselves whether this is not altogether true, whether *human* rights are not still, in many cases, *citizens*' rights.[7]

A publication arose from the Funchal proceedings. The preface, by Leuprecht, noted:

> The subjects discussed at the Colloquy are among the most crucial questions on protection of human rights in present day society. Indeed one of the major challenges facing Council of Europe member States lies in their citizens' capacity to accept aliens both as different and in the full sense of partners.

[5] Leuprecht, personal communication, 6 July 2011. Leuprecht became Deputy Secretary General of the Council of Europe in 1993. He resigned in 1997 following Russia's accession during the war in Chechnya, an accession which in his view could only lead to a watering down of the values proclaimed to be the *raison d'être* of the Council of Europe. The colloquy's proceedings were published as follows: Directorate of Human Rights, Council of Europe *Human Rights of Aliens in Europe. Proceedings of the Colloquy on 'Human Rights of Aliens in Europe'* (Dordrecht: Martinus Nijhoff, 1985), hereafter referred to as Colloquy.

[6] For a list of participants: Colloquy 465–474.

[7] Colloquy 24, emphasis in the original.

> It is clear that in Europe today a human rights problem exists in connection with the situation of aliens, be they migrant workers, refugees or others. Aliens encounter, as regards the effective enjoyment of human rights, serious difficulties which do not confront nationals in the same way.
>
> We are aware of the difficult economic situation in most European countries but we are firmly convinced that it is in these specific circumstances that human rights must be preserved to a greater extent than at any other time.[8]

Reading the proceedings three decades later, one is struck by the extent to which the problems and experience have remained the same over the intervening period: doors closing to migrants and their relatives; difficulties in substantiating the need for asylum; increased racism in the face of a deepening economic crisis; individuals expressing the wish to contribute to society but feeling excluded and debased; and the lack of awareness and acceptance for different ways of being and acting. There is nonetheless one conspicuous difference, and this is the lack of reference to security, which is of course very much a post-9/11 concern.

Another difference is the idea vocally expressed in 1983 that a firm and progressive move towards integrating aliens in the human rights framework is both possible and desirable. Although complete integration was recognised not to be possible immediately, the idea was optimistically and enthusiastically put forward that the Colloquy would get things moving in this direction. Leuprecht's Preface expressed the hope that the Colloquy would 'lead to political action with a view to securing a better observance of the human rights of aliens in Europe so that no one should be an alien in the Europe of human rights'. A seven-page list of recommendations ended the publication,[9] (which one would be hard pushed to find expressed in governmental circles today). To quote a few of these recommendations:

- Delete Article 16 of the European Convention on Human Rights.
- Establishment of the principle of right of entry.
- Refusals must be regarded as exceptional.
- Gradual abolition of visas.
- Recognition that expulsion is an exceptional measure, considering the seriousness of its consequences (which are sometimes greater than in the case of custodial sentences).
- The provision of judicial proceedings for expulsion.
- Possibility of lodging an appeal with a higher body in the event of '*refoulement*' at the frontier and refusal to issue or renew residence or work permits.

The recommendations, Leuprecht assures me, directly emanated from the debates held at Funchal and conveyed the 'feeling' which had dominated during these three days.[10]

[8] Colloquy v. [9] Colloquy 457–463.

[10] Leuprecht, personal communication of 11 July 2011. Some recommendations were obviously borrowed from the submitted reports. (The fourth I quote for example comes from the report submitted by Luis Silveira 'Colloquy' 155.) Participants were clearly invited to make suggestions: Colloquy 75.

For them to have made their way into a publication of the Council of Europe suggests that they were not regarded as beyond the pale, as the foolish or unrealistic dreams of a nascent Open Borders movement.[11]

This is not to deny that they were controversial.[12] The Council of Europe was and remains a complex structure containing different trends. Not everyone approved the Funchal debates. For example, Stefan Trechsel, who belonged to the Commission, found them to be missing the point. He started his observations to the Colloquy by saying:

> No one, I think, will dispute that the European Convention on Human Rights was not designed to deal with [these issues]. Many of the criticisms made here so far are basically criticisms of the fact that the Convention does not secure an individual's right to enter a country—or to continue to reside in one—which is not his own. But here we face a fact which has to be accepted even by those who would prefer a different solution... [T]he bodies which watch over the application of the European Convention on Human Rights, particularly the Commission, have laboured a great deal to extract from the Convention the maximum protection possible in order to fill the gap.[13]

There had admittedly been some friendly settlements in cases lodged by migrants in the first 30 years of the Convention system.[14] In addition, respondent states had occasionally revoked deportation orders or issued residence permits, which had led the Commission to strike cases off its list without this being reported.[15] The long delay in having the Commission refer a case involving a migrant to the Court, and the even longer wait before a migrant would win a case before the European Court of Human Rights,[16] nonetheless indicate that the 'maximum protection possible' offered in practice to aliens under the Convention was in reality minimal.[17]

Of the 590 applications lodged at the Commission the previous year, a Portuguese diplomat remarked, 156 had been filed by foreigners; he optimistically interpreted these figures as demonstrating that 'foreigners are just as protected and welcome in the Commission as nationals'.[18] Alternatively, one might have proposed that the Strasbourg institutions were repeatedly refusing to address problems affecting migrants. As the then Registrar of the European Court,

[11] To some extent, the last two recommendations are now part of law in some domestic jurisdictions (including the UK).

[12] Leuprecht reminisced that some diplomats had remarked to him, not necessarily in the friendliest way, on the 'surprise' he had prepared for them (personal communication, July 2011).

[13] Colloquy 187.

[14] For an early example, see *Alam and Khan v. the United Kingdom*, appl. 2991/66, PCom Report (EComHR), 17 Dec. 1968, discussed in Chapter 4.

[15] Andrew Drzemczewski, 'The Position of Aliens in Relation to the European Convention on Human Rights: A General Survey', in Colloquy 351–427 at 361.

[16] Foreign applicants had won before, but not on specifically migrant issues.

[17] This was not lost on the young academic who authored the comprehensive report submitted to the Funchal Colloquy: Drzemczewski 'The Position of Aliens'. Drzemczewski, then still based in a London polytechnic, was about to embark on a diverse and distinguished career within the Council of Europe.

[18] Colloquy 179.

Marc-André Eissen, noted in his address, the Court had 'scarcely dealt at all with the problem of the rights of aliens'.[19]

The Funchal Colloquy celebrated the referral of *Abdulaziz, Cabales and Balkandali* to the Court, which had happened just the previous week.[20] When *ABC* was eventually decided, the ruling would offer little to migrants, as we have seen in Chapter 4. Another five years would then pass before a victory for migrant rights would finally appear for the first time in the Strasbourg case law. This was *Berrehab*, the 127th judgment of the Court.[21] From then it would take yet another 25 judgments and one year for *Soering* to emerge (the 152nd).[22] The situation could not have presented itself more differently in the Inter-American system. There the early Advisory opinion 4/84 on naturalisation provisions (reviewed in Chapter 5) was followed by pronouncements which invariably confirmed that the Inter-American Court was determined to approach migrants first as subjects of human rights rather than as the objects of state sovereignty.

Chapter 9 reviews two advisory opinions delivered by the Inter-American Court in 1999 and 2003. The first concerns the right to consular assistance;[23] the second, the labour rights of irregular migrants, where the Inter-American Court famously declared the equality of human beings to be *jus cogens*, with enormous implications for migrants.[24] Chapter 10 focuses on a judgment on the merits of—this time—a contentious case, concerning the discrimination faced by stateless children of Haitian origin born in the Dominican Republic, adopted in 2005.[25] In these three rulings, the Inter-American Court shows itself true to the foundational instinct of the Inter-American system by treating migrants as human beings who enjoy the same human rights as everyone else.

19 Colloquy 189. 20 Colloquy 191.

21 I have attained these figures by counting the judgments listed by chronological order in: Barbara Mensah, *European Human Rights Case Summaries 1960–2000* (London: Cavendish, 2002) Section II.

22 As for *ABC*, it was the Court's 74th judgment (14th concerning the United Kingdom).

23 *The Right to Information on Consular Assistance in the Framework of the Guarantees of the due Process of Law*, Advisory Opinion OC-16/99 (IACtHR), 1 Oct. 1999.

24 *Juridicial Condition and Rights of the Undocumented Migrants*, Advisory Opinion OC-18/03 (IACtHR), 17 Sept. 2003.

25 *The Girls Yean and Bosico v. Dominican Republic*, Preliminary Objections, Merits, Reparations and Costs, Judgment (IACtHR), 8 Sept. 2005.

6

Shattering Lives: The Normalisation of Deportation

(After *Berrehab*)

Human rights set limits to what can be done to a human being: some things are not acceptable and should not be done. One of these, one might think, might be separating someone from their parents, spouses, children, and the whole of their social world by forcibly expelling them from the country where they live.

Yet, it has long been state practice to expel foreigners who have been convicted of crimes after they have finished serving their jail sentences. Many prospective deportees have knocked on Strasbourg's doors, arguing that their removal violated—or would violate, if implemented—Article 8 ECHR which guarantees respect for family and private life. The public are never very sympathetic to human rights victims who are criminals, but it should go without saying that the point of human rights is that they apply to all human beings, including offenders and ex-offenders. One might have thought that once a person had 'paid' for his crime, it would be wrong to make him pay again by deporting him. From one perspective, expelling a foreigner just when he was supposed to come out of jail raises an issue of discrimination between nationals and non-nationals, made all the more serious because, as we have seen in Chapter 5, the ECtHR systematically refuses to place states' rules governing the attribution of nationality under scrutiny. However, the European Court does not share this view: it has never accepted that deportation could be problematic under Article 14 ECHR, which prohibits discrimination. What the Court has done, though, for over 25 years, is to recognise that deportation constitutes an 'interference' with family and/or private life which it deems, in some circumstances, sufficiently serious to breach Article 8.

Berrehab v. the Netherlands is generally remembered as the first Strasbourg case regarding expulsion.[1] It is indeed the first case in which the Court found that a removal breached Article 8. However, by the time *Berrehab* was decided in 1988, ninety applications had been lodged at Strasbourg concerning deportation.[2] (This

[1] *Berrehab v. the Netherlands*, appl. 10730/84, Judgment (ECtHR), 21 June 1988.

[2] Mark Villiger, 'Expulsion and the Right to Respect for Private and Family Life (Article 8 of the Convention)—An Introduction to the Commission's Case-Law', in F. Matscher and H. Petzold (eds) *Protecting Human Rights: The European Dimension. Studies in Honour of Gérard J. Wiarda*

chapter uses the terms 'expulsion', 'removal', and 'deportation' interchangeably as their exact meanings across national jurisdictions vary.) For almost three decades, the Commission had declared these applications inadmissible, with the earliest such decision dating back to 1959.[3] This makes it clear that the Strasbourg system was not quick to reach a verdict of violation in a removal case.

One of the reasons why *Berrehab* managed to interrupt the flow of inadmissibility decisions is that the first applicant in this case was not a criminal but a law-abiding father whose divorce from his Dutch wife meant that he lost his right of residence in the Netherlands and, as a consequence, regular contact with his daughter, the second applicant (whom he had seen four times a week until his return to Morocco).

Berrehab created an opening in the case law, which was immediately taken up, so much so that commentators ventured to suggest, on the basis of verdicts adopted in its wake in the early 1990s, that a presumption had been established in Convention law against the deportability of 'second-generation' migrants.[4] In this period, the Commission and the Court seemed determined to question whether the interest of the deporting state was stronger than the expellees' Article 8 rights. Even so, verdicts of violation were not adopted on the basis of the *principle* that a long-settled migrant should in general, for the purpose of considering deportation, be treated like a national and thus, barring exceptional circumstances, not be considered deportable. Outcomes depended on the balancing exercise which the Strasbourg Court performed on a case-by-case, factual basis. It did not take long before verdicts of non-violation first appeared and then became common place. By 1996, a Strasbourg judge who favoured a principled approach against the expulsion of 'integrated aliens' felt it necessary to refer to the case law as 'a lottery'.[5]

This chapter agrees with this judge that the Court's unprincipled reasoning produced a haphazard, inconsistent, and ultimately weak case law. This is not how the Strasbourg case law is generally pictured in the media. Listening to politicians and journalists, one would think that the European Court is repeatedly preventing states from carrying out any of their deportation plans. Leaving aside the fact that most deportees never get to Strasbourg, those who do stand before a Court which is highly divided. However, clear disagreement on the Strasbourg bench does not mean that a Strasbourg mainstream cannot be identified: this being that rulings mostly go against the expellees. In this respect, one should not forget that the Court's pro-state stance is illustrated not only by verdicts of non-violation but

(Cologne: Carl Heymanns Verlag, 1988) 657–662. Other applications against expulsion alleged a violation of Article 3 ECHR. On this type of complaint, see Chapter 7.

[3] *A. v. Belgium*, appl. 312/57, Decision (EComHR), 9 Jan. 1959 (communicated to the author by the Strasbourg Court's Archives service).

[4] Ryszard Cholewinski, 'Strasbourg's "Hidden Agenda"? The Protection of Second-Generation Migrants from Expulsion under Article 8 of the European Convention on Human Rights' (1994) *Netherlands Quarterly of Human Rights* 287–306.

[5] Dissenting opinion of Judge Martens in *Boughanemi v. France*, appl. 22070/93, Judgment (ECtHR), 24 Apr. 1996.

also by decisions of inadmissibility which are adopted in a summary fashion and which never surface in the public domain. All in all, Strasbourg rulings which find deportation in breach of Article 8 are exceptional.

The ultimate consequence of this case law is that the European Court has not been in a position to stem the increasingly harsh deportation regime which European states have put in place in the last two decades.[6] The view expressed in this book is that deportation is a practice which in itself is problematic under human rights law. One should also not forget that the measures required to enforce either deportation at the end of a prison sentence or administrative removal are often deeply inhumane. Inmates have often been eagerly waiting the day of their release and are surprised, along with their families, when they are kept in jail at the end of their sentence, this time under immigration powers. As for those who have committed no crime, they are routinely taken away from their homes, without any notice, in frightening early morning raids and incarcerated in detention centres which offer fewer guarantees and rights than prisons. All are left unable to claim their personal belongings before their forced departure; subjected to physical restraint which, in some cases, has led to suffocation and death; sent to a place where they have little contact and may not even be able to communicate proficiently in the prevailing language; sometimes left with less chance of survival as the medical treatment upon which they depended in their country of residence is not accessible in their new location; and separated from other people who are important to them and to whom they are important, including their children. These consequences are no less real for being (hopefully) unintended.[7]

The European Court of Human Rights has hardly commented upon these measures. Of course, the Court is not responsible for its docket, as only applicants can bring cases. It must be considered, however, that the Court's reluctance to formulate a general principle against the expulsion of second-generation and other long-term migrants cannot but have facilitated the emergence of increasingly harsh state practices by failing to provide any break against the idea that deporting people can be understood as acceptable and routine. Had the Commission opposed

[6] Nicholas De Genova and Nathalie Peutz, *The Deportation Regime: Sovereignty, Space, and the Freedom of Movement* (Durham, NC: Duke University Press, 2010); Matthew Gibney, 'Asylum and the Expansion of Deportation in the United Kingdom' (2008) *Government and Opposition* 43, 146–167.

[7] These practices have been documented in e.g. Amnesty International, 'Out of Control: The Case for a Complete Overhaul of Enforced Removals by Private Contractors' (2011); Liz Fekete, *A Suitable Enemy: Racism, Migration and Islamophobia in Europe* (London: Pluto, 2009) Chapters 5 and 6; Liz Fekete and Frances Webber, 'Foreign Nationals, Enemy Penology and the Criminal Justice System', *IRR European Race Bulletin* no. 69, Autumn 2009. On death after expulsion due to ill health, compare *D. v. United Kingdom*, appl. 30240/96, Judgment (ECtHR), 2 May 1997 (would-be violation of Article 3 in the case of the exceptional circumstances of an applicant who was in the very final stage of AIDS, and thus already dying, and who would have received no medical or social support whatsoever in St Kitts, where he was due to be deported) and *N. v. the United Kingdom*, appl. 26565/05, GC Judgment (ECtHR), 27 May 2008 (non-violation in the case of a cancer sufferer whose death would follow within months if she were to be deported to Uganda, her country of origin, with a powerful dissenting opinion of Judges Tulkens, Bonello and Spielmann). In the end the applicant in *N.* was deported and she died shortly afterwards.

deportation in the early decades of the system's existence or had the Court been more forceful in the violation verdicts it pronounced in the post-*Berrehab* case law of the 1990s, this robust approach might have made it less easy for abhorrent policies and practices to develop. Instead these have grown largely unchecked. This is why this chapter is entitled 'the normalisation of deportation'.

The chapter starts by spending some time reviewing the Commission's early case law. This is important because these decisions introduced arguments which have become the accepted way for the Court to approach migrant cases to this day. The chapter then explains how *Berrehab v. the Netherlands* came to interrupt the flow of inadmissibility decisions. Having done this, it notes that the Strasbourg case law only ever represents the tip of the iceberg of potential complaints, putting the (inevitably) small case law in perspective. Another socio-legal element which is stressed is that deportation is life shattering for most deportees. With this historical and social background delineated, the chapter turns to an analysis of the Court's approach. It first notes that the confrontation between the state interest in expelling and the individual interest in continuing his life as it was remains unresolved, explaining the emergence and persistence of diametrically opposed reactions: many judges (and indeed commentators) find expulsion *either* entirely legitimate *or* morally repugnant. In turn, this tension explains that the Court has failed to adopt a principled approach and has produced in this area a case law which is fact dependent and characterised by a lack of transparency and consistency. This is illustrated by two Grand Chamber judgments of 2005 and 2008: *Üner v. the Netherlands* (which follows the framework of the 'Strasbourg reversal' noted in Chapter 4) and *Maslov v. Austria* (which avoids it).[8] If the Court is divided, the prevalent view nonetheless favours state sovereignty. This explains that the 'Strasbourg reversal' has taken a stronger hold in the case law as the years have gone by, despite an undercurrent always fighting against it. Avenues which could have informed the Court's legal reasoning, had it been so minded, towards finding expulsion objectionable in principle are explored. The chapter ends by asking whether the operation of distinguishing between human beings by reference to their nationality might one day be regarded as abjectly discriminatory, on a par with racial discrimination.

I. The First Thirty Years: The Commission Declares Expulsion Cases Inadmissible

The first application where an applicant complained at Strasbourg that his expulsion violated the Convention appears to have been lodged against Belgium in 1957.[9] The applicant in this case was an Italian national who had been born in Belgium in 1915, presumably the son of one of the many Italian 'guest-workers' who

[8] *Üner v. The Netherlands*, appl. 46410/99, GC Judgment (ECtHR), 18 Oct. 2006; *Maslov v. Austria*, appl. 1638/03, GC Judgment (ECtHR), 23 June 2008.

[9] *A. v. Belgium* decision. This is the earliest application cited in Villiger 'Expulsion'.

came to work in Belgium in the early twentieth century.[10] After World War II, the applicant, only known in the publicly available records of the Commission as A., was convicted of acts of collaboration with the Nazis and sentenced to death by a military court. Although the Commission speaks in its report of 'war crimes', this term did not have then the significance it has today. A.'s offences were probably not at the serious end of the scale: his sentence was commuted to imprisonment in 1951 and he was released from jail six years later. Two weeks after his release, he was expelled from Belgium on the basis of an order which had been adopted in 1952. A. turned to the Commission where he explained that his wife could not leave Brussels because of her job there, which enabled her financially to sustain their teenage son and her invalid mother; the expulsion, he argued, separated his wife and son from him. On 9 January 1959, the Commission decided that Article 8 ECHR was applicable, but that the expulsion was justified under its second paragraph (without further elaboration). The Commission declared the application 'manifestly ill-founded' and thus inadmissible.

On the same day, the Commission decided an application which had been formally lodged in 1958 in the same way. This application had long been in preparation: three years before, the applicant had already contacted the President of the Commission, but at that time the would-be respondent state, Luxembourg, had not yet accepted the optional right of individual petition.[11] The applicant was the wife of a German national who had been expelled from Luxembourg in 1950 (thus separating him from his wife and two children) after having been condemned to ten years' imprisonment for crimes also arising from his actions during the war.[12]

Like *Alam and Khan* reviewed in Chapter 4, these two applications indicate that migrants' legal representatives were quick to grasp the protective potential that the European Convention on Human Rights offered them. Their dismissal confirms another point which has also already been made, namely, that it would not be easy for migrants to persuade the Strasbourg institutions to interpret the Convention in a way which would transform this potential into tangible reality.

Admittedly, it was not only migrants but all applicants whose complaints were initially refused by the Commission. For the first five years of its existence, the Commission did not declare a single individual application admissible.[13] Both the

[10] As recalled in Chapter 2. [11] On this right, see Chapter 3 (pp. 70 and 73).

[12] *JT-B v. Luxembourg*, appl. 381/58 (communicated to the author by the Strasbourg Court's Archives' service).

[13] The first where it did so, *De Becker v. Belgium*, appl. 214/56, Judgment (ECtHR), 27 Mar. 1962, concerned, like *A.* reviewed earlier, the emotionally charged and legally controversial way in which 'war crimes' had been dealt with in Belgium. Lodged in September 1956, *De Becker* was declared admissible in June 1958. The applicant was a former editor of the Belgian daily newspaper *Le Soir* who complained that he had been prohibited *for life* from participating in *any* activity related to the running of *any* publication, due to his condemnation (initially to death, but then commuted to life imprisonment) for having 'furthered the enemy's policies and designs' during the war. The Strasbourg institutions worked slowly in order to maximise the chances of seeing a solution emerge which would avoid having a state being declared in violation of the Convention at Strasbourg: Ed Bates, *The Evolution of the European Convention on Human Rights: From its Inception to the Creation of a Permanent Court of Human Rights* (Oxford: Oxford University Press, 2010) Chapter 4. Eventually addressing the message emanating from Strasbourg, the Belgian authorities expedited the adoption

Commission and the Court were treading with extreme caution in the early years of the Convention system, not wanting states parties to torpedo the Convention project by rejecting the right of individual petition and the Court's jurisdiction (which remained optional until Protocol no. 11). From the mid-1960s and especially in the early 1970s, they nonetheless took significant steps towards controlling the contracting parties.[14] Strikingly, these 'bold' steps did not involve migrant cases.

Expulsion cases were consistently found inadmissible for around three decades. The Commission did this quickly and without much ado, as the principles it had started to identify took hold and their implications were worked out. For example, an application lodged on 13 June 1965 was declared inadmissible the following month. In this case, the Commission argued that family life was not violated since the applicant, the German wife of an Austrian national condemned seven times in Germany for 'minor' offences (not qualified any further in the Commission's decision), could follow her husband to Austria if she so wanted. The Commission felt that this conclusion was the more warranted since the couple had married after the husband had been prohibited from residing in Germany so that his wife had built her family life with full awareness of the risk of her husband's expulsion.[15] The argument according to which the spouse could follow the person who was to be expelled became recurrent. It was, for example, applied again to a German national who, having lost his job in 1968, was expelled from Switzerland two years later.[16] This particular application was dismissed in July 1976.

This date is significant in that the Commission's case law in other areas had been developing in significant ways by that time. To cite three cases which became and remain prominent in the Strasbourg case law, by July 1976, the Commission had communicated *Airey v. Ireland* to the respondent state,[17] had found *Marckx v. Belgium* admissible,[18] and was shortly to adopt its report in *Tyrer v. the United Kingdom*.[19] These are cases which touched upon sensitive social issues, respectively: limited access to court for people with little financial means, difference of treatment between children born in and outside wedlock, and corporal punishment in schools. The Convention institutions had clearly not been created in order to assess these types of issues. This deterred neither the Commission nor the Court from interpreting the Convention in wider terms than those originally agreed by the states parties to the Convention. The *Tyrer, Marckx*, and *Airey*

of a law which built in qualifications to the forfeiture of rights following treasonous acts. This allowed the Court to strike the case off its list on 27 March 1962. The case had nonetheless established that the Strasbourg institutions understood it to be within their remit to examine the compatibility of domestic legislation with the Convention: Bates *The Evolution* 207–213.

[14] Bates *The Evolution*.

[15] *E.L. v. Germany*, appl. 2535/65, Decision (ECtHR), 16 July 1965 (communicated to the author by the Strasbourg Court's Archives service).

[16] *X. v. Switzerland*, appl. 7031/75, PCom Decision (EComHR), 12 July 1976.

[17] The Commission communicated *Airey v. Ireland*, appl. 6289/73 on 1 October 1975.

[18] The Commission found *Marckx v. Belgium*, appl. 6833/74, admissible on 29 September 1975.

[19] *Tyrer v. the United Kingdom*, appl. 5865/72, was lodged in 1972 and the Commission adopted its report on it on 14 December 1976.

judgments, which date from 1978 and 1979, remain at the heart of European Convention law as we know it today. They introduced into this law the double idea that the Convention is a 'living instrument' which need not be interpreted by reference to the restrictive intention of its drafters and that it should yield 'practical and effective', rather than 'theoretical or illusory', rights.[20]

In the rapid and long-lasting construction of European human rights law of the 1970s, migrant cases are conspicuous by their absence. Further research might usefully be conducted into the ninety applications concerning expulsion which Mark Villiger has noted the Commission had received by the late 1980s.[21] Pending confirmation from a detailed examination of these cases, it appears that the initial closure of the European Convention's system to the issue of expulsion originally affected mostly white Western European applicants who pursued an individual project of migration rather than having been part of a large movement affecting whole families and communities—the very first, Italian, applicant could have been an exception.[22] Soon, the development of European Community law would severely restrict the circumstances under which a national of a state belonging to the European Community could be expelled from another state of the European Community.[23] This was reflected in the case law: Western European applicants complaining about their treatment by immigration authorities disappeared from the Strasbourg case law (but appeared in the Luxembourg case law of the European Court of Justice). As nationals of states belonging to the European Community benefited from the stress put by the European Community on freedom of movement, it is migrants from the global 'South' who started to turn to Strasbourg. They were faced with the restrictive principles which the Commission had identified in its early case law. One application, lodged in 1980, illustrates this point.

It is worth reproducing the full summary of its facts, as published by the Commission:

The applicant, a citizen of Pakistan, entered the United Kingdom in 1974 with a permission to enter for one month provided he did not take up any work. At the expiring of this period, he stayed on in the United Kingdom and took up employment. Upon his arrest in 1977, he revealed to the immigration authorities that his father had been lawfully settled in the United Kingdom since 1961 and his mother, brother and three sisters since 1975 and he had just concluded a civil marriage with a Pakistan citizen settled in the United Kingdom since 1975. He was then released. In August 1978, notice of the decision to deport the applicant was served on him. The applicant appealed to the Adjudicator, to whom he explained that he had in the meanwhile concluded a religious marriage according to muslim [*sic*] law; that he now lived with his wife and that she was pregnant. The applicant's wife stated that it was only after the religious ceremony that she had learned

[20] *Tyrer* judgment, para 31; *Airey* judgment, para 24.

[21] Villiger 'Expulsion'.

[22] On the history of the establishment of the Italian community in Belgium, see: Anne Morelli (ed.) *Histoire des étrangers et de l'immigration en Belgique: De la pré-histoire à nos jours* (Brussels: Couleurs Livres, 2004).

[23] Regulation (EEC) No. 1612/68 of the Council of 15 October 1968 on freedom of movement for workers within the Community.

that her husband was illegally residing in the United Kingdom. The Adjudicator did not believe this statement and considered that he was faced with a marriage of convenience and deliberate deceipt [*sic*]. This refusal was confirmed in March 1979 by the Immigration Appeal Tribunal.

A deportation order was made and the applicant was placed in detention awaiting deportation. He immediately made an application for a writ of Habeas Corpus which was refused. The deportation was however postponed since the applicant's solicitor had on the instructions of the applicant's family, withheld his passport and the Pakistan authorities were not willing to deliver another passport.

The applicant was finally deported in October 1981.[24]

The applicant's passport being withheld by a solicitor so as to impede the deportation process shows how dated this application is. In other respects, the application features elements which are still very much part of today's world: the fact that keeping families divided and constraining an individual's choice of spouse through immigration laws is regarded as acceptable, the assumption that migrants are deceitful, the suspicion that their marriage is not genuine, and the recourse to deportation as well as to pre-deportation detention.

One of the reasons why these features are so enduring is that they have never been denounced as violating human rights principles. In particular, the Commission did not feel that the facts of this case revealed anything which would have warranted the application to be examined on its merits. Its decision reported:

The Commission refers to its constant jurisprudence that there is no right to enter or reside in a particular country guaranteed as such by the Convention.... However, the Commission has also held that, in view of the right to respect for family life ensured by Article 8 the exclusion of a person from a country in which his close relatives reside may raise an issue under this provision of the Convention....

In the present case the Commission notes, however, that the applicant was deported for having defied immigration controls and that his marriage was contracted at a time when the applicant was aware that he was at risk with his irregular immigration status. There do not appear to be any insurmountable obstacles to the applicant's wife and child following him to Pakistan. The applicant's wife is not a United Kingdom citizen, but was brought up in Pakistan, only acquiring a right of abode in the United Kingdom in 1975. The applicant's child, although having United Kingdom citizenship by birth in the United Kingdom, is of an adaptable age.

In the circumstances of the present case, even though the applicant's deportation constitutes an interference with his right to respect for family life under Article 8, the Commission must attach significant weight to the reasons for the applicant's deportation. It finds with regard to the second paragraph of Article 8 that there are no elements concerning respect for family life which might outweigh valid considerations relating to the proper enforcement of immigration controls.[25]

[24] *X. v. the United Kingdom*, appl. 9088/80, Decision (EComHR), 6 Mar. 1982 (communicated to the author by the Strasbourg Court's Archives service).

[25] *X.* decision, para 1.

Two points in this reasoning stand out (a third will be mentioned later). The first is that the Commission implies that the applicant's wife could easily follow him to Pakistan as she was from Pakistan. The previous discussion suggests that the principle underlying this conclusion was first developed by the Commission in respect of German–Austrian families where the husband had presumably migrated as a single individual. The extension of this principle to members of transnational diasporas seems logically faultless. It nonetheless puts migrants belonging to diaspora communities at a disadvantage compared to the 'isolated' migrant given the Commission's underlying assumption that members of transnational communities could easily go back to their original place and settle there. Not only is this assumption asserted without supporting evidence, but it indirectly benefits those migrants whose spouse does not share 'their culture' and is thus not expected to adapt to life in an alien place. Although apparently pursued purely rationally, the Commission's discourse has racial and class implications which are left unspoken.

The second point is that the Commission considers the enforcement of immigration controls (mentioned at the very end of the quoted passage) a sufficient reason to justify deportation under Article 8. As already mentioned in Chapter 4, this reasoning can be criticised from a postcolonial perspective. Upendra Baxi has caustically observed that the crossing of sovereign frontiers was 'a done thing in the era of colonization'.[26] That era gone, the former colonial subjects who wanted to travel the globe were told that they needed authorisation to do so. Were this authorisation not forthcoming, they were told that they had no right to settle in the West so that the restrictions imposed on their movement were entirely legitimate. Like all others in this area, the Commission's decision did not explain in what sense exactly the deportation of the applicant served the legitimate interests of the state. A detailed reasoning was manifestly not considered to be necessary. Thus, the sentence which immediately followed the passage quoted, simply identified the 'prevention of disorder' as the aim which rendered the applicant's deportation 'necessary in a democratic society' under paragraph 2 of Article 8. How the deportation of the applicant contributed to preventing disorder is not explained—the Commission presumably believed the link to be obvious.

In the instant case, the Commission also found no violation of either Article 14 prohibiting discrimination or Article 3 prohibiting inhuman or degrading treatment. To quote its decision again:

> [T]he Commission considers that the difference in immigration rights between a Commonwealth citizen [under the Immigration Act 1971] and an alien in the United Kingdom has an obvious objective and reasonable basis i.e. in acknowledging the right of a country to limit the number of foreign persons who are entitled to reside in its territory, a State may reasonably give priority to the citizens of those countries with whom it has the closest links.

[26] Upendra Baxi, 'Afterword: The Struggle for *Sans Papiers* Human Rights', in Marie-Bénédicte Dembour and Tobias Kelly (eds) *Are Human Rights for Migrants? Critical Reflections on the Status of Irregular Migrants in Europe and the United States* (Abingdon: Routledge, 2011) 222–232 at 225.

Furthermore, the Commission finds that the measures taken against the applicant were in no way based on race, but on the particular circumstances of his case.[27]

On 6 March 1982, the Commission declared the application inadmissible for being manifestly ill-founded. The idea that former colonial powers might have special obligations towards populations who used to be their former subjects probably never entered the Commission's consciousness.

II. The Court Steps In: *Berrehab*'s Breakthrough

On 14 November 1983, Mr Berrehab, his ex-wife, and their daughter lodged an application with the European Commission of Human Rights. On 7 October 1986, the Commission found, by 11 votes to two, that Mr Berrehab's expulsion from the Netherlands constituted a violation of the respect of family life guaranteed by Article 8 ECHR. The Commission referred the case to the Court, thus finally interrupting its long-established practice of declaring expulsion cases inadmissible. As the case which achieved this breakthrough, *Berrehab* deserves attention.

The circumstances of the case can be summarised as follows. In October 1977, aged 25, Mr Berrehab had married Mrs Koster, a Dutch national. Three months later, he received permission to stay in the Netherlands 'for the sole purpose of enabling him to live with his Dutch wife'. He was issued a work permit two months later. In May 1979, the spouses were divorced on grounds of the irretrievable breakdown of their marriage. Rebecca Berrehab was born three months later. Rebecca lived with her mother, but she enjoyed regular contact with her father. In December 1979, Mr Berrehab's application for renewal of his residence permit was refused, on the ground that a renewal would be against the public interest, given that he was no longer living with his Dutch wife. Mr Berrehab's appeals against this decision were dismissed. A deportation order followed, which was executed in January 1984. Rebecca and her mother spent the two months of the following summer in Morocco. On 28 August 1984, Mr Berrehab applied to the Dutch Embassy in Rabat for a three-month residence permit. This was refused, but a one-month visa was subsequently granted—at a date which is not specified in the judgment, although the date of Mr Berrehab's departure to the Netherlands, 27 May 1985, makes it appear likely that the Commission's admissibility decision of 8 March 1985 might have played a role in the granting of this one-month visa. Having arrived in the Netherlands, Mr Berrehab requested an extension of his visa until 27 August. This was initially refused, but then granted on appeal before the Raad van State. On 14 August 1985, Mr Berrehab remarried Mrs Koster. Four months later, he was granted permission to reside in the Netherlands 'for the purpose of living with his Dutch wife and working during that time'.[28]

[27] *X.* decision, para 2.

[28] *Berrehab* judgment, paras 7–13.

The fact that the granting of this permission did not incite the Commission to strike off the case from its list suggests that the Commission was by then determined to test the Convention's requirements regarding the expulsion of aliens before the Court. The expellee was a devoted father who had done nothing wrong—not even flouted immigration rules—and whose expulsion, triggered by his divorce, separated him from his young Dutch daughter. *Berrehab* must have seemed a good case to refer to the Court if the intention was now to see the principle of state sovereignty softened in immigration matters. The government nonetheless had the audacity to argue that the two months which Rebecca had spent in Morocco in summer 1984 indicated that the expulsion had not prevented family life from continuing.[29] This argument did not impress the Court. On 21 June 1988, by six votes to one, the Court ruled that the interference with family life had been disproportionate. The Court observed that the case concerned the expulsion, following the breakdown of his marriage with a Dutch national, of 'a person who had... lawfully lived [in the Netherlands] for several years, who had a home and a job there, and against whom the Government did not claim to have any complaint'. The refusal of the residence permit and the ensuing expulsion had threatened to break the 'very close ties' which existed between Mr Berrehab and his daughter—whom he had visited four times a week. In these circumstances, the 'disproportion between the means employed and the legitimate aim pursued' meant that Article 8 had been violated.[30]

One could endlessly speculate about the exact reasons why this case achieved what dozens of cases had not managed to achieve previously. The circumstances of the case, which involved a law-abiding and caring father, may have appeared particularly compelling.[31] Of possible significance is the involvement of Mrs Koster in the case. Very often aliens lack the financial and cultural capital necessary to make effective judicial claims, whether at Strasbourg or even beforehand before the domestic courts (where domestic remedies must be exhausted for an application to be admissible at Strasbourg). In this case, Mrs Koster was listed as an applicant alongside her ex-husband and daughter in the original application. The Commission decided that she could not claim the status of victim in its decision of admissibility. Despite this, Mrs Koster presumably continued to support Mr Berrehab in the pursuit of the case. Finally, the timing of the application may also have been favourable: the *Berrehab* application was lodged four weeks after the holding of the Funchal Colloquy which had rung alarm bells within

[29] *Berrehab* report, para 34.

[30] *Berrehab* judgment, para 29.

[31] Compare with *Yousef v. the United Kingdom*, appl. 14830/89, Report (EComHR), 30 June 1992. In this case, the Commission stressed that 'Article 8 does not impose a general obligation on states to allow access to children of a broken marriage': para 42. It distinguished *Yousef* from *Berrehab*. In *Yousef*, the applicant had had limited access to his child of one supervised visit per week (because there was a fear that otherwise his unfavourable immigration status would have led him to leave the UK with his son), he was unemployed and had in the past a minor criminal conviction: para 43. His subsequent relationship with another British woman, with whom he also had a child, seems to have counted against him. The Commission unanimously thought that the facts of this case disclosed no violation of the Convention.

the Council of Europe about the poor treatment of aliens under the European Convention system—as noted in the introduction to Part II of this book.

III. The Tip of the Iceberg

Following the opening constituted by *Berrehab*, the Court started to decide numerous cases about the expulsion, following criminal conviction, of 'second-generation' migrants. A commentator wondered in the late 1990s why Article 8 was invoked by migrants far more often in order to oppose an expulsion measure rather than in order to seek family reunification.[32] Amongst the millions of migrants living in Europe, it is true that many face the difficulty of seeing a relative being prevented from joining them whilst relatively few are ordered to be expelled. Convention law itself, however, can go a long way in explaining the small number of cases relating to family reunification and the relatively high number of cases related to expulsion following criminal conviction in the Strasbourg case law. On the one hand, the Court never departed from the strong signal it gave in the 1980s in the *Abdulaziz, Cabales and Balkandali* case (*ABC*) that it was not ready to countenance the proposition that a right to be joined by one's family can be read into the European Convention (as discussed in Chapter 4). On the other hand, after *Berrehab* and then, 30 months later, *Moustaquim v. Belgium* (concerning the expulsion of a teenager of the 'second generation' following his repeated low-level criminal offending), the Court never completely closed the door to the possibility that the expulsion of a settled migrant could be found, in the specific circumstances of the case, to breach Article 8. Putting an argument to this effect is not necessarily the non-starter that it virtually always is in reunification cases. In countries where there is not a rigid division between the criminal and immigration branches of the legal profession, an additional factor may be that an individual who has gone through the criminal process is more likely to be followed by a lawyer, thus increasing his chances of being advised about the possibility of pursuing his case at Strasbourg, compared to the law-abiding migrant who suffers from being separated from his family outside the legal process.

The Strasbourg case law inevitably offers a distorted picture of the legal and human problems which people experience.[33] It nonetheless points to troublesome areas. The expulsion of aliens following criminal conviction clearly is one such area. In the decade between 1991 and 2001, the Strasbourg Court decided 12 Article 8 expulsion cases, ten of which were directed against France, and the remaining two against Belgium.[34] Such a configuration might reflect the fact that,

[32] Henri Labayle, 'L'article 8 de la Convention européenne des droits de l'homme et le droit de l'étranger au respect de sa vie privée et familiale', in Hugues Fulcheron (ed.) *Les étrangers et la Convention européenne de sauvegarde des droits de l'homme et des libertés fondamentales* (Lyon: L.G.D.J., 1999) 83–108 at 87.

[33] I am therefore wary of the picture according to which law offers a 'mirror' of society. Things are more complicated than that.

[34] *Moustaquim v. Belgium*, appl. 12313/86, Judgment (ECtHR), 18 Feb. 1991; *Beldjoudi v. France*, appl. 12083/86, Judgment (ECtHR), 26 Mar. 1992; *Nasri v. France*, appl. 19465/92,

at the time, France was expelling thousands of aliens every year. Neighbouring Belgium was expelling some 100 convicted foreigners a year at the beginning of that decade and only a few individuals by its end.[35] Question marks nonetheless remain as to why the case law was directed against these two states. Why not other states, such as Norway, for example?

On a research visit to Norway in 1997, I was told that the Norwegian government was following a policy whereby aliens who had been criminally convicted once, for however small a misdemeanour, were automatically expelled.[36] When I enquired about the absence of (known) applications to Strasbourg, a lawyer practising in Oslo explained that the legal costs incurred in order to meet the requirement of exhausting national remedies made it difficult to envisage applications to Strasbourg originating from migrants living in Norway unless and until the European Court accepted the argument that domestic proceedings were ineffective (and thus did not need to be exhausted) which the Court had not done. In comparison, he believed that it was easier for migrants to lodge applications against Sweden, given the lack of obvious judicial remedies against expulsion which existed there, thus circumventing the need to undertake a long and costly judicial journey at national level.[37] The presence or absence of associations on the ground (e.g. CIMADE in France) might also have been a significant factor.

Today, the UK has replaced France as the most common respondent state in the expulsion case law. This, again, is not entirely surprising. On the one hand, possibly partly in response to the Strasbourg case law, France has changed its laws governing the expulsion of aliens, thus protecting many legally settled migrants against the criminal sanction, which exists in its system, of '*interdiction judiciaire*

Judgment (ECtHR), 13 July 1995; *Boughanemi v. France*, appl. 22070/93, Judgment (ECtHR), 24 Apr. 1996; *C. v. Belgium*, appl. 21794/93, Judgment (ECtHR), 27 June 1996; *Bouchelkia v. France*, appl. 23078/93, Judgment (ECtHR), 29 Jan. 1997; *Mehemi v. France*, appl. 53470/99, Judgment (ECtHR), 26 Sept. 1997; *El Boujaïdi v. France*, appl. 25613/94, Judgment (ECtHR), 26 Sept. 1997; *Boujlifa v. France*, appl. 25404/94, Judgment (ECtHR), 21 Oct. 1997; *Dalia v. France*, appl. 26102/95, Judgment (ECtHR), 19 Feb. 1998; *Baghli v. France*, appl. 34374/97, Judgment (ECtHR), 30 Nov. 1999; *Ezzouhdi v. France*, appl. 47160/99, Judgment (ECtHR), 13 Feb. 2001, in French only.

[35] Two in 1999, six in 2000 and only one in 2001: Xavier Rolin, 'La double peine, une punition de la nationalité' (2002) *Revue du droit des étrangers* 118, 203–216 at 204. See also Halil Dogan, Kees Groenendijk, and Elspeth Guild, 'Sécurite de résidence des immigrés de longue durée', *Etude Comparative de la Législation et de la Pratique des Pays Européens* (Strasbourg: Council of Europe, 1998) 24–28. In 2003, Bertrand Tavernier spoke of 20,000 people being expelled from France in the previous five years: http://www.mrax.be/Campagnes/Doublepeine/interview.htm, accessed 9 June 2011.

[36] As confirmed by the facts of *Nunez v. Norway*, appl. 55597/09, Judgment (ECtHR), 28 June 2011, para 6: 'The applicant...was arrested on suspicion of shoplifting [in March 2006]. The next day she accepted a summary fine (*forelegg*) for theft of goods to the estimated value of NOK 5,098 (EUR 600). On the same date it was decided to deport the [21-year-old] and to prohibit her from re-entry for a period of two years'. The applicant came back under a false name and with a false passport, leading in time to a second expulsion, which was the one contested at Strasbourg. The European Court of Human Rights did not question the authorities' characterisation of the applicant's offences as 'very serious'. On the criminalisation of migrants, see Chapter 11.

[37] This point seems to be confirmed by *Bulus v. Sweden*, appl. 9330/81, PCom Decision (EComHR), 19 Jan. 1984.

du territoire français' (being prohibited from the French territory). Going in the opposite direction, the British government abandoned its fairly relaxed attitude towards the deportation of convicted criminals, following the 'revelation' in 2006 that 1,000 or so foreigners had been released from jail without having been considered for deportation, which was presented as a scandal in the press and which led the then Home Office Secretary to resign. Since then, the number of foreign prisoners deported by the UK at the end of their sentence has shot up dramatically.[38] Legislation was introduced in 2007 which made it mandatory for non-EU citizens sentenced to over 12 months in prison to face deportation action, subject to an appeal on ECHR grounds. The deportation of non-citizens convicted of crime has now become the expected norm in political debate, with the main parties vying for the speed at which and the quantities in which this can be achieved. As part of this process, there is an ongoing effort on the part of government to curtail prospective deportees' ability to claim an Article 8 defence against their predicament.

It is difficult to understand, from a socio-legal point of view, the origin of the cases which make up the case law, but one thing is clear: for every case which reaches Strasbourg, many others do not. At the Funchal Colloquy of 1983, one participant commented that thousands of people were expelled from Europe *every month*.[39] Given the ever-increasing coordination and control exercised by the state in this area, the numbers must surely have increased since then. The great majority of individuals who are expelled do not go to Strasbourg. This is so despite the devastating consequences which deportations entail for those directly affected by them, the deportees, and their families, as we shall now see.

IV. The Human Meaning of Deportation: Shattered Lives

In most jurisdictions, the deportation which befalls a convicted criminal who comes to the end of his custodial sentence is not legally considered to be a penal sanction.[40] It is classified instead as an administrative measure which pertains to immigration policy. In many cases, however, people who are deported experience their expulsion as a sanction which is heavier than any custodial sentence they have served, when they are in effect banished from the place where they have constructed their life, whether from birth or later.[41] Even if the expulsion is limited to

[38] Gibney 'Asylum' 146–167.

[39] João Pereira Bastos, 'Comment', in Directorate of Human Rights (ed.) *Human Rights of Aliens in Europe: Proceedings of the Colloquy on 'Human Rights of Aliens in Europe'* (Dordrecht: Martinus Nijhoff, 1985) 178–179 at 179. Bastos was Permanent Representative of Portugal to the Council of Europe. He gave a number of precise figures, which suggests this information is reliable. Many of the expulsions to which he refers could have been triggered by the then economic crisis and unemployment situation.

[40] In France, however, the expulsion of an alien can be either a penal sanction ordered by a judge or an administrative measure adopted by the executive.

[41] Ines Hasselberg, 'An Ethnography of Deportation from Britain', 2013 PhD thesis, University of Sussex.

a defined period (e.g. ten years), the visa which would allow the expellee to return and reside legally again in the territory of the expelling country is unlikely ever to be granted at the end of this ten-year period, given the applicant's past criminal record. Unable to face life in a country which they do not consider theirs, many expellees fall into serious depression. A significant number come back illegally to the country which has ordered them away, and are then condemned to conduct their life in limbo. Whether they stay in the country of which they have the nationality but which feels alien to them, or whether they come back to where their ties are, deportation has often shattered their lives.

The Strasbourg Court indirectly recognised this in the first case it decided in the expulsion of a second-generation migrant following a criminal conviction, *Moustaquim v. Belgium*, in 1991.[42] The applicant had arrived in Belgium in 1965 as a toddler, with his mother, in order to join his father. Two decades later, he was deported, after having been imprisoned on multiple occasions as a teenager—though mostly for short, often fortnightly, periods. On having to leave Belgium, he did not go to Morocco, his country of nationality, but to Spain, and from there to Stockholm, where he lived at times legally and at other times illegally, living, in the words of the Strasbourg judgment, 'by his wits and by taking the odd undeclared job in Greek and Italian restaurants'.[43] A Stockholm psychiatrist diagnosed him as 'suffering from depression brought about by the disruption of his family ties'.[44] The government, by contrast, expressed doubts as to the existence of any family ties worth taking into consideration, in view of the number of occasions on which he had run away and been imprisoned.[45] He was separated from his family for five years.

The most compelling stories of Strasbourg applicants I have read come from journalist Michael Goldhaber who set out to capture the real lives behind some of the most famous judgments of the Court.[46] Ali (as Goldhaber calls him) is one of the applicants Goldhaber traced and interviewed. The journalist's story sheds a very different light on Ali's expulsion than the *Mehemi v. France* judgment which concerns him. Ali's parents were originally from a village in Algeria. They established themselves in Lyon in the mid-1950s. Ali's father, who had previously fought in the French army for four years in Vietnam, worked as a bricklayer and his mother as a housekeeper in a home for the elderly. Ali and his four siblings were born in France. When Ali was deported to Algeria in 1993, France was advising its citizens to leave its former colony, then in the grip of a civil war. Ali explained to Goldhaber what happened to him there:

> Ali…was struggling with his own hysteria. Ali had never been to Algeria in his life and didn't have a single connection there. The French police randomly put him on a flight

[42] A royal order suspending Mr Moustaquim's deportation order was issued on the very day that the Commission referred the case to the Court in December 1989: *Moustaquim* judgment, para 33. The Court was obviously not prepared to strike the case off its list.

[43] *Moustaquim*, para 21. [44] *Moustaquim*, para 23. [45] *Moustaquim*, para 35.

[46] Michael D. Goldhaber, *A People's History of the European Court of Human Rights* (New Brunswick: Rutgers University Press, 2007).

to the small city of Constantine. When he arrived, the Algerian police saw that he was lost, so they dropped him at a hotel. Ali was able to pay the room rate indefinitely, with money from his family that he'd hidden in his toiletries bag. He could not work, because he was refused Algerian working papers. He could not travel, because he was refused an Algerian passport. He was depressed and rapidly lost weight. (He would ultimately lose fifty pounds). He spent his time listening to the droning of Arabic state television. There was an 11 PM curfew, but he didn't mind it, because there was nowhere to go. The telephone was his lifeline to the outside world. His relatives called so often that the hotel receptionist became friends with everyone in his family. After three months Ali began to hatch escape plans. First he went to Algiers and then to Oran, hoping to stow away on a boat bound for France or Spain. The only thing Ali found in either city was political unrest. In the cafés, all the talk was of God and assassination.

Everyone except the French regarded Ali as French. Fundamentalists set up false roadblocks to extort money from travellers, and Ali feared that they would slit his throat. Ali had no identification except his French deportation papers. He knew a bit of Arabic, but his accent was thick, so he remained quiet, which itself drew attention. In Algiers, Ali was picked up by the military police, who threw him in a jail cell crowded to bursting with Islamists. After release, Ali found another dive hotel and hatched a desperate new plan of escape.

In early 1995, Ali's younger brother pilfered his older brother's identity papers and sent them to Algeria with a friend. Ali bribed an Algerian bureaucrat to alter the photo and tried his luck. He made it to Paris—only to be stopped at Orly Airport and returned to Algiers. There was nothing left but wait for Strasbourg.

On September 26, 1997, the European Court of Human Rights found Ali's deportation [to be in violation of Article 8 ECHR].

Although France complied with the court order and let Ali return in February 1998, his travails were not entirely over. Ali was displeased with the conditions France imposed on his return. He was refused a pardon and given a compulsory residence requirement. He was forbidden to travel outside Lyon or to leave his home at night, and he was required to report to a parole officer. At first he was given renewable work papers that were good only for six months. Beginning in 2001, his work papers were renewable after one year. Ali complained that he couldn't find work because of the questions raised by his work permit. One of his brothers had to create a company to hire him as a taxi driver. Eventually, he was able to find odd jobs as an electrician through a temp agency. Ali brought a second case to the European Court of Human Rights to protest the conditions of his return, but in October 2003 the court ruled that his rights had not been violated.[47]

In the light of this account, the remark by a legal scholar that Mr Mehemi's family life in France seemed 'rather thin' (*'passablement anecdotique'*) appears gratuitous.[48] Uncharacteristically the Court in its judgment reverted to overtly emotional grounds by quoting a letter which Mr Mehemi's wife had written to the President of the French Republic. The letter could hardly be taken to refer to a man with no family in France. It read:

[47] Goldhaber *A People's History* 59–61. The ruling referred to at the end of the quotation is: *Mehemi v. France (No. 2)*, appl. 53479/00, Judgment (ECtHR), 10 Apr. 2003.

[48] Labayle 'L'article 8' 106, note 2.

I would not ask you to plead in my favour for a reduction of my husband's sentence... but I beseech you to help me have his expulsion from French territory quashed. He was sentenced to six years' imprisonment—so be it. That must be the way of it because he committed a crime and I know perfectly well that he must pay for it... But I cannot bring myself to accept his expulsion, and for good reason. Please understand me, Mr President, or at least try to: since my husband went to prison my children have not been themselves; they are suffering terribly and are constantly having to be examined by psychologists. But it is not just my children and I who are suffering: there is also the whole of my husband's family, particularly his mother, who is 67 years of age and a diabetic. She sees her grandchildren all the time and whenever they ask her where 'Dad' is and when he will be coming back she cannot help bursting into tears. This situation is having a terrible effect on her physical and mental health.

Things cannot go on like this. I do not want my family and the future of my children to be destroyed, because what future can I give them without their father at their side?...[49]

What persuaded the Court to find a verdict of violation in the *Mehemi* case is not clear. On the same day, the Court adopted a verdict of non-violation in *El Boujaïdi v. France*. If length of sentencing provides a good ground of comparison, then Mr Mehimi's offences, related to his involvement in a Moroccan hashish ring, were more serious than those for which Mr El Boujaïdi had been convicted. It is impossible to say which of the following facts might have played a role in persuading the Court to judge in favour of Mr Mehemi (the only time the Court did so in the eight removal Article 8 cases upon which it ruled between 1996 and 1999): that his wife was Italian (and thus possibly not expected to follow him to Algeria); that they had three young children who, moreover, had French nationality; or that Mr Mehemi had been born French but had lost this nationality because his parents had not made the declaration which would have meant he would have remained French in the post-1962 era of independent Algeria. The judgment offers no clue in this regard.

The circumstances of Mr Mehemi's life after his expulsion recounted by Goldhaber were not alluded to in the Court's judgment. It is possible that the Court had not heard them because Mr Mehimi's legal representative did not know of them either (after an expulsion, lawyers tend to lose contact with their clients). By contrast, it appears that Mr Mehemi's wife's letter must have struck a chord with some judges as the Court chose to reproduce it in its judgment. If so, it is a pity that, in other cases, the Court has not considered the fact that the expulsion of a long-term migrant must be presumed to be dramatic both for the expellee and for his family.[50]

The French film-maker Bertrand Tavernier has documented the experiences of deportees in a poignant documentary entitled *Histoires de vies brisées* [*Stories of lives which have been shattered*].[51] The film, which came out in 2001, galvanised the movement against '*double peine*' (being punished twice) in France. Tavernier

[49] *Mehemi* judgment, para 15.

[50] Hasselberg 'An Ethnography'.

[51] For a short description of the film, see <http://www.autourdu1ermai.fr/fiches/film/fiche-film-154.html>, accessed 21 July 2011.

interviewed 11 people who were on hunger strike in his native city of Lyon. Legally classified as aliens, these people appeared entirely local to him. In his words: 'I suddenly felt like I was seeing again the kids with whom I used to play, I was rediscovering the places of my childhood'. His interviewees spoke about the emotional but also physical wounds deportation inflicts. One interviewee could not hold back his tears. Hardly able to talk, he kept repeating that the French authorities were murderers. He recalled the friends with whom he used to talk and eat in a way which suggested that their enforced deportation to the civil war in Algeria had cost them their lives—literally. Tavernier believes his film encouraged Nicolas Sarkozy, the then Minister of the Interior, to declare before the Parliamentary Assembly that double punishment was problematic and had to be stopped.[52]

V. The Expulsion of Foreign Criminals: An Issue which Attracts Diametrically Opposed Positions

The first cases concerning the expulsion of criminal aliens which came before the Court ended either in a friendly settlement (which led the case to be struck off the Court's list) or in a verdict of violation of Article 8 ECHR.[53] This trend led commentators to surmise in the early 1990s that the Court was en route to establishing a principle according to which the expulsion of second-generation migrants would in general contravene Article 8. For some, this was a positive move, to be celebrated. For example, Ryszard Cholewinski argued:

> Western European countries have still not come to terms with their [growing] populations of second-generation migrants [who are] educationally, socially and culturally disadvantaged in relation to national youth, [which] creates conditions leading to criminality... Nationality is not a justifiable criterion to treat this group differently from nationals.... The fundamental precepts of customary international law regarding the expulsion of non-nationals are changing.[54]

Cholewinski talked of a 'hidden agenda' being pursued by the Court towards the protection of second-generation migrants from expulsion. At the opposite end, others felt the Court was overstepping its jurisdiction and illegitimately encroaching on state sovereignty. For example, leading French scholars wrote a case note in which they regretted the Court's 'exponential reading' of Article 8 and argued:

> The Court's judgment does nothing to help progress the debate on foreigners. Obviously a case decided on its facts, [the judgment nonetheless] lends legitimacy to the idea that, whatever the danger he represents for society, the second-generation migrant is entitled to

[52] 'Banissons la double peine', <http://www.mrax.be/Campagnes/Doublepeine/interview.htm>, accessed 21 July 2011.

[53] *Djeroud v. France*, appl. 13446/87, Judgment (ECtHR), 23 Jan. 1991 (ending on a friendly settlement); *Moustaquim* judgment; *Beldjoudi* judgment; *Lamguindaz v. United Kingdom*, appl. 16152/90, Judgment (ECtHR), 23 June 1993 (ending on a friendly settlement).

[54] Cholewinski 'Strasbourg's "Hidden Agenda"' 305.

remain on the territory of the State which has welcomed him in. It is far from certain that this is the best way to persuade State parties to fulfil their obligations...[55]

The hard-felt and irreconcilable convictions which underlay these two quotations were found not only among commentators but also within the Court. In the 'old' Court, it quickly became clear that some judges would never come to accept the position adopted by the Court in the early 1990s. Judge Valticos was one of them. He wrote in a dissenting opinion:

The deportation of aliens... is a prerogative of States, and its use is restricted in the Convention only in well-defined cases [exhaustively listed in Article 5(1)(f) of the Convention and Protocol nos 4 and 7]. This is not one of them.[56]

Judge Martens led the opposite camp. He explained, also in a dissenting opinion (to the first judgment concluding on a non-violation of the Convention):

[The Court] should start from the idea that *integrated aliens*—that is: aliens who have lived all, or practically all their lives within a state—*should no more be expelled than nationals.*[57]

The judicial result of this opposition between equally principled positions is that one side has never managed to win over the other side on a long-term basis. This has had two interrelated consequences. The first is that the Strasbourg case law has stayed away from affirming principles, instead preferring to make purportedly factual pronouncements. The second is that the case law has progressed in a 'yo-yo' manner, alternating between verdicts of violation and verdicts of non-violation.[58] This history is reviewed in the next section.

VI. The Absence of a Principled Approach by the Court and the Ensuing Judicial Lottery

Boughanemi v. France, decided on 24 April 1996, constituted the fourth Strasbourg judgment on the merits in a case involving the expulsion, following criminal conviction, of a second-generation migrant.[59] It was the first verdict of non-violation in such a case. Judge Martens' dissenting opinion bemoaned the absence of a principled approach, which 'obliges the Court to make a well-nigh impossible

[55] Henri Labayle and Frédéric Sudre, 'Chronique de jurisprudence' (2013) *Revue française de droit administratif* 982.

[56] Dissenting opinion of Judge Valticos in *Beldjoudi* judgment, emphasis added.

[57] Dissenting opinion of Judge Martens in *Boughanemi* judgment, emphasis added.

[58] The difficulty to adhere consistently to one principle given the presence of the opposing view is noticeable in other jurisdictions too, whether national or international, which is then reverberated in commentaries. See e.g. Sara A. Rodriguez, 'Exile and the Not-So-Lawful Permanent Resident: Does International Law Require a Humanitarian Waiver of Deportation for the Non-Citizen Convicted of Certain Crimes?' (2005–6) *Georgetown Immigration Law Journal* 483–541 (with the author responding 'no' to the question she asks) and Michelle Foster, '"An 'Alien' by the Barest of Treads"—The Legality of the Deportation of Long-Term Residents from Australia' (2009) *Melbourne University Law Review* 483–541.

[59] After *Moustaquim, Beldjoudi*, and *Nasri*.

comparison between the merits of the case before it and those which it has already decided'.[60] Indeed, how does one compare different patterns of offending behaviour and different family ties? Should involvement in a pub fight that results in someone being killed be considered more or less serious than dealing in Class B drugs? In the weighting exercise operated by the Court, should being the father of one young child conceived after the applicant was sentenced to jail and warned that he might be deported be considered less worthy of consideration than having two teenagers born well before the offending pattern started? Does it matter in this balancing exercise which nationality the children are? And how does one compare the seriousness of the offence with the depth of the family ties at risk of being broken? Also, if the expulsion is ordered when the applicant is 22, not in a relationship, and childless, does this mean he has no family life worth protecting? (The Court would say 'yes', but it has only made this answer clear after having recognised that a long-term migrant has, whatever his circumstances, a private life in the expelling country which needs to be taken into consideration.)

The number of factors which are of potential relevance to the Court's balancing exercise is high, and how they relate to each other far from clear. This comes out, for example, from a table published in 2003 which I compiled in an effort to compare the various circumstances of the 12 relevant cases which the Court had decided up to 2001.[61] The table listed: the nationality of the applicant; his age on arrival in the expelling state; how old he was at the time of the offence(s); the nature of his crimes (which was not always easy to summarise when the applicant's criminal record was long and varied); the length of his custodial sentences (again, an exercise which often proved difficult due to the varied picture which emerged at different levels of jurisdictions); the number of siblings in the expelling country and their nationality (given that this was something the Court then always mentioned);[62] whether the applicant was in a relationship, either then or before, and, if so, of which nationality was his partner and whether the relationship started before or after the order of expulsion; and finally how many children the applicant had, whether they had been born before or after the expulsion order, and of which nationality they were.[63] The whole exercise is bewildering. Can those who argue that the case law is consistent explain why a decision of inadmissibility such as *Djaïd v. France* and a verdict of non-violation such as *Baghli v. France* can be reconciled, in concrete terms, with a verdict of violation such as *Ezzouhdi v. France*?[64]

[60] Dissenting opinion of Judge Martens in *Boughanemi* judgment, para 4.

[61] Marie-Bénédicte Dembour, 'Human Rights Law and National Sovereignty in Collusion: The Plight of Quasi-Nationals at Strasbourg' (2003) *Netherlands Quarterly of Human Rights* 63–98 at 70; 'Etrangers ou quasi-nationaux? Le choix des droits de l'homme' [Observations sous *Ezzouhdi*] (2002) *Revue trimestrielle des droits de l'homme* 52, 963–982 at 982.

[62] That the Court has stopped doing so must be commended, as it does not make sense to draw positive or negative inferences from the fact that the applicant's parents and/or siblings have acquired or not the nationality of the expelling state.

[63] Dembour 'Human Rights Law'.

[64] These are the three cases I compared in: Dembour 'Etrangers' 961–963. For views which argue that the case law is consistent, see: Luzius Wildhaber, in Paul Mahoney et al. (eds) *Protecting Human Rights: The European Dimension. Studies in Memory of Rolv Ryssdal* (Cologne: Carl Heymanns

No doubt wishing to respond to the critique that its case law was lacking in coherence, the Court endeavoured to identify the relevant criteria to be applied when examining the question of whether an expulsion which 'interferes' with the family and/or private life of the applicant is 'necessary in a democratic society' (to use the words of Article 8), i.e. whether the expulsion is 'proportionate' to the aim pursued by the state (to use the words developed by the Court in its reasoning). The Court renewed its efforts to achieve systematisation in the *Boultif v. Switzerland* case decided on 2 August 2001, which concerned not the most common scenario in the Strasbourg Article 8 expulsion case law of a second-generation migrant but that of a relatively recently arrived foreigner who had married a national of the defendant state. The Court said:

> In assessing the relevant criteria in such a case, the Court will consider [1] the nature and seriousness of the offence committed by the applicant; [2] the length of the applicant's stay in the country from which he is going to be expelled; [3] the time elapsed since the offence was committed as well as the applicant's conduct in that period; [4] the nationalities of the various persons concerned; [5] the applicant's family situation, such as the length of the marriage; and other factors expressing the effectiveness of a couple's family life; [6] whether the spouse knew about the offence at the time when he or she entered into a family relationship; and [7] whether there are children in the marriage, and if so, their age. Not least, the Court will also consider [8] the seriousness of the difficulties which the spouse is likely to encounter in the country of origin, though the mere fact that a person might face certain difficulties in accompanying her or his spouse cannot in itself exclude an expulsion.[65]

The Court then applied these criteria wholesale, without explaining how each one of them was dealt with in the particular circumstances. It is possible, even likely, that such a detailed discussion was omitted from the judgment because there was no agreement within the Court as to how each of these eight criteria (which I have numbered for ease of discussion later) made the case lean either towards or against a violation of the Convention.

The concrete result in *Boultif* was a unanimous verdict of violation. Three of the seven judges—amongst them Judge Wildhaber, then President of the Court—wrote a concurring opinion where they suggested that what persuaded them to vote for a violation was the fact that seven years had elapsed since the applicant had committed the offence which led to his expulsion without him having re-offended, thus probably indicating 'rehabilitation'.[66] Had they not done this, it would have been far more difficult to understand, from the judgment, why a verdict of violation had been reached. In fact, some might have thought

Verlag, 2000) 1535–1538; Daniel Thym, 'Respect for Private and Family Law under Article 8 ECHR in Immigration Cases: A Human Right to Regularize Illegal Stay?' (2008) *International and Comparative Law Quarterly* 87–112 at 112. For a denunciation of the inconsistency of the case law, see: Marie-Françoise Valette, '"Double peine": Les fausses notes de la jurisprudence de la Cour européenne des droits de l'homme' [Observations sous *Üner*] (2007) *Revue trimestrielle des droits de l'homme* 1101–1119.

[65] *Boultif v. Switzerland*, appl. 54273/00, Judgment (ECtHR), 2 Aug. 2001, para 48.

[66] Concurring opinion of Judges Baka, Wildhaber and Lorenzen in *Boultif*.

that the decisive factor could have been that the applicant was married to a white European woman who would have been expected to find it difficult to settle in her husband's country of origin.[67] Such an interpretation does not appear warranted, however, given that the concurring judges were very clear that the Court's verdict was not due to a position of principle but arose because of the particular circumstances of the case—with the applicant's 'rehabilitation' corresponding to the third *Boultif* criterion, having carried particular weight, at least for them if not for the other judges.

The highly casuistic (case-by-case) approach of the Court—which Judge Martens had predicted in 1996 would prove a 'lottery for national authorities and a source of embarrassment for the Court'—made it impossible for the case law to settle.[68] After *Boultif*, the case law continued to evolve in a haphazard way, with some verdicts of violation and some verdicts of non-violation.[69]

In 2005, the appeal request of an applicant whose case, *Üner v. the Netherlands*, had been found by a Chamber not to disclose a violation of the Convention was allowed to proceed. Presumably this was in the hope that a judgment carrying the authority of the Grand Chamber would make it possible to settle the case law once and for all. The Grand Chamber decided *Üner* on the basis of the *Boultif* criteria and an additional two criteria, identified as:

– [9] the best interests and well-being of the children, in particular the seriousness of the difficulties which any children of the applicant are likely to encounter in the country to which the applicant is to be expelled; and
– [10] the solidity of social, cultural and family ties with the host country and with the country of destination.[70]

In its judgment of 18 October 2006, the Grand Chamber decided that the applicant could be expelled—as the Chamber had done the previous year. The majority reached this verdict without explaining how they carried out in practice the

[67] Hanspeter Mock, '"Selon que vous serez marié ou misérable"... —Eloignement des étrangers délinquants: le mariage, une meilleure garantie que l'intégration contre la "double peine"?' [Observations sous *Boultif*] (2002) *Revue trimestrielle des droits de l'homme* 483.

[68] The 'lottery' reference (at para 4 of Judge Martens' dissenting opinion in *Boughanemi*) is probably due to the fact that although *Boughanemi* was the first verdict of non-violation adopted by the Court, it was far from the first case where an applicant expelled after criminal conviction had lost his Article 8 claim at Strasbourg. See e.g. for Commission's decisions taken in the years directly prior to *Boughanemi: C. v. the United Kingdom*, appl. 13718/88, Decision (EComHR), 15 July 1988; *Aziz Patel v. the United Kingdom*, appl. 16009/90, PCom Decision (EComHR), 6 Sept. 1991; *T. v. the Netherlands*, appl. 16531/90, Decision (ECtHR), 16 Jan. 1991; *Tosun v. Germany*, appl. 19710/92, Decision (ECtHR), 11 Jan. 1995.

[69] Compare e.g. *Benhebba v. France*, appl. 53441/99, Judgment (ECtHR), 10 July 2003, in French only (non-violation) and *Mokrani v. France*, appl. 52206/99, Judgment (ECtHR), 15 July 2003, in French only (violation).

[70] *Üner* GC judgment, para 58. The second new criterion appears to have been inspired by previous dissenting opinions. See e.g. the dissenting opinion of Judges Costa and Tulkens in *Baghli* and of Judge Baka in the Chamber's *Üner* judgment where Judge Baka remarked that the applicant must 'have incomparably much closer family and social ties with the Netherlands than with Turkey' and that 'even an ability to speak a country's language does not in itself constitute a strong tie with that country'.

balancing exercise which led them to the conclusion that Mr Üner's expulsion was proportionate to the interference with his Article 8 rights.[71]

The judgment was not unanimous. Three of the 17 judges, including the President of the Court, Judge Costa, dissented. Theirs was first of all a position of principle:

> [I]n general terms, we believe that foreign nationals—in any case those who, like Mr Üner, have been residing legally in a country—should be granted the same fair treatment and a legal status as close as possible to that accorded to nationals.[72]

They suggested that the case was atypical, but did not say why they thought that.[73] Perhaps this was because the applicant, married to a Dutch national, had conceived his second child during a marital visit in jail? Or because he had arrived in the Netherlands at the relatively mature age of 12? Or because he was caught illegally helping a friend to grow cannabis on the Dutch territory which he said had happened because he took the opportunity to visit his family as he was back in Europe for the Grand Chamber's hearing, and needed to fund his travel?

Whatever their reason for finding the case atypical, the dissenters examined the *Üner* facts in the light of the '*Boultif* plus two' criteria. They noted that [1] the applicant had committed the offence which led to his expulsion during a fight, thus without any bearing on state security (had the latter been the case, they accepted this would warrant a departure from the general rule they were advocating); [2] the applicant had spent 17 years in the Netherlands where he had arrived aged 12; [3] five years had passed since the offence took place without the applicant's conduct in prison having appeared to cause a problem; [4] his partner and children were Dutch; [5 and 6][74] the couple's relationship had begun seven years before the expulsion; and [8] his partner would have faced considerable difficulties in settling in a country which was completely alien to her.[75] For the dissenting judges, the application of all the criteria identified as relevant by the Court (except for criterion [7], which was inapplicable as the applicant was childless) seemed 'to point to a violation of Article 8'.[76]

Given the strength of this dissenting opinion, it should come as no surprise that the authority lent by the Grand Chamber to the *Üner* judgment was not sufficient to settle the case law. One year later, another appeal was allowed to come before the Grand Chamber. On 23 June 2008, the Grand Chamber confirmed the Chamber's ruling in *Maslov v. Austria* that for Austria to expel the applicant for offences committed when he was a teenager would be a violation of Article 8. Again, the Court was divided; there was one dissenting opinion, this time from

[71] Valette '"Double peine"' stresses this fact in a section entitled 'L'introuvable application des critères dégagés' 1113–1119.

[72] Joint dissenting opinion of Judges Costa, Zupančič and Türmen in *Üner* GC judgment, para 5.

[73] Costa et al. in *Üner* GC, para 3.

[74] Although this is only one consideration, it applies to both the criteria I numbered 5 and 6 in my previous discussion of *Boultif*.

[75] Costa et al. in *Üner* GC, para 14.

[76] Costa et al. in *Üner* GC, para 15.

the national judge. Amongst other things, Judge Steiner noted that the offences committed by the applicant were 'considerable' in number, committed over a 'lengthy period' (15 months), with some having included the threat or use of violence;[77] the applicant did not seem to have solid ties in Austria, having dropped out of school and failed to undergo drug therapy;[78] having spent the first six years of his life in Bulgaria, he could be presumed to have some basic knowledge of Bulgarian;[79] and although the residence ban had been imposed when he was still a minor, the authorities did not proceed with his expulsion until he was 21.[80] In Judge Steiner's view, there had therefore been no violation of Article 8.

On face value, the two Grand Chamber judgments, adopted with an interval of 18 months, have produced contradictory outcomes. Legally it is nonetheless possible to reconcile them. It could be said, for example, that *Üner* lays down the general rule and that *Maslov*, which concerned a deportee who was a minor at the time of the offending, deals with a (probably fact-dependent rather than absolute)[81] exception to the general rule. Interestingly, however, commentators tend to cite *either* one *or* the other judgment—not both.[82] Meanwhile, the case law has continued to develop haphazardly. Since *Maslov*, only the occasional case has ended in a verdict of violation. Interestingly, this has normally not been because the applicant was a minor.[83] Specifically referring to the UN Convention

[77] Dissenting opinion of Judge Steiner in the Chamber's *Maslov* judgment, para 3, to which she refers in her dissenting opinion in the Grand Chamber's judgment.

[78] Steiner in the Chamber's *Maslov* judgment, para 5.

[79] Steiner in the Chamber's *Maslov* judgment, para 6.

[80] Steiner in the Chamber's *Maslov* judgment, para 8.

[81] Maarten den Heijer, post entitled 'Juvenile offender must be reintegrated, not expelled', on Antoine Buyse's EHCR blog, dated 24 June 2008: <http://echrblog.blogspot.com/2008/06/grand-chamber-judgment-maslov-v-austria.html>, accessed 8 June 2014.

[82] Only *Üner* is included in Vincent Berger, *Jurisprudence de la Cour européenne des droits de l'homme* (Paris: Sirey, 2009). By contrast Foster 'An "Alien"' cites only *Maslov*. So did the 'factsheet' on 'expulsions and extraditions' produced by the Press Unit of the European Court of Human Rights dated June 2011 (section on Article 8, p. 8). The most recent factsheet on this topic, dated July 2013, refers to *Maslov* but not to *Üner*, with *Balogun* appearing as the example of a non-violation verdict: <http://www.echr.coe.int/Documents/FS_Expulsions_Extraditions_ENG.pdf>, accessed 9 June 2014.

[83] A HUDOC search completed on 15 March 2014 for judgments with the words 'Üner' and 'Maslov' produced nine verdicts of violation, including the following six: *Omojudi v. the United Kingdom*, appl. 1820/08, Judgment (ECtHR), 24 Nov. 2009 (unanimous), where the applicant was not a second-generation migrant but was married with relatively older children who could not be expected to relocate; *A. W. Khan v. the United Kingdom*, appl. 47486/06, Judgment (ECtHR), 12 Jan. 2010 (unanimous), where the government had submitted that 'the main focus of the applicant's private life was his mother and siblings and that there was no evidence to suggest he had any deeper ties within the community', thus leaving the applicant with no family life to protect under the Convention as the aforementioned were all adults and, apparently, had no private life worth mentioning either: paras 28 and 30 of the judgment; *Bousarra v. France*, appl. 25672/07, Judgment (ECtHR), 23 Dec. 2010 (unanimous), in French only; *Nunez*, cited in n 36 previously; *A.A. v. the United Kingdom*, appl. 8000/08, Judgment (ECtHR), 20 Sept. 2011 (unanimous), in English only, where the Court praised the applicant's 'commendable efforts to rehabilitate himself and to reintegrate into society' in the seven years since his release from prison: para 68; and *Udeh v. Switzerland*, appl. 12020/09, Judgment (ECtHR), 6 Apr. 2013 (five votes to two), where the applicant had committed the main offence after his children had been conceived, so that his wife, a Swiss national, could not have known about the offence when she entered into the family relationship. The last three violation verdicts, arguably more about residence permit refusals, are reviewed in Chapter 13.

on the Rights of the Child, in one case a Chamber judgment has stressed the negative effects on young children of their separation from their mother due to her expulsion—an argument which remains to be made in respect of a father.[84] Far more cases, however, have resulted in either a Chamber's decision of inadmissibility or a verdict of non-violation.[85] No doubt an even greater number of applications have been summarily declared inadmissible under *Üner*'s authority, and thus without leaving any trace whatsoever in the annals of the Court—given that case files are destroyed 12 months after the applicant is sent the letter informing him of a summary inadmissibility decision adopted by committees of three or, increasingly, single-judge formations. In conclusion, the idea that states can expel aliens has a much stronger hold on the Strasbourg case law than the wish to see migrants being treated like nationals whenever possible.

VII. The Strasbourg Reversal Takes Hold

There is only one way to justify the deportation of people who have lived all or most of their lives in the place from which they are removed, and that is to say that they are not nationals, so that the rule according to which a state does not deport its nationals does not apply to them. This statement is unimpeachable if

[84] *Nunez* judgment, para 84. The Court said that the interests of the children needed to be taken into consideration even if they were not applicants to the case.

[85] The HUDOC search mentioned in the penultimate note produced 25 non-violation verdicts/inadmissible decisions, as follows: *Joseph Grant v. the United Kingdom*, appl. 10606/07, Judgment (ECtHR), 8 Jan. 2009 (unanimous); *Onur v. the United Kingdom*, appl. 27319/07, Judgment (ECtHR), 17 Feb. 2009 (unanimous); *Ousman Mbengeh v. Finland*, appl. 43761/06, Decision (ECtHR), 24 Mar. 2009 (unanimous); *Esmail Narenji Haghighi v. the Netherlands*, appl. 38165/07, Decision (ECtHR), 14 Apr. 2009 (by majority); *Ayodji Yesufa v. the United Kingdom*, appl. 7347/08, Decision (ECtHR), 16 Jan. 2010 (unanimous); *Mutlag v. Germany*, appl. 40601/05, Judgment (ECtHR), 25 Mar. 2010 (unanimous); *Jahed Tofur Miah v. the United Kingdom*, appl. 53080/07, Decision (ECtHR), 27 Apr. 2010 (unanimous); *Ilirian Saliu v. France*, appl. 48878/09, Decision (ECtHR), 15 June 2010 (unanimous); *Anam v. the United Kingdom*, appl. 21783/08, Decision (ECtHR), 7 June 2011 (unanimous); *Lukic v. Germany*, appl. 25021/08, Decision (ECtHR), 20 Sept. 2011 (unanimous); *Trabelsi v. Germany*, appl. 41548, Judgment (ECtHR), 13 Oct. 2011 (unanimous); *A.H. Khan v. the United Kingdom*, appl. 622/10, Judgment (ECtHR), 20 Dec. 2011 (unanimous); *Kostadinovic v. Bulgaria*, appl. 4512/02, Decision (ECtHR), 4 Jan. 2012 (unanimous); *Balogun v. the United Kingdom*, Judgment (ECtHR), 10 Apr. 2012 (five votes to two); *Samsonnikov v. Estonia*, appl. 52178/10, Judgment (ECtHR), 3 July 2012 (five votes to two); *Abdi Ibrahim v. the United Kingdom*, appl. 14535/10, Decision (ECtHR), 18 Sept. 2012 (unanimous); *Onyejiekwe v. Austria*, appl. 20203/11, Decision (ECtHR), 9 Oct. 2012 (unanimous); *M.S. v. the United Kingdom*, appl. 56090/08, Decision (ECtHR), 16 Oct. 2012 (unanimous); *Cakir v. Romania*, appl. 13077/05, Decision (ECtHR), 13 Nov. 2012 (unanimous); *Kissiwa Koffi v. Switzerland*, appl. 38005/07, Judgment (ECtHR), 15 Nov. 2012 (five votes to two); *Shala v. Switzerland*, appl. 52873/09, Judgment (ECtHR), 15 Nov. 2012 (four votes to three); *El-Habach v. Germany*, appl. 66837/11, Decision (ECtHR), 22 Jan. 2013 (unanimous); *Shala v. Germany*, appl. 15620/09, Decision (ECtHR), 22 Jan. 2013 (unanimous); *Savasci v. Germany*, appl. 45971/08, Decision (ECtHR), 19 Mar. 2008 (unanimous); *Vasquez v. Switzerland*, appl. 1785/08, Judgment (ECtHR), 16 Nov. 2013 (six votes to one). See also *Gezginci v. Switzerland*, appl. 16327/05, Judgment (ECtHR), 9 Dec. 2010, in French only, concerning the expulsion of an irregular, very long-term, worker who was not a criminal, but became an invalid and thus dependent on social services, with a dissenting opinion by Judge Spielmann rallied by Judge Jebens.

one subscribes to this logic. It is indeed the logic which informs the reasoning of the Strasbourg Court, as this section will show.

In *Üner*, the Grand Chamber operated the Strasbourg reversal. The first point it made (after reporting the facts, the law, and the arguments of the parties) was the following:

> The Court reaffirms at the outset that a State is entitled, as a matter of international law and subject to its treaty obligations, to control the entry of aliens into its territory and their residence there [with *ABC* the first authority cited here]. The Convention does not guarantee the right of an alien to enter or to reside in a particular country and, in pursuance of maintaining public order, Contracting States have the power to expel an alien convicted of criminal offences. However, their decisions in this field must, in so far as they may interfere with a right protected under paragraph 1 of Article 8, be in accordance with the law and necessary in a democratic society, that is to say justified by a pressing social need and, in particular, proportionate to the legitimate aim pursued.[86]

Such phrasing subsequently appears in migrant case after migrant case, almost as a litany. A close reading of the case law nonetheless reveals that the reasoning of the Court has evolved over the years. Almost imperceptibly, the reasoning has affirmed more and more categorically the principle of state sovereignty. To start with, the Commission's argument was not emphatic at all. To quote one of its earliest decisions:

> The Commission has no doubt that in the present case the expulsion order adopted against the applicant falls within the category of the restrictions and limitations laid out in paragraph 2 of Article 8 ECHR; that, henceforth, no violation of this article can be found.[87]

By the 1980s, the Commission's language had changed significantly, but without yet mentioning states' powers. Returning to a decision referred to above:

> The Commission refers to its constant jurisprudence that there is no right to enter or reside in a particular country guaranteed as such by the Convention.... However, the Commission has also held that, in view of the right to respect for family life ensured by Article 8 the exclusion of a person from a country in which his close relatives reside may raise an issue under this provision of the Convention... [88]

As we have already seen in Chapter 4, the state controlling power was specifically mentioned in the *ABC* case, where the Court stated:

> [The Court] cannot ignore that the present case is concerned not only with family life but also with immigration and that, as a matter of well-established international law and subject to its treaty obligations, a State has the right to control the entry of non-nationals into its territory.[89]

[86] *Üner* GC judgment, para 54.

[87] *A. v. Belgium*, p. 4 of the document communicated by the Strasbourg Court's Archives Service (last paragraph before the operating part of the decision).

[88] *X.* decision, para 1.

[89] *Abdulaziz, Cabales and Balkandali v. the United Kingdom*, appls 9214/80, 9473/81, 9474/81, PC Judgment (ECtHR), 28 May 1985, para 67.

Yet in subsequent judgments, the upfront reference to family life generally disappears, with the consequence that the Court's reasoning starts with, and gives primacy to, the 'well-established principle of international law' according to which states can control the entry and residence of aliens. As already noted, this formulation relegates human rights as an exception which limits the principle of state sovereignty—instead of human rights being the overarching principle which is somewhat limited by state sovereignty.

In Chapter 4, we have seen that in the area of family reunification this reversal prevented the Court from developing a vision of migrants as human beings entitled to see their family join them where they live. In the area discussed in the present chapter, the reversal prevents the Court from approaching the phenomenon of expulsion as a dramatic measure which shatters the lives of the migrants it affects, so that it should only be allowed to happen in strictly defined circumstances—such as when the national security of the expelling state absolutely demands it.

This section would not give an accurate picture of the case law, however, if it were not stressing that the reference to the 'well-established' principle of state power to control immigration matters was nowhere to be seen in early verdicts of violation, including the *Berrehab* judgment. The more the Strasbourg reversal took hold, the more it would become expected to find a reference to the principle in any migrant ruling. However, in *Maslov*, it had disappeared from the Grand Chamber's judgment (but not the Chamber's one).[90] A remark Judge Tulkens made at the end of a public lecture she gave at the University of Sussex in 2010 suggests that its removal must be due to the strong determination on the part of some judges to resist the Court's reflex to 'cut-and-paste' from earlier case law as they draft new judgments. The result is a salutary move which allows the Court to start its reasoning from the idea that the expelled migrants are first of all human beings with human rights and, incidentally, legally aliens over whom the state has powers of exclusion when these remain acceptable under human rights principles.

VIII. Taking a Stance against Expulsion: A Series of Legal Tools which Remain Unused

Legally it would be entirely feasible for the Court to denounce the routine expulsion of settled migrants as an affront to human rights. In a review which does not seek to be exhaustive, this section identifies some legal avenues through which this could be achieved.

Convention concepts have long been recognised to be autonomous from the meaning attributed to them in the various states of the Council of Europe.[91] This principle has allowed the Court to refuse restrictive interpretations presented by

[90] *Maslov* judgment, para 33.

[91] Ever since *Engel and others v. the Netherlands*, appls 5100/71, 5101/71, 5102/71, 5354/72, 5370/72, PC Judgment (ECtHR), 8 June 1976.

the states of their obligations under the Convention in all kinds of areas.[92] With respect to the case law presently reviewed, it would not have been difficult at all, theoretically, to associate the long-term foreign resident with a national, who is by definition non-deportable. The Commission opened the way to doing so when it remarked in its report on the second case which came before the Court (*Beldjoudi v. France*, decided in 1992) that the applicant's 'nationality link [to Algeria], though a legal reality, in no way [reflected] the real situation in human terms'.[93] This observation implies that the applicant's real link was to the expelling state. Ten years before *Beldjoudi* was decided, the Secretary-General of the Council of Europe had already spoken up at the Funchal Colloquy for those 'who are regarded as "alien" without genuinely belonging to another community'. He had remarked: 'People talk about second and even third generation migrants—how many generations does it take to gain acceptance?'[94] No doubt it is the same reflection which motivated Judge Martens, in his dissenting opinion of 1996 to the *Boughanemi* judgment, where he called for protection against expulsion for 'integrated aliens', which he defined as 'aliens who have lived all, or practically all their lives within a state'.[95] Although the phrase 'integrated aliens' may not have been the most inspired choice to refer to people who are often talked about by reference to their 'integration' problems, the idea was clear. Judges Costa and Tulkens said of the applicant that he was 'virtually a French national' in their dissenting opinion to *Baghli v. France* in 1999. The idea is that the 'quasi-national', who has failed to become a national either because he or she did not accomplish the necessary formalities in good time or because of unduly restrictive nationality laws, should be treated as a national when it comes to expulsion. Had the political will been there, it would have been possible implicitly or explicitly to rely on the idea that European Convention concepts are autonomous to inscribe this principle within European human rights law. But the will within the European Court of Human Rights obviously was not there, at least not at sufficient level.

Interestingly, perhaps as a response to the Strasbourg's occasional verdicts of violation, some countries have adopted laws which do protect those I call 'quasi-nationals'. For example, the French Code on the entry and residence of aliens, amended in 2004, provides that the criminal penalty of interdiction to the French territory cannot be pronounced in respect of a foreigner to whom any of the following circumstances apply: arrival before the age of 12; 20-year residence; ten-year residence and a marriage, entered before the deportation sanction was pronounced, with a French national or an alien who has lived in France

[92] Valette '"Double peine"' 1111, is similarly grieved that the Court develops Article 8 obligations in other areas but not this one. She gives the example of the obligation for states to facilitate the establishment of paternity in *Mikulić v. Croatia*, appl. 53176/99, Judgment (ECtHR), 7 Feb. 2002.

[93] *Beldjoudi v. France*, appl. 12083/86, Report (EComHR), 6 Nov. 1990 (concluding on a violation), para 64.

[94] Directorate of Human Rights, Council of Europe, *Human Rights of Aliens in Europe. Proceedings of the Colloquy on 'Human Rights of Aliens in Europe'* (Dordrecht: Martinus Nijhoff, 1985) 25.

[95] Martens in *Boughanemi*.

since at least the age of 12; or ten-year residence and parenthood of a minor child with French nationality. By the time the Grand Chamber of the Strasbourg Court ruled on *Üner*, another seven European countries had adopted a legislative framework protecting second-generation immigrants against deportation on the basis of their criminal record or activities. They were, the Court noted, Austria, Belgium, Hungary, Iceland, Norway, Portugal, and Sweden.[96]

Either as cause or consequence, these developments are part of a wider European trend. In 2000, the Committee of Ministers of the Council of Europe adopted a recommendation on the non-expulsion of long-term immigrants. Admittedly non-binding, Recommendation (2000) 15 provides, inter alia, that '[a]fter twenty years of residence, a long-term immigrant should no longer be expellable' and that '[l]ong-term immigrants born on the territory of the member state or admitted to the member state before the age of ten, who have been lawfully and habitually resident, should not be expellable once they have reached the age of eighteen'.[97] The following year, the Parliamentary Assembly of the Council of Europe recommended that the Committee of Ministers invite the governments of member states 'to take the necessary steps to ensure that in the case of long-term migrants the sanction of expulsion is applied only to particularly serious offences affecting state security of which they have been found guilty' and 'to guarantee that migrants who were born or raised in the host country and their under-age children cannot be expelled under any circumstances'.[98]

It would have been open to the Court to rely upon this 'growing consensus' against the expulsion of long-established migrants to restrict the margin of appreciation it grants states in this area. The Court has resorted to this notion in the past in respect of sensitive and controversial issues such as recognition of the gender of transsexuals. But there was obviously no wish to do this here. Without specifically using the notion of the 'growing consensus', in *Üner*, Judges Costa, Zupančič, and Türmen nonetheless observed that they regretted that the Court had not drawn 'the correct inferences' from the aforementioned as well as other European and international texts which they listed. In their view, Article 8 ECHR would have been best construed in the light of these texts.[99]

Furthermore, an even more radical route offered itself to the Court, and this was to have said bluntly that expelling an alien following a criminal conviction is a discriminatory practice which, as such, can virtually never be justified.[100] (A real threat to national security could be an exception to this principle.) Given that such a conclusion has little chance of being followed at present, as a middle step towards it, the autonomy of Convention concepts could be relied upon to reject states' arguments that the expulsion is an administrative measure rather than a punishment. Were the expulsion recognised to be a punishment (which is what it feels like to those who are expelled and which is how it is openly discussed by

[96] *Üner* GC judgment, para 39. [97] Committee of Ministers Rec (2000) 15.
[98] PACE Recommendation 1504 (2001).
[99] Costa et al. in *Üner* GC judgment, para 9.
[100] Some applicants specifically tried this route, as we shall see in Chapter 8, Section VI.

some governments in domestic political debates), there should immediately arise a question of why the national is punished only once, but the person legally categorised as an alien twice. Article 14, which prohibits discrimination notably on grounds of nationality, could then be persuasively brought in. The end of the dissenting opinion in *Üner* points in this direction, while refraining, however, from specifically mentioning Article 14. To quote,

> [T]he only way in which the finding of a non-violation can possibly be justified [given that the application of virtually all the 'Boultif criteria' was favourable to the applicant] is by lending added weight to the nature and seriousness of the crime.... we believe a question of principle to be at stake, [namely] the discriminatory punishment imposed on a foreign national in addition to what would have been imposed on a national for the same offence.[101]

Over its long existence, the Strasbourg Court has equipped Convention law with a myriad of tools in order to pursue a human rights agenda. This obviously required legal imagination. However, it is difficult not to conclude that such imagination has been singularly lacking when it comes to counteracting the power to expel criminal migrants which states have arrogated themselves. This is something which the dissenting judges in *Üner* were very close to saying. To quote them again:

> True, the Convention is a living instrument which must be interpreted in the light of present-day conditions. But we would have liked to see this dynamic approach to case-law tending towards increased protection for foreign nationals (even criminals) rather than towards increased penalties which target them specifically.[102]

IX. The Elephant in the Room: Despicable Discrimination

The dissenters put their finger on it: deportation is an increased penalty which targets foreign nationals specifically. They did not add that this kind of penalty verges on being inhumane, by relegating those which the law characterises as 'aliens' outside the society to which, like it or not, they belong. The judges also did not hint at the racism which underlies deportation. This, of course, is not an aspect which is generally acknowledged. It cannot be, because racism today is officially unacceptable and therefore tends to be hidden from mainstream discourse. Every so often, however, it resurfaces, sometimes quite explicitly. To give an example, on 10 June 2011 the UK Human Rights blog reported a decision adopted by the Court of Appeal of England and Wales under the title 'When deporting foreign criminals is in the public interest'. This post attracted the following comment: 'European human rights are for Europeans, not sub-human crooks from lesser areas of the world. Send more back; this will make our country

[101] Costa et al. in *Üner* GC, paras 16 and 17.

[102] Costa et al., para 18.

worth living in again.'[103] A few hours later, this comment was deleted and replaced by another repeating the words of the Immigration Minister Damien Green, who had themselves been quoted in the UK blog's report:

> 'We will not accept foreign nationals.... [*sic*] breaking our laws. Those who commit serious offences should be removed at the earliest possible opportunity. We will do all we can to protect the public from those who abuse their right to be here.' HEAR, HEAR![104]

Obviously, the person who wrote both the deleted comment and the one which now remains on the blog felt that the words of the minister encapsulated their sentiments.

What is interesting, though, in the second sanitised passage is that it implicitly makes a distinction between those who 'abuse their right to be here' (the foreigners) and those who, however bad they behave, do not *as such* abuse their right to be here because their right to be here is absolute (the insiders with British citizenship, which gives them an inalienable right of abode). Even assuming that the distinction between insiders and outsiders morally holds, the problem remains as to how the recognition of being a member of the expelling community can be denied to people who have long resided in a particular place.

Early applicants used to complain of violations of Articles 3 and 14 of the Convention.[105] This line of argument having obviously no chance of succeeding, these complaints no longer tend to be made. However, it is instructive to examine how they were dismissed in the past. Regarding Article 3, prohibiting inhuman or degrading treatment, the Strasbourg Court rejected the claim in *Nasri v. France*, the second case which came before the Court about the expulsion of a second-generation migrant following criminal conviction (decided in 1995). The applicant in this case was a deaf-mute who had arrived in France aged four, was illiterate, and had never been taught sign language. His removal from France would have condemned him to a life where he had no chance of being understood through any form of language, his family being the only people who had developed a means of understanding him. The Court ruled that his deportation would violate Article 8 of the Convention. Only one dissenting judge (Judge de Meyer) found a violation of Article 3. If the Article 3 complaint failed in *Nasri*, with such extreme facts, a wider attempt to argue that the expulsion is discriminatory and as such inhuman and degrading, would obviously fail too. Commentators have observed that the Court would clearly have wished to stay away from a ruling on Article 3 because it entails an *absolute* prohibition rather than being amenable to

[103] This comment was posted at 9:47 am on 10 June 2011. It disappeared later during the course of that day.

[104] <http://ukhumanrightsblog.com/2011/06/10/when-deporting-foreign-is-in-the-public-interest/>, accessed 19 July 2011.

[105] As well as of Articles 7 and 13 ECHR. See e.g. applicant's claims to the Commission (not the Court) in *Moustaquim*. For an interesting and inspired judgment in a different jurisdiction (the United States) which found an expulsion to be contrary to right after right, though these findings were admittedly reversed on appeal, see: *Beharry v. Reno*, 183 F. Supp. at 603, cited (disapprovingly) in Rodriguez 'Exile'.

a proportionality test like Article 8.[106] This may well be true, but the blank refusal ever to consider that Article 3 is violated when a migrant is 'removed' from the place where his life has developed is hardly a victory for human rights.

The Court has also invariably dismissed any claim related to Article 14. Taking the *Moustaquim* judgment of 1991 as an example:

> Mr. Moustaquim claimed to be the victim of discrimination on the ground of nationality, contrary to Article 14 taken together with Article 8, *vis-à-vis* juvenile delinquents of two categories: those who possessed Belgian nationality, since they could not be deported; and those who were citizens of another member-State of the European Communities, as a criminal conviction was not sufficient to render them liable to deportation.
>
> The Government made no observations on the matter [presumably indicating that the government did not think that this argument had any possibility of success].[107]
>
> Like the Commission, the Court would reiterate that Article 14 safeguards individuals placed in similar situations from any discriminatory differences of treatment in the enjoyment of the rights and freedoms recognised in the Convention and its Protocols.
>
> In the instant case the applicant cannot be compared to Belgian juvenile delinquents. The latter have a right of abode in their own country and cannot be expelled from it; this is confirmed by Article 3 of Protocol No. 4.
>
> As for the preferential treatment given to nationals of the other member-States of the Communities, there is objective and reasonable justification for it as Belgium belongs, together with those States, to a special legal order.
>
> There has accordingly been no breach of Article 14 taken together with Article 8.[108]

Applicants before the allegedly more progressive Commission had also vainly invoked Article 14. For example, a petition declared inadmissible—one might say as a result of the lottery identified by Judge Martens—seven months after the *Moustaquim* judgment, had argued:

> The applicant submits that the Home Secretary's decision amounts to an additional and drastic punitive action, only possible because of the applicant's financial inability to afford naturalisation in 1981 [when he had applied for British citizenship but not proceeded with his application, due to the cost involved of £250, a sum which he did not then possess]. The order to deport amounts to a discriminatory difference in treatment between the applicant and his co-defendants [all convicted of having imported a Class A controlled drug]. It also amounts to a discriminatory difference in treatment between the applicant and his brother, who is imprisoned for a similar offence, but who cannot be deported because he possesses British nationality.[109]

The Commission did not directly address these points and instead replied that:

> [T]here is no evidence in the case-file to substantiate the applicant's claim that the non-British co-accused in his case do not, or will not, also face deportation in family circumstances comparable to his.[110]

[106] Labayle 'L'article 8' 96, note 1.

[107] *Moustaquim* judgment, para 48.

[108] *Moustaquim*, para 49, reference omitted.

[109] *Patel v. the United Kingdom*, appl. 16009/90, Decision (EComHR), 6 Sept. 1991, p. 5 of 7.

[110] Patel, p. 7 of 7.

The fundamental problem with this type of reasoning is that it takes for granted that nationality is an objective ground of distinction, without questioning whether the criteria for bestowing (and, as a result, withholding) nationality are legitimate, as already noted in Chapter 5. In all these cases, nowhere do the Strasbourg institutions ask themselves—and the respondent state—why an applicant has not become a national of his country of residence, even though his remaining legally alien is what makes his deportation possible.

Sociologically it can be seen that nationality is a constructed concept rather than an objective fact. Going further, as I have argued elsewhere, one can say that nationality is a 'legal fiction' which does not tell 'the truth', but must be associated with mystification, deception, and even lies. It obliterates the similarity, if not the identical nature, of two situations by suggesting that there are different 'kinds' of people (e.g. a French man is not an Algerian man), thereby justifying that one cannot be deported whilst the other can. Only language is responsible for this difference. It is the legal fiction which creates a difference where there is a factual similarity: 'a man is a man is a man'. From this perspective, the chief function of nationality is to mask discrimination.[111]

When I originally submitted the paper where I made this argument to a prestigious scholarly journal, publication was refused on the grounds that it offered 'very little reasoning of any utility to the Strasbourg judges', given that 'citizenship and nationality remain valid concepts for the great majority of people'. The point of the article, however, was precisely to raise the idea that we should all stop taking nationality as a neutral concept. Since then, the Open Borders movement has grown. So far, it remains unlikely, however, that the European Court would be ready to take a lead in going against the grain of the current received wisdom and to point out that the current justification according to which the deportation of convicted foreigners is for 'the public good' may constitute a mystifying distortion of its real rationale.[112]

X. Conclusion

Despite numerous applications by migrants who were complaining that their actual or threatened deportation was in breach of Article 8 ECHR, it took 30 years for a case, *Berrehab v. the Netherlands*, to be thought by the European Commission of Human Rights and ruled by the European Court of Human Rights to reveal such a violation. Three decades is a long time. Admittedly, in their early years the Strasbourg institutions had avoided formally declaring states in violation of the Convention, as they were acutely aware that states still had to be persuaded either to become or to remain full participants in the system

[111] Dembour 'Human Rights Law' 93–94.

[112] Apart from the fundamental problem of inequality, there is also the question of whether deportations are not sometimes counterproductive, feeding into a climate where extremely confrontational attitudes are already divisive and resulting in wars and terrorism.

by accepting the jurisdiction of the Court and the right of individual petition. Nonetheless, this started to change in the mid-1970s across a number of various issues. It took almost another two decades for a similar development to take place in respect of immigration issues.

One might suggest that this is because the text of the Convention bestowed no rights on the immigrant *qua* immigrant. In other areas, however, the absence of clear provisions did not prevent the Commission and the Court from developing Convention law in remarkable ways. The real reason why the Strasbourg institutions refrained for an unusually long time to find violations of the Convention in migrant cases is most probably because a majority of commissioners and judges shared the general reticence in European society to regard aliens as endowed with the same human rights as citizens—which of course also explains why the Convention did not speak of asylum or of guarantees against arbitrary expulsion in the first place.

When the case law did start to develop, it did so from the premise that states are entitled to control the entry and residence of aliens. Human rights came to be seen as if they were moderating this principle, rather than the other way around. This logic does not favour the human rights of migrants. Instead of starting with the principle that migrants are human beings entitled to their Article 8 rights, the most common Strasbourg reasoning regards Article 8 rights as potentially limiting the sovereign discretion which the state enjoys of whether or not to grant aliens access to its territory. Inevitably, this goes hand-in-hand with a casuistic approach. To this day, the Court weighs the various circumstances of each case rather than making statements of principles. In turn, its case law is highly unpredictable, as it is never clear in advance how the various elements presenting themselves in any one given case will be 'weighted'.[113]

The Court's reluctance over the last 30 years to develop a principled approach in regard to the expulsion of foreign nationals with criminal convictions has had disastrous consequences. It does not take much imagination to realise that the lives of the individuals concerned are gravely affected after their removal from the place where they have built their lives. It is also important to think beyond the applicants who have come before the Court. Thinking beyond the specific issue of whether or not the deportation of a non-citizen violates his Article 8 rights, it is also in terms of the unchecked development by states of increasingly inhumane deportation policies and practices that the absence of a principled approach by the Court has been, from a human rights perspective, catastrophic.

The question arises as to how something as inhumane as the 'removal' of someone from where his family and social links are, can be found acceptable in the absence of an extreme circumstance such as a proven threat to national security. The answer is found in nationality laws, which are extremely useful in this respect as they make a distinction, generally regarded as entirely legitimate, between insiders and outsiders. This chapter, by contrast, has suggested that nationality

[113] A similar conclusion applies in respect of the case law related to the refusal of a residence permit, examined in Chapter 13.

laws may well come to be regarded at some time in the future as having caused illegitimate discrimination, by providing a logically highly questionable legitimacy to the idea that some people can be forcibly removed, however comparable their offending behaviour is to that of those who are legally granted the privilege to remain.

On the positive side, it is comforting that, despite the overall tendency for the Strasbourg Court to give precedence to the principle of state sovereignty over that of human equality, the Court has not spoken with one voice on this issue. Some Strasbourg judges have always argued that long-term migrants needed to be treated, as far as possible, like nationals. Occasionally they have even persuaded their colleagues to vote with them for a verdict of violation. This is a feature of the case law which is encouraging, showing as it does that the ideal of equality will not be easily defeated.

7

The Sleeping Beauty Awakens Late: An Absolute Prohibition with Many Buts

(Around *Soering*)

In his well-researched and elegantly written book, *The Evolution of the European Convention on Human Rights*, Ed Bates explains how the Convention remained dormant until the mid-1970s. He recalls that a member (and later Vice-President) of the European Commission of Human Rights referred to the first quarter century of the system as the Convention's 'sleeping beauty' years,[1] an image prompted by the fact that up to 1974 the European Court of Human Rights had delivered rulings in only nine cases on the merits, with four of those concerning pre-trial detention;[2] shortly afterwards, the Court began to pass judgments of critical importance, such as *Tyrer v. the United Kingdom, Marckx v. Belgium*, and *Airey v. Ireland*.[3] The result is that the late 1970s are rightly remembered as the period when the Convention's potential started to be duly appreciated and actively used.[4] Without disputing this story, this book adds another layer to it, which is that it took another decade before the sleeping beauty opened its eyes to the human rights of migrants. However, this was not a decisive awakening: in the area of migrant rights, the beauty was prone to fall back to sleep.

Soering v. United Kingdom,[5] upon which this chapter focuses, undoubtedly constituted a moment of startled awakening and great promise for migrants' rights. Delivered in 1989 by the European Court of Human Rights sitting in its plenary formation, *Soering* affirmed the obligation under Article 3 ECHR for a contracting state not to send a person to a place where this person might be subjected to

[1] Ed Bates, *The Evolution of the European Convention on Human Rights: From its Inception to the Creation of a Permanent Court of Human Rights* (Oxford: Oxford University Press, 2010) 10 and 257 (quoting Jochen Frowein).

[2] Bates 257.

[3] *Tyrer v. the United Kingdom*, appl. 5856/72, Judgment (ECtHR), 25 Apr. 1978; *Marckx v. Belgium*, appl. 6833/74, PC Judgment (ECtHR), 13 June 1979; *Airey v. Ireland*, appl. 6289/73, Judgment (ECtHR), 9 Oct. 1979.

[4] This timing is not coincidental. See Samuel Moyn, *The Last Utopia: Human Rights in History* (Cambridge, Mass.: University of Harvard Press, 2010); Jan Eckel and Samuel Moyn (eds) *The Breakthrough: Human Rights in the 1970s* (Philadelphia: University of Pennsylvania Press, 2014).

[5] *Soering v. the United Kingdom*, appl. 14038/88, PC Judgment (ECtHR), 7 July 1989.

torture or inhuman or degrading treatment or punishment. The case concerned an extradition request to the UK: the applicant, a young German national, was sought by the State of Virginia in the United States to be put on trial for murder. The European Court ruled that there was a real risk that the applicant would be sentenced to death, which at the time the Court found was not objectionable as such under the European Convention, but would involve the applicant being subjected to the 'death-row phenomenon', which the Court found would most likely constitute inhuman and degrading treatment in the particular circumstances of the case. This led the Court to rule that for the UK to extradite the applicant to the State of Virginia would entail a violation of Article 3 of the Convention.

It was immediately clear that this ruling could be of enormous import beyond extradition cases. If the Court so wished, on the basis of the principle established in *Soering*, it could prevent the return of failed asylum seekers and other migrants (e.g. recognised refugees threatened with expulsion following criminal conviction) to places where they might be at risk of encountering conditions proscribed by Article 3. Indeed, in time, this is exactly what happened. However, what is striking is the slow pace at which this evolution took place and the Court's continued reluctance to this day to find violations of the Convention in what I call 'Article 3 return cases'.

This chapter studies in detail the early case law in this area in order to understand why this development was so slow and timid. It identifies the ideas which allowed the Commission and the Court to turn down the majority of cases which came before them. These ideas were like seeds. Once they had germinated and given way to full-blown principles, alternative ways of approaching the issues brought by applicants facing return would be less likely to take root. As a result, the early pronouncements of the Strasbourg institutions actually continue to bear a preponderant influence on the voluminous 'post-*Soering*' case law which the Court has been producing in the last ten years or so. The main argument of this chapter is that these jurisprudential seeds were favourable to the state, and that today they still put the applicant at a relative disadvantage.

The reader may be surprised by the perspective developed in this chapter, given that Article 3 famously lays down an *absolute* prohibition: the resort by the state to torture or ill-treatment is *never* condoned in the European human rights system. The Court has affirmed and reaffirmed that a state can *never* return a person to torture or ill-treatment—even if this person is a suspected or convicted terrorist. The significance of this strong position is of course of tremendous import, as this chapter will acknowledge. It remains, however, that the great majority of applicants in Article 3 return cases lose their fight against expulsion. This is in a context where European states have not stopped, from the 1980s onwards, making it ever more difficult for asylum to be claimed in Europe, in a process which has been, if not positively encouraged, at least not actively discouraged by the European Union through directives, regulations, and other legislative and policy measures. The number of 'removals' has dramatically increased—and the more migrants have been threatened with expulsion, the more migrant cases have reached Strasbourg. And the European Court of Human Rights has not been keen to find violations of the Convention. To give just one statistic in this introduction, by 2000, the Court had adopted no more than three verdicts of violation in Article 3 return cases,[6] even though hundreds of applicants had been knocking on the doors of Strasbourg with this type of complaint.

A close study of the case law makes it possible to understand the formal legal reasons which explain why so few cases have succeeded, bringing us back to the principles developed by the Commission and the Court in the early years of the system. Admittedly, some of these principles have been altered over the years, as will also be documented in this chapter. My suspicion is that these alterations will have been called for by judges who were not satisfied with the results which the case law was producing for the majority of applicants in Article 3 return cases. The previous chapter has already introduced the idea that there exists an undercurrent within the Court which has always wanted and continues to want to restrain the possibility of states deporting 'quasi-national' migrants to their state of formal nationality after they have served a prison sentence. In the same way, I expect that the Court has always comprised judges concerned about the way failed asylum seekers and other migrants were allowed to be deported to a country where they were saying that they were at risk of ill-treatment proscribed by Article 3. Nonetheless, this study demonstrates that there has been relatively little will amongst the body of the European Court of Human Rights to alleviate the predicament of those who increasingly became 'failed' asylum seekers. Of course, there have been exceptions. (Amongst these, the resounding example of *M.S.S. v. Belgium and Greece*[7] is discussed in Chapter 12.)

The present chapter reviews the Strasbourg case law in Article 3 return cases in order to demonstrate its limitations.[8] As in other chapters, it starts by paying attention to decisions by the former Commission. It then attempts to explore why *Soering*, lodged by a young white European and concerning an extradition to the United States, became the leading case, while other applications, for example from rejected asylum seekers from Sri Lanka, might have appeared at first sight to be as, or even more, promising. To do this, the chapter reviews in detail early cases which failed to lead to a violation of the Convention, especially *Cruz Varas v. Sweden* and *Vilvarajah v. the United Kingdom*.[9] This study leads to the identification of a number of jurisprudential seeds which have typically worked in favour of the state and against the applicant. The following elements are identified: the Court commonly doubts the credibility of the applicant;

[6] See Table 7. 1 below (p. 235). See in addition. *D. v. the United Kingdom*, appl. 30240/96, Judgment (ECtHR), 2 May 1997, which concerned an expulsion to a lack of medical care, should be added to this list, however.

[7] *M.S.S. v. Belgium and Greece*, appl. 30696/09, GC Judgment (ECtHR), 21 Jan. 2011.

[8] For a legal account which makes it clear how this case law fits with other international and European mechanisms, see: Jeremy McBride, *Access to Justice for Migrants and Asylum Seekers in Europe* (Strasbourg: Council of Europe, 2009). For a more conventional account of the Strasbourg case law in this area, see: Nuala Mole, *Asylum and the European Convention on Human Rights* (Strasbourg: Council of Europe, 2010).

[9] *Cruz Varas and Others v. Sweden*, appl. 15576/89, PC Judgment (ECtHR), 20 Mar. 1991; *Vilvarajah and Others v. the United Kingdom*, appls 13163/87, 13164/87, 13165/87, 13447/87, 13448/87, Judgment (ECtHR), 30 Oct. 1991.

tends to accept wholesale the story told by the state; is disinclined to scrutinise national asylum determination procedures; accepts evidence up to the moment of the judgment; initially refrained from declaring binding its interim measures towards a stay of expulsion; and has adopted an unduly restrictive view of the notion of 'inhuman or degrading treatment' contained in Article 3, including insisting that, in situations of general conflict, the individual returned must be personally at risk of injury. The chapter goes on to remark that it would have been entirely possible, from a legal perspective, to adopt alternative, pro-migrant, positions on all these points. This not having been the case, it becomes entirely understandable that by the end of 2000 the Court had adopted only three verdicts of violation in cases lodged by asylum seekers. The chapter continues by observing that, however limited its record, the Court must nonetheless be praised for having steadfastly affirmed the principle that a return to serious ill-treatment is prohibited, whatever the circumstances, including when national security considerations are involved. The chapter's final note is less positive and highlights areas where human rights standards could usefully have been developed through an expanding case law, had the Court played a more active role in stemming the political tide against asylum seekers and other migrants which has engulfed Europe since the 1980s.

I. Who Remembers *KCL*? The European Commission's Unpromising Case Law

The aim of this chapter is to highlight the long-standing premises upon which the case law concerning Article 3 return cases have been built, almost inadvertently, i.e. without commentators necessarily noting these premises. It therefore makes sense not to start with the leading cases before the Court, which are always cited, but rather with their little-known antecedents before the Commission.

A cursory survey of the case law of the European Commission of Human Rights regarding claims made by aliens under Article 3 against either expulsion or extradition suggests that trends identified in previous chapters about the Commission's migrant case law apply here too. Two points in particular are striking. The first is that, right from the early days of the system, applicants came forward with applications to the Commission requesting that the compatibility of a forced return with Article 3 be checked. The second is that the Commission was extremely reluctant to find that the Convention had been violated in such cases.

A search on HUDOC for decisions of the Commission in English related to 'Article 3' and containing the word 'asylum' up to July 1989 (the month of the Court's judgment in *Soering*) produces 50 results. Of these 50 cases, a mere five were declared admissible (including the well-known *Vilvarajah and Others v. the United Kingdom* case, reviewed later in this chapter). Three further cases were struck out. The remaining 42 were declared inadmissible. Inevitably, more cases must have met this fate as some decisions would have been in French only; some relevant decisions would not have appeared in the search because they would not have contained the exact word 'asylum'; others would never have been entered into the HUDOC database; and most importantly many complaints would have been summarily declared inadmissible by committees of three Commission members.[10] What these imperfect statistics indicate is that the Commission had dealt with dozens if not hundreds of cases raising a point not wholly dissimilar to *Soering* and especially *Vilvarajah* by the time the Court had decided its first leading case in this area.

The first case in this sample was lodged in 1961. It was again directed against Belgium (the respondent state in other 'first' cases discussed in previous chapters). The applicant, originally from Hungary, said he was a recognised refugee under the 1951 Convention relating to the Status of Refugees. Belgium had given him 30 days to leave the territory. The Commission's decision on (in)admissibility does not record the motivation for this order, but the statement that he would have represented a threat to public order suggests that he might have been a presumed or convicted criminal. Why the applicant thought that his expulsion would contravene Article 3 is not completely clear either. A surgical operation preventing travel is mentioned, as well as a withdrawal by the Belgian authorities of his identity card, leaving him unable to work and to establish himself in another country. The Commission considered that the applicant was essentially requesting the right to live in Belgium. It noted that a right of residence for aliens was not inscribed in the Convention. It then added:

> Considering, nonetheless, that the application appears to raise the question of whether the expulsion of an alien can, in certain exceptional conditions, constitute inhuman and degrading treatment under Article 3 of the Convention; it is however not necessary to examine this question in this case [given that the applicant] cannot reasonably submit that he is a victim of a treatment contrary to Article 3 as, per the information he himself provided to the Commission, his expulsion has not yet taken place.[11]

The Commission declared the application inadmissible on 29 May 1961. The seed of a potential violation of Article 3 in a return case was nonetheless already planted. Admittedly this early interpretation required the applicant to have actually been removed and to have already suffered the treatment contrary to Article 3 for a claim to be arguable. By the time *Soering* was decided, it was settled that a risk which would materialise in the future could also be considered to infringe Article 3.[12]

The *Amekrane v. the United Kingdom* case would have highlighted the merits of this new interpretation. The case was lodged with the Commission in December

[10] Admittedly, some decisions which appeared in the search I made on HUDOC may not be relevant to the present discussion. This need not concern us as far more decisions would not have appeared which would have been relevant.

[11] *JP v. Belgium*, appl. 984/61, Decision (ECtHR), 29 May 1961, in French only.

[12] Marc Bossuyt has long been, and remains, fiercely opposed to this case law, which he regards as unduly activist. See e.g. amongst his many writings, 'The Court of Strasbourg Acting as an Asylum Court' (2012) *European Constitutional Law Review* 8, 203–245.

1972, by Mr Amekrane's widow (who was a German citizen).[13] Mr Amekrane, a Lieutenant Colonel in the Moroccan Air Force, had been involved in a putsch aimed at deposing the Moroccan king. When the putsch failed on 16 August 1972, Mr Amekrane went to Gibraltar where he requested that the British authorities grant him political asylum. He was, however, taken into custody instead and sent back to Morocco on 17 August 1972, where he was condemned to death and then executed by a firing squad the following January. The Commission declared the complaint admissible nine months later. In July 1974, it recorded that a friendly settlement had been reached which involved the payment of a sum of money—without, however, the British government officially admitting that the Convention had been violated in this case.[14] This is probably the Commission's best-known Article 3 return case.

A few other applicants also benefited from having gone before the Commission. For example, a national from Hong Kong married to a Dutch national was arrested in January 1979 with half a kilo of heroin in his possession. Convicted for drug offences, K.C.L., as he appears in the Commission's decision, was sentenced to four years' imprisonment in the Netherlands. His residence permit, which happened to expire two months after his arrest, was not renewed, and he was to be deported to Hong Kong. He claimed at Strasbourg that his deportation would contravene Article 3 ECHR because it would expose him to serious reprisals (varying from being killed to being shot in the knee) for his actions as an informant to the Amsterdam police. The Commission gave notice of the case to the respondent government on 12 October 1981. One month later, the Agent of the Government informed the Commission that 'on account of and for the duration of his marriage to a Dutch woman, [the applicant] is entitled to remain in the Netherlands for an indefinite period'. The Commission struck the application out of its list of cases.[15]

This decision is not as straightforward as may first appear, for the Commission could have chosen to carry on with the examination of the case. This is what it did in *Tyrer v. the United Kingdom*. In this case, on attaining 'full age', the applicant withdrew his application concerning the corporal punishment he had received in the Isle of Man following an incident at school. His request that the Strasbourg proceedings be abandoned was rejected by the Commission in view of the 'general questions' which the case raised.[16] *Tyrer*, decided by the Court in April 1978, is now considered one of the leading Strasbourg judgments. Had there been the will, the unknown *K.C.L.* case might have become a leading case too. The numerous Article 3 return cases lodged at Strasbourg throughout and beyond the years of the Commission belie its statement according to which the *K.C.L.* application failed to raise issues 'of a general character affecting the observance of the Convention'.

[13] See the discussion of *Berrehab v. the Netherlands*, appl. 10730/84, Judgment (ECtHR), 21 June 1988, in Chapter 6 p. 171 on the possible significance of his wife's nationality.

[14] *Amekrane v. the United Kingdom*, appl. 5961/72, PCom Report, 19 July 1974.

[15] *K.C.L. v. the Netherlands*, appl. 9538/81, Decision (EComHR), 17 Dec. 1981, Doc. E 53.050 06.2 communicated to the author by the Strasbourg Court's Archives service.

[16] *Tyrer* judgment, para 24.

On the contrary, it clearly raised issues of tremendous implications. These issues were also controversial. It is difficult not to think that the Commission delayed the need to determine them for as long as it could.

The least one can say is that the sleeping beauty which was the Convention system kept its eyes resolutely closed in regard to migrant issues far longer than it did in other areas. For a long time, the Commission refused to be persuaded to hold an applicant' claim that her actual or threatened expulsion entailed a risk of treatment contrary to Article 3. It is only in *Nasri v. France*,[17] decided five years after the Court's judgment in *Soering*, that the Commission found for the very first time, in 1994, a violation of Article 3 in a return case. (In *Soering*, five members of the Commission thought that the extradition of the applicant would contravene Article 3, but a majority of six did not.) Interestingly, Mr Nasri was not an asylum seeker, but a second-generation migrant (as discussed in Chapter 6). The fact that he was a deaf-mute is what made his deportation after his conviction for a gang rape controversial in respect not only of Article 8 but also of Article 3 in the opinion of the Commission (but not the Court). Asylum seekers and refugees arguing that their return would expose them to treatment contrary to Article 3 would have to wait even longer before finding protection under the Convention.

II. *Soering*: The Court Finally Steps In

A case was eventually fast-tracked (to use today's language) through the various stages of the Strasbourg proceedings in 1988 to 1989. This was *Soering v. the United Kingdom*, which would see the Court establish the principle that a state cannot send an individual to another state where that individual faces a real risk of ill-treatment contrary to Article 3. The applicant in *Soering* was not an asylum seeker coming from a troubled region of the world or a second-generation migrant whose parents had sought to improve their economic lot in Europe; he was a young German national who, in an alleged episode of '*folie à deux*', had killed the parents of his girlfriend in Virginia, United States. The State of Virginia requested his extradition from the UK, where he had fled. Mr Soering claimed at Strasbourg that if the British authorities were to extradite him, they would act in a way contrary to Article 3 by exposing him to the risk of having to endure the 'death-row phenomenon', which he deemed to be 'inhuman and degrading treatment'. He filed his application with the Commission in July 1988. The case was communicated to the British government one month later, and on the same day, the President of the Commission indicated to the UK that it was desirable for the applicant not to be extradited until his case had been examined. The case proceeded in record time: it was declared admissible in November 1988, the Commission adopted its report on the merits two months later, and the Plenary Court (to which the Chamber had relinquished jurisdiction immediately after

[17] *Nasri v. France*, appl. 19465/92, Judgment (ECtHR), 13 July 1995.

being assigned the case) rendered its judgment on 7 July 1989, just one year after Mr Soering had first contacted Strasbourg.

The fast-tracking of the case suggests that the Strasbourg institutions had been very keen to have the point of principle on the compatibility or otherwise of an individual's forced return to a place where she might suffer inhuman and degrading treatment legally determined. Lawyers often comment that the 'perfect' case to establish a particular legal point never comes along. Something in the circumstances of real cases is always wrong. Inevitably, a case is selected which is not ideal but which is hopefully good enough to make the point. In at least three respects, *Soering* might have appeared as unpromising in seeking to persuade the Strasbourg Court to extend the application of Article 3. First, it concerned an extradition process benefiting from judicial guarantees rather than a removal summarily decided by administrative authorities. Second, it seemed to put into question the quality of the penal process of no less an ally than the United States. Third, it turned around the application of a criminal sanction, the death penalty, which is explicitly allowed for in Article 2 ECHR and thus apparently legitimate under the Convention (despite a subsequent Protocol to the Convention which requires its abolition in peace time).

By the time *Soering* came along, the Commission had long been asserting that 'if conditions are such that there exists a serious risk of treatment in breach of Article 3, the deportation or extradition of an individual to face such conditions incurs the responsibility...of the Contracting State'. It thus reiterated this principle in its report on *Soering*.[18] Following its previous practice, the Commission also went on to find that in the particularly circumstances of this case, the applicant did not face such a risk. In this regard, the Commission noted that 'the death penalty scheme in Virginia [contained] numerous safeguards against arbitrariness' so that there was 'no indication that the machinery of justice to which the applicant would be subjected [was] an arbitrary or unreasonable one'.[19] This finding, however, was adopted by a very close majority of six votes to five.

The British government itself referred the case to the Court.[20] Presumably it did so in the hope of seeing the Commission's perspective overturned and of winning the case not only on its facts but also on the legal principle. The government argued that interpreting Article 3 so as to impose responsibility on a contracting state for acts which would occur later and outside its own jurisdiction would strain its language intolerably.[21] The judges failed to be convinced. In vain, the government also highlighted the dangers of an extension of Article 3, which would lead to international agreements (on extradition) being interfered with; alien systems of law and conditions existing in foreign states having to be evaluated; and criminals left untried, at large, and unpunished.[22]

[18] *Soering v. the United Kingdom*, appl. 14038/88, Report (EComHR), 19 Jan. 1989, para 98.
[19] *Soering* report, para 151.
[20] As did the Commission.
[21] *Soering* judgment, para 83.
[22] *Soering*, para 83.

Reasoning in a principled way and building on previous pronouncements,[23] the Court stated:

> Article 3 makes no provision for exceptions and no derogation from it is permissible under Article 15 in time of war or other national emergency. This absolute prohibition of torture and of inhuman or degrading treatment or punishment under the terms of the Convention shows that Article 3 enshrines one of the fundamental values of the democratic societies making up the Council of Europe... It would hardly be compatible with the underlying values of the Convention... were a Contracting State knowingly to surrender a fugitive to another State where there were substantial grounds for believing that he would be in danger of being subjected to torture, however heinous the crime allegedly committed. [In] the Court's view this inherent obligation not to extradite also extends to cases in which the fugitive would be faced in the receiving State by a real risk of exposure to inhuman or degrading treatment or punishment proscribed by [Article 3].[24]

Such endorsement of the possible responsibility of a contracting state for treatment meted out by another government ensured that *Soering* would take its place among the leading cases of the European Court of Human Rights. To this day *Soering* remains a founding authority and inescapable reference.

Having set the principle, the Court still had to decide whether in the particular circumstances of the *Soering* case the extradition of the applicant would *actually* constitute a violation of Article 3. The Court started its reasoning on this point with the by then already established principle that '[w]hat amounts to "inhuman or degrading treatment or punishment" depends on all the circumstances of the case'.[25] The Court formed the view that, in the particular case of *Soering*:

> having regard to the very long period of time spent on death row in... extreme conditions, with the ever present and mounting anguish of awaiting execution of the death

[23] *Soering*, para 87, started by stating: 'In interpreting the Convention regard must be had for its special character as a treaty for the collective enforcement of human rights and fundamental freedoms.... Thus, the object and purpose of the Convention as an instrument for the protection of individual human beings require that its provisions be interpreted and applied so as to make its safeguards practical and effective'. Lawyers familiar with the European Convention will recognise this language for having been introduced in the crucial judgments of the late 1970s.

[24] *Soering* judgment, paras 87 and 88.

[25] *Soering*, para 89. Some commentators have objected that the assessment of an absolute prohibition should never be allowed to be relative. I personally side with the Court on this point. The prohibition laid out in Article 3 ECHR is absolute. This means that treatment contrary to it can never be condoned for any reason—including national security. However, whether such treatment in fact exists is an assessment which is relative, depending as it does on taking into consideration many various factors—including, e.g., the age of the alleged victim. Few would dispute that it is *always* inhuman to confine for long hours, let alone days, a young child in a small cell with barely any human contact; it may not always be inhuman, however, for an adult to be subjected to this treatment. For a more elaborate discussion of the meaning of, and relationship between, the adjectives 'absolute' and 'relative', see: Marie-Bénédicte Dembour, *Who Believes in Human Rights? Reflections on the European Convention* (Cambridge: Cambridge University Press, 2006) Chapter 4. Natasa Mavronicola states it very well in: Mavronicola, 'What is an "Absolute Right"? Deciphering Absoluteness in the Context of Article 3 of the European Convention on Human Rights' (2012) *Human Rights Law Review* 12, 723–758.

penalty, and to the personal circumstances of the applicant, especially his age [he was not 18 at the time of the crime] and mental state at the time of the offence [a possible episode of '*folie à deux*'], the applicant's extradition to the United States would expose him to a real risk of treatment going beyond the threshold set by Article 3. A further consideration of relevance is that in the particular instance the legitimate purpose of extradition [punishing a crime] could be achieved by another means [extradition to and trial in Germany] which would not involve suffering of such exceptional intensity or duration.[26]

In other words, even though Mr Soering could not be extradited to the United States without this violating Article 3 ECHR, it was entirely possible that the extradition of another fugitive to the same place would not contravene Article 3—as happened recently when the Court controversially allowed the deportation of six suspected Islamic terrorists from the UK to the United States.[27]

It is important to stress that in *Soering* the unanimous Court was at pains to emphasise that its 'finding in no way [put] in question the good faith of the United Kingdom Government' which had refrained from extraditing the applicant all through the Strasbourg proceedings, in accordance with the interim measures indicated by the Commission and the Court, and which had referred the case to the Court.[28] Earlier in the judgment, the Court had also endorsed the positive comments of the Commission on the guarantees which the criminal justice process of the United States.[29] It nonetheless rejected the value of the assurance which the United Kingdom had received from the Virginian authorities. The question of the value to attribute to a memorandum of understanding between a Convention's member state and a state which does not enjoy a good record in refraining from practising torture of course has since been hotly debated at Strasbourg—with the case of *Othman (Abu Qatada) v. the United Kingdom* long proving particularly controversial in the UK.[30]

In the *Soering* case, the assurance was worded as follows: '[S]hould Jens Soering be convicted of capital murder as charged . . . a representation will be made in the name of the United Kingdom to the judge at the time of sentencing that it is the wish of the United Kingdom that the death penalty should not be imposed or carried out'.[31] The British government explained that it would

[26] *Soering* judgment, para 111.

[27] *Babar Ahmad and Others v. the United Kingdom*, appls 24027/07, 11949/08, 36742/08, 66911/09, 67354/09, Judgment (ECtHR), 10 Apr. 2012. By contrast, a year later, the Strasbourg Court found that the extradition of a mentally ill prisoner accused of terrorism to an American 'supermax' high security prison would breach Article 3: *Aswat v. the United Kingdom*, appl. 17299/13, Judgment (ECtHR), 16 Apr. 2013.

[28] *Soering* judgment, para 111. [29] *Soering*, para 111.

[30] *Othman (Abu Qatada) v. the United Kingdom*, appl. 8139/09, Judgment (ECtHR), 17 Jan. 2012. On memoranda of understanding, see: Haritini Dipla, 'The Contribution of the European Court of Human Rights to the Absolute Ban on Torture: The Practice of Diplomatic Assurances', in Dean Spielmann, Marialena Tsirli, and Panayotis Voyatsis (eds) *The European Convention on Human Rights: A Living Instrument. Essays in Honour of Christos L. Rozakis* (Brussels: Bruylant, 2011) 155–179; Lena Skoglund, 'Diplomatic Assurances Against Torture: An Effective Strategy?' (2008) *Nordic Journal of International Law* 77, 319–354.

[31] *Soering* report, para 114.

have been impossible under US law for the Virginian authorities to provide an assurance phrased in stronger terms. The value of this assurance, the British government said, needed to be assessed within the diplomatic context of the relationship existing between the United States and the UK; this relationship would be seriously undermined if the death penalty were to be imposed on Mr Soering.[32] Two of the six Commission members who concluded that there would be no violation of Article 3 in this case put great weight on this argument. In their concurring opinion, they said that, in the light of the assurance received by the British authorities, they did not believe that there was any real risk that the applicant would be sentenced to death, and thus exposed to the 'death-row phenomenon'.

At the public hearing of the case held by the Court, the British Attorney General nonetheless conceded that there was a 'significant risk' that the applicant might be convicted of capital murder as charged.[33] I expect that it is this statement by the Attorney General which swung the case. In its judgment, the Court observes that 'the effectiveness of [the Virginia Attorney's] undertaking has not yet been put to the test'.[34] This suggests that the Court was not ready to wait and see what would happen to the applicant after he had been extradited to find out whether a violation of Article 3 would occur.[35] The government argued that, were the Court to accept (wrongly in its view) that an extradition could give rise to an issue under Article 3, such an extension of Article 3 should be limited to these 'occasions in which the treatment or punishment abroad is certain, imminent and serious'.[36] The government asked the Court to require at the very least 'a very high degree of risk, proved beyond reasonable doubt, that ill-treatment will actually occur'.[37] This proposition (which the Court did not explicitly rebut) is illogical, for a risk can *never* be proved beyond reasonable doubt: it is in the nature of a risk not to be certain.[38] The admission by the British Attorney General that the applicant might well become subject to the death-row phenomenon was presumably sufficient proof for the whole Court that the applicant's extradition could put him at risk of ill-treatment. The applicant was eventually extradited to the United States, but not until further assurances that he would not be condemned to the death penalty were sought and received. He remains incarcerated there, having been found guilty (he says wrongly) of the murders with which he was charged.[39]

[32] *Soering* report, paras 115 and 116.

[33] *Soering* judgment, para 94.

[34] *Soering* judgment, para 97.

[35] Somewhat surprisingly, the British government does not appear to have specifically argued before the Court that a violation of Article 3 could not be found in anticipation. At least this argument is not recorded in the judgment.

[36] *Soering* judgment, para 83.

[37] *Soering* judgment, para 83.

[38] Thomas Spijkerboer, 'Subsidiarity and "Arguability": The European Court of Human Rights' Case Law on Judicial Review in the Asylum Cases' (2009) *International Journal of Refugee Law* 21, 48–74.

[39] See most recently and movingly, amongst his multiple and perceptive writings: Jens Soering, *One Day in the Life of 179212: Notes from an American Prison* (New York: Lantern Books, 2012).

III. *Cruz Varas*' First Seed: The Court need not Believe the Applicant

The first Article 3 return case decided by the Court after *Soering* was *Cruz Varas and Others v. Sweden*—in March 1991. Admittedly, 20 years on, *Cruz Varas* is no longer recurrently invoked by the Court explicitly. Even so, my contention is that, along with *Vilvarajah* (discussed later), it came to embody the Court's default position in Article 3 return cases lodged by so-called failed asylum seekers. As a result, lawyers for applicants in such cases are still implicitly waging a battle against this early case law today. It is, therefore, worth studying *Cruz Varas* in great detail.

The applicants were a man, his wife, and their young child. All three were Chilean. The first applicant had been politically active in socialist, pro-democracy circles. When President Allende was overthrown and General Pinochet took power in 1973, Mr Cruz Varas was in his mid-twenties. He came to Sweden in 1987, where his wife and two-year-old son joined him shortly afterwards. Once in Sweden, he claimed asylum but did not immediately reveal all the reasons which substantiated his claim. The doctors who treated him believed his allegations that he had been tortured, including that he had been raped. The Swedish authorities did not find his allegations credible. Not having been a prominent member of any party or trade union, there was no public record of either his political activities or the ill-treatment, torture, and intimidation he had suffered. His claim to asylum was rejected at all three levels of the Swedish asylum determination procedure. He and his family lodged an application at Strasbourg in October 1989. The following day, the Commission indicated to the Swedish government that it would be desirable not to deport the applicants to Chile until the Commission had had the opportunity of examining the application during its next session. Having received this indication, the Swedish government nonetheless proceeded to deport the applicant. This was at a time when Chile was taking its first steps towards democracy. Mr Cruz Varas stayed in Chile for three weeks. During this time, although nothing happened to him personally, he thought that an attack against his brother-in-law was in reprisal for hosting him. He left Chile and went to Argentina. His wife and child having gone into hiding in Sweden as he was taken away for removal, they were not deported. The Cruz Varas family lodged an application at Strasbourg complaining of a violation of Articles 3, 8, 6, 13, and 25 of the Convention. This was three months after the Court delivered its judgment in *Soering*. Their complaints were found either inadmissible or unfounded.

Like *Soering*, *Cruz Varas* was lodged to the Court both by the Commission and by the respondent state and the Court sat in its plenary formation to hear it. The first complaint to be examined was the one related to Article 3. The Court confirmed that the principle established in *Soering* applied in expulsion cases. On the facts, however, it did not find a violation of Article 3. One of the reasons for this ruling was that the first applicant had not given the same story to the Swedish authorities from one interrogation to another. As the months went by,

Mr Cruz Varas had recounted more episodes of ill-treatment and torture, as well as involvement in subversive political activities. This, according to the Court, fatally undermined his credibility.

Mr Cruz Varas' legal representative had submitted to the Court that:

> [I]n assessing the allegations concerning his political and clandestine activities the Court should take into account the fact that asylum-seekers can rarely provide documentary proof of such matters. Indeed his activities were of such a nature that they could not be supported by documentary evidence. The Court should also have regard to the fact that those who have been tortured may feel apprehensive towards any authorities and be afraid to give a full and accurate account of their case. He contended that against this background he should be entitled to a 'relaxation' of the burden of proof and given the benefit of the doubt, particularly in view of the medical evidence he had adduced.[40]

By contrast, the government argued that 'his version of events was not credible', that 'he had said nothing to the authorities about having been tortured until [a late date]' and that 'the contents of his story were... contradictory and... lacking in credibility in various respects'.[41] The government pointed out that 'the evidence they had gathered since his expulsion [supported] their belief that he had not been politically active... or persecuted by the police'.[42]

The Court sided with the government. In its words:

> [E]ven if allowances are made for the apprehension that asylum-seekers may have towards the authorities and the difficulties of substantiating their claims with documentary evidence, the first applicant's complete silence as to his alleged clandestine activities and torture by the Chilean police until more than eighteen months after his first interrogation... casts considerable doubt on his credibility in this respect... These doubts are reinforced by the fact that he was legally represented at all stages throughout the proceedings and that he must have been aware of the importance of bringing to the attention of the authorities any element which supported his asylum claim. His credibility is further called into question by the continuous changes in his story following each police interrogation and by the fact that no material has been presented to the Court which substantiates his claims of clandestine political activity on behalf of or in collaboration with members of the FPMR... On the contrary the evidence points in the opposite direction (see paragraphs 41–43 above).[43]

Without going into all the factual details given in the judgment, I find this a strange conclusion. Paragraph 43 of the judgment referred to an affidavit by the President of the Human Rights Commission of the city, Villa Alemana, where the first applicant lived. She had reported that 'she was not aware of any explosions in Villa Alemana directed at railway lines and electric power lines which occurred in the period 1983–86'.[44] This went against the first applicant's allegations to have had a role in such activities. However, in the part of the judgment which describes the particular circumstances of the case without attempting to assess them, it is recorded that the applicants submitted 'a Chilean newspaper cutting

[40] *Cruz Varas* judgment, para 71. [41] *Cruz Varas*, para 72.
[42] *Cruz Varas*, para 72. [43] *Cruz Varas*, para 78. [44] *Cruz Varas*, para 43.

of 17 October 1984 describing an attempt to blow up a power line in a town ten kilometres outside Villa Alemana'.[45] The Court does not mention this clipping at all when it evaluates the credibility of the applicant later in the judgment.

Obviously I am not in a position to assess the veracity of the applicant's allegations. It is disturbing, however, to note that such veracity was rejected by the Court after the Commission had accepted, 'on the basis of the material before it, that Mr Cruz Varas [had] been subjected in the past in Chile to treatment contrary to Article 3... and that the only plausible explanation is that this treatment has been carried out by persons for which the then Chilean regime was responsible'.[46] This was a unanimous finding by 13 Commission members who had held a hearing at which the doctor who had treated Mr Cruz Varas had appeared as a witness. (By contrast, the Court declined to hear any witnesses.[47])

The doctor had explained that beads of sweat had been dripping from Mr Cruz Varas' lips and forehead when, after much difficulty, he had revealed—for the first time given that he had not even told his wife—the sexual torture to which he had been subjected. In the doctor's view, this reaction indicated that he had lived through this situation.[48] The Court might have replied that it did not share the doctor's belief that Mr Cruz Varas had necessarily been raped. This would have been a controversial but nonetheless potentially understandable conclusion. Instead, the Court chose to infer that it was *not plausible* that Mr Cruz Varas had been raped because he had failed to mention this crucial fact to the authorities for 18 months.[49] Such a categorical inference is inappropriate and callous: psychological and sociological research do not cease to document how victims of sexual abuse may not talk about what has happened to them for years if not decades; when victims finally talk (if they do), a new and extremely difficult ordeal starts again for them if they are not believed.[50] Yet, a 2005 decision of inadmissibility suggests that the Court has not yet learnt the lessons of this research.[51]

Mr Cruz Varas' doctor had given other reasons for believing the applicant. For example, he had explained that it would have been strange for the collar bone fracture which Mr Cruz Varas had suffered not to have healed properly if it had been the result of accidental blunt force, given that such a wound is easy to treat.[52] This and further elements meant that for this expert with 20 years' experience in assessing scars and wounds in patients, the picture drawn by Mr Cruz Varas was

[45] *Cruz Varas*, para 46.

[46] *Cruz Varas, Bustamento Lazo and Cruz v. Sweden*, appl. 15576/89, Report (EComHR), 7 June 1990, para 83

[47] *Cruz Varas* judgment, para 8. [48] *Cruz Varas* report, para 50.

[49] Compare how the Inter-American Court dealt with an allegation of rape in *Vélez Loor v. Panama*, Preliminary Objections, Merits, Reparations and Costs, Judgment (IACtHR), 23 Nov. 2010, analysed in Chapter 131 (p. 386).

[50] See e.g. C. Van Velsen, C. Gorst-Unsworthy, and S. Turner, 'Survivors of Torture and Organized Violence: Demography and Diagnosis' (1996) *Journal of Traumatic Stress* 9, 181–193; Jane Herlihy and Stuart W. Turner, 'Asylum Claims and Memory of Trauma: Sharing our Knowledge' (2007) *British Journal of Psychiatry* 5.

[51] *Ovdienko Iryna and Ivan v. Finland*, appl. 1383/04, Decision (ECtHR), 31 May 2005.

[52] *Cruz Varas* report, para 51.

'clear-cut', 'typical for Chile', and very probably true.[53] For the Court, however, there was 'no element in the material before [it], apart from the first applicant's allegations', which provided 'direct evidence' for the conclusion that the only plausible explanation for the treatment which Mr Cruz Varas had evidently suffered was that it had been 'carried out by persons for whom "the Chilean regime" was responsible'.[54]

The crucial difficulty is: how was Mr Cruz Varas expected to prove that the story he was telling was true? A rape is unlikely to have been recorded anywhere. Even scars which appear entirely compatible with an account of beatings or torture do not clearly and unequivocally indicate their source—they may have been caused by an accident or even been self-inflicted, although this latter possibility is far less likely than immigration authorities appear to believe. Very often, the only thing victims can present is their words. Therefore a central question of the asylum determination process is almost always: is the asylum seeker credible?[55] That is, do the authorities tasked with granting or withholding refugee status or the Court *believe* the person in front of them who is seeking asylum? By nature, credibility is a matter of subjective rather than objective assessment. To say it differently, one cannot *prove* one's credibility beyond reasonable doubt; one can only *appear* credible.[56]

Mr Cruz Varas' legal representative tried to defend the credibility of his client. For example, he explained that at one point during an interview Mr Cruz Varas had mentioned that his dog had been killed. The interviewer asked him whether it had been poisoned. No, Mr Cruz Varas had replied, he had found the dog impaled on a metal fence that surrounded the house where he lived. The legal representative observed that surely Mr Cruz Varas would have answered 'yes' to the question put to him if he had been fabricating his story.[57] The legal representative's efforts to convince the Court of the credibility of his client were nonetheless to no avail. The Court dismissed the Commission's findings of facts regarding the credibility of Mr Cruz Varas, as it was free to do, even though the then Convention system recognised that the establishment and verification of facts was primarily a matter for the Commission.[58]

The Court proceeded to write its judgment in a way which cast doubts on the veracity of the applicant's account. For example, the supposedly neutral section which recounts the 'facts subsequent to the expulsion' includes a passage which states that the applicant '*claims* that his brother-in-law was attacked in the street and badly injured by unknown persons'.[59] The Court could have said

[53] *Cruz Varas* report, paras 49, 57, and 53. [54] *Cruz Varas* judgment, para 77.

[55] As apparent from: James A. Sweeney, 'Credibility, Proof and Refugee Law' (2009) *International Journal of Refugee Law* 21, 700–726; Robert Thomas, 'Assessing the Credibility of Asylum Claims: EU and UK Approaches Examined' (2006) *European Journal of Migration and Law* 8, 79–86.

[56] Tobias Kelly explains this beautifully in: Kelly, *This Side of Silence: Human Rights, Torture, and the Recognition of Cruelty* (Philadelphia: University of Philadelphia Press, 2011).

[57] *Cruz Varas* report, para 31.

[58] *Cruz Varas* judgment, para 74. On fact-finding missions, see: Philip Leach, *Taking a Case to the European Court of Human Rights* (Oxford: Oxford University Press, 2011) 35.

[59] *Cruz Varas* judgment, para 38, emphasis added.

'states' rather than 'claims'. Elsewhere the Court operates a slip to less emotive language, again as a way of discrediting the story of the applicant: while the applicant had explained in his original application that he had 'fled' Chile after three weeks,[60] the judgment simply records that he had 'left Chile for Argentina'.[61] The Court thus continually distances itself from the account given by the applicant. Problematically in my view, it does not exercise the same kind of distancing when it comes to the story presented by the State, as we shall see later.

In summary, the *Cruz Varas* case planted the seed within the Strasbourg jurisdiction of not believing the applicant even when they would be, by the nature of the situation they recount, extremely unlikely to be in a position to prove their allegations. It remains true today that in most cases (although not all), the Court does not proceed in a way which gives the applicant in Article 3 return cases the benefit of the doubt as to the veracity of the facts they are recounting.

IV. A Seed is not the Whole Story: Conflicting Tendencies in the Strasbourg Case Law

There are exceptions. Sometimes the Court decides that the applicant is credible or that she must at least be given the benefit of the doubt. The earliest case where this occurred is *Hatami v. Sweden*, a case upon which the Court rendered judgment in 1998. In this case, the applicant claimed that he had been detained and tortured in Iran for being a Mujahedin. The Swedish Aliens Appeals Board clearly did not believe him. To quote the decision of this Board:

> [The applicant] has stated that after being released from prison he was ordered to report to the police and subject to surveillance by the [Iranian] authorities, and it is therefore the opinion of the Board that it is not credible that he should have applied for a visa with a false passport; because of the rigorous checks when leaving Iran it is unlikely that [the applicant] would take such a risk, trying to leave Iran with a false passport. According to the evaluation by the Board, [the applicant] has applied for a visa with a legal passport, which indicates that he was not subjected to any special interest by the authorities. The Board also questions that [the applicant] should have visited a foreign embassy in Teheran, which is guarded by Iranian police, if he had been wanted.[62]

The Commission conducted a fact-finding mission in order to interview Mr Hatami in Sweden in May 1997. Its delegates 'found that the applicant's statements were on the whole consistent and credible and that his demeanour and comportment were convincing and sincere'.[63] This in turn led the Commission to express in April 1998 the unanimous view that the applicant's deportation to Iran would, if carried out, amount to a violation of Article 3 of the Convention.[64]

[60] *Cruz Varas; His Family v. Sweden*, appl. 15576/89, Decision (ECtHR), 7 Dec. 1989, p. 3 of 8 (last sentence in the section on 'The facts').

[61] *Cruz Varas* judgment, para 38.

[62] Reproduced in *Hatami v. Sweden*, appl. 32448/96, Judgment (ECtHR), 9 Oct. 1998, para 14.

[63] *Hatami*, para 25.

[64] *Hatami*, para 25.

Five months later, Mr Hatami was granted permanent residence in Sweden.[65] The Court struck out the case.

Dana Baldinger has remarked that the Court simply demands 'evidence capable of proving' the Article 3 risk, pointing to an extremely 'open and flexible criterion for the admissibility and admission of evidence'.[66] She observes that '[t]he Court has noted in a number of cases that it must take into account two particularities of asylum cases: the difficulty of substantiating asylum claims with direct documentary evidence and the difficulty of doing this within a short time frame'.[67] The *Bahaddar v. the Netherlands* judgment of 1998 can be quoted to this effect, as Baldinger does in a footnote:

> It should be borne in mind in this regard that in applications for recognition of refugee status it may be difficult, if not impossible, for the person concerned to supply evidence within a short time, especially if—as in the present case—such evidence must be obtained from the country from which he or she claims to have fled. Accordingly, time-limits [imposed by national procedures] should not be so short, or applied so inflexibly, as to deny an applicant for recognition of refugee status a realistic opportunity to prove his or her claim.[68]

However, this hefty principle did not help the applicant in this case: seven out of the nine judges found that the difficulties the applicant encountered did not absolve him from not having respected the domestic time limits. The applicant's legal representative had been waiting to obtain further evidence from Bangladesh because the authenticity of the documents originally submitted had been disputed. As a result she was three months late in submitting the grounds for her client's appeal against the decision which rejected his asylum claim, plus she had not requested an extension as she could have done. The appeal was declared inadmissible first in the Netherlands, and then at Strasbourg, for failure to exhaust national remedies.

The conclusion which Baldinger draws from her comprehensive study of the way in which the Strasbourg Court does or does not accept evidence in asylum cases, is that the Court does not often apply *in concreto* the general principle that asylum seekers should benefit from flexibility and a relaxation in the evidentiary burden they face.[69] She seems to have found the approach adopted by the Court, acting by unanimity, in the 2005 case of *Mawajedi Shikpohkt and Mahkamat Shole v. the Netherlands* particularly harsh. To quote Baldinger:

> The basic story of the Iranian applicant was that she came from a family which had always opposed the sitting Iranian regime, that she had taken over oppositional activities from her stepfather, including the distribution of oppositional pamphlets, and that she had

[65] *Hatami*, para 17.

[66] Dana Baldinger, *Rigorous Scrutiny versus Marginal Review: Standards on Judicial Scrutiny and Evidence in International and European Asylum Law* (2013 doctoral dissertation submitted to Radboud University Nijmegen and printed by Wolf Legal Publishers) 252.

[67] Baldinger 254.

[68] *Bahaddar v. the Netherlands*, appl. 25894/94, Judgment (ECtHR), 19 Feb. 1998, para 45.

[69] Baldinger *Rigorous Scrutiny* 255.

received a written threat that had caused her to go into hiding. She had substantiated her claim before the national authorities and the ECtHR with an impressive amount of evidentiary material. The ECtHR found it problematic that she had not, however, submitted the written threat, or the oppositional material she had stated she had distributed.[70]

Such strictness by the Court is obviously not to the liking of all judges. For example, in *Bahaddar*, two judges (as well as the Commission) were of the view that the gravity of the applicant's circumstances outweighed the failure to respect technical procedural formalities, especially given that the applicant had never intended to circumvent the subsidiary character of the Convention system, on the contrary having given the Dutch authorities plenty of opportunities to put matters right through the Dutch system by having the case heard, investigated, and decided at several levels by several administrative and judicial authorities.[71]

To end this section on a positive note, by contrast, *R.C. v. Sweden* is an example where the Court found in 2010, at a majority of 6 to 1, that the applicant's basic story had been consistent throughout the proceedings and accepted the general conclusions of a medical report that the marks of injuries on the applicant's body could have originated from torture; the Court concluded that the applicant had sufficiently substantiated his Article 3 claim.[72]

V. *Cruz Varas*' Second Seed: The Court Normally accepts the Facts as Presented by the Respondent State

The facts at issue in Article 3 return cases are typically disputed. Most often the applicant states that she has suffered ill-treatment at the hands of the state where she is about to be deported (sometimes this does not happen because past ill-treatment is not part of the problem).[73] The state then replies that this story is not credible. In every case, the applicant alleges that the deportation either already has (if removal has already taken place) or would put her (if it has not yet happened) at risk of being subjected to ill-treatment. The deporting state then puts forward the view that this risk is not 'real'. Whether the Court is ready to follow either the applicant or the respondent state on these two sets of facts typically leads it either to find or not to find a violation of the Convention. Now, the Court's default position is to follow the state—against the applicant. This is partly due to the lack of credibility which the Court typically believes affects the applicant, as explained previously. But, as the present section argues, this element must itself be understood to be part and parcel of the wider institutional

[70] Baldinger 255.

[71] Dissenting opinion of Judge Foighel and dissenting opinion of Judge Morenilla in *Bahaddar* judgment.

[72] *R.C. v. Sweden*, appl. 41827/07, Judgment (ECtHR), 9 Mar. 2010. The judges of the majority were Josep Casadevall, Bostjan Zupančič, Alvina Gyulumyan, Ineta Ziemele, Luis López Guerra, and Ann Power; the dissenting judge was Elisabeth Fura.

[73] See e.g. *N. v. Finland*, appl. 38885/02, Judgment (ECtHR), 26 July 2005.

framework constituted by the European Convention system. Two aspects of this framework must be highlighted. The first relates to the burden of proof which normally falls on the applicant. The second concerns the fact that the European Court of Human Rights must avoid acting like a court of fourth instance. These two factors were not explicitly mentioned by the Court in *Cruz Varas*. However they would have played a role in favour of the state. And once their pertinence had been accepted in this case, even if only implicitly, the tendency afterwards would have been to continue to pay respect to them in subsequent Article 3 return cases, making it difficult and time-consuming to replace them with ideas and principles more favourable to the applicant.

The first principle worth considering is that the applicant must prove the merits of her case. This is how things should be: given that the applicant is the person who complains that someone else (the respondent state) has done something wrong, it is up to her to substantiate her claim. Lawyers say that the burden of proof falls on the applicant. In other words, it is not for the respondent state to prove that it has not acted wrongly every time an applicant alleges that it has. This principle is logical and helps to secure the continual support of contracting states to the Convention system. It is not difficult to see, however, that it also makes it easy for a state to absolve itself when an applicant is not in a position to present the proof of what she alleges.

In 2008, the Court explicitly recognised this difficulty and stated in the crucial case of *Saadi v. Italy* (discussed more fully later):

> It is in principle for the applicant to adduce evidence capable of proving that there are substantial grounds for believing that, if the measure complained of were to be implemented, he would be exposed to a real risk of being subjected to treatment contrary to Article 3... Where such evidence is adduced, it is for the Government to dispel any doubts about it.[74]

Another way to express this statement is to say that once an applicant has satisfied the Court that her case is 'arguable' (i.e. that there is some plausibility to her case, even though one does not know yet whether or not it thoroughly stands on its merits), the Court *shifts* the burden of proof to the state which now has to demonstrate that the applicant has no case if it (the state) is to win. The Court has now done this at least 22 times since *Saadi*.[75]

This shift has potential consequences which cannot be underestimated. It theoretically puts the applicant in a much stronger position. This does not mean, however, that all the evidentiary problems she faces disappear. For one, the applicant must still convince the Court that she has an arguable case. This may be a very arduous task. In law, one says that the *initial* burden of proof remains hers.

One of the reasons why the burden of proof born by the applicant has always been and remains heavy even after *Saadi* has to do with the principle according to

[74] *Saadi v. Italy*, appl. 37201/06, GC Judgment, 28 Feb. 2008, para 129. The Inter-American Court did this immediately: *Velásquez-Rodríguez v. Honduras*, Merits, Judgment (IACtHR), 29 July 1988.

[75] As suggested by a HUDOC search for the quoted sentences.

which the European Court of Human Rights should normally refrain from acting as a court of fourth instance. Put simply, this principle means that the Court is not an appeal tribunal which should take it upon itself to look at all the facts anew. Given the requirement that the applicant exhausts national remedies before turning to Strasbourg, a comprehensive examination of the facts will normally have been undertaken by the domestic courts, at first, second, and possibly third instances; it is not for the Strasbourg Court to reassess them again. The principle is one facet of the subsidiary character of the Convention system. It enshrines a deferential attitude towards states (without the cooperation of which the system would collapse) and limits the task of the Court (which does not have the resources to go over every factual claim from all angles).

Importantly the principle that the Court should refrain from acting like a court of fourth instance is not absolute. It *never* prevents the Court from reviewing the facts when the Court deems this exercise necessary. But when does the Court deem this exercise necessary? The short answer is: not very often in Article 3 return cases.

Against the argument that I have been developing it might be argued that there are many cases where the Court has substituted its own appreciation of the situation for that of the domestic authorities. I am of course aware of this. A good example of such a case is *N. v. Finland*, which was decided in 2005. In this case, the Court delegated two of its members to go and collect oral evidence from the applicant and another three persons in Finland. The applicant originated from the Democratic Republic of the Congo (DRC), formerly Zaire. He had indicated that he had been a secret agent in President Mobutu's Division Spéciale Présidentielle (DSP). He said that he had infiltrated dissident student associations at Zairian universities as well as the regime's opponents in the Netherlands where he had posed as an asylum seeker from 1993 to 1994 before being deported after his asylum claim was rejected by the Dutch authorities. He argued that, if he were to be returned now—a decade later—by Finland to the DRC, he would be at risk of reprisals from relatives of those critical of the Mobutu regime whom he had denounced, the more so since the Finnish newspapers had widely reported his unsuccessful appeal before the Supreme Administrative Court, thus alerting the whole Congolese community in Finland to the reasons underlying his asylum claim, which would then inevitably be relayed to the Congo. At every level of the Finnish administrative and judicial procedure the information provided by the applicant had been found unreliable. The Strasbourg Court, having regard to the overall impression formed by its two delegates, was more mixed in its assessment:

> The Court has certain reservations about the applicant's own testimony before the Delegates which it considers to have been evasive on many points and is not prepared to accept every statement of his as fact [especially as to the way he had travelled to Finland]. The Court finds however that the applicant's account of his background in the DRC must, on the whole, be considered sufficiently consistent and credible.[76]

[76] *N. v. Finland* judgment, paras 154 and 155.

Given the absolute character of the prohibition proscribed in Article 3, the nature of the applicant's work in the DSP could not invalidate the Court's conclusion that a return to the DRC would put the applicant at risk of ill-treatment and thus contravene the Convention.[77] The case of *Hatami v. Sweden*, which we saw in the previous section was struck out by the Court in 1998 following the issue by the respondent state of a residence permit after the Commission had concluded its own investigations, is another exception to the application of the principle according to which Strasbourg does not normally reassess the factual basis of a case as established by the domestic authorities.

However, it remains substantially the case that it is extremely rare for the Court to go against the domestic assessment of the facts. So why conduct fact-finding missions in *Hatami* and *N.* but not in other cases? I am not aware of an answer to this question which would point to objective case-selection criteria. Thinking further, for example, about the way in which *Hatami* triggered the privilege of a complete reassessment by the Commission, it is worth noting that many other Iranian failed asylum seekers did not benefit from a re-investigation by a Strasbourg organ.[78] A HUDOC search for admissibility decisions in English related to 'Article 3' and containing the word 'Iranian', up to 11 July 2000 (the date of the Court's first verdict of violation of Article 3 in a return case lodged by an Iranian applicant, *Jabari v. Turkey*),[79] produced 44 results. Aside from *Hatami* and *Jabari*, only two of these 44 cases were declared admissible.[80] There would have been further decisions (in French or by committees of three) involving applications by failed asylum seekers arguing that their return to Iran would expose them to ill-treatment. This is without even considering asylum seekers originating from other countries. My suspicion is that many of these applicants might well have appeared equally credible to the delegates who interviewed Mr Hatami (or indeed N.), if only they too had been interviewed by them.

In her most interesting study of the way facts are determined in asylum cases by international judicial or quasi-judicial bodies, Baldinger regrets that the Strasbourg Court has not developed an elaborate doctrinal position as to when it will accept the facts as assessed by the domestic authorities and when it will determine them afresh.[81] She suggests that the Strasbourg Court may well be internally divided as to which of these two avenues should be followed.[82] This indeed appears likely. In the previous chapter, we saw that some judges would have wished to see long-settled migrants treated as quasi-nationals who should not be subject to deportation after having served a prison sentence, but that these judges never managed to turn their view into an uncontested principle of the Strasbourg

[77] *N. v. Finland*, para 166.

[78] The Court now conducts fact-finding missions very rarely: Philip Leach, Costas Paraskeva, and Gordana Uzelac, 'Human Rights Fact-Finding: The European Court of Human Rights at a Crossroads' (2010) *Netherlands Quarterly of Human Rights* 28, 41–77 at 42.

[79] *Jabari v. Turkey*, appl. 40035/98, Judgment (ECtHR), 11 July 2000.

[80] *Tarighi Wageh Dashti v. Greece*, appl. 24453/93, PCom Decision (EComHR), 9 Dec. 1994; *M.A.R. v. the United Kingdom*, appl. 28038/95, PCom Decision (EComHR), 16 Jan. 1997.

[81] Baldinger *Rigorous Scrutiny* 248.

[82] Baldinger 249.

case law. Likewise, in all likelihood, there are judges who would personally be inclined to give migrants who explain why they fear a return to their country of origin the benefit of the doubt. Occasionally, these judges will manage to convince their colleagues to side with them. This would thus produce the type of jurisprudential lottery which Judge Martens had denounced in the mid-1990s in respect of the Article 8 removal case law, but which must also operate in Article 3 return cases. To put it bluntly, Mr Hatami and N. were lucky;[83] for no particularly good reason numerous failed asylum seekers who also applied to Strasbourg have not enjoyed the same luck.

Admittedly neither is it the Court's function nor does it enjoy the necessary resources to re-examine the entirety or near-entirety of the factual basis of the numerous Article 3 return cases it sees. Accepting this valid objection without requesting that something else be done on a different plane nonetheless leaves entirely unresolved the problem both of the lottery and of the practical failure of the Strasbourg Court to achieve the aim of ensuring that the absolute prohibition on forced returns to proscribed treatment is applied in practice. This problem could have been tackled outside the framework of Article 3. Most naturally the Court could have made use of Article 13 in order to scrutinise domestic asylum determination procedures in-depth, thus insisting upon their robustness and diligence.[84] The next section documents the fact that the Court has not done this.

VI. *Cruz Varas*' Third Seed: The Court's Long Reticence at Scrutinising National Determination Procedures

Article 13 provides that there must be an effective domestic remedy for any arguable violation of the Convention. In other words, anyone who believes that she has suffered a violation of the Convention must be able to raise her complaint before a national authority. Given the inapplicability of Article 6 to immigration matters (as explained in Section IX), Article 13 provides the most promising route to have the quality of the domestic proceedings examined at Strasbourg. In *Cruz Varas*, the applicants had attempted to activate Article 13 and had complained of its violation in their original application to the Commission. They had argued that the procedure before the National Immigration Board had not fulfilled the requirements of Article 13.[85] The Commission found this complaint manifestly

[83] There are of course more recent examples too, which have not relied on a fact-finding mission. See e.g. *S.F. and Others v. Sweden*, appl. 52077/10, Judgment (ECtHR), 15 May 2012, where the Court found that uncertain aspects did not undermine the overall credibility of the Iranian applicant's 'basic story'.

[84] Thomas Spijkerboer reaches the same conclusion through a more technical legal analysis which observes that the subsidiary nature of Strasbourg's control should in theory prevent the Court from conducting a more in-depth judicial review than the review exercised by domestic courts. Typically the opposite occurs when the Court finds a violation of Article 3 in a return case: Spijkerboer 'Subsidiarity and "Arguability"' 48–74.

[85] *Cruz Varas* decision, point 4 under the section entitled 'The Law'.

ill-founded and thus inadmissible.[86] It justified this finding by reference to the fact that the case had been examined at three different levels of jurisdiction in Sweden—without one word on the quality of these proceedings.

The Article 13 avenue having been closed, the only route for examining the quality of the national procedures was through Article 3. In *Cruz Varas*, five members of the Commission were of the opinion that there had been a violation of Article 3. Amongst the multiple reasons which they cited for this finding was the view that not only the burden of proof should have been shifted to the state (thus anticipating by almost two decades the Court's eventual pronouncement in *Saadi v. Italy*) but also the fact that the examination of the situation by the respondent state had been defective. To quote them:

> In view of the fact that the Commission has found that Mr. Cruz Varas has been subjected to treatment contrary to Article 3 of the Convention in the past in Chile and in view of the particular circumstances of this case including the situation in Chile, it was for the Government to show that, at the time of the expulsion, there was no longer any risk that Mr. Cruz Varas would be treated contrary to Article 3 if sent back to Chile. In this respect we take into account that the respondent Government have proved to be in a position to carry out quickly an extensive investigation in Chile but that this investigation was carried out only after the expulsion [had taken place].[87]

This was a rather damning observation to make. By contrast, the Court seemed to praise the domestic proceedings. To quote:

> The Court...attaches importance to the fact that the Swedish authorities had particular knowledge and experience in evaluating claims of the present nature by virtue of the large number of Chilean asylum-seekers who had arrived in Sweden since 1973. The final decision to expel the applicant was taken after thorough examinations of his case by the National Immigration Board and by the Government.[88]

A vast experience in dealing with an issue does not in itself guarantee that the process undertaken in order to do this is qualitatively sound.[89] Let us remember *Hatami*. Asking in what sense the national authorities' examinations had been 'thorough' would have been both legitimate and most appropriate. The Court did not address this question.

As we shall see in more detail in Chapter 12, the Court has proved extremely reticent in scrutinising the national procedures to which states resort in order to determine who is and who is not a refugee (or, more broadly, someone worthy of international protection). To anticipate this discussion, although cases have occasionally surfaced where the Court has found a violation of Article 13 because of averted deficiencies in the domestic procedures, there is still no sign

[86] *Cruz Varas* decision, point 4 under the section entitled 'The Law'.

[87] *Cruz Varas* report, dissenting opinion of MM. Trechsel, Weitzel, Mrs Thune, MM. Rozakis and Loucaides.

[88] *Cruz Varas* judgment, para 81.

[89] The first quoted sentence was repeated by the Court (with the necessary adaptations) in its *Vilvarajah* judgment, para 114. The Court refrained from repeating it afterwards, perhaps indicating that it realised that its statement was not persuasive.

that the Court is intent on denouncing in any systematic fashion the ways in which states have undermined the possibility for asylum seekers to become recognised refugees under the 1951 UN Refugee Convention. The erosion of the asylum regime started in the 1980s, with the imposition of visa requirements on nationals who originated from countries which until then had been free from such requirements and the introduction of carrier sanctions that were meant to dissuade air-travel companies from bringing to Europe people who were not properly documented. At the same time a discourse was developing that condemned 'bogus' asylum seekers, thus legitimising these new governmental measures.[90] Reading the case law of the European Court of Human Rights, one would not be aware that these tremendous changes were taking place. Even in the far-sighted judgment of *M.S.S. v. Belgium and Greece*, decided in January 2011 and reviewed in Chapter 12, the double finding of a violation of Article 13 was comparatively timid, certainly in respect of Belgium.

VII. *Cruz Varas*' Fourth Seed: The Court Examines the Article 3 Complaint *Ex Nunc*

Turning now to an important technical point: an Article 3 return case inevitably brings up the question as to the moment at which the Court (or the Commission) should assess the planned or executed return's compatibility with the Convention–should this moment be the one at which the authorities planned the return, or the one at which the return was executed (if it was), or the one at the point of assessment by the Court? In answer to this question, the Court said in *Cruz Varas*:

> Since the nature of the Contracting States' responsibility under Article 3 (art. 3) in cases of this kind lies in the act of exposing an individual to the risk of ill-treatment, the existence of the risk must be assessed primarily with reference to those facts which were known or ought to have been known to the Contracting State at the time of the expulsion; the Court is not precluded, however, from having regard to information which comes to light subsequent to the expulsion. This may be of value in confirming or refuting the appreciation that has been made by the Contracting Party or the well-foundedness or otherwise of an applicant's fears.[91]

Strikingly this is not a univocal answer; it leaves the Court with options of how to proceed in the circumstances of any particular case.

In the next Article 3 return case which the Court decided, *Vilvarajah and Others*, one could say that the Court turned this flexibility not only to the disadvantage of the applicant (and thus to the advantage of the state), but also in a way which appears rather at odds with its *Cruz Varas* statement. In *Vilvarajah*, it

[90] See e.g. Frances Webber, *Borderline Justice: The Fight for Refugee and Migrant Rights* (London: Pluto, 2012).

[91] *Cruz Varas* judgment, para 76.

was not seriously disputed—even if the Court put it in the language that it was 'claimed'—that three of the five applicants had actually suffered inhuman treatment after they had been deported by the UK to Sri Lanka. Evidence demonstrating this had been collected by the applicants' London-based legal representatives who had made the trip to Sri Lanka precisely for the purpose of collecting such evidence, which had then persuaded the British courts to overturn the initial administrative decision and to invite the three applicants back to the UK. Still the Strasbourg Court did not find a violation of Article 3. It justified its verdict of non-violation with the idea that 'there existed no special distinguishing features in [the applicants' personal circumstances] that could or ought to have enabled the Secretary of State to foresee that they would be treated in this way'.[92] We shall come back to this point below. What can be noted for now is that evidence which had surfaced sufficiently early for the Strasbourg Court to be able to consider it and which would clearly have favoured the case of the applicants if it had been taken into consideration was dismissed by the Court as irrelevant.

Since *Cruz Varas* and *Vilvarajah*, it has become accepted that the Court assesses Article 3 return cases *ex nunc* (from now) rather than *ex tunc* (from then). As the Court has since explained, it assesses the reality of the risk that a removal may be contrary to the standards of Article 3 'in the light of the material before it at the time of its consideration of the case', irrespective of the moment at which relevant information before it has surfaced.[93] As Thomas Spijkerboer has argued, this makes sense given that the purpose of an Article 3 complaint is to assess whether the deportation has involved or, more often these days, would involve if implemented, a real risk of ill-treatment for the applicant.[94] The position would be different if the aim of the Strasbourg proceedings were to decide on the legality of the administrative decision to deport. In this scenario, the assessment by the Court should take place by reference to the circumstances which existed at the moment of the adoption of this decision (*ex tunc*).[95] This is therefore the test which applies to Article 13 complaints (see Chapter 12).

In the context of this section, what is important is that an examination *ex nunc* appears sensible in order to deal with an Article 3 complaint. This principle can favour either the applicant or the state. On the one hand, the Court will not refuse, as a matter of principle, to consider an allegation by the applicant that her home country had subjected her to torture just because this allegation was submitted too late according to domestic procedure.[96] Having said this, the Court nonetheless often finds that late allegations negatively affect the applicant's credibility.[97]

[92] *Vilvarajah* judgment, para 112.

[93] *D. v. the United Kingdom*, appl. 30240/96, Judgment (ECtHR), 2 May 1997, para 50; *Bensaid v. the United Kingdom*, appl. 44599/98, Judgment (ECtHR), 6 Feb. 2001, para 35; *Ovdienko* decision, point 3.

[94] Spijkerboer 'Subsidiarity and "Arguability"' 53.

[95] Spijkerboer 53.

[96] In *Hilal v. the United Kingdom*, appl. 45276/99, Judgment (ECtHR), 6 Mar. 2001, a one-month delay was accepted.

[97] Baldinger gives the examples of *Nasimi v. Sweden*, appl. 38865/02, Decision (ECtHR), 16 Mar. 2004 as well as the *Ovdienko* decision.

Documents which an applicant submits in order to support her allegations will be considered by the Court, however late their submission.[98] Of course, the state may contest their authenticity or value, in which case the Court may be persuaded to reject their evidentiary probity.

On the other hand, the *ex nunc* principle may also favour the state. A typical scenario is that the state argues that the current situation of the country where it wants to deport the applicant has now improved, making the risk of ill-treatment upon return insignificant. The Court seems constantly to ignore the volatile character of the unstable political situations to which applicants are returned at a so-deemed auspicious moment in the history of the relevant country.[99] In the absence of a long-averted period of stability, this way of proceeding has to be objectionable. This was not lost on the five Commission members who did not agree with the report of the majority of the Commission in the *Cruz Varas* case. They remarked:

> As regards the political situation in Chile it is correct that at the relevant time, [when Mr Cruz Varas was deported] in October 1989, certain steps had been taken to restore democracy and respect for human rights. However, the change which had taken place at the relevant time was unstable and the country was still in a transitional stage towards democracy and in fact the political regime had not changed. It is to be recalled that no democratic election had taken place at that time. The subsequent development in Chile cannot be taken into account when examining Mr. Cruz Varas' complaints in the present case.[100]

Surprisingly this important feature of the Court's case law does not seem to have attracted commentary even by the most acute observers of the Convention system.[101]

VIII. *Cruz Varas*' Fifth (but now Dead) Seed: Strasbourg Requests for the State to Stay Deportation are not Binding

In *Cruz Varas*, the first applicant had been deported a few hours after the Commission had indicated by phone and fax which was relayed to the appropriate person in the Swedish government, that it was desirable that the government should not proceed with the deportation until the case had been examined.[102]

[98] Baldinger 278.

[99] See e.g. *Venkadajalasarma v. the Netherlands*, appl. 58510/00, Judgment (ECtHR), 17 Feb. 2004, where the Court agreed with the government that 'the current situation' then prevailing in Sri Lanka made it unlikely that the Tamil applicant would run a real risk of being subjected to ill-treatment upon return.

[100] Trechsel et al. in *Cruz Varas* report. Judge De Meyer, the only member of the Court to find a violation of Article 3 in the case, concurred with this dissenting opinion. He observed that in October 1989 the situation in Chile 'was still not wholly reassuring', with the presidency for example still in the hands of General Pinochet: *Cruz Varas* judgment, separate opinion of Judge De Meyer.

[101] e.g. Baldinger says nothing about it.

[102] *Cruz Varas* report, paras 66–70.

The indication had been made under Rule 36 of the Commission (which has now become Rule 39 of the Court) in order to prevent 'irreparable harm' taking place, without prejudging how the case would eventually be decided.

For the Commission, the disregard for its indication amounted to a violation of the provision of the Convention which makes it an obligation for contracting states not to hinder the right of individual petition (formerly Article 25, now Article 41).[103] By the narrowest of majorities, the Court took another view. As far as the majority of the Court was concerned, nothing in the Convention suggested that the indication, adopted under a rule of procedure drawn up by the Commission itself, was meant to give rise within the Convention system to a binding obligation for the state which received it.[104] This ruling was adopted by ten votes to nine.

That so many judges and almost all the Commission (only one of its members dissented) thought that a state acted in violation of the Convention when it was returning an applicant in complete disregard for an interim measure did not result in a quick change in the case law. Only in 2005, in *Mamatkulov and Askarov v. Turkey*, did the Court, sitting as a Grand Chamber, declare for the first time an interim measure binding and its disrespect to be a violation of Article 41. This jurisprudence immediately settled.[105]

IX. *Cruz Varas*' Confirmations: Article 3's High Threshold, Non-Violation of Article 8 and Inadmissibility of Any Article 6 Complaint

Without much surprise, the Court reaffirmed in *Cruz Varas* a number of points which were very much part of the Strasbourg case law by the time the Grand Chamber adopted its judgment in this case in March 1991. Three such points are worth mentioning.

The first is that in order to fall within the scope of Article 3, ill-treatment must attain a 'minimum level of severity', which necessitates the undertaking of a 'relative' assessment which 'depends on all the circumstances of the case'.[106] This pronouncement first appeared in a Court's judgment in the *Ireland v. the United Kingdom* case, decided in 1978 and concerning the conflict in Northern Ireland, especially the treatment of presumed Irish Republican Army (IRA) terrorists.[107]

[103] Fourteen members of the Commission shared this opinion; only one, Mr Sperduti, dissented: *Cruz Varas* report, para 122.

[104] *Cruz Varas* judgment, para 98.

[105] Elisabeth Lambert-Abdelgawad, *Preventing and Sanctioning Hindrances to the Right of Individual Petition Before the European Court of Human Rights* (Mortsel: Intersentia, 2011). The Inter-American Court did this immediately: Laurence Burgorgue-Larsen and Amaya Úbeda de Torres, *The Inter-American Court of Human Rights: Case Law and Commentary* (Oxford: Oxford University Press, 2011) Chapter 9.

[106] *Cruz Varas* judgment, para 83.

[107] *Ireland v. the United Kingdom*, appl. 5310, PC Judgment (ECtHR), 18 Jan. 1978, para 162.

The principle applies across the board of the many various situations where Article 3 is argued by applicants (not necessarily migrants). Applying the principle to the circumstances of the *Cruz Varas* case, the Court accepted that the applicant had been suffering from post-traumatic stress disorder prior to his expulsion and that his mental health had 'appeared' to deteriorate following his return to Chile (note yet again the distancing language).[108] However, as far as the Court was concerned, the expulsion had not 'exceeded the threshold set by Article 3', for no substantial basis had been shown for his fears.[109] This finding was adopted by 18 votes to one. The Commission had been more divided: it had reached the same conclusion by eight votes to five. For the dissenters 'having regard to the real risk of treatment contrary to Article 3 which existed at the relevant time, Mr Cruz Varas' personal and reasonable fears and anxiety for such treatment if expelled, and his bad state of health, his expulsion involved such serious hardship that it attained the level of severity which made Article 3 applicable'.[110]

As for the arguably traumatising effect of the expulsion on Mr Cruz Varas' four-year-old child, it was not mentioned in the Article 3 complaint.[111] The applicants had nonetheless argued that the expulsion had entailed a separation of the family in breach of Article 8. Both the Commission and the Court rejected this claim. In their view, no evidence had been adduced to demonstrate that family life could not be pursued in Chile. Accordingly, responsibility for the separation was not imputable to Sweden but to the actions of the second and third applicants who had gone into hiding (in Sweden) after the first applicant had been taken into custody in Sweden to facilitate his deportation to Chile. The two bodies reached this finding unanimously. They reaffirmed that Article 8 does not guarantee migrant families the right to live together in the country where one of their members happens to be, as per *Abdulaziz, Cabales and Balkandali* (see Chapter 4).[112]

Last but not least, the inadmissible character of an Article 6 complaint with regard to immigration proceedings was yet again repeated.[113] The applicants had argued in their original application to the Commission that the examination of their requests for a residence permit was a determination of their civil rights, so that they should have been entitled to a procedure which satisfied the

[108] *Cruz Varas* judgment, para 83. [109] *Cruz Varas* judgment, para 83.

[110] Trechsel et al. in *Cruz Varas* report.

[111] Children and their 'best interests', to use the phrase of the UN Convention on the Rights of the Child, have long remained peripheral to the Strasbourg case law. See Eva Brems (ed.) *Diversity and European Human Rights: Rewriting Judgments of the ECHR* (Cambridge: Cambridge University Press, 2013), Part I on 'Children'.

[112] *Cruz Varas* judgment, para 88; *Cruz Varas* report, paras 97 and 100. The Commission continued by observing that the alternative of taking the whole family into custody to ensure the expulsion was not above reproach as it would mean a considerable increase in the number of individuals deprived of their liberty and notably children. This remark shows, if needed, that perspectives on immigration detention have changed tremendously in the last two decades: *Cruz Varas* report, para 101. On immigration detention in the Strasbourg case law, see Chapter 11.

[113] Early applicants commonly alleged that Article 6 had been violated, as noted in passing in Chapter 3 in relation to *East African Asians v. the United Kingdom*, appl. 4403/70 and 30 others, PCom Report (EComHR), 14 Dec. 1973 and in Chapter 4 (pp. 102–3) in relation to *Alam and Khan v. the United Kingdom*, appl. 2991/66, PCom Report (EComHR), 17 Dec. 1968.

requirements of a fair trial under Article 6.[114] The Commission responded that it had 'constantly held that a decision as to whether an alien should be able to stay in a country is a discretionary act of a public authority' which thus falls outside the scope of Article 6; the Commission found no reason to depart from this case law,[115] and declared the complaint inadmissible. To my knowledge the only complaint related to this point which has ever been declared admissible is *Maaouia v. France*, a case which was brought before the 'new' Court soon after it was established in November 1998.[116] Perhaps unwisely, the Chamber originally assigned *Maaouia* relinquished jurisdiction to the Grand Chamber, which proceeded to confirm the Commission's long-established stance.[117] A fully authoritative precedent was therefore created, with the unfortunate result that a change on this absolutely crucial point for the defence of migrants' rights is still awaited today.[118] Baldinger argues that Article 6 ECHR is now fully applicable to *national* asylum court proceedings via Article 47 of the EU Charter of Fundamental Rights.[119] For the Strasbourg Court to overturn *Maaouia* would be the next logical step.[120] Some judges who belong to the Strasbourg 'undercurrent' are known to think that the time is becoming ripe for this to happen.[121]

X. Back to the Commission and enter *Kozlov* and *Varfolomejev*: When is Inhuman 'Inhuman'?

Current Strasbourg case law often remains rooted in decisions of the erstwhile Commission which have long been forgotten. This book has been able to draw this lesson from its assumption that researching the Commission's case law is invariably rewarding. This perspective has led to the unearthing of a couple of

[114] *Cruz Varas* decision, point 3 under the section entitled 'The Law'.

[115] Cruz Varas decision, point 3 under the section entitled 'The Law'.

[116] *Maaouia v. France*, appl. 39652/98, GC Judgment (ECtHR), 5 Oct. 2000.

[117] The Chamber was obviously sympathetic to the case, or it would not have declared it admissible.

[118] This jurisprudence has a tremendous impact on migrants' lives. Given this it is surprising how difficult it is to find academic commentary on it. One exception is: Ian Bryan and Peter Langford, 'Impediments to the Expulsion of Non-Nationals: Substance and Coherence in Procedural Protection under the European Convention on Human Rights' (2010) *Nordic Journal of International Law* 79, 457–479. See also C. W. Wouters, *International Legal Standards for the Protection from Refoulement* (Antwerp: Intersentia, 2009) 344–345. Pieter Boeles had made a cogent argument for the application of Article 6 to immigration proceedings before *Maaouia* settled the point in the opposite way: Boeles, *Fair Immigration Proceedings in Europe* (The Hague: Martinus Nijhoff, 1997).

[119] Baldinger *Rigorous Scrutiny* 210–233.

[120] The more so ever since the Court extended the application of Article 6 to a dispute regarding the salaries of police officers—an area which could have been construed as belonging by nature to administrative law: *Vilho Eskelinen and Others v. Finland*, appl. 63235/00, GC Judgment (ECtHR), 19 Apr. 2007.

[121] Judge Tulkens, personal communication (May 2011). *Maaouia* is currently a major battleground in the UK because of cuts to legal aid. Were domestic judicial challenges to the British government's policies to fail, one assumes that the European Court of Human Rights will have the opportunity to revisit *Maaouia*, if it so wishes.

decisions which the Commission adopted a few months after the Plenary Court delivered its judgment in *Cruz Varas*. What these two decisions indicate is that the Strasbourg institutions were set to interpret the notion of treatment proscribed by Article 3 restrictively. As a result, the sacrosanct principle according to which return to proscribed treatment is prohibited would be confined in its actual application to rather limited situations.

Article 3 prohibits 'torture' and 'inhuman or degrading treatment', with the latter concept initially very much seen as a milder version of the former. Neither notion is immediately clear. Famously, in the *Ireland v. the United Kingdom* case, the techniques of sensory deprivation used by the British government against IRA suspects were thought by the European Commission of Human Rights to amount to torture, but not by the Court.[122] As for the notion of 'inhuman or degrading treatment', it was originally conceived in the Convention and by the Strasbourg institutions as something approaching but not quite reaching the threshold of physical or mental torture. This conception has had tremendous implications for the way the case law on Article 3 return cases has (or, rather, has not) developed, as the present and next sections demonstrate.

The *Kozlov v. Finland* application was lodged with the Commission in July 1990.[123] The applicant was a citizen of the Soviet Union who had been called up for military service in 1988 when he had turned 18. Having notified the Soviet authorities that he felt unable to continue his military service because it caused him moral and ethical problems, Mr Kozlov had been sent to a military hospital where he was injected with sulphuric substances. On his release from hospital, his military passport was stamped with an indication that he was mentally ill, thus preventing him from continuing his studies, working, choosing his domicile, obtaining a passport, and participating in public elections. In June 1990, Mr Kozlov hijacked a small aircraft and, without having hurt anyone or used any weapon, arrived in Finland where he claimed asylum. His application was rejected and, in July 1990, he was sent back to the Soviet Union which had requested his extradition. The day before, he had slashed himself with a razor blade. Back in the Soviet Union, he was sentenced to five years' imprisonment with 'hard discipline'. His lawyer argued at Strasbourg that his trial, held in March 1991, had not satisfied fairness requirements (Mr Kozlov had been placed in a cage with metal bars, with his defence counsel sitting five metres away from him, thus preventing communication between the two during the proceedings).[124] On 28 May 1991, the Commission declared the *Kozlov* application inadmissible:

[122] *Ireland v. the United Kingdom* paras 165–168 (for the Court's opinion). Think also of the discussions surrounding 'waterboarding' in the United States.

[123] *Kozlov v. Finland*, appl. 16832/90, Decision (EComHR), 28 May 1991.

[124] This practice has recently been examined by the Court in a number of cases. See e.g. *Khodorkovskiy v. Russia*, appl. 5829/04, Judgment (ECtHR), 31 May 2011, and comments by Strasbourg Observers, http://strasbourgobservers.com/2011/06/20/khodorkovskiy-in-a-cage/, accessed 26 August 2014. *Svinarenko and Slyadnev v. Russia*, appls 32541/08, 43441/08, Judgment (ECtHR), 11 Dec. 2012 was referred to the Grand Chamber, which confirmed on 17 July 2014 the conclusion that 'the applicants' confinement in a metal cage in the courtroom amounted to degrading treatment prohibited by Article 3' (para 139).

> In the present case, the Commission considers that the information which was available to the Finnish Government at the time of the extradition with regard to the personal situation of the applicant and the development in the Soviet Union did not show that the applicant, upon his extradition, would run a substantial risk of being exposed to treatment contrary to Article 3 (Art. 3) of the Convention. The information which has subsequently been provided by the applicant's lawyer about the applicant's trial, conviction and sentence cannot be considered to show that the applicant has been, or is likely to be, submitted to treatment of punishment *of such gravity* as to be deemed 'inhuman' or 'degrading' within the meaning of Article 3 (Art. 3) of the Convention.[125]

Three months later, the Commission reached the same conclusion in a very similar case.[126] This time, the applicant had requested to be examined by doctors in Finland, who found him mentally healthy. On his return to the Soviet Union Mr Varfolomejev was tried and given a four-year suspended sentence. His invalidity classification, based on his mental illness as diagnosed prior to his escape to Finland, was not revoked, however, so that he was not able to work.

Finland had only ratified the European Convention the year before, in May 1990 and these were the very first decisions of the Commission concerning it (showing, once again, that lawyers defending migrants were quick to perceive the Convention as a potentially useful instrument for their clients). Throughout the Cold War, Finland was the only European non-USSR country to return Soviet nationals to the USSR, a practice which Amnesty International had denounced in successive reports.[127] It is therefore intriguing that the Commission did not find it in breach of the European Convention. Far from it, in the second case the Commission praised the 'considerable care' the Finnish government had displayed 'in order to preclude a real risk that the applicant would be exposed to treatment contrary to Article 3'. Presumably Finland had learnt its lesson from the first case and had put more conditions on the extradition of Mr Varfolomejev than on that of Mr Kozlov. A close reading of the Commission's decision suggests that the Finnish authorities had insisted that Mr Varfolomejev should not be prosecuted or punished for any offence other than the hijacking,[128] that a Finnish psychiatrist should be allowed to participate in any further mental examination undertaken in the Soviet Union, and that the Finnish government should receive information regarding any criminal proceedings directed against the applicant after he was extradited. As we have seen, Mr Varfolomejev escaped the fate of Mr Kozlov of not only being sent to prison but also being subjected to 'hard discipline' while there. He remained labelled, however, as a paranoid schizophrenic.

[125] *Oleg Kozlov v. Finland*, appl. 16832/90, Decision (EComHR), 28 May 1991, emphasis added.

[126] *Varfolomejev v. Finland*, appl. 17811/91, Decision (EComHR), 2 Sept. 1991.

[127] Amnesty International, 'Finland, Protection of Refugees: Correspondence between Amnesty International and the Government of Finland', 30 September 1987 (AI Index: EUR 20/01/87); Amnesty International, 'Finland: Summary of Amnesty International's Concerns', October 1990 (AI Index: EUR 20/04/90).

[128] At that time, 'flight abroad, or refusal to return from abroad to the USSR' was regarded as a treasonable offence and was punishable by imprisonment for a term of 10 to 15 years with or without additional exile for a term of two to five years, or by death (Marjorie Farquharson, personal communication of 5 October 2011).

A talented Master's degree student who reviewed the nascent case law of the Strasbourg institutions in Article 3 return cases was not impressed by these decisions. Ralf Alleweldt asked the question: how could declaring mentally healthy individuals mentally ill and thus preventing them inter alia from working, studying, marrying, and founding a family not be found manifestly to constitute degrading or inhuman treatment?[129] The Commission did not provide any explanation. Realpolitik considerations might have played a part, such as a wish to avoid antagonising the USSR which was then engaging on a reform path—though a path which one applicant argued had 'not yet reached the military, prisons or mental hospitals'. There would also have been the politically and emotionally sensitive issue of the hijacking possibly being considered a criminal offence—even though the United Nations High Commissioner for Refugees (UNHCR) submitted an opinion to the effect that hijacking need not be considered a serious crime barring the granting of refugee status, when it is not carried out through violent means and is the only available means of escaping persecution on the grounds of political opinion.[130] Another possible explanation for these decisions is more simply that the Commission might not have found the treatment to which the applicants were subjected, however objectionable, close enough to torture to come within the ambit of Article 3. The European context, where Europe was bracing itself against asylum seekers coming from the hotspots of the world, may also have played a role. The first case was decided unanimously, the second by (undisclosed) majority.

An unduly restrictive interpretation of the required 'minimum level of severity' obviously empties the protection offered by Article 3 of much of its substance. At times, the Court has opened up this interpretation, such as in the *D. v. the United Kingdom* case, reviewed later. Most often the finding that the 'minimum level of severity' required to engage Article 3 is not reached is left unreasoned. The complaint is simply declared inadmissible for referring to a situation which 'manifestly' falls outside the scope of Article 3. In order to circumvent this difficulty, applicants have sometimes argued that their removal would be contrary to another article of the Convention, on the grounds that the removal would lead them to be subjected to an unfair trial (Article 6) or prevented from practicing their sexuality (Article 8),[131] religion (Article 9), or freedom of expression (Article 10).[132] The difficulty they have faced is that none of these provisions lay down absolute prohibitions. The Court has usually taken the view that because the rights provided in Articles 6 and 8 to 10 entail positive obligations which are

[129] Ralf Alleweldt, 'Protection Against Expulsion Under Article 3 of the European Convention on Human Rights' (1993) *European Journal of International Law* 4, 360–376 at 364.

[130] Varfolomejev, 'The Facts' part.

[131] For an insightful review of the way in which lesbian, gay, bisexual, transgender, queer (LGBTQ) individuals find it difficult to substantiate their claims for asylum in Canada, but with findings easily transferrable elsewhere: see Sharalyn R. Jordan, 'Un/Convention(al) Refugees: Contextualising the Accounts of Refugees Facing Homophobic or Transphobic Persecution' (2009) *Refuge: Canada's Periodical on Refugees* 26(2), 165–182.

[132] For more details, see: Nuala Mole, *Asylum and the European Convention on Human Rights* (Strasbourg: Council of Europe, 2008) 52–61.

by nature relative, they do not lend themselves to prohibiting return. Recently, however, the case law has moved on this front. Amidst much publicity, in January 2012, the Court ruled that the deportation of Abu Qatada from the UK to Jordan would infringe Article 6 of the Convention.[133] The impact of this jurisprudential development—perhaps adopted by the unanimous Court in the hope that a finding on Article 6 would be more acceptable to the UK than one on Article 3[134]—remains to be seen at the time of writing. What is certain is that the ruling did not abate the ire of the British government towards the Court.

XI. *Vilvarajah*: Randomly Inflicted Ill-Treatment does not Qualify for Article 3 Protection

War creates movements of population. As a Belgian, I should know that. Apparently, fleeing the deliberate killing of civilians and the destruction of homes by the German army, a staggering one million people left Belgium during World War I, amounting to almost one-sixth of the total population of the country. I was not aware of this until I read Nadine El-Enany's thesis.[135] By contrast, memories of the 1940 'evacuation' of Belgians to France populated my childhood. My father's family spent that summer in southern France. The family left their home one morning, without any preparation. Part of the journey was undertaken under German bombardment. My father always recalled the welcome, which never ceased to amaze him, with which they had been received and hosted for a whole three months by people they had never previously met. The notebook in which one of my ageing uncles gathered the recollections of his life contains the reproduction of the identity card he had been given. It bore his name and was stamped in capital letters '*RÉFUGIÉ*'. The journey had been traumatic, but once the family was temporarily settled, the children were nonetheless able to develop fond memories of a hot summer playing in the countryside.

[133] *Othman (Abu Qatada) v. the United Kingdom*, appl. 8139/09, Judgment (ECtHR), 17 Jan. 2012.

[134] The memorandum of understanding between the UK and Jordan was accepted by the Court as providing sufficient protection for the applicant from a violation of Article 3, due to the specific circumstances of its conclusion, its detail, and formality, and the modalities of monitoring the Jordanian authorities' compliance with the assurances. This, however, did not solve the problem of the Jordanian judiciary's use of evidence obtained under torture. The primary witness in the Jordanian state's case against Abu Qatada had given his evidence under torture, and there was widespread belief that other evidence had been similarly obtained. The Court thus ruled that use of such evidence would constitute a 'flagrant denial' of the substance of the right contained in Article 6. The UK government was forced to negotiate a further memorandum with the Jordanian authorities which addressed the Court's concerns regarding torture evidence. When this memorandum was concluded Mr Qatada voluntarily agreed to return to Jordan to face trial, rather than pursuing a further challenge.

[135] Nadine El-Enany, 'Refugee Law in the United Kingdom and the European Union: The Constitutive and Subversive Effects of Immigration and Border Control', 2011 PhD Thesis, European University Institute 43.

A few decades later and in a different part of the world, Sri Lanka started to produce its own *réfugiés*, notably after the killing in 1983 of 13 Sri Lankan soldiers by a Tamil liberation group triggered pogroms against Tamil communities. *Vilvarajah and Others v. the United Kingdom*, decided in October 1991, is the first of many judgments by the Strasbourg Court which testify to this situation. The Strasbourg case law shows that the generosity from which my father's family benefited in the early months of the Belgian invasion by the Nazi regime is not reproduced wherever and whenever people flee violence and devastation.

Two applications, lodged in 1987, generated the *Vilvarajah* case. The applicants were five young Tamils whose (unrelated) families had sent them on a journey which brought them to the UK earlier that year. Their relatives had feared that, as young males, they would be likely to be particularly targeted by the authorities as presumed members of the separatist Liberation Tigers group. The families had already suffered indiscriminate violence at the hands of the Sri Lankan army, taking the form of the destruction of homes, murders, detention, and beatings. The applicants' claims for asylum in the UK were rejected shortly after their arrival on the grounds that the events they recounted were 'random and part of the army's general activities directed at discovering and dealing with Tamil extremists'. As such, these events were ruled not to constitute evidence of personal, targeted persecution in the sense of the UN Refugee Convention.[136] The appeal against such a ruling not being suspensive, the UK returned the applicants to Sri Lanka in February 1988—at a time when some other European countries such as the Federal Republic of Germany and Italy were heeding the UNHCR's advice not to return Tamils to Sri Lanka.[137] When the applicants' legal representatives visited Sri Lanka in order to collect evidence as to what had happened to their clients upon their return, three recounted having suffered ill-treatment, including beatings with iron bars, hanging, and electric-shock treatment. In March 1989, this evidence persuaded the British adjudicator who was deciding their out-of-country asylum appeal to rule in their favour. The three were then allowed to return to the UK at the expense of the government.[138] As the Commission observed, the facts were not seriously in dispute, only their interpretation was.[139]

The Commission adopted its report in the case on 8 May 1990. By seven votes to seven, with the President's casting vote, the Commission found no violation of Article 3. It is worth quoting first the eminently sensible opinion of the minority:

> We are of the opinion that... the applicants faced a real risk of severe ill-treatment on return... [I]t was likely that they would be caught up in the troubles and exposed to a genuine risk to life and limb. There were no unambiguous signs of any amelioration of this civil disorder... Indeed the UNHCR had continuously urged that these people, including the present applicants, should not be forced to return, a plea supported by Amnesty

[136] Quoted in *Vilvarajah* judgment, para 13. [137] *Vilvarajah* judgment, para 76.

[138] This particular fact is mentioned by Judge Russo in his dissenting opinion in the *Vilvarajah* judgment.

[139] *Cruz Vara* report, para 141.

International and other humanitarian organisations.... Our opinion is further confirmed by the decision of the independent adjudicator on 13 March 1989 in these cases.[140]

These seven Commission members also mentioned two aggravating factors: the young age of the fourth applicant (born in 1970) and the fact that the fourth and fifth applicants had been sent back without their identity cards, thus making any travelling within Sri Lanka even more hazardous given the existence of numerous security check points on the roads.

For the other seven members who formed the majority of the Commission, by contrast, the decision of the UK to return the applicants was not unreasonable or arbitrary: although the applicants had undoubtedly been exposed to the possibility of ill-treatment, the applicants could not be said to have faced greater personal risks than the rest of the Tamil population, so that Article 3 had not been violated.[141]

The Court followed this view and elaborated on it as follows:

> The evidence before the Court concerning the background of the applicants, as well as the general situation, does not establish that their personal position was any worse than the generality of other members of the Tamil community or other young male Tamils who were returning to their country. Since the situation was still unsettled... there existed the possibility that they might be detained and ill-treated as appears to have occurred previously in the cases of some of the applicants... A mere possibility of ill-treatment, however, in such circumstances, is not in itself sufficient to give rise to a breach of Article 3.[142]

The fact that three applicants had in fact been subjected to ill-treatment following their return was neither here nor there. In the words of the Court: 'Be that as it may... there existed no special distinguishing features in their cases that could or ought to have enabled the Secretary of State to foresee that they would be treated in this way'.[143] Even the fact that two applicants had been returned without identity documents did not sway the Court to castigate the British authorities. This was 'open to criticism', the Court said, as it was 'likely to make travelling more difficult... because of numerous checkpoints' but 'this fact alone [could not be said to have] exposed them to a real risk of treatment going beyond the threshold set by Article 3'.[144]

Only the Italian judge, Judge Russo, found a violation of Article 3. The other eight judges did not. By seven votes to two, the Court also failed to find a violation of Article 13. The Commission had found a breach of this provision by 13 votes to one.

The real reason for the non-violation verdict may have been expressed by the government in an argument which the Court left unanswered:

[140] *Vilvarajah, Skandarajah, Sivakumaran, Navratna Singam, Rasalingam v. the United Kingdom*, appls 13163/87, 13164/87, 13165/87, 13447/87, 13448/87, Report (EComHR), 8 May 1990, partly dissenting opinion of MM. Trechsel, Emacora, Gözübuyuk, Campinos, Mrs Thune, Mr Rozakis and Mrs Liddy, as regards the issue under Article 3 of the Convention.

[141] *Vilvarajah* report, para 143.

[142] *Vilvarajah* judgment, para 111.

[143] *Vilvarajah*, para 112.

[144] *Vilvarajah*, para 113.

[I]n determining whether a State's responsibility is in fact engaged in any particular case, a balance is to be struck between the demands of the general interest of the community and the requirements of the protection of the individual's fundamental rights. The consequences of finding a breach of Article 3 . . . in the present case would be that all persons in similar situations, facing random risks on account of civil turmoil in the State in which they lived, would be entitled not to be removed, thereby permitting the entry of a potentially very large class of people with the attendant serious social and economic consequences.[145]

As for the first sentence, the Court would later reject the argument, put forward yet again by the British government, to the effect that balancing the applicant's individual interest with that of the community was appropriate in Article 3 return cases (see later). As for the second sentence, I wonder whether it might obliquely reveal the real reason why the Court refused to find a violation of Article 3 in *Vilvarajah*, namely its fear that many individuals would be able to rely on the precedent *Vilvarajah* would create if the applicants succeeded on this occasion and that this would entail an 'opening of the floodgates' in times of acute crises around the world.

The Court would certainly prove most careful in not opening the Strasbourg gates too widely. To this day, returns to a situation of general violence are rarely found to entail a violation of Article 3, as Tamil, Afghan, Congolese, and Palestinian applicants have repeatedly found.[146] With *NA. v. the United Kingdom*—yet another Tamil case—decided in July 2008, the Court took the opportunity of explaining its case law in this area.[147] On this occasion, the Court accepted that the fierce deterioration of the situation in Sri Lanka was leading to egregious human rights violations. Still, it reaffirmed the principle that the applicant had to demonstrate 'special distinguishing factors' indicating why he would be at risk of ill-treatment upon return if a violation of Article 3 is to be found.[148] In this particular case, the applicant managed this, but other Tamils would not.[149] For the Court, the important point was, first, that 'the domestic authorities . . . [had not concluded] that . . . *all* Tamils returning to Sri Lanka [were at risk]' and, second, that nothing in the information submitted required the Court to reach, of its own motion, a different conclusion.[150] The Court expressly refuted the idea that its insistence on the existence of further distinguishing factors personal to the applicant rendered 'illusory' the protection offered by Article 3.[151] It appears to be hardly coincidental that this confirmation of a very high test was adopted by a Chamber formed from the Section of the Court then presided over by Judge Bratza. As we shall discuss in Chapters 8 and 12, on more than one occasion Judge Bratza took the opposite view to that of the resolutely pro-migrant Judge Tulkens, who was then presiding over another Section of the Court.

145 *Vilvarajah*, para 105.

146 For specific references to case law, see: Baldinger *Rigorous Scrutiny* 244, note 269.

147 *NA. v. the United Kingdom*, appl. 25904/07, Judgment (ECtHR), 17 July 2008, paras 108–117.

148 *NA.*, para 128.

149 One case in point is the Tamil applicant in *E.G. v. the United Kingdom*, appl. 41178/08, Judgment (ECtHR), 31 May 2011. Note Judges Garlicki and Kalaydjieva's dissenting opinion in this case, which was decided by a Chamber drawn from the Fourth Section.

150 *NA.* judgment, para 125, emphasis added.

151 *NA.*, para 128.

At the time of writing, there has only been one case where the Court has been persuaded to accept that the applicants were at risk of a violation of Article 3 if returned on account of a general situation of violence. This is *Sufi and Elmi v. the United Kingdom*, decided by the same Fourth Section on 28 June 2011.[152] In this case, which concerned a return to Somalia, the Court considered that 'the large quantity of objective information overwhelmingly indicates that the level of violence in Mogadishu is of sufficient intensity to pose a real risk of treatment reaching the Article 3 threshold to *anyone* in the capital'.[153] Even before this factual finding was overturned,[154] a Belgian asylum lawyer with whom I discussed *Sufi and Elmi* found the case depressing. Yes, he said, the applicants' representatives had made a stellar job of collating report after report and of assessing the situation on the ground in Somalia, almost kilometre by kilometre. But how was the run-of-the-mill lawyer expected to be able to do this? Especially at a time of legal aid cuts. And, most importantly, what were the consequences of this approach for failed asylum seekers or other expelled migrants who were not able to access the level and quality of legal representation which the applicants in *Sufi and Elmi* had enjoyed?

XII. An Important Aside: Why the Leading Case of *Soering*, not *Vilvarajah*?

Before moving on with our discussion, let us return briefly to *Vilvarajah*. The case was lodged in 1987—more than half a year before *Soering*. It was far more representative of the type of returns which were generating applications at Strasbourg than *Soering*. Why then did it not get selected as the case to fast-track in order to produce a leading case?

Admittedly *Vilvarajah* was not the ideal case to obtain the principle that a return could be problematic under Article 3 established by the Court. But neither was *Soering*, as we have seen. Of course, Mr Soering had excellent lawyers—but the *Vilvarajah* applicants benefited from the very best legal representation too.[155] On the face of the Commission's report, *Soering* might even have been thought to be slightly less promising than *Vilvarajah*. In *Soering*, a majority of Commission members failed to find a violation of Article 3. Admittedly this was a majority of only 6 against as many as 5, but this was still the majority. In *Vilvarajah*, the 14 Commission members who examined the case were equally divided; it took the casting vote of the

[152] *Sufi and Elmi v. the United Kingdom*, appls 8319/07, 11449/07, Judgment (ECtHR), 28 June 2011.

[153] *Sufi and Elmi*, para 248.

[154] *K.A.B. v. Sweden*, appl. 886/11, Judgment (ECtHR), 5 Sept. 2013. The significance the Court attributes to this ruling is demonstrated by the fact that *K.A.B* is one of only two Article 3 expulsion cases mentioned in its 'Annual Report 2013', <http://www.echr.coe.int/Documents/Annual_report_2013_ENG.pdf>, accessed 17 May 2014, pp. 86–87.

[155] Mr Soering was represented by Colin Nicholls QC, and R. Spencer and F. Gardner, Solicitors; the *Vilvarajah* applicants by Richard Plender QC, Nicholas Blake, Counsel, (the late) David Burgess and Christopher Randall, Solicitors, all specialists in refugee and immigration matters and stars of the legal profession in the UK.

President to get the Commission's view to be that Article 3 had not been violated. Moreover, the British government had expected to lose the *Vilvarajah* case. (This was so much so that proposals for the introduction, for the first time in the UK, of a suspensive right of appeal for failed asylum seekers were published prior to the Strasbourg hearing in the case; these proposals were integrated in the British legislation in 1993.) The question is nagging: why *Soering*, not *Vilvarajah*?

It is easy to imagine that the Court would have wanted to avoid establishing the application of Article 3 in a return case in an area as politically sensitive as asylum had become in the late 1980s. At the height of the Cold War, Western Europe had warmly welcomed the few defectors who had managed to make it from behind the Iron Curtain. Then, each defection was a celebration. Even refugees from the right-wing Latin American dictatorships who had landed in Europe in the 1970s were integrated into the labour force and within the population with relative ease. By the end of the next decade (as Mr Cruz Varas discovered when he came to Europe in 1987), the aura surrounding seeking asylum had vanished. In addition, some internal conflicts, notably in Sri Lanka and Iran, were producing a large number of asylum seekers. Suddenly, now that Europe no longer wanted labour migrants, the perception was that the refugee regime was being abused and that it was unable to cope with the pressures which it was experiencing. Barriers were erected everywhere. This climate of anti-asylum seekers may have influenced Strasbourg Commission members and judges.

Could it also be that the Strasbourg judges could consciously or unconsciously imagine the applicant in *Soering*—a white European young man—being a son, nephew, friend, or acquaintance, a loose association which could somehow have contributed not only to the decision to fast-track the *Soering* case but also to the outcome of the verdict? We shall never know. We can nonetheless speculate that a Strasbourg judge might find it easier to empathise with the horror of being on death row in the United States than of being subjected to torture as a Tamil in Sri Lanka—or reduced to slave status in Mauritania[156] or subjected to female genital mutilation in Nigeria,[157] to draw on only two examples from the subsequent applications which were rejected.

XIII. An Alternative Pro-Migrant Case Law: The Leading Case of my Imagination

Granted, the European Convention has never specifically guaranteed a right to asylum. However, an activist court would have had no problem with circumventing this difficulty, just as the Strasbourg Court had done in *Marckx* (when it was faced with national discrimination between 'natural' and 'legitimate' children), *Airey* (when the applicant complained that without legal aid she did not have the means to separate from her husband), and many other cases which at first sight have raised issues squarely outside the Convention's remit.

156 *Ould Barar v. Sweden*, appl. 42367/98, Decision (ECtHR), 19 Jan. 1999.
157 *Collins and Akaziebie v. Sweden*, appl. 23944/05, Decision (ECtHR), 8 Mar. 2007.

One only needs to turn to the dissenting opinions of judges and Commission members to think about what an alternative, resolutely pro-migrant case law might have looked like in Article 3 return cases. The seeds planted by this imaginary leading case would have seen the Court:

(a) refraining from rushing to dismiss the allegations of the applicant (and at the very least reporting them in a truly neutral tone);
(b) approaching the respondent state's allegations with a degree of caution and looking at reversing the burden of proof onto the state;
(c) taking every opportunity to subject national determination procedures to scrutiny (as the best chance of affecting systemic changes in a deficient asylum process);
(d) assessing Article 3 complaints *ex nunc* and Article 13 complaints strictly *ex tunc*;
(e) being strong at ordering interim measures and insisting from the start that these were binding on the respondent state;
(f) understanding 'inhuman or degrading treatment' by reference to the common understanding of these words rather than through implicit reference to the UN Refugee Convention.

Crucially their various lines of action would not even have needed to be incrementally adopted as the case law was slowly developing. The experience of the Inter-American system (discussed in subsequent chapters) suggests that they could have all happened at once.

XIV. The Court's Reluctance to Proceed to Verdicts of Violation

Instead of a multi-prong, activist approach to the problem of seeing Europe closing its doors to refugees, the Strasbourg Court trod cautiously. The result is that its recognition of the removal of an individual violating Article 3 when it places this individual at risk of ill-treatment—however crucial—has in practice had a much more limited impact than could have been expected. In order to start substantiating this point, Table 7.1 shows in chronological order the results of a HUDOC search for judgments related to 'Article 3' and containing the word 'asylum', up to 31 December 2000.[158] The year 2000 is not particularly significant. It has been selected because it is a round number which appears suitable, following as it does the *Soering* Grand Chamber judgment by over a decade, thus

[158] 'False negatives' such as *Soering, Djeroud v. France*, appl. 13446/87, Judgment (ECtHR), 23 Jan. 1991, and *Beldjoudi v. France*, appl. 12083/86, Judgment (ECtHR), 26 Mar. 1992 have been eliminated. *Bahaddar* has been added, producing what appears to be a comprehensive list as no other relevant case is mentioned by Peer Lorenzen in *Actes du 2e Colloque sur la Convention européenne des Droits de l'Homme et la protection des réfugiés, des demandeurs d'asile et des personnes déplacées [Strasbourg, 19–20 mai 2000]* (Strasbourg: Council of Europe, 2001) 26, note 3.

Table 7.1 Post-*Soering* Judgments in Cases Introduced by Failed Asylum Seekers or Refugees (until 31 December 2000)

Name of case	Date of Judgment	Origin of applicant	Violation of Article 3?
Cruz Varas and Others v. the United Kingdom	20/04/1991	Chile	No
Vilvarajah and Others v. the United Kingdom	30/10/1991	Sri Lanka (Tamil)	No
Vijayanathan and Pusparajah v. France	27/08/1992	Sri Lanka (Tamil)	Not considered (no longer at imminent risk of removal)
Chahal v. the United Kingdom	**15/11/1996**	**India (Sikh)**	**Yes**
Ahmed v. Austria	**17/12/1996**	**Somalia**	**Yes**
H.L.R. v. France	29/04/1997	Columbia	No
Paez v. Sweden	30/10/1997	Peru	Not considered (residence permit granted)
Bahaddar v. the Netherlands	19/02/1998	Bangladesh	No (inadmissible)
Hatami v. Sweden	09/10/1998	Iran	Not considered (friendly settlement)
Abdurrahim Incedursun v. the Netherlands	22/06/1999	Turkey (Kurd)	Not considered (residence permit granted)
Aspichi Dehwari v. the Netherlands	27/04/2000	Iran	Not considered (residence permit granted)
G.H.H. and Others v. Turkey	11/07/2000	Iran	Not considered (applicants now living in the United States)
Jabari v. Turkey	**11/07/2000**	**Iran**	**Yes**

Source: HUDOC database.

allowing sufficient time for the Court to have had a real opportunity to develop its case law. The selected cut-off year offers the additional advantage of including the early months of the 'new' Court, which serves to highlight that it did not adopt a significantly different approach from that pursued by the 'old' Court.

Only three out of the 13 cases listed in Table 7.1 ended with a verdict of non-violation of the Convention, with a fourth case declared inadmissible. This automatically suggests a 70 per cent rate of success for the applicants. Such a promising result might at first sight appear to contradict the main argument developed in this chapter. What must be taken into consideration, however, is that these four judgments would have a major impact on the development of subsequent case law, including by leading committees of three to declare cases inadmissible on the basis of the principles they had erected.

There is no need to reiterate here the principles which the Court developed in *Cruz Varas*, *Vilvarajah*, and *Bahaddar*, as they already have been extensively reviewed and exposed to be overall in favour of the state. The fourth case, *H.L.R. v. France*, recognised that it was not just actions by public officials in the returned country which could give rise to a violation of Article 3.[159] This principle in theory extends the protection offered to migrants threatened with return. On the facts, however, the applicant was unsuccessful. He had been found smuggling drugs while in transit through Roissy Airport. After his trial in France, he argued that a return to Columbia would expose him to vengeance by the drug traffickers he had denounced and exposed to the French police. By 19 votes to ten, the Commission agreed that his return would entail a violation of Article 3. By contrast, a majority of 15 judges were of the view that the applicant had not demonstrated that he was at 'real risk' of ill-treatment with the scenario he feared, for example, not mentioned in Amnesty International reports.[160] Six judges took the opposite view. This case shows yet again the crucial importance of principles and practice related to the burden and standard of proof.

Understanding when the Court accepts that there is a violation of Article 3 in a return case has the potential of either invalidating or supporting the thesis developed in this chapter. Table 7.1 contains three verdicts of violation. Starting with the latest, the applicant in *Jabari v. Turkey* had been granted refugee status by the authority competent to do so in Turkey, namely the Ankara branch office of the UNHCR, which had concluded that removing her to her home country (Iran) might expose her to being stoned to death, whipped, or flogged on account of her adultery.[161] It is useful at this stage to note that a refugee determination by the UNHCR is not a definite guarantee that the Strasbourg Court will find a return to be in violation of the Convention. Baldinger cites the case of *Y v. Russia*,[162] decided in 2008, as a counter-example. Nonetheless, the same author observes that the Court normally relies on the determination made by the UNHCR.[163] When state authorities have themselves acknowledged the reality of the risk of ill-treatment upon return, it seems to me that the Court never goes against this finding. This, I would argue, is what happened in the first verdict of violation listed in Table 7.1, *Chahal v. the United Kingdom*.[164] In this case the domestic authorities said that they had been *balancing* the risk of persecution with the national security risk posed by the applicant, a Sikh activist who was suspected of having participated in terrorist activities. *Chahal* has become notorious for the response of the Strasbourg Court, to the effect that since the prohibition of returning an applicant to ill-treatment is absolute, the balancing exercise undertaken by the British authorities was not allowed. [165] What is important for the present discussion, however, is that the government's phrasing of its argument seemed to implicitly acknowledge that the applicant was indeed at risk of persecution. The last

[159] *H.L.R. v. France*, appl. 24573/94, GC Judgment (ECtHR), 29 Apr. 1997, para 40.

[160] *H.L.R.*, para 42.

[161] That the applicant was a woman is worth noting given the under-representation of female applicants in this area even though they constitute a significant part of the migrant population.

[162] *Y. v. Russia*, appl. 20113/07, Judgment (ECtHR), 4 Dec. 2008. In this case one of the Chinese applicants, a couple, was a Falun Gong practitioner who had been granted refugee status by the UNHCR office in Moscow.

[163] Baldinger *Rigorous Scrutiny* 250, and references cited therein.

[164] *Chahal v. the United Kingdom*, appl. 22414/93, GC Judgment (ECtHR), 15 Nov. 1996.

[165] Compare the argument put by the government in *Vilvarajah*, but not specifically responded to by the Court, that 'a balance [needed] to be struck between the demands of the general interest of the

relevant case on the list, *Ahmed v. Austria*, was even clearer on this front: the Austrian Ministry of the Interior had granted the applicant, a Somali citizen, refugee status (but forfeited this status after he was convicted of attempted robbery).

The common point between the three verdicts of violation listed in Table 7.1, therefore, is that in each of these cases either the domestic authorities themselves or the UNHCR had recognised that the applicant might be persecuted if returned to his or her country of origin. Interestingly, the same factor can be said to have been at play in *Soering*. The reader may recall that at the Court's hearing, the Advocate General had recognised that the applicant might experience the death-row phenomenon if he was returned. In my view, this 'detail' might have been the crucial element which swung the case.

If I am right, this means that applicants with the best chance of winning their case at Strasbourg would be those in respect of whom the state has acknowledged, perhaps inadvertently or by relying on the UNHCR to make determinations in respect of asylum claims lodged in their country, that they are actually at risk of ill-treatment upon return. A recent variation of this scenario is the case of *I.K. v. Austria* where the Court found that the expulsion of the applicant of Chechen origin to Russia would entail a violation of Article 3 as the applicant's mother had been granted the status of refugee in domestic appeal proceedings and that there was no indication in the file that the applicant would be at a lesser risk of persecution upon return to Russia than his mother.[166] Such a scenario is by its nature not going to be a common occurrence, as the very fact that proceedings are taking place at Strasbourg is in the great majority of cases precisely because the authorities are denying the reality of this risk. Admittedly applicants sometimes manage to prove the reality of this risk outside this scenario, as for example occurred in the cases of *NA* and *Sufi and Elmi*. The odds are nonetheless greatly stacked against the applicants to manage to prove their case.

The six remaining cases in Table 7.1 also deserve some commentary. They did not give rise to a ruling on Article 3 by the Court because the applicants had ceased to be at immediate risk of removal by the respondent state. In these cases (which include *Hatami*, discussed earlier) the defendant government would have anticipated losing before the Court. However, it is impossible to be certain of the outcome which would have been reached had the cases proceeded to a judgment on the merits.[167] That said, the case law does not appear to suggest that many verdicts of violation would have been found.

community and the requirements of the protection of the individual's fundamental rights': reported in *Vilvarajah* judgment, para 105.

[166] *I.K. v. Austria*, appl. 2964/12, GC Judgment (ECtHR), 28 Mar. 2013.

[167] Today the Court refrains from disclosing to the parties, prior to the delivery of the judgment, its provisional view as to whether or not there has been a violation of the Convention: Helen Keller, Magdalena Forowicz, and Florenz Engi, *Friendly Settlements Before the European Court of Human Rights: Theory and Practice* (Oxford: Oxford University Press, 2010) 31. By contrast in the era of the 'old' Court, pre-1998, when the Commission was responsible for negotiating and concluding friendly settlements, the Commission shared with the parties its provisional view on the merits of

Equally importantly, the six struck-out outcomes mean that the Court did not seize the opportunity of using any of these cases to produce a general effect.[168] In the absence of any judgment formally finding it in violation of the Convention, none of the respondent states in these cases was under an obligation to change the way it determined asylum and other protection claims.

The Court's reluctance to pronounce on the merits in asylum seeker return cases was extremely frustrating for migrants' defenders. In 2000, Nuala Mole, Director of the AIRE Centre in London, noted at a colloquium on the European Convention and asylum that, in the previous three years alone, the Convention institutions had received more than 100 complaints related to expulsion and Article 3.[169] The great majority of these applications were summarily rejected, without any reasoning, by committees of threes. The state of affairs where little case law reached the annals of the Court started to change half a decade later. Even so, violation verdicts remain exceptional, rather than run of the mill, as we shall have the occasion to note in Chapter 12 which discusses the tremendously important and positive case of *M.S.S. v. Belgium and Greece*.[170]

XV. Is a Return to No Medical Care Compatible with Article 3? The One-Off Case of *D. v. the United Kingdom*

The review of the post-*Soering* case law up to the new millennium would not be complete without discussing *D. v. the United Kingdom*, decided in 1997. In this case, the Court ruled that the deportation to the Caribbean island of St Kitts of an AIDS sufferer in the very last stages of the disease would contravene Article 3.

the case: Keller et al. 18. Keller and her co-authors nonetheless note that the invitation by the 'new' Court's Registry for the state to settle the case amounts to an indication that it considers the case clear-cut: Keller et al. 31, note 97.

168 Compare with the way in which the Strasbourg Court carried out the examination of *Berrehab v. the Netherlands*, appl. 10730/84, Judgment (ECtHR), 21 June 1988 and *Moustaquim* v. *Belgium*, appl. 12313/86, Judgment (ECtHR), 18 Feb. 1991 after the applicants in these two cases had received a residence permit, as reviewed in Chapter 6 (pp. 171 and 175 n. 42)., respectively. Also worth comparing is the way the Inter-American Court chooses to carry on with the case even when the situation of the individual victims has been resolved. See e.g. *The Girls Yean and Bosico v. Dominican Republic*, Preliminary Objections, Merits, Reparations and Costs, Judgment (IACtHR), 8 Sept. 2005 case, discussed in Chapter 10 (Section III).

169 Nuala Mole, 'Exposé', in *Actes du 2e Colloque sur la Convention européenne des Droits de l'Homme et la protection des réfugiés, des demandeurs d'asile et des personnes déplacées [Strasbourg, 19–20 mai 2000]* (Strasbourg: Council of Europe, 2001) 39–50 at 43.

170 It is striking that many applicants who could have taken their case to Strasbourg have decided instead to lodge a complaint with the UN Committee Against Torture, which is not empowered to give binding judgments but expresses views instead on violations of the Convention Against Torture (CAT). Presumably this is because they (rightly) assessed that this Committee was more likely to rule in their favour than the European Court of Human Rights. On the CAT's case law in this area, see: Baldinger *Rigorous Scrutiny* Chapter 4. The UK has not ratified the Protocol permitting individuals to bring a complaint against it before the CAT committee.

The applicant, known only as D., had spent most of his life in St Kitts. He had arrived in the UK in 1993 and was found to be carrying a substantial amount of cocaine with a street value estimated at £120,000. The following year, while in prison, he was diagnosed with AIDS. Prior to his release on licence in 1996, directions for his removal to St Kitts were issued. He applied to Strasbourg. The government argued that:

> [T]he applicant had no valid claim under Article 3 (art. 3) in the circumstances of the case since he would not be exposed in the receiving country to any form of treatment which breached the standards of Article 3 (art. 3). His hardship and reduced life expectancy would stem from his terminal and incurable illness coupled with the deficiencies in the health and social-welfare system of a poor, developing country. He would find himself in the same situation as other AIDS victims in St Kitts.[171]

The Court refused this argument. It stated that the fact that the risk of ill-treatment stemmed from 'factors which cannot engage either directly or indirectly the responsibility of the public authorities of [the receiving] country, or which, taken alone, do not in themselves infringe the standards of... Article 3' was not a reason for it not to examine the applicant's claim.[172] The Court added: 'To limit the application of Article 3 (art. 3) in this manner would be to undermine the absolute character of its protection'.[173] Turning to the circumstances of the case, the Court was sensitive to the fact that D. had no remaining family or social network in St Kitts and that he would have no guaranteed access to any medical support there. Moreover, by the time his application was examined, he was 'clearly weak and close to death'.[174] The Chamber of nine judges unanimously found that a deportation to St Kitts in these very particular circumstances would violate the Convention.

Since then other applicants have often claimed before the Court that their deportation would condemn them to a serious deterioration of their medical condition or even to an early death, but to no avail.[175] The Court gave a very clear signal that *D. v. the United Kingdom* was an exceptional case which would remain so when a Grand Chamber decided the case of *N. v. the United Kingdom* in 2008.[176] By that time, N., a failed asylum seeker, had been living in the UK for ten years. Suffering from AIDS like D., she was nonetheless in a stable condition due to the treatment she was receiving in the UK. This factor and other factual circumstances persuaded the Grand Chamber to distinguish *N.* from *D.* A majority of 14 judges found no reason to declare that N.'s deportation would infringe the Convention. N.'s death followed, as predicted, within months of her return to Uganda. In all likelihood, she would still be alive as I write these lines had she been allowed to remain in the UK.

In a tightly argued opinion, Judges Tulkens, Bonello, and Spielmann strongly dissented with their colleagues in *N.* Two of their remarks concerning 'general

[171] *D. v. the United Kingdom* judgment, para 42. [172] *D.*, para 49.
[173] *D.*, para 49. [174] *D.*, para 41.
[175] See the Court's own review of its relevant case law in *N. v. the United Kingdom*, appl. 26565/05, GC Judgment (ECtHR), 27 May 2008, paras 35–41.
[176] *N.* judgment.

principles' merit special attention. They noted that in previous cases, such as *Pretty v. the United Kingdom*, the Court had accepted that Article 3 could be engaged when treatment for which contracting states could be held responsible would aggravate the suffering flowing from 'naturally-occurring illness'.[177] The three dissenting judges therefore did not understand why ill-treatment emanating from illness (as opposed to acts by public authorities) should be considered only if it reached a 'higher threshold'[178]—the test used by the Court in Article 3 return cases involving concerns about level of health care in the returning country ever since *Bensaid v. France*.[179] Second, the dissenting judges lamented the suggestion of the Grand Chamber in *N.* that the Convention is directed at the protection of civil and political rights, a statement which they said ignored the 'social dimension' of an 'integrated' human rights approach which the Court itself had pioneered in the late 1970s with its *Airey v. Ireland* judgment.[180]

The fact that the dissenting judges chose to cite non-migrant cases (*Pretty* and *Airey*) in support of their arguments is noteworthy. In so doing, they implicitly refused to condone the message which implicitly runs through much of the jurisprudence of the Court that the reasoning in cases brought by migrants must start from the overarching principle that states have the right to control the entry and residence of aliens. Obviously, as far as these dissenting judges are concerned, the overarching human rights principles hold throughout the whole of the case law, whatever the status (national or alien) of the applicant.

N. has brought to an end, for the foreseeable future, any possibility of a Chamber reaching a verdict of violation in an Article 3 removal case relating to reasons of ill-health. This is clear from *Yoh-Ekale Mwanje v. Belgium* where the Chamber to which the case was assigned had to follow the precedent set by the Grand Chamber in *N.* and found, in December 2011, that the return of the applicant to Cameroon, where she was expected to die within 12 months due to lack of appropriate health care, would not entail a violation of Article 3 of the Convention.[181] Led by Judge Tulkens, six of the seven judges who sat on the bench wrote a partially concurring opinion where they expressed the hope that the Court would revise its jurisprudence as the current stance did not make sense to them: from a *human* perspective, there was no difference between being at death's door (as in *D.*)[182] and being condemned to death within 12 months (as

177 Dissenting opinion of Judges Tulkens, Bonello and Spielmann in *N.*, para 5.

178 Tulkens et al., para 5.

179 *Bensaid* judgment; *Ovdienko* decision, point 3; *Ahmed v. Austria*, appl. 25964/94, GC Judgment (ECtHR), 17 Dec. 1996, para 43.

180 Tulkens et al. in *N.*, para 6.

181 *Yoh-Ekale Mwanje v. Belgium*, appl. 10486/10, Judgment (ECtHR), 20 Dec. 2011, in French only.

182 In fact, Caroline Sawyer reports that 'D's treatment continued to be successful over many years': Sawyer, 'Stateless in Europe: Legal Aspects of *De Jure* and *De Facto* Statelessness in the European Union', in Caroline Sawyer and Brad K. Blitz (eds) *Statelessness in the European Union: Displaced, Undocumented, Unwanted* (Cambridge: Cambridge University Press, 2011)

in *N.* and the case before them).[183] The judgment in *Yoh-Ekale Mwanje*, and thus the opinion of these six judges, has not been translated into English. Despite the best efforts of these judges to express their opposition to the way in which the European Convention is interpreted and applied, *N.* stands for the foreseeable future.[184]

XVI. Glass Half Full? From *Chahal* to *Saadi v. Italy*, National Security does not Dampen the Prohibition of a Return to Torture

This chapter has sought to understand why it has proved so difficult for a meaningful post-*Soering* case law to develop. It must be stressed, however, that there is one front where the European Court of Human Rights has held fast to human rights principles: the absolute character of the prohibition of Article 3. In particular this has led the Court to reject all suggestions put to it by states that there are circumstances where torture or treatment recognised to be contrary to Article 3 can or indeed should be condoned due to national security considerations.

Chahal v. the United Kingdom was decided in 1996. The first post-*Soering* verdict of violation reached by the Court, it saw the Court unequivocally rejecting the idea that such considerations could enter the assessment made by the state concerning the appropriateness of proceeding with a return which might be in breach of Article 3. To its credit, the Court went on to confirm the absolute nature of the prohibition inscribed in Article 3 in the post-9/11 era of the so-called 'War on Terror', despite strong pleadings by states to change its position.

For a while, everyone assumed that *Chahal* would be revisited in the case of *Ramzy v. the Netherlands*, which originated in an application lodged in 2005. The applicant was an Algerian national born in 1982 who was first arrested in the Netherlands as a teenager when he was caught in a lorry attempting to cross to the UK. He sought asylum, declaring that he had been raised in an orphanage and had left Algeria because of the dangerous situation

69–107 at 97, note 107. It would be interesting to know why the Court got the facts wrong in *D.* and whether this mistake influenced its subsequent approach in similar cases. It remains that the principles which are now applied are problematic.

[183] Partially concurring opinion common to Judges Tulkens, Jočienė, Popović, Karakaş, Raimondi and Pinto de Albuquerque in *Yoh-Ekale Mwanje*.

[184] One recent example of such an application is *S.H.H. v. the United Kingdom*, appl. 60367/10, Judgment (ECtHR), 29 Jan. 2013, where the applicant, an Afghan national, had been seriously injured during a rocket launch in Afghanistan in 2006, leading to several amputations. The Court ruled that Article 3 did not imply an obligation on states to provide all illegal migrants with free and unlimited health care and that the applicant had not demonstrated that he was at personal risk of treatment proscribed by Article 3 if returned to Afghanistan. For further details, see Chapter 12 (p. 437).

there. This claim for asylum, as well as two subsequent ones, was rejected. The applicant remained illegally in the Netherlands. In June 2002, he was arrested for participation in a criminal organisation: 'pursuing the aims of aiding and abetting the enemy in the conflict opposing, on the one hand, the United States of America, the United Kingdom and their allies—including the Netherlands—and, on the other, Afghanistan (under Taliban rule until January 2002) and/or the Taliban and their allies (Al-Qaeda and/or other pro-Taliban combatants) and which organisation was further involved in drug-trafficking, forgery of (travel) documents, providing third persons with forged (travel) documents, and trafficking in human beings'.[185] In 2003, the applicant and his co-defendants were acquitted of all charges. The applicant was immediately put in aliens' detention for expulsion purposes. On his release from detention, he was ordered to leave the Netherlands. An exclusion order was then imposed on him on the grounds that he was a threat to national security and that this was in the interests of the Netherlands' international relations. Various appeals on a variety of points to different bodies were made throughout the years. Ultimately, the government having won before the Dutch courts, the applicant lodged an application with Strasbourg against his expulsion on 15 July 2005.

The European Court of Human Rights declared *Ramzy* admissible on 27 May 2008. At 46 pages, this was an unusually long and detailed admissibility decision. No less than four governments—Lithuania, Portugal, Slovakia, and the UK—had intervened in the case and submitted memorials to the Court. A number of NGOs had been authorised by the Court to do so too. Comments were sent by the AIRE Centre, Interights (also acting on behalf of five other organisations), Liberty, and Justice (based in London). The stakes were obviously very high. *Ramzy* was heralded as the case where the Court would decide whether or not to reiterate its *Chahal* pronouncement.

Nothing of the kind happened. The case which settled this point switched and became *Saadi v. Italy* (not to be confused with *Saadi v. the United Kingdom*, an altogether different case discussed in Chapter 11). *Saadi v. Italy* had been lodged in September 2006. The Section of the Court to which it had been allocated relinquished jurisdiction to the Grand Chamber on 29 March 2007. When the organisations which had intervened in *Ramzy* realised what was going on, it was too late for them to intervene. The British government—probably tipped off about this new development—was luckier: it 'requested leave to intervene as third party in good time'.[186] At the public hearing which took place on 11 July 2007, the British government was represented by no less than five people. The NGO world was not represented at all and was worried. In fact, it did not need to be. As became clear, the Court was in no mood to relax its view on the absolute character of the prohibition proscribed in Article 3.

[185] *Ramzy v. the Netherlands*, appl. 25424/05, Decision (ECtHR), 27 May 2008, para 13.

[186] Concurring opinion of Judge Myjer, joined by Judge Zagrebelsky in *Saadi* judgment.

The applicant in *Saadi v. Italy* was a Tunisian national who had arrived in Italy in the late 1990s and who was arrested on suspicion of international terrorism in 2002. He was acquitted by the Italian Assize Court which only found evidence that he and his co-defendants had links with Islamic fundamentalist circles, not that they had begun to put into practice plans for committing acts of violence. By contrast, a Tunisian court sentenced Mr Saadi in his absence to 20 years' imprisonment for membership of a terrorist organisation. Italy wanted to deport him to Tunisia. He said that he would face treatment contrary to Article 3 if he was returned to Tunisia. On a request from the Italian Embassy in Tunis, the Tunisian government sent a written note confirming that 'Tunisian laws in force guarantee and protect the rights of prisoners in Tunisia and secure to them the right to a fair trial'. Such an assurance seemed rather hollow in the light of concurrent reports by Amnesty International and other organisations that ill-treatment in prisons as well as unfair trials against political prisoners were occurring in Tunisia in that period (which the world became aware of as the 'Arab Spring' started to unfold in 2011).

Before the Strasbourg Court, the Italian government focused on matters of evidence. It relied on a decision by the Strasbourg Court to reject as manifestly ill-founded an application previously lodged by a Tunisian national and on the use of the conditional tense throughout the Amnesty International report, arguing that there was no certainty as to the conditions that existed in Tunisia.[187] It also contended that the situation in Tunisia was largely comparable to that of certain countries of the Council of Europe and better than many countries (including Algeria) where the Strasbourg Court had refused to countenance that expulsion might see applicants being subjected to ill-treatment.[188]

The submissions of the British government were much broader, attacking directly the 'rigidity' of the principle enunciated by the Court in *Chahal*, which 'had caused many difficulties for the Contracting States by preventing them in practice from enforcing expulsion measures'.[189] The UK argued that a terrorist might not yet have committed any offence or that it might not be possible to bring criminal charges for lack of evidence, but that this individual might still represent a danger to the lives of the members of the community in the midst of which he lived. Therefore, the British government contended, 'the applicant's rights must be weighted against the interests of the community as a whole'.[190]

The Court flatly refused this argument:

> The Court notes first of all that States face immense difficulties in modern times in protecting their communities from terrorist violence...That must not, however, call into

[187] *Saadi* judgment, paras 106 and 108. [188] *Saadi*, para 110.

[189] *Saadi*, para 117.

[190] *Saadi*, para 28. To make this point, the government relied on a distinction between negative and positive obligations which, quoted earlier (p. 231), need not detain us here. The idea of a balance between individual and communal interests had already been put forward by the British government in the *Vilvarajah* case: *Vilvarajah* judgment, para 105.

question the absolute nature of Article 3.... Since protection against the treatment prohibited by Article 3 is absolute, that provision imposes an obligation not to extradite or expel any person who, in the receiving country, would run the real risk of being subjected to such treatment. As the Court has repeatedly held, there can be no derogation from that rule.[191]

The Court reaffirmed *Chahal*:

[I]t is not possible to weigh the risk of ill-treatment against the reasons put forward for the expulsion in order to determine whether the responsibility of a State is engaged under Article 3, even where such a treatment is inflicted by another State. In that connection, the conduct of the person concerned, however undesirable or dangerous, cannot be taken into account...[192]

This pronouncement looks set to stay.[193]

As to *Ramzy*, the Court struck out the case from its list on 20 July 2010. Perhaps this was because the applicant's representatives did not know where he was (which is not unusual in Article 3 return cases).[194]

XVII. Glass Half Empty? *Sivanathan*

While the Court has thankfully refused to dilute the principle of the absolute prohibition of return to treatment proscribed by Article 3, an implicit dilution nonetheless happens all too frequently in practice.[195] One only has to think again about *Hatami* and ask: why was this case successful but not others? The principle is unequivocal: no individual can be returned to proscribed treatment. In practice, however, one could say that the principle is subjected to a rather large number of factual 'buts'.

A person seeking international protection *can* be returned if she cannot convince the authorities that she would now be at real risk of proscribed treatment. This may be as a result of one of many causes. Perhaps she cannot produce the hard evidence which incontrovertibly points to the persecution she suffered in the past and the story she tells is not immediately credible. Perhaps she does not seem to stand out and there is no reason to believe that she would be at personal risk in a situation of general violence, or the situation in her country of origin looks rather promising at the time the assessment regarding the potential violation of the Convention is being made, or there is one place in her country of origin where it appears that she could be returned without real risk of ill-treatment, however alien this place may be to her, and so on.

[191] *Saadi*, paras 137 and 138.

[192] *Saadi*, para 138.

[193] See e.g. *A. v. the Netherlands*, appl. 4900/06, Judgment (ECtHR), 20 July 2010; *Labsi v. Slovakia*, appl. 33809/08, Judgment (ECtHR), 15 May 2012.

[194] This seems also to have happened in, e.g., *Cruz Varas*.

[195] Compare Hemmes Battjes, 'In Search of a Fair Balance: The Absolute Character of the Prohibition of *Refoulement* under Article 3 ECHR Reassessed' (2009) *Leiden Journal of International Law* 22, 583–621.

There is a saying that it is better to let one criminal go free than to have one innocent person jailed. If we really believed in and were committed to the absolute character of the prohibition of torture and inhuman or degrading treatment proscribed in Article 3 ECHR, wouldn't we wish to err on the side of caution in this area too? Will the day come when we shall accept that it is better to welcome ten asylum seekers without a legal refugee claim than to send one person back to torture? Obviously the consequences of this principle would be tremendous. It would be close to endorsing free movement across borders. Is it not, however, the only logical way to respect the principle of the absolute prohibition of torture and inhuman treatment to which we say that we are so attached?

We are far from endorsing such a principle at the moment. At present it is the state which is most often given the benefit of the doubt (with exceptions). This is so even though states dispose of resources far superior to those available to irregular migrants to prepare their submissions to Strasbourg. Because states are presumed by the Court to be credible actors (which applicants are not), if they say something, their word carries weight. To give an example which I have not explored in detail in this book, diplomatic assurances are not easily disregarded.[196] This phenomenon goes beyond the migration field: 'the whole structure of the Convention rests', to quote the Court, 'on the general assumption that public authorities in the member States act in good faith'.[197] It nonetheless has a particular importance when applicants are particularly vulnerable to being abused by states, which is the case of irregular migrants.

One case which graphically demonstrates the point is *Sivanathan v. the United Kingdom*, a case which yet again concerns a Sri Lankan national of Tamil ethnicity. The applicant, whose claim for asylum in the UK had been refused, lodged an application with the Strasbourg Court on 31 August 2007 as he feared being removed to Sri Lanka. An interim measure under Rule 39 of the Rules of the Court was granted indicating to the British authorities that he should not be expelled until further notice. The Agent of the Government informed the Court by letter dated 21 April 2008 that the applicant had returned to Sri Lanka at his own request on 5 September 2007. The relevant Section Registrar of the Court asked for a copy of the document which the government had said in his letter the applicant had signed to the effect that he was returning to Sri Lanka out of his own free will. The government replied that

[196] *T.I. v. the United Kingdom*, appl. 43844/98, Decision (ECtHR), 7 Mar. 2000 and *K.R.S. v. the United Kingdom*, appl. 32733/08, Decision (ECtHR), 2 Dec. 2008 are discussed in Chapter 12. See also e.g. *Olaechea Cahuas v. Spain*, appl. 24668/03, Decision (ECtHR), 3 July 2003; *Mamatkulov and Askarov v. Turkey*, appls 46827/99, 46951/99, GC judgment (ECtHR), 4 Feb. 2005 (and the dissenting opinion of Judges Bratza, Bonello and Hedigan); *Abu Salem v. Portugal*, appl. 26844/04, Decision (ECtHR), 9 May 2006; *Saoudi v. Spain*, appl. 22871/06, Decision (ECtHR), 19 Sept. 2006; *Othman (Abu Qatada) v. the United Kingdom*, appl. 8139/09, Judgment (ECtHR), 17 Jan. 2012.

[197] *Khodorkovskiy* judgment, para 899.

the document which Mr Sivanathan had signed had been kept at Heathrow Airport for two months before being destroyed and that due to an administrative oversight the copy which should have been lodged in his main UK Border Agency file had not been. The Court accepted all this. It thus considered that 'in these circumstances, the applicant may be regarded as no longer wishing to pursue his application'.[198]

His lawyer could not understand why Mr Sivanathan had returned to Sri Lanka of his own free will, five days after his application to Strasbourg had been lodged. Despite this, it was the end of the matter. The *Sivanathan* case was struck out of the Court's list of cases, a decision which the Fourth Section of the Court took by unanimity. A report of the Parliamentary Assembly of the Council of Europe expressed concern about the 'decision by the Court to retrospectively exonerate the United Kingdom for removal of an individual from its jurisdiction despite a Rule 39 measure being in force'.[199] The case is so extraordinary that Mr Sivanathan's lawyer asked for the Court to restore it to its list.

What *Sivanathan* graphically demonstrates is the 'inequality of arms' between the applicant and the respondent state, and the credibility which the Court is ready to lend to the state. It is also striking that the case was destined to be entirely forgotten, never mentioned again, irrelevant. The common fate of asylum seekers in Europe?

XVIII. The Missing Case Law

The holes in the case law go further than the failed asylum seekers who could or indeed should, on the current mainstream interpretation of the European Convention, have been allowed to remain in Europe. I shall highlight three areas.

First, from a human rights perspective, the dearth of case law related to the way asylum seekers and irregular migrants are treated in twenty-first century Europe is surprising. There is no judgment, for example, on the way too many irregular migrants are driven to their death as they try to reach Europe;[200] the way in which unaccompanied minors are left to fend for themselves;[201] or the violence

[198] *Sivanathan v. the United Kingdom*, appl. 38108/07, Decision (ECtHR), 3 Feb. 2009.

[199] PACE report on Rule 39 indications, para 50.

[200] See e.g. the report authored by Tineke Strik, 'Lives Lost in the Mediterranean Sea: Who is Responsible?' submitted to the Committee on Migration, Refugees and Population of the Parliamentary Assembly of the Council of Europe, Doc. 12895 dated 5 April 2012, which led to Resolution 1872 (2012) adopted on 29 March 2012; 'Borders, Deaths and Resistance' (2014) *Statewatchjournal: Reflections on the state and civil liberties in Europe* 23(3/4). See also the research project led by Thomas Spijkerboer on 'The Human Costs of Border Control', presented at <http://www.rechten.vu.nl/en/research/top-research/vici-spijkerboer/sub-projects/index.asp>, accessed 13 March 2014.

[201] Nathalie Griesbeck, Motion for a European Parliament Resolution on the Situation of Unaccompanied Minors in the EU (2012/2263(INI)), Committee on Civil Liberties, Justice and Home Affairs. See also the research project entitled 'In Whose Interests? Exploring Unaccompanied Minor's Rights through the Lens of Migration and Asylum Processes (MinAs)', presented at http://minas.splet.arnes.si, accessed 15 November 2014.

with which deportations are conducted.[202] These practices are well documented. It is not to the credit of the European Convention system that they have not been brought before the Court. Admittedly, the Court is not responsible for its docket in that it cannot examine on its own motion an issue which is not part of a case which has been lodged before it. However, the way the Court decides the cases which do come before it either encourages or on the contrary discourages applications which have the potential of taking the case law further. The record of the Strasbourg Court in managing to stem the vertiginous deterioration of the asylum regime in Europe is simply abysmal.

Second, the level at which the debates are conducted means that only the surface of things is touched upon. The fact that one is concerned with survival issues makes it impossible even to start to consider the cultural dimension of what is happening to migrants in Europe today. In particular, there is no time to think about whether the safety net which is provided (if it is) is respectful of the dignity, including cultural sensibility, of those who manage to access it.[203]

Third, as the focus remains on distinguishing between those who deserve protection because of political persecution and those who do not, it is impossible to move the debate beyond the terms set during the Cold War. As a political scientist has recently remarked 'it is doubtful that only those fleeing political persecution have very strong claims to entry'.[204] For Ryan Pevnick, those fleeing 'abject poverty, rampant disease, or incompetent governance' should also be entitled to entry, even at some cost to the host society, as long as that cost does not threaten the host community's standard of living.[205] We are nowhere near discussing this view in the European Convention system.

XIX. Conclusion

This chapter has attempted to understand why the beautiful words of the leading pronouncement of *Soering* produced only three Strasbourg verdicts of violations up to the end of 2000. Granted, the European Convention was not created with migrants in mind, as we have seen in Chapter 2. However, the original intention of the drafters did not stop the Court from interpreting the Convention in other

[202] Michael M. Collyer, 'Deportation and the Micropolitics of Exclusion: The Rise of Removals from the UK to Sri Lanka' (2012) *Geopolitics* 17, 276–292; Nicholas De Genova and Nathalie Peutz (eds) *The Deportation Regime: Sovereignty, Space and the Freedom of Movement* (London: Duke University Press, 2010).

[203] This is leaving aside that people do not want to be refugees, they want to be members of the community where they live. This was already noted in the Funchal Colloquy by Augusto Perez-Lindo: Directorate of Human Rights, Council of Europe *Human Rights of Aliens in Europe. Proceedings of the Colloquy on 'Human Rights of Aliens in Europe'* (Dordrecht: Martinus Nijhoff, 1985) 91-97 at 96. For a pertinent critique of the very way in which refugee law is conceptualised: see Simon Behrman, 'Legal Subjectivity and the Refugee' (2014) *International Journal of Refugee Law* 26, 1–21.

[204] Ryan Pevnick, *Immigration and the Constraints of Justice: Between Open Borders and Absolute Sovereignty* (Cambridge: Cambridge University Press, 2011) 91.

[205] Pevnick 91 and 103.

areas in a novel way which would make the rights provided real and effective, rather than theoretical and illusory. The reply that the Convention offers no right to political asylum in the Convention does not therefore really explain anything. The propensity of 'the beauty to fall back to sleep' in Article 3 return cases is more likely to have been triggered by the general tide against asylum seekers which engulfed Europe in the mid-1980s and the fear that an opening of the 'flood gates' would see Europe 'invaded' by migrants.

Only viewed from this perspective can the case law and its underlying principles start to make sense, though not in a way which could make Europe proud. Some scholars believe that Europe's commitment to protecting political refugees is so central to its self-understanding that it would be impossible to renege on it.[206] If the absolute nature of the prohibition of return to torture or to other treatment accepted as being against Article 3 ECHR was taken seriously, one would have expected to see the European Court of Human Rights extremely resolute in upholding both substantive claims that a return would violate Article 3 and complaints under Article 13 that asylum domestic procedures are deficient. This chapter has put forward the controversial view that the Court does neither.

For good reasons, the role of the European Court of Human Rights is conceptualised as subsidiary: the state should be given a chance to wash its dirty linen, as it were, out of the international glare; in any case, an international court would not have the resources to tackle every possible issue which would be raised in all the members states which belong to a regional system; furthermore, solutions developed at local level are generally preferable because they are likely better to fit the requirements of the specific situation. The view that the European Court of Human Rights should not normally act like a court of fourth instance is also a good rule. However, when facts are disputed, as they typically are in Article 3 return cases, this becomes highly problematic.

For the Court not to reinvestigate the facts in an overall procedural set up which favours the state, means that the system turns away applicants without having provided them with a real opportunity to put across their case. In 2008, the Court started to say that it would distribute the burden of proof between the applicant and the state. The initial burden nonetheless remains on the applicant. It is a very heavy one since the Court says it accepts great flexibility regarding the standard of proof but is in fact very strict. Although I have not noted this in the body of the chapter, what I call the 'Strasbourg reversal', whereby the Court starts its reasoning on migrant cases by enunciating that 'Contracting States have the right, as a matter of well-established international law and subject to their treaty obligations including Article 3 (art. 3), to control the entry, residence and expulsion of aliens', is also affecting the Article 3 return case law.[207]

[206] Carl Levy, 'Refugees, Europe, Camps/State of Exception: "Into the Zone", the European Union and Extraterritorial Processing of Migrants, Refugees, and Asylum-Seekers (Theories and Practice)' (2010) *Refugee Survey Quarterly* 92–119, at 98.

[207] This principle was not mentioned in either *Soering* or *Cruz Varas*, but appeared in *Vilvarajah: Vilvarajah* judgment, para 102. For later examples, see e.g. *N. v. Sweden* judgment, para 158; *Ovdienko* decision, point 3; *Saadi* judgment, para 124.

Recently some judges have started to express strong disagreement with judgments reached by the Court in this area. Interestingly the lines of the internal battles which one imagines have always taken place within the Court were not immediately as clearly drawn in the Article 3 return case law as in the Article 8 case law concerning the deportation of convicted criminals. A number of possible explanations for this contrasting situation come to mind. First, the apparent robustness of the Article 3 case law may have played a role: the theory that admits no exception to the principle that no one can be returned to torture or ill-treatment may obscure the need for spelling out these differences of view. Second, the Article 3 case law typically deals with facts which are not clearly ascertained: the applicant will, for example, allege having been tortured in the past and of being at risk of torture in the future, but the state is likely to say that there is no evidence to support these allegations. Possibly this makes it more difficult for judges, however sympathetic to the plight of failed asylum seekers and other migrants, to adopt a resolute stance given the uncertain factual basis on which they would have to do so. Third, the population of foreign convicted criminals is relatively small by comparison to the pool of asylum seekers and other migrants seeking a life in Europe. The potential numbers involved may have unconsciously persuaded some judges not to express their discomfort with the case law in the clearest possible way.

In a conversation where we were discussing one of the verdicts of non-violation discussed in this chapter, one judge probably put the majority view when he told me: 'This Court cannot be the saviour of the world'. This judge commented that the principles upon which the case law is built are both morally sound and politically necessary if the Court is to maintain its credibility with the contracting states. In his view, which I take to reflect the dominant view at the Court, the verdict we were discussing did not raise any problem from a human rights perspective. This, I respectfully contend, is a questionable position which relies on too narrow an understanding of human rights.

Apart from dissenting opinions and occasional verdicts of violation, one saving grace of the reviewed case law is nonetheless that the Court has always refused to countenance the idea that a return to torture or treatment contrary to Article 3 would sometimes be acceptable, for example due to national security considerations. To have explicitly accepted that a balancing exercise could take place in this area would have been an even greater loss to human rights than the current situation. However, it remains the case that Europeans should not feel morally comfortable with the way the Strasbourg case law on Article 3 return cases has been developing. More will be said on this in Chapter 12.

8

Social Protection? All are Equal, But Some More So than Others

(After *Gaygusuz*)

As I was planning this book, it was clear that one chapter would need to be devoted to *Gaygusuz v. Austria*.[1] My thought originally was that the strand of jurisprudence emanating from this unanimous judgment of 1996 could only attract praise. *Gaygusuz* found that the denial of a social security benefit to the applicant on the sole ground that he had not been a national of the state where he had worked legally for over ten years had breached Article 14 of the European Convention on Human Rights (taken together with Article 1 of Protocol no. 1 guaranteeing enjoyment of possessions). This conclusion came after the Court posited the general principle that 'very weighty reasons would have to be put forward [by a respondent state] before the Court could regard a difference of treatment based exclusively on the ground of nationality as compatible with the Convention'.[2] In my application for research funding, I did not criticise *Gaygusuz*. I proposed instead to explore when the Court accepted and when it refused the legitimacy of treating a foreigner differently *qua* foreigner. Five years on, this question remains pertinent. I would now dispute, however, that *Gaygusuz* is the all-important equality affirming judgment which it is widely taken to be in international human rights law.[3] For a supposedly crucial judgment, *Gaygusuz* has produced a quantitatively meagre case law which is qualitatively rather bland, in that it mainly endorses what had already become a truism in Europe by the 1990s, namely, that it is possible and desirable to open a social security system to workers originating from outside the national community, at least when they are legally settled and contributing to this system.

[1] *Gaygusuz v. Austria*, appl. 17371/90, Judgment (ECtHR), 16 Sept. 1996.

[2] *Gaygusuz*, para 42.

[3] See e.g. Daniel Moeckli, 'Immigration Law Enforcement after 9/11 and Human Rights', in Alice Edwards and Carla Ferstman (eds) *Human Security and Non-Citizens: Law, Policy and International Affairs* (Cambridge: Cambridge University Press, 2010) 484; Françoise Tulkens, 'L'évolution du principe de non-discrimination à la lumière de la jurisprudence de la Cour européenne des droits de l'homme', in Jean-Yves Carlier (ed.) *L'étranger face au droit* (Brussels: Bruylant, 2010) 193–210 at 202.

The limits of the *Gaygusuz* pronouncement must be understood by reference to a contradiction at the heart of the political philosophy of liberalism; between the drive towards universalism (all human beings have human rights) on the one hand, and the attraction of particularism or closure (only those who are recognised as belonging to the polity have citizenship rights) on the other hand. In *Gaygusuz*, the Court did not signal how it envisaged this tension to be navigated in European human rights law, beyond ruling out the denial of social benefits to legally settled migrants. The post-*Gaygusuz* case law shows, however, that despite valiant attempts from some quarters of the Court to denounce the inequality suffered by migrants, in many respects the Strasbourg migrant jurisprudence has tended towards the latter pole.

The first part of this chapter is concerned with the *Gaygusuz* judgment and the case law which has developed directly in its wake. The review of the judgment shows that it was not originally considered by the Court as a leading case. Some observers nonetheless immediately thought that the Court's transposition of the 'very weighty reasons' pronouncement into the nationality sphere could mark the beginning of a highly significant case law. One factor to take into consideration in order to explain why the case was regarded as straightforward by the Court at the same time as it was heralded as potentially groundbreaking by commentators is that immigration is often assumed to put an established social security system at risk. A second factor is the liberal contradiction between universalist and particularist (enclosing) impulses. In *Gaygusuz*, the Court seems to have navigated this contradiction by implicitly accepting that the very weighty reasons proviso applied to the applicant because he was a legally settled migrant and because of the field to which the case was related—although this was not explicitly stated. Interestingly the Court sided towards closure in three cases decided in 2000 which involved either extradition or deportation. Set against this background, post-*Gaygusuz* verdicts of violation appear as ripples rather than revolutionary developments. This is due to the areas into which the post-*Gaygusuz* case law did not venture.

Following this, the chapter leaves *Gaygusuz* behind and begins to offer a critical analysis of a series of individual cases which, each in their own way, raise questions about how the Strasbourg Court either approaches or ignores discrimination complaints made by migrants. First, the *Timishev v. Russia* judgment of 2005 is reviewed, with the question being asked of why the Court did not find in it a violation of Article 14 in conjunction with Article 2 of Protocol no. 1, about education. Second, the same question, transposed to Article 14 in conjunction with Article 8, is raised in respect of *Moser v. Austria*, a 2006 judgment about an 'illegal' mother who had had her newborn baby taken away from her. A 'radical' suggestion is then introduced into the chapter, namely, that migrants are routinely discriminated against on the grounds of nationality and that this entails a regular violation of Article 14 which is not noticed. Having made this suggestion, the chapter continues to review case law. The 2009 judgment of the Second Section in *Anakomba Yula v. Belgium* is celebrated for having extended the 'very weighty reasons' requirement to a distinction of treatment between regular and irregular migrants. This is contrasted with two judgments of 2011 by the Fourth Section which intimate that immigration status is not a questionable criterion of distinction and which are taken to represent the Strasbourg 'mainstream': *Ponomaryovi v. Bulgaria* and *Bah v. the United Kingdom*. The chapter concludes by regretting the way in which the Court tends to downscale the difficulties migrants encounter. It illustrates this tendency by reference to two cases—the *Zeïbek v. Greece* judgment of 2009 and *Ponomaryovi*—where the Court focused on a comparatively small issue rather than embracing the bigger problems of, respectively, the withdrawal of nationality by the state and the inability of the applicant to obtain a valid residence permit, which correspond to the two forms of legal status through which migrants could most securely access social protection.

I. The Short and Straightforward *Gaygusuz*

Mr Gaygusuz was a Turkish national who had come to Austria in 1973 when he was in his early twenties. He worked there with some interruptions for just over a decade, at which point his poor health led him to claim social security benefits. As his entitlement to unemployment benefits expired, he applied for an advance on his pension in the form of emergency assistance under the Unemployment Insurance Act. Two days later, his application was rejected on account of his Turkish nationality, and he returned to Turkey the following September. Had he been Austrian, he would have received this emergency money. He complained of this refusal before the upper Austrian Regional Labour Office and then before the Constitutional Court, which referred the case to the Administrative Court, which decided that the complaint fell outside its jurisdiction.[4]

Mr Gaygusuz applied to the European Commission of Human Rights in May 1990. The Commission registered his application five months later and declared it admissible in January 1994. There was nothing particularly unusual in this sequence as the spiralling docket was already causing problematic delays (spurring the negotiation of Protocol no. 11 which eventually came into force in 1998). The Strasbourg institutions could nonetheless have fast-tracked *Gaygusuz* if there had been the will to do so.[5]

[4] Amazingly, the Austrian government would plead at Strasbourg at the admissibility stage that: 'the Administrative Court was bound to state that it had no jurisdiction because of the nature of the applicant's complaints [so that] its decision should be disregarded, with the result that the applicant has failed to comply with the six months time-limit' within which applications must be brought to Strasbourg. The Commission responded that 'it was the Constitutional Court, not the applicant, which remitted the case to the Administrative Court' and rejected the government's rather bad-faith argument that the applicant was in the wrong for having waited for this decision before turning to Strasbourg.

[5] As we have seen in Chapter 7 (p. 203), they did this in *Soering v. the United Kingdom*, appl. 14038/88, PC Judgment (ECtHR), 7 July 1989.

The absence of references in the Commission's admissibility decision suggests that the issue at the core of *Gaygusuz* had never previously been examined—at least not in a registered case. The existing case law would not have offered the applicant any guidance as to which reasoning might find favour with the Strasbourg institutions. Without any elaboration, he relied on Articles 6 and 8, as well as, 'in the alternative', Article 1 of Protocol no. 1. It is this 'alternative' which proved successful.

On the merits, the government advanced before the Commission that Article 6 was not applicable to the case at all. The Commission agreed. In its view, apart from in criminal proceedings, Article 6 applied only in civil proceedings in which there exists a 'dispute' over a 'right'. The Commission found that 'the applicant did not have—even arguably—a right in ordinary domestic law to the benefit he claimed'.[6] Thus, Article 6 did not apply.[7] However, the Commission accepted that the benefits in question fell 'within the ambit' of Article 1 of Protocol no. 1. As a result, Article 14 prohibiting discrimination in the enjoyment of a right provided by the Convention was deemed applicable. It became the provision around which the case turned even though it had not been mentioned in the Commission's admissibility decision.

The government argued that 'the legislature [had] considered it admissible to limit the benefit to Austrian citizens only, and that it did so in the expectation that other States would look after the emergency needs of their own citizens'; it also referred to 'the difficult financial situation', without further detail.[8] The Commission did not think that the government had justified the difference in treatment. For the Commission, the salient point was that 'foreign citizens [were] permitted to enter and to work in a country, and they [were making] payments into the prevailing systems of insurance on the same basis as nationals'.[9] Denying them the benefits of this insurance had no 'objective and reasonable' justification as would have been required under the existing Strasbourg case law for the difference in treatment to be acceptable under Article 14 of the Convention. The Commission found it established that the applicant had been treated differently from an Austrian in otherwise the same position from at least July to September 1987. The Commission concluded, unanimously, that there had been a violation of Article 14 taken together with Article 1 of Protocol no. 1. It finally found that the application raised no separate issue in connection with Article 8.

Having rendered its report on the merits, the Commission let the matter rest. This would normally have meant that the Committee of Ministers would have examined the case under former Article 32 of the Convention.[10] However, the

[6] *Gaygusuz v. Austria*, appl. 17371/90, Report (EComHR), 11 Jan. 1995, para 35.

[7] One Commission member, Mrs J. Liddy, dissented on this point. Since then the relationship between Article 6 and Article 1 of Protocol no. 1 has received much attention and the concepts at the heart of these two provisions are regarded as having to be congruent with each other.

[8] *Gaygusuz* report, para 46. [9] *Gaygusuz* report, para 46.

[10] On this mechanism, see Andrew Drzemczewski, 'Decision on the Merits [Article 32, ECHR]: By the Committee of Ministers', in Ronald St John Macdonald et al. (eds) *The European System of Human Rights Protection* (Boston: Dordrecht, 1993) 733.

applicant brought the case before the Court, as was then possible under Protocol no. 9, and the Court's Screening Panel did not reject it.[11]

The Court delivered its judgment in September 1996. It was extremely short. Article 14 could only apply if the benefit denied to the applicant came within the scope of Article 1 of Protocol no 1. The Court noted that entitlement to emergency assistance was linked to the payment of contributions to the unemployment insurance fund; there was no entitlement to this benefit where such contributions had not been made.[12] In the past, the Court had already decided that 'pecuniary rights' fell within the ambit of Article 1 of Protocol no. 1. Here the Court characterised emergency assistance as a 'pecuniary right', thus triggering the applicability of Article 14.[13]

In little more than a page and a half, the Court summarised the arguments of the parties, expressed its own reasoning, and gave its conclusion on whether Article 14 of the Convention in conjunction with Article 1 of Protocol no. 1 had been complied with. The Court reiterated two founding principles of its case law on Article 14: first, a difference of treatment is discriminatory if it has no objective and reasonable justification, if it does not pursue a legitimate aim, or if there is a lack of proportionality between the means employed and the aim sought; and, second, contracting states enjoy a certain margin of appreciation in assessing whether and to what extent differences in otherwise similar situations justify a difference in treatment. In a formulation borrowed from the section of the *Abdulaziz, Cabales and Balkandali* judgment related to sex discrimination,[14] the Court added to this that 'very weighty reasons would have to be put forward before the Court could regard a difference of treatment based exclusively on the ground of nationality as compatible with the Convention'.[15]

The Court's application of this new principle to the facts of the case could hardly have been more concise. To quote:

> The Court notes in the first place that Mr Gaygusuz was legally resident in Austria and worked there at certain times . . . paying contributions to the unemployment insurance fund in the same capacity and on the same basis as Austrian nationals.
>
> It observes that the authorities' refusal to grant him emergency assistance was based exclusively on the fact that he did not have Austrian nationality . . . [16]

The Court concluded, without any further elaboration, that it found the arguments put forward by the Austrian government 'unpersuasive'.[17]

[11] *Gaygusuz* judgment, para 2.

[12] *Gaygusuz* judgment, para 39.

[13] Today, this would probably also trigger the application of Article 6. The partially dissenting opinion of Mrs Liddy to the Commission's report in *Gaygusuz* was prescient.

[14] *Abdulaziz, Cabales and Balkandali v. the United Kingdom*, appls 9214/80, 9473/81, 9474/81, PC Judgment (ECtHR), 28 May 1985, para 57 (*ABC* judgment). See Section IX of Chapter 4.

[15] *Gaygusuz* judgment, para 42.

[16] *Gaygusuz*, paras 46 and 47.

[17] *Gaygusuz*, para 50.

II. The Anticipated Significance of *Gaygusuz*

Gaygusuz was not considered a leading case by the Court itself. It was decided by the Strasbourg institutions on the basis of an entirely written procedure (without any oral hearing); it was referred to the Court by the applicant (not the Commission); decided at that level by a Chamber (not the Grand Chamber); and by unanimity (suggesting that the issues were not perceived to be particularly controversial).[18] The case, however, immediately struck a number of observers as of potentially great significance. The following year, it became the object of an academic colloquium which gathered a dozen experts from seven countries and led to a publication entitled *Social security, non-discrimination and property*.[19] Paul Lemmens (now the Belgian judge at Strasbourg) wondered at this colloquium whether the judgment might prove 'the starting point for the drafting of a whole new code of social security law'.[20]

The days when the fathers of the Convention had been determined to leave outside the European Convention any right susceptible to being interpreted as having an economic and social dimension seemed a distant memory. This position had made it impossible to include the rights to property and education in the text of the original Convention, even though they had been intensely discussed in 1949 to 1950. A formulation deemed sufficiently apt at avoiding the risk of having the intended civil and political content of these rights interpreted in a social and economic way was nonetheless found shortly afterwards, allowing Protocol no. 1 to be opened to signature and ratification in 1951. Article 1 of Protocol no. 1 protects the right to the 'peaceful enjoyment' of one's possessions, a formulation designed to indicate the absence of any right to material goods arising from state economic and social programmes. For the same reason, rather than guaranteeing the actual provision of education, Article 2 of Protocol no. 1 prohibits the 'denial' of the right to education.

However, the supposedly essential and irretrievable legal distinction between civil and political rights on the one hand and economic and social rights on the other was never completely endorsed by the Strasbourg Court. Right from the start, the Court accepted that although the Convention did not make it a duty for states to provide any particular social provision, if a state chose to make such provision, then it could not limit access to it in a way which was discriminatory, defined as a difference of treatment lacking in reasonableness and proportionality. The Court stated this principle in the third judgment on the merits which it rendered. This was the *Belgian Linguistic* case, decided in 1968.[21] The Court noted

[18] Paul Lemmens, 'The Decision of 16 September 1996 in the Gaygusuz Case Situated in the Case Law of the European Court of Human Rights', in Stefaan Van den Bogaert (ed.) *Social Security, Non-Discrimination and Property* (Antwerp: Maklu, 1997) 25.

[19] van den Bogaert (ed.) *Social Security*.

[20] Lemmens 'The Decision' 33.

[21] *'Relating to certain aspects of the laws on the use of languages in education in Belgium' v. Belgium*, appls 1474/62, 1677/62, 1691/62, 1769/63, 1994/63, 2126/64, PC Judgment (ECtHR), 23 July 1968. This was the second judgment against Belgium. Chapter 6 (p. 165) mentioned the first: *De Becker v. Belgium*, appl. 214/56, Judgment (ECtHR), 27 Mar. 1962. Belgium decidedly continues

that Article 14 offers protection against discrimination which occurs in respect of rights and freedoms which are set forth in the Convention, making it clear that it is not a standalone provision. The Court also stated, however, that Article 14 can be engaged without the substantive provision of the right alleged to be provided in a discriminatory manner having itself been violated. This pronouncement was crucial. It made it possible for any matter related to ('within the ambit of') a right mentioned in Articles 2 to 13 of the Convention or its additional Protocols to be examined by the Court for its compatibility with the Convention under Article 14.

One decade after the *Belgian Linguistic* case, the Court confirmed that it rejected the idea of a clear break between 'civil and political' and 'economic and social' rights in *Airey v. Ireland*, its 25th judgment.[22] *Airey*, decided in 1979, concerned the right to fair trial, a seemingly very clear political and civil right. Even so, the Court was ready to interpret Article 6 ECHR as encompassing the right to *access* to justice, which it found had been denied to the applicant who could not afford the costs of the judicial procedure which would have allowed her to obtain a legally recognised separation from her abusive husband.

Article 1 of Protocol no. 1 especially lent itself to having economic and social rights encroaching into the Convention system. From an early period, the European Commission of Human Rights countenanced that contributory social security benefits came under the scope of Article 1 of Protocol no. 1 and could be examined under Article 14.[23] Part of the grounds for *Gaygusuz* was thus laid out early on, even though the question of whether the Convention could be interpreted in a way which reaches economic and social rights would always remain controversial.[24]

Gaygusuz was not just about social security, but also about foreigners. This mix could have proved particularly controversial. Interestingly, the case does not seem to have triggered much debate within the Court as it was being processed. That said, it provoked sufficient excitement outside Strasbourg to attract a colloquium entirely devoted to it, which would both explore the opening of the Strasbourg system to social security issues and challenge the view that immigration and welfare are not easily compatible. Is there any sense, then, that the case

to appear in this book as having had a fair number of lawyers aware of, and willing to resort to, the Strasbourg system right from its inception.

[22] *Airey v. Ireland*, appl. 6289/73, Judgment (ECtHR), 9 Oct. 1979.

[23] See *Mrs X v. the Netherlands*, appl. 5763/72, Decision (EComHR), 18 Dec. 1973; *Müller v. Austria*, appl. 5849/72, Report (EComHR), 16 Dec. 1974. *Gaygusuz* was the first Court's confirmation of this. For later judgments, see e.g. *Van Raalte v. the Netherlands*, appl. 20060/92, Judgment (ECtHR), 21 Feb. 1997 and especially *Stec and Others v. the United Kingdom*, appls 65731/01, 65900/01, GC Judgment (ECtHR), 12 Apr. 2006. For a perceptive and critical review of this case law, see: Ingrid Leijten, 'From *Stec* to *Valkov*: Possessions and Margins in the Social Security Case Law of the European Court of Human Rights' (2013) *Human Rights Law Review* 13, 309–349.

[24] See e.g. *N. v. the United Kingdom*, appl. 26565/05, GC Judgment, 27 May 2008, discussed in the previous chapter. For a cogent argument that human rights must extend to social and economic matters, see: Sandra Fredman, *Human Rights Transformed: Positive Rights and Positive Duties* (Oxford: Oxford University Press, 2008).

was revolutionary? This chapter's answer is that it could have been, but only if it had been applied extensively, which it has not.

III. Immigration and Welfare: A Viable Relationship

It is a received idea that the state sets up a social security system for the people who belong to it and that any such systems might not survive being open to outsiders. This view has a long history. To quote a recent article:

> In his book *Beyond the Welfare State*, the famous Swedish [and Nobel laureate] economist Gunnar Myrdal stated—back in 1960—that, in its essence, the welfare state is protectionist and nationalist... Welfare states... can only function properly when the dividing line between insiders and outsiders is crystal clear, because anyone who contributes to one is also a potential beneficiary, and vice versa. In addition, the welfare state has been designed to redistribute scarce resources between individuals, between generations and sometimes also between regions. These transfers always take place from those who are better off to those who are less well off *within* a given society and *within* one and the same system.[25]

Policy and academic literature ceaselessly seems to endorse the idea that immigration undermines the existence of a strong welfare state. So much so that, until the banking and austerity crises, one might have suspected that it was immigrants who were putting the future of European welfare states under threat. In fact, it has always been very difficult to calculate whether migrants are net beneficiaries of, or net contributors to, welfare systems, and there is a great deal of evidence pointing to their contributions.[26]

Moreover, while it is not necessarily easy for a national social security system to accommodate the movement of contributors/beneficiaries from other states, this is not an unfeasible goal and indeed exactly what European Union law forces EU states to do. Originally European Community law did this in order to facilitate the movement of workers, but this is now increasingly done in order to promote the idea and reality of European citizenship. Irrespective of motivation, EU practice is the living proof that it is wrong to affirm that welfare states 'can only function properly when the dividing line between insiders and outsiders is crystal clear', as affirmed in the quote above.

The Common Market was built from the 1950s onwards on the idea that the tendency for a state to wish to privilege its own nationals over nationals belonging to other member states of the European Community (EC) needed to be eliminated. By the time *Gaygusuz* was decided, EC (now EU) law had been developing for four decades. It was a very strong legal instrument and the

[25] Hans Entzinger, 'Open Borders and the Welfare State', in Antoine Pécoud and Paul de Guchteneire (eds) *Migration without Borders: Essays on the Free Movement of People* (Oxford: Berghan 2007) 119-134 at 119, emphasis in the original.

[26] See e.g. Carlos Vargas-Silva, 'Briefing: The Fiscal Impact of Immigration in the UK', available at: <http://www.migrationobservatory.ox.ac.uk/sites/files/migobs/briefing%20-%20the%20fiscal%20impacy%20of%20immigration%20in%20the%20uk_0.pdf>, accessed 18 June2014.

principle of the prohibition of national discrimination had become one of its mantras. This new legal habitus (to borrow a sociological term coined by Pierre Bourdieu) may well have played a conscious or unconscious role in enabling the Strasbourg Court to suggest, apparently without a second thought, that discriminating on grounds of nationality is at first sight not only unnecessary but also sufficiently abhorrent to need to be justified by 'very weighty' reasons.[27]

IV. Universalism and Closure: A Contradiction at the Heart of Liberalism

The 'very weighty reasons' proviso found in *Gaygusuz* had been borrowed by the Court from its *Abdulaziz, Cabales and Balkandali* Grand Chamber judgment, where it had appeared in the section which dealt with discrimination on grounds of sex. In *ABC*, the Court had offered a brief explanation for its pronouncement, as follows: 'it can be said that the advancement of the equality of the sexes is today a major goal in the member States of the Council of Europe'.[28] The Court could similarly have affirmed in *Gaygusuz*: 'it can be said that the advancement of the equality of nationals and non-nationals is today a major goal in the member States of the Council of Europe'. That it refrained from doing so and proceeded to the next point is not surprising: the statement would not have rung true.

As was stated at the beginning of this book, human rights rest on the proposition that all human beings are equal. Affirming equality regardless of nationality should therefore be uncontroversial. It is because it is such an obvious point that the Court was able to make its 'very weighty reasons' proviso and reach a verdict of violation in *Gaygusuz*. However, the idea that we are all equal despite our various nationalities is also deeply controversial. It is because the principle does not at all correspond to our world order that the Court could not possibly have borrowed the *ABC* formulation that equality is a major goal in Europe and integrated it into *Gaygusuz*. Far from a goal of equality between nationalities driving Europe today, what we witness is an intent to devise rules which exclude some people from being able to access liberal European polities.

As pointedly argued by Phillip Cole in his work, *Philosophies of Exclusion*, there is an irresolvable contradiction between liberalism's universalistic impulse and

[27] Another potential influence would have been the conclusions reached by the UN Human Rights Committee in a number of cases concerning social security benefits from the mid-1980s: Frédéric Sudre, 'La portée du droit à la non-discrimination: de l'avis d'Assemblée du Conseil d'Etat du 15 avril 1996, Mme Doukouré, à l'arrêt de la Cour européenne des droits de l'homme du 16 septembre 1996, Gaygusuz c Autriche' (1997) *Revue française de droit administratif* 13, 966–975 at 970–971. Although the European Court tends to work in isolation from other international human rights bodies, Judge Cançado Trindade also suggests that the decisions of the Human Rights Committee influenced the Strasbourg judges in *Gaygusuz*: Concurring opinion of Judges Cançado Trindade, García Ramírez, Salgado Pesantes and Abreu Burelli in *Juridical Condition and Rights of Undocumented Migrants*, OC-18/2003 (IACtHR), 17 Sept. 2003, para 61.

[28] *ABC* judgment, para 78.

its 'concealed particularism'.[29] Cole explains that liberalism is committed to the moral equality of all human beings but that it insists at the same time that the riches of the liberal community can be denied to those it classifies as 'outsiders' through the application of a criterion, nationality status, which is, from a liberal perspective, entirely arbitrary, arising as it does from an accident of birth.

This contradiction besets legal codes. One of its telling manifestations is the United Nations' International Convention on the Elimination of All Forms of Racial Discrimination. The first paragraph of the first Article of this Convention defines 'racial discrimination' in very broad terms; the second paragraph goes on to provide: 'This Convention shall not apply to distinctions, exclusions, restrictions or preferences made by a State Party to this Convention between citizens and noncitizens'. In the European Convention system, the contradiction expresses itself in a case law which has always been imbued with respect for the sovereign right of states to control the entry and residence of aliens (the principle with which the Strasbourg Court starts many migrant cases) but then suddenly states in 1996, without any explanation or qualification, that 'very weighty reasons' would have to be advanced for the state to be justified in treating human beings differently on the grounds of their nationality.

V. A Belated Answer to the Austrian Government: *Gaygusuz* Applies to the Legally Settled Migrant

Although the Court does not say it as such, in its view, immigration control was always going to be one of the very weighty reasons which would justify a difference of treatment between nationals and non-nationals. Indeed, the judgment in *Gaygusuz* is more circumscribed than a cursory reading may suggest. What the Court reproached in this case was the practice whereby the state, *having exercised its legitimate privilege to control immigration by specifically admitting Mr Gaygusuz on its territory*, then went on to discriminate against him. In support of this argument, one can note that before reaching the conclusion that Article 14 had been violated, the Court referred to Mr Gaygusuz's legal status, his work at certain times in Austria, and the fact that he had contributed to the unemployment insurance fund.[30]

Reading this judgment in the twenty-first century when irregular migration has become a major concern, one feels that, were *Gaygusuz* decided today, the Court might hammer home this message even further. Today one can easily imagine that the Court might choose to note that the applicant had *entered* Austria legally, that he had been living there as a legal resident *throughout* his stay, and that he had worked there, *legally*, for over ten years. Back in 1996, however, the Court did not even preface its conclusion that there had been a violation with words,

[29] Philip Cole, *Philosophies of Exclusion: Liberal Political Theory and Immigration* (Edinburgh: Edinburgh University Press, 2000) 2.

[30] *Gaygusuz* judgment, para 46.

commonly found in its case law, to the effect that 'The Court finds that *in the specific circumstances of the present case* the difference in treatment was unjustified' (emphasis added). In fact, the Court did not give any inkling as to why the difference of treatment constituted a prohibited discrimination in this particular case, let alone providing any general guidance as to when a difference of treatment on the grounds of nationality might be acceptable and when it would be unacceptable.

The Court also left unanswered the argument presented by the Austrian government that 'the difference in treatment [between the applicant and Austrian nationals] was based on the idea that the State had special responsibility for its own nationals and must take care of them and provide for their essential needs'.[31] This defence was not far-fetched, but in line with widespread thinking, including as we have seen by a Nobel laureate. Still, the Court confined itself to saying that it found such arguments 'unpersuasive'. Why did the Court not elaborate further? One possible answer is that the government's argument was so blatantly unacceptable that it did not call for any response (as per the European Community's *habitus*); another, that the issue was so sensitive that the Court preferred to stay away from even starting to discuss it (as per the assumed idea that immigration puts a social security system at risk). These two factors may not appear at first sight to go hand in hand. However, both could have played a role in enticing the Court not to elaborate on its views on the relationship between welfare and immigration.[32]

The simplest and least controversial argument that the Court could have offered in reply to Austria's defence might have been that, once a state accepts a foreigner into its labour force, it must accept that this individual soon becomes part of the group of people for which it has responsibility, irrespective of nationality. Admittedly this would not have been a highly sophisticated response. Lawyers would have asked questions, including: what evidence must there be that a state has accepted a foreigner as a worker? Do members of the worker's family also become part of the social security system? When does such integration start and what are its limits? Sociologically inclined commentators could have discussed how the judgment highlighted the unavoidable impact of migration and globalisation on the character of the national labour market, the identity of social security system's participants, and even the concept of national belonging. If many questions had remained unanswered, the elaboration proposed above, however unsophisticated, would nonetheless have contributed to circumscribing the judgment.

[31] *Gaygusuz*, para 45.

[32] Only Judge Matscher could be said not to have been completely silent on this relationship. Disagreeing with the amount of pecuniary damage allocated by the Court to the applicant, he asserted: 'The background to the whole case is a typical instance of abuse of the Welfare State, a very widespread trend in all our societies'. As far as he was concerned, it was regrettable that the Court was reinforcing this trend by making an 'excessive' allocation to the applicant. It is to be noted, however, that Judge Matscher specified that his remark was not specifically directed at foreigners: Partly dissenting opinion of Judge Matscher in *Gaygusuz*, 18.

VI. Reining in *Gaygusuz*: Three Cases Reaffirm Closure

As it was, the *Gaygusuz* judgment was phrased in surprisingly general terms.[33] Obviously the Court had not meant to suggest that everyone, irrespective of nationality, would now be entitled under the Convention to access social protection on the same conditions as nationals. Indeed, it did not take long before the Court seized an opportunity to begin to reaffirm the closure side of the contradiction at the heart of liberalism. With *M.S. v. Germany*,[34] decided in 2000, the Court reined in *Gaygusuz's* 'universal' pronouncement.

M.S. was lodged by a citizen of the former Yugoslavia who was residing in Germany with his German family—his wife and two children. The US Embassy in Germany requested his extradition because he was suspected of having raped a woman in Texas. He complained at Strasbourg about the detention in which he was held whilst awaiting extradition, on the grounds that 'he [had] been discriminated against in that German citizens are protected against extradition to a foreign country and the ensuing adverse effects on their family life while he as a foreigner was not, although he had been strongly integrated into German society'.[35] Applying the *Gaygusuz* 'very weighty reasons' proviso and referring to international law and state responsibility, the Court found that 'nationality is a distinction which, in the circumstances of the present case, must be considered as being based on an "objective and reasonable justification"'.[36] The *M.S.* application was unanimously declared inadmissible in January 2000.

A further two decisions adopted in the following months confirmed this stance.[37] *Özturk* and *Aftab* were both lodged against Norway. Clones of each other, they contested the deportation of a foreign national after criminal conviction. In each case, the children of the main applicant were included in the application. It was put to the Court that the father's implemented expulsion had amounted to a violation of Article 14, in conjunction with Article 8, as 'an unjustified difference of treatment of them as children, compared with other Norwegian children whose parents were nationals of countries within the EU and the EEA'.[38]

[33] This is in contrast to the Court's typical casuistic approach which very often makes it difficult to predict whether the solution reached in a previous case will apply to a new case which, however similar, is also always different. Applicants and lawyers must thus come back over and over again to Strasbourg to find out what the Convention requires: Marie-Bénédicte Dembour, 'What it Takes to Make a Case: The Backstage Story of *Muskhadzhiyeva v Belgium* (Illegality of Children's Immigration Detention)', in Elisabeth Lambert-Abdelgawad (ed.) *Preventing and Sanctioning Hindrances to the Right of Individual Petition to the European Court of Human Rights* (Brussels: Intersentia, 2011) 75-104 at 82.

[34] *M.S. v. Germany*, appl. 44770/98, Decision (ECtHR), 20 Jan. 2000, in English only.

[35] *M.S.*, para 4. [36] *M.S.*, para 5.

[37] *Saban Özturk and Others v. Norway*, appl. 32797/96, Decision (ECtHR), 21 Mar. 2000; *Mohammed Aftab and Others v. Norway*, appl. 32365/96, Decision (ECtHR), 4 May 2000. See also the earlier *Theodora Ajayi and Others v. the United Kingdom*, appl. 27663/95, Decision (ECtHR), 22 June 1999 (where the second applicant, from Nigeria, had taken paid employment in breach of her six-month leave to remain, leading to her expulsion from the UK and the family relocating to Ireland where her husband, a British national, could exercise his European Community free movement rights and be joined by her and of course their British children).

[38] *Özturk*, para 3; *Aftab*, paras 6–7.

It was also pointed out that 'the parent in question was not likely to re-offend and would be of valuable assistance and support to the children if allowed to return to Norway'.[39] This did not sway the Court. The two benches (identical except for one judge) declared the applications inadmissible. They did so only by majority, however, indicating yet again the presence of a jurisprudential Strasbourg undercurrent.

VII. Post-*Gaygusuz* Ripples

Inevitably the Court must navigate the liberal contradiction between universalism (as represented by *Gaygusuz*) and closure (as represented by the three cases discussed in the previous section). The relative paucity of the post-*Gaygusuz* case law suggests that it has done this in a way which favours closure.

A search conducted on the Court's HUDOC database on 17 March 2014 for decisions and judgments containing the words 'very weighty reasons' and 'on the ground of nationality' (as well as '*considérations très fortes*' and '*fondée sur la nationalité*') returned ten results, apart from *Gaygusuz* and *M.S.* These ten rulings respectively concerned the denial of a non-contributory disability allowance to the adult adoptive son of a French national,[40] the impossibility for a foreigner to join a social security scheme specifically designed for farmers in Poland,[41] the refusal to count periods of work spent abroad towards a pension whilst a Latvian national in the same situation would have had those periods taken into account,[42] the denial by Greece of a large-family benefit to a Muslim woman in Thrace[43] and then to two refugees from Syria and Lebanon,[44] the denial of a complementary pension subscribed to by a colonial subject prior to Algerian independence (the second verdict of non-violation after *M.S.* in this particular HUDOC search),[45] barring access to secondary education to Russian youngsters who had long been settled in Bulgaria and suddenly found themselves without a valid residence permit on their 18th birthdays,[46] the refusal by the British authorities to allocate priority social housing to a Somali family where the child held a conditional visa only (which led to the last verdict of non-violation in this search),[47] and the refusal of social therapy or relaxations in the conditions of detention to a prisoner in Germany against whom a final expulsion order was in force.[48] As this brief

[39] *Özturk*, para 3; *Aftab*, paras 6–7.
[40] *Koua Poirrez v. France*, appl. 40892/98, Judgment (ECtHR), 30 Sept. 2003.
[41] *Luczak v. Poland*, appl. 77782/01, Judgment (ECtHR), 27 Nov. 2007.
[42] *Andrejeva v. Latvia*, appl. 55707/00, GC Judgment (ECtHR), 18 Feb. 2009.
[43] *Zeïbek v. Greece*, appl. 46368/06, Judgment (ECtHR), 9 July 2009, in French only.
[44] *Saidoun v. Greece*, appl. 40083/07, Judgment (ECtHR), 28 Oct. 2010, in French only; *Fawsie v. Greece*, appl. 40080/07, Judgment (ECtHR), 28 Oct. 2010, in French only (as well as Armenian). These two cases are clones of each other.
[45] *Si Amer v. France*, appl. 29137/06, Judgment (ECtHR), 29 Oct. 2009, in French only.
[46] *Ponomaryov and Ponomaryov v. Bulgaria*, appl. 5335/05, Judgment (ECtHR), 21 June 2011, in English only.
[47] *Bah v. the United Kingdom*, appl. 56328/07, Judgment (ECtHR), 27 Sept. 2011.
[48] *Rangelov v. Germany*, appl. 5123/07, Judgment (ECtHR), 22 Mar. 2012.

description shows, for a long time the post-*Gaygusuz* case law maintained itself within the social security field understood in a narrow sense.[49] The field of application of non-discrimination on grounds of nationality would always have been expandable beyond this sphere, however, as the recent *Rangelov* judgment relating to the detention regime in Germany demonstrates.

In this case law, the European Court generally concluded on a violation of the Convention because of a breach of Article 14 taken together with either Article 1 of Protocol no. 1 or Article 8. The exceptions in this respect were the Bulgarian and German cases which were respectively found to be linked to either Article 2 of Protocol no. 1 (right to education) or Article 5 (detention).[50] The verdicts of violation were most often taken by unanimity, with the two and a half exceptions in this respect worth reviewing.

The first dissenting opinion arose in *Koua Poirrez v. France*, itself the first verdict of violation due to discrimination on grounds of nationality which the Court reached after having rendered *Gaygusuz*—after an interval of seven years. Judge Mularoni objected to the idea that a non-contributory social benefit such as a disability allowance could be a 'possession' within the meaning of Article 1 of Protocol no 1. In her view, the case went 'to the heart of Article 8 of the Convention', so that it was to this provision that Article 14 should have been linked (a suggestion largely taken up in the subsequent case law). Thus, the dissenting opinion in *Koua Poirrez* did not object as such to the finding that discrimination had taken place.

Of more significant note for our purposes is the 'half exception' constituted by the majority decision regarding admissibility in *Luczak v. Poland*. The applicant in this case was a French national who had returned to Poland, bought a farm, and had then been denied access to the farmers' social security scheme.[51] Developing a more circumscribed reasoning than in either *Gaygusuz* or *Koua Poirrez*, the Court considered that 'in the instant case the Government [had] not provided any convincing explanation of how the general interest [had been] served by refusing the applicant's admission to the farmers' scheme'.[52] It thus found a violation of Article 14 in conjunction with Article 1 of Protocol no. 1.[53] Retrospectively, the case appears to constitute a clear-cut and inevitable application of *Gaygusuz*. Originally, however, it had been declared admissible only by majority.[54] Neither the identity of the dissenting judges nor their number (nor a fortiori the grounds on which they are dissenting) is ever indicated in an admissibility decision. It is possible that the dissent originated from a judge who shared Judge Mularini's concerns as to the exact provision which should be considered applicable in conjunction with Article 14. The dissent at admissibility stage may also have been related, however, to the perception that the Court was moving too far in the direction of protecting social and economic rights or the belief that the Court was not well placed to regulate the tension between providing limited welfare resources

[49] But not access to health care.

[50] For more details and a table, see Dembour '*Gaygusuz* Revisited'.

[51] *Luczak* judgment, paras 8–12. [52] *Luczak*, para 59. [53] *Luczak*, para 60.

[54] *Luczak v. Poland*, appl. 77782/01, Decision (ECtHR), 27 Mar. 2007.

and integrating aliens in the social security system, leading the dissenting judge(s) to find the Polish government's arguments at first sight persuasive.

The last exception to the unanimity pattern in verdicts of violation arose in the Grand Chamber judgment of *Andrejeva v. Latvia*. The case involved an applicant who was a 'permanently resident non-citizen' of Latvia, having settled there as a 12-year-old national of the former USSR, well before the country's independence in 1990. When the time came to draw her pension, the Latvian authorities calculated it on the basis of the work she had undertaken in Latvia and excluded USSR postings she had undertaken outside Latvia. Had she been Latvian all these postings would have been considered. To the Latvian government's argument that she could have acquired Latvian nationality, the Court responded that 'dismissing [the] victim's claims on the ground that he or she could have avoided the discrimination by altering one of the factors in question—for example by acquiring a nationality—would render Article 14 devoid of substance'.[55] Sixteen judges found that it was clear that Latvia was 'the only State which, objectively, [could] assume responsibility for her in terms of social security'.[56] Thus there was a breach of Article 14 of the Convention in conjunction with Article 1 of Protocol no 1.[57] Judge Ziemele wrote a very long partly dissenting opinion. According to her, the Court had ignored the relevant international law context in which the Latvian State Pensions Act had been formulated, namely, the way in which Latvia had been a victim of Soviet aggression.[58] The dissent to the verdict of violation thus arose in a geopolitical historical context such that the non-national applicant seeking equality of treatment with nationals of the host country was associated with past oppression.

Except for these cases, verdicts of violation due to discrimination on grounds of nationality have always been adopted by unanimity. This might suggest that the Court's position is very strong in this sphere and that it will simply not tolerate discrimination between nationals and non-nationals. Such a conclusion needs to be qualified, however, in that the *Gaygusuz* case law merely confirms what was already accepted as a truism in the mid-1990s, namely, that it is wrong to exclude from social security provisions people who have been accepted into the national economy and have contributed to it in an entirely legal way.

VIII. What a Revolutionary Post-*Gaygusuz* Case Law would have Looked Like

At the colloquium devoted to *Gaygusuz* in early 1997, an expert who examined the European situation observed:

> Fundamentally, social security schemes *do* include non-nationals in their coverage if these persons [fulfil] the prerequisites under which the scheme becomes applicable

[55] *Andrejeva* GC judgment, para 91. [56] *Andrejeva*, para 88.
[57] *Andrejeva*, para 87.
[58] Partly dissenting opinion of Judge Ziemele in *Andrejeva*, paras 4 and 5.

(i.e. residence, employment or tax liability). Thus, in principle, nationality is of no relevance.[59]

What von Maydell was saying is that nationality rarely constitutes a prerequisite for awarding social security benefits. He noted the exceptional situations which derogated from this principle,[60] but these were abnormal. It is these exceptions—such as denying access to a social security scheme to a foreign farmer or a maternity benefit to a foreign mother—which the *Gaygusuz* case law has typically caught. This is important, but hardly a revolution in twenty-first-century Europe.

For the post-*Gaygusuz* case law to have been of great significance, it would have needed to go beyond the comparatively rare problem of direct discrimination. *Gaygusuz* could, for example, have had a great impact in the field of 'indirect discrimination'. As von Maydell explained:

> Aside from the—not very numerous—cases of explicit legal differentiation ['direct discrimination'] between non-nationals and nationals, discrimination against non-nationals nevertheless occurs in practice because these persons more often than nationals do not, or to a lesser extent, [fulfil] the benefit preconditions applicable to all persons. If, for example, the award of benefits is geared to employment or residence periods completed in the national territory, both non-nationals and nationals are able to furnish proof of these periods, but the periods completed by non-nationals will inevitably be shorter. Similar [indirect] discrimination may result if family benefits are paid only to dependents residing in the domestic territory.[61]

Moreover, as von Maydell had also observed, the *Gaygusuz* principle could have been instrumental in helping migrants denied access to social security and/or assistance because they do not have a work permit or their residence is deemed 'illegal'.[62] The Court did not venture down this path, as we shall see in detail in Chapter 13. This is to say that the Strasbourg case law ultimately endorses the fact that social protection is for some and not for others.[63]

IX. When Discrimination is not Discussed: *Timishev* and Other Non-Existent Cases on Education

For a supposedly 'leading' case,[64] *Gaygusuz* has left very little case law in its wake. This is so even though it would have lent itself to be applied in all kinds of

[59] Bernd von Maydell, 'Discrimination in Domestic Social Security Law of the Member States of the European Union', in Van den Bogaert (ed.) *Social Security* 93, emphasis in the original. The study by von Maydell covered the then EU countries.

[60] von Maydell 93. [61] von Maydell 96. [62] von Maydell 97.

[63] That the Court would do so may appear uncontroversial. However, it is not accepted across the whole political spectrum. E.g. economist and member of the French Green Party Yann Moulier-Boutang believes that a social security system is feasible even in an open borders policy. See Yann Moulier-Boutang, 'Le revenu garanti ou salariat affaibli, condition structurelle d'un régime vivable de capitalisme cognitif' (2007) 27 *Multitudes* 97; Yann Moulier-Boutang, *Cognitive Capitalism* (Cambridge: Polity Press, 2012).

[64] Tulkens 'L'évolution' 202.

situations, beyond social security conceived in a rather limited way. This restraint may be linked to the fact that when a verdict of violation of the Convention is reached in respect of the denial of a substantive right 'taken alone', the Court is often disinclined to adopt a verdict of violation of Article 14.[65]

Timishev v. Russia illustrates this trend. The applicant was a Russian national of Chechen ethnicity who used to live in Groznyy until his house was destroyed as a result of a military operation. From 1996 he lived in Nalchik in the Kabardino-Balkaria Republic as a forced migrant. In two applications lodged at Strasbourg in 2000, he complained about having been denied: (a) access to court; (b) freedom of movement; (c) child benefits; (d) admission to school (for his children who were not specifically named as applicants in their own right in the application); and (e) the issuance of a passport.[66] The first and last of these complaints were declared inadmissible; the one concerning the child benefits was struck out following payment.[67] The other two complaints were upheld. Regarding the liberty of movement, Article 2 of Protocol no. 4 was found to have been violated both alone and in conjunction with Article 14. However, although the denial of education was ruled to be a violation of Article 2 of Protocol no. 1 taken alone, Article 14 was not mentioned in relation to this provision.

The Court reasoned:

> There is no doubt that the right to education guarantees access to elementary education which is of primordial importance for a child's development.... [T]he Convention and its Protocols do not tolerate a denial of the right to education. The Government confirmed that Russian law did not allow the exercise of that right by children to be made conditional on the registration of their parents' residence. It follows that the applicants' children were denied the right to education provided for by domestic law. Their exclusion from school was therefore incompatible with the requirements of Article 2 of Protocol No. 1.[68]

It is difficult to think that in this case the children were not denied access to school because of their (or their father's) migratory status. One might say that the universality of the phrasing according to which the right of *every* child to access elementary education is affirmed renders any discriminatory complaint redundant. This might be so only if one were satisfied that the Court always pushes the logic of rights 'taken alone' to its full. Moreover, the recognition that discrimination has taken place is often very important for group dynamics at play in society, not to mention the applicant himself.

The question therefore remains salient: why didn't the Court say anything about the possible discriminatory angle of the violation of Article 2 of Protocol no. 1? It is impossible to say from the judgment. Perhaps discrimination was not

[65] As noted by many commentators including: Samantha Besson, 'Evolutions in Non-Discrimination Law with the ECHR and ESC Systems: It Takes Two to Tango in the Council of Europe' (2012) *American Journal of Comparative Law* 60, 147–180 at 157.

[66] *Timishev v. Russia*, appls 55762/00, 55974/00, Decision (ECtHR), 8 July 2003.

[67] Timishev decision of 2003; *Timishev v. Russia*, appls 55762/00, 55974/00, Decision (ECtHR), 30 Mar. 2004.

[68] *Timishev v. Russia*, appls 55762/00, 55974/00, Judgment (ECtHR), 13 Dec. 2005, paras 65 and 66.

pleaded in regard to the lack of access to education,[69] or the evidence of discrimination was scant, or—more likely—the Court found it unnecessary to examine this point.

Access to education can be problematic for migrants. It is therefore somewhat strange that the issue has not attracted more case law than *Timishev* and *Ponomaryov and Ponomaryov v. Bulgaria*, reviewed later. For example it appears unlikely that no legally settled migrant would ever have complained of a violation of Article 14 due to the lack of recognition of his professional qualifications, for this situation commonly affects refugees who were part of the professional elite in their home country and prevents them from participating in their new community to their full ability. *Gaygusuz* could also have been relied upon by children who are denied access to appropriate primary or secondary education, an issue which again affects thousands of non-Convention-recognised refugees.[70] Would this be because such complaints have been summarily declared inadmissible? As summarily rejected applications leave no trace and are thus not researchable, it is impossible to say, but this appears possible.

X. Discrimination goes Unseen? From *Moser* to *K.A.B.* and *Zhou*, or When Children are Taken Away from their Parents

The holes in the case law related to discrimination on grounds of nationality are manifold. One area which is particularly poignant is the situation where children are separated from their parents for no good reason. The Court has reached three verdicts of a violation of Article 8 in such cases, when the parent was a migrant. It refrained from investigating whether this latter fact may have played a role in the fact that a violation of the right to family life had arisen at all.

In *Moser v. Austria*, decided in 2006,[71] the applicants were a mother and her young son. The mother, a citizen of the Republic of Serbia, had been living in Austria since 1991 and had been granted a residence and work permit until 1997. In 1999, she was issued a five-year residence prohibition for illegal employment. In 2000, she gave birth to her son, the second applicant, in hospital. The next day the Vienna Youth Welfare Office ordered that her son should not leave the hospital with her since 'her unclear personal and financial situation and lack of a residence permit would endanger the child's welfare'.[72] The child was placed with

[69] One would need to read the whole file of the case in the Archives of the Court to confirm this point.

[70] See e.g. Halina Grzymala-Moszczyńska and Magdalena Trojanek, 'Image of the World and Themselves Built by Young Chechens living in Polish Refugee Centres. Intercultural Conflict', in Katarzyna Górak-Sosnowska (ed.) *Muslims in Poland and Eastern Europe: Widening the European Discourse on Islam* (Warsaw: University of Warsaw, 2011) 69–88. See also *Muskhadzhiyeva and Others v. Belgium*, appl. 41442/07, Judgment (ECtHR), 19 Jan. 2010, where the issue of the lack of access to education during the detention of the applicant children was noted but not examined by the Court.

[71] *Moser v. Austria*, appl. 12643/02, Judgment (ECtHR), 21 Sept. 2006.

[72] *Moser*, paras 1 and 7–10.

foster parents and his custody transferred to the Youth Welfare Office. In the six months following his birth, the mother was given the opportunity to see him twice—but she actually saw him only once, briefly. Contact afterwards was even more limited.

The applicants 'complained of discrimination on account of their nationality, alleging that they would have been placed in a mother-child centre if they had been Austrian nationals or nationals of another member state of the European Union'.[73] The government responded that such placement was a social service provided by legislation which applied to all persons resident in Vienna.[74] The Court accepted that placement was not dependent on nationality. As a result it found no violation of Article 14.[75] In the absence of an expressly discriminating text and given the reluctance by the Court to reverse the burden of proof onto the state (as noted in Chapter 7), discrimination would have been barely possible for the applicant to prove.

By contrast, the applicants succeeded in their complaints regarding Articles 8 and 6 of the Convention taken alone. The Court found that their right to have their family life respected under Article 8 had not been respected because the government had not taken positive action 'to explore possibilities which would have allowed the applicants to remain together, for example by placing them in a mother-child centre' or to clarify the applicant's residence status, a situation 'aggravated by the fact that no measures were taken to establish and maintain the contact between the applicants while the [custody] proceedings were pending'.[76] Moreover neither the procedural requirements inherent in Article 8 nor Article 6 had been respected, as the mother had not had any involvement in the Juvenile Court proceedings.[77] From the facts of the case, one forms the impression of a woman who just did not know to whom she could turn in the hope of regaining access to her son. Ms Moser was probably lucky to come into contact with a lawyer who took pains to examine her case carefully, thereby identifying diverse stages where the mother should have been given the opportunity to be involved in the proceedings. At Strasbourg, he stressed that there had not been a single hearing where she was given the chance to put her views across to the judge, who had therefore only ever heard the authorities' side of the story.

By the time the European Court adopted its judgment, four and a half years after the application had been lodged, the second applicant was six years old. Under 'Damage', the judgment awarded a mere €8,000 to the mother and *nothing* to the boy about whom 'the Court does not find that the deficiencies of the custody proceedings had any direct effect'. The applicants had claimed a greater amount of compensation for the second than for the first applicant (€50,000 and €30,000).[78] This made sense, judging from scholarly research such as *Why Love Matters* and *The Primal Wound* which document the long-term effects on a person of the absence of bonding with their birth

[73] *Moser*, para 75. [74] *Moser*, para 77. [75] *Moser*, paras 78 and 79.
[76] *Moser*, paras 70 and 71. [77] *Moser*, paras 72 and 80. [78] *Moser*, para 106.

mother.[79] Had a house been at the centre of the case, a survey would have been undertaken to assess the damage caused. One cannot help wondering why there was no relevant expertise put forward in this case. Why did the Court decide that it should itself simply come up with a sum which it declared to be 'on an equitable basis'[80] but which did not seem to rely on anything other than its own past practice and present mood? What was clearly needed was a plan to make it possible for contact to be re-established between mother and child. This is a case where the limitation of the reparations ordered by the Strasbourg Court, discussed in Chapter 10,[81] is particularly glaring. This, however, is a digression which takes us away from the issue of discrimination in social protection at the core of the present chapter.

Moser is not a one-off. In *K.A.B. v. Spain*,[82] decided in March 2013, the applicant was the father of a child who had been put into care at 13 months old, when his mother was deported to Nigeria. The applicant had tried to resist this process, claiming that he was the father. However, he had not been heard. The Strasbourg Court reproached the domestic court for not having taken into account the applicant's vulnerability and for having held him fully responsible for the loss of contact with his son—clearly the last thing he had wanted. By six votes to one, the Court found a violation of Article 8 and allocated €8,000 for non-pecuniary damages. In *Zhou v. Italy*,[83] decided in January 2014, the first applicant was a Chinese national who had given birth to the second applicant while in Italy. She was leaving him in the care of neighbours as she was going to work. For reasons not specified in the Strasbourg judgment, the authorities objected to this arrangement. They considered that she had abandoned the child and gave him up for adoption. The Court found a violation of Article 8 and allocated the mother €40,000 in damages. Nothing was said in either of these cases about reuniting, or at least having contact re-established, between the parent and the child. Of particular significance in the context of this chapter is the fact that the way in which the foreignness of the applicants may have played a role in the unfolding of the adoption proceedings was not touched upon at all.

When a universal right is denied because of a prohibited discriminatory process, two violations of the Convention occur: a violation of the right taken alone

[79] Sue Gerhardt, *Why Love Matters: How Affection Shapes a Baby's Brain* (Hove: Brunner-Routledge, 2004); Nancy Verrier, *The Primal Wound: Understanding the Adopted Child* (London: British Association for Adoption and Fostering, 2009).

[80] *Moser* judgment, para 109.

[81] We shall see in Chapter 10 that the Inter-American Court adopts a very different approach to the issue of reparations. In a case like *Moser*, one could imagine it positively wondering which steps are called for and must be required from the state in order to make it possible for mother and child to be reunited. In the European system, by contrast, the Court simply *declares* the violation. With some exceptions, it does not believe that it is within its remit to think about how the violation must be redressed. After the European Court of Human Rights has declared the violation, the execution of the verdict is left to be supervised by the Committee of Ministers. This Committee representing governmental interests, it can hardly be presumed to have the applicant's interest at heart in achieving as complete a reparation as possible.

[82] *K.A.B. v. Spain*, appl. 59819/08, Judgment (ECtHR), 26 Mar. 2013.

[83] *Zhou v. Italy*, appl. 33773/11, Judgment (ECtHR), 21 Jan. 2014.

on the one hand and a violation of the prohibition of discrimination taken together with this right on the other.[84] From the perspective not only of the applicant but also of preventing a repetition of the violations, both aspects—the discriminatory treatment and the denial of the substantive right—may be equally important. More often than not, however, the discriminatory nature of the treatment is not recognised by the Court—as the quantitatively limited case law on Article 14 demonstrates. Then, only the denial of the substantive right, taken alone, gives rise to a verdict of violation of the Convention (if it does so at all).

XI. A Radical Suggestion: Migrants are Discriminated Against and this Amounts to Inhuman and Degrading Treatment

The applicants in *M.S.* and *Moser* complained of a violation of Article 14 to no avail. Other applicants have refrained from relying on Article 14, one might say wisely as this particular complaint is more or less bound to fail and perhaps to irritate the Court. However, theoretically, virtually the whole migrant case law could be reconstructed as instances of discrimination.

To take one example discussed in Chapter 7: it would not have been wise for the applicant in *N. v. the United Kingdom*[85] to argue before the Strasbourg Court that sending her back to Uganda to face an early death while she could have carried on living in the UK thanks to the anti-viral drugs which kept her AIDS in check was discriminatory because the UK would never have inflicted similar treatment on one of its citizens, even one who had happened to have developed strong connections with a different country. The argument would simply have failed, even though being sent to your death may be conceived of as the ultimate discrimination.

This book advances the argument that there is something highly objectionable in the way in which we take for granted that human beings can be treated differently according to the nationality (or lack of nationality) they happen to hold. Such difference in treatment may one day come to be regarded as itself being inhuman and degrading. When that day comes, if it comes, it will appear that many of the applicants whose cases have been recounted in this book had actually suffered a violation of Article 14 of the European Convention, but that this went unseen at the time the cases were processed. Going further, this violation could then be construed as inhuman and degrading treatment, itself a breach of Article 3.

[84] By contrast, in *Gaygusuz* it was the discriminatory denial of a benefit offered by the state as it were of its own free will rather than because Convention law so required which led to the finding that the Convention had been violated. There could have been no violation of Article 1 of Protocol no. 1 taken alone.

[85] *N. v. the United Kingdom*, appl. 26565/05, GC Judgment (ECtHR), 27 May 2008.

XII. Extending *Gaygusuz* to an Irregular Migrant: *Anakomba Yula v. Belgium*

Until and unless such a revolution in thinking comes about, the best we can hope for is that some inroads into the otherwise rather close Strasbourg case law will take place. *Anakomba Yula v. Belgium*, a case decided in 2009 by the Second Section of the Court, provides an example of the kind of inroad I have in mind.

Mrs Anakomba Yula was a Congolese national whose last child had not been fathered by her (Congolese) husband but by a (Belgian) national. Before the child could be recognised by her biological father, a judicial action contesting paternity had to be pursued successfully against the mother's husband in the civil courts. This procedure must be lodged within one year of the birth of a child. Mrs Anakomba Yula requested judicial assistance towards its costs (which were estimated at €1,400 if a blood analysis was required). This was refused on the ground that Mrs Anakomba Yula was not a regular migrant in Belgium at the time of her application. She was told that she should first regularise her residence, for which she might benefit from judicial assistance, and then return for the action to contest paternity. However, there was no time for this, as the action to contest paternity had to be brought within one year of the birth of the child. Mrs Anakomba Yula instigated the procedure for contesting her daughter's paternity and won, but she was required to pay the costs (which turned out to be €288). She argued at Strasbourg that she had suffered from a violation of Article 14 taken together with Article 6.

The Belgian government must have anticipated in *Anakomba Yula* that the Court would be unlikely to condone a difference of treatment based on nationality.[86] It argued instead that a migrant's irregular status need not be a suspect criterion justifying a difference of treatment.[87] It advanced a number of arguments in support of the non violation of Article 14, including the fact that Article 6 does not require free access to a tribunal and that there had been no interference with the applicant's right to justice as she had evidently been able to pursue her claim and had done so at relatively little cost. Regarding the condition of regular residence for granting judicial assistance, the government contended that it had pursued the legitimate aims of restricting public funding to aliens with a certain degree of connection with Belgium and of discouraging illegal immigration, while doing so in a proportionate manner as other benefits (e.g. free access to a lawyer) remained open to aliens who were denied judicial assistance.[88]

The Second Section of the Court presided over by Judge Tulkens rejected these arguments. It noted the serious nature of the family law issues at stake, where domestic tribunals were taking decisions which affected a number of people throughout their lives. As a result, only 'very weighty reasons could justify

[86] Even though the *Gaygusuz* pronouncement remained at the time to be confirmed by the Grand Chamber in *Andrejeva*.

[87] *Anakomba Yula* judgment, para 29.

[88] *Anakomba Yula*, para 29.

a difference of treatment between the applicant who did not have a residence permit and people who did have such a permit'.[89] Adopting a casuistic reasoning, the Court listed a number of circumstances specific to the case: the applicant's residence permit had expired a mere six weeks before the birth of her daughter; before it expired, the applicant had already started the procedure for her regularisation; and the procedure to contest paternity could not wait. In other words, not used by the Court, the applicant was a 'quasi-regular migrant' who was requesting assistance with regard to the crucial matter of establishing kinship. The Court said that it was on the basis of all the elements it had reviewed that it was finding a violation of Article 6 taken together with Article 14 (significantly listed in the judgment in that order).[90]

As can readily be seen, *Anakomba Yula*, adopted in March 2009, was not phrased in a way which affirmed the equality of all human beings—whether migrants with a residence permit, migrants without a residence permit, *or* people who do not require a residence permit (nationals, EU citizens, and some others). It nonetheless reads like an extension of *Gaygusuz*. The judgment—the first to find a violation of the Convention because of a difference of treatment between regular and irregular migrants—has not been translated into English. From a positive perspective, this could suggest that its findings were regarded as 'going without saying'. It also means, however, that it has little jurisprudential value and that the extension it proposed of the *Gaygusuz* principle was not secure, as subsequent judgments would confirm.

XIII. Immigration Status not a Criterion of Potentially Objectionable Distinction: *Ponomaryovi*'s Retreat

In sharp contrast to *Anakomba Yula* stands *Ponomaryov and Ponomaryov v. Bulgaria*. In this case, the Fourth Section of the Court found a violation of Article 14 taken in conjunction with Article 2 of Protocol no. 2. Despite this outcome, *Ponomaryovi* seems to signal a significant retreat from the confident pronouncement of equality which characterised *Gaygusuz*.

Ponomaryovi was initially lodged by a teenager who, on his 18th birthday, had lost his regular migrant status in Bulgaria. He and his younger brother had arrived in Bulgaria at a young age as their mother, a Russian national, settled there after her marriage to a Bulgarian national. On the basis of her marriage, the mother was granted a permanent residence permit, which in turn entitled her children to reside in Bulgaria. From their legal majority, however, the children were required to obtain their own independent permit. As he reached his 18th birthday in 2004, the eldest son was first told that he would have to leave Bulgaria, get a visa, return to Bulgaria, and obtain a temporary residence permit,

[89] *Anakomba Yula*, para 37, my translation.

[90] *Anakomba Yula*, para 39.

and only then apply for a permanent residence permit. Some time later, he was told that he could apply from within Bulgaria, but would need to pay BGN1,300 (Bulgarian levs) to obtain his permit.

Unable to pay this amount and having unsuccessfully applied for the fee to be waived, he complained at Strasbourg that the situation whereby he was prevented from getting a residence permit due to his indigence contravened Articles 8 and 14 of the Convention. The day after he lodged this application at Strasbourg, the Bulgarian Ministry of Education wrote to his school to enquire whether it had received the fees he owed to it as an alien without a residence permit.[91] The school required the young man to pay the equivalent of €800 in fees or face being barred from attending his final year of school and getting his school certificate. Two years later, his younger brother encountered similar difficulties and also turned to Strasbourg. The European Court declared their Article 8 complaint inadmissible but accepted the claim relating to the right to education.[92]

Repeating the *Belgian Linguistic* case, the Court observed that 'although [the Convention] cannot be interpreted as imposing a duty on the Contracting State to set up or subsidise particular educational establishments, any State doing so will be under an obligation to [offer] effective access to them'.[93] The only question before the Court, the Fourth Section stressed, was not whether secondary education should be free but 'whether, once a State has voluntarily decided to provide such education free of charge, it may deny that benefit to a distinct group of people'.[94] The applicants had suffered a difference of treatment exclusively due to their nationality and immigration status.[95] In what could be regarded as the opposite outcome to the one reached in *Timishev*, the Court ruled that there had been a violation of Article 14 of the Convention taken together with Article 2 of Protocol no. 1 on the right to education (without adding that there had been a violation of this provision taken alone).

Although it found a violation of Article 14, the Fourth Section did not produce a judgment which read in any way like *Gaygusuz*. First, the Court stated that 'a State may have legitimate reasons for curtailing the use of resource-hungry public services—such as welfare programmes, public benefits and healthcare—by short-term and illegal immigrants, who, as a rule, do not contribute to their funding'.[96] This was an unnecessary remark, reminiscent of a popular anti-immigration discourse. Second, again without this being relevant to the circumstances of the case, the Court specifically endorsed the preferential treatment of nationals of member states of the European Union which 'may be said to be based on an objective and reasonable justification, because the Union forms a special legal order'.[97] This seeming justification is entirely tautological: it simply refers to what has been set up in law, without addressing the fundamental contradiction of

[91] *Ponomaryov and Others v. Bulgaria*, appl. 5335/05, Partial Decision (ECtHR), 18 Sept. 2007, 4, in English only. The applicant invoked Article 34 of the Convention in a letter to the Court dated 3 May 2005: *Ponomaryovi* decision of 2007, 10.

[92] *Ponomaryov and Others v. Bulgaria*, appl. 5335/05, Final Decision (ECtHR), 10 Feb. 2009.

[93] *Ponomaryovi* judgment (2011), para 49.

[94] *Ponomaryovi*, para 53.

[95] *Ponomaryovi*, para 50.

[96] *Ponomaryovi*, para 54.

[97] *Ponomaryovi*, para 54.

liberalism which professes universalism, but practises closure. Third, the Court, having made general remarks about the special place of the right to education in the human rights framework, stated that, '[f]or the Court, the State's margin of appreciation in this domain increases with the level of education'.[98] The Court went on to legitimise the practice, which it described as 'commonplace', of charging aliens higher fees at university level. Yet again, one wonders why such a controversial remark was considered apposite and included in the judgment.[99]

A fourth element which distinguishes *Ponomaryov* from *Gaygusuz* is the casuistic approach expressly favoured by the Fourth Section. Paradoxically in view of the wide-of-the-mark statements noted earlier, the Court opined that '[i]t must confine its attention, as far as possible, to the particular circumstances of the case before it'.[100] Two paragraphs spelt out 'the specific circumstances of the present case' which led to the verdict of violation.[101] The first distinguished the applicant brothers from 'individuals arriving in the country unlawfully and then laying claim to the use of its public services, including free schooling'.[102] A positive point for the applicants was that 'the authorities had no substantive objection to their remaining in Bulgaria' and had not seriously envisaged their deportation. As a result, 'considerations relating to the need to stem or reverse the flow of illegal immigration'[103] could not have played a role, which the reader is led to assume might otherwise have been taken into consideration by the Court. The second paragraph stressed that the applicants could not be said to have 'tried to abuse' the Bulgarian educational system.[104] In support of this assertion, the Court noted that it was not the choice of the applicants to settle in Bulgaria where they had arrived when they were very young following the marriage of their mother to a Bulgarian national, that they spoke fluent Bulgarian, and that they could not be expected to go and live in another country. One cannot help wondering whether the Fourth Section was setting out the ground for denying secondary education (or another public service) to young people whose circumstances would not be as compelling, from the point of view of the Court, as these.

Although reaching a verdict of violation, the Court allocated a mere €2,000 to each of the applicants instead of the €50,000 they had claimed. Without any

[98] *Ponomaryovi*, para 56.

[99] The legitimacy of setting different university fee levels for home state and other students does not go without saying. See e.g. Saïla Ouald Chaib, 'Immigration, Education and Integration. A Cloudy Combination. (*Anatoliy Ponomaryov and Vitaliy Ponomaryov v. Bulgaria*)', 7 July 2011, <http://strasbourgobservers.com/2011/07/07/immigration-education-and-integration-a-cloudy-combination-anatoliy-ponomaryov-and-vitaliy-ponomaryov-v-bulgaria/>, accessed 18 March 2014. When the UK began to initiate differentiated fees in a small way in 1967, the British government so much feared that this might be challenged under the Race Relations Act that it specifically introduced a reservation which would ensure that the problem would not arise. Almost half a century on, the inequality of treatment between home state and overseas students is mostly regarded as natural in the UK. This does not mean that it should be regarded as fair, and some people remain shocked by this practice especially if they are outsiders to the system and have not been socialised in it.

[100] *Ponomaryovi* judgment, para 59.

[101] *Ponomaryovi*, para 63.

[102] *Ponomaryovi*, para 60.

[103] *Ponomaryovi*, para 60.

[104] *Ponomaryovi*, para 61.

discussion, the Court seemed to accept as legitimate the fees that Bulgaria had been charging migrants deemed not to have a special relationship with the country for the purpose of obtaining residence permits.[105] In the Court's view, these fees were not related to the violation, suffered by the applicants, of Article 14 taken together with Article 2 of Protocol no. 1.[106] The Court went on to observe that it was not clear whether the applicants had actually ever paid the fees the school had requested. It did not seem to occur to the judges that either the school fees would have been paid or the applicants would have suffered presumably even greater damage by being prevented from completing their secondary education.

XIV. From *Ponomaryovi* to *Bah*: The Strasbourg Mainstream?

Ponomaryovi was decided by the Fourth Section in June 2011 under the presidency of Judge Bratza. Three months later, the same Section confirmed its orientation in *Bah v. the United Kingdom.* Ms Bah, a Sierra Leonean national, had arrived in the UK in 2000 and unsuccessfully claimed asylum, although she was granted indefinite leave to remain in 2005. Had she become a recognised Convention refugee, the Strasbourg case would not have arisen. But because she was not a refugee, when her young son joined her in 2007, he was granted only conditional leave to remain in the UK.[107] The condition on his leave to rema in was that he must not have recourse to public funds. After her son's arrival, Ms Bah's landlord asked that they move from the room that she had been renting in Southwark, London. Ms Bah applied to Southwark Council for assistance in finding housing. As she was unintentionally homeless and with a minor child, she would normally have been allocated social housing with reasonable preference. However, the council decided that because of her son's conditional status, Ms Bah could not be classified as being in priority need. She complained of a violation of Article 14 of the Convention taken in conjunction with Article 8.[108]

[105] Bulgaria is not alone in this practice. Immigration fees in the UK are also high, with the settlement fee now costing £1,093 and a Tier 1 in-country visa £1,601: <https://www.gov.uk/government/uploads/system/uploads/attachment_data/file/279536/Fees_Table_April_2014.pdf>, accessed 24 April 2014. There are a couple of cases where the Court found a violation of the Convention due to the level of the fee set for obtaining a residence permit. One such is *G.R. v. the Netherlands*, appl. 22251/07, Judgment (ECtHR), 10 Jan. 2012. The violation found was of Article 13 (rather than Article 8, as contended by the applicant). This was due to the 'extremely formalistic attitude of the Minister' who required the applicant to prove his inability to pay the fee of €830 through additional documents which should have been unnecessary as the applicant's family's receipt of social assistance should in itself have satisfactorily indicated the 'disproportion between the administrative charge in issue and the [family's] actual income': *G.R.*, paras 54 and 55. The context of this case is reviewed in Chapter 13. See also *Hode and Abdi v. the United Kingdom*, appl. 22341/09, Judgment (ECtHR), 6 Nov. 2012, in English only, finding a violation of Article 14 read together with Article 8 in a case where refugees were treated differently from foreign workers and students. Also of relevance: *O'Donogue and Others v. the United Kingdom*, appl. 34848/7, Judgment (ECtHR), 14 Dec. 2012, about marriage approval.

[106] *Ponomaryovi* judgment, para 70.

[107] *Bah* thus acts as a reminder that despite what is commonly assumed, failing to be granted Convention refugee status has potentially important repercussions for the individuals concerned even when they benefit from another protection status.

[108] *Bah* judgment, paras 6–7, and 3.

The government submitted to the Strasbourg Court that immigration status was an entirely legal criterion which did not give rise to discrimination falling foul of Article 14 or, in the alternative, that discrimination based on immigration status flowed from the state's need to control and monitor immigration and was therefore different from discrimination based exclusively on nationality which it accepted was 'plainly suspect'.[109] The government further argued that it was both reasonable and proportionate, under the wide margin of appreciation which the state should enjoy in this area, for scarce resources to be allocated in preference to those with the greatest level of connection to the UK, as shown by their fixed and permanent rights to be there.[110] The government added that it was justifiable to treat EEA nationals more favourably than others due to the nature of the 'special legal order' formed by the European Union.[111]

The applicant objected that the underlying ground of discrimination in this case was nationality even if the official ground was immigration status.[112] This was rejected by the Court which was persuaded that it was the applicant's son's 'conditional legal status, and not the fact that he was of Sierra Leonean national origin, which resulted in his mother's differential treatment under the housing legislation'.[113] The applicant also observed that the government's position did not make sense since EEA nationals cannot be presumed to have a greater degree of connection to the UK than persons with indefinite leave to remain.[114] In view of the longstanding case law on the European Union having created a special legal order,[115] this argument had very little chance to stand. The Court did not even specifically respond to it.

In a unanimous judgment, the Fourth Section found that there had been no violation of Article 14 taken together with Article 8. On the positive side, it did not accept the principle put forward by the respondent state that immigration status can never amount to a ground of illegitimate distinction for the purposes of Article 14.[116] However, in this particular instance, it accepted the account of the government according to which the applicant had hardly suffered in practice from the difference of treatment.[117] On the reasonableness of the distinction, the Court said:

> [T]here is nothing arbitrary in the denial of priority need to the applicant when it would be based solely on the presence in her household of her son, a person whose leave to enter the United Kingdom, granted only a few months before the applicant's request for housing assistance, was expressly conditional upon his having no recourse to public funds. *By bringing her son into the United Kingdom in full awareness of the condition attached to*

[109] *Bah*, paras 25 and 26. [110] *Bah*, paras 26–27. [111] *Bah*, para 28.
[112] *Bah*, para 29. [113] *Bah*, para 44. [114] *Bah*, para 31.
[115] *Moustaquim v. Belgium*, appl. 12313/86, Judgment (ECtHR), 18 Feb. 1991, para 49; *C. v. Belgium*, appl. 21794/93, Judgment (ECtHR), 7 Aug. 1996, para 38.
[116] *Bah* judgment, para 45, relying on *A. and Others v. the United Kingdom*, appl. 3455/05, GC Judgment (ECtHR), 19 Feb. 2009, paras 182–190.
[117] For this account, see *Bah*, para 51. One wonders whether such an approximate presentation of the facts would ever be so readily accepted when it is put forward by the applicant. For a discussion of the burden of proof (in Article 3 cases but transposable here), see Chapter 7.

his leave to enter, the applicant accepted this condition and effectively agreed not to have recourse to public funds in order to support her son. The Court upholds the Government's argument that it is justifiable to differentiate between those who rely for priority need status on a person who is in the United Kingdom unlawfully or on the condition that they have no recourse to public funds, and those who do not, and finds that the legislation in issue in this case pursued a legitimate aim, namely *allocating a scarce resource fairly* between different categories of claimants.[118]

In this passage, the applicant seems to be blamed for her decision to bring her child to the UK. At the very least, the onus of the situation in which she finds herself seems to be put on her, as if it were the result of her individual actions and had nothing to do with her structural position, let alone a problematic world order.[119] This is a clear example of the Court working with what Lourdes Peroni has called an 'abstract subject'.[120] But what was the applicant supposed to do? Return to Sierra Leone? Leave her son there? What were her choices? The reference to a fair allocation of resources at the end is similarly grating. Fair to whom? Why would the applicant's son be less entitled to housing than a British child? From which perspective? Taking into account which historical context? It may seem strange to raise these questions at a time when the British government does not cease to cut the 'benefits' to which the population, and especially the poor, used to be entitled. (It already seems apposite to use the past tense.) These questions, however, remain as pertinent as ever, for their answers are not obvious. How scarce are the resources of 'the nation'? Why are they so scarce? Why are there so many cuts today? The quoted passage condones rather than questions the idea that there are not enough resources for everyone so that some people must be excluded. A human rights perspective could be expected to work at encouraging states to adopt policies which are fairer across the whole board.

The *Bah* and *Ponomaryovi* rulings of the Fourth Section suggest that it may not be very difficult for states to justify a difference of treatment on the ground of immigration status. In line with the state bias which generally characterises the Strasbourg migrant case law, I expect that these judgments announce the flavour of the future Strasbourg case law in this area. The fact that each has been translated in the second official language of the Court lends further weight to the suggestion that they represent the mainstream. One should take heart, however, in the different tone which also surfaces at Strasbourg, and can sometimes be seen such as in a case like *Anakomba Yula*. Whilst it cannot be a coincidence that the latter judgment exists only in French, it nonetheless demonstrates the strength of the undercurrent which deems it both legally and socially possible for

[118] *Bah*, para 50, emphases added.

[119] As Betty de Hart comments about the *ABC* judgment, 'this way of reasoning transforms the actions of the state…into the consequence of choice by [the applicants]': de Hart, 'Love Thy Neighbour: Family Reunification and the Rights of Insiders' (2009) *European Journal of Migration and Law* 11, 235–252 at 238.

[120] Lourdes Peroni, 'Opening Up the European Convention Human Rights Subject: An Inclusive, Multilayered Framework for Adjudicating Religious and Cultural Claims', 2012–2013 PhD thesis, University of Ghent.

European human rights law to be more attentive to the plight of migrants and which endeavours to make the value of equality of all human beings respected more fully.

XV. The Court's Regrettable Minimisation Strategy: *Zeïbek* and *Ponomaryovi*

It nonetheless remains that the Article 14 case law has not developed in a way which encompasses a broad equality agenda across nationalities. This failure is probably linked to a relative inability by the judges who constitute the Strasbourg benches to put themselves in the shoes of the applicants and to think about the problems they face in a holistic way. Too often, it seems to me, the Court looks at one aspect of the predicament suffered by the applicant and ends up analysing the particular problem which it declares admissible without seeking to connect it to 'the bigger picture' of which it is only a part. This section offers two examples of such disconnections or 'minimisation' found in the post-*Gaygusuz* case law, with one related to state-engineered statelessness, the other to the loss of a valid residence permit—thus corresponding to the two routes through which a person can access a proper legal status and, in turn, social protection.[121]

In *Zeïbek v. Greece*, which has briefly been mentioned earlier in the presentation of the post-*Gaygusuz* case law, the applicant was a not a migrant but a woman who belonged to the Muslim minority living in Thrace. This population of mainly peasants, many of them illiterate, has endured a long history of neglect and discrimination at the hands of the Greek authorities.[122] This history is obliquely referred to in the judgment when it recalls an earlier application of the Zeïbek family to the European Commission of Human Rights regarding the way the Greek authorities had deprived them of their Greek nationality in 1984, after a visit to Mrs Zeïbek's father in Istanbul.[123] In 2000, Mrs Zeïbek had had her Greek nationality reinstated, and so had three of her four children. Her eldest daughter, however, did not regain her nationality, as a result of which Mrs Zeïbek did not qualify for the large-family benefit at issue in her 2006 application. Without commenting on the apparently arbitrary way in which one daughter continued to be denied Greek nationality, the Strasbourg Court unanimously found a violation of Article 1 of Protocol no. 1, taken both alone and with Article 14. By contrast, it did not find that Article 8, either taken alone or in conjunction with Article 14, had been breached. Given what must have been at stake not only for the Zeïbek

[121] Neither of these 'passports to social protection' are well protected at Strasbourg. As we have seen in Chapter 5 (Section VI), the Strasbourg Court has long refrained from ruling on nationality issues. Although the Court has started to develop a case law on residence permit refusals, it has done so timidly, with devastating consequences for the legal protection of those who are left 'in limbo'. This is examined in Chapter 13.

[122] Vemund Aarbakke, 'The Muslim Minority of Greek Thrace', 2000 DPhil thesis, University of Bergen.

[123] *Zeibek* judgment, para 7.

family but also for the Muslim Greek minority in Thrace, this ruling can only be characterised as a missed opportunity. One must also regret that the first *Zeibek* application about a deprivation of nationality which resulted in statelessness—the bane of international law—was rejected by the Court on an entirely formal reasoning.[124] This application was declared inadmissible for failure to exhaust domestic remedies. The Commission accepted that the Greek Council of State had not had the opportunity to examine the complaint because it had not been lodged within the legal period of 60 days from the notification of the deprivation of nationality. Such formalism hardly considers the difficulties which a population kept in poverty and social exclusion encounters in pursuing judicial claims, easily turning its members into remediless victims of human rights violations.[125]

Our second case is *Ponomaryovi*, already introduced at length previously. What is of note for the current discussion is that what had originally brought the applicants to Strasbourg was the fact that they had suddenly found themselves without a residence permit. Had they been granted a residence permit, their legal status would have been secure and they could have continued to attend school. Thus, the violation of Article 1 of Protocol no. 1 (found in conjunction with Article 14) would not have arisen. The Court declared the part of their application relating to their lack of access to a residence permit inadmissible. Thus its exclusive focus was the way in which the brothers had been denied access to school. Of course the denial of education was highly problematic. However, it was the symptom of a bigger problem. One could say that the Court washed its hands of this other problem.

The brothers noted that an alien who would have been recognised to 'have at least one ancestor of Bulgarian origin and have a Bulgarian national consciousness' would have paid no more than 0.5 per cent of the fee they themselves were charged for their residence permit.[126] Such discrepancy, they argued, breached Article 14 of the Convention. The applicants also alleged that 'in fixing the amount of the fees the State had failed to treat them differently from aliens who were adult and had employment and income, in breach of Article 14 of the Convention'. In the view of the Court, 'making it easier for persons having particularly strong ties with Bulgaria to settle and remain in the country' was a legitimate aim. The Court recognised that 'the difference in the fees due was considerable' but stated that 'there are in general persuasive social reasons for giving special treatment to those who have a special link with a country'.[127] The 12 years that the brothers had spent in Bulgaria since their early childhood obviously did not amount to a special link in the eyes of the Court and the Article 14 complaint regarding the refusal of the residence permit was unanimously declared manifestly ill-founded in 2007. The argument related to their youth was not specifically answered by the Court.

[124] On the lack of attention paid by the European Court of Human Rights on nationality issues, see Chapter 5.

[125] On the Western Thrace case law, see Konstantinos Tsitselikis, 'Minority Mobilization in Greece and Litigation in Strasbourg' (2008) *International Journal of Minority and Group Rights* 15, 27–48.

[126] *Ponomaryov* decision of 2007, 9.

[127] *Ponomaryov* decision of 2007, 12.

The applicants had also argued that their difficulties in accessing a residence permit were a violation of Article 8, taken alone. The Court gave notice of this complaint to the government.[128] When the Court examined this issue in 2009, it noted that the brothers had now been granted a residence permit (for which they had each paid around BGN 1,400 after borrowing the money). The Court concluded, again by unanimity, that this particular matter had been 'resolved'.[129] It reached this conclusion without addressing the issue of the level of the fee the brothers had been charged at a time when they were 18, and in education, and after having spent most of their lives in Bulgaria. It simply repeated its long-standing and recently reconfirmed case law according to which 'Article 8 cannot be construed as guaranteeing, as such, the right to a particular type of residence permit'.[130]

To end with the shortcomings of the Court's approach to the *Ponomaryovi* case, it must finally be noted that the Court took no notice of the complaint regarding Article 34, which requires states not to hinder the right of individual petition. To reiterate, the day after the eldest of the Ponomaryovi brothers lodged his application at Strasbourg, his school was contacted and informed that he should not be admitted to class until and unless he paid school fees as an alien. Instead of asking the state to explain how this came about in order to be able to ascertain whether that action had been taken as a reprisal for lodging the initial complaint at Strasbourg, the Court ignored the Article 34 complaint.[131]

The line between legality and illegality can be very fine, as the applicants in *Ponomaryovi, Moser*, and *Anakumba Yula* all experienced. The Strasbourg Court does not seem alert to this reality. It has also not demonstrated that it is intent on discouraging states from making it difficult for a stateless or so-called illegal migrant to secure his European Convention rights.

XVI. Conclusion

After *Gaygusuz* was adopted in 1996, there was excitement in some quarters that this judgment might signal a whole new way of approaching the treatment of non-nationals by states, including in the particularly sensitive sphere of social security. Verdicts of violation which followed in its wake were mostly adopted by unanimity. This might have been taken to indicate that the Strasbourg Court was ready to speak with one voice about the fact that discrimination on the sole grounds of nationality is unacceptable under the Convention. Such a conclusion

[128] *Ponomaryov* decision of 2007, 11. [129] *Ponomaryovi* decision of 2009, 13.

[130] *Ponomaryovi* decision of 2009, 13. See Chapter 13 for an analysis of the Strasbourg case law regarding residence permit refusals.

[131] Nothing in either of the two decisions of admissibility or the judgment on the merits in *Ponomaryovi* indicates that the Court responded in any way to the complaint of a violation of Article 34 made by the first applicant. On the approach adopted by the Court towards Article 34 complaints, see Elisabeth Lambert-Abdelgawad (ed.) *Preventing and Sanctioning Hindrances to the Right of Individual Petition before the European Court of Human Rights* (Antwerp: Intersentia, 2011).

would neglect the fact that, with the recent exception of *Rangelov* on the detention regime, these verdicts all target a form of discrimination which is nowadays barely practised in Europe, namely, the denial of social security benefits to legally settled migrants.

The reason why *Gaygusuz* did not mark the beginning of an abundant, diverse, and highly significant case law by the Strasbourg Court is partly due to the fact that the denial of social protection to legally settled migrants is a relatively rare phenomenon.[132] However, it is also the result of a choice by the Court not to extend its *Gaygusuz* pronouncement beyond the sphere of social security (with rare exceptions) and beyond the situation of the legally settled migrant (with one exception). This chapter has provided examples of cases where the Court either did not examine or specifically rejected discrimination complaints made by migrants. In addition, it appears likely that applications alleging a violation of Article 14 on grounds of nationality have been summarily declared inadmissible.

Out of this weak record emerges a concern that the Court seems rarely attuned to, or interested in, the difficulties which migrants encounter. These difficulties are particularly acute for people who enjoy neither the nationality of their host state nor a valid residence permit. Such lack of legal status can often bar them from being able to access social protection, understood in a wide sense. Problematically the Strasbourg Court—or at least its mainstream, for an undercurrent going in the opposite direction is discernable—seems to display a tendency to downscale applicants' difficulties. Too often the Court prefers to focus on and examine one relatively small and self-contained issue, rather than approaching the situation of the applicant in a holistic manner. This is not conducive to a case law which is effective at ensuring that all human beings enjoy social protection and are treated with dignity.

Having painted a relatively detailed picture of the Strasbourg Court in the last three chapters, it is now time to continue to discover how the Inter-American Court approaches migrant cases. Chapter 9 looks at two of its advisory opinions, whilst Chapter 10 focuses on a contentious case.

[132] It is open to debate whether this is changing. Tom Southerden alerts me to the fact that foreigners who successfully fight either deportation or removal on Article 8 grounds in the UK are now no longer automatically entitled to public funding.

9

The Voice of the Inter-American Court: Equality as *Jus Cogens*

(Advisory Opinions 16/99 and 18/03)

Chapter 5 discussed in detail the first ruling of the Inter-American Court of Human Rights on an issue of direct relevance to migrants. The reader will recall that this case consisted of an advisory opinion dating back to 1984 about the human rights compatibility of Costa Rica's proposed changes to naturalisation rules. In this opinion the Inter-American Court made pronouncements which it is difficult to imagine the European Court of Human Rights making. The present chapter continues to review the history of the Inter-American migrant case law, focusing on the next two cases from the Inter-American Court. They are Advisory opinion no. 16 on 'the right to information on consular assistance in the framework of the guarantees of the due process of law'[1] and Advisory opinion no. 18 on 'the juridical condition and rights of undocumented migrants'.[2]

On both occasions, the requests for these opinions emanated from Mexico, which wanted to raise issues about the treatment of its nationals in the United States. The United States not being party to the American Convention on Human Rights, Mexico could not bring a contentious case against its northern neighbour. It filed requests for an advisory opinion on consular assistance in 1997 and on the labour rights of irregular migrants in 2002. The Inter-American Court was then under the presidency of Judge Cançado Trindade, famous for his erudite, passionate, and lengthy concurring opinions. The Court accepted that it had jurisdiction in the two cases. In the first, it ruled in 1999 that for a detained foreigner not to be informed of the possibility of receiving consular assistance is a human rights violation, which amounts to a violation of the right to life if it occurs within penal proceedings that result in the death penalty. In the second case, the Court ruled in 2003 that the principle of equality and/or non-discrimination means that workers cannot be deprived of their labour rights because of their irregular

[1] *The Right to Information on Consular Assistance in the Framework of the Guarantees of the due Process of Law*, Advisory opinion OC-16/99 (IACtHR), 1 Oct. 1999.

[2] *Juridical Condition and Rights of the Undocumented Migrants*, Advisory opinion OC-18/03 (IACtHR), 17 Sept. 2003.

migrant status, a principle which the Court declared to be *jus cogens*, i.e. holding universally whether or not states have elected to be bound by it.

The wide-ranging and unequivocal conclusions reached by the Inter-American Court in these two cases are without counterpart in the European system. On the one hand, as we shall see, the Strasbourg Court has ruled that giving a foreign detainee information about consular assistance is not an obligation under Article 6 ECHR in the sole relevant case recorded in HUDOC. On the other hand, as documented in the previous chapter, it has not pushed the non-discrimination principle very far. How can such different outcomes be arrived at in systems which, on the surface, seem to tackle more or less the same issues and might be expected to do so in more or less the same way? This chapter seeks to address this question by comparing the overall orientation of the two courts. In order to ground this exercise, it offers a detailed review, with an abundance of quotes, of Advisory opinions 16/99 and 18/03, paying close attention not only to the main rulings but also to the concurring opinions they attracted, as these reveal the driving forces which were at work at the Inter-American Court in the period of their adoption. A comparison is then offered with the Strasbourg Court, which relies on what has already been said about the European system in previous chapters.

Lawyers tend to oppose judicial activism to judicial restraint. On this continuum, compared with each other, the Inter-American Court lies on the side of activism; the European Court, on that of restraint. The orientation of each court naturally translates into substantive rulings which are either more or less generous to migrants' rights. These results are supported by choices regarding interpretative techniques which are congruent with the courts' overall more activist or deferential approaches. The following four aspects are discussed in this chapter: the breadth of the courts' normative interpretation; the scope of the legal sources upon which they rely in their reasoning; the intended reach of their rulings; and their attitude towards civil society participation. Not surprisingly, the techniques adopted by the Inter-American Court favour a *pro-homine* approach, whilst those followed by the European Court defer more to the state's declared interest.

This chapter starts by offering a brief history of the presence of Mexicans in the United States, as background context. Advisory opinions nos 16 and 18 are then closely reviewed, with special attention given to: how the Inter-American Court declared itself competent to deliver Advisory opinion no. 16; the way it declared the right to consular information a human right; the fact that neither the International Court of Justice in *Avena* and *LeGrand* nor the European Court of Human Rights in the little known *Kimmel* case followed the Inter-American Court's lead; the way Advisory opinion no. 18 considerably enlarged the human rights of migrants by declaring the principle of equality and non-discrimination *jus cogens*; and the four concurring opinions this ruling attracted (out of a bench of seven judges). The chapter then makes a comparison along the four aspects identified in the previous paragraph, in order to highlight the way the Inter-American Court is far more activist than the comparatively far more restrained Strasbourg Court. The risks associated with the kind of visionary jurisprudence for which the

Inter-American Court has become renowned are finally reviewed, without being judged to be necessarily pertinent.

I. Mexicans in the United States: A Brief History

The background of the two advisory opinions (16 and 18) is best understood as related to the history of Mexican labour in the United States, a country which famously built itself upon immigration, so much so that it is 'generally seen as the most important of all immigration countries'.[3]

By the turn of the twentieth century, almost one million immigrants were entering the United States annually.[4] Up to the mid-1920s, both Europeans and Latin Americans (but not Asians) were free to enter the country.[5] The 'Mexican back-door' provided an ideal tap of cheap labour, which could be turned on or off as economic needs required. Its advantages were identified by an official US Commission which reported in 1911 that:

> Because of their strong attachment to their native land... and the possibility of their residence here being discontinued, few [Mexicans] become citizens of the USA. The Mexican immigrants are providing a fairly adequate supply of labor.... While they are not easily assimilated, this is of no great importance as long as most of them return to their native land. In the case of the Mexican, he is less desirable as a citizen than as a laborer.[6]

At the end of the 1920s there were over 1.4 million Mexicans in the United States.[7] The Bracero Program (1942–1964) saw five million of them working on US farms and ranches, under a temporary status which made it difficult for them to disrupt the Euro-American control and domination of American agribusiness.[8] The Mexican 'braceros'—as they became known—were meant to replace the 'illegal' workers of the past. Far from solving the problem of illegal immigration, however, the Bracero Program is considered to have entrenched it, particularly via the practice of catching so-called 'wetbacks' and taking them back to the border so that they could be 'dried out' for immediate enrolment in the programme.[9]

In the 1970s, migration to the United States continued to grow—in marked contrast to what was then happening in Europe.[10] Restrictionism nonetheless became the order of the day from the early 1980s in the United States too.[11] By

[3] Stephen Castles and Mark J. Miller, *The Age of Migration: International Population Movements in the Modern World* (Basingstoke: Palgrave Macmillan, 2009) 84.

[4] Kitty Calavita, 'Mexican Immigration to the USA: The Contradictions of Border Control', in Robin Cohen (ed.) *The Cambridge Survey of World Migration* (Cambridge: Cambridge University Press, 1995) 237–244 at 236.

[5] Castles and Miller *The Age of Migration* 85.

[6] Quoted in Calavita 'Mexican Immigration' 236.

[7] Mae M. Ngai, *Impossible Subjects: Illegal Aliens and the Making of Modern America* (Princeton: Princeton University Press, 2004) 130.

[8] Ngai 131 and 138; Calavita 'Mexican Immigration' 237.

[9] Ngai 147.

[10] Castles and Miller *The Age of Migration* 97.

[11] Calavita 'Mexican Immigration' 238.

then previous American practices and policies had set the stage for the presence of high levels of documented and undocumented immigrants, especially but not only from Mexico.[12]

While 'Latinos' continued to provide a useful source of cheap labour, they also increasingly became perceived as a threat to social cohesion. As made clear by a recent book entitled *The Latino Threat*,[13] the fears were multiple. They relate amongst others to language (with Spanish overriding English in places), demands upon social services, and criminality and security. From the perspective of so-called 'sending countries', however, what is clear is that their citizens have had a hard time in the United States. This is the context in which to understand Mexico's requests to the Inter-American Court, the way these requests were supported by other OAS states, and the responses which they received from the Court—which involved judges who came from 'sending countries' and may thus be thought to have been sympathetic to the Latino experience of being an immigrant in the United States.

II. The Inter-American Court Asserts its Jurisdiction to Deliver Advisory Opinion No. 16

In December 1997, the United Mexican States (Mexico) submitted a request to the Inter-American Court for an advisory opinion concerning 'the issue of minimum judicial guarantees and the requirement of the due process when a court sentences to death foreign nationals whom the host State has not informed of their right to communicate with and seek assistance from the consular authorities of the State of which they are nationals'.[14]

This mouthful, which appears in the first paragraph of the opinion which the Inter-American Court delivered in 1999, was no doubt carefully drafted. The Court would have had to decline jurisdiction had the case been framed in a way which called for detailed discussion of cases that involved a state not party to the American Convention on Human Rights, hence the avoidance in this summary of any reference to the United States. The death penalty framing is probably the result of the push for litigation having come from 'abolitionists'. It is of course impossible to say whether Mexico would still have brought the request to the Court if it were not execution which awaited its nationals. Whatever the case, the death penalty framing served to emphasise the gravity of the matter, thereby implicitly justifying the request for an interpretation of the law, even if restricting the issue of consular information to death penalty cases was not really logical.[15]

[12] Calavita 237–238.

[13] Leo R. Chavez, *The Latino Threat: Constructing Immigrants, Citizens, and the Nation* (Chicago: Stanford University Press, 2008).

[14] AO 16/99, para 1.

[15] As Judge García-Ramírez explained, '[t]he consequences of a violation of the right to consular information when a human life is at stake are infinitely more serious than in other cases—even though, technically speaking, they are the same': Concurring opinion of Judge García-Ramírez in AO 16/99, para 3.

As for the reference to judicial guarantees and due process, it located the request squarely within the human rights field, and thus within the Inter-American Court's substantive jurisdiction.

Mexico thus requested the Inter-American Court to interpret 'several treaties concerning the protection of human rights in the American States'.[16] This was in line with the unusually broad interpretative competence which the American Convention grants the Inter-American Court. To quote: 'The member states of the Organization [of American States] may consult the Court regarding the interpretation of this Convention *or of other treaties* concerning the protection of human rights in the American states'.[17] Mexico asked the Court to clarify the human rights significance of one provision in particular of the Vienna Convention on Consular Relations (hereafter, Consular Convention). Adopted by the United Nations in 1963, the Consular Convention is mostly concerned with privileges and immunities of consular officers.[18] It talks about sending and receiving states, listing their rights and obligations.[19] However, its Article 36 refers to the 'nationals of the sending State' and makes clear that these must be notified of their right to access consular officers when they are detained in 'the receiving State'.[20] Mexico told the Inter-American Court that there were ten states in the United

[16] AO 16/99, para 1.

[17] ACHR, Article 64 (1), emphasis added. Which 'other treaties' are subject to the consultative jurisdiction of the Court was the point of an advisory opinion rendered by the Inter-American Court in September 1982: *'Other treaties' subject to the consultative jurisdiction of the Court (Art. 64 American Convention on Human Rights)*, Advisory opinion OC-1/82 (IACtHR), 24 Sept. 1982.

[18] 596 UNTS 261. The Consular Convention entered into force in 1967.

[19] Annemarieke Vermeer-Künzli, 'Where the Law Becomes Irrelevant: Consular Assistance in the European Union' (2011) *International and Comparative Law Quarterly* 965–995, 983.

[20] Article 36 of the Consular Convention provides:

1. With a view to facilitating the exercise of consular functions relating to nationals of the sending State:
   (a) consular officers shall be free to communicate with nationals of the sending State and to have access to them. Nationals of the sending State shall have the same freedom with respect to communication with and access to consular officers of the sending State;
   (b) if he so requests, the competent authorities of the receiving State shall, without delay, inform the consular post of the sending State if, within its consular district, a national of that State is arrested or committed to prison or to custody pending trial or is detained in any other manner. Any communication addressed to the consular post by the person arrested, in prison, custody or detention shall be forwarded by the said authorities without delay. The said authorities shall inform the person concerned without delay of his rights under this subparagraph;
   (c) consular officers shall have the right to visit a national of the sending State who is in prison, custody or detention, to converse and correspond with him and to arrange for his legal representation. They shall also have the right to visit any national of the sending State who is in prison, custody or detention in their district in pursuance of a judgement. Nevertheless, consular officers shall refrain from taking action on behalf of a national who is in prison, custody or detention if he expressly opposes such action.
2. The rights referred to in paragraph 1 of this article shall be exercised in conformity with the laws and regulations of the receiving State, subject to the proviso, however, that the said laws and regulations must enable full effect to be given to the purposes for which the rights accorded under this article are intended.

States where Mexican nationals had been sentenced to death without the Mexican consular authorities having been informed at all or in good time of the criminal proceedings which were being conducted against its nationals. It detailed six such cases.[21]

However, the problem which prompted Mexico to turn to the Inter-American Court clearly went far beyond these six cases. It reflected a general practice in the United States not to inform detainees of their consular rights. When Mexico filed a contentious application to the International Court of Justice at The Hague just a few years later, it referred to no less than 51 Mexican nationals sentenced to death in the United States without having been informed of their right to seek consular assistance.[22] The magnitude of the US disregard for Article 36 of the Consular Convention (which it had ratified in 1969) was also reflected in the fact that six states (El Salvador, the Dominican Republic, Honduras, Guatemala, Paraguay, and Costa Rica) chose to intervene and support Mexico's submissions before the Inter-American Court, at a time when contentious cases on the same question were simultaneously pending before the Inter-American Commission on Human Rights.[23] In addition, Paraguay started proceedings before the International Court of Justice in respect of one of its own nationals (Angel Breard) in 1998. (Paraguay discontinued these proceedings following Mr Breard's execution.[24]) And the problem was not restricted to nationals of Latin American countries: Germany filed a case against the United States at the International Court of Justice in 1999, concerning two of its nationals (the LaGrand brothers).[25] Hundreds of foreign nationals were awaiting execution in the United States without ever having been informed of their right to seek consular assistance.[26]

Returning to the procedure before the Inter-American Court, the United States participated in it by submitting written comments and appearing at the public hearing which the Court held in June 1998. Regarding the jurisdiction of the Court, the United States argued that the Consular Convention was a global treaty which did not lend itself to regional interpretation, that the Court should defer consideration of Mexico's request until the International Court of Justice had rendered its decision in the *Breard* case, and that the request was 'patently an attempt to subject the United States to the contentious jurisdiction of this Court'.[27] It was also the US view that the Consular Convention was a multilateral treaty 'of the traditional type concluded to accomplish reciprocal exchange of rights for the mutual benefit of the contracting States' so that it could not be considered a treaty

[21] AO 16/99, para 46.

[22] *Case Concerning Avena and Other Mexican Nationals* (*Mexico v. United States of America*) [2004] ICJ Rep 12.

[23] AO 16/99, paras 19, 51, and 52.

[24] *Case Concerning the Vienna Convention on Consular Relations* (*Paraguay v. United States of America*) [1998] ICJ Rep 248.

[25] *LaGrand Case* (*Germany v. United States of America*) [2001] ICJ Rep 466.

[26] William A. Schabas 'The ICJ Ruling Against the United States: Is it Really About the Death Penalty?' (2002) *Yale Journal of International Law* 27, 445–452 at 447.

[27] AO 16/99, paras 13–14 and 26–27.

'concerning' the protection of human rights falling within the interpretative jurisdiction of the Inter-American Court.[28]

The Inter-American Court rejected all these points. It stressed that it would 'not rule on charges of evidence alleged against a State' but would 'throw light on the meaning, object and purpose of international human rights norms'.[29] It welcomed the examples given by Mexico and other states for demonstrating that this issue was 'not mere academic speculation', warranting the delivery of an advisory opinion which was of potentially great benefit to the international protection of human rights.[30] The Court rejected the idea that it could be 'restrained from exercising its advisory jurisdiction because of contentious cases filed with the International Court of Justice'.[31] As for the Inter-American Commission, it specifically invited the Court to hear the request.[32] Both the sending state and the host state in the referred cases were members of the OAS, signatories of the American Declaration, and party to the Consular Convention.[33] The Court, 'mindful of the permissive scope of its advisory function, unique in contemporary international law',[34] agreed to answer the questions which Mexico had submitted.[35]

III. The Inter-American Court Declares Consular Information a Human Right

Having established its jurisdiction, the Inter-American Court proceeded with interpreting Article 36 of the Consular Convention. The first point it noted is that the Convention bestowed foreign nationals with individual rights.[36] Did these rights *concern* the protection of human rights?[37] If the Court said no, there would obviously be no advisory opinion. But the Court was not tempted by a negative answer. As far as it was concerned, it was 'self-evident' that the purpose of notification of the possibility of consular assistance is to enable an 'effective' defence, which is why the Consular Convention provides that the notification must be 'prompt'. According to the Court, in the absence of a more precise text, this means that 'notification must be made at the time the accused is deprived of his freedom, or at least before he makes his first statement before the authorities'.[38] The Court concluded that such notification is obviously part of the body of international human rights law.

The Inter-American Court not only recognised that this interpretation rested on an evolutive conception of human rights but also praised the dynamism at the heart of its own reasoning, which had allowed, in its own words, 'great headway' to be made in the way human rights law regulates relations between states and those human beings who find themselves under their jurisdiction.[39] The Court

[28] AO 16/99, paras 15 and 28.
[29] AO 16/99, para 47.
[30] AO 16/99, para 49.
[31] AO 16/99, paras 61 and 52.
[32] AO 16/99, para 19.
[33] AO, para 42.
[34] A warranted description: Laurence Burgorgue-Larsen, 'Les méthodes d'interprétation de la Cour interaméricaine des droits de l'homme: Justice in context' (2014) *Revue trimestrielle des droits de l'homme* 97, 23–71 at 66.
[35] AO 16/99, para 64.
[36] AO 16/99, para 84.
[37] AO 16/99, para 85.
[38] AO 16/99, para 106.
[39] AO 16/99, paras 114 and 115.

returned to the idea, already present in its previous case law, that procedural requirements for judicial guarantees must be effective and appropriate.[40] In a paragraph crucial for the subject of this book, which preceded the Inter-American Court's later stress on the need to compensate migrants' vulnerability, the Court stated:

> To accomplish its objectives, the judicial process must recognize and correct any real disadvantages that those brought before the bar might have, thus observing the principle of equality before the law and the courts and the corollary principle prohibiting discrimination. *The presence of real disadvantages necessitates countervailing measures* that help to reduce or eliminate the obstacles and deficiencies that impair or diminish an effective defense [*sic*] of one's interests. Absent those countervailing measures...one could hardly say that those who have the disadvantages enjoy a true opportunity for justice and the benefit of the due process of law equal to those who do not have those advantages.[41]

This, the Court continued, is 'why an interpreter is provided when someone does not speak the language of the court, and why the foreign national is accorded the right to be promptly advised that he may have consular assistance'.[42] What must be considered is '*the real situation* of the foreign nationals facing criminal proceedings'.[43] For the Court, 'it is obvious that notification of one's right to contact the consular agent of one's country will considerably enhance one's chances of defending oneself'.[44]

The Court thus brushed aside the arguments presented by the US government. One was that: 'Consuls are unlikely to be able to provide assistance to all their nationals detained abroad [so that] it would be illogical to consider such assistance to be one of the requirements of the due process.'[45] Another was that: 'It is not the purpose of Article 36 of the Vienna Convention to establish minimum standards for criminal proceedings' so that this Convention could not possibly be taken to have created an individual human right essential to criminal due process.[46] The Inter-American Court ruled that Article 36 of the Consular Convention is linked to, and expands the scope of protection of, the right to due process of law notably recognised in Article 14 of the International Covenant on Civil and Political Rights (signed and ratified by the United States).[47] Its unanimous conclusion was that the right to consular information is a human right. By six votes to one, it added that if a violation of the right to consular information occurred in criminal proceedings which resulted in the

[40] AO 16/99, para 119.

[41] AO 16/99, para 119, emphasis added, reference omitted. This passage is consonant with, and in this sense announces, the emphasis on vulnerability which the Court will put in AO 18/03.

[42] AO 16/99, para 120. [43] AO 16/99, para 121. [44] AO 16/99, para 121.

[45] AO 16/99, para 28. Inelegancies in the English translation (e.g. failing to drop the 'the' in the expression 'requirements of the due process') are the product of the Inter-American Court not having sufficient budget to pay professional translators. The Council of Europe experienced the same problem in its early days, as noted in Chapter 2 (p. 39).

[46] AO 16/99, paras 27–28. [47] AO 16/99, para 122.

death sentence, then the right not to be deprived of life 'arbitrarily' was also breached.

No doubt aware that the Court was breaking new ground in a way which was bound to be controversial, two of its judges, one its then President, the other a President-to-be, elaborated their position in concurring opinions. Judge Cançado Trindade divided its characteristically long opinion into three major points. The first of these scorned 'the excesses of a degenerated legal positivism'.[48] It celebrated the evolutive interpretation pursued by the Court which 'disauthorized' a traditional understanding of human rights law as deriving from 'the free will of the States' and found instead 'an answer to the problem of the foundations and the validity of general international law in the *universal juridical conscience*'.[49] This made it possible to put at the core of international law 'the final addressee of juridical norms: the human being'.[50]

Judge Cançado Trindade went on to denounce the 'double standards' manifestly practised by the United States which had argued two decades previously before the International Court of Justice, in the case filed against Iran about US Embassy officials held hostage in Tehran, that the situation had occurred 'in the grossest violation of consular norms *and accepted standards of human rights*'.[51] Implicitly naming the United States, Judge Cançado-Trindade wryly observed: '[T]he real commitment of a country to human rights is measured, not so much by its capacity to prepare unilaterally... governmental reports on the situation of human rights in other countries, but rather by its initiative and determination to become a Party to human rights treaties, thus assuming the conventional obligations of protection therein.'[52]

Judge Cançado Trindade's last point concerned the crucial importance of crystallising the right to information on consular assistance 'in a world torn by distinctions between nationals and foreigners [where borders] open themselves to capital, inversions and services but not necessarily to the human beings'.[53] Judge Cançado-Trindade observed that the application of the principle of non-discrimination is 'of great potential (not sufficiently developed to date) and of capital importance in the protection of human rights'. (This point can retrospectively be taken to have announced the subsequent declaration in Advisory opinion no. 18 of the principle of equality as *jus cogens*.) The right to information on consular assistance, according to Judge Cançado-Trindade, contributes to extending 'the protecting shield of Law to those who find themselves in a disadvantaged situation—the foreigners under detention—and who, thereby, stand in greater need of such

48 Concurring opinion of Judge A.A. Cançado-Trindade in AO 16/99, para 12.
49 Cançado-Trindade, paras 3, 13, and 14, emphasis in the original.
50 Cançado-Trindade, para 12.
51 Cançado-Trindade, paras 18–19 and 22, emphasis in the original.
52 Cançado-Trindade, para 22.
53 Cançado-Trindade, para 23.

protection, above all in social circles constantly threatened or frightened by police violence'.[54]

An emphasis on the need to create real conditions of equality is also expressed, in less abstract terms, by Judge García-Ramírez in his concurring opinion. For the purposes of this book, the central paragraph of this opinion reads:

> Aliens facing criminal prosecution—especially, although not exclusively, those who are incarcerated—must have the facilities that afford them true and full access to the courts. It is not sufficient to say that aliens are afforded the same rights that nationals of the State in which the trial is being conducted enjoy. Those rights must be combined with others that enable foreign nationals to stand before the bar on an equal footing with nationals, without the severe limitations posed by their lack of familiarity with the culture, language and environment and the other very real restrictions on their chances of defending themselves. If these limitations persist, without countervailing measures that establish realistic avenues to justice, then procedural guarantees become rights 'in name only', mere normative formulas devoid of any real content. When that happens, access to justice becomes illusory.[55]

Another point upon which Judge García-Ramírez elaborates is the reasons why the violation of the right to consular information in death penalty cases also breaches the right to life. Judge Jackman had dissented on this point (and on this point only, otherwise voting with the Court on declaring the right to consular information a human right). Judge Jackman found it 'difficult to accept that, in international law, in every possible case where an accused has not had the benefit of consular assistance, the judicial procedure leading to a capital conviction must, *per se*, be considered to be *arbitrary*'. He failed to be persuaded by the way in which the Court held an 'immaculate' conception of due process, which he said is 'not justified by the history of the precept in either municipal or international law'. In his concurring opinion, Judge García-Ramírez implicitly responds to this argument by explaining that '[t]o contend that a supposedly fair outcome... is sufficient to vindicate the procedure used to obtain that outcome... is tantamount to arguing that a lawful outcome justifies unlawful procedure'.[56] He argues that the effects of the violation of the Consular Convention have to be systematic rather than examined on a case-by-case basis. Otherwise, he explains, the system of rights and guarantees would be dangerously relativised.

For Judge García-Ramírez, Advisory opinion no. 16 was 'cutting edge'. At the same time it was also 'merely confirming many of the laws already on the books to perfect the criminal justice system'.[57] Indeed, it seems something of a paradox that the right to consular assistance benefited individuals well before international law earnestly started to recognise human rights in the second part of the twentieth century, but nonetheless proved a late and controversial addition to the body of human rights law.

[54] Cançado-Trindade, para 28.
[55] Concurring opinion of Judge García-Ramírez in AO 16/99, p. 2.
[56] García-Ramírez, 2. [57] García-Ramírez, 1 and 3 respectively.

IV. Other Courts Deny Consular Information is a Human Right: *LaGrand, Avena* and the Unknown *Kimmel*

The 'truly pioneering'[58] finding by the Inter-American Court on 1 October 1999 that consular information could not but be part of the evolving human rights corpus has not been emulated elsewhere. The International Court of Justice and the European Court of Human Rights have both declined to declare consular information a human right. Reviewing this case law further highlights the exceptional character of the stance adopted by the Inter-American Court.

Seven months before Advisory opinion no. 16 was adopted, Germany brought before the International Court of Justice the contentious case of *LaGrand* concerning two brothers of German nationality sentenced to death in the United States without having ever been informed of their right to communicate with German consular officials. Karl LaGrand was executed on 24 February 1999. On 2 March, Germany filed actions both in the International Court of Justice against 'its close ally, the United States' and in the US Supreme Court to stay the imminent execution of Karl's brother Walter. The Supreme Court dismissed the proceedings. By contrast, the International Court of Justice issued within hours of receiving this plea, without having held a hearing and on its own motion, an Order on provisional measures.[59] This was a first in its history. The order requested the United States not to execute Walter LaGrand pending a final decision in the proceedings. Walter was nonetheless executed the next day. Fifteen months later, the International Court ruled that the provisional measure it had issued should have been considered legally binding, so that the United States had been in breach of international law when it had ignored the Court's order. The International Court of Justice also held that the United States had violated its obligations to both Germany and the LaGrand brothers under the Consular Convention. In the Court's view, it was 'immaterial ... whether the LaGrands would have sought consular assistance from Germany, whether Germany would have rendered such assistance, or whether a different verdict would have been rendered'. The important point was that the Consular Convention 'conferred these rights, and that Germany and the LaGrands were in effect prevented by the breach of the United States from exercising them, had they so chosen'.[60]

[58] Antônio Augusto Cançado-Trindade, 'The Humanization of Consular Law: The Impact of Advisory Opinion No. 16 (1999) of the Inter-American Court of Human Rights on International Case-Law and Practice' (2007) *Chinese Journal of International Law* 6, 1–16 at 8.

[59] Monica Feria Tinta, 'Due Process and the Right to Life in the Context of the Vienna Convention on Consular Relations: Arguing the *LaGrand* Case' (2001) *European Journal of International Law* 12, 363–366 at 363.

[60] *LaGrand* judgment, para 74.

The International Court of Justice never referred to Advisory opinion no. 16 of the Inter-American Court in the *LaGrand* judgment. Germany had argued that the right to consular information was a human right, but the International Court remained silent on this point.[61] *LaGrand* also did not go as far as the Inter-American Court in its identification of the consequences of the violation of the right to consular information. Although it imposed on the United States the obligation to review and reconsider convictions and sentences which had been reached in violation of the Consular Convention, this was far short of requiring that convictions of defendants denied the right to consular assistance be overturned. It was accepted that the result was that remedies would depend on the circumstances of the cases at hand.

In practice, as commentators had expected, the United States did not even review these cases. It simply turned a blind eye to the *LaGrand* judgment.[62] The US Supreme Court observed that freeing all victims of the violations of the Consular Convention was not a realistic form of reparation, given the pervasiveness of these violations.[63] One can say that with one or two exceptions, the United States simply ignored the *LaGrand* judgment of June 2001.

In March 2004, the internationalisation of the issue continued with the International Court of Justice's decision in the *Avena* case, which had been filed by Mexico.[64] The Court ruled that under the Consular Convention a detainee must be informed of consular rights 'once it is realized that the person is a foreign national, or once there are grounds to think that the person is probably a foreign national', which may be indicated by unfamiliarity with the English language or appearance.[65] A violation of the Consular Convention was found to have occurred only in three out of the 51 cases which had been put before the Court: these were the only cases that had become final. It adjudged that in all the other cases the United States must provide, by means of its own choosing, meaningful and effective review and reconsideration of the convictions and sentences. In an unusual step the International Court of Justice added that 'the fact that in this case the Court's ruling has concerned only Mexican nationals cannot be taken to imply that the conclusions reached by it in the present judgment do not apply to other foreign nationals finding themselves in similar situations in the United States'.[66]

[61] Some commentators thought this was the right approach to take. 'Any other interpretation would have overstated the importance of consular assistance in proceedings before national courts': Christian J. Tams, 'Consular Assistance: Rights, Remedies and Responsibility: Comments on the IJC's Judgment in the *LaGrand* Case' (2002) *European Journal of International Law* 13, 1257–1259 at 1258; also Vermeer-Künzli 'Where the Law' 989. Others, quoting Judge Cançado Trindade, would have regretted the missed opportunity of contributing to 'the process of humanization of international law' and remarked on the continued 'ghettoization' of international human rights law which is 'no longer consistent with reality': Tinta 'Due Process' 365.

[62] William J. Aceves, [Case note on *LaGrand*] (2002) *American Journal of International Law* 96, 210–218 at 218.

[63] Joan Fitzpatrick, 'The Unreality of International Law in the United States and the LaGrand Case' (2002) *Yale Journal of International Law* 22, 427–443 at 432.

[64] Laurence Burgorgue-Larsen and Amaya Úbeda de Torres, *The Inter-American Court of Human Rights: Case Law and Commentary* (Oxford: Oxford University Press, 2011) 95.

[65] *Avena* judgment, para 63. [66] *Avena*, para 151.

As in *LaGrand* it declined to rule on whether the right to consular information was a human right—and it did not refer to Advisory opinion no. 16.

Again, the United States did not review domestic proceedings in the light of the *Avena* ruling, nor did it change its practice.[67] What it did instead was to denounce in March 2005 the Optional Protocol to the Consular Convention which makes the jurisdiction of the International Court of Justice compulsory for disputes related to the Consular Convention. The United States had been party to this Protocol since 1969, presumably because, with more consuls than any other country in the world, it had a lot to gain from the strict observance of the right of consular access.[68] The US antipathy to the International Court of Justice, which can be traced back to the condemnation of the United States in the mid-1980s for supporting the Contras in Nicaragua, thus came to manifest itself even in the consular field where one would have thought that the United States had much to benefit from an enforceable convention.[69]

Not just the avowedly state-centred International Court of Justice but also the European Court of Human Rights have refrained from following the lead of the Inter-American Court on the human rights status of the right to consular information. Admittedly, in all its history, the European Court has rarely had the opportunity to discuss this status. A HUDOC search suggests that virtually no applicant has complained at Strasbourg of a denial of their right to consular information in breach of the European Convention.[70] The one clear exception is the applicant in *Kimmel v. Italy*, a case which the European Court of Human Rights ruled inadmissible six months after the International Court of Justice had rendered its *Avena* judgment.

[67] Carsten Hoppe, 'Implementation of *LaGrand* and *Avena* in Germany and the United States: Exploring a Transatlantic Divide in Search of a Uniform Interpretation of Consular Rights' (2007) *European Journal of International Law* 18, 317–336 at 324.

[68] John Quigley, 'LaGrand: A Challenge to the U.S. Judiciary' (2002) *Yale Journal of International Law* 27, 435-440 at 435.

[69] Schabas 'The ICJ Ruling' 448. Some have suggested that US citizens should be denied any right to consular information in retaliation for the US practice of neglecting to inform foreign detainees of this right: Frederic L. Kirgis, '*International Law in the American Courts*—The United States Supreme Court Declines to Enforce the I.C.J.'s *Avena* Judgment Relating to a U.S. Obligation under the Convention on Consular Relations' (2008) *German Law Journal* 9, 619–638. This kind of retaliation would be to the detriment of individuals and not something I would personally wish to advocate. The lack of respect by a state of its international duties should not result in permission granted by other states to violate the human rights of individuals belonging to the defaulting state—or their individual rights if the status of the right to consular information as a human right is contested.

[70] This text was drafted on the basis of a search conducted in early 2012 for 'consular assistance' (in English) and 'assistance consulaire' (in French). Reconducted on 23 April 2014, the search brought up three judgments and one decision. Amongst these, the more famous is *Öcalan v. Turkey*, appl. 46211/99, Judgment (ECtHR), 12 Mar. 2003 (where the complaints did not concern lack of access to consular assistance). This dearth of case law may be due to a mixture of factors, including the fact that any complaint regarding consular assistance is summarily dismissed by the Strasbourg Court as inadmissible and/or that information on consular assistance is often provided by European states, with those who miss out on this right either not in a position or not with an intent to complain about this failure.

Kimmel concerned the allegedly poor defence that the applicant, a Polish national without a fixed residence in Italy, had received in criminal proceedings there. The applicant had been charged and convicted on 5 August 1999 for resisting police officers (whom she claimed had assaulted her first). She lodged an application with the Strasbourg Court in January 2000. The following May, she was sentenced by an Italian tribunal in her absence to an eight-month suspended sentence. She complained at Strasbourg that these penal proceedings had been in breach of Article 6 ECHR on a number of grounds, including poor legal representation. Amongst other points, she contended that the Polish consulate had not been informed of her arrest and detention in August 1999. The Strasbourg Court's partial decision of admissibility of 2003 records that the applicant wrote to the Polish Embassy 'numerous letters' following her release, that the Polish Embassy had requested clarification from the Italian government, and that the Italian Minister of Justice had responded that the director of the prison where she had been detained had reported that she had 'declared not to want to contact anyone and not to wish to avail herself to her country's consular assistance'.[71]

The final Strasbourg decision as to admissibility, adopted in September 2004, simply states:

> As regard the failure by the Italian authorities to inform the Polish Embassy of the proceedings, the Court observes that Article 6 does not impose such an obligation. Moreover, it appears from the note of the Italian ministry of Justice dated 11 April 2001 that the applicant had declared not to want to contact anyone and not to wish to avail herself of her country's consular assistance.[72]

This paragraph contains all the reasoning ever offered by the European Court of Human Rights on consular information as (not) being a human right. The least one can say is that it is not sophisticated. Despite the second sentence's careful opening of 'it appears', its wording suggests that the European Court is endorsing the version presented by the Italian state. This is disturbing given that the applicant had complained that 'no response would have been given to the requests for information which had been put forward [to the Italian government] by the Polish Embassy and that the Embassy had not been duly informed of the proceedings'.[73] Judging from the summary of the government's arguments included in the inadmissibility decision, the Italian government did not respond to this part of the applicant's complaints. As we know from the above quotation, a note denying the pertinence of the complaint was produced by the Italian government in April 2001. However, nothing is said about the history leading to this note materialising. In the absence of an investigation about the note's history and given that the facts were disputed by the parties, the question arises as to why the Strasbourg Court favoured the version of the respondent government over that of

[71] *Kimmel v. Italy*, appl. 32823/02, Partial Decision (ECtHR), 10 Apr. 2003, in French only, p. 3.

[72] *Kimmel v. Italy*, appl. 32823/02, Final Decision (ECtHR), 2 Sept. 2004, in French only, p. 9, my translation.

[73] *Kimmel* final decision, p. 6, my translation.

the applicant. This was not necessary in order to dismiss the case on the basis that consular information is not part of Article 6 ECHR.

Obviously, had the European Court opted for as dynamic and teleological an interpretation of human rights law as did the Inter-American Court, it could have found that Article 6 ECHR implicitly encompasses the right to consular information. Wishing to start going in this direction but not as far, it could also have left the point open, to be decided in the future. Instead, it appeared to settle the point by declaring that Article 6 does not impose an obligation of consular information.

Ever since *Airey v. Ireland*, the European Court has adopted dynamic and progressive interpretations of Article 6 which go far beyond the originally intended text of this provision. The impact of the Strasbourg Court on criminal procedure in Europe has been tremendous.[74] Why not in this area? Could it be that the apparently anodyne inadmissibility ruling in *Kimmel* indicates that the European Court of Human Rights is not as vigorous at defending the rights of accused migrants as those of other accused? Admittedly the *Kimmel* case was relatively benign: it did not involve serving a prison sentence, let alone the death penalty as in the American cases. This does not make the Court's pronouncement less peremptory in character.

At the time of writing, all that the European Court of Human Rights has said about the relationship between consular assistance and the fair trial guarantees of Article 6 is to deny that the one is part of the other. From a human rights and/or migrant perspective, this textual observation is neither forceful nor promising.[75]

V. Equality as *Jus Cogens*: Advisory Opinion No. 18 on the Rights of Undocumented Migrants

In stark contrast to the timidity of the European Court, the Inter-American Court has not hesitated to adopt visionary rulings. This is perhaps no better illustrated than by Advisory opinion no. 18, which will now be reviewed.

In May 2002, Mexico turned again to the Inter-American Court for another interpretation request spurred on by the treatment of Mexican nationals in the United States. This time it was the fate of undocumented migrant workers, then conservatively estimated to include three million Mexicans in the United States, which prompted the request.[76] Two months before, the US Supreme Court had ruled in *Hoffman Plastic Compounds v. National Labor Relations Board* that an undocumented migrant worker illegally dismissed for attempting to create a

[74] Andrew Ashworth, Alison Macdonald, and Ben Emmerson, *Human Rights and Criminal Justice* (London: Sweet & Maxwell, 2012).

[75] It should be noted that Article 6 specifically includes the right to an interpreter, which has produced some case law. For a short introduction, see D. J. Harris, M. O'Boyle, E. P. Bates, and C. M. Buckley, *Law of the European Convention on Human Rights* (Oxford: Oxford University Press, 2009) 327–329. However, as already observed, Article 6 has been construed as not applying to immigration and asylum proceedings.

[76] Out of a population of a then estimated 5.3 million undocumented workers in the United States: AO 18/03, para 34 (brief submitted by the Delgado Law Firm).

union was not entitled to back pay for work done prior to his dismissal. As one lawyer observed before the Inter-American Court, 'this decision create[d] a clear legal exception to the guarantees granted to other workers'.[77] Mexico asked the Inter-American Court whether such 'deprivation of the enjoyment and exercise of certain labor rights [was or not compatible] with the obligation of the American States to ensure the principles of legal equality, non-discrimination and the equal and effective protection of the law embodied in international instruments for the protection of human rights'.[78] The Inter-American Court could not have given a more resounding response, as we shall see.

The first part of the advisory opinion offers a short presentation of Mexico's request. Its second part documents in 80 pages the written and oral submissions which the Inter-American Court received from 12 American States (although not the United States),[79] the Inter-American Commission, the UNHCR, as well as no less than nine civil society organisations.[80] The third part sees the Court affirming its competence to hear the case, a point which—in the absence of the United States which had obviously formed the opinion that participating in the proceedings was pointless—no intervening party contested. The next 20 pages of the advisory opinion are devoted to the substance of the request, which is dealt with in four steps.

The first step can be summarised as follows: human rights must be respected and guaranteed by all states.[81] Crucial to their protection are the principles of non-discrimination and equality (as evidenced by the fact that they are found in numerous international human rights documents).[82] Non-discrimination and equality are two aspects of the same principle, a principle so fundamental that it is part of *jus cogens*, meaning that the principle 'may be considered peremptory under general international law, inasmuch as it applies to all States, whether or not they are party to a specific international treaty, and gives rise to effects with regard to third parties, including individuals'.[83] As a result of this, 'States must abstain from carrying out any action that, in any way, directly or indirectly, is aimed at creating situations of *de jure* or *de facto* discrimination'.[84] In addition 'States are obliged to take affirmative action or reverse or change discriminatory situations that exist in their societies to the detriment of a specific group of people'.[85]

In a second step, the Inter-American Court applies the *jus cogens* principle of equality and non-discrimination to migrants. In this part of the reasoning the Court highlights the intrinsic vulnerability of most migrants, stating:

> Migrants are generally in a vulnerable situation as subjects of human rights; they are in an individual situation of absence or difference of power with regard to non-migrants

77 AO 18/03, para 38 (brief submitted by Javier Juárez, of the Law Office of Sayre and Chavez).

78 AO 18/03, para 1.

79 The intervening states included: Honduras, Nicaragua, El Salvador, Costa Rica, Uruguay, Paraguay, the Dominican Republic, Brazil, Panama, Argentina, and Peru, as well as Canada.

80 The Court held a public hearing at its seat in February 2003 as the United States was preparing to attack Iraq, a factor which coloured the atmosphere of the hearing: Judge Cançado Trindade, personal communication.

81 AO 18/03, para 73.

82 AO 18/03, para 86, note 33.

83 AO 18/03, para 100.

84 AO 18/03, para 103.

85 AO 18/03, para 104.

(nationals or residents). This situation of vulnerability has an ideological dimension and occurs in a historical context that is distinct for each State and is maintained by *de jure* (inequalities between nationals and aliens in the laws) and *de facto* (structural inequalities) situations. This leads to the establishment of differences in their access to the public resources administered by the State.[86]

The Court does not hesitate to identify broad sociological causes for, and consequences of, this situation:

Cultural prejudices about migrants also exist that lead to reproduction of the situation of vulnerability; these include ethnic prejudices, xenophobia and racism, which make it difficult for migrants to integrate into society and lead to their human rights being violated with impunity.[87]

Returning to a more legal reasoning, the Court rules (in a phrasing which the reader will note puts right the 'Strasbourg reversal' operated by the European Court of Human Rights in migrant cases):

[T]he regular situation of a person in a State is not a prerequisite for that State to respect and ensure the principle of equality and non-discrimination... This does not mean that [states] cannot take any action against migrants who do not comply with national laws. However... when taking the corresponding measures, States should respect human rights and ensure their exercise and enjoyment to all persons who are in their territory, without any discrimination owing to their regular or irregular residence, or their nationality, race, gender or any other reason.

Consequently, States may not discriminate or tolerate discriminatory situations that prejudice migrants. However, the State may grant a distinct treatment to documented migrants with respect to undocumented migrants, or between migrants and nationals, provided that this differential treatment is reasonable, objective, proportionate and does not harm human rights.[88]

The Court then links the situation of vulnerability inherent in being a migrant to the need to provide due process and a 'genuine and not merely formal' access to justice to all migrants in respect of all (not just criminal) matters.[89]

The third step of the reasoning applies these principles to undocumented migrant workers (rather than migrants generally). Its central idea is that:

On assuming an employment relationship, the migrant acquires rights as a worker, which must be recognized and guaranteed, irrespective of his [*sic*] regular or irregular status in the State of employment.

...States and individuals, such as employers, can abstain from establishing an employment relationship with migrants in an irregular situation.

[86] AO 18/03, para 112. On the concept of vulnerability in the Inter-American jurisprudence, see Rosmerlin Estupiñan-Silva, 'La vulnérabilité dans la jurisprudence de la Cour interaméricaine des droits de l'homme: Esquisse d'une typologie', in Laurence Burgorgue-Larsen (ed.) *La vulnérabilité saisie par les juges en Europe* (Paris: Pedone, 2014) 89–113.

[87] AO 18/03, para 113.

[88] AO 18/03, paras 118 and 119.

[89] AO 18/03, paras 124–126. The notion of vulnerability is not unproblematic, however. See Martha Fineman and Anna Grear (eds) *Vulnerability: Value and Critique* (London: Ashgate, 2013).

However, if undocumented migrants are engaged, they immediately become possessors of the labor rights corresponding to workers and may not be discriminated against because of their irregular situation. This is very important, because one of the principal problems that occurs in the context of immigration is that migrant workers who lack permission to work are engaged in unfavourable conditions compared to other workers.[90]

The Court infers from this a very large international responsibility for states, which is engaged not only in what lawyers refer to as a vertical (state–individual) relationship but also in a horizontal one (from private person to private person):

States are obliged to ensure that, within their territory, all the labor rights stipulated in its laws... are recognized and applied. Likewise, States are internationally responsible when they tolerate actions and practices of third parties that prejudice migrant workers.[91]

The Court goes on to state that conflicts of norms which result from the many domestic and international instruments which regulate labour rights must be solved by applying 'the norm that best protects the individual, in this case the worker'.[92] The Court notes that certain rights 'assume a fundamental importance and yet are frequently violated, such as: the prohibition of obligatory or forced labor; the prohibition and abolition of child labor; special care for women workers, and the rights corresponding to: freedom of association and to organize and join a trade union, collective negotiation, fair wages for work performed, social security, judicial and administrative guarantees, a working day of reasonable length with adequate working conditions (safety and health), rest and compensation'.[93]

The philosophy of the Court is perhaps best encapsulated in the following paragraph:

Workers have the right to engage in a work activity under decent, fair conditions and to receive a remuneration that allows them and the members of their family to enjoy a decent standard of living in return for their labor. Likewise, work should be a means of realization and an opportunity for the worker to develop his [*sic*] aptitudes, capacities and potential, and to realize his ambitions, in order to develop fully as a human being.[94]

It is only in the fourth and final step of its reasoning that the Court comes to acknowledging the legitimacy of state migratory policies, nonetheless stressing the respect due to international instruments for the protection of human rights. The final paragraphs of the reasoning underlying Advisory opinion no. 18 again vividly demonstrate the difference in approach between the Inter-American and Strasbourg Courts regarding migrant issues and the power of states to regulate their residence and status. It is useful to quote them at some length:

[I]n the exercise of their power to establish migratory policies, it is licit for States to establish measures relating to the entry, residence or departure of migrants who will be engaged as workers in a specific productive sector of the State, provided this is in accordance with measures to protect the human rights of all persons and, in particular, the human rights of the workers.... States may [grant or deny] general work permits or permits for certain

90 AO 18/03, paras 134–136.
91 AO 18/03, para 153.
92 AO 18/03, para 156.
93 AO 18/03, para 157.
94 AO 18/03, para 158.

specific work, but they must establish mechanisms to ensure that this is done without any discrimination.

Therefore it is not admissible for a State of employment to protect its national production, in one or several sectors by encouraging or tolerating the employment of undocumented migrant workers in order to exploit them, taking advantage of their condition of vulnerability in relation to the employer in the State or considering them an offer of cheaper labor, either by paying them lower wages, denying or limiting their enjoyment or exercise of one or more of their labor rights, or denying them the possibility of filing a complaint about the violation of their rights before the competent authority.[95]

The conclusion of the Court remains broad:

The Court considers that the State must not subordinate or condition the observance of the principle of equality before the law and non-discrimination to achieving the goals of its public policies, whatever they may be, including those of a migratory nature. This general principle must be respected and guaranteed always. Any act or omission to the contrary is inconsistent with the international human rights instruments.[96]

VI. The Concurring Opinions

Four of the seven judges appended concurring opinions to this unanimous opinion. These opinions make very clear from where the wind was blowing when the Inter-American Court adopted Advisory opinion no. 18/03.

The first concurring opinion was signed by the President of the Court, Judge Cançado Trindade. It is a dozen pages longer than the ruling of the Court itself (if one excludes the 80-page summary of the submissions of the multitude of intervening parties).[97] Judge Cançado Trindade starts by noting that the case has generated the greatest mobilisation so far seen in the Inter-American Court's history.[98] This, to him, underscores the fact that Advisory opinion no. 18 deals with a matter which interests 'millions of human beings', indeed 'the whole international community, and... humanity as a whole'.[99] Such importance leads Judge Cançado Trindade to be particularly prolific (even for him) and to present his reflections on every single one of the following aspects: 'a) the *civitas maxima gentium* and the universality of the human kind; b) the disparities of the contemporary world and the vulnerability of the migrants; c) the reaction of the universal juridical conscience; d) the construction of the individual subjective right of asylum; e) the position and the role of the general principles of Law; f) the fundamental principles as *substratum* of the legal order itself; g) the principle of equality and non-discrimination in the International Law of Human Rights; h) the emergence

[95] AO 18/03, paras 169 and 170. [96] AO 18/03, para 172.

[97] Such a lengthy reporting of the proceedings would be unlikely today, as the Inter-American Court has vowed to respond to calls for its judgments to be readable by a wider public, notably by attempting to make them shorter.

[98] Concurring opinion of Judge A.A. Cançado Trindade in AO 18/03, para 1.

[99] Cançado Trindade, para 2.

and the scope of the obligations *erga omnes* of protection (their horizontal and vertical dimensions)'.[100]

Suffice it here to note (as in Advisory opinion no. 16) the central attention and sympathetic treatment accorded the vulnerable human being, as demonstrated, for example, by the following sentence: 'The drama of the refugees and the undocumented migrants can only be effectively dealt with amidst a spirit of true human solidarity towards the victimized'.[101] For Judge Cançado Trindade, 'the Law' (a word he writes with a capital letter) 'does not emanate from the inscrutable "will" of the States, but rather from human conscience';[102] 'new forms of exploitation of man by man [do not show that] Law does not exist [but that it] is being ostensibly and flagrantly violated, from day to day, to the detriment of millions of human beings, among whom the undocumented migrants all over the world'.[103]

Judge García Ramírez' ten-page concurring opinion stresses the extreme vulnerability of undocumented migrants 'who are very often almost totally helpless'[104] as they participate in processes which 'produce a form of subsidy for the most developed economies'.[105] In Judge García Ramírez' words, '*OC-18/2003* rejects the opinion suggesting there should be restrictions and reductions in the rights of the individual when he [*sic*] crosses the borders of his own country and moves abroad, as if this journey eroded his human condition and took away a migrant's dignity and, therefore, his rights and freedoms'.[106] In a phrasing at the antipode of the 'well established principle' favoured by the European Court of Human Rights, Judge García Ramírez explains that the advisory opinion 'does not deny the possibility of [states] establishing differences between categories of subjects', but that non-compliance with migratory policies 'should not produce effects in areas that are unrelated to the matter of the entry and residence of migrants'.[107] He insists that economic and social rights 'have the same status as the so-called "civil and political rights"[;] they are all part of the contemporary statute of the individual'.[108] Thus, Judge García Ramírez continues, all these rights 'have the same rank and demand equal respect'; even if they should not be confused, they are interrelated, as demonstrated by the right to work which, as a subsistence factor, is related to the right to life.[109] In a characteristically realist vein, Judge García Ramírez observes that '[a]nnouncing rights without providing guarantees to enforce them is useless'.[110] This leads him to stress the importance of an effective access to justice, without which many other rights are easily denied.[111] He concludes:

> It would be unrealistic to believe that the opinion of a jurisdictional body [such as the Inter-American Court]—even though it is supported by... hundreds of millions... could,

[100] Cançado Trindade, para 3. [101] Cançado Trindade, para 15.
[102] Cançado Trindade, para 87. [103] Cançado Trindade, para 88.
[104] Reasoned concurring opinion of Judge Sergio García Ramírez in AO 18/03, para 9.
[105] García Ramírez, para 6. [106] García Ramírez, para 23.
[107] García Ramírez, para 24. [108] García Ramírez, para 27.
[109] García Ramírez, para 28. [110] García Ramírez, para 36.
[111] García Ramírez, paras 36–39.

in the short term, reverse obsolete tendencies that are rooted in deep prejudices and sizeable interests. However, when combined, these forces can play their role in man's effort to move mountains.[112]

Turning to the third concurring opinion appended to Advisory opinion no. 16, Judge Abreu Burelli echoes the concern for the 'tragedy' which each case of forced migration represents. He invites the international community to 'concern itself with investigating the real causes of migration and ensure that people are not forced to migrate'. His own emphasis is on the establishment of a just society through the 'strengthening of a genuine democracy that fully guarantees the dignity of the human being'.[113]

The fourth concurring opinion, by Judge Salgado Pesantes, discusses a number of points identified earlier. Its particular focus is on the difference between the concepts of (legitimate) distinction and (prohibited) discrimination. It is not exactly clear, however, where Judge Salgado Pesantes draws in practice the line between the two. To quote:

> Equality before the law means that [undocumented migrant workers] must be treated in the same way as documented migrants and nationals before the law of the receiving country.... The condition of undocumented worker can never become grounds for not having access to justice and due process of law, for failing to receive earned salaries, for not having social security benefits and for being the object of various forms of abuse and arbitrariness.[114]

Like Judge García Ramírez but perhaps in even stronger words, Judge Salgado Pesantes denounces the way in which 'grave violations of rights, as in the case of the undocumented migrant workers, end up by seriously affecting the *right to life*'.[115]

VII. The State and the Individual Interests: Different Positionings

The readiness of the Inter-American Court to put the human being at the centre of its reasoning is remarkable. This *pro-homine* approach characterises its whole case law, not just that relating to migrants. What it means in the migrant cases, however, is that the Inter-American Court thinks of migrants first as human beings. By contrast, as noted in previous chapters, the European Court of Human Rights thinks of migrants first as foreigners (if they are). This difference between the two courts is fundamental. It is worth elaborating on it a little, even at the risk of some repetition.

112 García Ramírez, para 43.
113 Concurring opinion of Judge Alirio Abreu Burelli in AO 18/03, Part IV.
114 Concurring opinion of Judge Hernán Salgado Pesantes in AO 18/03, para 12.
115 Salgado Pesantes, para 15, emphasis in the original.

The European Court of Human Rights operates what I have called 'the Strasbourg reversal' in most (not all)[116] migrant cases. This reversal has the effect of giving precedence to the 'well-established principle of international law' according to which states are entitled, as part of the exercise of their sovereignty, to control the entry and residence of aliens. This principle, which embodies state interests, is often the first thing which the Strasbourg Court mentions after having summarised the facts, relevant law, and arguments of the parties in decisions concerning migrant issues. Human rights come second, laying down limits to the general principle of state control of immigration. The predominant value thus seems to be implicitly identified as state sovereignty rather than the protection of the human being.

There is no hint of such a reversal in the Inter-American case law. For the Inter-American Court, the human being comes first. As Judge Cançado Trindade repeatedly explained in his concurring opinions until he left the Inter-American Court in 2006, he saw the whole point of human rights jurisprudence as the humanisation of international law. In Advisory opinion no. 18, the Inter-American Court starts by discussing human rights generally, then the human rights of the migrant as a vulnerable human being, then those of the irregular migrant worker, and finally comes to consider state migratory policies, which it finds legitimate *as long as* they respect human rights.

Do these respective approaches necessarily produce different results? The short answer is no. It is not because the reasoning starts with human rights that a verdict of violation of human rights will follow. Inversely, it is not because reasoning starts with the state's privilege to control foreigners that a violation of human rights will never be found. Nonetheless, if one accepts that the migrant case law (whether in the Inter-American or the European system) reflects an irresolvable tension between individual and state interests, it is clear that the balance is slightly weighted, to begin with, towards the individual in the *pro-homine* approach and towards the state in the sovereignty approach. This is not to say that the 'second' interest (whichever it is in each system) cannot be ultimately assessed to be stronger than the 'first' (again, whichever it is in each system).

Should the discussion be left at suggesting that the tension between the state and the individual interests is inevitable, however? It is arguably conceptually simplistic and politically counterproductive to claim that this tension can never be put to rest. In an enriched vision and practice, one should be able to consider that the two interests are often congruent. Take for example the issue raised in Advisory opinion no. 18/03. One could ask: who benefits from allowing irregular

[116] As noted in the introduction to Part II of this book (p. 155), the principle for example does not appear *at all* in leading judgments of the 1990s. Judge Tulkens has spoken in public lectures about her efforts to get the principle deleted from the reasoning of judgments in which she participated. This was prompted by her having read a scholarly article denouncing the Strasbourg reversal (without calling it as such), namely: Sylvie Saroléa, 'Quelles vies privée et familiale pour l'étranger? Pour une protection non discriminatoire de ces vies par l'article 8 de la Convention européenne des droits de l'homme (C.E.D.H.)' (2000) *Revue québecoise de droit international* 19, 247–285 (Tulkens, personal communication, March 2014).

migrant workers not to receive pay for work they have actually done? The question involves so many stakeholders in such different positions, with such a myriad of interests which are not easily calculable, that it does not lend itself to a straightforward answer. What is clear, however, is that whether one believes that the denial of labour rights to irregular migrants is in the 'state' interest or against it very much depends upon one's overall political and economical ideology. Turning to the issue raised in Advisory opinion 16/99 and assuming the correctness of the facts reported by the applicant in *Kimmel*, one could also ask: who benefits and who loses from a form of justice which is delivered without a firm obligation to inform a foreigner accused of a crime of her right to contact her consul?

In sum, it is simplistic to posit that there exists a stark opposition between the individual and state interests. All the issues examined in this book could be re-evaluated in a way which envisages their potential congruence. For example, one could argue that it is against the interests of the state/'national community' to have families separated through immigration restrictions or expulsion because such enforced separation causes a tremendous social loss, on a number of levels, and thus negatively affects not just the families directly concerned by these measures but society at large.

VIII. Inter-American Activism and European Restraint: Four Key Indicators

Courts are regularly *either* applauded *or* criticised for their activism and/or restraint.

To simplify, a court is said to be 'activist' when it takes the text it must apply to the instant case, reads it, and finds within it meanings which had not been intended by those who had originally adopted the words the court is now applying/interpreting. By comparison, a non-activist court shows restraint: it is more attached to the actual wording of the text upon which it is called to rule. A court which exercises self-restraint is therefore more inclined than an activist court to respect the intention of the non-judicial body which is at the source of the legal text. In international law, states are the source of conventions, agreements, and other legal texts. The result is that a non-activist international court tends to be 'deferential' both to the words stated in the law and to the will of states.

Observers who approve of an activist stance typically commend a court for showing 'courage' or 'boldness', whilst deploring its 'timidity' or 'caution'. By contrast, those who think a court should not go too far (wherever 'too far' is) speak highly of judicial 'prudence' and 'deference', with 'boldness' becoming a negative characteristic and 'caution' a word of praise in their assessment.

Activism and self-restraint are not pure essence. They are relative terms which exist on a continuum. Relative to each other, the Inter-American Court is clearly more activist than the European Court which is comparatively more deferential.[117] These overall tendencies manifest themselves in a series of choices operated by the two courts, notably regarding: (a) their comparatively more generous or more limited interpretation of human rights provisions; (b) the broader or more restricted range of provisions upon which they base their reasoning; (c) the more general or more particular reach of the rulings they take; and (d) their stronger or weaker support for civil society participation in the proceedings before them.

The judicial interpretation of human rights provisions

As expressed by its former President, the aim of the Inter-American Court is precisely to liberate itself from a narrow interpretation of legal obligations defined by the will of states. Given this philosophy, it is not surprising that the Inter-American Court has not hesitated to broaden the scope of the provisions which it is called to interpret. As a result, it works with an understanding of rights which is far more generous to rights bearers than what states might have thought these rights were meant to cover when they originally signed up to them. That this is a feature of the Inter-American jurisprudence will continue to be explored in subsequent chapters.

This state of affairs can be contrasted to what is happening in the European system of human rights protection. In its migrant case law, the Strasbourg Court has not been quick to read rights into provisions of the European Convention which were absent in the original text. To return to examples which have already been discussed at length, it only started to find a forced removal to torture or inhuman and degrading treatment in breach of the Convention in 1989; it is yet to express an unequivocal principle to the effect that the deportation of 'quasi-nationals' born or settled at a young age in their country of residence cannot take place except in the most extraordinary circumstances; it has never identified a set of criteria under which family reunification should be allowed to take place; it has refused to scrutinise any legislative provision related to the granting of nationality; and it has refrained from suggesting that the right to consular information could be part of fair trial guarantees. The list could go on.

The normative basis of the courts' reasoning

One factor which helps the Inter-American Court reach a broad normative scope is that it feels no restraint in citing a wide range of international instruments, whether or not these are legally binding. In Advisory opinion no. 18, for example, there is a footnote which lists more than 30 international instruments in support of the statement according to which the principles of equality and

[117] For some, the Strasbourg Court is nonetheless far too activist. This is, for example, the case of Marc Bossuyt, whose views on the Strasbourg migrant case law stand directly opposed to mine. See Bossuyt, 'Judicial Activism in Strasbourg' paper, dated 16 September 2013, available at <http://www.openeurope.org.uk/Content/Documents/Judicial_Activism.pdf>, accessed 8 June 2014.

non-discrimination are at the heart of human rights law.[118] One gets the impression that for the Inter-American Court, every provision that supports its typically wide interpretation of human rights law is one which is worth quoting. Although this was not captured in the review presented earlier (as it omitted references), Advisory opinion no. 18 contains an abundance of references to the decisions of various bodies. The most frequently cited body after the UN Human Rights Committee is the European Court of Human Rights. Occasional references are also found, in a non-exhaustive list, to the African Commission of Human and People's Rights, the International Court of Justice, the United Nations General Assembly, and the UN Committee on the Elimination of Racial Discrimination.

The European Court could not operate more differently. Even though it sometimes includes international or European documents in the section devoted in its rulings to relevant texts, it has only recently started to go outside the European Convention in its actual reasoning.[119] Even the widely ratified UN Convention on the Rights of the Child was long absent from its reasoning. Although this is now changing, compared to what one sees in Inter-American rulings, the reluctance by the European Court to rely upon instruments beyond the European Convention continues to be marked.

Lawyers might be tempted to understand this stark methodological difference between the two courts by reference to their constitutive texts. The European Court of Human Rights is laid out in the European Convention as the final interpreter of this Convention and of no other instrument. By contrast, Article 64 ACHR provides that the Inter-American Court can be consulted by OAS member states 'regarding the interpretation of the American Convention or of other treaties regarding the protection of human rights in the American states'. This, however, does not explain everything, as the readiness by the Inter-American Court to pick and cite not just treaties but an extremely diverse range of legal instruments extends to the judgments it adopts in contentious cases (as we shall see in Chapter 10). Article 62 ACHR, which regulates the contentious jurisdiction of the Inter-American Court, speaks of 'matters relating to the interpretation or application of *this* Convention' (emphasis added). The broad approach adopted by the Inter-American Court is not just a mere matter of text; it also needs to be understood by reference to its comparatively stronger 'activist' stance.

The intended general or particular reach of the ruling

The Inter-American Court displays a strong appetite for wide-ranging rulings. Going hand in hand with this, it also rules in any one case on a large number

[118] AO 18/03, para 86, note 33.

[119] Magdalena Forowicz, *The Reception of International Law in the European Court of Human Rights* (Oxford: Oxford University Press, 2010); Françoise Tulkens, Sébastien Van Drooghenbroeck, and Frédéric Krenc, 'Le soft law et la Cour européenne des droits de l'homme' (2012) *Revue trimestrielle des droits de l'homme* 91, 433-489.

of points, which some might be inclined to consider are hardly germane to the case before it. For example, in Advisory opinion no. 16, the Court did not stop at saying that the right to consular information was a human right; it added that its violation in death penalty proceedings was also a violation of the right to life. In Advisory opinion no. 18, it intimated that many policies which distinguish between migrants and nationals, or documented and undocumented migrants, would fall foul of the equality principle. Of course, it is always possible to go further, and this applies to the Inter-American Court too. The Court has, for example, been criticised for missing the opportunity of finding a violation of the right to education in the *Yean and Bosico* case, as we shall see in Chapter 10.

By contrast, when the European Court reaches a verdict of violation, it often does so by reference to the very particular circumstances of the case to which this verdict relates. Its jurisprudence thus tends to be casuistic, that is, adopted on a case-by-case basis. Furthermore, it generally manifests a reluctance to ruling on every complaint brought by the applicant. Its predilection for deciding the issues before it in a narrow manner can be seen as yet another manifestation of its overall deferential stance.

One might be tempted to relate the Inter-American Court's willingness, if not determination, to embrace as wide a field as possible and to draw numerous implications and consequences from them, to a wish to make the most of the few cases which come before it (at most two dozen a year). It is too simplistic, however, to explain this tendency by a purely instrumental motivation. The Inter-American Court acquired a reputation for philosophical and abstract thinking during the presidency of Judge Cançado Trindade and not without reason. As passages quoted previously illustrate, the Court was not averse to offering general observations which would not have been out of place in a sociological essay. The Court's refusal to limit itself to a strict legal reasoning helped it to fulfil the role which it saw for itself, namely contributing to the *development*, rather than the mere application, of human rights law. To this day, although in different ways, the Inter-American Court does not want to restrict its pronouncements to the case at hand. It allows itself to think 'abstractly' about the definition and scope of the human rights upon which it pronounces. Moreover it strives to identify the 'concrete' means necessary to ensure their respect as well as the types of reparation that its findings of violation in contentious cases require (as will be demonstrated in the next two chapters). By contrast, the European Court of Human Rights adopts rulings which tend to be very much focused on the circumstances of the case before it, preventing a broad subsequent application of the principles it has identified.

Civil society participation

In harmony with its activist orientation, the Inter-American Court is interested in hearing the views of human rights activists. As noted in Chapter 5, some of these actually work in its midst as interns. Another manifestation of this opening is that anyone can submit a third party intervention to the San José Court.

The only proviso is that the intervention must reach the Inter-American Court in time: either the date set on the Court's website for cases falling under its advisory jurisdiction or two weeks after the public hearing in a contentious case. As a result, third party interventions are often numerous, as happened in the cases reviewed in this chapter. And the Court gives them attention. For example, it always organises a public hearing of third party interveners before preparing its advisory opinion. It should also be noted that the Court regularly holds hearings outside its seat, throughout Latin America. With such hearings supported by the host state, they of course represent a way for the Court to conduct its work at a relatively low cost. However, these extramural hearings are also valued by the Court for their symbolic and social dimensions. In my conversations with them, the judges never failed to stress that they represent an opportunity to enter in contact with, and become known by, a range of American people beyond state officials. This is not to deny that the Court is criticised by some for being aloof and insufficiently cognizant of the reality of the societies at the heart of the cases upon which it rules.[120] One should also not ignore the fact that the Court is inaccessible to all but the tiniest number of prospective applicants. Its determination not to stay comfortably distant is nonetheless noteworthy and contrasts with the practice prevalent at Strasbourg.

At first sight, the European Court is more approachable than the Inter-American Court: any individual can lodge an application. However, it also projects the image of a statist institution, which considers that the important players are state representatives. For example, any state can submit a third party intervention while a private party needs to request the authorisation of the Court.[121] The deadlines for doing so are also much tighter than in the Inter-American system. Another example of this statist tendency is the list of invitees at the European Court's annual celebration for the opening of the judicial year, an event at which state officials are heavily represented. This is not to suggest that the European Court is completely closed to civil society. For example, in *Hirsi v. Italy*, as many as seven NGOs submitted third party interventions. This, however, was a rather exceptional presence.

IX. The Dangers of a Visionary Jurisprudence: Real Risks or False Alarm?

Especially under the presidency of Judge Cançado Trindade, the Inter-American Court acquired the reputation of producing a 'visionary' jurisprudence. Some commentators used this adjective as a compliment; others as a rebuke. The former believed the Court was to be congratulated for its audacity and the

[120] Par Engstram and Andrew Hurrell, 'Why the Human Rights Regime in the Americas Matters', in Mónica Serrano and Vesselin Popovski (eds) *Human Rights Regimes in the Americas* (Tokyo: United Nations University Press, 2010).

[121] As to who has taken up this opportunity and with what results, see: Laura Van den Eynde, 'An Empirical Look at the Amicus Curiae Practice of Human Rights NGOs Before the European Court of Human Rights' (2013) *Netherlands Quarterly of Human Rights* 31, 271–313.

positive development of human rights law it fostered. The latter thought that the Inter-American Court was going too far and thus running the risk of jeopardising the system of human rights protection in the Americas by losing sight of its state addressees.

For Harvard Law Professor Gerald Neuman, for example, the Court was in danger of not paying sufficient attention to 'the consent of the regional community of states as a factor in the interpretation of a human rights treaty'.[122] Put in simplistic terms that Neuman does not use, one could summarise the thrust of his article as: the Court goes it alone and leaves states behind. The first problem is that a gap therefore emerges between the law as states have consented to it and the law as posited by the Court. The second problem is that the Court does not care about this gap, even though states are the parties which sign treaties and give the Court its legitimacy and means of existence. If anything, the Court celebrates the gap, by implicitly elevating the supposedly 'universal juridical conscience' to the status of the most legitimate source of international law, thus above state consent.

Indeed, as clearly indicated by his multiple concurring opinions (not just those reviewed in this book), Judge Cançado Trindade saw it as the mission of the Inter-American Court to liberate itself from the will of the states in order to be able to distil the true meaning of international law from a deeply humanistic juridical conscience. As we have seen in this chapter, this method has resulted in a norm being declared *jus cogens* on the basis of a wide variety of instruments, some of which are binding but many not,[123] all treated as if they *equally* testified to an evolution capable of influencing the interpretation of state's obligations under international law.[124] Advisory opinion no. 18 can be said to have 'obviated state consent altogether'.[125] In it, the Court was ready to give equal weight to the bare appearance of a proposition in a UN resolution and the recommendation of an expert body, as to a carefully drafted principle which had been the subject of intense negotiations before being adopted. In doing so, 'the Court is converting global soft law into regional [American] hard law'.[126] Neuman warns against the possibility that this 'could lead to unpredictable and detrimental consequences across the entire range of international law'.[127] He does not identify these 'unpredictable' dangers, but one presumes they concern overt or covert state rebellion.

A good starting point for reflecting on the risk of state rebellion is an article written by Neuman's Harvard colleagues James Cavallaro and Stephanie Erin Brewer in 2008. Cavallaro has recently become a judge at the Inter-American Court. Prior to this, he had a long experience of representing applicants alleged victims before the Court. As 'friends of the Court', he and Erin Brewer wanted it to be as effective as possible. As such, in their article they recommended that the Court stay in tune with 'local' factors, as they feared that being 'out of touch with

[122] Gerald L. Neuman, 'Import, Export, and Regional Consent in the Inter-American Court of Human Rights' (2008) *European Journal of International Law* 19, 101–123 at 102.

[123] Neuman 119. [124] Neuman 114. [125] Neuman 102.

[126] Neuman 111. [127] Neuman 122.

realities on the ground' might cost the Court its effectiveness.[128] Their discussion has a number of strands. One is that it is very easy for states to ignore the Court's more philosophical rulings, especially when these do not 'mesh with parallel civil society developments and broad societal understanding of a given issue'.[129] They do not dispute the fact that the Court should not refrain from issuing opinions simply because these are unlikely to go down well in a reigning political climate. But they ask the Court to be as concrete as possible. They take the example of Advisory opinion no. 18. In this case '[t]he Court could have decided the issue before it on the grounds that certain labor rights are fundamental... and that among these is workers' entitlement to full remedies for unjust termination due to union activities regardless of immigration status [rather than framing] its reasoning within a broad and philosophical framework of non-discrimination'.[130] They regret that 'rather than issuing the most readily implementable decision possible, the Court has produced one that may appear far too removed from daily life to attract widespread public support or institutional cooperation'.[131]

Cavallaro and Brewer go on to observe that Advisory opinion no. 18 has not 'brought about clear improvements in the treatment of migrant workers in the region'.[132] As an example, they cite the labour laws of Mexico which continue to forbid non-Mexicans from holding leadership positions in trade unions. They conclude that 'the opinion may reflect a Court focused on an idealized view of human rights law rather than on the development of jurisprudence most relevant to the challenging and often domestically unpopular field of migrant workers' rights'.[133]

Their reflections, however, cannot but spur the following question: had the Court specifically focused on back pay and trade union rights, would this more restricted opinion have persuaded Mexico to change its laws and/or practices? This appears extremely unlikely. In my view, it is therefore important to think about the kind of 'effectiveness' which the Court was seeking to achieve in this case. In his concurring opinion, Judge García Ramírez had specifically commented upon the fact that Advisory opinion no. 18 had no prospect of being implemented immediately. In his words, the opinion would hopefully play a role 'in man's effort to move mountains'. The Inter-American Court was obviously seeking to influence the development of state practice in the long term, possibly in a diffuse way. If so, is it useful to condemn it for its lack of immediate and clearly discernible impact?

Having said this, were there to be evidence that the Court's approach is counterproductive, then it would obviously be important to invite the Court to change its attitude.[134] The next chapter will discuss the problems of lack of full implementation of the Court's judgments and state denunciations of the Inter-American

[128] James L. Cavallaro and Stephanie Erin Brewer, 'Reevaluating Regional Human Rights Litigation in the Twenty-First Century: The Case of the Inter-American Court' (2008) *American Journal of International Law* 768–827.

[129] Cavallaro and Brewer 821.

[130] Cavallaro and Brewer 822.

[131] Cavallaro and Brewer 823.

[132] Cavallaro and Brewer 823–824.

[133] Cavallaro and Brewer 824.

[134] Or, most crucially, the OAS to ensure the Inter-American Court has the means to function properly, given that many of the regrettable trends which Cavallaro and Brewer point out are a matter of resources.

system. These are problems which cannot be ignored and they would obviously be extremely concerning if they were very serious—which, so far, they do not seem to have been.

The 'unpredictable and detrimental consequences' envisaged by Neuman when he criticises the philosophical and visionary character of the jurisprudence of the Inter-American Court could take lesser forms than straightforward state rebellion, such as starving the Court of funding. This hypothesis does not lack pertinence. The Court has long depended for its survival and expansion of activities on allocations from as diverse sources as the European Union, Norway, Spain, and even some individual OAS members. Such a situation is far from satisfactory. Moreover it could get worse. However, there is no guarantee that the OAS would be more generous towards a less 'visionary' and more 'practical' court. Compared to the Inter-American Court, the European Court has been very deferential to states. This has not translated into either state gratitude or generous funding, as the attitude of the British government especially demonstrates. Admittedly, the European Court is in a much better financial position than the Inter-American Court, but this does not prevent it from constantly pleading, often unsuccessfully, for funding.

When reflecting upon the possible negative repercussions of an activist jurisprudence, commentators may have in mind not only states which are currently party to the American Convention, but also those that might consider joining. It would of course be of enormous benefit to the Inter-American system to count the United States amongst its members. With the kind of pronouncements which the Inter-American Court has made in the past and is still making today, the US resolve to stay away from the American system of human rights protection is assuredly not going to lessen any time soon. What would persuade the United States to join, however? As we have seen, it is not ready to comply even with the rulings of the state-orientated International Court of Justice. In *LaGrand* and *Avena*, the International Court had merely requested that domestic cases where violations of the right to consular information had occurred be internally reviewed. The response of the United States was to denounce the Protocol to the Consular Convention. In my view, the Inter-American Court would be ill advised to dilute its strong pronouncements in the hope that this more deferential approach might persuade some states to submit to its jurisdiction.[135]

X. Conclusion

Advisory opinion no. 16 on consular information was adopted in 1999 and Advisory opinion no. 18 on labour rights in 2003. Clearly, the former prepared

[135] Canada's declared reason for not joining is that it fears that the American Convention would not allow it to stick to its views regarding the status of the foetus. Informal conversations with Canadian legal academics suggest that there is not enough interest amongst Canadian human rights activists and others for a system which they feel they do not need.

the ground for the latter. Clearly too, far from merely consolidating previous case law, especially the declaration of the principle of equality as *jus cogens* represented a huge leap in human rights law. There is no doubt that this amazing step, variously praised or criticised, owes a lot to the then President of the Court.[136]

In comparison to the Inter-American Court, the European Court has always trod 'cautiously'. It either does not wish (because it shares European states' views on migration) or does not dare (because it fears that it would lose the indispensible state support which it needs) interpreting the provisions of the European Convention in as broad a way as the Inter-American Court has done in respect not only of the American Convention but also of human rights law more generally.[137]

Was the Inter-American Court right to be as 'audacious' as it was under the leadership of Judge Cançado Trindade? This book sides for a positive answer on the grounds that timidity in the human rights field yields terrible results for the protection of the human being. One might object that the expansive humanist and visionary principles identified by the Inter-American Court were never sustainable in the legal or real world, and that they are therefore useless. True, neither Advisory opinion no. 16 nor Advisory opinion no. 18 changed the world. But even if these have not yielded immediate practical effect, they remain references in human rights law, upon which human rights lawyers can rely.

Some will retort that this is all very good in the abstract but that there is a risk that the Inter-American Court's boldness might prove counterproductive and damage its effectiveness. However, as Judge Cançado Trindade observed, 'the alternative to utopia is desperation'.[138] Besides, the author of this book cannot help but think that a human rights court which is faithful to the human rights idea is formidable, in the best sense of the word. The energy it projects is refreshing, exhilarating, promising, galvanising, and powerful.

[136] Judge Cançado Trindade is now writing separate opinions at the rather different International Court of Justice. His opinions are now dissenting rather than concurring. A prolific academic, he has also written multiple scholarly works, including *International Law for Humankind: Towards a New Jus Gentium* (The Hague: Martinus Nijhoff, 2010).

[137] The closest pendant to Advisory opinion 18/03 is, in the European system, *Paulet v. the United Kingdom*, appl. 6219/08, Judgment (ECtHR), 13 May 2014. In *Paulet*, which was decided after this chapter was completed, the Strasbourg Court found a violation of Article 1 of Protocol no. 1 due to the confiscation by the respondent state of the savings the applicant had made out of employment he had secured through having presented a false French passport to his employer. However, the Strasbourg Court found a violation because of the narrow scope of review which had been exercised by the Court of Appeal. Having found that the confiscation was in the public interest, the domestic judges had not gone on to assess 'whether the requisite balance [had been] maintained in a manner consonant with the applicant's right' under Article 1 of Protocol no. 1 when the confiscation sanction had been taken (para 67). The procedural nature of the violation incited the Strasbourg Court not to allocate the applicant the total sum of his confiscated savings (over £21,000) as pecuniary prejudice. The Court allocated him only £2,000, moreover as non-pecuniary rather than pecuniary damage (para 73). Judge Kalaydjieva, joined by Judge Bianku, dissented on this point.

[138] Cançado Trindade in AO 18/03, para 42.

10

Reparations are a Big Issue: Taking Human Rights One Step Further

(*Yean and Bosico*)

Advisory opinions nos 16 and 18 saw the Inter-American Court of Human Rights adopt a broad, humanistic, visionary jurisprudence regarding migrants, but could this spirit survive a contentious case? The test came when two girls of suspected foreign origin complained to the Inter-American Commission that their country of birth had arbitrarily denied them a birth certificate, leaving them stateless and without legal recognition, and the Commission took their case to the Court. This case, *The Girls Yean and Bosico v. the Dominican Republic*,[1] no longer concerned an abstract interpretation of human rights law in the Americas. If the Inter-American Court upheld the alleged victims' complaints, its judgment would have an effect far beyond the two victims (the older one an adult by the time the Court delivered its judgment). Given the island's history, the Dominican Republic could be expected to fiercely resist a judgment which called upon it to change its approach towards the thousands of people of Haitian origin settled on its territory. The stakes were high not only for the parties to the case but also for the Court itself.

The Inter-American Court delivered its judgment in *Yean and Bosico* in September 2005. This chapter reviews the various rulings which the case generated as well as the decisions of the Court in 'the matter'—also involving Haitians in the Dominican Republic—which eventually became the *Benito v. the Dominican Republic* case, pending before the Court as this book went to press.[2] The review is undertaken in order to highlight further differences between the European and Inter-American Courts regarding the former's greater restraint and the latter's activism. This chapter continues this comparison, with the focus now shifting more towards process, including the ordering of reparations.

[1] *The Girls Yean and Bosico v. Dominican Republic*, Preliminary Objections, Merits, Reparations and Costs, Judgment (IACtHR), 8 Sept. 2005.

[2] Case 12.271 *Benito Tide Méndez and Others v. Dominican Republic*, submitted by the Inter-American Commission to the Court on 12 July 2012. A third case concerning the treatment of Haitians in the Dominican Republic, *Nadege Dorzema et al. v. Dominican Republic* (IACtHR), 24 Oct. 2012, is reviewed in Chapter 14.

In *Yean and Bosico*, the reparations ordered followed the finding of three sets of violations. The first of these concerned the denial of the rights to nationality and equal protection in respect of children who, the Court assesses, are by definition vulnerable;[3] the second was the denial of the right to a name and to juridical personality, again in respect of children; and the third was the inhumane treatment suffered by the children's closest next of kin (their mothers and one sister) due to their fear that the children might be deported. The Court's principled and unwavering approach also comes across in a number of additional, more 'procedural', ways, however. Particularly notable is the fact that the Court rejects the argument by the Dominican Republic according to which the granting of birth certificates to the two alleged victims (at a time when the case was pending before the Inter-American Commission) was sufficient grounds to close the case. Equally remarkable is the imposition of wide-ranging reparation measures designed both to compensate the victims and to avoid the repetition of the violations.

Although the judgment is far-reaching on paper, in practice it has failed to produce the results which the activists involved in the case were hoping for. The Dominican Republic had been very keen on migrant rights when they enhanced the position of its own nationals, as its third party interventions to the Inter-American Court in the proceedings related to Advisory opinions nos 16 and 18 show. No doubt it then had in mind Dominicans who settled in the United States (the largest New York migrant community). It took a different view of migrant rights when these would benefit those it insists on conceptualising as 'transient', rather than permanent settlers. While the compensation awarded to the *Yean and Bosico* victims was eventually paid, the Dominican Republic transformed its legislation and policies regarding birth registration in the opposite way from the one it had been ordered by the Court to follow. The case is still lingering in the Inter-American system, with no prospect of an early resolution. The Inter-American Court, which itself supervises the execution of its judgments by states, is unlikely to be in a position to close the *Yean and Bosico* case any time soon.

As with any other international court, the Inter-American Court cannot rely on the support of an executive branch in order to get its judgments implemented. The Court would have been aware that the Dominican Republic would not welcome its judgment. These factors did not entice it either to accept the 'friendly settlement' proposed by the state or to order narrow reparation measures. The question arises: was such determination to keep to a human rights context a wise course of action on its part? Some might think that the Court was foolish; others may on

[3] This follows in the wake of 'Juridical Condition and Human Rights of the Child', Advisory opinion no. 17/02 (IACtHR), 28 August 2002. Referring to the phrase 'best interests of the child' found in Article 3 of the Convention on the Rights of the Child, the Court stated: 'The principle of equality reflected in Article 14 of the American Convention on Human Rights does not impede adopting specific regulations and measures regarding children, who require different treatment due to their special conditions. This treatment should be geared toward protection of children's rights and interests' (para 137, opinion's point 3).

the contrary applaud it for resisting the state and going exactly where the human rights logic led it.

The choices which the Inter-American Court of Human Rights made in *Yean and Bosico* are very different from those which one might expect the European Court of Human Rights to make if it was presented with a similar scenario.[4] This chapter will discuss how the Strasbourg Court is more inclined to strike off cases when the respondent state has taken steps to address the situation of the individual applicants, even when this leaves an important underlying issue unresolved. It will also highlight the declaratory nature of the Strasbourg judgments, a consequence of which is that the Strasbourg Court to this day refrains from addressing the reparation implications of its verdicts (with only limited exceptions). As a result, it is relatively easy for the Committee of Ministers of the Council of Europe—the body in charge of supervising the execution of the judgments of the European Court of Human Rights—to reach the point where it can close a case through a final resolution which indicates that the respondent state has executed the judgment.

What can we make of this? On the one hand we can begin to understand why the execution record of the European and Inter-American systems is reputed to be, overall, good and poor respectively. On the other hand we can also see that comparing the execution records of the two systems is not instantly meaningful, given that the systems work in different contexts and follow different modes of operation. One point is nonetheless clear: the current opposition which the European Court of Human Rights faces from a number of states, including the UK, indicates that an international court's reward for the adoption of a deferential stance is not an automatic gain in compliance from states. On the basis of the European experience, one perhaps should not hasten to predict that the Inter-American system of human rights protection would necessarily gain if its Court were to emulate the restraint which so manifestly characterises the actions of the Strasbourg Court in migrant cases.

In short, this chapter pursues the double aim of presenting the principled approach of the Inter-American Court throughout the various stages of the proceedings of a contentious case and of comparing this approach to that of the European Court of Human Rights. It starts by highlighting the context of the two main cases under review through a brief discussion of the history of the relationship between Haiti and the Dominican Republic. It proceeds with a brief introduction of the provisional measures which were ordered by the Inter-American Court in 2000 in the matter of the *Haitians and Dominicans of Haitian origin in the Dominican Republic* (hereafter, the '*Haitians*' matter). The chapter then turns to the *Yean and Bosico* case, which it analyses in depth, and explores what one might expect would happen in a similar case under the European system. The way the Inter-American Court dealt with the Dominican

[4] Perhaps the closest Strasbourg case to *Yean and Bosico* is *Kurić and Others v. Slovenia*, appl. 26828/06, GC Judgment (ECtHR), 13 July 2010, briefly discussed at pp. 144–145.

objection according to which a friendly settlement should have closed the case is recounted and then contrasted with the way the Strasbourg Court could be expected to approach a situation where the respondent state has resolved the situation of the claimants. The next section reviews the multiple violations which the Inter-American Court found by relying on its previous case law but developing it further, including by introducing some (albeit far from fully fledged) remarks about the right to education.

The chapter continues by discussing issues of reparations and execution which are often neglected in legal commentaries. The wide scope of reparations typically ordered by the Inter-American Court is stressed and contrasted to the European Court's approach. The Dominican resistance to implementing *Yean and Bosico* is then noted. This is followed by a section which questions the *bien-fondé* of the reputation the European system enjoys of having managed to secure an overall unproblematic execution record, while observing that any comparison between the execution records of the judgments of the European and Inter-American Courts must take into consideration the higher demands made by the Inter-American Court upon defendant states. The next section challenges—on the basis of the European experience—the idea that judicial restraint produces state respect. The chapter ends by returning to the 'Haitian' matter and highlights the approach of the Inter-American Court to provisional measures.[5]

I. Haitians in the Dominican Republic

It is never easy for two states to share an island. This, in particular, applies to the Republic of Haiti and the Dominican Republic, which respectively occupy the western one-third and eastern two-thirds of the second-largest island in the Caribbean Sea (after Cuba). Tellingly the two countries do not refer to this island in the same way. Haiti calls it Haiti; the Dominican Republic, Hispaniola.[6]

Haiti gained its independence from France in 1804, following a slave revolution in the economically thriving colony of Saint-Domingue. The republic took its name from the island's indigenous name. Its 1805 Constitution declared all its citizens black. Fearing an invasion by the European colonial powers from the other side of the island, the Republic of Haiti occupied the eastern part of the island in 1822. The Haitian occupation lasted 22 years until the Dominican Republic achieved its independence in 1844—from a previous colony. The new state defined itself in opposition to its neighbour and previous master. It was not to be African, black, or heathen. This legacy is enduring. To this day Dominicans stress their Spanish, white, and Catholic heritage. In line with this, they tend to favour light over dark colour of skin and to deny their own African descent, for

[5] For a discussion of provisional measures in the Strasbourg system, see Chapter 12 (pp. 434–436).

[6] Bridget Wooding and Richard Moseley-Williams, *Needed but Unwanted: Haitian immigrants and their descendants in the Dominican Republic* (London: CIIR, 2004) 18–19.

example describing themselves as *indiola* (rather than *mulatto*, the term commonly used in the rest of the region).[7]

Arguably, Haiti never recovered from the international isolation in which it was kept after it achieved its black-led independence. Its subsequent internal history was marred with political violence—as well as dictatorships under the Duvaliers (first François, who ruled from 1957 to 1971 and then Jean-Claude, who ruled from 1971 to 1986, and who were respectively known as 'Papa' and 'Baby Doc'). Additionally suffering from earthquakes, Haiti holds the unfortunate distinction of being the poorest country in the western hemisphere.[8] In comparison, the Dominican Republic fares better, even though it has also known dark political periods, including a dictatorship under the presidency of Rafael Leonidas Trujillo (1927–1961). Sugar plantations had been developed with foreign capital in the late nineteenth century. Links with the United States brought in income, but not equal distribution; the Dominican Republic is a highly unequal society.

The strong economic disparity between the two countries and Haiti's endemic poverty has meant that Haitians have always sought work in the economically better-off Dominican Republic. Until the sugar industry collapsed in the mid-1980s due to a dramatic fall in prices on the world market, Haitians came to do the very hard job of cutting sugarcane. They lived in rudimentary and isolated settlements erected on the plantations, called *bateyes*. Today Haitians are mostly found in other sectors of the Dominican economy: various types of labour-intensive agriculture as well as construction and tourism. They have the lowest paid jobs that Dominicans shun. Like immigrants elsewhere, they are both needed and unwanted[9] and suffer from deep-seated prejudice.

The single most atrocious episode against Haitians in the Dominican Republic occurred in 1937, when President Trujillo ordered their slaughter—nonetheless sparing from this order the indispensible cane-cutters. Thousands were killed.[10] A less dramatic form of state-implemented discrimination is the continual refusal to register the birth of people who are presumed, with or without good reason, to be of Haitian origin, as happened to the victims in the *Yean and Bosico* case.

Poor black people who live in the Dominican Republic are assumed to be Haitians—even though many are Dominicans. People taken or mistaken for Haitians not uncommonly deny this origin to try to evade the prejudice that it attracts. People's identities are often publicly disputed. In a context where corruption makes it possible to buy documents, official documentation is rarely sufficient to convince the Dominican authorities that a person is not of Haitian origin.[11]

[7] Strictly speaking the term '*indiola*' does not make sense if it is meant to refer to the indigenous population, decimated within 50 years of Columbus' arrival: David Howard, *Coloring the Nation: Race and Ethnicity in the Dominican Republic* (Oxford: Signal Books, 2001) 41.

[8] Wooding and Moseley-Williams *Needed but Unwanted* 26.

[9] To quote the title of the report by Wooding and Moseley-Williams.

[10] While the 1935 census had recorded 52,675 immigrants, the 1950 census recorded only 29,500: Wooding and Moseley-Williams *Needed but Unwanted* 22.

[11] Steven Gregory, *The Devil Behind the Mirror: Globalization and Politics in the Dominican Republic* (Berkeley: University of California Press, 2007) 171.

The Dominican Republic is a society where the undocumented are not necessarily migrants, but are assumed to be so.

In 1994, an academic publication advanced the figure, now frequently cited, of 500,000 Haitians living in the 8.5 million-strong Dominican Republic. The authors of this study reached this figure by adding together immigrants born in Haiti (245,000) and the projected number of descendants of Haitian immigrants who had been recorded in the censuses carried out through the twentieth century (260,000).[12] This latter figure has been criticised for being inflated and for risking endorsing the idea that some people, although legally entitled to the Dominican nationality because they were born there, are not 'properly' Dominican.[13] In *Nadege Dorzema*, it is reported that around one million people of Haitian origin are living in the Dominican Republic.[14]

What Haitians and Dominicans of Haitian origin mistaken for Haitians fear most from the state on a day-to-day basis is deportation. Massive deportation operations were conducted in 1991, 1996, and 1999.[15] Smaller-scale deportations happen all the time. Public transport vehicles are, for example, checked, and black people who are unable to prove convincingly that they are not illegal migrants are arrested and deported immediately to Haiti, without a chance to contact their families or to pick up their belongings.[16] Many will have lived in the Dominican Republic all their lives, possibly leaving their children there without warning. The *Nadege Dorzema* case (reviewed in Chapter 14) testifies to the violence which can accompany these deportations and which occurs without any respect for due process.

In time, deportees often make their way back to the Dominican Republic. They do so 'under the wire'. This latter image should not be taken literally: there is no fence separating the two countries. Entering the Dominican Republic from Haiti presents no obstacle for those with sufficient economic means to travel. Harassment comes once inside the Dominican borders.

II. The Inter-American Court Orders Provisional Measures in 2000

In November 1999, the Inter-American Commission on Human Rights received a complaint about mass expulsions from the Dominican Republic to Haiti of people selected on the basis of the colour of their skin. The petitioners estimated that 20,000 individuals had been deported during November 1999. Both Haitians and Dominicans of Haitian origin were affected. The Commission issued a precautionary measure and requested the Dominican Republic 'to cease

[12] Wooding and Moseley-Williams *Needed but Unwanted* 33.

[13] Wooding and Moseley-Williams 33.

[14] *Nadege Dorzema*, para 39.

[15] D. Baluarte, 'Inter-American Justice comes to the Dominican Republic: An Island Shakes as Human Rights and Sovereignty Clash' (2006) *Human Rights Brief* 13, 25–28 at 26.

[16] Wooding and Moseley-Williams *Needed but Unwanted* 10.

the "mass expulsions" and that, in case these continued, they should be done according to the requirements of due process'. The Dominican Republic rejected this precautionary measure, and the Commission brought the matter before the Inter-American Court.

Article 63 (2) of the American Convention provides:

> In cases of extreme seriousness and urgency, and when necessary to avoid irreparable damage to persons, the Court shall adopt such provisional measures as it deems pertinent in matters it has under consideration. With respect to a case not yet submitted to the Court, it may act at the request of the Commission.[17]

The Inter-American Court, no doubt prompted by the murder of witnesses during the proceedings related to the first contentious case it heard, has always made innovative and imaginative use of this unusual provision in international law.[18] The Court, for example, has convened the parties at hearings in order to help it to assess the appropriateness of adopting and/or maintaining provisional measures. Moreover, the Court supervises the implementation of its provisional orders. To assist it in this task, it typically requests that the parties submit reports at regular intervals of a few months apart.

In the matter of *Haitians and Haitian-origin Dominicans in the Dominican Republic*, the Inter-American Court summoned the state and the Commission to a public hearing which took place at the seat of the Court on 8 August 2000. The parties took this hearing seriously: eight individuals appeared for the Dominican Republic, seven for the Commission. There were also two witnesses who had been proposed by the Commission: Father Pedro Ruquoy, a Belgian priest who had worked for more than two decades with the Haitian and the Haitian-Dominican communities in the Dominican Republic and Ms Solange (or Solain) Pie (or Pierre),[19] a social worker who was directing the NGO Movimiento de Mujeres Dominínico-Haitianas (MUDHA). The state had objected to these witnesses, arguing that they were not experts but directly implicated in the cases pending before the Commission. The Court rejected this objection and ordered the Dominican Republic to facilitate their exit from and re-entry into its territory.[20]

In its brief, the Commission had petitioned the Court 'to adopt the provisional measures for the State to...suspend mass expulsions-deportations...be cause they risk the life and physical integrity of deported people, as well as their separated relatives, particularly children under age who are left abandoned' as well as 'to establish [deportation procedures respectful of due process] including minimum period of notice, access to family members, adequate hearings, and

[17] This is the official English text. The order of 14 September 2000 in the '*Haitians*' matter used more convoluted phrasing (at p. 11, para 2), which, presumably, originates in the person who translated this order into Spanish. This is worth mentioning in that it highlights the 'shoestring' conditions in which the Inter-American Court is working.

[18] Laurence Burgorgue-Larsen and Amaya Úbeda De Torres, *The Inter-American Court of Human Rights: Case Law and Commentary* (Oxford: Oxford University Press, 2011) 197.

[19] In Dominican society where people of Haitian origin commonly speak both French creole and Spanish and where documentation is sparse, having variant names is common.

[20] '*Haitians*' matter, provisional measures, Order (IACtHR), 7 Aug. 2000.

decisions legally adopted by competent authorities'. The Court found this request too broad. It insisted that the specific individuals who were to benefit from the measures of protection be named. Moreover, it refused to make what it regarded to be a decision on the merits which went beyond preventing 'irreparable damage'.

Ten days after the hearing, the Court decided on the basis of what it had heard to require the Dominican Republic: to protect the life and personal integrity of seven individuals (including the two witnesses who had testified at the hearing); to refrain from deporting two of them; to allow the immediate return of another two to its territory; to investigate the situation of the remaining individual as well as some others; and to allow as soon as possible the family reunification of two of these individuals who had been separated from their underage children. Despite not wanting to anticipate its decision on the merits of the case, the Court nonetheless also required the state and the Commission to provide it 'with detailed information on the situation of border community or "batey" members who may be subject to forced repatriations, deportations or expulsions'.[21]

For the then President of the Court, Judge Cançado Trindade, who appended (yet again) a concurring opinion, the right balance had been reached. He explained:

> There is a difference between to request [*sic*] provisional measures of protection for a community of an 'indeterminate' character, and to request them for a community or group whose members can be *individualized*. [Here] the Tribunal has duly individualized them, without failing to singling [*sic*] out the context of their situation, in further requiring from the State detailed information on the situation [prevailing where people] may find themselves involved in the problem dealt with herein. . . . I cannot, thus, fail to express my hope that the measures which the Dominican Republic comes to take . . . are reverted to the benefit of all the other persons—not indicated nominally in the petition of the Inter-American Commission—who find themselves in the same situation of vulnerability and risk.[22]

Judge Cançado Trindade also expressed his satisfaction that provisional measures had been granted in relation to rights other than life and personal integrity, namely, rights 'to personal liberty, to the special protection of the children in the family . . . and to circulation and residence'.[23] He noted that this was the first time in its history that the Court had proceeded in this way, and approved of this development, given the absence of any 'juridical or epistemological impediment' and 'the necessity to develop . . . new means of protection inspired in [*sic*] the reality of the intensity of human suffering itself'.[24]

Most importantly Judge Cançado Trindade addressed the underlying global economic and political causes of the circumstances of the case. Only in a legal sense was the case about the way in which the Dominican Republic expelled Haitians. Judge Cançado Trindade did not hesitate to name the real cause of the 'human tragedy' revealed by the case as the deep inequality engulfing our

[21] '*Haitians*' matter, provisional measures, Decision (IACtHR), 18 Aug. 2000, point 10.

[22] Concurring opinion of Judge A. A. Cançado Trindade in '*Haitians*' matter decision of 18 August 2000, paras 21, 22, and 24.

[23] Cançado Trindade, para 15.

[24] Cançado Trindade, paras 14 and 15.

increasingly global world. In his words, the 'globalized' world opened frontiers to capital, investments, goods, and services but not necessarily to human beings,[25] with 'wealth ... increasingly concentrated in the hands of a few ones, at the same time that those marginalized and excluded regrettably increase, in a growing (and statistically proven) way'.[26] From this emerges the 'perfectly avoidable' new phenomenon of 'uprootedness, mainly of those who seek to escape from hunger, from illnesses and from misery'.[27] 'The lessons of the past seem to have been forgotten, the sufferings of previous generations appear to have been in vain. The current "globalizing" frenzy, shown as something inevitable and irreversible,—constituting in reality the most recent expression of a perverse social neodarwinism,—appears entirely devoid of all historical sense'.[28] The problem 'concerns the whole human kind' and 'encompasses the totality of human rights'.[29] Unfortunately 'the States have not yet accepted a right to *immigrate* and to *remain* wherever one happens to be'.[30] 'In spite of being a problem which affects the whole *international community*... uprootedness continues to be treated in an atomized way by the States, with the outlook of a legal order of a purely inter-State character, without apparently realizing that the Westphalian model of such international order is... definitely exhausted.'[31]

The Dominican Delegation had pointed out that it should not fall upon the shoulders of one state to find a solution to a problem of global economic disparity which concerns the whole international community.[32] Judge Cançado Trindade accepted this. In his words, '[t]he problem of uprootedness ought to be considered in a framework of action oriented towards the erradication [*sic*] of social exclusion and extreme poverty,—if one indeed wishes to reach its causes and not only to fight its symptoms'.[33] Most lawyers would reject the idea that the remit of the Inter-American Court extends to force or at least to invite states to devise new social and economic practices which encourage solidarity rather than greed and selfishness. Judge Cançado Trindade was exceptional. The type of analyses he produced through his tenure at the Inter-American Court—reminiscent of what the '99% movement' is now saying—have not been reproduced by any other judge at the Inter-American Court.

Already then, it was accepted that what the Court could do in the matter before it was limited. At this particular stage in the proceedings, when there was not even a case pending before the Court,[34] the only thing the Court could do was

25 Cançado Trindade, paras 1 and 3.
26 Cançado Trindade, para 3.
27 Cançado Trindade, para 4.
28 Cançado Trindade, para 3.
29 Cançado Trindade, para 6.
30 Cançado Trindade, para 8, emphases in the original.
31 Cançado Trindade, para 11, emphasis in the original.
32 Cançado Trindade, para 2.
33 Cançado Trindade, para 7.
34 Only in July 2012 did the Inter-American Commission bring a case before the Court: *Benito Tide Méndez and Others v. Dominican Republic*. Judgment was delivered after the manuscript of this book had been sent to the press. The case was renamed: *Expelled Dominicans and Haitians v. the Dominican Republic*, Preliminary Objections, Merits, Reparations and Costs, Judgment (IACtHR), 28 Aug. 2014. See Chapter 14's postcript for a brief review (p. 502).

to accept, to some extent, the Commission's request for the order of provisional measures. At the end of this chapter, we shall return to these measures in order to comment on their (lack of) impact.

III. No 'Friendly Settlement' in *Yean and Bosico*

By contrast to the '*Haitians*' matter, *Yean and Bosico* quickly became a judicial case, properly lodged before the Inter-American Court. It arose from the same social context, highlighting the problem that thousands of children who grow up in the *bateyes* and the most deprived areas of the Dominican Republic do not have a birth certificate. Getting the birth of their children registered is understandably not the priority of poverty-stricken mothers who can ill-afford the costs. But the result is that legally these children do not exist. They do not have a name and they are stateless. As a result, secondary school is also closed to them. When they become adults, they typically still have no legal existence and transmit their precarious status to their children. MUDHA decided to try to do something about this issue.

In March 1997, MUDHA's lawyer Genaro Rincón Miesse took a group of 20 children of Haitian origin born in the Dominican Republic to register their birth.[35] The Yean and Bosico children were part of this group. At that time Dilcia Yean was ten months old and Violeta Bosico 12 years old. The children were presented to the Civil Status Registrar of Sabana Grande de Boyá. Their mothers submitted their own identity papers (they were Dominican) as well as a certificate from where their child had been born to prove the birth had taken place. According to Rincón Miesse, the registrar refused to accept the documentation presented to her 'because children of Haitian immigrants could not be declared, since their parents were in the country illegally [and if] the parents are Haitian, the children are also Haitian, since the parents are in transit'.[36] Attempts to have the rejection of these birth certificates overturned came to no avail. As a result, the children were also prevented from confirming the Dominican nationality to which they were legally entitled given that the Dominican Republic follows the principle of *jus soli*. Dominican law provides that nationality is granted to all persons born on its territory, except if their parents are diplomats or migrants 'in transit'. The Yean and Bosico children should therefore have been entitled to Dominican nationality. They were born on Dominican territory and they were not children of migrants in transit: the judgment states that their mothers were Dominican (and their fathers—not in contact with them—Haitian). On this account, there was no reason for the Yean and Bosico children to be denied a birth certificate, and thus Dominican nationality, except racial prejudice.

35 *Yean and Bosico* judgment, para 5.

36 *Yean and Bosico*, para 86 a) 1) p. 26.

In October 1998, a petition on behalf of the children was submitted to the Inter-American Commission on Human Rights through their representatives Rincón Miesse and Solain Pierre (or Pie)—whom we encountered earlier as one of the recipients of the provisional measures ordered by the Court in the '*Haitians*' matter.

As should happen in a contentious case, the Inter-American Commission put itself at the disposal of the parties in order to reach a friendly settlement. The Dominican Republic appears to have taken this opportunity to try to have the case closed. It granted the two children birth certificates in September 2001.[37] However, the children's representatives argued that this measure did not go far enough. They submitted that there could be no resolution of the case 'until [all] the alleged human rights violations [had] been acknowledged and totally repaired'.[38] The Inter-American Commission accepted this argument in the proceedings before it. So did the Inter-American Court when the case reached it. To the preliminary objection raised by the Dominican Republic that the alleged victims should not have rejected the friendly settlement accepted by the state, the Court replied that 'in order to reach a friendly settlement there must be a basic consensus among the parties, which shows their willingness to end the dispute on the merits of the matter and the possible reparations and this has not occurred in the instant case'.[39]

IV. Friendly Settlements in the European System

The same approach might not have been followed by the European Court of Human Rights. The Strasbourg Court increasingly resorts to friendly settlements: a scholarly publication mentions that a staggering 43 per cent of judgments handed down in 2008 consisted of friendly settlements or 'arrangements' between the parties.[40] Moreover, when a settlement falls through because the applicant refuses to accept it, the Strasbourg Court now closes the case on the basis of a 'unilateral declaration' by the respondent state if it deems the refusal of the applicant unreasonable.[41] These various techniques—which are mostly applied in so-called repetitive cases and/or in areas where the case law is 'well

[37] *Yean and Bosico*, para 25. [38] *Yean and Bosico*, para 68.

[39] *Yean and Bosico*, para 72. The Court also rejected the other two preliminary objections raised by the defendant state. The Dominican Republic had claimed that national remedies had not been exhausted and that the complaint related to an event which had taken place prior to the state's acceptance (in March 1999) of the contentious jurisdiction of the Court. The Court rejected the latter objection because of the continuing nature of the alleged violation. Compare with the inadmissibility decision in the Slovenian 'Erased' case, reviewed in Chapter 5 (pp. 144–145). See also Damian A. Gonzalez-Salzberg, 'Do Preliminary Objections Truly Object to the Jurisdiction of the Inter-American Court of Human Rights? An Empirical Study of the Use and Abuse of Preliminary Objections in the Court's Case Law' (2012) *Human Rights Law Review* 12, 255–286.

[40] Helen Keller, Magdalena Forowicz, and Lorenz Engi, *Friendly Settlements before the European Court of Human Rights: Theory and Practice* (Oxford: Oxford University Press, 2010) 75.

[41] Keller et al. p. 67. The first case where this practice was introduced was *Akman v. Turkey*, appl. 37453/97, Judgment (ECtHR), 26 June 2001.

established'[42]—have been developed as case management tools.[43] Their beneficial effect is hardly in doubt from a case management perspective, even if some negotiations (conducted by the Registry, never the judges themselves) can occasionally be time-consuming. Their value, however, is not as obvious from a human rights standards perspective.

A study on the growing practice of friendly settlements in the Strasbourg system has suggested that through its encouragement of, if not desperation for, friendly settlements, the European Court is 'neglecting its genuine function of authoritative definition and protection of human rights'.[44] The authors of the study—Helen Keller,[45] Magdalena Forowicz, and Lorenz Engi—observe that a friendly settlement rarely includes an acknowledgement that the European Convention has been violated and therefore does not signal an obligation for the state to change its ways. This may be satisfactory for the individual applicant—although even this is questionable, for example, when what he gains is a residence permit for a short period.

The same authors stress the danger of a 'monetarization of human rights' whereby 'human rights violations [would stand] for little more than an occasion for earning, or paying money, respectively'.[46] Such a concern, however, does not appear so germane in the immigration field where applicants typically seek the adoption of concrete, particular, individual immigration measures, such as the revocation of a deportation order or the granting of a residence permit, rather than monetary compensation.[47]

A friendly settlement results in the Strasbourg Court (or previously, the Commission)[48] not pronouncing itself on important questions. During my stay at the Vrije Universiteit Amsterdam, I was repeatedly told of the 15 or so 'Dutch hidden cases' which had raised issues similar to *Said* and *Salah Sheekh*.[49] These cases revealed the structural nature of the problems affecting asylum determination procedures in the Netherlands. They never made it into the limelight, however, as the Court struck them out following the conclusion of friendly settlements.[50]

[42] This fact indicates that the backlog of the Strasbourg Court is perhaps not as unmanageable as the raw figure of over 160,000 pending cases at one time suggested. This is something Judge Tulkens repeatedly argued, but without many people accepting her argument, during her tenure at the Court (personal communication, April 2012).

[43] Keller et al. *Friendly Settlements* 10.

[44] Keller et al. 85.

[45] Who has since become the judge at Strasbourg in respect of Switzerland.

[46] Keller et al. *Friendly Settlements* 85.

[47] Keller et al. 21–22 and 41. One cannot assume, however, that this will not change. Chapter 13 reviews a number of cases where compensation was ordered for non-pecuniary damages in migrant cases.

[48] As in the *Amekrane* case discussed in Chapter 7 (pp. 200–201): *Amekrane v. the United Kingdom*, appl. 5961/72, PCom Report (EComHR), 19 July 1974.

[49] *Said v. the Netherlands*, appl. 2345/02, Judgment (ECtHR), 5 July 2005; *Salah Sheekh v. the Netherlands*, appl. 1948/04, Judgment (ECtHR), 11 Jan. 2007.

[50] As confirmed by Dana Baldinger by personal communication of 12 May 2014. For one example of these 'hidden cases', see e.g. *Mir Isfahani v. the Netherlands*, appl. 31252/03, Decision (ECtHR), 31 Jan. 2008. The UNHCR third party intervention makes clear that the virtual impossibility for an asylum seeker either to prove his refugee status (given the level of evidence required) or to appeal the original decision in a meaningful way (given the lack of review of factual assessment) was not at all specific to the applicant: *Mir Isfahani*, pp. 9–10 of 12.

To give another example, one lawyer who worked for a time as a case worker in the AIRE Centre recalled to me her disappointment when a case she had hoped would become leading in respect of Article 3 returns to her client's country of origin morphed into an insignificant friendly settlement. The British government, eventually recognising the potential strength of the case, offered the applicant a five-year residence permit as a refugee. There was no guarantee that the Court would adopt a verdict of violation. The legal representative felt she was in no position to advise her client to refuse the settlement.[51]

Keller and her co-authors rightly observe that the two parties invited to settle are rarely on an equal footing: 'The applicant is generally a one-shot player, whereas the Government Agent is a repeat player. In terms of influence, experience and resources, the Government is in a much more favourable position than the individual applicant'.[52] Even the AIRE Centre, which has proved a formidable player in Strasbourg proceedings, is nowhere near a position of strength equal to that enjoyed by states. The European Court does not seem to be attentive to this factor. This can be illustrated by one small example: when a case is struck out, legal costs are almost never awarded to the applicant, however much work has been put into preparing the Strasbourg application, not to mention the exhaustion of domestic remedies beforehand.[53]

This is not without consequences in an area such as refugee law and immigration which does not attract many legal practitioners and in which NGOs barely survive (if they survive at all). Additionally, it is often extremely difficult for lawyers to identify and successfully pursue cases which concern clients whose legal status is uncertain and who, because of this, have a tendency to 'disappear'—either because they are put in detention or deported, or because they lose hope of seeing any timely legal resolution of their case.[54] The practice of striking out what may well be the most promising migration cases because the state is ready to settle is thus particularly undermining of human rights.

Keller and her co-authors note that when the applicant refuses a friendly settlement, the Court sometimes appears to penalise the applicant for having continued the case by awarding a lower level of compensation in the judgment on the merits than would have been expected in a case of this kind and was offered in the settlement. By contrast, they found no evidence of a state being 'penalised' for not having followed a settlement through.[55] There is nothing wrong with the

[51] *K. v. the United Kingdom*, appl. 29696/07, Judgment (ECtHR), 8 Sept. 2009.

[52] Keller et al. *Friendly Settlements* 7.

[53] There have been exceptions to this trend, but they are rare. See e.g. *El Majjaoui and Stichting Touba Moskee v. the Netherlands*, appl. 25525/03, GC Judgment (ECtHR), 20 Dec. 2007 (struck out following the delivery of a work permit, but €5,000 granted to the applicant for costs and expenses).

[54] Marie-Bénédicte Dembour, 'What it Takes to Have a Case: The Backstage Story of *Muskhadzhiyeva v. Belgium* (Illegality of Children's Immigration Detention)', in Elisabeth Lambert-Abdelgawad (ed.) *Preventing and Sanctioning Hindrances to the Right of Individual Petition Before the European Court of Human Rights* (Cambridge: Intersentia, 2011) 75–104 at 87–89; Jeremy McBride, *Access to Justice for Migrants and Asylum Seekers in Europe* (Strasbourg: Council of Europe Publishing, 2009) 39.

[55] Keller et al. *Friendly Settlements* 65.

European Court of Human Rights trying to close cases quickly. The problem is that it seems to be doing so in a way which sides with state interests rather than with applicants.

The likelihood is that in a case comparable to *Yean and Bosico* where the defendant state had granted the alleged victims birth certificates, and thus a route to nationality, Strasbourg applicants would be encouraged, if not forced, to settle.[56] This would mean that the opportunity for as penetrating and wide-ranging a verdict of violation as the one pronounced by the Inter-American Court in this case would be lost. Admittedly the Inter-American Court deals only with a few cases per year. Moreover, the institution which initially receives the individual applications in the Inter-American system, i.e. the Commission, is seeking to develop the adoption of friendly settlements.[57] This inevitably involves closing cases in a way which, if it solves the situation for the victim, nonetheless fails to provide a full analysis of the situation and to create new standards. More research is required before meaningful comparison can be made between the two systems. What can be advanced at this stage is that the European system could do more to deal with repetitive cases in a way which advances a strong human rights agenda. One could wish, for example, that the Strasbourg Court would invent a system whereby repetitive cases are treated in a summary fashion which allows, after the adoption of a lead case, a presumption that a state remains in violation of the Convention.

V. *Yean and Bosico*'s Merits: Multiple Inter-Related Violations

As we have seen in the previous chapter, the Inter-American system encourages the involvement of civil society in its proceedings. Typically originating from NGOs, activists, and university-based legal clinics, *amici curiae* help the Inter-American Court to develop its case law by researching and providing a progressive line of reasoning in a particular area. In the *Yean and Bosico* case, no less than ten *amici curiae* were submitted.[58] This may have contributed to the host of violations of the American Convention which the Court found in this case.

The background to these violations, the Court noted, was the alleged victims' vulnerability as girl children.[59] Vulnerability has become a concept *en vogue*, both in legal and social discourse.[60] Social and legal theorists have remarked that it

[56] There is no Strasbourg case law on birth certificate and nationality. But see Chapter 13 (pp. 468 and 478) for illustrations of the Strasbourg trend to strike out a case after a residence permit is delivered (with some exceptions noted at pp. 461, 468, 476–477).

[57] The Inter-American Commission's Strategic Plan for 2011–2015 mentions the aim of achieving 75 friendly settlements in 2013, 2014, and 2015 (for a total of 171 reports per year): <https://www.oas.org/en/iachr/docs/pdf/IACHRStrategicPlan20112015.pdf>, accessed 9 May 2014, point 2.4, at p. 16.

[58] *Yean and Bosico* judgment, para 53. In a contentious case, an *amicus curiae* can be submitted by anyone, without prior submission, until two weeks after the public hearing.

[59] *Yean and Bosico*, para 134.

[60] Martha Albertson Fineman and Anna Grear (eds) *Vulnerability: Reflections on a New Ethical Foundation for Law and Politics* (Aldershot: Ashgate, 2013); Laurence Burgorgue-Larsen (ed.) *La vulnérabilité saisie par les juges en Europe* (Paris: Pedone, 2014).

has tended to replace the language of exclusion—to mixed effects, including sometimes a negation of individual agency and an assignment of responsibility to the individual in a neo-liberal framework.[61] The Inter-American Court has long referred to vulnerability.[62] In its reasoning, such references signal the need for the state to be aware of, and thus be ready to adopt measures which are apt to counteract, the weakness with which vulnerable human beings find themselves.

In *Yean and Bosico*, the first violation the Court found related to the right to nationality, which is guaranteed by Article 20 of the American Convention, the opening paragraphs of which read:

1. Everybody has the right to a nationality.
2. Everybody has the right to the nationality of the State in whose territory he was born if he does not have the right to any other nationality.

The Court considered it a determined fact that the Yean and Bosico children 'had no nationality until September 25, 2001'.[63] This was a serious situation given that nationality is 'a requirement for the exercise of specific rights'.[64] The Court stated:

> The determination of who has a right to be a national continues to fall within a State's domestic jurisdiction. However, its discretionary authority in this regard is gradually being restricted with the evolution of international law, in order to ensure a better protection of the individual in the face of arbitrary acts of States. Thus, at the current stage of the development of international human rights law, this authority of the States is limited, on the one hand, by their obligation to provide individuals with the equal and effective protection of the law and, on the other hand, by their obligation to prevent, avoid and reduce statelessness.[65]

The last sentence hints at what lawyers call positive and negative state obligations.[66] The Court was very concerned with the statelessness in which the alleged victims were left, as it induces a 'condition of extreme vulnerability'.[67] The Court recalled its earlier rulings according to which the principle of equal protection and non-discrimination must be respected 'irrespective of a person's migratory status in a State'.[68] It now elaborated on this aspect in the following way:

(a) The migratory status of a person cannot be a condition for the State to grant nationality, because migratory status can never constitute a justification for depriving a person of the right to nationality or the enjoyment and exercise of his rights;

[61] Marc-Henry Soulet, 'La vulnérabilité, une ressource à manier avec prudence', in Burgorgue-Larsen (ed.) 7–27.

[62] Rosmerlin Estupiñan-Silva, 'La vulnérabilité dans la jurisprudence de la Cour interaméricaine des droits de l'homme: Esquisse d'une typologie', in Burgorgue-Larsen (ed.) 89–113.

[63] *Yean and Bosico* judgment, para 132.

[64] *Yean and Bosico*, para 137.

[65] *Yean and Bosico*, para 140.

[66] See further, Laurence Burgorgue-Larsen and Amaya Úbeda de Torres, *The Inter-American Court of Human Rights: Case Law and Commentary* (Oxford: Oxford University Press, 2011) Chapter 22.

[67] See particularly *Yean and Bosico* judgment, para 142.

[68] *Yean and Bosico*, para 155.

(b) The migratory status of a person is not transmitted to the children, and

(c) The fact that a person has been born on the territory of a State is the only fact that needs to be proved for the acquisition of nationality, in the case of those persons who would not have the right to another nationality if they did not acquire that of the State where they were born.[69]

With (a) this paragraph repeats Advisory opinion no. 18; with (b) it addresses the Dominican context where lack of recognition of people of Haitian origin affects generation after generation; and with (c) it draws out the concrete implications of the previous two points, identifying a new right to nationality if one would otherwise be stateless.[70]

The Court went on to observe that 'a foreigner who develops connections in a State cannot be equated to a person in transit'.[71] This echoed the Commission's argument that 'those who live for 10, 15 or more years in a country cannot be described as transients'.[72] The Court concluded that under no circumstances could the Dominican legislative exception to *jus soli* have been applied to the Yean and Bosico children whose mothers were Dominican and who were born in the Dominican Republic.[73]

The Court then turned its attention to the issue of the birth certificate. Not surprisingly given the number of people, including Dominicans, who do not register their children at birth, the Dominican Republic has a procedure in place for late registration. The requirements are different depending on whether this late registration takes place prior to or after the age of 13.[74] In the latter case, the documentation required is more substantial, and thus more difficult to collect. Amongst other documents, it comprises a certificate from the medical institution where the child was born (or from the mayor in rural areas); a certificate from the church or parish if the child has been baptised; a certificate from all the registry offices from the child's place of birth; and a copy of the parents' marriage certificate if they are married. As the Inter-American Court implicitly remarks, this documentation does not appear to be geared towards checking the sole fact that a birth has taken place in the Dominican Republic.

In the particular case of the Yean and Bosico children, the registrar had been presented with their birth certificates and their mothers' identity cards. Applying to them the legislation related to children over 13, although they were significantly younger, the registrar deemed this documentation insufficient. The Court ruled that this had imposed a disproportionate and undue burden of proof on the

[69] *Yean and Bosico*, para 156, reference omitted.

[70] *Yean and Bosico* can therefore be seen as developing further Advisory opinion no. 4/84, reviewed in Chapter 5.

[71] *Yean and Bosico* judgment, para 157.

[72] *Yean and Bosico*, para 111 b).

[73] *Yean and Bosico* judgment, para 158.

[74] Cavallaro and Brewer note that the public hearing had been instrumental in highlighting the importance of the documentation issue: James L. Cavallaro and Stephanie Erin Brewer, 'Reevaluating Regional Human Rights Litigation in the Twenty-First Century: The Case of the Inter-American Court' (2008) *American Journal of International Law* 768–827 at 805, note 174. We shall see in the next chapter that the tendency is to shorten the length of hearings (which nonetheless remain much longer than at Strasbourg) (p. 362, n. 7).

victims.[75] As a result, the state had 'acted arbitrarily...in a way that was contrary to the superior interest of the child [and] discriminatory', resulting in the children being kept stateless and thus placing them in a situation of extreme vulnerability.[76]

The Court observed that this treatment had to be situated within the context of the vulnerable situation of the Haitian population and Dominicans of Haitian origin in the Dominican Republic, which had been specifically reported upon by the United Nations Committee on the Rights of the Child and the United Nations Commission on Human Rights[77] (in an illustration of the propensity of the Inter-American Court to rely on other bodies to advance a human rights agenda, as noted in Chapter 9). All this led the Court to find a violation of the right to nationality (Article 20 of the American Convention) and the right to equal protection (Article 24), in relation to the rights of the child (Article 19) and also in relation to the obligation to respect the Convention's rights (Article 1 (1))—to the detriment of the children Dilcia Yean and Violeta Bosico.[78]

In a parallel formulation, the Court went on to find a violation of the rights to juridical personality (Article 3) and to a name (Article 18), still in relation to Article 19 and also in relation to Article 1 (1) of the American Convention, again to the detriment of the two children.[79] This was a crucial finding. Here, rather than reviewing it in detail, suffice it to say that the children did not exist in law and that they also officially had no name.[80]

The Court also noted that the vulnerability to which the children were exposed as a result of the lack of nationality and juridical personality came to be reflected in the fact that Violeta Bosico was prevented from attending school for a year (until the precautionary measures ordered by the Inter-American Commission soon after the application was lodged saw her readmitted to school).[81] During that year, in order to carry on with her education, Violeta attended evening classes for adults. Article 19 of the American Convention provides that 'Every minor child has the right to the measures of protection required by his condition as a minor on the part of his family, society and the state'. The Court interpreted this provision as entailing the obligation for the state to 'provide free primary education to all children in an appropriate environment and in the conditions necessary to ensure their full intellectual development'.[82] This statement is included in the Court's *reasoning*. It is conspicuously not reproduced in the *operative* part of the judgment

[75] *Yean and Bosico* judgment, paras 163–165. See Chapter 7 on the burden of proof in Article 3 return cases in the European system.

[76] *Yean and Bosico*, para 166.

[77] *Yean and Bosico*, paras 168–170.

[78] *Yean and Bosico*, paras 174 and 260, point 2.

[79] *Yean and Bosico*, paras 187 and 260, point 3. The Court accepted to examine the complaint of a violation of Article 18 which had not been alleged by the Inter-American Commission, because the victims' representatives pleaded it on the basis of the facts presented by the Commission: *Yean and Bosico* judgment, para 181.

[80] The right to juridical personality is not mentioned as such in the European Convention. Even in a case as poignant as the Slovenian 'Erased' case, the European Court has not been ready to find it subsumed under Article 3 or 8 ECHR, as reviewed in Chapter 5 (pp. 144–145).

[81] *Yean and Bosico* judgment, paras 8 and 86 a) 1) p. 26.

[82] *Yean and Bosico*, para 185.

where the Court recaps at the end of its judgment the violations it has found and the reparation measures it orders. In other words, the denial of education is not confirmed as a violation of the Convention in the *Yean and Bosico* case.

For Amaya Úbeda de Torres, this omission was a 'missed opportunity'. Úbeda de Torres regrets that the Court did not assert the education rights of children belonging to a disadvantaged group despite the arguments which the Commission had put to this effect.[83] Presumably the Inter-American Court thought that the time was not yet ripe in the state of its jurisprudence to take the bold step of relying on the rather vaguely phrased Article 19 to assert the right to primary education, especially in a case where neither applicant was of primary school age. Probably uncomfortable with the idea of leaving the issue completely unaddressed, the Court nonetheless included some remarks on the right to education in its reasoning.

The Inter-American Court found a violation on a third count. Expanding upon the reasoning offered by the victims' representatives, it concluded that the right to humane treatment embodied in Article 5 of the American Convention had been violated to the detriment of the mothers, as well as one sister, of the two children.[84] This was due to the 'uncertainty and insecurity' generated by the fear that, without birth certificates proving their Dominican nationality, the children might be expelled from the Dominican Republic.[85] While the Court does not elaborate further on this point, it is clear that the frequency of deportations of people considered to be of Haitian origin from the Dominican Republic persuaded the Court that such a fear was not unfounded.

The judgment was unanimous. Judge Cançado Trindade appended a separate opinion which, at six pages long, was one of his shorter productions. He stressed both the idea that no issue belongs intrinsically to the sphere reserved to the state and the broad scope of the general protection obligations of the American Convention. He also approved of the way in which the Court 'ha[d] interrelated the violated rights (right to nationality and rights of the child, right to a name and to juridical personality, and the right to equal protection and the right to humane treatment), instead of dealing with them in an unduly compartmentalized way'.[86] This was not a point upon which Judge Cançado Trindade's concurring opinions touched in Advisory opinions nos 16 and 18. In *Yean and Bosico*, the former Court's President (Judge García Ramírez was now presiding) stated that he 'would greatly regret if, in future (*tempus fugit*), the Court moved away from this case law which maximises the protection of human rights under the American Convention'.[87] This remark may be taken to indicate that some of the five judges who took part in the *Yean and Bosico* judgment were not immediately convinced by the interrelated

[83] Burgorgue-Larson and Úbeda de Torres *The Inter-American Court* 574.

[84] *Yean and Bosico* judgment, paras 206 and 260, point 4. By contrast, the Strasbourg case law on violations of human rights suffered by direct victims' next of kin—inspired by developments in the Inter-American system—remains comparatively limited.

[85] *Yean and Bosico*, para 205.

[86] Separate opinion of Judge A. A. Cançado Trindade in *Yean and Bosico*, para 22.

[87] Cançado Trindade, para 22.

approach adopted by the Court in this case.[88] Judge Cançado Trindade seems to be warning against, and already regretting, a likely change of orientation. As we shall see in Chapters 11 and 14, subsequent jurisprudence in migrant cases does not indicate that the Inter-American Court has operated a major volte-face, although there is a perceptible retreat from the broadest pronouncements which characterised what could be called the Cançado Trindade era.

From its very first judgments in contentious cases, the Inter-American Court showed itself to be resolutely innovative and forward-looking in regard to reparations.[89]

The Court takes to heart the twin ideas that the damage done to the victim must be repaired and that further violations must be avoided. Pecuniary compensation, although remaining central to its orders, features as one element amongst an array of other, often more exacting, measures which render the concept of reparations meaningful. Thus, the Inter-American Court has become renowned for ordering defendant states to investigate and prosecute the actors responsible for the denounced human rights violations; to train the officials in charge of implementing state policies so that they become aware of and respect human rights; to publicly acknowledge responsibility for the wrongs which have been committed; or to honour victims, for example by naming a street in their memory or instituting a commemorative public holiday. The *Yean and Bosico* case is no exception to the Court's tendency to take full advantage of a case before it in order to address a problematic situation through relevant and pointed reparations.

In *Yean and Bosico*, the Inter-American Court recalls the *raison d'être* of its approach to reparations:

> Whenever possible, reparation of the damage caused requires full restitution (*restitutio in integrum*), which consists in the re-establishment of the previous situation. If this is not possible, as in the instant case, the international court must determine measures to ensure the damaged rights [*sic*], repair the consequences of the violations and avoid new violations, and also establish compensation for the damage caused. The responsible State may not invoke provisions of domestic law to modify or fail to comply with its obligation to provide reparation, all aspects of which (scope, nature, methods and determination of the beneficiaries) are regulated by international law.[90]

The Dominican Republic had pleaded that:

> It would be a financial impossibility for the State to pay [the damages claimed by the representatives] because, should they be awarded to the applicants, based on the principle of non-discrimination it would have to make financial reparation to all the other

[88] The Dominican Republic had appointed Ambassador Rhadys Abreu de Polanco Judge ad hoc. The Inter-American Court refused this appointment on the grounds of incompatibility and conflict of interests due to the role Rhadys Abreu de Polanco had played in the proceedings before the Inter-American Commission. The Court invited the Dominican Republic to designate another judge ad hoc, but the Dominican Republic did not do so: *Yean and Bosico* judgment, paras 37, 40, and 41. Today no national judge sits in a contentious case brought by a private party. Rhadys Abreu became a judge of the Inter-American Court in 2007, a position she held until 2012.

[89] Burgorgue-Larsen and Úbeda de Torres *The Inter-American Court* 224.

[90] *Yean and Bosico* judgment, para 210.

citizens who have carried out similar measures, and this would seriously undermine the Dominican Republic's financial reserves.[91]

This argument could appear disingenuous: the Dominican Republic would never have entertained the idea of compensating all the individuals who had suffered the same fate as the applicants. In fact, the Yean and Bosico children are likely to be the only victims of the set of human rights violations linked to the denial of birth certificates in the Dominican Republic who will ever have their case decided by the Inter-American Court.

As Lisa Laplante has explained in respect of Inter-American case law emerging from Peru, in the context of a numerically restricted case law, the Inter-American Court is intent on making examples of the few cases which reach it, including by compensating the victims fully.[92] In *Yean and Bosico*, the Court awarded each of the two children the sum which the representatives had requested in their respect as non-pecuniary damages: US$8,000. (By contrast, although some of the children's relatives were recognised to have been treated inhumanely, in their case the Court considered the judgment itself constituted a form of reparation and therefore awarded them no monetary compensation.[93])

The Inter-American Court went on to order what it calls measures of satisfaction and guarantees of non-repetition. In this respect, the Court integrated most of the suggestions made by the Inter-American Commission and the children's representatives. The Dominican Republic was ordered:

(a) to publish, within six months of the judgment, parts of the judgment (as specified by the Court) in the official gazette and in another newspaper with national circulation in the Dominican Republic;
(b) to organise, in the same time period, a public act acknowledging the defendant state's international responsibility and apologising to the victims, to be disseminated in the media;
(c) to adopt in its domestic law within a reasonable time a simple, accessible, and reasonable procedure for acquiring Dominican nationality based on a late declaration of birth.[94]

The last point was discussed at great length in the reasoning part of the judgment. There the Court specified that 'there must be an effective recourse for cases in which the request is refused'.[95] It also explained:

The Court finds that, when establishing the requirements for late registration of birth, the State should take into consideration the particularly vulnerable situation of Dominican children of Haitian origin. The requirements should not constitute an obstacle for

[91] *Yean and Bosico*, para 220.

[92] Lisa J. Laplante, 'Entwined Paths to Justice: The Inter-American Human Rights System and the Peruvian Truth Commission', in Marie-Bénédicte Dembour and Tobias Kelly (eds.) *Paths to International Justice: Social and Legal Perspectives* (Cambridge: Cambridge University Press, 2007) 216–242.

[93] *Yean and Bosico* judgment, paras 226 and 229.

[94] *Yean and Bosico*, para 260, points 6–8.

[95] *Yean and Bosico*, para 239.

obtaining Dominican nationality and should be only those essential for establishing that the birth occurred in the Dominican Republic. In this regard, the identification of the father or the mother of the child cannot be restricted to the presentation of the identity card; rather, for this purpose, the State should accept another appropriate public document, since the said identity card is only held by Dominican citizens. Moreover, the requirements should be specified clearly and be standardized, and their application should not be left to the discretion of State officials, in order to guarantee the legal certainty of those who use this procedure and to ensure an effective guarantee of the rights embodied in the American Convention, pursuant to Article 1 (1) of the Convention.

The State should also take the permanent measures necessary to facilitate the early and opportune registration of children, irrespective of their parentage or origin, so as to reduce the number of individuals who resort to the procedure of late registration of birth.

The Court also finds that the State should implement, within a reasonable time, a program to provide training on human rights, with special emphasis on the right to equal protection and non-discrimination, to the State officials responsible for registering births, during which they should receive guidance on the special situation of children, and a culture of tolerance and non-discrimination is fostered.[96]

The use of the conditional tense in these quotations is not significant given that the Spanish and authentic version of the judgment says '*debe*' ('must' rather than 'should'). It has also been explained to me that the fact that these additional pointers are included in the reasoning rather than in the operative part of the judgment is not determinant either, as the judgment is read as a whole and the Court listens to the arguments of both parties before deciding whether a judgment has been complied with.[97]

Interestingly, the *Yean and Bosico* judgment includes some statements about primary education. To quote: 'The State should comply with its obligation to guarantee access to free primary education for all children, irrespective of their origin or parentage'.[98] As we have already seen in respect of the merits of the complaints of violation, the Court seems to have wanted to smuggle in the primary education issue in its reasoning but without referring to it in the operative part of its judgment. This is what it does here too in regard to reparations.

This relative restraint should not be taken as a sign that the Inter-American Court was timid on the reparations front. Of all the reparation measures which had been requested by the Commission, only one was not ordered by the Court, namely, that the state initiates 'a serious and exhaustive investigation into the actions of the officials of the Dominican Civil Status Registry and the Public Prosecutor's Office who violated the fundamental rights of the children Dilcia and Violeta'.[99] Presumably the Court considered that the responsibility for the violations it found in this case, although serious and denying the human rights of individuals of Haitian origin, was exclusively attributable to the state. In other words, it would have found it unfair to make this responsibility also fall on the shoulders of officials who had carried out their functions without committing acts

[96] *Yean and Bosico*, paras 240–242.

[97] Interviews with members of the Registry of the Inter-American Court, September 2012.

[98] *Yean and Bosico* judgment, para 244.

[99] *Yean and Bosico*, para 231.

of such brutality or obvious inhumanity that it would have been incumbent upon them to resist, out of their own conscience, acting in such a way. The Court would have assessed that what was needed in this case was for the Dominican government explicitly to instruct its officials to register the birth of all children in a way which respected both the law and their human rights.

Some measures requested by the children's representatives were likewise not granted by the Court. These included ordering the state to 'send civil status registrars to register the children in the communities where they live', 'reduce birth registration costs', and 'eliminate the requirement to present birth certificates for school enrolment'.[100] Obviously such practices, if implemented, would have been useful, but the Court must have thought that it could not instruct changes that amounted to the creation of 'an ideal world'. It therefore would have decided to limit itself to order a course of reparations intended to eliminate the practice of *preventing* people of Haitian origin from being issued a birth certificate, rather than positively *facilitating* access to a birth certificate and to school. This is already a tall order given the climate of widespread prejudice prevalent in the Dominican Republic against Haitians and black people.

VI. The *Declaring* Role of the Strasbourg Court and the Development of the Pilot Procedure

There is a sense in which the Inter-American Court could have imposed even wider reparation measures than it did in the *Yean and Bosico* case: it is always possible to do more in respect of human rights. Having said this, the Inter-American Court clearly goes much further than the European Court of Human Rights in this regard. This is because the European Court on the whole still abides by the principle according to which its judgments are 'declaratory' in nature, thus leaving it little scope to specify what a defaulting state must do to become Convention-compliant again. As we shall see in the next section, the tentative encroachments admitted today on the declaratory nature of the Strasbourg judgments do not always even work out to the advantage of recognised victims of human rights violations.

The Strasbourg Court's jurisdiction has long been conceptualised as being restricted to *declaring* whether or not the European Convention has been violated. Commentators have traced back this perspective to the Convention's *travaux préparatoires* which debated and rejected the possibility of extending the Court's competence to drawing out the implications of verdicts of violation.[101] One exception

[100] *Yean and Bosico*, para 232 (g), (h), and (i).

[101] Philippe Frumer, 'La réparation des atteintes aux droits de l'homme internationalement protégés—Quelques données comparatives' (1996) *Revue trimestrielle des droits de l'homme* 329–352 at 329–330; Christian Tomuschat, 'Just Satisfaction under Article 50 of the European Convention on Human Rights', in Paul Mohoney et al. (eds.) *Protecting Human Rights: The European Perspective. Studies in Memory of Rolv Ryssdal* (Cologne: Carl Heymanns Verlag, 2000) 1409–1430 at 1412.

to this principle has always been accepted: this is the power to attribute to the applicant pecuniary damages, called 'just satisfaction' in the Convention.[102] Such a conceptual construction has commanded that the Strasbourg Court refrains from indicating what the respondent state should do in order to respect its Convention obligations. Any invitation by the applicant for the Court to impose a particular course on the state has been accordingly met with rebuttal.

In 1979, the Court explained its approach in the *Marckx* case (its 24th judgment) in the following terms:

> [In the present case, the Court] is enquiring whether or not the application [of the contested national legislation to the applicants] complies with the Convention... Admittedly, it is inevitable that the Court's decision will have effects extending beyond the confines of this particular case, especially since the violations found stem directly from the contested provisions and not from individual measures of implementation, but the decision cannot of itself annul or repeal these provisions: the Court's judgment is essentially declaratory and leaves to the State the choice of the means to be utilised in its domestic legal system for performance of its obligation under [the Convention to comply with the judgment].[103]

This philosophy continues to be affirmed today. A report issued in 2012 by the Committee of Ministers of the Council of Europe, the body tasked with supervising the execution of the judgments of the European Court of Human Rights under the European Convention,[104] for example, explains:

> [J]udgments in general remain silent [as regards the nature and scope of execution measures other than the payment of just satisfaction]. These measures have thus, in principle,... to be identified by the state itself under the supervision of the Committee of Ministers.... This situation is explained by the principle of subsidiarity, by virtue of which respondent states have in principle freedom of choice as regards the means to be employed in order to meet their obligations under the Convention.[105]

This stance has long been controversial. One judge of the Court, S. K. Martens (whose critique of the 'lottery' character of the quasi-national case law we encountered in Chapter 6) contested in the mid-1990s the view that the judgments of the Court should limit themselves to declaring whether or not a violation of the Convention had occurred.[106] In the same period, some commentators also invited

[102] Though different understandings are possible. Compare Andrew Drzemczewski, 'L'exécution des "décisions" des instances internationales de contrôle dans le domaine des droits de l'homme', in *La Protection des Droits de l'Homme et l'évolution du droit international. Colloque de Strasbourg, 1997* (Société française pour le droit international, 1998) 215–270 at 241, no. 107, with S. K. Martens, 'Individual Complaints under Article 53 of the European Convention on Human Rights', in Rick Lawson and Matthijs de Blois (eds.) *The Dynamics of the Protection of Human Rights in Europe: Essays in Honour of Henry G. Schermers* (The Hague: Martinus Nijhoff, 1994) 253–292 at 275–283.

[103] *Marckx v. Belgium*, appl. 6833/74, PC Judgment (ECtHR), 13 June 1979, para 58.

[104] On execution in the European system, see Elisabeth Lambert-Abdelgawad, *The Execution of Judgments of the European Court of Human Rights* (Strasbourg: Council of Europe, 2008).

[105] Conseil de l'Europe, Comité des Ministres, 'Supervision of the execution of judgments and decisions of the European Court of Human Rights: Annual report, 2011' (Council of Europe, April 2012), paras 15–16.

[106] Martens 'Individual Complaints' 269 ff. The most insightful and politically aware doctrine also saw the absence of an insistence on execution as problematic: Christian Tomuschat, 'Quo

the European Court to emulate the Inter-American Court and the Human Rights Committee which did not hesitate to discuss the consequences of their findings of human rights violations, even when such a power was not directly allocated to them.[107]

The Strasbourg Court started to take cautious steps in this direction. One first blow to the theory according to which the Strasbourg Court cannot give injunctions to the respondent state regarding the execution of its judgments was delivered in 1995, when the Court made it clear that restitution in nature would be preferable to pecuniary compensation. Until then, the theory had always been that *restitutio in integrum* (whereby the victim should be restored to the situation which would have existed were it not for the violation of the Convention) should be sought whenever possible—but that it was not within the Court's remit to assess whether such restitution was feasible and how best it could be achieved. In a case decided in 1995, which concerned property, the Court implicitly encouraged the respondent state to opt for restitution of the expropriated building which was at the centre of the litigation, by fixing the compensation for non-restitution at a high level.[108] This move did not go unnoticed.[109] In a judgment adopted five years later, the Court stated that 'the respondent State remains free to choose the means by which it will discharge its legal obligation [to abide by the judgment] under Article 46 of the Convention, provided that such means are compatible with the conclusions set out in the Court's judgment'.[110] Again this passage was noteworthy in a context where the European Court had strictly adhered to a purely declaratory stance for close to four decades.

It took the crisis of an ever-expanding Strasbourg case law, which risked making the Court 'a victim of its own success', to persuade the Council of Europe that it might be useful for Strasbourg judgments to be more forthcoming as to what was required to eliminate declared violations of the Convention. In the context of this crisis, the hope was that fully implemented judgments would translate into fewer victims lodging complaints at Strasbourg, thus alleviating the pressure on the Court. The idea surfaced in 2000 that it would be advantageous to see a more effective synergy develop between the Court, the Committee of Ministers, and national authorities regarding execution.[111] Once expressed, the idea immediately took hold. Since then, it has invariably been included in

Vadis, Argentorum? The Success Story of the European Convention on Human Rights—and a few Dark Stains' (1992) *Human Rights Law Journal* 13, 401–406.

[107] Gérard Cohen-Jonathan, *La Convention européenne des droits de l'homme* (Paris and Aix-en-Provence: Economica and Presses universitaires d'Aix-Marseille, 1989) 60–62.

[108] *Papamichalopoulos v. Greece*, appl. 14556/89, Judgment (ECtHR), 31 Oct. 1995. See also *Hentrich v. France*, appl. 13616/88, Judgment (ECtHR), 3 July 1995, para 71.

[109] See e.g. Frumer 'La réparation' 336.

[110] *Scozzari and Giunta*, appls 39221/98, 41963/98, Judgment (ECtHR), 13 July 2000, para 249.

[111] It was expressed both by the Parliamentary Assembly and at the Rome ministerial conference celebrating the 50th anniversary of the Convention: Reforming the European Convention on Human Rights: A Work in Progress (Strasbourg: Council of Europe, 2009) 11.

any ministerial conference and other gatherings discussing 'the future' (understood to mean the effects of the caseload and backlog) of the European Court of Human Rights.[112]

The recognised need to have the Convention *implemented* in the member states spurred various developments, including the elaboration of the so-called pilot-judgment procedure. The Strasbourg Court developed this procedure in the last decade as it was confronted with numerous, identical applications which a particular 'structural' or 'systemic' problem was generating in a particular member state. Under the pilot procedure, the Court selects and examines one exemplary case, while putting on hold pending cases which relate to the same problem. In its pilot-judgment, the Court indicates to the state that it must adopt general measures apt to resolve the situation. The Court occasionally specifies what these measures are, but often it does not, only stating that the required measures must be adopted within six months or one year. The Committee of Ministers then prioritises the supervision of the execution of these judgments over that of other judgments.

The Court rendered its first pilot-judgment in June 2004 in the *Broniowski v. Poland* case, where the underlying systemic problem concerned the lack of a compensation scheme for people who had been displaced over the Bug River after World War II. In the wake of *Broniowski*, the Polish government submitted a 'plan of action' for the payment of compensation. This plan was accepted by the Committee of Ministers and included the provision that Bug River claimants would not recover more than 20 per cent of their original property's current value. Although not all the people affected were satisfied with this, their efforts to go back to Strasbourg to complain about this ceiling were to no avail: the Court dismissed their applications.[113]

The pilot procedure was clearly developed as a case management tool. It signals that a particular situation requires urgent action and that everyone—the Court, the respondent state, and the Committee of Ministers—must devote efforts to resolve the situation without delay; it allows applications which have already been lodged to be put on hold; and it aims at avoiding a future flood of applications from the myriad of people who are affected by the problem at the centre of the case to which the pilot procedure is applied. The procedure's primary function is to help the Court to survive the potentially asphyxiating problem of its ever-expanding caseload.

VII. The Strasbourg Court's Incursions into Execution and the *Hirsi Jamaa* Indication

The European Court of Human Rights now allows itself to discuss execution in a way which would have been unimaginable in the first decades of its existence, but its remarks

[112] See e.g. the 'Brighton Declaration' issued by the High Level Conference on the Future of the European Court of Human Rights, April 2012, paras 26–29.

[113] Keller et al. *Friendly Settlements* 73.

in this regard—which occur both within and outside the context of pilot procedures—do not appear to be primarily motivated by a determination to try to ensure that human rights violations are repaired to the full. In the field of migration, *Hirsi Jamaa and Others v. Italy*, decided by a Grand Chamber in February 2012, illustrates this point.[114]

The applicants in *Hirsi* were 'irregular' migrants who had tried to reach Europe by crossing the Mediterranean. Intercepted by the Italian authorities, they apparently agreed to board an Italian military ship after having been told that it would take them to Italy. Instead, they were returned to Tripoli, Libya. This was done without the applicants' identity being taken, let alone having given them access to an asylum procedure. The European Court found multiple violations of the European Convention.

The Court responded to Italy's objection that the majority of the powers of attorney signed by the 24 applicants contained formal defects by stating that it would consider valid a simple written authority as long as it was not shown that it was made without the applicants' understanding and consent.[115] Without this response, the case would obviously not have been able to proceed.[116] This step taken, the Court did not hesitate to find a violation of Article 3. It took note of 'the numerous reports by international bodies and non-governmental organisations [which] paint a disturbing picture of the treatment meted out to clandestine immigrants in Libya at the material time',[117] and it found that 'the Italian authorities knew or should have known that, as irregular migrants, [the applicants] would be exposed in Libya to treatment in breach of the Convention'.[118] This was so even though no information had been provided on the individual, specific treatment which the applicants had suffered; all but six of whom had lost contact with their representatives by the time the case was heard by the Court. The Court also brushed aside as irrelevant the allegation by the Italian state (disputed by the applicants) that none of them had requested international protection on board the military ships. The Court considered that 'it was for the national authorities, faced with a situation in which human rights were being systematically violated... to find out about the treatment to which the applicants would be exposed after their return'.[119] This made it clear that it is not just in the face of formal requests for asylum that the obligation of *non-refoulement* of irregular migrants arises. The Court went on to find a violation of Article 4 of Protocol no. 4 which prohibits the collective expulsion of aliens. This was only the second time in its history that it had reached such a conclusion. It finally found a violation of Article 13, dismissing the candid argument by the Italian government that 'because the events in the instant case had taken place on board ships, it had been impossible to guarantee the applicants the right of access to a national court'.[120] These findings on the merits, all adopted unanimously, are remarkable. Procedurally they depart from the Strasbourg tendency to require the migrant applicants to prove their case

[114] *Hirsi Jamaa and Others v. Italy*, appl. 27765/09, GC Judgment (ECtHR), 23 Feb. 2012.

[115] *Hirsi Jamaa* judgment, paras 45 and 52.

[116] Compare *Hussun and Others v. Italy*, appls 10171/05 et al., Judgment (ECtHR), 19 Jan. 2010, in French only.

[117] *Hirsi Jamaa* judgment, para 123.

[118] *Hirsi Jamaa*, para 131.

[119] *Hirsi Jamaa*, para 133.

[120] *Hirsi Jamaa*, para 191.

and to let the respondent state off the hook. Substantively they seem to put into question the very idea and practice of intercepting irregular migrants on the high seas and summarily returning them to their point of embarkation.

On the face of the part of the judgment on the merits of the applicants' complaints, *Hirsi* has tremendous implications for Italy but also for other states as well as for EU policy, including operations conducted by Frontex (the EU border control). One could say that these operations appear to be in need of stark revision.[121] However, the indication made by the Court as to reparations gives a rather different message. The Court asked the Italian government to 'take all possible steps to obtain assurances from the Libyan authorities that the applicants will not be subjected to treatment incompatible with Article 3 of the Convention or arbitrarily repatriated'.[122] This in a judgment where the Court concluded a violation of Article 3 precisely because the applicants had been returned to Libya and because Libyan promises regarding the respect of human rights, including the prohibition of inhuman and degrading treatment, were considered hollow.

The *Hirsi* indication is troubling in that it reads like a concession to the respondent state which goes rather a long way to annulling the consequences which one would have expected to follow naturally from the multiple violations which the European Court of Human Rights had found. It comes across as an instance of double-talk, if not outright hypocrisy. One way to understand it is that the Court, fearing the open-border implications of its verdict of violation, would have felt the need to reassert the interests of state immigration control. According to Jan Schneider, case management concerns might also have motivated the Court. It might have wanted to ensure that it had a way of dealing with a surge in applications from migrants intercepted at sea, should such a surge materialise—notwithstanding the enormous difficulties which migrants would encounter in making an application to Strasbourg after having been *refoulés* outside Europe.[123]

The best way to repair the violations declared in *Hirsi* would have been to invite the applicants to come back to Italy, to enable them to have any claim they chose to make against expulsion duly examined. This is what Judge Pinto de Albuquerque thought. To quote just one sentence of his very long opinion, 'The Italian Government has a positive obligation to provide the applicants with practical and effective access to an asylum procedure in Italy'.[124] That the Court did not impose such a course of action on Italy is not surprising. It could, however, have opted to remain silent on the issue of reparation, thus leaving it to the Committee of Ministers to interpret the execution implications of the judgment. Instead, the Court specifically chose to

[121] Maarten den Heijer, 'Reflections on *Refoulement* and Collective Expulsion in the *Hirsi* Case' (2013) *International Journal of Refugee Law* 25, 265–290. For a more tempered assessment, see: Mariagiulia Giuffré, 'Watered-Down Rights on the High Seas: *Hirsi Jamaa and Others v. Italy* (2012)' (2012) *International and Comparative Law Quarterly* 61, 728–750.

[122] *Hirsi Jamaa*, para 211.

[123] Jan Schneider, personal communication of 29 February 2012.

[124] Incidentally, one can note that Judge Pinto de Albuquerque's opinion was written in a style reminiscent of that espoused by Judge Cançado Trindade in that it was long and erudite, and put human rights at the very centre of its principled reasoning, without flinching from drawing the implications of what a human rights ethos requires, however costly these implications.

make an indication as to how Italy and, by extension, any other state located at the border of the European Union which routinely intercepts irregular migrants at sea and returns them to their point of departure, might successfully avoid being found to be in violation of the Convention. Bewilderingly the Court's suggested method was for the respondent state to secure assurances of adequate treatment by the state to which migrants were returned after having been intercepted at sea.[125]

VIII. The Dominican Republic Digs its Heels: Did the Inter-American Court Request Too Much in *Yean and Bosico*?

By contrast, the reparation measures ordered by the Inter-American Court seem to be motivated by a broad human rights agenda, where the Court thinks about the precise measures which need to be adopted in order to ensure that the human rights violations it denounces in its judgments do not recur. Its rather uncompromising stance towards states means that its verdicts are likely to be resisted, especially in cases which touch upon issues that the defendant state finds particularly sensitive.[126] This is exactly what happened in the *Yean and Bosico* case. At the time of writing, the Dominican Republic has not yet yielded to the orders it has received from the Court in the first judgment adopted against it.

Cavallaro and Brewer have noted that the judgment met with a 'backlash'.[127] In December 2005, three months after the Inter-American Court rendered its decision, the Supreme Court of the Dominican Republic ignored the *Yean and Bosico* judgment when it ruled the Dominican Law on Emigration constitutional and found the refusal to grant Dominican nationality to children of undocumented workers unproblematic.[128] A few months later, the Dominican Secretary of Foreign Relations issued a document stating that the government questioned the procedures and outcome of the Inter-American case.[129]

Four times now, the Inter-American Court, acting in its execution supervisory role, has formally enjoined the Dominican Republic to respect its orders to publicise the *Yean and Bosico* judgment and to transform its legislation and policy.[130] So far, this has been in vain. The backlash which *Yean and Bosico* attracted was

[125] The Italian authorities indicated to the Committee of Ministers in March 2013 that 'they have not been able to obtain such assurances due to objective difficulties arising from developments in Libya', which prompted the Committee to invite them to 'consider other possible actions, in particular in response to possible requests made by the applicants' representatives': Council of Europe, Committee of Ministers, 'Supervision of the Execution of Judgments and Decisions of the European Court of Human Rights. 7th Annual Report of the Committee of Ministers 2013', at 103.

[126] Pursuing an interesting and different line of thought, Alexandra Huneeus notes that execution which requires the actions of many different types of state actors will be difficult to implement: Huneeus, 'Courts Resisting Courts: Lessons from the Inter-American Court's Struggle to Enforce Human Rights' (2011) *Cornell International Law Journal* 44, 493–533.

[127] Cavallaro and Brewer 'Reevaluating' 790.

[128] Burgorgue-Larsen and Úbeda de Torres *The Inter-American Court* 569.

[129] Cavallaro and Brewer 'Reevaluating' 790.

[130] *Yean and Bosico Girls v. the Dominican Republic*, Monitoring of Compliance with Judgment, Orders (IACtHR), 28 Nov. 2007, 18 May 2009, 27 Aug. 2010, and 10 Oct. 2011.

predictable given the social context prevailing in the Dominican Republic and the number of people who could potentially benefit from proper implementation of the judgment. Do these difficulties of execution mean that the Inter-American Court should have taken a different tack?

As we have noted in the previous chapter, the Inter-American Court has been criticised for not being sufficiently in tune with state concerns and dangerously so—the suggestion being that the Court is going too far for its own good. It is true that few of the contentious cases decided by the Court have been fully complied with.[131] Scholars are divided. Some appear to suggest that the Inter-American Court might be well inspired to be less ambitious and more realistic. Others would like to see it aware of and tackling more angles. Looking at the gender dimensions of the reparations the Court orders, Ruth Rubio-Marín and Clara Sandoval acknowledged the road already travelled but encourage the Court to go further. They conclude their study as follows: 'When the shortcomings are... structural, triggering systemic transformation is both a necessary and a legitimate task for an international human rights tribunal'.[132]

In the Inter-American system, the assertion that 'compliance requires changing the status quo'[133] seems accepted. This is something the Court is proud of, with its former President having explained that the Court often manages to achieve much through one single ruling which is taken on board not only by the state to which it is directly addressed but also by other states and especially judges in the region, in a kind of domino effect.[134]

IX. The European System's Not–So-Impeccable Execution Record

For a long time, it was accepted that the European system enjoyed an impeccable execution record. This led the President of the Strasbourg Court, Judge Ryssdal, to observe in 1996:

> [T]o date judgments of the European Court of Human Rights have, I would say, not only generally but always been complied with by the Contracting States concerned. There have

[131] 'At the end of 2011, 124 out of the 136 contentious cases decided by the Court up to then, were not complied with or only partially complied with': Jan Schneider, 'Implementation of Judgments: Should Supervision be Unlinked from the General Assembly to the Organization of American States?' (2013) *Inter-American and European Human Rights Journal* 5, 198–216 at 199.

[132] Ruth Rubio-Marín and Clara Sandoval, 'Engendering the Reparations Jurisprudence of the Inter-American Court of Human Rights: The Promise of the Cotton Field Judgment' (2011) *Human Rights Quarterly* 33, 1062–1091 at 109.

[133] Courtney Hillebrecht, 'The Domestic Mechanisms of Compliance with International Human Rights Law: Case Studies from the Inter-American Human Rights System' (2012) *Human Rights Quarterly* 34, 959–985 at 961.

[134] Concrete examples related to amnesties, the obligation to investigate human rights violations, the right to an effective remedy and non-discrimination, and the rights of indigenous people can be found in: Diego García-Sayán, 'The Inter-American Court and Constitutionalism in Latin America' (2011) *Texas Law Review* 89, 1835–1862.

been delays, perhaps even some examples of what one might call minimal compliance, but no instances of non-compliance.[135]

It is unlikely that such an optimistic and categorical assessment would be heard within the walls of the Council of Europe today. With the massive expansion of the Council of Europe in the 1990s, culminating in the accession of Russia in 1996—not to forget the acceptance of right of individual petition by Turkey in 1990, problems affecting execution started to appear. The perception nonetheless lingers that the judgments of the European Court are overall well executed. In 2011, the then President of the Court, Judge Costa, was quoted in *Le Monde* saying that apart from a couple of regrettable cases, the implementation of the rulings of the Court run smoothly.[136] Such an assumption of 'everything is well' permeates academic circles. For example, it was recently argued that the good compliance which the Strasbourg judgments attract enhances the European Court's reputation, which in turn enables it to render judgments which are increasingly 'costly' for states to implement.[137] However, the idea of such a virtuous cycle is not entirely convincing.

Admittedly, in its first 25 years, the Strasbourg system presented a near-impeccable execution record. A turning point was reached in the mid-1990s when, shortly after Judge Ryssdal made the statement reproduced earlier, it became clear that the European system was beginning to face some serious problems of execution.[138] A few years later, in 2000, the Parliamentary Assembly of the Council of Europe was sufficiently worried about this trend to decide that it should take some steps towards monitoring compliance.[139]

The first big problem to emerge was the implementation of the judgment of *Loizidou v. Turkey*, in which Turkey had been ordered to pay the applicant 300,000 Cypriot pounds for the loss of access to her property in Northern Cyprus.[140] By the time Mrs Loizidou received her compensation five years after the judgment, in December 2003, a number of countries were appearing to ignore the implications of the verdicts of violation adopted against them. Even if they were paying individual applicants the damages ordered by the Court, they were refraining from adopting the general measures which would have prevented the repetition of the denounced violations.

[135] Rolv Ryssdal, 'The Enforcement System Set Up Under the European Convention on Human Rights', in Mielle K. Bulterman and Martin Kuijer (eds) *Compliance with Judgments of International Courts* (The Hague: Martinus Nijhoff, 1996) 49–69 at 67.

[136] '[Mis a part deux ou trois cas regrettables,] tout se passe correctement': interview published in *Le Monde* on 5 November 2011 and available on: <http://libertes.blog.lemonde.fr/2011/11/05/jean-paul-costa-respect-sans-melange/>, accessed 22 May 2012.

[137] Shai Dothan, 'Judicial Tactics in the European Court of Human Rights' (2011) *Chicago Journal of International Law* 12, 116–142.

[138] Andreas von Staden, 'Rational Choice within Normative Constraints: Compliance by Liberal Democracies with the Judgments of the European Court of Human Rights', version dated 13 February 2012, Figure 2, page 12 (on file with the author).

[139] Andrew Drzemczewski and James Gaughan, 'Implementing Strasbourg Court Judgments: The Parliamentary Dimension', in Wolfgang Benedek et al. (eds) *European Yearbook on Human Rights* (Antwerp: European Academy Press, 2010) 233–244 at 235–236.

[140] *Loizidou v. Turkey*, appl. 15318/89, GC Judgment (ECtHR), 28 July 1998.

Russia was, and remains, the biggest defaulter in this respect. Judgments pointing to serious violations of the Convention pertaining amongst other things to the right to life and freedom from torture remain unexecuted, leading to calls for the application of political sanctions against it. Also of note is the attitude of the government of David Cameron in the UK which, in a very different context, has been vocal in expressing its dissatisfaction with judgments of the Court against it, including the issue of prisoners' voting rights, with the British Parliament specifically refusing to implement the relevant judgment in 2011.

An excellent piece of research which has examined the measures which followed the 12,263 compliance-relevant decisions which had been adopted by the Strasbourg Court up to 2010 demonstrates that lack of execution goes beyond these emblematic and well-known situations.[141] Given this, how can one explain the smooth execution record of the first 25 years?

Three factors come to mind. First, in that period the Court was dealing almost exclusively with issues of 'fine tuning' which arose in states that were overall democratic. Until the accession of the 1990s, the system was spared encounters with massive and extreme violations of human rights, such as disappearances and brutal repression of dissent, in regimes which were not intent on seeing those practices eradicated. Second, in a context that was overall sympathetic to human rights, the European Court did not feel the need to push for a resolutely militant human rights agenda in areas which states considered highly sensitive, such as migration control. In this area, conceived as embodying the last bastion of state sovereignty in an increasingly supranational era, the Court refrained from making broad pronouncements. It trod very carefully, issuing a verdict of violation here and there, but mostly endorsing the 'well-established principle of international law' regarding state control, thus largely avoiding the issue of execution in that area. Third, the body in charge of supervising the execution of the Court's judgments, namely the Committee of Ministers, was easily satisfied. Up to the 1980s, promises by a state that it would take remedial measures were deemed sufficient to warrant the adoption of a resolution which marked the end of the Committee's supervision of the execution of a judgment and definitely closed the case.[142]

Notable changes have occurred in all these respects in the last 15 to 20 years. First, the European system now has to deal with situations which denote most serious and systematic violations of human rights. Second, as the legal protection of migrants has steadily deteriorated, the Court has been persuaded to rein in some of the most objectionable aspects of their treatment. Third, over the years, the Committee of Ministers has taken steps which have enabled it to tighten its control of execution.[143] The days when it was sufficient for a state merely to promise that something would be done to close a case are definitely over. It is therefore not surprising that difficulties of execution have become visible in the European system.

[141] von Staden 'Rational Choice'. [142] von Staden 'Rational Choice' 16.
[143] Lambert-Abdelgawad *The Execution* 36.

Interestingly the predominant story remains that the European system functions well overall, as per President Costa's interview in *Le Monde*. This perception affects the way most academic studies are conducted. For example, von Staden's research relies on the assumption that 'a final decision by the Committee of Ministers indicates that a state has properly complied with a Strasbourg judgment against it'.[144] This is justified by reference to statements by insiders of the Council of Europe that 'supervision by the Committee has worked well for the most part' or that the Committee applies 'sufficiently high thresholds'.[145] Care is taken by von Staden to present this assumption as a *working* assumption.[146] Nonetheless nowhere does he suggest that this assumption is possibly defective or would at the very least deserve to be carefully examined. To my knowledge there exists to date no scholarly study which critically assesses the quality of the concrete measures which the Committee of Ministers endorses as constituting adequate execution of Strasbourg verdicts of violation.

As its name indicates, the Committee of Ministers is a political body made of state representatives. Members of the Committee are unlikely either to favour strong human rights standards or to adopt a severe stance towards a state—their peer. While a state will avoid altogether disregarding a judgment which goes against it, it will nonetheless seek to minimise the way in which it complies with it. As von Staden recognises, states will be inclined towards the least 'costly' implementation option, i.e. the one which requires the least change on their part.[147] In such cases, can one say the judgments have been implemented? Opinions are likely to differ on this question.

X. 'Execution' and 'Execution': A Rare Comment from the Strasbourg Court in *Emre (No.2)*

Where does the line fall between compliance and non-compliance? This is almost always open to interpretation; there is 'execution' and 'execution'. In theory, a defective execution can give rise to a *new* violation of the Convention.[148] However, if the Committee of Ministers has adopted a final resolution closing a case, the Court would openly have to go against the Committee to acknowledge this; in the opposite scenario where the Committee had not yet pronounced on the execution of the case, for the Court to pronounce a new verdict of violation could be frowned upon as encroaching upon the functions of the Committee. This context is not propitious for applicants who would wish to argue before the Court that the way a state is choosing to execute a judgment entails a new violation of the Convention.

144 von Staden 'Rational Choice' 17.

145 von Staden 17. 146 von Staden 17. 147 von Staden.

148 It should be noted that when the Committee of Ministers considers that the supervision of the execution of a judgment is hindered by a problem of interpretation of the judgment, under Article 46 (3) ECHR introduced by Protocol no. 14 the Committee may refer the matter to the Court for a ruling on the question of interpretation.

In the review of the Strasbourg case law related to the deportation of foreigners who have been convicted of a crime (presented in Chapter 6), we have seen that Mr Mehemi's application to the effect that France had committed a new violation of the Convention when it assigned conditions to his permission to return to France had failed.[149] Recently, Mr Emre was luckier. His expulsion from Switzerland to Turkey following criminal convictions had been found by the Court to be in breach of Article 8 ECHR in May 2008.[150] One year later, a Swiss tribunal quashed the permanent exclusion order which the Strasbourg Court had found in violation of the Convention and replaced it with a ten-year one (running from the original exclusion date of June 2003). Mr Emre came back before the Strasbourg Court, arguing that the new judicial order constituted a new violation of the Convention.

The Court, in a Chamber presided over by Judge Tulkens, accepted this in *Emre (No. 2)*. A majority of five judges rejected the government's argument according to which the pertinent issue was whether the new order constituted a proper execution of the May 2008 judgment and was thus for the Committee of Ministers to decide.[151] Their short reasoning noted that the Committee of Ministers had not yet started to supervise the execution of the May 2008 judgment, without explaining the implications of that fact.[152] A one-off, *Emre (No. 2)* vividly illustrates both the potentially extremely controversial nature of decisions concerning execution and the risks of minimal execution which must be associated with attributing the task of supervising that execution to a political body of state representatives.[153]

There seems to be a common assumption that the European system enjoys a better execution record than the Inter-American system. It is difficult to compare the two systems, however, given the very different ways in which they operate. Any assessment needs to take into account the fact that the Inter-American Court is both very precise and very demanding on the reparations it orders in contentious cases, while the Committee of Ministers of the Council of Europe is comparatively lax, even if it makes more stringent demands than 20 years ago. One should therefore expect it to be politically more difficult to reach the point where a case is closed in the Inter-American as compared to the European system.[154] Given the stringent demands made by the Inter-American Court on defendant states, the fact that it manages to close cases at all is impressive. From a human rights perspective, it is not clear that the Inter-American execution record has much to envy of the European experience.

[149] *Mehemi v. France (No. 2)*, appl. 53479/00, Judgment (ECtHR), 10 Apr. 2003, (p. 176).

[150] *Emre v. Switzerland*, appl. 42034/04, Judgment (ECtHR), 22 May 2008.

[151] *Emre v. Switzerland (No. 2)*, appl. 5056/10, Judgment (ECtHR), 11 Oct. 2011. The two dissenting judges were Judges Malinverni and Thór Björgvinsson.

[152] *Emre (No. 2)*, para 42.

[153] e.g. in *Nunez v. Norway*, appl. 55597/09, Resolution (CM), 11 June 2013, the case was closed after the applicant was granted a three-year residence permit (it was nonetheless specified that in their assessment of a potential request for renewal, the Norwegian authorities would take due account of their obligations under Article 8).

[154] Burguorgue-Larsen's analysis of the Inter-American case law against impunity for the most serious crimes/human rights violations supports this conclusion: Laurence Burguorgue-Larsen, 'Le

XI. Judicial Restraint in the European System Not a Guarantee of State Respect

As this book has repeatedly demonstrated, the Inter-American Court is bold in its pursuit of human rights, the European Court far more cautious and partial to state interests. Do these different attitudes have adverse or advantageous implications for the judicial authority which characterises these two courts? An authoritative doctrine suggests that the activism of the Inter-American Court engenders the risk that states parties to the American Convention might want to disengage from it and perhaps even leave the system altogether.[155] If this hypothesis is correct, one might assume that its reverse would also hold, namely, that the more deferential European Court would have been more successful in gaining state respect. In fact, neither of these two propositions seems to be borne out in practice. On the one hand, the Inter-American Court's strategy has not led to disastrous consequences for the Inter-American system of human rights protection. On the other hand, the politics of 'appeasement'[156] pursued by the European Court has not had the effect of winning the praise of states.

Some states clearly choose not to implement the unambiguous orders that they have received from the Inter-American Court. One example is the Dominican Republic which has not yet fully complied with the *Yean and Bosico* judgment. Is it possible that the activist jurisprudence of the Court will take it into even more troubled waters and that one should not dismiss the possibility that the entire Inter-American system of human rights protection could collapse due to repeated state denunciations? Are these risks real? And if they are, are they worth taking? These are difficult questions, and not really for a lawyer to answer. What is nonetheless clear is that at the moment, the system does not appear to be collapsing.

Following displeasure with the stance of the Inter-American Court on the death penalty, the Republic of Trinidad and Tobago denounced the American Convention in May 1998, which became effective one year later.[157] Peru tried to withdraw its recognition of the Court's contentious jurisdiction in July 1999 with immediate effect (which the Court refused). It reintegrated into the system in 2001, as soon as President Fujimori's successor took office. Most recently, Venezuela denounced the Convention in September 2012, a decision which came into force in 2013. At a general level, the recent exercise in 'strengthening' the

bannissement de l'impunité: Décryptage de la politique jurisprudentielle de la Cour interaméricaine des droits de l'homme' (2012) *Revue trimestrielle des droits de l'homme* 3–42.

[155] Cavallaro and Brewer 'Reevaluating' 817.

[156] Helen Fenwick, 'Post 9/11 UK Counter-Terrorism Cases in the European Court of Human Rights: A "Dialogic" Approach to Rights' Protection or Appeasement of National Authorities?', in Fergal F. Davis and Fiona de Londras (eds) *Critical Debates on Counter-Terrorism Judicial Review* (Cambridge: Cambridge University Press, 2014); 'An Appeasement Approach in the European Court of Human Rights?', UK Constitutional Law Association blog, available at <http://ukconstitutionallaw.org/2012/04/05/helen-fenwick-an-appeasement-approach-in-the-european-court-of-human-rights/>, accessed 14 June 2014.

[157] Schneider 'Implementation' 201.

Commission was widely perceived as an effort by states to weaken the institution, and thus the whole Inter-American system of human rights protection.[158] This would have been a potentially serious development, although civil society mobilisation succeeded in averting the worst effects. As already mentioned, it is true that neither the OAS nor individual American states are giving the Inter-American system of human rights protection sufficient material resources for its proper functioning, forcing the Court to rely on unconventional sources (e.g. the Spanish and Norwegian states, as well as the European Union) to fund its existence and activities.[159] This state of affairs is undoubtedly problematic. However, nothing suggests that a more cautious attitude by the Inter-American Court would result in better funding. Even if it did, it is not clear that caution should be the way forward given the tremendous losses for the human rights ideal and practice that this new judicial strategy would entail.

Turning to the European system, the fear of losing state support seems to have been at the core of the development of the European Court of Human Rights throughout its history. To this day, this fear subsists. The British government has been amongst the most intimidating states in this respect. It has made it very clear that it resented the *East African Asians* case in the 1970s, warned that it might not renew the optional protocols in the 1980s, and took offence at the verdict of violation regarding the shooting of Irish Republican Army (IRA) terrorists in Gibraltar in the 1990s.[160] Expressing disgruntlement has been taken to a new level by the government of David Cameron, which has not ceased to complain about some judgments (especially on prisoners' voting rights and the deportation of Abu Qatada) and led a call for the European Court of Human Rights to stop interfering with so-called domestic matters. The hostility which the UK government has displayed must, from its perspective, have borne some fruit. The Court has been noted to react with a policy of 'appeasement', avoiding verdicts of violation altogether or at least toning them down. During his presidency of the Court from 2011 to 2012, the British judge, Sir Nicolas Bratza, did not cease to provide objective responses to the vitriolic attacks on the Court by the British government. One point he made was that the Court adopted very few verdicts of violation against the UK.[161] It

[158] Douglas Cassel, 'Regional Human Rights Regime and State Pushback: The Case of the Inter-American Human Rights System' (2011–2013)' (2013) *Human Rights Law Journal* 33, 1–10. See also the special issue on 'The Future of the Inter-American System of Human Rights' in (2012) *Human Rights Brief* 20(2).

[159] Schneider 'Implementation' 206.

[160] Ed Bates, *The Evolution of the European Convention on Human Rights: From its Inception to the Creation of a Permanent Court of Human Rights* (Oxford: Oxford University Press, 2010) 247, 427, and 434 respectively.

[161] Nicolas Bratza, 'The Relationship between the UK Courts and Strasbourg' (2011) *European Human Rights Law Review* 505–512 at 507. In *Balogun v. the United Kingdom*, appl. 60286/09, Judgment (ECtHR), 10 Apr. 2012, the Court did not find in breach of Article 8 the deportation of a young adult who was convicted of drug offences. The applicant had arrived in the UK at the age of three. He was barely an adult, having just turned 18, at the time of his last offence. He said that he had now overcome his drug addiction, a claim which seemed supported by the fact that he had had no dealings with the police since his release from prison five years previously. There was not very much to justify his deportation, but the Court did not find it disproportionate.

seems that for the greater part of the British political class and the media, even one is too many. In January 2014, Judge Spielmann, who had succeeded Judge Bratza in the presidency of the Court, appeared on the BBC current affairs programme *Hard Talk*.[162] He similarly had to defend the Court from extremely negative and ill-informed views about the way in which the Court was alleged to be constantly and gratuitously infringing national sovereignty. Such poisonous dynamics are not without implications for the way a timid European Court of Human Rights conducts itself, and opts to continue its timid approach. Needless to say, this potentially becomes a vicious circle.

These few remarks do not offer a comprehensive analysis of what is going on either in the European or the Inter-American systems. What they indicate, however, is that the comparatively deferential approach of the European Court has not shielded it from criticism; a position of strength has not been its reward for its propensity to acknowledge state interests and refrain from adopting a perspective resolutely in favour of human rights. By contrast, there is great merit in the Inter-American Court having sought to remain true to the human rights project. This has not put its existence under immediate threat, even if it has generated state resistance and has done nothing to convince other potentially key states, such as the United States and Canada, to join the system.[163]

XII. Provisional or Perennial Measures? The Inter-American Court Cannot Act Alone

No court can, on its own, ensure respect of human rights law. This can only arise as the result of a convergence of actions from a variety of bodies. The '*Haitians*' matter with which we started this chapter can be used to illustrate the relative powerlessness of the Inter-American Court, when it is left unsupported in its role of human rights defender. Let us recall that, in August 2000, the Inter-American Court ordered the Dominican Republic to adopt provisional measures in respect of the matter concerning *Haitians and Dominicans of Haitian origin in the Dominican Republic*. This order was not a magic wand which sorted out the situation once and for all. The Court revised its orders in this matter in late 2000 (twice), May 2001, October 2005, February 2006, July 2009, December 2011, and February 2012. The fact that so many revisions were needed is a clear indication that all was not well.

Beneficiaries of the provisional measures not uncommonly reported that the safe conduct which they had received in order to be protected from deportation had simply been torn up and thrown away by military authorities at a

[162] See <http://www.bbc.co.uk/iplayer/episode/b03q0b61/HARDtalk_Dean_Spielmann_President_of_the_European_Court_of_Human_Rights/>, accessed 8 April 2014.

[163] In an ironic twist, the United States has apparently nonetheless made aid to Columbia dependent on Columbia's implementation of judgments against it by the Inter-American Court: Jan Schneider, personal communication.

checkpoint.[164] Those at the forefront of the fight for the rights of Haitians—Father Ruquoy and Ms Pierre (Pie)—received threats against their lives and personal security. In such instances, the Court would order the Dominican Republic to investigate 'the facts that prompted the adoption, maintenance and extension' of the provisional measures and to punish those responsible. There is no evidence that this actually happened.

This is not to say that the Dominican Republic altogether ignored the orders of the Court. It would go through some motions, but without much effect. For example, it would communicate the names of the authorities in charge of supervising the implementation of the measures, but the representatives of the beneficiaries would report that these persons were either not yet or no longer in place. To give another example, the state would create the mechanism requested by the Court to coordinate and supervise the implementation of the ordered measures,[165] but then it would not ensure that the body met at regular intervals, prompting the Court subsequently to request to be informed of 'the scheduling of the next meetings and the measures to be implemented'.[166]

For someone familiar with the European system, the level of detail in which the Inter-American Court is involved is astonishing (and obviously only possible because of the small number of cases with which it deals). The Court requests to be informed of developments every few months, it listens to what the parties report, it assesses the problems which are put before it, and it tries to act in an effective way. All this happens within the legal framework provided by the American Convention. Every time the ordered provisional measures are reviewed, the Court verifies that the three conditions provided by Article 63 (2)—extreme gravity, urgency, and the necessity to avoid 'irreparable damage to persons'—remain fulfilled. The provisional measures have always been conceived of by the Inter-American Court as legally binding. They are understood to serve a double purpose: one is 'precautionary'—safeguarding the effectiveness of the jurisdictional function itself; the other 'protective'—protecting the substantive human rights of human beings (which, if violated, could not be repaired *ad integrum* at a later stage).[167]

Years and years of ordering provisional measures in the '*Haitians*' matter belied the supposedly provisional character of these orders. The Inter-American Court repeatedly made it clear that it wished for the Commission to process the case at its level and then to lodge it before the Court, but without any means to force the hands of the Commission on this. (Eventually, in June 2012, this 'matter' became the *Benito v. the Dominican Republic* case after the Commission formally submitted it to the Court for judicial examination of its merits). And so the Court went on monitoring the situation and exercising light pressure, adjusting the

[164] '*Haitians' matter*, Order (IACtHR), 2 Feb. 2006, p. 11, para 10 e).

[165] '*Haitians*' order of 2 Feb. 2006, p. 14, para 9 j).

[166] '*Haitians*' matter, Order (IACtHR), 1 Dec. 2011, p. 6, para 20.

[167] Concurring opinion of Judge Cancado Trindade in '*Haitians*' matter, provisional measures, 18 August 2000, paras 17 and 18, as well as Order of 1 December 2011, p. 2, para 4.

provisional measures ordered along the way. For example, in February 2012, it dropped 'Ms Solain Pie or Solain Pierre or Solange Pierre' from the list of beneficiaries,[168] having been informed of the death of this intrepid human rights defender.[169] In September 2012, the Court rescinded the provisional measures in favour of the children of Solange Pierre and three other individuals, finding that the requests for maintaining them were too general to demonstrate a situation of extreme gravity and urgency.[170]

What impact all these provisional orders have had and continue to have in practice is impossible to assert without researching this question through proper fieldwork in the Dominican Republic and the careful assessment of a variety of experiences and opinions.[171] What is clear is that the judges of the Inter-American Court have been trying to do what they can in order to protect a certain, admittedly limited, number of people involved in the matters and cases which are brought before them. What they can achieve without external support is always going to be limited.

XIII. Conclusion

This chapter has focused on *Yean and Bosico*, the first contentious case brought by migrants which was decided by the Inter-American Court. The case was of potential relevance to a huge population of Haitians and people taken to be Haitians in the Dominican Republic and concerned a most sensitive issue for the defendant state: the granting of birth certificates and thus nationality to people who are presented by this state as being merely 'in transit'. The political significance of the case cannot be overstated in a context where there is a lingering fear amongst Dominicans that one day Haiti might collapse and her population of eight million pour over the border. The Inter-American Court must have approached the proceedings of this case in full awareness that Dominicans were never going to be easily persuaded to entrench the rights of persons of Haitian origin in their territory. This awareness does not seem to have affected its determination to advance a full human rights agenda at every single stage of the proceedings.

Thus, it refused to consider that the mere granting of birth certificates to the alleged victims would justify the imposition of a friendly settlement; it found numerous and interrelated violations of human rights; it ordered precise and wide-ranging reparation measures; it continues to insist to this day that the defendant state must execute its judgment in *Yean and Bosico*. For over a decade, it also

[168] *'Haitians'* order of 29 February 2012, operative part, para 1.

[169] Although she had sometimes felt the need to leave the Dominican Republic for her own safety and that of her children, her death did not appear to have occurred in suspicious circumstances. Her dedication to the human rights cause was formally recognised by a Robert F. Kennedy Human Rights Award in 2007: Cavallero and Brewer 'Reevaluating' note 66.

[170] *'Haitians'* matter, Order (IACtHR), 7 Sept. 2011.

[171] Father Ruquoy seems to have been dissuaded from returning to the Dominican Republic after he visited his (presumably) native Belgium in 2005/6.

carried on ordering supposedly provisional measures of protection in the 'matter' which concerned the deportation of 'Haitians' in the Dominican Republic, striving to protect the lives, personal integrity, and right to be with their families of an admittedly limited number of individuals.

The Inter-American and European systems of protection of human rights have evolved in largely different contexts, which makes them difficult to compare. It has nonetheless been noted that a case like *Yean and Bosico* would most likely have met a very different fate had it been before the European Court of Human Rights. Were a similar case to have been lodged at Strasbourg, it is reasonable to think that the Court would have been tempted to strike it out after the applicants had been granted birth certificates. Had this not happened and the case had proceeded to be assessed on its merits, the Strasbourg Court would have been unlikely to find as broad and interrelated violations of human rights as did the Inter-American Court. Even if it had found some Convention violations, the Strasbourg Court would certainly not have been as demanding as the Inter-American Court was in the reparations it ordered. As a result, it would have been easier for the Committee of Ministers of the Council of Europe to bring the case to a close through a final resolution.

The relative institutional ease with which this final point would have been reached does not mean, however, that human rights law is necessarily in better shape in the European rather than the American system. In this regard, it is important to observe once again that the pronouncements of the European Court in migrant cases do not go very far. This timidity is not compensated for by the guarantee that at least a deferential stance produces a ready acceptance of occasional verdicts of violation by states. On the contrary, some states, such as the UK, seem intent on contesting the authority of the Strasbourg Court in a rather fundamental way. The Court has not dared to show itself to be strong, and it has arguably retreated further. Once the Court is perceived to be weak, however, there is a danger that this might generate more and more attacks from states, with such 'appeasement' leading to the exact opposite of what it is intended to achieve. Alongside the development of procedures primarily designed to manage Strasbourg's ever-expanding caseload, this does not bode well for a principled defence of human rights.

The Inter-American system runs into other difficulties. The persistent opposition of the Dominican Republic to the message conveyed by the *Yean and Bosico* judgment vividly demonstrates the limits of what the Inter-American Court can achieve in isolation from other institutions and social actors. Obviously a judicial pronouncement can never be expected to work like a magic wand that produces instantaneous effects as soon as it is waved. In and of itself, a verdict of human rights violation is unable to transform the situation it denounces: being just words, it cannot do this. Something else always needs to happen. In the absence of a political context receptive to its rulings, the Inter-American Court is relatively powerless.

PART III
PROSPECTS

Part I and Part II of this book have examined the way in which the migrant case law of the European and Inter-American Courts was initiated and then consolidated on rather different paths. One of the things that this third and final part may be expected to do is to ask whether the identified trends are likely to continue or whether a convergence is in sight. Given how difficult it is to predict the future, this is done in a modest way: by reviewing recent case law in order to conclude that, so far, the two courts are largely maintaining their respective course.[1]

When I initially designed the structure of this book, the only aspect which was clear about Part III is that it would have to include a chapter on the *Vélez Loor v. Panama* case.[2] *Vélez Loor* saw the Inter-American Court insisting that immigration detention must be a 'last resort' surrounded by procedural guarantees. When the judgment came out in 2010, I had assumed that it would be the last Inter-American ruling this book would tackle. Since then, however, the Inter-American migrant case law has developed substantially. *Nadege Dorzema v. the Dominican Republic*, about the forced and violent—indeed, fatal—deportation of Haitians or presumed Haitians, contrary to all humanitarian considerations and outside any legal process, was decided in 2012.[3] The ruling in *Pacheco v. Bolivia*, concerning a family of asylum seekers from neighbouring Peru, followed in 2013.[4] In July 2011, the four members of the South American economic and political union of MERCOSUR—namely, Argentina, Brazil, Paraguay, and Uruguay—requested an advisory opinion about the treatment of migrant children, raising nine questions.[5] This advisory opinion came out shortly

[1] This conclusion echoes the findings of Diego Acosta Arcarazo and Andrew Geddes (about migration governance rather than regional human rights jurisprudence) in 'Transnational Diffusion or Different Models? Regional Approaches to Migration Governance in the European Union and Mercosur' (2014) *European Journal of Migration and Law* 16, 19–44.

[2] *Vélez Loor v. Panama*, Preliminary Objections, Merits, Reparations and Costs, Judgment (IACtHR), 23 Nov. 2010.

[3] *Nadege Dorzema et al. v. the Dominican Republic*, Merits, Reparations and Costs, Judgment (IACtHR), 24 Oct. 2012.

[4] *Family Pacheco Tineo v. Plurinational State of Bolivia*, Preliminary Objections, Merits, Reparations and Costs, Judgment (IACtHR), 25 Nov. 2013, in Spanish only at the time of writing.

[5] Request for Advisory Opinion on Migrant Children before the Inter-American Court of Human Rights of 6 April 2011, <http://www.corteidh.or.cr/solicitudoc/solicitud_eng.pdf>, accessed 29 May 2014.

after the manuscript of this book had been submitted to the press.[6] So did the judgment in *Expelled Dominicans and Haitians v. the Dominican Republic* (which became the new name of the *Benito Tide Méndez* case, itself the follow-up to the '*Haitians*' matter which gave rise to provisional measures, as examined in Chapter 10).[7]

My original plan for Part III was to take *Vélez Loor* as its starting point and to make the issue of immigration detention, as addressed by the San José and Strasbourg Courts, a test case for assessing the potential development of the two regional bodies of jurisprudence. This focus, however, soon appeared too narrow. This was both because of the surge in the Inter-American migrant case law and because of the diversity of Strasbourg case law which cried out to be studied. Admittedly, the abundance of the Strasbourg jurisprudence made its comprehensive study an unattainable goal. Granted choices were to be made, it still remained that Part III could not be entirely focused around the issue, however serious and topical, of immigration detention.

The summary of *M.S.S. v. Belgium and Greece* included in an early draft of Chapter 7 failed to do justice to this Grand Chamber judgment, which had declared the application of a central mechanism of EU migration policy—'Dublin II'—in breach of the European Convention on a number of fronts.[8] *M.S.S.* clearly required a fuller analysis than could ever be offered in a chapter designed to trace the history of the whole of the Article 3 returns case law. Similarly, a draft of Chapter 8, which the reader will recall focuses on *Gaygusuz* and examines social protection, ended with a review of the case law concerning residence permit refusals. Such refusals affect hundreds of thousands of so-called irregular migrants in Europe. The lack of secure legal status they signal leads to the lack of access to a number of 'goods', including legal work, health care, and other social benefits, not to mention bank accounts, driving licences, etc. The stalemate in which the affected people find themselves can persist indefinitely. I initially thought of including a review of the complaints which had arisen from this situation in Chapter 8, but it made this chapter far too long. Moving the discussion of both *M.S.S* and the Strasbourg residence permit refusals case law to Part III proved an obvious solution.

This seemed the more appropriate since the cases relevant to these two strands of discussion were all very recent, and thus fitted well with the project of examining 'prospects'. Recounting the history of how Part III came about makes it clear that the chapters devoted to *M.S.S.* (Chapter 12) and the residence permit refusals (Chapter 13) are a direct continuation of Chapters 7 and 8, respectively. They are preceded by a chapter devoted to *Vélez Loor* (Chapter 11) (a stand-alone rather than a direct continuation of another chapter) and followed by a chapter about the most recent Inter-American case law (Chapter 14), which, amongst other things, takes the history recounted in Chapters 9 and 10 forward.

[6] *Rights and Guarantees of Children in the Context of Migration and/or in Need of International Protection*, Advisory Opinion OC-21/14 (IACtHR), 19 Aug. 2014, in Spanish only at the time of writing.

[7] *Expelled Dominicans and Haitians v. the Dominican Republic*, Preliminary Objections, Merits, Reparations and Costs, Judgment (IACtHR), 28 Aug. 2014, in Spanish only at the time of writing.

[8] *M.S.S. v. Belgium and Greece*, appl. 30696/09, GC Judgment (ECtHR), 21 Jan. 2011.

The resulting four-chapter structure of Part III offers a number of advantages. First, it continues the chronological organisation adopted in the first two parts of the book: *Vélez Loor* dates from 2010; *M.S.S.* from January 2011; *I. v. the Netherlands*—which is central to the analysis presented on the residence permits refusals case law—consists of two decisions of inadmissibility dating from late 2011 and 2012;[9] the most recent Inter-American case law is... most recent (with two rulings even post-dating the submission of the manuscript of the book for publication). Second, it 'sandwiches' the Strasbourg chapters between Inter-American chapters, which can be taken to highlight the counterpoint function which the Inter-American case law fulfils in this book. Last but not least, it allows for the best (*M.S.S.*) and the worst (the condoning of lack of proper legal status) of the Strasbourg migrant case law to be juxtaposed.

As with previous Inter-American chapters, Chapter 11 on *Vélez Loor* is used as an opportunity to review relevant Strasbourg case law; it shows the stark contrast in the way the two Courts approach immigration detention. Chapter 12 celebrates the jurisprudential leaps which *M.S.S.* effected, whilst berating the time it took for the Strasbourg Court to take this course and its lack of determination to carry the protective impulse forward in subsequent case law. Chapter 13 examines Strasbourg decisions of inadmissibility regarding residence permit refusals, including cases where there is no dispute that the applicants cannot be returned to their country of origin. Its main argument is that the Strasbourg Court ends up condoning rightlessness—which is no small paradox for a court designed to protect the rights of every human being. Chapter 14 returns to the Inter-American Court. On my instructions, its author, Lourdes Peroni, has kept it short. Its main aim is to inform the reader of the latest developments in the Inter-American jurisprudence. It does not provide a comprehensive review of all the aspects of the cases discussed. Instead it focuses on the discrimination reasoning in *Nadege Dorzema*; the declared need for solid procedural guarantees in *Pacheco*, and the likelihood that what was at time of writing the awaited advisory opinion on the rights of migrant children would produce strong pronouncements on procedural guarantees in asylum and migration proceedings that involve children. Peroni's identification of different equality and due process 'routes' travelled by the Inter-American Court provides a perfect lead to Chapter 15, the concluding chapter, as will become clear in due course.

European migration law experts will no doubt regret that some migrant case law by the new Strasbourg Court will have been omitted from this book. The volume of this case law made this inevitable. I shall nonetheless briefly introduce five cases to which I had thought at some stage of devoting a full chapter.

The first of these is *Maaouia v. France*, which was briefly described in Chapter 7.[10] The reader is invited to re-read the paragraphs devoted to this judgment, fully taking on board its foundational status.[11] For an inordinately long time, countless applications will either have been declared inadmissible or

[9] *I. v. the Netherlands*, appl. 24147/11, Decisions (ECtHR) 18 Oct. 2011 and 10 Jul. 2012.
[10] *Maaouia v. France*, appl. 39652/98, GC Judgment (ECtHR), 5 Oct. 2000.
[11] See Chapter 7, p. 224.

failed to be lodged at all by legal representatives all too aware that any Article 6 complaint regarding immigration proceedings has virtually no chance of being heard at Strasbourg, precisely because of *Maaouia*.[12] Although there is hope in many circles that the Strasbourg Court may revisit this jurisprudence, the poisonous effects of the verdict will have influenced the European legal landscape throughout the early part of the twenty-first century. This is because of the typically far-reaching effects of verdicts of non-violation by the Grand Chamber, which make the absence of a right under the Convention particularly glaring. The lessons of a Grand Chamber's verdict of non-violation are often applied to all similar cases, almost automatically. In other words, once the Grand Chamber has pronounced negatively in a categorical way, it can be very difficult to undo what has been done.[13] Verdicts of violation rarely have the same categorical impact. In a system which favours a casuistic reasoning, these verdicts 'merely' open avenues, the exact direction of which typically remains to be explored, thus preventing one verdict of violation from giving rise to further verdicts of violation in the same automatic and categorical way as happens with negative Strasbourg verdicts.

The second case to which I would have liked to devote a chapter is *Al-Nashif v. Bulgaria*.[14] This case is interesting on more than one count: it involved a family of Palestinian origin who settled in Bulgaria and thus seemed to point to little-discussed historical patterns of migration established during the Cold War; the detention and expulsion of the first applicant, a Muslim teacher, appeared to have been motivated by Islamophobia, thus touching upon one of the most pressing issues in Europe, namely, the problematic relationship which Europeans entertain with Islam; the authorities justified their treatment of the claimant by invoking unsubstantiated 'national security' reasons, in a way which the Strasbourg Court had no difficulty finding arbitrary. The outcome is undoubtedly welcome but nonetheless raises the spectre of a Court which may be more distrusting of Eastern than of Western European states. As if this was not enough, *Al Nashif* marked the beginning of a long series of verdicts of violation in similar circumstances, demonstrating here the powerlessness of Strasbourg to halt a problematic practice.[15]

[12] Add to this that the *Maaouia* effect is far-reaching. It could be said to encompass e.g. *I.R. and G.T. v. the United Kingdom*, appls 14876/12 and 63339/12, Decision (ECtHR), 28 January 2014 (inadmissibility under Articles 8 and 13 of complaints regarding 'closed material' proceedings before the Special Immigration Appeals Commission).

[13] A recent example where this is happening is *N. v. the United Kingdom*, appl. 26565/05, GC Judgment (ECtHR), 27 May 2008. This is probably why the Second Section opted for appending a six-strong separate opinion in *Yoh-Ekale Mwanje v. Belgium*, appl. 10486/10, Judgment (ECtHR) 20 Dec. 2011 rather than relinquishing this case to the Grand Chamber. By contrast *Üner v. the Netherlands*, appl. 46410/99, GC Judgment (ECtHR), 18 Oct. 2006, did not have this effect, no doubt because it touched upon an issue which had always seen the Court divided.

[14] *Al-Nashif v. Bulgaria*, appl. 50936/99, Judgment (ECtHR), 20 June 2002.

[15] The latest report of the Committee of Ministers on the supervision of the execution of judgments and decisions of the Strasbourg Court notes that general measures are still awaited before *Al Nashif* and later similar cases can be closed: 7th Annual Report 2013, 101–103.

Yet another case law which would have deserved special treatment in this book is that related to trafficking and/or forced labour. For a long time, the only case which fell into this category was *Siliadin v. France*.[16] This changed with the *Rantsev v. Cyprus and Russia* judgment,[17] about trafficking. *Rantsev* would not have existed without the relentless efforts of the father of the victim, a young Russian woman who had been enrolled to work as an 'artist' in a cabaret in Cyprus and fell to her death from a balcony after possible sequestration by her employers. Mr Rantsev would not give up. He kept asking the authorities in both the country his daughter had left and the country to which she had gone to investigate her death. He instigated the necessary domestic judicial proceedings (funding them by selling his flat, as a result of which he lived in a car). He hand-wrote a long petition in Russian to Strasbourg. Miraculously the latter did not end up being summarily rejected as inadmissible. After the judgment was rendered, he put energy into publicising the Strasbourg verdict so that others could benefit from the denunciation of multiple breaches of the Convention relating to the problem of trafficking through the development of new jurisprudential lines.

It would also have been appropriate to reproduce in this book the results of research I conducted around *Mushkhadzhiyeva v. Belgium*, a case related to children's immigration detention.[18] My research highlighted the difficulties which irregular migrants' legal representatives encounter in bringing cases about even the most problematic treatment. In fact, one might venture to say that the more problematic the treatment, the more difficult it is to locate a victim who is well placed to complain about it and be at the centre of judicial proceedings. This is not the place to repeat the article I have published elsewhere on *Muskhadzhiyeva*'s 'backstage story'.[19] My plea for the Strasbourg Court to apply the rules governing admissibility with flexibility and to adopt wide-ranging judgments rather than rulings which focus on the narrow circumstances of the instant case[20] nonetheless remains entirely apposite, as the concluding chapter will stress.

Last but not least, *El-Masri v. 'the former Yugoslav Republic of Macedonia'* would have warranted special attention.[21] This was one of only two cases which the President of the Court mentioned in the speech he gave on the occasion of the

[16] *Siliadin v. France*, appl. 73316/01, Judgment (ECtHR), 26 July 2005.

[17] *Rantsev v. Cyprus and Russia*, appl. 25965/04, Judgment (ECtHR), 7 Jan. 2010. For an interesting review, see: Vladislava Stoyanova, 'Dancing on the Borders of Article 4: Human Trafficking and the European Court of Human Rights in the *Rantsev* Case' (2012) *Netherlands Quarterly of Human Rights* 30, 163–194.

[18] *Muskhadzhiyeva v. Belgium*, appl. 41442/07, Judgment (ECtHR), 19 Jan. 2010, in French only.

[19] Marie-Bénédicte Dembour, 'What it Takes to Make a Case: The Backstage Story of *Muskhadzhiyeva v. Belgium* (Illegality of Children's Immigration Detention)', in Elisabeth Lambert-Abdelgawad, *Preventing and Sanctioning Hindrances to the Right of Individual Petition to the European Court of Human Rights* (Brussels: Intersentia, 2011) 75–104.

[20] Dembour 76.

[21] *El-Masri v. 'the former Yugoslav Republic of Macedonia'*, appl. 39630/09, GC Judgment (ECtHR), 13 Dec. 2012.

opening of the judicial year 2013. This is how Judge Spielmann presented it: 'For the first time, the Court found against a State for taking part in an extraordinary rendition of prisoners to the CIA, putting an end to the impunity with which such operations had, for a long time, been carried out. Above all, our Court is the first in the world to have classified as torture the actions committed by the CIA in the context of such operations, even though it was the respondent State that was found responsible for the violation on account of the express or tacit approval of its authorities'.[22] *El-Masri* is generally regarded as being concerned with the fight against terrorism rather than about migration. Needless to say, the two issues often have repercussions on each other.[23]

[22] Judge Spielmann's speech is reproduced in the Court's '2013 Annual Report', <http://www.echr.coe.int/Documents/Annual_report_2013_ENG.pdf>, accessed 18 May 2014, pp. 25–30. The reference to *El-Masri* is at p. 28.

[23] See for another example the five cases involving extradition to the United States where no violation of Article 3 was found: *Babar Ahmad and Others v. the United Kingdom*, appls 24027/07, 11949/08, 36742/08, 66911/09, 67354/09, Judgment (ECtHR), 10 Apr. 2012.

11

Migrants, Not Criminals: The Continual Elaboration of Strong Human Rights Norms in the Inter-American System

(*Vélez Loor*)

The next case related to migration which the Inter-American Court of Human Rights decided after *Yean and Bosico* is *Vélez Loor v. Panama*.[1] At its heart lies the phenomenon of 'crimmigration', a term coined by Juliet Stumpf a decade ago in order to capture the way in which both the general public and state authorities increasingly think of irregular migrants as criminals and treat them as such.[2]

Mr Vélez Loor, an Ecuadorian national, was caught by the police in the Republic of Panama without a valid visa in November 2002. There followed a ten-month detention in terrible circumstances. Seeking redress through various means after being released and deported to his native country, Mr Vélez Loor eventually petitioned the Inter-American Commission on Human Rights in early 2004. Five years later, the Commission submitted his case to the Court, no doubt because it wanted to test the legal issues which arose from such a detention, without any due process, for a criminal offence related to migratory status. Mr Vélez Loor's own determination to pursue the case was motivated by his desire to seek redress for the conditions of detention to which he had been subjected, which he said had included acts of torture.

Anyone who, like me, attended the public hearing held by the Court in August 2010 perceived that something had gone seriously wrong in the ten-month detention which Mr Vélez Loor had endured in Panama. The state acknowledged this prior to the hearing and in its submissions to the Court. It recognised its responsibility for violations of the American Convention arising, on the one hand, from the governing legislation which provided for the automatic detention of illegal migrants who had been deported in the past and, on the other hand, from the

[1] *Vélez Loor v. Panama*, Preliminary Objections, Merits, Reparations and Costs, Judgment (IACtHR), 23 Nov. 2010.

[2] Juliet P. Stumpf, 'The Crimmigration Crisis: Immigrants, Crime, and Sovereign Power' (2006) *American University Law Review* 56, 367–419.

structural deficiencies in its national prison system. How far, however, would the Inter-American Court, under the leadership of a new president and with two recently elected judges, be ready to use the case to make a ruling with general implications about the very principle of immigration detention? This was the question on the lips of many people in San José at the end of the hearing. The short answer, at least from a European perspective, is far.

In its judgment of November 2010, the Inter-American Court established the principle that the American Convention prevents resorting to imprisonment as a means of punishing migration offences. Moreover, whilst immigration detention is not prohibited in all circumstances, exacting conditions must be met for it to be compatible with the American Convention. It must always be based on an examination of the individual circumstances of the migrant person, which means it can never be automatic. It must be subject to judicial supervision, and the individual concerned must have access to legal representation provided by a qualified lawyer (not an NGO, however specialised in the field) and be informed of the possibility of requesting consular assistance.

This is a far cry from the relaxed requirements which the European Court of Human Rights has found to apply to immigration detention. The leading case of the Strasbourg case law in this area is *Saadi v. the United Kingdom* (not to be confused with *Saadi v. Italy*), which was decided by a Grand Chamber in January 2008.[3] In this case, the European Court ruled that immigration detention could be used for administrative convenience, namely, helping the process of determining asylum claims by having the asylum seeker at hand for any interview. The contrast between *Saadi* and *Vélez Loor* could hardly be starker.

Dr Saadi was an asylum seeker from Iraq who had presented himself to the British authorities on arrival at Heathrow Airport. Admittedly his conditions of detention were very different from those experienced by Mr Vélez Loor. His detention lasted only seven days, i.e. the period of time deemed appropriate for allowing the 'fast-track' processing of asylum claims related to countries categorised as unlikely to produce refugees—the outcome of which is that these claims are almost always rejected; and the regime of detention was relatively relaxed. It was still detention, however. The three dissenting judges expressed their indignation at the majority's perspective by ending their dissenting opinion with the question: 'Is it a crime to be a foreigner?'

What this chapter does, then, is to contrast the *Vélez Loor* judgment with some selected cases from the abundant Strasbourg jurisprudence on immigration detention. It notes that the European Court of Human Rights verges towards adopting a reasoning which resembles that of the Inter-American Court when circumstances are particularly bad, for example when a five-year-old is separated at the airport from the adult accompanying her and detained with adults for four weeks.[4] Even then, however, the European Court refrains from making any broad

[3] *Saadi v. United Kingdom*, appl. 13229/03, GC Judgment (ECtHR), 29 Jan. 2008.

[4] *Mubilanzila Mayeka and Kaniki Mitunga [Tabitha] v. Belgium*, appl. 13178/03, Judgment (ECtHR), 12 Oct. 2006, para 58.

pronouncement about the requirements of human rights. The result is that judgment after judgment is required before it can be understood when a particular practice, for example the immigration detention of children, is or is not acceptable under the European Convention on Human Rights. By contrast, in the very few judgments it adopts, the Inter-American Court is keen to state what the law means and entails in a general way.

Having said this, the type of pronouncement which President Cançado-Trindade used to make is no longer seen and activists informally report finding it far more difficult to persuade the Inter-American Court both to adopt verdicts of violation and to set states exacting standards. For an external observer such as myself, there nonetheless remains a perception that the Inter-American Court conceives its role as encompassing the need to render explicit the standards which are contained within the law.

The first part of this chapter is devoted to the *Vélez Loor* case, including various aspects of the case's hearing, the general reasoning adopted by the Court, and its actual findings. This leads to a section which recapitulates the exacting conditions which the Court says must be met for immigration detention to be lawful under the American Convention. The approach adopted by the Strasbourg Court on immigration detention is then shown to be very different. In short, in the European system, immigration detention has been allowed to develop largely unchecked. The question is, from where does the contrast between the two systems arise? An answer is phrased in terms of text, context, judges, and judicial *habitus*. The latter aspect is expounded through a section which characterises the approach of the Inter-American Court as realist, humanist, and thorough. The next section observes that the European Court displays the same characteristics in cases when it reaches a 'tipping point', such as the case of the five-year-old referred to earlier. This, however, should not be taken to signal that the Strasbourg case law on children's detention is strong and principled, as the following section demonstrates. The chapter ends by returning to *Vélez Loor*. It explains that the judgment has not been a panacea for the victim and that the Court refrained from taking up the representatives' invitation to understand what had happened to Mr Vélez Loor by reference to a context of general discrimination against migrants.

I. Mr Vélez Loor has his Day in Court

The Commission submitted the *Vélez Loor* case to the Court as per the American Convention in October 2009.[5] It requested the Court to declare the state responsible for the violation of: Articles 5 (the right to humane treatment/personal integrity), Article 7 (the right to personal liberty), Article 8 (the right to a fair trial/judicial guarantees), and Article 25 (the right to judicial protection), in

[5] For the criteria under which the Commission now must refer a case to the Court, see: Laurence Burgorgue-Larsen and Amaya Úbeda de Torres, *The Inter-American Court of Human Rights: Case Law and Commentary* (Oxford: Oxford University Press, 2011) 36–37.

connection with the obligations established in Articles 1 (1) and 2 of the American Convention, as well as some provisions of the Inter-American Convention to Prevent and Punish Torture (hereafter, Convention against Torture) related to the duty to investigate allegations of torture. Mr Vélez Loor was represented by the Center for Justice and International Law (CEJIL) and three months later, CEJIL submitted its first brief in the case to the Court. It basically alleged the same violations as the Commission, with one notable difference: it submitted that Panama should be held responsible not only for having failed to *investigate* allegations of torture but also for actual *acts* of torture.[6]

The Court convened a hearing in the case at its seat for one and a half days on 25 and 26 August 2010.[7] When the news of the hearing came, four weeks prior to its taking place, CEJIL contacted its client who was now living in Bolivia with his new wife. Given his lack of papers, Mr Vélez Loor made his way up to his native country by bus in about two weeks. Once in Ecuador, he obtained a visa without difficulty which allowed him to fly to Costa Rica for the hearing. During this time, CEJIL was frantically preparing the case, and one assumes the same is true of Panama: in order to expedite cases relatively quickly, the Court imposes a tight time frame on the proceedings without being able, I am told, to plan its work much in advance.

As the alleged victim, Mr Vélez Loor was the first person to be heard on 25 August. It was clear as one was listening to him that what he wanted most was to denounce the ill-treatment he had suffered at the hands of the Panamanian authorities. The representative of the Commission first questioned him. She started by asking him to recount what had happened to him on 11 November 2002. He soon came to a crucial point of his story, quoted in the judgment:

> [F]rom the moment that I was detained... the police opened fire with rifles..., and they forced me to fall down on the floor; they closed in, stood on my arms, made me spread my arms in the form of a cross on the floor, stood on the palms of my open hands, and stripped me of my belongings. Later on, they took off my shoes and socks, put shackles on my arms and my feet, and forced me to walk barefoot... up to a small barracks of the village of Nueva Esperanza of the Province of Darién.... What they did afterward [was] hang me from a pole... from my right arm, where I remained for nearly eight hours.[8]

Mr Vélez Loor was taken to the nearby small town of Meteti by helicopter the next morning. He explained that he was made to lie down by the door of the helicopter, still handcuffed, and warned that things would get complicated for him if he complained about his treatment. It is not disputed that after a week he was

[6] On the role attributed to the individual in the proceedings before the Inter-American Court: Burgorgue-Larsen and Úbeda de Torres 40–47.

[7] These days, most hearings take place over one day, to the regret of observers who argue that gradually shortening them decreases the opportunities for the Inter-American Court to understand potentially crucial elements in the cases before it. The situation at Strasbourg is very different, with hearings now the exception rather than the rule and consisting almost exclusively of pleadings by the legal representatives of the parties.

[8] Quoted in *Vélez Loor* judgment, para 233.

transferred to La Palma detention centre for criminals. The conditions there were deplorable. Mr Vélez Loor explained to the Court that:

> [A]ll of the prisoners that were in a migratory situation [made the decision to] stage a peaceful strike, holding hands, [and] a ton of police arrived and began to drag us by the feet, and as we were caught, they began to beat us with clubs and sticks... and in that beating that they gave us, they broke my skull.[9]

At this stage, the Commission's representative interrupted to ask whether he had been informed of the charges against him and the possibility of contacting the Ecuadorian consulate.

At mid-morning, CEJIL carried on with the examination. Mr Vélez Loor was transferred to La Joyita prison on 18 December 2002. He was asked how he felt when he arrived. He responded: 'I felt that my life was over'. CEJIL asked whether he had refused medical attention. No, he said, he thought he was going to die in prison, without his family knowing where he was. He needed urgent medical assistance, he insisted. The fact that some of the state reports noted that he would have refused assistance was absurd. He reported having sewn his lips and gone on a hunger strike on 1 June 2003, which he said led to the most severe act of torture he had suffered:

> [The police] took me to the maximum security cellblock 12, walking, far from the other blocks... then a police officer... said: 'bring that guy over here; why have you sewn closed your mouth?' Well, I did not say anything because I had my mouth stitched closed; at that moment they began to spray gas in my face; I felt that I had to force open my lips; I ripped open my lips so that I could breath, and I bled everywhere, and from there they took off my clothes... left me naked and put cuffs... on my feet; [they laid me on the floor and] began to walk around in a circle, first hitting them [*sic*] with thick clubs over the soles of the feet, and then walking on the backs of the naked detainees while opening up bottles of teargas and pouring it on their naked bodies and spraying them with water... it was maddening; it was like fire on the skin. From there, they went around again, made [us] turn faceup [*sic*], and came walking on [our] bellies.... From there... they took me to a small room that they call '*la discoteca*'... [and] they continued spraying me with that powder... from there, they locked me up in a small cellblock... there they continued spraying me with gas [and] a police officer comes with taunts, laughing, and he tells me: 'ah, you want to have sex with me?' And laughing... he kicks me with his boots, then, there he inserts a powder in my anus with the eraser-end of a pencil, and he kicks me...[10]

Throughout most of this testimony, Mr Vélez Loor was looking at the state representatives, as if he was telling them: this is what you have done to me, and now you will pay for it. As he explained to me afterwards, the last thing he wanted was to appear like a broken victim. With his suit, his glasses, and his upright demeanour, he did not.[11] Some of us who were attending the hearing could not

[9] Quoted in *Vélez Loor*, para 233. [10] *Vélez Loor* judgment, para 233.

[11] For a photograph of him at the hearing, see CEJIL's press release of 26 February 2013, <http://cejil.org/comunicados/corte-idh-declara-incumplimiento-de-panama-en-sentencia-de-persona-migrante>, accessed 18 May 2014.

help wondering whether his defiant attitude might make the Court less inclined to rule in his favour.

The last thing CEJIL asked was how he thought the State of Panama could remedy the violations committed against him. Mr Vélez Loor responded that he hoped that the violations which had been committed against him would be recognised and measures adopted so that they would never happen again. Further, he wanted the crimes he suffered to be investigated and for the state to be ordered to publish the violations that it had committed against him. He explained to me later that evening that he wished for the judgment to receive worldwide publicity. He had in mind a film which would educate people, through his story, about the mechanisms of protection in the Inter-American human rights system. At that time, he felt very positive about the proceedings. He had had his day in court.

II. The Position of the State of Panama and the Rest of the Hearing

The defendant state had already acknowledged having infringed some provisions of the American Convention prior to the hearing. Panama recognised that deficiencies had affected the order of 6 December 2002 whereby, in an automatic application of Decree Law 16 of 1960, the Director of the National Migration Office had sentenced Mr Vélez Loor to a two-year prison term for having re-entered the country after having been warned against doing so in 1996.[12] The state had also accepted that the same December 2002 order had not complied with due guarantees in that Mr Vélez Loor had not been notified of the charges against him, had not been able to prepare any defence, and had not been notified of the order which had been taken against him.[13] Whilst rejecting all allegations of torture, the state had finally acknowledged that the detainee's right to integrity had been negatively affected by serious deficiencies in the national prison system relating to the provision of water supply, overcrowding, the systems for classifying prisoners, and the re-socialisation and education programmes.[14]

These acknowledgements were repeated at the public hearing and again in the state's final written arguments to the Court. In its ruling on the case, the Court stressed that it valued this 'partial acknowledgment by the State', which made 'a positive contribution to the development of [the instant] proceedings and to the exercise of the principles that inspire the American Convention'.[15] However, neither this acknowledgement nor Panama's efforts to remedy the situation by replacing the 1960 legislation with a new Decree Law in 2008 induced the Court to close the case.[16] As far as the Inter-American Court was concerned there remained a number of factual and principled issues in dispute which therefore required adjudication.[17]

[12] *Vélez Loor* judgment, para 94. [13] *Vélez Loor*, paras 58 and 60.

[14] *Vélez Loor*, para 197. [15] *Vélez Loor*, para 69.

[16] Things might well have proceeded differently in the European system. See Chapter 10 (pp. 322–326).

[17] These issues are listed in the *Vélez Loor* judgment, para 67. The state had also raised a number of preliminary objections and matters which need not detain us here. See *Vélez Loor* judgment, paras 13–56.

In this context, another strategy pursued by the Panamanian state was to paint Mr Vélez Loor as a not entirely innocent victim. Accordingly, its cross-examination of him was direct and confrontational. Mr Vélez Loor was first asked where he had entered Panama—his answer involved the Darién Province. He was then asked how many times he had been deported from Panama. He replied 'three times'—in September 1996, January 2002, and finally September 2003, the latter being when the contentious detention discussed before the Court was brought to an end. Next, Mr Vélez Loor was asked what he was doing in Panama when he was apprehended in November 2002. He responded that he had been 'in transit' to the United States. The state asked him about the likelihood of migrants choosing to cross the country through as impenetrable and high risk an area as the jungle of the Darién Province. Mr Vélez Loor's representatives raised an objection which was sustained by the President of the Court as the question did not relate to the object of Mr Vélez Loor's testimony.[18] Everyone nonetheless understood that Mr Vélez Loor's presence where he had been apprehended required an explanation which had not been provided. The state carried on with questions about remedies which would have been open to Mr Vélez Loor, the medical attention he had received, and the contacts he may have had with his consulate whilst in detention.

After Mr Vélez Loor, the next person to be heard was Mrs Maria Cristina Gonzáles Batista, the Director of the Migration and Naturalization Service of the Panamanian Minister of Home Affairs at the time of the hearing, a witness proposed by the state. Two experts followed: one for the Inter-American Commission, namely, Gabriela Rodríguez Pisarro who was the UN special rapporteur on the rights of migrants from 1999 to 2005, and the other for the alleged victim, Dr Marcelo Flores Torrico who had medically examined Mr Vélez Loor over five days in July 2008. The next morning, the Court listened to the arguments of the parties regarding the preliminary objections, the merits, and the reparations.

III. The Question Asked in Summer 2010: What will the New Court Decide?

CEJIL, which litigates the majority of the cases which come before the Inter-American Court, had issued a press release in August 2010 explaining that the *Vélez Loor* case represented an 'historical opportunity' for the Court to concretise the principles which its advisory opinion on the juridical condition and rights of undocumented migrants had established seven years earlier.[19] The organisation asked members of civil society, human rights organisations,

[18] As defined in the Resolution of the President of the Court dated 30 July 2010 in the case.

[19] <http://cejil.org/comunicados/caso-Vélez-loor-vs-panama-primer-caso-contencioso-sobre-inmigrantes-en-el-continente>, accessed 18 May 2014.

and academics to write to the President of the Court and to stress the unique opportunity which the case represented for a jurisprudence deepening the rights of migrant persons in Latin America.[20] This bizarre call from a seasoned participant in Inter-American proceedings remained without effect: I am told no one contacted the Court.[21] It nonetheless reflects the great trepidation which CEJIL felt as it awaited the ruling of the Court in its new formation—comprising two new judges and a newly elected president. Many people with whom I spoke in August 2010 feared that the Court might veer in a direction which would renege on its previous jurisprudence.

The questions Judge Franco asked Mr Vélez Loor after he had been re-examined by the state, about his identity document and his expired tourist visa, suggested state powers might be given more consideration by the Court than in the past. Judge Franco also said he 'wanted to understand' whether Mr Vélez Loor had anticipated that he might be arrested and detained and what he had thought might happen. Did Mr Vélez Loor want to stay and work in Panama? A few days later, another judge jokingly commented to me that one might perhaps say that Mr Vélez Loor's profession was to be an illegal migrant. This did not appear to me to augur well for a judgment building on Advisory opinion no. 18. In the event, however, the *Vélez Loor* judgment further entrenched the rights of undocumented migrants. CEJIL recognised this by qualifying the decision as 'historic'.[22]

IV. The Beginnings of a San José Reversal? The Inter-American Court Grapples with the Same Tension as the Strasbourg Court

The part of the *Vélez Loor* judgment which deals with the merits of the case starts with four paragraphs which explain the Court's reasoning in general terms. These are reproduced immediately below, with the numerous references the Court provides for its pronouncements nonetheless omitted, except for a short mention when they consist in case law previously reviewed in this book (for obvious reasons) or in international documents (as they signal the Court's determination to adopt a broad interpretation of human rights law, as noted in Chapter 9). To quote:

> 97. This Tribunal has already stated that, in exercise of its power to adopt migratory policies [Advisory opinion no. 18], States may establish mechanisms to control the entry into and departure from their territory of individuals who are not nationals, as long as they are compatible with the norms of human rights protection established in the American

[20] <http://cejil.org/comunicados/caso-Vélez-loor-vs-panama-primer-caso-contencioso-sobre-inmigrantes-en-el-continente>.

[21] Pablo Saavedra, personal communication.

[22] <http://cejil.org/categoria/pais/panamá>, accessed 18 May 2014.

Convention [see the '*Haitians*' matter]. Also, even though States enjoy a margin of discretion when adopting their migratory policies, the goals of such policies should take into account respect for the human rights of migrants [Advisory opinion no. 18; UN Special Rapporteur].

98. In this respect, the Court has established that from the general obligations to respect and guarantee rights, derive special duties, which can be ascertained based on the particular needs of protection of the legal person, considering the personal condition or the specific situation of the person. In this respect, migrants who are undocumented or in an irregular situation have been identified as a group in a vulnerable situation [UN General Assembly, cited in Advisory opinion no. 18] given that 'they are the most vulnerable to potential or actual violations of their human rights' [UN Special Rapporteur] and they suffer from, as consequence of their situation, a lack of protection of their rights at a high level and 'differences in their access... to the public resources administered by the State [in relation to nationals or residents]' [Advisory opinion no. 18]. Evidently, this situation of vulnerability has 'an ideological dimension and occurs in a historical context that is distinct for each State and is maintained by *de jure* (inequalities between nationals and aliens in the laws) and *de facto* (structural inequalities) situations' [Advisory opinion no. 18]. Moreover, cultural prejudices about migrants lead to reproduction of the situation of vulnerability, which make it difficult for migrants to integrate into society [Advisory opinion no. 18]. Finally, it is worth mentioning that the human rights violations committed against migrants many times go unpunished due to, *inter alia*, the set of cultural elements which justify it, the lack of access to power structures in a given society and the legal and factual impediments which make the effective access to justice illusory [UN Special Rapporteur].

99. Pursuant to the principle of effectiveness and the need of protection in those cases of people or groups in situation of vulnerability, this Tribunal shall interpret and give essence to the rights enshrined in the Convention, according to the evolution of the international *corpus juris* existing in relation to the human rights of migrants, taking into account that the international community has recognized the need to adopt special measures to ensure the protection of the human rights of this group [Advisory opinion no. 18; UN World Summit; UN International Conference; UN General Assembly].

100. This does not mean that [states] cannot take any action against migrants who do not comply with the State legal system. However, it is important that, when taking the corresponding measures, States should respect human rights and ensure their exercise and enjoyment to all persons who are in their territory, without any discrimination owing to their regular or irregular residence, or their nationality, race, gender, or any other reason. [Advisory opinion no. 18] Likewise, the evolution of this aspect of international law has placed certain limits on the application of migratory policies that must always be applied with strict regard for the guarantees of due process and respect for human dignity, [Advisory opinion no. 18; African Commission of Human Rights and Peoples] whatever the legal situation of the migrant may be.

Paragraph 97 is formulated à la Strasbourg: it mentions first the power of states to control migrants and human rights only afterwards. This is most likely a sign that the Inter-American Court in *Vélez Loor* was no longer as open to the rights of migrants as it had been in Advisory opinion no. 18. The paragraphs which follow nonetheless seem to annul the negative effect of this reversal in reasoning. Paragraph 98 identifies undocumented migrants as persons who are in a vulnerable situation as such (without requiring any other circumstance, such as being an asylum seeker).[23] Paragraph 99 explains that this will have consequences for the Court's interpretation of the rights enshrined in the American Convention. Paragraph 100 seems to reverse the initial reversal by putting the human rights guarantees due to migrants *before* the right of states to pursue migratory policies. So, in this reasoning, is the Inter-American Court stressing or limiting states' human rights obligations?

In order to consider this question, it is worth noting that there is nothing which prevents a reversal à la Strasbourg and a human rights reasoning à la President Cançado-Trindade from ending up at the same middle point.[24] These two perspectives nonetheless represent two different ways of approaching a tension which involves the poles of state control on the one hand and human rights on the other, neither of which can completely disappear from consideration as long as the tension remains. Moreover, each of the two perspectives entails a default position which is likely to attribute more weight to one pole than the other. Admittedly this is not a given, so that the actual way in which the tension is managed in practice is always an empirical question. The details of what the Inter-American Court said in the *Vélez Loor* case therefore need to be reviewed before a conclusion can be reached as to how the Inter-American Court resolved the tension between state control and human rights in this particular case.

V. *Vélez Loor*'s Findings: Immigration Detention Subjected to Safeguard after Safeguard

A lengthy point-by-point analysis of the various defects which marred Mr Vélez Loor's ten-month detention follows the general reasoning which the Court had provided.

The first act analysed by the Court is Mr Vélez Loor's initial arrest on 11 November 2002. This arrest had been effected by the police as there was no specific immigration authority in the (inhospitable) area in question. The Court observes that 'the measures restricting the personal liberty applied to Mr Vélez Loor were not related to the commission of a criminal crime, but responded to an irregular migration status'.[25] Article 7 (5) of the American Convention provides that: 'Any person detained shall be brought promptly before a judge or other officer authorized by law to exercise judicial power and shall be entitled to trial within a reasonable time or to be released…'. The Court notes that contrary to the European Convention, the American

[23] Compare with *M.S.S. v. Belgium and Greece*, appl. 30696/09, GC Judgment (ECtHR), 21 Jan. 2011.

[24] See also Thomas Spijkerboer, 'A Distributive Approach to Migration Law: Or the Convergence of Communitarianism, Libertarianism, and the Status Quo', in Roland Pierik and Wouter Werner (eds) *Cosmopolitanism in Context: Perspectives from International Law and Political Theory* (Cambridge: Cambridge University Press, 2010) 249–274, especially at 269–270.

[25] *Vélez Loor* judgment, para 106.

Convention does not provide for any circumstance where this guarantee would be limited.[26] Therefore, under the American Convention, all detention is subject to judicial control. Such control must be prompt and carried out 'in such a way as to guarantee compliance with the law and the detainee's effective enjoyment of his rights, taking into account his special vulnerability'.[27] The judicial officer who undertakes the control must fulfil requirements of impartiality and independence. The Court stresses that this must include 'the authority to order the release of the person if his or her detention is illegal or arbitrary'.[28] In the instant case, Mr Vélez Loor had been put 'at the disposal of the Office of Immigration and Naturalization' under Decree Law 16 of 1960. The Court understands this to mean that there was no requirement that the detained person be heard by the competent authority which, per force, was not in a position to evaluate the explanations provided by that person.[29] In an interesting phrasing which indicates that a high burden of proof falls on the state, the Court concludes: '[T] he State has not provided sufficient elements that demonstrate that it has complied with the terms established in Article 7 (5) of the Convention'.[30]

Next, the Court examines the arrest warrant of 12 November 2002, which had ordered Mr Vélez Loor's arrest 'for having entered the country illegally and for reasons of security and public order in order to apply to him any of the measures established in Decree Law no. 16 of 1960'.[31] The Court states that an arrest, even when made for security and public order reasons, must comply with all the guarantees laid down in Article 7 of the Convention. In particular, the reason why the detaining measure is necessary must be objectively substantiated; it cannot consist of a mere listing of applicable norms.[32] Also, the measure must indicate how long it will last, as the absence of a temporal limit 'favors the undue duration of the detention of immigrants, thus becoming a punitive measure'.[33] In the instant case, the arrest warrant did not provide a term of duration. It also appears to have been 'automatically issued after the initial arrest, without consideration of the particular circumstances'.[34] This leads the Court to consider it 'arbitrary'.[35] There is therefore a violation of Article 7 (3) of the Convention, which provides: 'No one shall be subject to arbitrary arrest or imprisonment'.

The Court then examines whether Mr Vélez Loor had effective remedies available to him in order to challenge the lawfulness of his detention. As we have seen, Article 7 (5) accepts that any officer with judicial authority can review the legality of the detention in the period immediately following the arrest. After this initial period, the detainee must have 'recourse to a competent court', as per Article 7 (6). The State of Panama had argued that a range of remedies had been available to Mr Vélez Loor.[36] The Inter-American

[26] *Vélez Loor*, para 107.
[27] *Vélez Loor*, para 107.
[28] *Vélez Loor*, para 107.
[29] *Vélez Loor*, para 109.
[30] *Vélez Loor*, para 111.
[31] *Vélez Loor*, para 114.
[32] *Vélez Loor*, para 116.
[33] *Vélez Loor*, para 117.
[34] *Vélez Loor*, para 118.
[35] *Vélez Loor*, para 118.

Court finds these to have been unsatisfactory. On the one hand, actual judges were not involved in the remedies provided through governmental channels, such as the Director of the National Migration Office and the Ministry of Interior.[37] On the other hand, the judicial remedy of *habeas corpus*, although satisfactory from this perspective, also breached the requirements of Article 7 (6) because it was not effective in practice.[38] In a case like this one which involves 'an alien who may not know the legal system of the country and who is in a particularly vulnerable situation given the deprivation of liberty', the Inter-American Court states that it is incumbent upon the recipient state to 'take into account the particular characteristics of the persons [*sic*] situation, in order for said person to have effective access to justice in equal terms'.[39] In particular, legal aid needs to be provided by a legal professional in order to satisfy the requirements of a procedural representation.[40] The Court specifies that 'the assistance that non-governmental organizations might exercise does not substitute for the State's obligation to offer free legal counsel'.[41] According to the Panamanian state, legal counsel could have been provided to Mr Vélez Loor free of charge and a number of remedies were open to him.[42] The Court finds this point not to have been sufficiently substantiated. In its words, 'the State has not proven how, in the specific circumstances in which Mr. Vélez Loor was imprisoned at La Palma Public Prison in Darién, these remedies were effective, taking into account the fact that he was an arrested alien who did not have legal counsel and without knowledge on the persons or organizations that could provide legal assistance'.[43] The way in which the Inter-American Court lays the burden of proof on the defendant state to show not only the existence of remedies in its legal system but also their concrete effectiveness is yet again striking: 'the existence alone of recourses is not sufficient without proof [by the state] of their effectiveness'.[44] The Court finds a violation of Article 7 (6).

The Court then turns to the proceedings before the National Office of Immigration and Naturalization which led to the issue, on 6 December 2002, of the order which sentenced Mr Vélez Loor to imprisonment. The compatibility of these proceedings with Article 8 of the Convention, on fair trial, is examined. The Court starts by recalling how it said in Advisory opinion no. 18 that 'the right to due process of law must be recognized as one of the minimum guarantees that should be offered to any migrant, irrespective of his migratory status'.[45] It now adds: 'This implies that the State must ensure every foreign person, even when said person is a migrant in an irregular situation, may exercise his or her rights and defend his or her interests effectively and in full procedural equality with other triable [*sic*] individuals'.[46] Referring to one of its previous decisions in a non-migrant

[36] *Vélez Loor*, para 121.
[37] *Vélez Loor*, para 127.
[38] *Vélez Loor*, para 129.
[39] *Vélez Loor*, para 132.
[40] *Vélez Loor*, para 132.
[41] *Vélez Loor*, para 137.
[42] *Vélez Loor*, para 131.
[43] *Vélez Loor*, para 139.
[44] *Vélez Loor*, para 139.
[45] *Vélez Loor*, para 143.

case, it recalls having 'sustained that the right to defense [*sic*] binds the State to treat the person, at all times, as a true party to the proceeding, in the broadest sense of this concept and not simply as an object thereof'.[47] Again citing Advisory opinion no. 18, the Court also recalls having 'considered that, in the administrative or judicial instances, where decisions may be taken by which an accused may be deported, expelled, or deprived of freedom, the provision of free public legal aid service is necessary to avoid the violation of the right to due process'.[48] The Court observes that Mr Vélez Loor had not been provided with the right to defence before the administrative instance which had applied a penalty of deprivation of liberty in December 2002, inevitably affecting all subsequent stages of the proceedings. Because of this, a violation of Article 8 of the American Convention occurred.[49]

Further violations of Articles 7 and 8 arise from the fact that the state has not proven it had complied with its obligation to notify Mr Vélez Loor of his right to seek consular assistance in order to assist his defence.[50] It was not disputed that at one stage the Ecuadorian consulate had been informed that Mr Vélez Loor was in custody. There was, however, a controversy regarding the date on which the consulate had been notified.[51] Moreover, Mr Vélez Loor said at the public hearing that he had never been aware whilst in detention that the consulate had been making representations on his behalf (eventually leading to his release and deportation in September 2003).[52] The state had provided no evidence that Mr Vélez Loor had either been informed of his right to communicate with the consulate of his country or put in a position to exercise his right to defence with consular assistance.[53]

The next point analysed by the Court concerns 'the power of States to impose a punitive penalty for the non-compliance with immigration laws, like the sanction of two years [*sic*] contemplated in... Decree Law 16 of 1960'.[54] The Court lays down a four-point test in order to assess whether a measure restricting liberty is not arbitrary and thus compatible with Article 7 (3) of the Convention: (a) the purpose of resorting to this measure must be compatible with the Convention; (b) this purpose must be achievable through the measure in question; (c) this measure must be necessary in order to achieve this purpose; and (d) it must also be strictly proportionate, meaning that 'the sacrifice inherent in the restriction of the right to liberty is not exaggerated or excessive compared to the advantages obtained from this restriction and the achievement of the purpose sought'.[55] The Court notes that it established earlier in the judgment that states have the authority to control and regulate the entrance and stay of foreign persons in their territory, so that it is possible that punitive custodial measures for the control of migratory flows are pursuing a lawful purpose under the American Convention.[56]

[46] *Vélez Loor*, para 143. [47] *Vélez Loor*, para 145.
[48] *Vélez Loor*, para 146, referring to AO 18, para 126.
[49] *Vélez Loor*, paras 147 and 148. [50] *Vélez Loor*, paras 149–160.
[51] *Vélez Loor*, para 156, [52] *Vélez Loor*, para 156. [53] *Vélez Loor*, para 160.
[54] *Vélez Loor*, para 163 (reference omitted).
[55] *Vélez Loor*, para 166 (reference omitted).

In the present case, however, taking into account the views of the UN Working Group on Arbitrary Detention and of the UN rapporteur on the human rights of migrants, the Court considers that 'the objective of imposing a punitive measure upon a migrant that reenters [*sic*] in an irregular manner to a country after a previous deportation order cannot be considered a lawful purpose in conformity with the Convention'.[57] Also, the measure was not needed. It is worth quoting the Court at some length on this point:

> [T]he detention of people for non-compliance with immigration laws should never involve punitive purposes. Hence, a custodial measure should only be applied when it is necessary and proportionate in the specific case [in order to protect fundamental legal rights from serious attacks that may impair or endanger them] and only for the shortest period of time. Therefore, it is essential for States to seek alternatives to detention whenever possible, which may be effective for the achievement of the purposes described. As a consequence, those migratory policies whose central focus is the mandatory detention of irregular migrants, without ordering the competent authorities to verify in each particular case and by means of an individualized evaluation, the possibility of using less restrictive measures of achieving the same ends, are arbitrary.[58]

The lack of notification of the order of 6 November 2002 is next considered by the Court. Whilst the state had acknowledged its responsibility in this regard, the Court notes that the lack of notification placed Mr Vélez Loor in a situation of uncertainty and made it unfeasible for him to exercise his right to appeal.[59] There is therefore also a violation of Article 8 (2) (h) of the Convention, which provides for 'the right to appeal the judgment [on any criminal, civil, or other matter] to a higher court'.[60]

The last element of the proceedings related to the arrest and detention of Mr Vélez Loor is his place of incarceration. According to the textual terms of the domestic legislation of 1960 which was applied to Mr Vélez Loor, as a migrant punished for an immigration offence Mr Vélez Loor should have been placed in the Penal Colony of Coiba. Since the adoption of this legislation, however, Coiba Island had been transformed into a tourist and ecological resort. As a result, Mr Vélez Loor had been placed in one of the country's penitentiary centres. The Supreme Court of Justice of Panama had condoned this practice in 2002 (in relation to another case).[61] For the Inter-American Court, such an extensive interpretation of criminal law had the effect of creating a heavier sanction than stipulated in Decree Law 16 of 1960. As such, it breached the principle of non-retroactivity of penal law inscribed in Article 9 of the American Convention.[62]

The place of Mr Vélez Loor's incarceration also raised the more general question of whether it is ever permissible for a state to detain persons deprived of their liberty because of their irregular immigration status with prisoners who have committed crimes or who are in custody pending criminal trial.[63] The Court

[56] *Vélez Loor*, para 169. [57] *Vélez Loor*, para 169.
[58] *Vélez Loor*, para 171 (references omitted). [59] *Vélez Loor*, para 180.
[60] *Vélez Loor*, para 181. [61] *Vélez Loor*, para 186.
[62] *Vélez Loor*, paras 187 and 188.

answers this question in the negative. Referring again to the 'particular vulnerable situation of migrants', which is 'even more critical when... migrants are held in penitentiary centers', it reasons that 'the State must abstain from acting in a way that favors, promotes, fosters, or deepens that vulnerability'.[64] It rules:

> Therefore, in the case their detention is necessary and proportionate, migrants must be held in facilities specifically destined for that purpose, according to their legal situation and not in common prisons... This principle of separation... attends to the distinct purposes of deprivations of liberty. Certainly, when dealing with convicted persons, the imprisonment conditions must tend to the 'essential aim' of the custodial measures that is the 'reform and social re-adaptation of the prisoners'. In cases of migrants, detention and imprisonment of persons solely for their irregular status should only be used as necessary and proportionately in the concrete case, only admissible for the shortest possible period of time and according to the legal purposes mentioned.[65]

Even though this was not at issue here, the Court specifies that such deprivation of liberty should avoid 'as far as possible, the disintegration of the family group' and be positively organised by the state in such a way that it 'does not entail a higher risk to the infringement of the rights, the integrity, and personal and family welfare of migrants'.[66] For the Inter-American Court, the fact that Mr Vélez Loor had been detained with people awaiting criminal trial and/or serving time for the commission of a crime entails in itself a violation of Article 5(1) and 5(2) of the American Convention, which respectively read: 'Every person has the right to have his physical, mental, and moral integrity respected' and 'No one shall be subjected to torture or to cruel, inhuman, or degrading punishment or treatment. All persons deprived of their liberty shall be treated with respect for the inherent dignity of the human person'.

The other complaints raised by Mr Vélez Loor all related to (lack of) humane treatment. Although some violations had been acknowledged by the state, controversies remained between the parties. One concerned the source of the problems in the supply of drinking water, which the state attributed to a poor infrastructure but the applicant to a deliberate practice instigated as a means of punishing prisoners. The Court refrained from deciding this question for lack of 'sufficient elements'.[67] Another controversy related to the level of medical care which Mr Vélez Loor had received in detention. The Court considered it proven that Mr Vélez Loor's apparent cranial fracture had been left untreated, which could have had a long-term negative effect on his health and which was 'contrary to the dignified treatment due'.[68] As for the allegations of torture brought by Mr Vélez Loor, the Court found that his representatives had not sufficiently proven the accusations of police abuse in order to allow the Court to deliberate on whether torture had occurred.[69] By contrast, the Court had no difficulty finding a violation of both the American Convention and the Convention against Torture for the state failure to

[63] *Vélez Loor*, para 206. [64] *Vélez Loor*, para 207.

[65] *Vélez Loor*, para 208, references omitted, inverted commas in the original.

[66] *Vélez Loor*, para 209. [67] *Vélez Loor*, para 217. [68] *Vélez Loor*, para 222.

[69] *Vélez Loor*, para 226. The Commission had not brought this allegation before the Court.

investigate the torture allegations which Mr Vélez Loor had brought to the attention of the Panamanian government soon after he was deported to Ecuador.[70]

The Court ordered a range of reparations, including payment for specialist medical and psychological treatment and care, publication of the judgment in different outlets, instigation of a criminal investigation in respect of Mr Vélez Loor's allegations, the establishment of proper immigration detention facilities, human rights training for officials dealing with migrants, and training related to the investigation of allegations of torture.[71]

VI. Recapitulation: Immigration Detention under the American Convention

Vélez Loor will mostly be remembered for the safeguards which the Inter-American Court identified as having to be in place when state authorities resort to immigration detention. Recapping, these safeguards are:

(a) the state can never use detention as a punitive measure for an immigration offence;

(b) alternatives to immigration detention must be sought. Given the inherent 'sacrifice' detention entails for the right to liberty and the requirement that its disadvantages remain strictly proportionate to its advantages, these alternatives must be used whenever possible. Detention can never become routine;

(c) any immigrant who is arrested and detained must be promptly brought before an officer authorised by law to exercise judicial power; this officer must hear the detainee and motivate the detention by reference to her particular circumstances;

(d) judicial remedies must subsequently be available to the detained migrant. These remedies must involve judges. They cannot just exist in the abstract but must be readily accessible in practice by any immigration detainee;

(e) the immigration detainee must be put in a position to exercise her right to defence. This necessarily entails that she is offered free legal representation by a qualified lawyer. Assistance by organisations which defend the rights of migrants is not sufficient;

(f) the immigrant detainee must be informed of her right to possible consular assistance;

(g) immigration detainees cannot be placed in a prison which hosts criminals and/or people on remand;

(h) special attention must be given to the position of families.

[70] *Vélez Loor*, paras 234–245.

[71] *Vélez Loor*, operative part of the judgment, paras 11–18.

VIII. A World Apart: The Strasbourg Court's Approach to Immigration Detention

The Strasbourg case law on immigration detention is voluminous. Decisions of inadmissibility and verdicts of non-violation go back to the early years of the European Commission of Human Rights. I do not propose to trace this history here.[72] Instead this section reviews four cases, including the two which are recognised to be leading in this area: *Chahal v. the United Kingdom*[73] and *Saadi v. the United Kingdom*. Another is *Kabongo v. Belgium*,[74] a decision of inadmissibility in a case, the circumstances of which are in some ways similar to those of *Vélez Loor*. The last, *Gebremedhin v. France*,[75] is rarely discussed in terms of immigration detention, no doubt because the Court concluded, without much discussion, that the applicant's detention had not violated the Convention. Together, these four cases, to which could be added many others, amply demonstrate that the European Court of Human Rights does not consider immigration detention to be, in principle, a problematic practice under the European Convention.

Chahal v. the United Kingdom has already been discussed in Chapter 7. Decided in November 1996 by a Grand Chamber, the case concerned the detention and deportation of a Sikh man suspected of involvement in a conspiracy to assassinate the Indian Prime Minister. As we have seen, the Court found that his deportation would violate Article 3 ECHR, and that he had had no domestic remedies in respect of this complaint. But the applicant had also complained that his detention had entailed a violation of Article 5(1) ECHR, which guarantees 'the right to liberty and security of person'. Article 5(1) provides that 'No one shall be deprived of his liberty save in [six enumerated] cases and in accordance with a procedure prescribed by law'. The sixth exception, '(f)', relates to immigration matters. It has two limbs relating respectively to entry and removal. *Chahal* is the leading case on the latter, i.e. to quote part of Article 5(1)(f), 'the lawful arrest or detention...of a person against whom action is being taken with a view to deportation or extradition'.

The first applicant in *Chahal* argued that his detention pending deportation had been of an excessive duration, thus ceasing to be 'lawful' and violating the Convention. Puzzlingly, the Court considered the relevant period of detention to be three and a half years rather than the six years the applicant had spent in prison up to the time of the judgment.[76] In the Court's view, this period was not excessive given the exceptional circumstances of the case: various levels of decisions regarding the asylum claim of

[72] For a brief history of this case law, see: Daniel Wilsher, *Immigration Detention: Law, History, Politics* (Cambridge: Cambridge University Press, 2012) 141–143.

[73] *Chahal v. the United Kingdom*, appl. 22414, GC Judgment (ECtHR), 15 Nov. 1996.

[74] *Ntumba Kabongo v. Belgium*, appl. 52467/00, Decision (ECtHR), 2 June 2005.

[75] *Gebremedhin [Gaberamadhien] v. France*, appl. 25389/05, Judgment (ECtHR), 26 Apr. 2007.

[76] As also noted by Wilsher *Immigration Detention* 241, n. 25.

an individual considered to be a national security risk. By 13 votes to six, the Grand Chamber concluded that Article 5(1)(f) had not been violated. In its reasoning, the Court stated:

> Article 5 para. 1 (f)...does not demand that the detention of a person against whom action is being taken with a view to deportation be reasonably considered necessary, for example to prevent his committing an offence or fleeing...
>
> [A]ll that is required under this provision...is that 'action is being taken with a view to deportation'.[77]

As Galina Cornelisse has remarked, it would have been difficult for Article 5(1)(f) to be interpreted in a way which would have given the state any more discretion.[78] This large discretion resulted from the Court not subjecting immigration detention to a necessity test, so that the state need not show that deportation would not be achievable without the prospective deportee being detained.[79] Other exceptions to the right to personal liberty inscribed in Article 5 are subject to a necessity test. For example, 'persons of unsound mind', 'alcoholics', and 'vagrants' cannot be detained just because they are of unsound mind, are alcoholics, or vagrants; they must present a threat to themselves or others for their detention to be lawful under Article 5(1)(e). In this respect, the Court has ruled that detention is 'only justified when other, less severe measures have been considered and found to be insufficient to [achieve] the public or individual interest which might require that the person concerned should be detained'.[80] By contrast, as long as a state has started deportation proceedings against a foreign national, under *Chahal* it is acceptable for that person to be detained. In this context, the fact that the Court unanimously found a violation of Article 5(4) in *Chahal* is meagre consolation. Article 5(4) provides: 'Everyone who is deprived of his liberty by arrest or detention shall be entitled to take proceedings by which the lawfulness of his detention shall be decided speedily by a court and his release ordered if the detention is not lawful'. Given the absence of a necessity test, a judge would have no reason to find the detention of a person to be deported unlawful under the Convention (as long as there is a real prospect that the deportation is being pursued and will take place).

Most commentators would carry on this account by jumping to *Saadi v. the United Kingdom*, which is the case where the Court, again sitting as a Grand Chamber, extended its conclusion regarding the lack of a necessity test in immigration matters to the first limb of Article 5(1)(f) which concerns the 'detention of a person in order to prevent his effecting an unauthorised entry into the country'. *Saadi*, decided in January 2008, is often presented, including by the Court itself, as 'the first case in which the Court [was] called upon to provide an interpretation

[77] *Chahal* judgment, para 112.

[78] Galina Cornelisse, *Immigration Detention and Human Rights: Rethinking Territorial Sovereignty* (The Hague: Martinus Nijhoff, 2010) 295.

[79] As noted by Cornelisse 292; Wilsher *Immigration Detention* 148.

[80] See e.g. *Witold Litwa v. Poland*, Judgment (ECtHR), para 78, quoted in Cornelisse 306

of [this provision]'.[81] Such a presentation, however, ignores previous cases upon which the Court chose not to rule or not to find a violation of Article 5(1)(f). One example is *Ntumba Kabongo v. Belgium*, which was ruled inadmissible by a Chamber in June 2005.

The applicant was a Congolese woman who, like Mr Vélez Loor, had been detained for ten months for lack of proper documentation—in her case, from February to December 1999. Her conditions of detention were nowhere near as awful as those experienced by Mr Vélez Loor in Panama three years later. Another distinguishing factor is that she was repeatedly offered the opportunity to leave her country of detention. In fact this became part of her complaint to Strasbourg. She had been taken a number of times to Brussels Airport. Each time, she refused to board the flight which the authorities had booked for her. The Belgian state explained to the Strasbourg Court that it had been unable to proceed with her forceful embarkation because of the level of protest, including by the airline pilots, against this practice which the death of a failed asylum seeker during a deportation attempt had generated in Belgium. So, every time, the applicant, also a failed asylum seeker, was taken back to detention. At each return to detention, the authorities restarted the calculation of her detained period, which thus was not treated as a prolongation of the previous period. The applicant argued at Strasbourg that this constituted arbitrary imprisonment, without a legal basis and for an unlimited period, contrary to Articles 3, 5(1), 5(4), 13, and 14 ECHR. For the Belgian authorities, it was her refusal to embark which had caused the contentious detention. By an undisclosed majority, the Chamber to which her case was assigned declared all the applicant's complaints inadmissible.[82] An opportunity for the European Court to examine and keep in check the growing practice by European states of detaining migrants for longer and longer periods, without strong legal guarantees, was lost. There was no reference to the inherent vulnerability of asylum seekers, let alone foreigners, in the decision.

We can turn to *Gebremedhin v. France* for another judgment confirming the lack of interest shown by the Court for strengthening the guarantees against deprivation of liberty in migrant cases. This case was lodged by an Eritrean journalist who would have wished, but did not manage, to apply for asylum immediately upon his arrival in France. The Court found a violation of Article 13 of the European Convention taken in conjunction with Article 3 (see Chapter 12 for an analysis of this aspect of the case). The applicant had also complained of a violation of the admission limb of Article 5(1)(f). Without any authorisation to enter France, the applicant was held in the waiting zone of Paris Charles de Gaulle Airport for at least 20 days, as recognised by the government, and possibly for an

[81] Joint partly dissenting opinion of Judges Rozakis, Tulkens, Kovler, Hajiyev, Spielmann and Hirvelä in *Saadi* judgment, opening paragraph; see also *Saadi*, para 58; PACE Report on 'The Detention of Asylum Seekers and Irregular Migrants in Europe' Doc. 12105 dated 11 January 2010, para 18, available at <http://assembly.coe.int/Documents/WorkingDocs/Doc10/EDOC12105.pdf>, accessed 6 July 2012.

[82] The Chamber was composed of Judges Rozakis, Loucaides, Tulkens, Lorenzen, Vajić, Spielmann, and Jebens.

additional two days, as submitted by the applicant. The French legislation allowed immigration detention in the airport's waiting zone for a maximum period of 20 days. The Court noted that the applicant had not produced 'any prima facie evidence to support his assertion that he [had] arrived...on 29 June 2005', whilst the government had 'stated [having] checked the passenger lists for [relevant flights and having found] no trace of a passenger by the [applicant's] name'.[83] Without requesting the state to produce the list of passengers of the flight which the applicant would *actually* have taken, the European Court concluded 'as the Government' that 'the only reliable document [was] the report drawn up by the airport and border police on 1 July stating that the applicant was questioned at 11 a.m. that day'.[84] The Strasbourg Court was thus satisfied that the maximum period of 20 days laid down in domestic law had not been exceeded.[85] Other arguments submitted by the applicant were equally dismissed. One was to the effect that the granting on 15 July 2005 by Strasbourg of a Rule 39 request against the applicant's removal to Eritrea had rendered his continued detention unlawful: the Court accepted the government's argument that he might have been sent to a country other than Eritrea; furthermore, the Court saw 'no reason to doubt the government's good faith in stating that the authorities had to conduct checks as to his identity before granting him leave to enter the country'.[86] According to the Court, 'the length of time for which the applicant was held in the waiting zone for that purpose did not exceed what was reasonable in the circumstances of the case'.[87] The Court unanimously ruled that there were 'no grounds for considering that...the applicant [had been] arbitrarily deprived of his liberty'.[88]

Saadi v. the United Kingdom has become the leading case on the first limb of Article 5(1)(f). This is the case where a Grand Chamber finally held a full discussion on the meaning to be attributed to the words 'detention of a person to prevent his effecting an unauthorised entry into the country'. The applicant was an Iraqi doctor who had fled the Kurdish Autonomous Region of Iraq in December 2000 after having treated and facilitated the escape of three fellow members of the Iraqi Workers' Communist Party who had been injured in an attack.[89] He had arrived at Heathrow Airport on 30 December 2000 and immediately claimed asylum. He was granted 'temporary admission' to stay at a hotel of his choice and was requested to return to the airport the following morning, which he did. On 31 December, he was granted yet another temporary admission of one day under the same conditions. The same thing happened on 1 January 2001.[90] When he reported to the airport for the third time, on 2 January 2001, he was detained and transferred to Oakington Reception Centre, established in order to expedite the asylum claims process which is expected to take no more than seven days.[91] There Dr Saadi was detained for seven days. He was refused asylum on 8 January. The next day, he was released and granted temporary admission pending the determination of the

[83] *Gebremedhin* judgment, para 70. [84] *Gebremedhin*, para 70.
[85] *Gebremedhin*, para 70. [86] *Gebremedhin*, para 75. [87] *Gebremedhin*, para 75.
[88] *Gebremedhin*, para 75. [89] *Saadi v. the United Kingdom*, GC, para 10.
[90] *Saadi*, para 10. [91] *Saadi*, para 11.

appeal he had lodged. Two years later, his appeal was allowed and he was granted asylum.[92] His legal representatives and two third party interventions—one from the AIRE Centre, the European Council on Refugees and Exile, and Liberty (jointly), the other from the UNHCR—argued that his detention had violated Article 5(1) ECHR. Given the wording of Article 5, the only possible way of finding that his detention had not violated the Convention was to find that it was covered by the first limb of the exception provided in Article 5(1)(f). The central question in the case therefore became the following: had Dr Saadi been detained in order to prevent him from effecting unauthorised entry to the UK?

This appeared doubtful since prior to his detention he had been authorised to enter the UK on the condition that he reported to the authorities the next day, which he had done for three days in a row. By four votes to three, the Chamber which decided the case in July 2006 nonetheless ruled that Dr Saadi's detention fell within the wording of Article 5(1)(f). On the applicant's appeal, the case was referred to the Grand Chamber. By 11 votes to six, the Grand Chamber reached the same conclusion in January 2008. In the majority's view, there was no reason to depart in respect of the first limb of Article 5(1)(f) from the conclusion the Court had reached in *Chahal* regarding its second limb: immigration detention is not subject to a necessity test.[93] The purpose of the Oakington detention regime was the speedy resolution of asylum claims expected to be resolvable (i.e. rejected) within one week. In 1999, this regime had made it possible to treat 13,000 applications, out of a total of 84,000 asylum applications made to the UK that year. Up to 150 interviews were scheduled per day. For the Court, the detention had not been arbitrary since: (a) the authorities had acted in 'good faith', pursuing a policy which was to benefit all asylum seekers by making it possible to determine asylum claims in a speedy manner; (b) the detention was 'closely connected' to the purpose of preventing unauthorised entry,[94] a qualification which applied to Dr Saadi's entry on the grounds that any entry is 'unauthorised' until a state has 'authorised' it; (c) the conditions of detention at Oakington had been relatively relaxed and thus appropriate for their purpose; and (d) the length of detention had not exceeded that reasonably required for the purpose pursued.[95]

Led by Judges Rozakis and Tulkens (the two national judges in the *M.S.S.* case of 2011 reviewed in Chapter 12), the six dissenting judges were incensed.[96] They relied on the case law of the UN Human Rights Committee in order to affirm the principle that 'asylum seekers who have presented a claim for international protection are *ipso facto* lawfully within the territory of a State'. They found the majority's argument according to which detaining an asylum seeker is in their interests as an 'exceedingly dangerous stance' and the assimilation of 'all asylum

[92] *Saadi*, para 15. [93] *Saadi*, para 73.

[94] Cornelisse has criticised this loose test of 'connexity' rather than causality.

[95] *Saadi* judgment, paras 74–80 and 65.

[96] Joint partly dissenting opinion of Judges Rozakis, Tulkens, Kovler, Hajiyev, Spielmann and Hirvelä in *Saadi*.

seekers to potential illegal immigrants' particularly disturbing. In a critique of the 'close connection' test, they insisted that detention must always be ordered *in concreto* in order to achieve one of the aims referred to in the Convention, which was not the case here as detention was pursued for 'a purely bureaucratic and administrative goal, unrelated to any need to prevent [the applicant's] entry into the country'. In their view, other less coercive measures should have been sought. They found support for this view in the Human Rights Committee's case law, European Union directives, and the Committee of Ministers Recommendation of 2003 (all listed in the part of the judgment entitled 'Relevant international law documents' which also refers to the UNHCR Executive Committee Conclusion 44 and to a report of the UN Working Group on Arbitrary Detention).[97] They asked whether 'it is permissible today for the European Convention on Human Rights to provide a lower level of protection than that which is recognised and accepted in the other organisations'.[98] Their indignation was palpable in their final words:

> Are we now also to accept that Article 5 of the Convention, which has played a major role in ensuring controls of arbitrary detention, should afford a lower level of protection as regards asylum and immigration which, in social and human terms, are the most crucial issues facing us in the years to come? Is it a crime to be a foreigner? We do not think so.

The Parliamentary Assembly of the Council of Europe (PACE) has expressly criticised the *Saadi* judgment.[99] In 2010, it also issued a forceful resolution on the detention of asylum seekers and irregular migrants in Europe.[100] This followed many previous pronouncements about the treatment of asylum seekers and migrants in Europe. For example, in 2002, PACE had declared: 'The Assembly insists that the Council of Europe's fundamental values will be threatened if nothing is done to combat the present climate of hostility towards refugees, asylum seekers and immigrants, and to encourage respect for their safety and dignity in all circumstances'.[101] This intervention had not remained without impact as the following year the Committee of Ministers adopted its first comprehensive Recommendation on the detention of asylum seekers.[102] In this document, the

[97] *Saadi* judgment, paras 31–40.

[98] On the discrepancy between the Strasbourg Court's jurisprudence and the standards promoted by other international institutions, see: Cathryn Costello, 'Human Rights and the Elusive Universal Subject: Immigration Detention Under International Human Rights and EU Law' (2012) *Indiana Journal of Global Legal Studies* 19, 257–303.

[99] PACE Doc. 12105, report of the Committee on Migration, Refugees and Population entitled 'The detention of asylum seekers and irregular migrants in Europe' and adopted on 11 January 2010, rapporteur: Ms Ana Catarina Mendonça, available at <http://assembly.coe.int/ASP/Doc/XrefViewPDF.asp?FileID=12435&Language=EN>, para 14, page 20.

[100] PACE Resolution 1707 (2010) on the detention of asylum seekers and irregular migrants in Europe, adopted on 28 January 2010.

[101] PACE Recommendation 1547 (2002) on expulsion procedures in conformity with human rights and enforced with respect for safety and dignity, adopted on 22 January 2002, point 8.

[102] CM Recommendation R (2003) to member states on measures of detention of asylum seekers, adopted on 16 April 2003.

Committee of Ministers itself referred to Conclusion 44 adopted by the Executive Committee of the UNHCR as early as the mid-1980s.[103] The Committee of Ministers recommended the following:

> Measures of detention of asylum seekers should be applied only after a careful examination of their necessity in each individual case. These measures should be specific, temporary and non-arbitrary and should be applied for the shortest possible time. Such measures are to be implemented as prescribed by law and in conformity with standards established by the relevant international instruments and by the case-law of the European Court of Human Rights.

Also from within the Council of Europe, the European Commissioner for Human Rights and the European Committee for the Prevention of Torture had made clear their opposition to the use of immigration detention as a first response and deterrent to migrants reaching Europe irregularly.[104]

The large array of these multiple interventions (not all of which are cited here) indicates that it would have been open to the European Court to rely on a growing European and international consensus in order to denounce routine immigration detention as an affront to human rights. Instead of this, the European Court of Human Rights sent the message that immigration detention does not in principle violate European human rights standards.

It may be retorted that drawing such a bleak picture is unwarranted, especially in view of the increasingly common verdicts of violation of Article 5(1)(f) reached by the Court, including: when measures of detention have no basis in domestic law;[105] when detention is maintained even in the absence of the prospect of actual deportation taking place;[106] when the decision on whether or not to authorise entry takes an inordinately long time (six months);[107] or when the detainees are children.[108] Admittedly, verdicts of violations of Article 5(4) (because of the lack of a judicial remedy against the detention measure) and of Article 3 (because of the 'inhuman and degrading' conditions of detention) are also frequent.[109] It remains, however, that all these assuredly crucial decisions leave intact the principle that part of the human population can be detained simply for lacking proper documentation.

[103] UNHCR Executive Committee Conclusion No. 44 (1986), Detention of Refugees and Asylum Seekers.

[104] Memorandum by Thomas Hammarberg, Commissioner for Human Rights of the Council of Europe, following his visits to the United Kingdom on 5–8 February and 31 March–2 April 2008, as cited in London Detainee Support Group, 'Detained Lives: The Real Cost of Indefinite Immigration Detention', report dated January 2009, p. 11.

[105] *Al-Nashif v. Bulgaria*, appl. 50936/99, Judgment (ECtHR), 20 June 2002, which marked the start of an abundant case law.

[106] *Mikolenko v. Estonia*, appl. 10664/05, Judgment (ECtHR), 8 Oct. 2009, in English only; *A and Others v. the United Kingdom*, appl. 3455/05, GC Judgment (ECtHR), 19 Feb. 2009.

[107] *Suso Musa v. Malta*, appl. 42337/12, Judgment (ECtHR), 23 July 2013. This arguably introduces something like a proportionality test.

[108] See text later in the chapter.

[109] See e.g. *A.A. v. Greece; M.S.S. v. Belgium and Greece*, appl. 30696/09, GC Judgment (ECtHR), 21 Jan. 2011; *Suso Musa* judgment.

IX. The Source of the European and Inter-American Chasm: A Matter of Text, Context, Judges and Judicial *Habitus*

According to the authoritative jurisprudential line of the European Court of Human Rights, immigration detention need not be a last resort, and the immigration detainee need not have access to judicial oversight such that the detained migrant is entitled to legal representation. The Inter-American Court takes the opposite view on each of these points. How can we explain the contrast in these respective approaches?

Lawyers' first reflex is often to examine whether a difference in judicial outcomes can be traced to the governing legal texts. On this front, it is readily observable that Article 5(1)(f) ECHR on immigration detention has no equivalent in Article 7 ACHR which applies to any detention. The fact that Article 7 ACHR refrains from exhaustively identifying the various situations where someone can be detained arguably makes it more difficult to distinguish between these various situations. The forceful dissenting opinions of Strasbourg minority judges in verdicts of non-violation of Article 5(1)(f) nonetheless demonstrate that the text of the European Convention does lend itself to be interpreted in a way which reins in immigration detention. If the Strasbourg Court had so wished, it could have insisted on applying both a necessity and a proportionality test to immigration detention—and indeed it sometimes does so.[110] It could also have used Article 5(4) ECHR to build in additional safeguards by guaranteeing oversight by judges in remedies which would have been demonstrably accessible to migration detainees. Ultimately the textual difference between Article 7 ACHR and Article 5 ECHR does not explain the stark jurisprudential gulf between the Inter-American and European Courts' positions on immigration detention.

The key question is: why has the Strasbourg Court refrained from insisting on strong safeguards against immigration detention? Article 5(1)(f) would have been drafted with the idea that it should be possible for states to detain immigrants about to be deported for short periods of time, without attracting the whole apparatus of due process. No one in the early days of the Convention system would have imagined that what was a relatively benign system of detention would become a general tool of 'migration management'. In the *East African Asians* case dating from 1970 and reviewed in Chapter 3, the longest period of detention to which applicants had been subjected was 45 days; it was often shorter.[111] The Commission's disregard for Article 5 complaints in this case would have occurred without any perception that soon immigration detention would no longer be counted in terms of weeks but in terms

[110] See e.g. *Yoh-Ekale Mwanje v. Belgium*, appl. 10486/10, Judgment (ECtHR), 20 Dec. 2011, in French only, especially para 124. *Yok-Ekale Mwanje* was a judgment of the Second Section presided over by Judge Tulkens.

[111] *'East African Asians' I, Samji Maji Lalji Patel and Others v. the United Kingdom*, appl. 4403/70 and 24 others, Decision (EComHR), 10 Oct. 1970, pp. 92–131 at 93–100.

of months, and then years, and that children would start being incarcerated too, until both these aspects became normalised.

The early case law of the Commission nonetheless created a path which continued to be trod after practices were transformed beyond recognition. The case law seemed clear, and the Court followed it. Circumstances gradually changed, so much so that from the late 1980s immigration detention became routine practice. The Court could have turned to the idea that the Convention was a 'living instrument' which needed to be constantly adapted to new circumstances to come up with a new interpretation of Article 5(1)(f). Instead, having probably forgotten the circumstantial origins of its inadmissibility and non-violation reflexes, it carried on applying the principles which had become entrenched in its case law.[112]

Outside the Court, there nonetheless seems to exist a consensus in the human rights community that subjecting the immigration detention regime to strict guarantees should be considered a staple of human rights and/or rule of law requirements. This consensus has been expressed not only by NGOs and independent experts but also from within the ranks of political institutions; not only in distant lands but also from within Europe; not just by close majorities but also through processes which reflect a broad consensus; not in the distant past but very recently.[113] In this context, it appears that the real reason why the Strasbourg Court is positioning itself at the opposite end of what the rest of the human rights world thinks about immigration detention must be due to its own political and sociological history. On the one hand, its perennial reflexes of trusting the old democracies of Western Europe and of deferring to state interests must play a role. On the other hand, the popular fear of 'hordes of migrants' disembarking in Europe and destabilising our ways of doing things and privileges also seems relevant. Preaching and practising equality becomes all the more challenging in a region which is structured on increasingly unequal lines and where the differentials between the haves and the have-nots, the status-endowed (especially citizens) and the status-deprived (especially irregular migrants) are becoming wider. Presumably the Strasbourg judges think: what would happen if we were not to detain migrants?

Strongly worded dissenting opinions attest to the fact that some Strasbourg judges do not think along these lines at all. Had these minority judges been in the majority, the Strasbourg migrant case law would look very different from how it looks today. As it is, the persistent undercurrent which they have kept alive has allowed continual resistance to the Strasbourg mainstream. This undercurrent has nonetheless never managed to become truly dominant at the Strasbourg Court. By contrast, the Inter-American Court started on a footing which pushed the human rights logic from the beginning. This entrenched default positions which would become difficult to dethrone later.

[112] For a review of cases other than those mentioned here, see: Wilsher *Immigration Detention* 143–157; Cornelisse *Immigration Detention*; Costello, 'Human Rights'.

[113] I borrow these four criteria from: Françoise Tulkens, Sébastien Van Drooghenbroeck, and Frédéric Krenc, 'Le Soft Law et la Cour européenne des droits de l'homme: Questions de légitimité et de méthode' (2012) *Revue trimestrielle des droits de l'homme* 433–489 at 473–481, in a contribution which usefully attempts to identify the weight to be given to various soft law instruments.

In other words, the contrasting approaches of the European and Inter-American Courts must be linked to the respective judicial *habitus* (to borrow Pierre Bourdieu's useful concept again) which they have developed. Each court has produced a particular *habitus*—a way of doing things and a way of thinking which becomes unreflectively followed. The reflexes derived from their respective *habitus* in turn have for effect that the courts tend to produce results which are in tune with their overall respective approaches. Their respective tendencies can thus be expected to endure over time, in a kind of self-fulfilling prophecy. Not surprisingly, then, there is a great deal of continuity in the overall jurisprudential lines adopted by the European and Inter-American Courts respectively. Given how important *habitus* is, the next section identifies three recurrent traits in the way the Inter-American Court deals with the cases before it.

X. The Realism, Humanism and Thoroughness of the Inter-American Court

Like any other text, the American Convention offers itself to various interpretations. The way the Inter-American Court chooses to approach its jurisprudential task must therefore be key to its widely protective pronouncements. This book has already stressed how the Inter-American Court always tries to make the most of a case which comes before it; how it is happy to rely on various instruments of international human rights law to find support for its progressive interpretations; and how it has no inclination to presume a state's statement should be given more credibility than one expressed by the applicant. This section identifies another three characteristics of its approach: its realism, humanism, and thoroughness.

The term 'realism' is used here in order to denote the way the judges of the Inter-American Court think in concrete terms. An illustration of this *habitus* is provided by Judge Macaulay's questioning of Ms González Batista, the witness presented by the state at the *Vélez Loor* public hearing. Judge Macaulay wanted to know how a migrant in detention in 2003 like Mr Vélez Loor would have been able to access the remedies which existed in law if he did not have the benefit of legal representation. Ms González Batista offered what could be characterised as textbook answers. These did not satisfy Judge Macauley who kept refining her question, until she finally exploded: 'But I'm locked up. I have virtually no contact with the outside world. How do I get my case heard? How do I get before a judge?'[114] The issue was taken up again at the close of the hearing as individual judges were indicating to the parties questions which they specifically wished to see developed in the final written pleadings which the parties were going to submit to the Court in the following weeks. Speaking last, Judge Garcia-Sayán, the Court's President, commented that the state had explained that it was very easy to lodge a *habeas corpus* application but that the representatives had said that the

[114] The quotes come from my field notes and may not be a literal transcription of the exact words used by Judge Macauley.

real conditions in arrest and detention made it *impossible* (Judge Garcia-Sayán stressed this word) to access this remedy. The President then said: 'Please tell us how it would have been possible for Mr Vélez Loor to ask for habeas corpus. Don't go into an explanation now, but tell us specifically *how* [in your written pleadings]'.[115] Disregarding the invitation to provide an explanation later, the state immediately volunteered an example of a Columbian citizen who had been detained for drug-related offences and who had filed a motion with the Supreme Court with the unskilled assistance of a third party. The state's subsequent written pleadings obviously failed to convince the Court that *any* detained migrant would have been in a position similarly to access this remedy.

Humanism is a second word which appears particularly pertinent to characterise the Inter-American Court's approach. One of the things which struck me during the *Vélez Loor* hearing is the attention which the Court paid to the people who stood before it, especially the victim. This was apparent in small gestures, such as allowing time at the opening of the hearing to take pictures. This mundane and apparently insignificant practice can be seen to stem from a recognition by the Court of the symbolic importance which appearing before it has for individuals—not only for the victim but also the representatives of the defendant state who, from what I saw, also bring cameras to hearings. Also striking is the fact that the Inter-American Court uses the actual name of the victim to refer to him or her in its judgments. In the Strasbourg system, this is never done and the applicant is always referred to more impersonally as 'the applicant' (perhaps significantly, not as 'the victim'). These various denominations are possibly linked to the fact that the alleged victim commonly appears before the Inter-American Court, making the person and their suffering comparatively more tangible to the members of the Court. By contrast, the Strasbourg Court has long ceased to hear applicants themselves.[116] This is not to deny that reading a judgment even by the Inter-American Court is not the best means to get to know the victim. Inevitably, legal discourse reconstructs a whole and complex person into a rather uni-dimensional legal party, and often violates this person's wishes and understandings,[117] as I shall document further later in relation to the *Vélez Loor* case. Despite this, there is less distancing at the Inter-American Court, and a seemingly greater propensity on the part of its judges to try to put themselves in the shoes of the people who appear before them, than at the European Court.

One of the ways in which the humanism of the Inter-American Court shows itself is in the care it seems to take in not demeaning the victim even when it remains to be persuaded by her claims. The European Court does not appear to have any reservations about suggesting that the applicants are not credible and

[115] The previous note applies here too.

[116] One of the last cases where it appears to have done so is: *Incal v. Turkey*, appl. 22678/93, Judgment (ECtHR), 9 June 1998.

[117] See e.g. James Boyd White, *The Legal Imagination* (Chicago: University of Chicago Press, 1973 and 1985) 114.

declaring their claims to be unfounded. When the European Court finds evidence adduced by the applicant to be lacking, it routinely concludes that there has been no violation of the European Convention. The Inter-American Court is not as trenchant. For example, in the *Vélez Loor* case it more subtly 'observes that the representatives did not offer sufficient and assorted [*sic*] evidence referring to the time of the facts that permits the Court to deliberate over the [torture allegations]'.[118] Such language allows the Inter-American Court not to side with the state. Admittedly the Inter-American Court does not say either that it believes Mr Vélez Loor, something which he found hurtful (as he told me in an email). The negative effect on Mr Vélez Loor of the lack of endorsement of his story by the Inter-American Court should not be underestimated. As the late Helen Bamber, founder of the Helen Bamber Foundation, repeatedly stressed, one of the most difficult experiences for victims of torture is that the story they report is not believed.[119] Nonetheless, the Inter-American Court at least reproduces Mr Vélez Loor's account of his allegations of torture word for word in its judgment,[120] and does not say that it does not believe him. It leaves the question open, rather than closing it by specifically giving the benefit of the doubt to the state.

Moreover, the Inter-American Court nowhere blames Mr Vélez Loor for his arrest and detention. Often, the European Court feels free to suggest that it is the migrant applicants who brought on themselves the misfortune from which they complain at Strasbourg, for example by bringing a child into the country without sufficient means (*Bah*)[121] or by not refraining from entering a relationship or starting a family when one person's legal immigration status was uncertain (*Omoregie*).[122] The implication which the Inter-American Court draws from Mr Vélez Loor's irregular migrant status goes in the opposite direction, for this status is taken to increase his vulnerability.

The way in which the Inter-American Court seems willing to attempt to respect and understand the human person before it also shows in its willingness and indeed determination to examine a case under the multitude of human rights angles the treatment complained of reveals. This translates into what I call its 'thoroughness', a characteristic which is amply demonstrated by the number of issues it examined in the *Vélez Loor* case, as reviewed earlier. By contrast, the European Court often resorts to saying that the examination of one complaint is unnecessary in view of the finding of violation it has reached under another provision. An array of findings of violation on the same matter but from a variety of perspectives is hardly ever purely repetitive; it normally makes clear the different ways in which a particular treatment is wrong, thus both offering recognition to the victim and at

[118] *Vélez Loor* judgment, para 226.

[119] On the Helen Bamber Foundation, see <http://www.helenbamber.org/>, accessed 16 May 2014.

[120] *Vélez Loor* judgment, paras 232–233.

[121] *Bah v. the United Kingdom*, appl. 56328/07, Judgment (ECtHR), 27 Sept. 2011, reviewed in Chapter 8.

[122] *Darren Omoregie and Others v. Norway*, appl. 265/07, Judgment (ECtHR), 31 July 2008, in English only. See further, Section IX Chapter 13.

the same time calling for a variety of transformations, thus enhancing protection. One might be tempted to explain the respective 'light touch' and 'thoroughness' of the European and Inter-American Courts by reference to their respectively highly voluminous and rather minimal dockets. A deeper explanation may concern the fact that the Inter-American Court of Human Rights was both too realist and too humanist to be willing to miss important opportunities to offer human beings both recognition and protection when it was first established, thus creating an enduring mindset. Interestingly, occasionally, the European Court also demonstrates realism, humanity, and thoroughness, as the *Tabitha* case, reviewed in the next section, illustrates.

XI. A Lone Five-Year-Old in Detention: *Tabitha* Proves an 'Inter-American Tipping Point' for the Strasbourg Court

Who would think of separating a five-year-old from the person with whom she is travelling, putting her in detention in an immigration centre with adults, and keeping her there for two months? Who would then return this child to a country where there is no certainty that any family member or friend would be waiting for her? Moreover, when this is a country from which it was alleged that her mother had fled? The Belgian authorities did this to a child named Tabitha in 2002. The case which ensued, *Mubilanzila Mayeka and Kaniki Mitunga v. Belgium*, more commonly known in activist circles as *Tabitha* (after the second applicant's first name), proved a tipping point for the European Court of Human Rights. The Strasbourg Court (in a bench which did not include Judge Tulkens)[123] found a string of violations of the European Convention, displaying a thoroughness more generally associated with the Inter-American Court. This result was made possible through judicial realist reasoning imbued with sympathy for the suffering which both the child and her mother (resident in Canada) endured. In this section, I review this exceptional judgment in the Strasbourg case law in order to highlight how, when 'tipped', the European Court reverted to adopting a human rights logic which is true to its claimed premise of guaranteeing rights to a human being, *qua* human being.

In *Tabitha*, the European Court of Human Rights stated that the second applicant's 'extremely vulnerable situation takes precedence over considerations relating to [her] status as an illegal immigrant'.[124] This unusual sentence, lifted by the European Court from the applicants' legal representative's submissions,[125] is perhaps the most often quoted passage of the *Tabitha* judgment. It has a positive

[123] For personal reasons, Judge Tulkens recused herself from the case. The ad hoc judge was Paul Martens.

[124] *Tabitha* judgment, para 55.

[125] The legal representative was Dirk Vanheule. Vanheule explained he had written it as part of his submissions to the Court in the case, after I quoted the sentence at a panel which he happened to be chairing during a research seminar (held at the University of Antwerp on 28 September 2012).

but also a negative side. Starting with the negative side, vulnerability is used here simply to gain the sympathy of the Court towards the applicant, without calling for counteracting measures which would ensure a level playing field.[126] On the positive side, the European Court accepts here to apply a logic which can be summarised in the words 'child first, migrant second'. The typical Strasbourg inversion is thus reversed. This allows the Court to apply a human rights reasoning which is reminiscent of those produced by the Inter-American Court. This will be discussed after a more detailed review of the facts of the case has been offered.

The first applicant, Tabitha's mother, had arrived in Canada in 2000 and had been granted refugee status one year later. She had asked her brother, K., a Dutch national living in the Netherlands, to go and collect Tabitha (the second applicant) from the Democratic Republic of the Congo where she was living with her ailing grandmother. K. was to look after Tabitha until the first applicant was able to join her daughter. On his arrival at Brussels National Airport on 17 August 2002, K. tried to persuade the immigration authorities that Tabitha, for whom he did not have the necessary travel and immigration papers, was his daughter. This did not work. Tabitha was refused leave to enter Belgium. Her uncle returned to the Netherlands.[127] Tabitha was taken into detention. The immigration office at the Canadian Embassy in the Netherlands (wrongly) informed the Belgian authorities that her mother had not yet been granted refugee status in Canada.[128] Tabitha's lawyer explained to the authorities that although Tabitha was treated with as much care as possible in detention and allowed to speak to her mother and uncle every day on the phone, her isolation and detention amongst adults she did not know put her at risk of psychological damage.[129] His requests to have her placed with foster parents or in an institution for children were not acted upon. On 16 October 2002, the *chambre du conseil* of the Brussels Court of First Instance ordered Tabitha's immediate release for being incompatible with the UN Convention on the Rights of the Child. On the same day, the Belgian authorities received formal confirmation that Tabitha's mother was actually a recognised refugee in Canada. The next day, Tabitha was put on a flight to Kinshasa which had been booked for her by the Belgian authorities the previous week. She travelled accompanied by a social worker from the detention centre. At Kinshasa Airport, she was placed in the care of the police. Late in the night, a secretary at the National Information of the DRC took her home.[130] That day, when her mother phoned the detention centre to speak to her daughter, she was informed that Tabitha was no longer there and she was advised to contact the Aliens Office, which in turn suggested that she speak to the UNHCR, from which she learnt that Tabitha had been deported to Kinshasa.[131] Tabitha left the DRC five days later following the intervention of the Belgian and Canadian

[126] On the dangers to be avoided when resorting to vulnerability, see: Lourdes Peroni and Alexandra Timmer, 'Vulnerable Groups: The Promise of an Emerging Concept in European Human Rights Convention Law' (2013) *International Journal of Constitutional Law* 11, 1056–1085.

[127] *Tabitha* judgment, paras 9–13.

[128] *Tabitha*, para 21.

[129] *Tabitha*, para 23.

[130] *Tabitha*, paras 30–32.

[131] *Tabitha*, para 32.

Prime Ministers, with the latter agreeing in principle to authorise the reunification of the family.[132]

These chilling facts led the Strasbourg Court to reason with what I have called in the previous section realism and humanism. For example, the Court states: 'The fact that the second applicant received legal assistance, had daily telephone contact with her mother or uncle and that staff and residents at the centre did their best for her cannot be regarded as sufficient to meet all her needs as a five-year-old'.[133] It is as if in this case, the facts speak for themselves. They need not be established and demonstrated further, for example through a medical certificate. To quote again:

> The Court considers that the measures taken by the Belgian authorities... were far from sufficient to fulfil the Belgian State's obligation to provide care for the second applicant.... The Court is in no doubt that the second applicant's detention in the conditions described above caused her considerable distress. Nor could the authorities who ordered her detention have failed to be aware of the serious psychological effects it would have on her. In the Court's view, the second applicant's detention in such conditions demonstrated a lack of humanity to such a degree that it amounted to inhuman treatment.[134]

The words 'lack of humanity' which appear in the last sentence are strong and unusual. A HUDOC search for decisions containing these words (as well as, in French, '*manque d'humanité*') produced only one result: the *Tabitha* judgment.[135] Of course, it may well be that other judgments express a similar idea in slightly different words. Still it remains that the Court clearly regarded the circumstances of the *Tabitha* case as epitomising treatment which is inhumane, in this case defying any sense of what human decency could countenance. The Court had reached a tipping point: it could no longer apply its normal reasoning by considering border controls before human rights; Tabitha's extreme vulnerability as a five-year-old separated from her uncle had to take precedence over her irregular status.

The Court found the treatment inflicted upon Tabitha so terrible and inhumane that it was driven to accept that her mother's rights under Article 3 had also been violated. It does so on account of both Tabitha's detention and her deportation. The reasoning, however, uses different words to those quoted previously. The Court does not say that the mother suffered a 'lack of humanity'. It more prosaically says that the 'threshold of severity' for a violation of Article 3 has been attained in her respect. To quote:

> The Court has no doubt that, as a mother, the first applicant suffered deep distress and anxiety as a result of her daughter's detention. In view of the circumstances of the case,

132 *Tabitha*, para 34. 133 *Tabitha*, para 52. 134 *Tabitha*, para 58.

135 This search was conducted on 3 July 2012. Repeated on 16 May 2014, it produced a second result: *Mahmundi and Others v. Greece*, appl. 140902/10, Judgment (ECtHR), 31 July 2012, in French only. The phrase appears at para 15, in the applicants' submissions (not the Court's reasoning). *Mahmundi* concerns the detention of various members of a family after they were rescued in the Mediterranean while they were trying to cross illegally. The Court found a violation of Article 3 (amongst other provisions) but not of Article 5(1).

the Court concludes that the level of severity required for a violation of Article 3 of the Convention was attained in the present case.[136]

Similar language is used for the deportation in respect of which the Court specifically notes the disregard for the first applicant's feelings, evidenced by the fact that the Belgian authorities did not trouble themselves to advise her of her daughter's deportation.[137] Again, humanism and realism underlay this observation.

This mode of reasoning inevitably leads the Court to find violation after violation of the Convention. No less than eight verdicts of violation are reached in this case, all unanimous. This high number must be something of a record in the Strasbourg jurisprudence for a case the facts of which were not particularly convoluted. Half of the verdicts relate to Article 3, as the Court examines separately the situation of the child and the mother, each time in respect of the detention on the one hand and the deportation on the other. The Court finds a violation of Article 3 in each of these four possible permutations. The Court goes on to find two violations of Article 8 in respect of both applicants (considered together) as a result of Tabitha's detention on the one hand and deportation on the other hand. The Court finally finds, in respect of Tabitha only, first a violation of Article 5(1) and then a violation of Article 5(4). These successive findings show the Strasbourg Court determined to make a point. Often, the Court seems to assume that a finding of violation under one ground makes it unnecessary to examine a complaint, related to the same facts, under a different ground. In this case, however, the European Court seems to want to take every opportunity to spell out the fact that the state's treatment is wrong, from whichever angle one looks at it.

In *Tabitha*, the Strasbourg Court is unmoved by the respondent government's suggestion that the applicants were somehow to blame for the predicament in which they found themselves. The Belgian government argued that 'the first applicant and the family had failed to cooperate with the competent authorities and had brought the situation of which they now complained upon themselves by treating certain matters as a "fait accompli"'.[138] To this argument, the Court simply replied: 'Article 3 makes no provision for exceptions'.[139] On the Article 8 complaint, the government stressed that 'the first applicant had sought to deceive the Belgian authorities with her brother's help'.[140] For the Court, however, the fact that 'the first applicant's conduct was questionable and does not appear to have been entirely fault-free [does not] deprive her of victim status in the instant case'.[141] This phrasing is interesting in the light of other case law where the European Court endorses a respondent state's characterisation of immigration deception as a 'serious offence'.[142] Here the Court finds this action merely

[136] *Tabitha* judgment, para 62. [137] *Tabitha*, para 70.

[138] *Tabitha*, para 47. On the '*fait accompli*' argument in the residence permit case law, see Chapter 13.

[139] *Tabitha*, para 48. [140] *Tabitha*, para 89. [141] *Tabitha*, para 84.

[142] See e.g. *Nunez v. Norway*, appl. 55597/09, Judgment (ECtHR), 28 June 2011, in English and with a Russian translation, para 72.

'questionable'.[143] Just like the Inter-American Court did in *Vélez Loor*, the European Court does not countenance in *Tabitha* the idea that the first applicant could have been responsible for what had happened to her daughter. The applicants are awarded exactly what they requested under Article 41 (which admittedly was far from extravagant): €35,000 between them in compensation for the damage and €14,036 for costs and expenses.

It is finally useful to examine the position which the Belgian state adopted during the Strasbourg proceedings. Basically, it stood its ground. It did not accept any responsibility for what had happened to Tabitha or her mother, only indirectly recognising that the way the applicants had been treated was far from ideal and needed to be avoided in the future. The main message put across by the Belgian government is that, at the material time, it could not have done things differently, and that it had now changed its procedures.[144] This is very different from the partial (if insufficient) admission of responsibility which Panama offered the Inter-American Court in the *Vélez Loor* case.

Nonetheless, it is only in regard to Article 8 (not Article 3) that the government brings into its reasoning the principle that states are entitled to control the entry of aliens onto their territory.[145] Interestingly, the Court does not put this principle at the very start of its reasoning in its discussion of the merits of the Article 8 complaints. Instead, the Court starts by making a number of general observations. After these, it turns to the question of whether the interference with family life was justified in this case, and it is only at this stage that the Court pays attention to the

[143] It is to be noted that Tabitha could have gone to Canada lawfully, as her mother was entitled as a recognised refugee to have her minor children join her. The judgment does not allude to the reasons why Ms Mubilanza Mayeka did not do so. One assumes that it may have to do with either ignorance of the law or lack of trust in the immigration regime.

[144] The European Court summarises the Belgian state's defence regarding the Article 3 complaints in *Tabitha* as follows:

> In [the state's] submission, it had not been possible for the child to be given permission to enter Belgian territory without any identity papers or a visa. Nor could she have been allowed to leave with her uncle, as he had not provided any evidence to show that he was her guardian or established that he was a relative. At that juncture the Canadian authorities had not offered a laissez-passer, and indeed none had been requested by the applicants. Had the first applicant travelled to Belgium, her daughter's detention and subsequent removal would, no doubt, have been avoided.
>
> The chances of finding accommodation in a more suitable centre were virtually non-existent and, above all, would not have guaranteed the child's supervision, or therefore, her protection. There had accordingly been a risk that she would disappear. Furthermore, although the place of detention was not adapted to the needs of a five-year-old, particularly for what turned out to be quite a lengthy period, the explanation for this lay in the exceptional circumstances of the case and in the fact that, since situations of this type were relatively rare at the time, adequate procedures and structures had yet to be established.
>
> Legislation had since been introduced in... 2002, which provided for the appointment of a guardian and for the minor to be taken into care. In addition, on 19 May 2006 [four months after the Strasbourg hearing of the case], the Cabinet had approved in principle a measure intended to prohibit the detention in a closed centre of unaccompanied foreign minors arrested at the border.

Tabitha judgment, paras 43–44

[145] *Tabitha*, para 74.

border control principle. Moreover, this principle is then presented merely as one factor amongst others worthy of consideration, as the initial word in the relevant passage indicates:

> *Furthermore*, the States' interest in foiling attempts to circumvent immigration rules must not deprive aliens of the protection afforded by these conventions or deprive foreign minors, especially if unaccompanied, of the protection their status warrants. The protection of fundamental rights and the constraints imposed by a State's immigration policy must therefore be reconciled.[146]

Thus, the European Court acknowledges the tension between human rights and the power of the state to control immigration, but in this case the second pole is mentioned in the middle of a longer reasoning, moreover related not to thc first but the fifth complaint examined by the Court. In other words, the European Court gives prominence to the guarantees provided by the Convention. This is yet another illustration of the way in which *Tabitha* reverses, and makes right, the unfortunate Strasbourg inversion characteristic of most of its migrant case law.

For all these reasons, *Tabitha* is a remarkable judgment. This is an excellent example of the European Court adopting a human rights logic in a migrant case. There are nonetheless two areas where the judgment could have been stronger. Whilst the UN Convention on the Rights of the Child is cited in the section on the 'relevant international law and practice',[147] this is the only international text which is cited and it is barely referred to in the reasoning of the Court.[148] In all likelihood, a judgment adopted today would read differently in this respect. *Tabitha*, adopted as late as 2006, nonetheless shows how long it has taken the European Court to start inscribing its jurisprudence in worldwide trends. A second matter of regret is the way in which the European Court does nothing regarding the fact that Tabitha was the daughter of a refugee, adding to her vulnerability. In these conditions, returning her to the DRC was particularly callous. As the applicants argued,

> [D]eporting the child of a person with recognised refugee status was contrary to the fundamental rule that asylum-seekers should not be expelled. There was, furthermore, a danger in such cases that the authorities in the country of origin would use the child's presence there to compel the refugee to return or even that they would seek to exact revenge on the child.[149]

The Court ignored this argument in its own reasoning.

XII. The European Court of the Rights of States? Subsequent Case Law on Children's Detention

However positive, *Tabitha* is very much a one-off judgment. Subsequent Strasbourg case law on children's immigration detention revert to the more typical

[146] *Tabitha*, para 81, emphasis added.
[147] *Tabitha*, para 39
[148] See *Tabitha*, paras 81 and 83.
[149] *Tabitha*, para 64.

Strasbourg judicial *habitus* of tending to let the state 'off the hook' and requiring strong evidence from the applicant. This section traces what happened in four cases: *Muskhadzhiyeva and Others v. Belgium*;[150] *Kanagaratnam and Others v. Belgium*;[151] *Popov v. France*;[152] and the decision on the application of Rule 39 in *Badalian v. France*.[153] The discussion, technical at times, traces how the decisions evolve. An analysis of the first three cases suggests that, with each new case, the Court is ready to broaden the scope of protection against the detention of children whose parents are in detention with them. In the fourth instance, concerning a Rule 39 request, the Court fails to push the logic of human rights protection where it should naturally lead. This suggests that ultimately the Strasbourg Court is all too ready to renege on the idea that children should not be put in detention—let alone maintained there for long periods—simply because they do not have the right papers.

Muskhadzhiyeva and Others v. Belgium concerned the one-month detention of four children and their mother whose asylum claim in Belgium had been rejected. Elsewhere I have described in detail the extraordinary circumstances which allowed the case to make its way to Strasbourg. In short, this involved the concerted and indefatigable efforts of a number of lawyers, activists, and associations in order to: gain access to detention centres and provide immigration detainees with legal representation; confront the rebuttal propounded by the Belgian courts that the children were not detained but merely accompanying their parents in detention; have an accredited lawyer (*huissier de justice*) to record the refusal by the director of a detention centre to allow the children outside for a specifically organised activity, thereby demonstrating the children were indeed detained; and research all the judicial remedies which might possibly be pursued and have multiple procedures lodged by lawyers who were committed to the cause. The outcome of this enormous expanse of energy were some 50 cases commenced in the lower courts in the 15 months that followed *Tabitha*, from which *Muskhadzhiyeva* eventually emerged at Strasbourg.[154]

In January 2010, the European Court found a violation of Article 3 in respect of the four Muskhadzhiyeva children, but not of their mother. It reached the same result in respect to Article 5(1). It found no violation of Article 5(4), despite the fact that detained migrants do not receive information about the judicial remedies which exist in Belgian law and do not have automatic access to lawyers.[155] The

150 *Muskhadzhiyeva v. Belgium*, appl. 41442/07, Judgment (ECtHR), 19 Jan. 2010, in French only.

151 *Kanagaratnam and Others v. Belgium*, appl. 15297/09, Judgment (ECtHR), 13 Dec. 2011, in French only.

152 *Popov v. France*, appl. 39472/07, Judgment (ECtHR), 19 Jan. 2012.

153 *Badalian v. France*, appl. 11593/12, pending at the time of writing.

154 Marie-Bénédicte Dembour, 'What it Takes to Make a Case: The Backstage Story of *Muskhadzhiyeva v. Belgium* (Illegality of Children's Immigration Detention)', in Elisabeth Lambert-Abdelgawad (ed.) *Preventing and Sanctioning Hindrances to the Right of Individual Petition to the European Court of Human Rights*, (Brussels: Intersentia, 2011) 75–104.

155 A comprehensive and detailed report issued by ten associations in 2006 noted that only 20 per cent of immigrants detained in Belgium had had their detention examined by a tribunal in 2003: Aide aux personnes déplacées, Caritas International Belgique, le Centre Social Protestant,

violation of Article 3 arose from the Court giving consideration to 'the young age of the applicant children [from seven months up to seven years], the period of their detention [over four weeks] and the state of their health, documented by medical certificates established during their detention'.[156] The complaint related to Article 8 was simply declared manifestly ill-founded.[157] It had been argued for the applicants that children experience extreme insecurity in immigration detention by having to face the reality that they are in jail despite having committed no crime, being confronted by the hopelessness of their parents who are unable to provide any certainty on the length of their stay, and often having to witness fights and sexual violence which are all too common in detention centres.[158] The Court did not seem to have the realism and humanism necessary to rule that such an experience was bound to be seriously detrimental, in the short and long terms, to the mental health of these children, thus affecting their ability to form healthy relationships and to build a decent life, as Article 8 presumably entitles them to do.[159]

On the positive side, the Court found that there was a violation of Article 3 in respect of all four children, not just one of them, Khadija, who showed a particularly high level of trauma and had medical certificates to verify this. This legal victory—which did not directly benefit the applicants who had 'disappeared' by the time the judgment was rendered and have probably never heard of the compensation which the Court awarded them[160]—was not a given. Nuala Mole, the Director of the AIRE Centre, commented to me that it would not have been a foregone conclusion for her to take the case to Strasbourg had she been the family's legal representative.[161] She would have feared that the Court might have been more inclined to follow the Grand Chamber's lead in *Saadi v. the United Kingdom* than *Tabitha*, given that the Muskhadzhiyeva children were accompanied by their mother. It is of course impossible to know what happened during the deliberations of the Chamber. What is clear is that the *Muskhadzhiyeva* judgment reads very differently from *Tabitha*. Gone is the sense that the Court is grappling with a form of treatment beyond the pale; a blanket condemnation of children's detention when the said children are not 'unaccompanied' is conspicuous by its absence. We can only presume that the reason why the Strasbourg Court did

le CIRE, Jesuit Refuge Service Belgium, la Ligue des droits de l'homme asbl, le MRAX, Point d'appui, le Service Social de Solidarité Socialiste, Vluchtelingenwerk Vlaanderen, 'Centres fermés pour étrangers: Etat des lieux', Octobre 2006, p. 31.

156 *Muskhadzhiyeva* judgment, para 63, my translation.

157 Muskhadzhiyeva, paras 98–99.

158 Jean-Yves Hayez, 'L'enfermement des enfants sans-papiers', webpage created 13 February 2008, available at: <http://www.jeanyveshayez.net/602-enfe.htm>, accessed 11 July 2012.

159 See also, expressing similar views: Wouter Vandenhole and Julie Ryngaert, 'Maistreaming Children's Rights in Migration Litigation: *Muskhadzhiyeva and others v. Belgium*', in Eva Brems (ed.) *Diversity and European Human Rights: Rewriting Judgments of the ECHR* (Cambridge: Cambridge University Press, 2013) 68–92.

160 The Muskhadzhiyeva family had lost contact with their legal representative by the time the Court made its ruling. When he tried to inform them of the judgment, Alexis Deswaef discovered that his clients had been deported to Poland under 'Dublin II' and had probably then made their way to France before being deported again and there was no further trace of the family.

161 Nuala Mole, personal communication of June 2010.

not go further than it did is because the majority of the judges on the bench could not help thinking that it was not possible to imagine returning to a world without immigration detention. As a lower Belgian judge remarked to the lawyer of the Muskhadzhiyeva family at the end of his oral pleadings: 'Do you realise the implications of what you are telling me? If I follow you, I would have to free every family in immigration detention. This would amount to positively inviting asylum seekers to come to Belgium'.[162]

Another case against Belgium concerning children in immigration detention had been lodged in 2009. The applicants in *Kanagaratnam and Others* were a mother and her three children who were put in detention immediately upon their arrival in Belgium when the children were about 13, 11, and eight.[163] Their detention lasted three and a half months. Four months after their release, they were granted refugee status. The Court's judgment in *Kanagaratnam* went further than *Muskhadzhiyeva* in a number of ways. In *Kanagaratnam*, the Court specifically said that the absence of a medical certificate recording the detrimental effect of the detention on the children was not conclusive.[164] It also ruled that the 'superior interest of the child' laid down in the UN Convention on the Rights of the Child had to prevail even in an expulsion case. Because of this, the Court continued, its reasoning had to start from the presumption of the children's vulnerability. In the instant case, this vulnerability arose from the fact that three applicants were children, as well as from their personal history. The government had argued that it had not been established that the mother had been experiencing difficulties in enacting her role of parent. The Court replied that the mother's inability to face the situation and to assume her maternal role was an '*objective* factor *inherent* in the living conditions existing in detention centers', which was aggravated in the instant case by her illiteracy. This is a principled statement, even if it immediately went on to be moderated by the Court's remark that it was also taking into account the length of the detention—almost four months.[165] Nonetheless, the ultimate conclusion was phrased in stronger words than in *Muskhadzhiyeva*: 'In view of the foregoing, the Court considered that, by putting the children applicants in a detention centre, the Belgian authorities had exposed them to feelings of anguish and inferiority and took, in full awareness of the implications of their actions, the risk to compromise their development'.[166] The high 'threshold' required for a violation of Article 3 was reached in respect of the children.[167]

It was not in respect of their mother, however.[168] The only violation which the Court found in her respect relates to Article 5(1)—regarding her continued detention following an initial period of two months which the Court found acceptable. (By contrast the whole period of detention of the children is found to violate Article 5(1).) The judgment quotes a report by the Jesuit Refugee Service, rather extensively, in the section entitled 'Relevant law and practice'. This report explains

[162] Quoted in Dembour 'What it Takes' 85.
[163] *Kanagaratnam* judgment.
[164] *Kanagaratnam*, paras 66 and 67.
[165] *Kanagaratnam*, para 67 my translation, emphasis added.
[166] *Kanagaratnam*, para 68.
[167] *Kanagaratnam*, para 69.
[168] *Kanagaratnam*, paras 71–72.

that the immigration detainees cannot choose what they eat, what they do during the day, or when they go outside for some fresh air. Although they typically find it difficult to sleep at night, they cannot rest during the day. They also cannot isolate themselves at any time to think alone about their situation. The report concludes that 'the strict framework to the group regime destroys any remnant of personal autonomy and reinforces the feeling of helplessness of the detainees'.[169] Had the Court been willing, one suspects that this could have been sufficient grounds for finding a violation of at least Article 8, if not Article 3, in respect of the mother.

Although *Kanagaratnam* goes further than *Muskhadzhiyeva*, it does not send an unequivocal message that children's immigration detention is abhorrent and has negative effects on the development of children. The section of the judgment which lays down the circumstances of the case, for example, ends with the following words:

> From 26 January 2009, the children applicants were placed within a schooling framework for one and a half hours per day. At the end of the detention, the teaching staff established for each child a report on their evolution during their stay in the centre. These documents report scholarly progress and a satisfactory emotional and social development.[170]

The Court accepts this information (which surely originates from the state's submissions) without subjecting it to any critical evaluation. One wonders about the children's 'scholarly progress', not only given the limited amount of schooling they received but also given the context in which this schooling took place. The same holds for the 'satisfactory emotional and social development' which they are reported to have shown. Such words make it difficult not to conclude that the Strasbourg Court is biased towards the state.

With *Popov v. France*, decided in January 2012, the Court goes one step further than in *Karagaratnam* against children's immigration detention. This case concerned the two-week detention of a family—two parents, one three-year-old and one infant—whose claim for asylum was eventually recognised. The Court found a violation of Article 3 in respect of the children, Article 5(1) and (4) in respect of all the applicants, and also of Article 8. The Article 8 verdict, the first in a case of this kind, was supported by references to the Convention on the Rights of the Child, a European directive, the European Parliament's Committee of Civil Liberties, Justice and Home Affairs (LIBE), the UNHCR, and two French organisations.[171] The Court specifically said that the automatic detention of children is unacceptable and that alternatives to their detention must be sought.[172] Another highlight of this case is a partly dissenting opinion by Judge Power-Forde which strongly defends the view that not just the children, but also their parents were subjected to inhuman treatment in violation of Article 3, for having had to watch helplessly the treatment meted out to their children.

Muskhadzhiyeva, Kanagaratnam, and *Popov* are Chamber decisions which exist only in French, signifying that the Court does not attribute much importance

[169] *Kanagaratnam*, para 38.
[170] *Kanagaratnam*, para 34, my translation.
[171] *Popov* judgment, paras 141–144.
[172] *Popov*, para 147.

to them. Nonetheless, given that the verdicts of violation were all reached by unanimity in these cases,[173] one would hope that they could constitute the basis of a solid jurisprudence against children's immigration detention, soon to be confirmed by a Grand Chamber judgment. This is not to say, however, that everyone at the Court is persuaded by the ignominy of this practice and determined to use all possible means to put an end to it. On 24 February 2012, the Badalian family introduced a Rule 39 request towards their release from immigration detention in France. (Rule 39 requests are requests for provisional measures. They are discussed in Chapter 12.) The Acting President of the Section to which the application was assigned refused the request. As the 'Combat pour les droits de l'homme' blog observes, the Court (or at least the Acting President who refused the request) was not ready to see *Popov* immediately impacting other cases. The blog entry reports that the family was released after about two weeks, but this was only after they agreed to enrol for voluntary return. The authors of the blog, Nicolas Hervieu and Serge Slama, remark that this transaction may have resulted from some kind of blackmail and was certainly at odds with a philosophy which proclaims the guarantee of absolute protection against inhuman and degrading treatment. Not without provocation, they refer to the Strasbourg Court as the European Court of the Rights of States.[174]

XIII. Don Jésus' Story (Continued): What Mr Vélez Loor did not get from the Inter-American Court

The least one can say is that the guarantees established by the Inter-American Court in *Vélez Loor* remain to be developed in the Strasbourg jurisprudence. This is not to suggest that the Inter-American Court is a perfect institution. It can always do more,[175] and thus will always be criticised for not doing enough. It will also almost inevitably fail to deliver a sense of complete justice even to those few individuals who are lucky enough to have had their case submitted by the Inter-American Commission. Let us take the example of the victim in the *Vélez Loor* case, whose full name is Mr Jesús Tranquilino Vélez Loor. During the hearing, CEJIL addressed him, midway between familiarity and formality

[173] See also *Rahimi v. Greece*, appl. 8687/08, Judgment (ECtHR), 5 Apr. 2011, in French only.

[174] Nicolas Hervieu and Serge Slama, 'Enfants en rétention: une tragédie franco-européenne en quatre actes', Blog Combats pour les droits de l'homme, posted on 6 March 2012, available at: <http://combatsdroitshomme.blog.lemonde.fr/2012/03/06/enfants-en-retention-une-tragedie-franco-europeenne-en-quatre-actes/>, accessed 14 July 2012.

[175] Or arguably should sometimes do less. For example, one of the reparations ordered in *Miguel Castro-Castro Prison v. Peru*, Merits, Reparations and Costs, Judgment (IACtHR), 25 Nov. 2006, was that the names of the inmates who were killed, many of whom were linked to the Shining Path terrorist group, should be added to 'The Eye that Cries', a monument dedicated to the memory of the victims of the dictatorship. This is felt in many Latin American circles to have been sociologically and politically detrimental, causing a lot of unnecessary resentment against the Inter-American Court: Philip Alston and Ryan Goodman, *International Human Rights: The Successor to International Human Rights in Context: Law, Politics and Morals* (Oxford: Oxford University Press, 2013) 1022-1023.

as the Spanish language allows, as Don Jesús. I shall do the same in this section which relies on the personal conversation and emails I had the privilege of having with him, helping me to understand the case beyond the account officially recorded in the judgment which bears his name.

Don Jésus was deported from Panama to Ecuador on 10 September 2003. He told me that at that time he could hardly walk. He went to his family but his wife did not believe that the reason why he had given her no news was because he had been detained for lack of documentation. The marriage was finished, and with it the opportunity to re-bond with his young daughter. He also learnt that he had missed the funeral of one of his parents who had died when he was in detention.

Almost physically and psychologically destroyed, Don Jésus was nonetheless determined to get justice. On 15 September 2003, he addressed a communication to the Commission on Human Rights of the National Congress of Ecuador, and five weeks later to the Ombudsman's Office of Ecuador. He also went to the Ecuadorian Comision Ecumenica De Derechos Humanos which refused his testimony and asked him whether he was crazy—because he was crying. He had a lawyer file a brief with the Panamanian Embassy in Ecuador in January 2004. Later that year, he also notified the Panamanian Ministry of Foreign Affairs of the treatment he had suffered. Still nothing happened.[176] But Don Jésus would not give up and kept trying to find ways of accessing justice. Eventually he stumbled across the Inter-American Commission on Human Rights as he was searching the web for organisations which might support him.

Within 24 hours of emailing the Inter-American Commission, he was told the number which had been assigned to his file and asked to provide a postal address as well as additional information. When the Commission suggested months later that he approach CEJIL to represent him, again he received a quick response: the forms arrived within three days. Don Jésus had been lucky that his complaint fell within an area—the treatment of irregular migrants—which both the Inter-American Commission and CEJIL wanted to prioritise, in the light of the appalling situation which was developing in Mexico and elsewhere. His communications would have identified his situation as the opportunity for these organisation to launch the leading case they were seeking .

In August 2010, in the evening after the Court's hearing had finished, Don Jésus explained to me that he used to be healthy and a keen horse-riding enthusiast, but since his release from detention, he was always in pain, especially his head, back, and arms. He had ulcers and problems with sleeping. Rather than just living his life, he felt he was now a survivor.

I contacted him after the judgment was delivered to ask what he thought of it. As a reflective person from a 'campesino' (peasant farming) family with a few years of education, he gave me a balanced answer. He acknowledged that the case

[176] This is recorded in the *Vélez Loor* judgment, para 235 and, along with other failures, would lead the Inter-American Court to find Panama in violation of the duty to investigate Mr Vélez Loor's allegations of torture.

had furthered the rights of migrants, but also expressed disappointment, especially at the lack of recognition for the torture he had suffered.

Still later, I asked him whether he had any objection to the account of his experience being presented in this book and to confirm that I could mention that he was living as an illegal immigrant in Bolivia, with access only to casual work. He said it was all fine. He added that he had received the payment ordered by the Court and the judgment had been published. However, the general measures of implementation remained to be executed.[177] As he had already told me in San José, his dream was to see a film made about his ordeal and the Inter-American proceedings.

XIV. Vulnerability rather than Equality: Where the Inter-American Court refused to go in *Vélez Loor*

As we have seen previously, the Inter-American Court did not hesitate to stress the vulnerability of an individual who is not only a migrant but also an irregular migrant, and not only an irregular migrant but in detention, in order to pronounce that immigration detention should include due process guarantees. However CEJIL would have wanted it to go further. CEJIL had argued that the violations which Jésus Vélez Loor had suffered had been 'framed within a generalized context of discrimination and criminalization of immigration' in order to reduce migration flows especially of irregular migrants.[178] In response, the Court reaffirmed the *jus cogens* character of the principle of equality and non-discrimination.[179] It also repeated from its previous case law that the confirmation of a single case of violation of human rights is not sufficient in itself to presume the existence of a widespread practice.[180] It considered an 'alleged context of generalized discrimination [to be] an issue of fact [for which] the alleging party must offer evidence'.[181] Mr Vélez Loor's representatives had referred to reports of UN rapporteurs and other reports by NGOs or private individuals.[182] The Court considered that these were not sufficient to consider the said context proven.[183] One will never know how the bench which adopted Advisory opinion no. 18 would have decided *Vélez Loor*. One nonetheless somehow expects that it would have been more open to the argument put forward by the victim's representatives.

Although the Court did not foreclose the possibility that it might find the point persuasive in the future were stronger evidence to be put before it, the level of proof which it requires appears to have gone up over the years. This is a phenomenon which legal representatives from a variety of NGOs I met during my visit to San José in 2012 told me was happening across the board of the case law. One

177 *Vélez Loor v. Panama*, Supervision of execution of judgment, Resolution (IACtHR), 26 Feb. 2013.

178 *Vélez Loor* judgment, para 246.

179 *Vélez Loor*, para 248.

180 *Vélez Loor*, para 249.

181 *Vélez Loor*, para 250.

182 *Vélez Loor*, para 250.

183 *Vélez Loor*, para 251.

example I was given related to allegations of torture: these were found not proven even in the case of *Cabrera García and Montiel Flores v. Mexico*, which had been heard in the same session as *Vélez Loor* and where the evidence appeared at first sight very strong.[184] The record of the Inter-American Court is therefore mixed, and the question of how it will want to go in the future open. On the positive side we shall see in Chapter 14 that it has continued to expand the human rights standards it has been developing in most recent migrant cases.

XV. Conclusion

Immigration detention is now a routine tool of migration management. The numbers are horrifying: to cite only one figure, it is said to affect annually one million children worldwide.[185] NGOs have continued to raise awareness of this worsening situation but to no avail.

The European Court of Human Rights has done little to counteract this trend. In the early days of the Strasbourg system, the Commission did not see any reason to express the opinion that Article 5(1)(f) ECHR had been violated. A path was created which may explain the hands-off approach which the Court adopted in cases such as *Chahal, Ntumba Kabongo, Gebremedhin*, and *Saadi v. the United Kingdom*. This is not to suggest that the Strasbourg Court has never found that immigration detention was wrong. There are plenty of examples where breaches of the Convention have been found. It is to say, however, that the Court has refrained from adopting a position of principle.

I remember that the first time I read about the actual circumstances in which immigration detention took place in the UK,[186] I thought that if only the public were made aware that immigration detainees did not benefit from the safeguards which apply in the criminal process,[187] that their periods of detention were recalculated at each transfer, making them 'indefinitely' long,[188] as well as of other shocking circumstances, then there would be a general outcry. I was obviously wrong to think that the main reason for the lack of outcry was that immigration detention was occurring out of sight. When it came into the limelight of the European Court of Human Rights, only a minority of judges exclaimed: 'Is it a crime to be a foreigner?'

[184] *Cabrera García and Montiel Flores v. Mexico*, Preliminary Exceptions, Merits, Reparation and Costs, Judgment (IACtHR), 26 Nov. 2010.

[185] Stephanie Grant, 'Immigration Detention: Some Issues of Inequality' (2011) *The Equal Rights Review* 7, 69–82 at 71.

[186] This draft became: Mary Bosworth, 'Human Rights and Immigration Detention in the United Kingdom', in Marie-Bénédicte Dembour and Tobias Kelly (eds) *Are Human Rights for Migrants?* (Abingdon: Routledge, 2011) 165–183.

[187] E.g. the British education inspection service—Office for Standards of Education, Children's Services and Skills (OFSTED)—does not extend to immigration detention centres: Bosworth 'Human Rights'.

[188] As noted by the documentary film *How Long is Indefinite?* by Alexis L. Wood (2013).

The case law which has emanated from the Inter-American Court of Human Rights on immigration detention could not have been more unequivocal in its declaration that it could be nothing more than a last resort, for use in exceptional circumstances, and only with fair trial guarantees in place. Saying that *Vélez Loor* was easy to achieve because Latin Americans would naturally be inclined to protect immigrants will not suffice. An anti-migrant discourse is not absent in the Americas, as we have seen through the Dominican Republic's attitude towards Haitians, discussed in Chapter 9. What has made the *Vélez Loor* ruling possible is the Inter-American Court's determination to question the version presented by the defendant state, its willingness to explore the details of the facts of the case, its sympathy for the victim, and its refusal to make her (the victim) bear responsibility for the actions of the authorities, which are their own.

Human rights is too complex a project for this book to make sweeping assessments that imply that the Inter-American Court always gets it right. Conversely, there is no denial that the Strasbourg case law contains many causes for celebration, even if one wishes the European Court would more often abandon its deferential attitude towards states. Chapter 12 discusses a case where it has done this magnificently.

12

Domestic Asylum Procedures Aside: Scrutinising Strasbourg's 'Scrutiny' (*M.S.S.*)

The eagerly anticipated Grand Chamber judgment in the *M.S.S. v. Belgium and Greece* case came out on 21 January 2011.[1] I first read it on a train journey and it was such music to my ears that I remember smiling all the way, sometimes hardly believing what I was reading. Not written in the style I had grown accustomed to expect from the European Court of Human Rights, it embodied a pro-applicant attitude which I had come to associate more readily with the Inter-American Court. On my journey back in the evening, I was sitting by chance across from an acquaintance who happens to be a migration expert. I poured out to him my excitement about the judgment. Even though I had not yet had the time to read its 117 pages, I had already sensed the jurisprudential leaps which the Court had been ready to make. My companion was almost taken aback. He seemed a bit concerned by what I was telling him the European Court had said and done. This chapter seeks to identify why the judgment is so out of the ordinary, why it comes across as a cause for either celebration or concern, and how it fits within the history of the Strasbourg case law.

The applicant in *M.S.S.* was an Afghan national who had left Kabul in early 2008 after, he said, escaping a murder attempt by the Taliban in reprisal for having worked as an interpreter for the international forces stationed in Kabul.[2] After arriving in Belgium in February 2009, he applied for asylum. A search for his fingerprints in the Eurodac database (of fingerprints of asylum seekers and immigrants) identified Greece as the first EU country which he had entered. As such, under a piece of European Union legislation informally known as 'Dublin II', the Belgian authorities deemed Greece the most appropriate country for examining his asylum application. Belgium expelled the applicant to Greece in June 2009. Once in Greece, his asylum claim was left unprocessed and he was at risk of an Article 3-proscribed return to Afghanistan. Multi-party litigation ensued

[1] *M.S.S. v. Belgium and Greece*, appl. 30696/09, GC Judgment (ECtHR), 21 Jan. 2011.

[2] *M.S.S.*, para 31. The judgment says that this is what he 'claimed'. On the significance of this vocabulary, see Chapter 7 (pp. 210–211).

at Strasbourg. Its three most important aspects for the purposes of this chapter concerned the quality of the Greek asylum procedures under Article 13; the possible responsibility of the Belgian government under Article 3 for having returned the applicant to a country where the asylum procedures were allegedly defective; and the quality of the domestic asylum procedures in Belgium itself. In addition, the applicant complained that the conditions under which he had been living in Greece, including being detained for two short periods and being homeless and forced to live in a park in Athens for almost two years, were inhuman and degrading, and thus contrary to Article 3. He claimed that this engaged responsibility under the European Convention on Human Rights, with the responsible state for these violations being not only Greece, but also Belgium (for having transferred him to these conditions).

Previous Strasbourg case law could have suggested that the case would simply be summarily rejected (by a committee of three as *M.S.S.* was lodged in June 2009, exactly one year before single-judge formations came into place). Instead it became a Grand Chamber judgment which questioned the 'Dublin II' mechanism[3] and brought most significant innovations to ECHR law. This was achieved thanks to a reasoning which embraced a consistent and far-reaching human rights logic, refraining from accepting state arguments wholesale and implicitly rejecting the relevance of the 'well-established' principle of international law which grants states the right to expel aliens (subject to certain exceptions).

Remarkably the judgment was adopted by a near-unanimous Grand Chamber. If the ruling was so obvious, why did it take so long for a case like *M.S.S.* to arise? What were the obstacles? Of equal importance, what were the favourable factors in a context which was not propitious to its emergence? Crucial too is the question of whether one can expect the most remarkable features of *M.S.S* to prove enduring. Finally one has to ask whether the reach of the judgment is sufficient to stem the tide of ever deteriorating asylum conditions in Europe.

The last question is particularly important. As it has been observed, '[s]ince the early 1980s, European States have virtually exhausted the repertoire of feasible restrictions to asylum systems—short of outright abandonment of the 1951 Geneva Convention'.[4] Chapter 7 indirectly suggested that, for the prohibition of a return contrary to Article 3 ECHR to be worthy of the claim of absoluteness which is attached to it, any procedure which is used to decide the question of whether a return is contrary to or, more crucially, actually *compliant with* Article 3, must be extremely robust. One aim of this chapter is accordingly to use *M.S.S.* as an opportunity to comment upon the contribution which the European Court of Human Rights has made—or not, as the case may be—in this area of tremendous significance. This chapter accordingly introduces the overall Strasbourg context of the *M.S.S.* litigation with a view to paying particular attention to the aspects

[3] Violeta Moreno-Lax, 'Dismantling the Dublin System: *M.S.S. v. Belgium and Greece*' (2012) *European Journal of Migration and Law* 14, 1–31.

[4] Christina Boswell, 'Europe and International Migration', in B. Marshall (ed.) *The Politics of Migration* (London: Routledge, 2006) 100.

of the case which pertain to the scrutiny of domestic procedures for determining asylum claims.

The greatest part of the chapter is taken up by explaining *M.S.S.* The following elements are reviewed: the 'Dublin' mechanism; the numerous violation headings; the way the Court lightened the applicant's burden of proof while at the same time making it clear that it expected the respondent states to have known better and to have behaved more appropriately; the judgment's reversal of the Strasbourg reversal; the way the respondent states relied on the previous lead *K.R.S.* case, but only to convince one single judge (Judge Bratza); the circumstances which made *M.S.S.* possible, including the identity of the two national judges (Judge Tulkens and Judge Rozakis); the Court's apparent irritation at the way the respondent states tried to blame the applicant for his situation; and the abysmal nature of the asylum procedure and living conditions in Greece which, because they were highly documented, meant that the Court could not carry on condoning transfers to Greece.

The chapter then proceeds on a different track and explains why it took so long for the judgment to appear, with reference to the underdeveloped Article 13 case law. The Court's lack of insistence on states developing robust domestic asylum procedures is then linked to the rise, up to 2011, of Rule 39 requests, whereby desperate applicants asked the Court to order the state not to proceed with their removal until their complaints under the Convention have been properly examined at Strasbourg. Ominously the Rule 39 caseload has virtually disappeared today, making one wonder where refused asylum seekers at risk of treatment contrary to Article 3 now turn. The chapter ends by making clear that the Court is ready to allow migrants to be returned to serious adversity, including in Afghanistan. This is in part because it requires an impossibly high level of documentation before accepting that the general situation is too dangerous for migrants to be returned there.

I. The Context: 'Dublin II'

In 1997, 'the Dublin Convention', informally named after the city where it was signed, was adopted by 12 (extended to 13, then 15) European states, acting outside the formal European Community structure. Its centrepiece consisted of the principle that the country through which an asylum seeker enters the territory of the signatories is in principle responsible for the examination of their asylum claim. In 2003, 'Dublin' was integrated into the European Union framework through the adoption of Regulation 2003/343/CE, which became known as 'Dublin II'.

Dublin's original aim had been to prevent asylum claims being submitted in numerous European states by individuals who were trying to find the national asylum system which might prove most beneficial to them. This kind of 'forum shopping' was generating duplication in administrative procedures, at a time when there was an outpouring of refugees from the wars raging in the former

Yugoslavia. It was felt that this could be avoided through the adoption of principles clearly allocating responsibility for determining the asylum claim of a particular individual to one specific country. Since these early days, however, 'Dublin' has become highly controversial and criticised from increasing quarters because of the pressure it puts on some member states located on the fringe of the EU borders. As can readily be seen, the system benefits those states—such as the UK, France, and the Netherlands—which have the good fortune of not being at the EU borders typically crossed by asylum seekers. Conversely the system puts at a marked disadvantage states which are in this situation, including Greece, Malta, and Italy, as well as Poland in the north. Today it is puzzling to read that 'Dublin' was initially adopted in an effort to facilitate asylum 'burden sharing' amongst European states.

Neither the original Dublin Convention of 1997 nor the Regulation adopted within the EU framework in 2003 had ever obliged an EU member state to return an asylum seeker to the first EU country they had entered. Under EU law, the Dublin principle instituted a mere facility rather than an obligation for the transferring member state, which was always free to disregard the principle. A so-called 'sovereignty clause' specifically allowed EU member states to carry on examining asylum claims themselves if they so wished. On the pressing recommendation of NGOs, especially the UNHCR, some states had actually refrained from transferring asylum seekers to Greece before the *M.S.S.* judgment came out because of the dire conditions which existed there.

II. The Extraordinary *M.S.S.*: A Brief Tour of the Judgment

For the European Court of Human Rights to denounce 'Dublin transfers' to Greece in *M.S.S.*, it logically had to be accepted that Belgium should have refrained altogether from applying the core principle of the Dublin Regulation and from sending the applicant back to Greece. The central question in *M.S.S.* was: under the European Convention, was Belgium under an obligation to refrain from transferring M.S.S. to Greece because of Article 3-proscribed conditions to which asylum seekers were subjected there? To get to a positive answer to this question, it first had to ascertain that the asylum situation in Greece was unacceptable. This the Court did through a series of findings.

First, the Court found that, as an asylum seeker, the applicant should not have been detained,[5] and certainly not in the inhuman and degrading conditions which had been reported to exist in Greece by multiple organisations. The Court paid attention to documents from numerous reliable sources, with one reporting, for example, overcrowding of such a level that detainees could not all lie down and sleep at the same time (even on the cell's bare floor), and such poor access to water that detainees were obliged to drink from the toilets.[6] While it was not

[5] *M.S.S.* judgment, para 216.

[6] *M.S.S.*, para 230.

disputed that the applicant had spent four and seven days respectively in detention, the government contested that the applicant had suffered the inhuman and degrading conditions denounced in general reports, since the documentation on which these reports had been based had not been collected at the exact period of the applicant's detention and might have related to a different cell from the one which he had been occupying. Thus the government argued that 'the applicant had adduced no evidence' supporting his claim that *he* had suffered conditions contrary to Article 3.[7] Unanimously, the Court refused this objection and found a violation of Article 3 in respect of the conditions of M.S.S.'s detention, thus adding to a growing body of Strasbourg case law concerning detention conditions in Greece.[8]

A second crucial and most innovative finding concerned the living conditions of the applicant in a park in the middle of Athens for many months: in a state of the most extreme poverty, in constant fear of being attacked, and without any prospect of the situation improving.[9] In a clear and largely unprecedented lightening of the burden of proof generally put on the applicant at Strasbourg, the Court, yet again on the basis of concordant reports, saw 'no reason to question the truth of the applicant's allegations'.[10] It proceeded to rule that the Greek authorities had to be held responsible under Article 3 ECHR for the inhuman and degrading conditions of these living conditions, given that the Greek government had taken no action to remedy them despite a clear obligation to do so under a number of laws, particularly the EU Reception Directive which Greece had transposed into its legal system.[11] This aspect of the judgment was reached by 16 votes to one.

The Court finally found, again by unanimity, that the Greek procedures for examining asylum claims were defective, and therefore in breach of Article 13.[12] This was because, although procedures for processing asylum claims assuredly existed in Greek law, *in practice* they did not ensure that the Greek authorities would seriously examine the arguable claim which M.S.S. had made that he could not be returned to Afghanistan without this being in violation of Article 3. The Court observed that a wide array of reputable organisations had long reported on the shortcomings of the Greek asylum procedure, in terms both of its accessibility and internal quality.[13] One detail from a report cited in the judgment gives an idea of the magnitude of the accessibility problem: 'At the present time about twenty applications are being registered per day, while up to 2,000 people are waiting outside to complete various formalities'—this as 'asylum applications can be lodged only on one day in the week'.[14] In addition the examination of actual asylum applications was defective due to various factors, including interviews held without an interpreter,[15] lack of training of the staff conducting these interviews,[16] lack of legal aid,[17] and an acute shortage of lawyers able to take up asylum cases.[18]

[7] *M.S.S.*, para 207.
[8] *M.S.S.*, para 234.
[9] *M.S.S.*, para 254.
[10] *M.S.S.*, para 255.
[11] *M.S.S.*, paras 250 and 263.
[12] *M.S.S.*, para 321.
[13] *M.S.S.*, para 300.
[14] *M.S.S.*, para 180.
[15] *M.S.S.*, para 181.
[16] *M.S.S.*, para 185.
[17] *M.S.S.*, para 301.
[18] *M.S.S.*, para 319.

The result was a near total absence of recognition of refugee status in Greece, as follows:

For 2008, the UNHCR report[ed] a success rate at first instance (proportion of positive decisions in relation to all the decisions taken) of 0.04% for refugee status under the Geneva Convention (eleven people), and 0.06% for humanitarian or subsidiary protection (eighteen people)... 12,095 appeals were lodged against unfavourable decisions. They led to 25 people being granted refugee status by virtue of the Geneva Convention and 11 for humanitarian reasons or subsidiary protection. Where appeals were concerned, the respective success rates were 2.87% and 1.26%. By comparison, in 2008 the average success rate at first instance was 36.2% in five of six countries which, along with Greece, receive[d] the largest number of applications (France, the United Kingdom, Italy, Sweden and Germany).[19]

From reading *M.S.S.* there is no doubt about the abysmal character of the situation of asylum seekers in Greece. These conditions led the Court to find Greece in violation of the Convention on three counts, as already reviewed: a violation of Article 3 in respect of the applicant's conditions of detention (unanimous); a second violation of Article 3 in respect of the applicant's living conditions (16 votes to one); and a violation of Article 13 taken in conjunction with Article 3 'because of the deficiencies in the asylum procedure followed in the applicant's case and the risk of his expulsion to Afghanistan without any serious examination of the merits of his asylum application and without any access to an effective remedy' (unanimous).[20] These findings in turn open the way for the Court to find Belgium also to have committed multiple violations of the Convention for having sent the applicant to a place where he was at 'real risk' of suffering treatment contrary to Article 3.

By 16 votes to one, the Court finds that the Belgian authorities were at fault for having refrained from verifying that the Greek authorities were actually applying their legislation on asylum, at a time when deficiencies in the Greek procedures had been widely denounced so that the Belgian authorities should have been aware of the need to do this. As such the risk of the applicant not having access to the Greek asylum procedure and being sent back by the Greek authorities was 'real and individual enough' to fall within the scope of Article 3.[21] Moreover, by transferring the applicant to Greece, the Court considers that Belgium had knowingly exposed him to proscribed conditions of detention and living conditions.[22] This further ruling was adopted by 15 votes to two.

As if this was not enough, the Court continues by unanimously finding Belgium in violation of Article 13 taken in conjunction with Article 3 because of the lack of effective remedy which had been available to the applicant in Belgium

[19] *M.S.S.*, para 126. The 'Geneva Convention' referred to by the Court corresponds to what this book has been calling the 'Refugee Convention'.

[20] *M.S.S.*, operative part of the judgment, point 7.

[21] *M.S.S.*, para 359. On the significance of the characterisation of the risk being 'real and individual enough', see Section XI Chapter 7.

[22] *M.S.S.*, para 367.

in order to contest his expulsion to Greece.[23] The reasons for this last finding will transpire as our discussion proceeds. Suffice it to say at this stage that this particular ruling required the Court to dismiss the claim by the respondent state that the remedies which existed in Belgian law were adequate. In turn, this required the Court to examine whether, in practice, the applicant was in a *real* position to access remedies theoretically open to him and, when the government argued that he had not even tried to access some remedies, whether these remedies could have made a real difference to his fate and enabled him to remain in Belgium and have his asylum application examined there. The Court answered these two questions in the negative.

III. The Court Distances Itself from the Respondent States

The reader will now have a sense of some of the reasons why *M.S.S.* is such an extraordinary judgment. Apart from the judgment wounding the 2003 Dublin Regulation, what is also striking is that the Court constantly refrains in this case from following what can be described as its usual practice of siding with the state and distancing itself from the applicant (as documented in previous chapters). The Court resorts to five techniques to achieve this.

The first technique is that, whenever facts are disputed (as was the case for all the complaints directed against Greece) the Strasbourg Court systematically lightens the burden of proof placed on the applicant. Each time the Court says it is doing this because of the abundance of information collected by international organisations.[24] The crucial move towards redistributing the burden of proof has not failed to attract the ire of some commentators.[25] Without this step having been taken, however, it is difficult to see how any violation could have been found in the case.

[23] *M.S.S.*, paras 362–397.

[24] Regarding the conditions of detention in Greece, the Court observes that '[I]t is not possible to establish with certainty exactly what happened to the applicant. However, the Court is once again obliged to note that the applicant's allegations are consistent with numerous accounts collected from witnesses by international organisations': *M.S.S.*, para 227. Regarding his living conditions in Athens, 'the Court sees no reason to question the truth of the applicant's allegations' for the same reason that they are consistent with the description provided in numerous reports: para 255. Regarding information about domestic asylum procedures which Greece said the applicant had received but which the applicant said he had not received, as well as an appointment he missed, the Court 'attaches more weight to the applicant's version because it is corroborated by a very large number of accounts collected from other witnesses by the [Council of Europe's] Commissioner [for Human Rights], the UNHCR and various non-governmental organizations': paras 304 and 311. For the same reason, the Court accepts that 'the applicant should not be expected to bear the entire burden of proof' in respect of the allegation that Belgium should have known the general situation which prevailed in Greece regarding the deficiencies of the asylum procedure: para 352.

[25] Marc Bossuyt, 'Belgium Condemned for Inhuman or Degrading Treatment Due to Violations by Greece of EU Asylum Law' (2011) *European Human Rights Law Review* 581–596; Cédric Raux, 'La politique d'asile de l'union européenne dans le viseur de la Cour européenne des droits de l'homme' (2011) *Revue trimestrielle des droits de l'homme* 88, 1023–1043 at 1038–1039.

The second technique is that the Court approaches the story presented by the respondent states from a realistic mindset which results in its expressing scepticism towards what it is being told. Examples are peppered throughout the judgment, but I shall provide three in respect of each state. The first concern Greece:

- to the government's criticism of the applicant for not having set the asylum procedure in motion by presenting himself to the relevant authorities within the prescribed time limit,[26] the Court responds that the time limit (three days) was 'a very short one considering how difficult it is to gain access to the [authorities] concerned';[27]
- the Court writes that it 'is not convinced by the Greek Government's explanations concerning the policy of returns to Afghanistan on a voluntary basis [because it] cannot ignore the fact that forced returns by Greece to high-risk countries have regularly been denounced by the third-party interveners [such as the UNHCR and the Greek Helsinki Monitor] and several of the reports consulted by the Court';[28]
- the Greek government claimed that, if needed, an application to the Supreme Administrative Court for judicial review following a rejection of the applicant's request for asylum would provide a safety net against any expulsion contrary to Article 3.[29] The Court is not convinced. In its words, the way the Greek authorities have 'taken no steps to ensure communication between the competent authorities and the applicant, [coupled with malfunctions in the notification procedure reported by the Commissioner and the UNHCR], makes it very uncertain whether the applicant will be able to learn the outcome of his asylum application in time to react within the prescribed time-limit'.[30]

Turning to Belgium:

- The Court disagrees with the Belgian Government's argument that, because he had failed to voice them at his interview, the Aliens Office had not been aware of the applicant's fears in the event of his transfer back to Greece at the time when it issued the order for him to leave the country.[31]
- The Court 'considers it established that in spite of the few examples of application of the sovereignty clause produced by the Government... the Aliens Office systematically applied the Dublin Regulation to transfer people to Greece without so much as considering the possibility of making an exception'.[32]
- An appeal with the Aliens Appeals Board for setting aside the order to leave the country had been faxed by the applicant's counsel at 10.25 a.m. on 29 May 2009.[33] The hearing of this appeal was then scheduled to take place

[26] *M.S.S.*, para 305.
[27] *M.S.S.*, para 306.
[28] *M.S.S.*, para 314.
[29] *M.S.S.*, para 316.
[30] *M.S.S.*, para 318.
[31] *M.S.S.*, para 346.
[32] *M.S.S.*, para 352.
[33] *M.S.S.*, para 21.

> at 11.30 am in Brussels on the same day.[34] Counsel's office was in Tongres, almost 100 kilometres away. The appeal was rejected on procedural grounds, namely the applicant's failure to appear.[35] The Court remarks that '[i]t fails to see how his counsel could possibly have reached the seat of the Aliens Appeals Board in time. As to the possibility of requesting assistance from a round-the-clock service, the Court notes in any event that the Government have supplied no proof of the existence of such a service *in practice*'.[36]

These examples, and others in the judgment, clearly show the Court unwilling to take the words presented to it by the states at face value.

Moving to a third point, the Court criticises the respondent states on a couple of occasions for not having thought better about the actual conditions of the applicant's situation. To quote, the Court 'does not see how the [Greek] authorities could have failed to notice or to assume that the applicant was homeless in Greece';[37] it 'considers that at the time of the applicant's expulsion the Belgian authorities knew or ought to have known that [the applicant] had no guarantee that his asylum application would be seriously examined by the Greek authorities'.[38]

Fourth, going one step further still, the Court chastises each state for not having taken the course of action which the situation required. It does not hesitate to state, for example, that 'the Greek authorities should not simply have waited for the applicant to take the initiative of turning to the police headquarters to provide for his essential needs';[39] it finds them 'responsible, because of their inaction, for the situation in which [the applicant] found himself for several months, living in the street, with no resources or access to sanitary facilities, and without any means of providing for his essential needs'.[40] The Court also regrets that 'the Greek authorities have not taken any steps to communicate with the applicant or reached any decision [on his asylum application]'.[41] To the Belgian government's argument that 'the applicant had not sufficiently individualized, before the Belgian authorities, the risk of having no access to the asylum procedure [in Greece]', the Court responds that 'it was in fact up to the Belgian authorities [to] verify how the Greek authorities applied their legislation on asylum in practice'.[42]

In a different register, a fifth technique is identifiable, namely, the readiness by the Court to find violation after violation of the Convention. One might colloquially say that the European Court goes in for the kill. Of all the complaints put forward by the applicant, only one appears to have been left unexamined by the Court: the allegation that Belgium would have violated Article 2 by expelling the applicant to Greece.[43] Article 2 concerns the right to life. As there is no indication that the applicant actually ever neared death, the Court's finding that there was no need to examine his Article 2 complaints against Belgium after having reached violation verdicts on Article 3 appears reasonable.

[34] *M.S.S.*, para 22. [35] *M.S.S.*, para 392.
[36] *M.S.S.*, para 392, emphasis added [37] *M.S.S.*, para 258.
[38] *M.S.S.*, para 358. [39] *M.S.S.*, para 259. [40] *M.S.S.*, para 263.
[41] *M.S.S.*, para 313. [42] *M.S.S.*, para 359. [43] *M.S.S.*, paras 3, 361, and 397.

Through these five techniques, the Court: (a) accepts the allegations of the applicant; (b) approaches the respondent states' allegation with a degree of caution, thus implicitly reversing the burden of proof onto the state; (c) seems to take every opportunity to scrutinise the conduct of the state; and (d) understands 'inhuman and degrading treatment' beyond the common understanding of what these words mean in the context of the UN Refugee Convention. These constitute lines of reasoning which section XIII of Chapter 7 highlighted as propitious to the development of a Strasbourg pro-migrant case law. To use the image of the title of this section, I would indeed consider *M.S.S.* to be very close to embodying what the leading case of my imagination would look like.

IV. Embracing a Human Rights Reasoning: The Reversal of the Reversal

Some commentators think the Court went too far in *M.S.S* by resolutely siding with the applicant and distancing itself from the states.[44] The point of human rights law is, however, to scrutinise state behaviour. For a human rights court to start from a position which distrusts the state, or at least demands that it justifies itself can or indeed should appear entirely natural. Admittedly, such an approach has not been at the core of the way the Strasbourg migrant case law has developed, as this book has demonstrated. This is exactly what makes the consistency of a judicial impulse which is suspicious rather than trusting of the state, such a remarkable and unusual position in the *M.S.S.* reasoning. As far as I am aware, such a determined resolve is new on the part of a Grand Chamber acting in a migrant case.

This resolve goes hand in hand with the conspicuous absence anywhere in the *M.S.S.* judgment of any reference to the supposedly 'well-established principle of international law', which is otherwise commonly encountered in the Strasbourg migrant case law. That the principle is nowhere to be seen results from the logic adopted by the Court: there is no obvious point in the development where it could be added: mentioning it would detract from the reasoning which the Court follows. In other words, it simply has no place in the reasoning deployed in *M.S.S*.

Admittedly, thanks to the perspective of judges sympathetic to the plight of the migrant applicant, the Strasbourg migrant case law has far from always contained a reference to this principle. What is further noticeable, however, is that in *M.S.S.* the Court implicitly and perhaps ironically stresses this absence by retaining the adjective 'well-established', but this time in order to qualify its own case law rather than a principle of public international law which has nothing to do with human rights. Thus, the Court's reasoning about the merits of the applicant's complaint regarding his exposure by Belgium to inhuman and degrading

44 Bossuyt 'Belgium Condemned'; Raux 'La politique d'asile'.

conditions of detention and living conditions in Greece starts with the following sentence:

> On the merits, the Court reiterates that according to its well-established case-law the expulsion of an asylum seeker by a Contracting State may give rise to an issue under Article 3, and hence engage the responsibility of the Convention, where substantial grounds have been shown for believing that the person concerned faces a real risk of being subjected to torture or inhuman or degrading treatment or punishment in the receiving country.[45]

The Strasbourg reversal is thereby stood on its head. The various points of law to be taken into consideration appear in the Court's reasoning using human rights logic with the starting point being a provision of the Convention rather than the state's prerogative to exclude without justification.

V. How the Court Overcame its own Case Law: From *T.I.* to *K.R.S.* to *M.S.S.*

M.S.S. is a most impressive achievement on a number of counts, as will be steadily revealed throughout this chapter. We have already seen that the judgment represented a full frontal attack on a major piece of EU legislation and that it adopted a resolutely human rights approach. Let us now add that this achievement was the most outstanding since the Strasbourg Court's own case law had specifically stood in the way of *M.S.S.*

In December 2008, the Court had decided *K.R.S. v. the United Kingdom*, a case which also concerned a Dublin transfer to Greece. *K.R.S.* had been a lead case, meaning that numerous similar applications to Strasbourg had been put on hold by the Court during its examination of the case. The applicant in *K.R.S.* had been an asylum seeker from Iran whom the UK wanted to transfer to Greece, as his first country of arrival in the European Union.[46] Citing the UNHCR's position paper advising EU member states to refrain from returning asylum seekers to Greece and various reports by NGOs, the applicant had argued that his removal to Greece would be in breach of Article 3.

In *K.R.S.*, the Court relied on its previous decision in the case of *T.I. v. the United Kingdom*. In *T.I.* the UK wanted to transfer a Tamil applicant to Germany. The applicant was claiming that, if this happened, he would be at risk of being transferred to Sri Lanka, given that at the time Germany tended to offer protection

[45] *M.S.S.*, paras 365; see also para 342. I am not aware that this kind of formulation had previously been used by the Court in a migrant case. However, *Shamayev and Others v. Georgia and Russia*, appl. 36378/02, Judgment (ECtHR), 12 Apr. 2005, summarises the first point of the Georgian submission regarding the Article 3 extradition complaint by saying that '[t]he Georgian authorities had acted in conformity with the Court's well-established case-law, according to which the State from which an individual is extradited has a duty to ensure that the extradited person will not be subjected to treatment contrary to Article 3 of the Convention': *Shamayev* judgment, para 324.

[46] *K.R.S. v. the United Kingdom*, appl. 32733/08, Decision (ECtHR), 2 Dec. 2008.

under Article 3 ECHR only if the prohibited treatment emanated from authorities acting in their official function, while T.I. feared excesses—not legally condoned but nonetheless widely reported—by individual officials. A majority of the Strasbourg Court was 'satisfied by the German Government's assurances that the applicant would not risk immediate or summary removal to Sri Lanka'.[47] The *T.I.* case was declared inadmissible for being 'manifestly ill-founded' in March 2000. (A few days later, the UK sent back to Germany a Kurd who was then transferred immediately to Turkey. The scenario which T.I. had feared and taken to Strasbourg had occurred, although not to the applicant in *T.I.* but to another individual.[48])

When *K.R.S.* came before the Court eight years later, the unanimous Court stuck to the *T.I.* reasoning. Thus, the Chamber said that '[t]he presumption must be that Greece will abide by its [international] obligations'. In the Court's view, it would be open to the applicant to lodge an application at Strasbourg directed against Greece if he found upon transferral to Greece that he was at risk of removal to Iran. On the possibility that the applicant might suffer treatment contrary to Article 3 while in Greece, the Court replied that although 'the objective information before it on conditions of detention in Greece is of some concern, [any claim in this respect] should also be pursued first with the Greek domestic authorities and thereafter in an application to this Court'.

On the basis of the *K.R.S.* unanimous lead decision as to admissibility, subsequent complaints about transfers to Greece had virtually no chance of being found admissible (with *M.S.S.* a startling exception, of course). In addition, Rule 39 requests from asylum seekers about to be transferred to Greece were also rejected. This book has hardly mentioned 'Rule 39' so far, despite its central importance to the migrant case law during the period during which the research for this book was conducted. Rule 39 of the Court allows it to grant an applicant interim relief to prevent irreparable harm from taking place. Thousands of requests were received in 2010 and 2011. By far the most common application is a request that the Court prohibit a state from removing someone to a place where they face a real risk of treatment prohibited by Article 3. If granted, since 2005, such an order is considered binding on the state which receives it.[49] The granting of interim relief does not mean that the Court will necessarily find a violation of the Convention when it decides upon the merits of the case. It nonetheless indicates to the respondent state that the Court is treating the case seriously. In *M.S.S.* the applicant had applied to the Court to have his transfer to Greece suspended through a Rule 39 request.[50] Following the *K.R.S.* precedent, the Court had refused this request.[51]

[47] *T.I. v. the United Kingdom*, appl. 43844/98, Decision (ECtHR), 7 Mar. 2000.

[48] Nuala Mole, 'Exposé', in *Actes du 2e Colloque sur la Convention européenne des Droits de l'Homme et la protection des réfugiés, des demandeurs d'asile et des personnes déplacées [Strasbourg, 19–20 mai 2000]* (Strasbourg: Council of Europe, 2001) 39–50 at 44.

[49] *Mamatkulov and Askarov v. Turkey*, appls 46827/99, 46951/99, Judgment (ECtHR), 4 Feb. 2005.

[50] *M.S.S.* judgment, para 31.

[51] *M.S.S.*, para 32.

Not surprisingly, this became a major argument used by the Belgian government in the Strasbourg *M.S.S.* litigation. Not without reason, the government argued:

Belgium had had no reason to apply the [sovereignty] clause [of the Dublin Regulation]. Indeed, the Court itself had not considered it necessary to indicate an interim measure to the Belgian Government to suspend the applicant's transfer.[52]

Not surprisingly, the Belgian government also relied on *K.R.S.* in its submissions.[53]

K.R.S. was understandably also central to the two state third party interventions which the Court received in the *M.S.S.* case. Both interventions strongly encouraged the Court to maintain its case law. The Netherlands argued that:

In keeping with the Court's decision in *K.R.S.*... it was to be assumed that Greece would honour its international obligations and that transferees would be able to appeal to the domestic courts and subsequently, if necessary, to the Court. To reason otherwise would be tantamount to denying the principle of inter-State confidence on which the Dublin system was based... and questioning the balanced, nuanced approach the Court has adopted... in assessing the responsibility of the States when they applied Community law.[54]

Pointing in the same direction, the UK's argument (again, as summarised by the Court) was more multi-stranded. It started as follows:

The Government of the United Kingdom emphasised that the Dublin Regulation afforded a fundamental advantage in speeding up the examination of applications, so that the persons concerned did not have time to develop undue social and cultural ties in a State. That being so, it should be borne in mind that calling to account under Article 3 the State responsible for the asylum application prior to the transfer, as in the present case, was bound to slow down the whole process no end. The Government of the United Kingdom were convinced that such complaints... should be avoided when the State responsible for handling the asylum application was a party to the Convention. In such cases, as the Court had found in *K.R.S.* decision [*sic*], the normal interpretation of the Convention would mean the interested parties lodging their complaints with the courts in the State responsible for processing the asylum application and subsequently, perhaps, to the Court.[55]

The Court was not convinced that the British argument accurately rendered the reality of Dublin transfers to Greece. One of the factors which persuaded the Court that the Convention's supposedly 'normal' interpretation did not work in practice was 'the very small number of Rule 39 requests for interim measures against Greece lodged by asylum seekers in that country, compared with the number lodged by asylum seekers in the other States'.[56]

[52] *M.S.S.*, para 327.

[53] *M.S.S.*, para 329. The Belgian government also relied on *Said Bashir, Shahla and Said Amir Quraishi v. Belgium*, appl. 6130/08, Decision (ECtHR), 12 May 2009, in French only. This case involved Afghan applicants whose Strasbourg application was declared inadmissible in view of the fact that they still had a remedy pending in Belgium against their transfer to Greece.

[54] *M.S.S.*, para 330. [55] *M.S.S.*, para 331. [56] *M.S.S.*, para 357.

This factor, by contrast, did not enter the British government's reasoning which continued its submissions by arguing that the *K.R.S.* interpretation:

> ... did not absolve the transferring States of their responsibility for potential violations of the Convention though it meant that their responsibility could be engaged only in wholly exceptional circumstances where it was demonstrated that the persons concerned would not have access to the Court in the State responsible for dealing with the asylum application. No such circumstances were present in the instant case, however.[57]

If not in Greece with its 0.1 per cent recognition rate at first instance and the small number of Rule 39 requests emanating from it, where could such circumstances ever be found? The British government's categorical conclusion appears almost risible after the *M.S.S.* judgment.

It remains the case that the authoritative Strasbourg case law presented the Court with a problem if it wished to overturn the *K.R.S.* 'normal interpretation of the Convention' in *M.S.S.* This difficulty was well put by Judge Bratza in his dissenting opinion in *M.S.S.*, which is worth quoting at some length:

> The majority's conclusion appears to me to pay insufficient regard to the unanimous decision of the Court concerning the return of asylum seekers to Greece under the Dublin Regulation in the lead case of *K.R.S. v. the United Kingdom*, which was delivered in December 2008, less than 6 months prior to the return of the present applicant, and which had been relied on not only by national authorities but by the Court itself in rejecting numerous requests for interim measures.[58] ...
>
> Whether or not, with the benefit of hindsight, the *K.R.S.* case should be regarded as correctly decided by the Court, Member States concerned with the removal of persons to Greece under the Dublin Regulation were, in my view, legitimately entitled to follow and apply the decision in the absence of any clear evidence of a change in the situation in Greece which had been the subject of examination by the Court or in the absence of special circumstances affecting the position of the particular applicant.[59] ...
>
> I am unpersuaded that any of the developments relied on in the [*M.S.S.* judgment] should have led the Belgian authorities in June 2009 to treat the decision as no longer authoritative or to conclude that the return of the applicant would violate Article 3 ... I have difficulty in seeing how it can be held against the Belgian authorities that they failed to take account of material which was already in the public domain at the time of the *K.R.S.* decision itself.[60] ...
>
> I have similar difficulty in seeing how, in June 2009, the presumption of Greek compliance which the Court had found to exist in December 2008 could be rebutted by the numerous reports and other information which became available in the second half of 2009 and in 2010 [to which the Court refers in its *M.S.S.* judgment].[61] ...
>
> I note [not only the refusal of the Rule 39 application in the present case but also] that it is acknowledged in the judgment ... that, at the time of refusing the application, the Court was 'fully aware of the situation in Greece' ... [O]f even greater significance in my view ... is the general practice followed by the Court at the material time in the light of the *K.R.S.* decision.... In the period between 1 June and 12 August 2009 alone, interim measures

[57] *M.S.S.*, para 331.
[58] Partly dissenting opinion of Judge Bratza in *M.S.S.* judgment, point 1.
[59] Bratza, point 6. [60] Bratza, point 8. [61] Bratza, point 9.

were refused by the Court in 68 cases of the return of Afghan nationals to Greece from Austria, Belgium, Denmark, France, the Netherlands, Sweden and the United Kingdom.

I find it quite impossible in these circumstances to accept that Belgium and other Member States should have known better at that time or that they were not justified in placing the same reliance on the Court's decision in *K.R.S.* as the Court itself.[62]

Judge Bratza's reasoning is impeccably logical. It also begs the question of how Strasbourg verdicts of non-violation which retrospectively appear to have been unwise can be overturned since they set a precedent on which states should be able to rely, from one case to the next, in order to decide which course of action to adopt. When, then, can the vicious circle which has been engineered and which constantly feeds itself through new case law, ever be stopped?[63]

One small entry the Court did not miss in *M.S.S.* was a letter from the UNHCR to the Belgian minister in charge of immigration, which contained an unequivocal plea for the suspension of transfers to Greece. The letter had been sent on 2 April 2009,[64] thus exactly between the *K.R.S.* decision and M.S.S.'s transfer by Belgium to Greece. The Court attached 'critical importance' to it.[65] The Court also mentioned that the European asylum system of the EU had entered a reform phase in December 2008 which included proposals for strengthening the protection of asylum seekers and implementing a temporary suspension of Dublin transfers to member states unable to offer them sufficient protection.[66]

The truth of the matter, however, is that the situation had only very marginally changed since *K.R.S.* The real problem preventing the Court from heeding the calls from throughout Europe to stop transfers to Greece was its own case law. Had the Court been sufficiently strict with transferring states in the past, when the situation in Greece was already abysmal and denounced in many quarters, the conundrum would not have arisen. As it was, there seemed to be no end to it. To some judges, it must have become increasingly pressing to find a way of breaking the self-perpetuating circle of the *K.R.S.* jurisprudence.

VI. *M.S.S.*: An Exceptional Situation, an Exceptional Applicant, an Exceptional Lawyer, an Exceptional Judge

Although unanimous, the *K.R.S.* decision was controversial even within the Court. It was an open secret, in particular, that the then President of the Second

[62] Bratza, point 14.

[63] Looking at it from the point of view of positive human rights norms, whilst Judge Casadevall has defended the principle of non-regression, Luzius Wildhaber, President of the Court from 1998 to 2007, rejects what he calls the 'one-way-street theory', on the basis that the Court could have been wrong and thus must be allowed to make amends, that many interests are at stake, and that democratic societies may change their values and laws: Luzius Wildhaber, 'Rethinking the European Court of Human Rights', in Jonas Christoffersen and Mikael Rask Madsen (eds) *The European Court of Human Rights between Law and Politics* (Oxford: Oxford University Press, 2011) 204–229 at 215–216.

[64] *M.S.S.* judgment, para 16.

[65] *M.S.S.*, para 349.

[66] *M.S.S.*, para 350.

Section, Judge Tulkens, was not happy with it. It became known in the corridors of the Court and beyond that her Section was not disinclined to grant Rule 39 requests, while the Fourth Section, presided over by Judge Bratza, hardly ever did this. In an oblique reference to this state of affairs, the lack of consistency in the approach to Rule 39 by the Court was, for example, specifically mentioned as something to be remedied in a report commissioned by the Committee on Migration, Refugees and Population of the Parliamentary Assembly of the Council of Europe (PACE).[67]

(This Committee would have deserved a greater place in this book. It has traditionally attempted, within the limited political leverage it commands in the European institutional landscape, to act as a progressive force for migrants. For example, the preparation of the report which I have just mentioned was prompted by the Committee's deep discomfort at the way asylum seekers were treated in Europe in general and within the *K.R.S.* jurisprudence in particular. In a sense, the Committee's report was PACE's way of asking the Court to revise its jurisprudence. By the time the report was formally adopted and it had given rise to a PACE resolution on the same topic,[68] *M.S.S.* had come out. Nonetheless PACE's activities and public position reinforced the legitimacy of the judgment.)

Returning to our main concern, M.S.S.'s request for a Rule 39 application would have gone to the Second Section, as the request was directed against Belgium and such requests normally went to the Section which comprised the national judge. (Since late 2012, they have been decided by a unique decision body, composed of three Section vice-presidents). In the relevant period, a Rule 39 request was normally considered by the President of this Section immediately after it was received at Strasbourg. However, in *M.S.S.* the request would not have gone to Judge Tulkens because she was a national judge in the case, a status which barred her from examining it. The request would thus most likely have gone to the Vice-President of the Second Section. For Rule 39 positive decisions to be effective—given that their aim is to prevent irreparable and imminent harm from taking place—they need to be given more or less 'on the spot'. Sometimes this is literally what happens: the judge stops whatever they are doing, examines the application, and makes their decision. In *M.S.S.* the applicant applied to the Court to have his transfer to Greece suspended on 11 June 2009. The Court refused to apply Rule 39 the next day.

This decision was no doubt adopted in the wake of *K.R.S.* It did not seem that the person who took this decision did so without discomfort, as instead of leaving the matter at that, the Court proceeded to write and inform 'the Greek Government that its decision was based on its confidence that Greece would honour its obligations under the Convention and comply with EU legislation on

[67] PACE Doc. 11978, report of the Committee on Migration, Refugees and Population on 'Preventing harm to refugees and migrants in extradition and expulsion cases: Rule 39 indications by the European Court of Human Rights', adopted on 2 October 2011, rapporteur David Darchiashvili, para 66.

[68] PACE Resolution 1788 (2011).

asylum'.[69] Greece was specifically required 'to inform the Court of the progress of any asylum claim made by the applicant in Greece as well as the place of detention, if he is detained on arrival in Greece'.[70] This unusual letter by the Court can only indicate that whoever refused the Rule 39 request did not trust that the applicant would be all right if the situation was not monitored closely. The fact that Greece did nothing to process M.S.S.'s asylum application even after it received the letter implicitly announcing that *M.S.S.* was destined to become high profile, only serves to demonstrate further the abyss of inefficiency into which Greek asylum determination procedures had fallen.

So the Rule 39 request was rejected on 12 June and M.S.S. was transferred to Greece three days later. What happened next, the *M.S.S.* judgment informs us, is that '[o]n 19 June 2009 the applicant's lawyer received a first text message (sms), in respect of which he informed the Court. It stated that upon arrival the applicant had immediately been placed in detention in a building next to the airport...'.[71] This apparently innocuous sentence is crucial, as it indicates that the applicant kept in contact with his Belgian lawyer. In the great majority of cases, deported migrants 'disappear' from the radar of the lawyers who used to represent them prior to their deportation. Either they are not in a situation which allows them to maintain contact with their lawyer or they simply feel they have no longer any incentive to do so. A lawyer with no contact with his client is in a very difficult situation to continue with a potential case.[72] The problems are multiple, for example lack of instructions, lack of documentation and evidence, and lack of financial reward. On the last point, it is worth noting that asylum cases are typically complicated and time-consuming; as an extremely dedicated asylum lawyer once commented to me, he too had a family to support and could not continually work for free. In *M.S.S.* both the Belgian lawyer and the applicant were exceptional in their determination to maintain contact with each other and to pursue the case at Strasbourg, however much they must have known that their chance of success at this final level was uncertain.

Potential obstacles to persuading the Court that M.S.S. had a case where every other asylum seeker transferred to Greece had previously failed, would have taken many forms. One can highlight, in a non-exhaustive list, the following factors: the applicant had neither been returned to Afghanistan nor been expelled from Greece (though he said he almost was);[73] he had twice tried to leave Greece, once with a false identity card;[74] there was no direct evidence that he had personally suffered inhuman and degrading treatment in Greece; the Greek authorities had issued him with a pink card which theoretically gave him access to the labour

[69] *M.S.S.* judgment, para 32. [70] *M.S.S.*, para 32. [71] *M.S.S.*, para 34.

[72] For an exception which worked, see *Muskhadzhiyeva and others v. Belgium*, appl. 41442/07, Judgment (ECtHR), 19 Jan. 2010, in French only, and my analysis of its non-legal background: Marie-Bénédicte Dembour, 'What it Takes to Make a Case: The Backstage Story of *Muskhadzhiyeva v. Belgium* (Illegality of Children's Immigration Detention)', in Elisabeth Lambert-Abdelgawad (ed.) *Preventing and Sanctioning Hindrances to the Right of Individual Petition to the European Court of Human Rights* (Brussels: Intersentia, 2011) 75–104.

[73] *M.S.S.* judgment, para 53. [74] *M.S.S.*, paras 43 and 53.

market (though his actual chances of finding work were arguably non-existent); educated and fluent in English, he did not fit the stereotype of the vulnerable asylum seeker and one might have said, like Judge Sajó who considered him to be 'in possession of considerable means', that he should not have expected undue exceptional support from the Greek state.[75]

There is never a perfect case, however, as we have already discussed in respect of the *Soering* case in Chapter 7. In an interview, Judge Tulkens told me that there was one feature in the *M.S.S.* case which made it stand out in a most encouraging way. The lawyer, Mr Chihaoui, had had the brilliant idea of directing the complaints not only at the transferring state, but *together* at the transferring and the receiving states.[76] This seems to have been the crucial factor which opened up possibilities for unblocking the case law and dethroning *K.R.S.* from its status of most authoritative precedent as lead, moreover unanimously adopted, decision.

My guess is that Judge Tulkens saw in the *M.S.S.* application a great opportunity to have *K.R.S.* overturned. The judicial deliberations being secret, it is impossible for those who did not attend them to know exactly what happened. But one can make informed guesses. The Chamber constituted out of the Second Section of the Court in order to examine *M.S.S.* relinquished the case to the Grand Chamber in November 2009.[77] One would expect that this Chamber would have wanted to see *K.R.S.* overturned. Presumably it was reasonably confident that the same result could be achieved before the Grand Chamber; otherwise it would not have wanted to take the risk of increasing the stakes, when it could have gone for the option of slowly building the case law in favour of the new approach at Chamber level. The documentation about the situation in Greece was abundant, the criticism of Dublin transfers to it loud, wide-ranging, and mounting. My guess is that the discomfort with the *K.R.S.* jurisprudence could already have been felt within a large part of the Court at the time of the relinquishment to the Grand Chamber.

Whether I am right or not, what is clear is that two opposite views, most fiercely expressed by Judge Bratza and Judge Tulkens respectively, would have clashed in

[75] Partly concurring and partly dissenting opinion of Judge Sajó in *M.S.S.*, p. 106. The applicant in *M.S.S.* can be seen and heard as he is interviewed in the excellent documentary *Dublin's Trap: Another Side of the Greek Crisis*, directed by Bryan Carter and released in 2012 <http://vimeo.com/38882993>, accessed 21 May 2014.

[76] Mr Chihaoui did this without the assistance of a Greek lawyer. He brought the following cases to Strasbourg (all rulings in French only except *Bouyid*): *Kanagaratnam v. Belgium*, appl. 15297/09, Judgment (ECtHR), 13 Dec. 2011; *Yoh-Ekale Mwanje v. Belgium*, appl. 10486/10, Judgment (ECtHR), 20 Dec. 2011; *Bouyid v. Belgium*, appl. 23380/08, Judgment (ECtHR), 21 Nov. 2013, referred to the Grand Chamber, finding that an 'isolated slap inflicted thoughtlessly by a police officer who was exasperated by the applicants' disrespectful or provocative conduct' when this 'apparently occurred in an atmosphere of tension between the members of the applicants' family and police officers in their neighbourhood', does not generate 'a sufficient degree of humiliation or debasement for a breach of Article 3 to be established' (para 51); *Firoz Muneer v. Belgium*, appl. 56005/10, Judgment (ECtHR), 11 Apr. 2013, finding the detention of a prospective 'Dublin referee' to Greece a violation of Article 5(4)—but not of Article 5(1)(f); *M. D. v. Belgium*, appl. 56028/10, Judgment (ECtHR), 14 Nov. 2013, with a similar outcome to *Firoz Muneer*; another three cases struck out in 2011, and one declared inadmissible in 2013.

[77] *M.S.S.* judgment, para 4.

the Grand Chamber. The stakes were high, and each perspective could expect to attract a number of supportive third party interventions. Indeed, this is what happened with submissions on the one hand from two states which have regularly been at the forefront of the migrant Strasbourg case law—the Netherlands and the UK;[78] and on the other hand by the AIRE Centre, Amnesty International, the Council of Europe Commissioner for Human Rights, the UNHCR, and the Greek Helsinki Monitor. Also of potential significance was the identity of the second national judge in this case, the Greek judge. Judge Rozakis had been a member of the Commission in the years of the 'old' Court, and in *Cruz Varas v. Sweden* and *Vilvarajah v. the United Kingdom*, he had been part of the minority of Commission members who thought that these cases entailed a violation of Article 3. In all likelihood he was also committed to adopting a pro-migrant stance in *M.S.S.*

Whatever happened in the deliberations, at the end of the day Judge Bratza's view on the legitimacy of the Belgian transfer to Greece was a lone (partly) dissenting opinion.[79]

VII. The States' Standard Arguments—And Possibly an Irritated Court

With hindsight, it would be easy to say that the respondent states were bound to lose in *M.S.S.* However, their defeat would not necessarily have been predicted when the case was first lodged, or one would surmise that Belgium would have refrained from transferring M.S.S. It is therefore interesting to review the arguments which the states put forward. We have already indirectly encountered one through the previous discussion and quotes: the applicant had not proved his case. It is worth highlighting another two which are standard state defences in the migrant case law: the applicant only had himself to blame for what had happened to him, and his complaint fell outside the ambit of the Convention in any event.

This strategy was most notably pursued by the Greek government with regard to the complaint related to living conditions. To quote:

> The [Greek] Government submitted that the situation in which the applicant had found himself...was the result of his own choices and omissions. The applicant had chosen to invest his resources in fleeing the country rather than in accommodation. Furthermore, he had waited until 18 December 2009 before declaring that he was homeless....[80]
>
> [S]ince June 2009, the applicant had had a 'pink card' that entitled him to work, vocational training, accommodation and medical care, and which had been renewed twice.[81]

[78] It is difficult to explain why this is so. It can be as much a matter of a particularly strong network of NGOs as a domestic situation which is objectively worse for migrants than that pertaining in other European countries.

[79] There were an additional three separate opinions: two 'concurring', as reviewed later (p. 425) and one 'partly concurring and partly dissenting', as reviewed in Section IV of Chapter 13.

[80] *M.S.S.*, para 240. [81] *M.S.S.*, para 241.

The Government argued that in such circumstances it was up to the applicant to come forward and show an interest in improving his lot. Instead, however, everything he had done in Greece indicated that he had no wish to stay there.[82]

In any event the Greek Government submitted that to find in favour of the applicant would be contrary to the provisions of the Convention, none of which guaranteed the right to accommodation or political asylum.[83]

These arguments appear elsewhere too but then separately from each other. The following quotes give a flavour of the way the respondent states repeatedly sought to blame the applicant for the situation that had evolved:

The applicant's attitude had to be taken into account: he had, in breach of the [Greek] legislation, failed to cooperate with the authorities and had shown no interest in the smooth functioning of the procedure...[84]

[The government] considered that the Greek authorities had followed the statutory procedure in spite of the applicant's negligence and the errors of his ways.[85]

[The Belgian authorities] alleged that the applicant had placed himself in an urgent situation by appealing to the Aliens Appeals Board only a few hours before his departure, when he had been taken into custody ten days earlier, under an order to leave the country.... Furthermore there was the fact that, in view of its urgency, the case had been scheduled for immediate examination but no one had attended the hearing, even though the applicant's counsel could have asked the permanent service of the legal aid office in Brussels to represent him before the Aliens Appeals Board.[86]

The Court responded by continually exonerating the applicant for having acted as he did. Further the Court did not hesitate to blame the respondent states for having acted as they did. To give two striking examples of such responses:

The fact that... the applicant had been trying to leave Greece cannot be held against him when examining the conduct of the Greek authorities with regard to the Convention and when the applicant was attempting to find a solution to a situation the Court considers contrary to Article 3...[87]

[The Court] wishes to emphasize that it cannot be held against the applicant that he did not inform the Belgian administrative authorities of the reasons why he did not wish to be transferred to Greece. It has established that the procedure before the Aliens Office made no provision for such explanations and that the Belgian authorities applied the Dublin Regulation systematically...[88]

Each responding government also tried to say that the Court should not have examined the case against it at all:[89]

According to the [Greek] Government, complaints concerning possible malfunctions of the legal aid system should not be taken into account because Article 6 did not apply to asylum procedures. In the same manner, any procedural delays before the Supreme

[82] *M.S.S.*, para 242. [83] *M.S.S.*, para 243. [84] *M.S.S.*, para 272.
[85] *M.S.S.*, para 273. [86] *M.S.S.*, paras 379 and 380. [87] *M.S.S.*, para 315.
[88] *M.S.S.*, para 366.
[89] With one exception: the Greek government seems to have granted conditions of detention would be examined. On this complaint, its main argument was that the applicant had not adduced any evidence pertaining to *his* personal conditions, as discussed earlier.

Administrative Court fell within the scope of Article 6 of the Convention and could therefore not be examined by the Court in the present case.[90]

Whereas:

> [The Belgian government] submitted that asylum seekers should lodge applications with the Court only against Greece...[91]

As we know, the Court was not impressed by these arguments.

The applicant did not claim substantial compensation for the non-pecuniary damages he had sustained in Greece—€1,000.[92] By contrast he claimed €24,900 for the decision of the Belgian authorities to transfer him to Greece.[93] The Court upheld this claim. Once legal costs were added, this meant that Greece had to pay the applicant €5,725, while Belgium had to pay €32,250.

At first sight, the discrepancy in these amounts might be surprising. It is clear, however, that it merely follows the claims made by the applicant himself. It may also be that the Court was more sympathetic to the plight of Greece than Belgium. To put it crudely, Greece was in a dire situation, while Belgium was not. In his concurring opinion, Judge Rozakis noted that 'almost 88% of the immigrants (and among them asylum seekers) entering the European Union today cross the Greek borders to land in our continent' so that there clearly was 'an urgent need for a comprehensive reconsideration of the existing European legal regime'.[94] The difficulty of this situation was expressly acknowledged by the Court at the outset of its reasoning. The Court nonetheless stated that, 'having regard to the absolute character of Article 3, that [situation] cannot absolve a state of its obligations under that provision'.[95] By contrast the Court stressed that it would have been easy for Belgium to respect the human rights of the applicant. The only thing it needed to do was to refrain from transferring him, which it 'had the means' to do.[96]

Keeping the Inter-American case law in mind, what is striking is that neither Belgium nor Greece showed any willingness to express any contrition about their actions before the European Court of Human Rights. As far as they were concerned, the case should simply have been dismissed. In view of previous Strasbourg case law, it cannot be said that they were entirely naïve in thinking this might be a possible outcome. However, on this particular occasion, this strategy might have backfired, at least as far as Belgium is concerned.

VIII. Awaiting the Repetition of *M.S.S.*

M.S.S. is a fantastic judgment. However, it may also show the abysmal level to which conditions must fall before the Court is ready to step in when the

[90] *M.S.S.*, para 277.

[91] *M.S.S.*, para 356. The Belgian government also argued that the applicant had failed to exhaust national remedies: *M.S.S.*, paras 335 and 378.

[92] *M.S.S.*, para 404.

[93] *M.S.S.*, para 407.

[94] Concurring opinion of Judge Rozakis in *M.S.S.* judgment.

[95] *M.S.S.*, para 223.

[96] *M.S.S.*, para 358.

issues touch upon immigration. What if instead of 0.1 per cent of protection claims being granted in Greece, the rate had been 5 per cent? What if instead of overcrowding such that not all detainees could lie down at the same time, detainees had to share a mattress? What if instead of being left without any support whatsoever, some minimal help had been extended? Because the Court decides on a case-by-case basis it is impossible to know. The conditions for asylum seekers in Malta and Italy are known to be very poor, if not quite as bad as in Greece. Are transfers to these countries equally proscribed under the Convention?

On 3 April 2013, the Court unanimously declared the case of *Mohammed Hussein and Others v. the Netherlands and Italy*, concerning a Dublin transfer to Italy, inadmissible.[97] One might say that this was the wrong test case to bring: following responses provided by the Italian government to the Court, it turned out that, contrary to her earlier allegations, the Somali applicant, a young mother with one child born in Italy and a second one born in the Netherlands, had been granted a three-year residence permit for subsidiary protection in Italy and had been provided with reception facilities, including medical care.[98] This appears to have been fatal to the case, although one might recall that in *M.S.S.* the applicant was in possession of a 'pink card'. Depending on the way in which they are integrated in the overall narrative of the judgment, the same facts can appear to be very different.

In *Mohammed Hussein*, the Court opted to 'reiterat[e] at the outset that Contracting States have the right as a matter of international law and subject to their treaty obligations, including the Convention, to control the entry, residence and expulsion of aliens'.[99] The part of the decision about the 'relevant practice in other countries' gave more space to a judgment of the Court of Appeal for England and Wales condoning a Dublin transfer to Italy than to the practice followed by lower courts in Germany and Belgium to suspend such transfers. Reports drawn by the UNHCR and the Commissioner for Human Rights were summarised in a way that highlights their reference to 'recent improvements to remedy some of the failings',[100] an arguably unduly optimistic reading of the reports as quoted by the Court earlier in its decision.[101] The Court added that 'all reports are unanimous in depicting a detailed structure of facilities and care to provide for the needs of asylum seekers'.[102] While correct, this statement did not refer at all to what happens in practice. It is also notable that neither the applicant's allegations that she had been raped in Italy nor the interests of her children entered the reasoning of the Court. This decision was followed by further inadmissible decisions which distinguished the situation in Italy from that found in *M.S.S.* with regard to Greece because in Italy there is no 'systematic failure'

97 *Samsam Mohammed Hussein and Others v. the Netherlands and Italy*, appl. 27725/10, Decision (ECtHR), 2 Apr. 2013.

98 *Mohammed Hussein*, paras 72 and 73.

99 *Mohammed Hussein*, para 65.

100 *Mohammed Hussein*, para 78.

101 *Mohammed Hussein*, paras 43–44.

102 *Mohammed Hussein*, para 78.

to provide support or facilities catering for asylum seekers, even if the reality is that their general situation and living conditions are in practice extremely difficult.[103] At the time of writing, a case is pending before the Grand Chamber on this question.[104] Four states and four NGOs have intervened; a hearing was held in February 2014.[105]

Three more cases are worth noting, all involving Austria. In *Sharifi*, the Court did not find it established that the Austrian authorities ought to have known in autumn 2008 that the serious deficiencies in the Greek asylum procedures reached the Article 3 threshold.[106] In *Ebrahimi*, a case regarding another transfer to Greece was avoided for 'want of an "applicant" '.[107] In *Mohamed*, a transfer to Hungary was found to be permissible: although UNHCR reports had identified problems with asylum claims in Hungary, the Court ruled that the applicant had not demonstrated a prima facie reason why he should be considered a refugee.[108]

It is too early to say whether the verdict of violation in *M.S.S.* is a one-off. What can be said is that the bar for finding that the threshold of ill-treatment proscribed by Article 3 is met looks set to remain high. Even in *M.S.S.* the Court said that it found the conditions of detention amounted to degrading treatment within the meaning of Article 3, having taken into account the fact that the applicant was an asylum seeker, who therefore was 'particularly vulnerable because of everything he had been through during his migration and the traumatic experiences he was likely to have endured previously'.[109] Does this mean that the conditions of detention would not have been degrading for *anyone* who would have had to endure them? I expect that some judges would be opposed to this idea but that

[103] *Daybegova and Magomedova v. Australia*, appl. 6198/12, Decision (ECtHR), 4 June 2013; *Mohammed v. Austria*, appl. 2283/12, Decision (ECtHR), 6 June 2013; *Abukeber v. Austria and Italy*, appl. 73874/11, Decision (ECtHR), 18 June 2013; *Alimi v. Austria and Italy*, appl. 53582/11, Decision (ECtHR), 18 June 2013; *Mohammed Hassan and Others v. The Netherlands and Italy*, appls 40524/10, 11746/13, 18764/11, 20355/12, 23696/12, 41993/10, 57531/10, 62865/12, 7903/13, 81839/12, Decision (ECtHR), 27 Aug. 2013; *Miruts Hagos v. the Netherlands and Italy*, appl. 9053/10, Decision (ECtHR), 27 Aug. 2013; *Hussein Diirshi and Others v. the Netherlands and Italy*, appls 2340/10, 18324/10, 47851/10, 51377/10, Decision (ECtHR), 10 Sept. 2013. *M.M. and Others v. Finland*, appl. 72861/11, Decision (ECtHR), 3 Sept. 2013, was struck out following the grant of a four-year residence permit.

[104] *Tarakhel and Others v. Switzerland*, appl. 29217/12, Legal Summary, 25 June 2012. The judgment of the Grand Chamber in this case was rendered on 4 November 2014 (just before this book went to press). The Court found that 'the current situation in Italy can in no way be compared to the situation in Greece at the time of the *M.S.S.* judgment', justifying the adoption of a different approach (para 115). It concluded that 'were the applicants to be returned to Italy without the Swiss authorities having first obtained individual guarantees from the Italian authorities that the applicants would be taken charge of in a manner adapted to the age of the children and that the family would be kept together, there would be a violation of Article 3 of the Convention' (para 122).

[105] The interveners were: the UK, the Netherlands, Sweden, and Norway; and the AIRE Centre, Amnesty International, and European Council for Refugees and Exiles (ECRE) (acting together) and Defense for Children.

[106] *Sharifi v. Austria*, appl. 60148/08, Decision (ECtHR), 5 Dec. 2013, para 38.

[107] The legal representative had not collected a duly signed authority form when the applicant was still in Austria and then lost contact after the transfer to Greece: *Ebrahimi v. Austria*, appl. 15974/11, Decision (ECtHR), 1 Oct. 2013, para 23.

[108] *Mohammed v. Austria*, appl. 2283/12, Judgment (ECtHR), 6 June 2013. In this case, however, a violation of Article 13 in conjunction with Article 3 was found.

[109] *M.S.S.* judgment, paras 231–232.

the reference to the 'particularly vulnerable' condition of the applicant would nonetheless have been one of the factors which made it possible for the Grand Chamber to adopt a unanimous ruling on this aspect of the judgment.[110]

Even more problematic is the sense one gets from the *M.S.S.* judgment that the rulings on Article 13 were triggered by the appalling conditions of detention and living endured by the applicant in Greece. Strictly speaking, the adequate or inadequate character of an asylum determination procedure is a question which should have nothing to do with a finding of a violation of Article 3. The way in which the *M.S.S.* judgment is structured (starting with verdicts of violation concerning first conditions of detention and then of living) therefore points to a potential weakness in the approach of the Court. On the positive side, the Court refrained from examining whether the expulsion of the applicant to his country of origin would entail a violation of Article 3, as the next section explains.

IX. Defective Asylum Domestic Procedures: The Strasbourg Story up to *M.S.S.*

In *M.S.S.* the Court accepted that the applicant had an 'arguable' claim that his expulsion to Afghanistan might entail a violation of Article 3.[111] This triggered the application of Article 13, which guarantees the right to an effective remedy before a national authority. In the event, the Court found a violation of Article 13 both by Greece and by Belgium. Remarkably, the Court did not feel it necessary to examine whether an expulsion to Afghanistan would actually have entailed a violation of Article 3. This is unusual. Generally, the Court examines whether there would be a violation of Article 3 in the case of return before turning to the examination of any complaint under Article 13—prompting Judge Villiger to opine in a separate opinion in *M.S.S.* that the question of whether the applicant's return to Afghanistan would have violated Article 3 should necessarily have preceded an examination of the Article 13 complaint against Greece.[112] The reason why the Strasbourg asylum case law has very much developed out of Article 3 complaints must be linked to the fact that avoiding a forced return is typically the paramount concern of asylum seekers. Nonetheless, expecting the Court to make rulings on the substance of the merits of Article 3 in return cases is problematic on two counts. The first, already discussed in Chapter 7, is that the Court neither has the means nor should it be its role to assess all return cases on a substantive basis. The second, explained in this section, is that a focus on Article 3 too easily leaves national asylum determination procedures unscrutinised. This is why the acceptance by the Grand Chamber that it did not need to be dragged into examining

[110] Reference to vulnerability was also made in respect of the living conditions complaint: *M.S.S.*, para 263.

[111] *M.S.S.* judgment, paras 286 and 298.

[112] Concurring opinion of Judge Villiger in *M.S.S.* judgment.

the actual merits of the asylum claim must be counted as one of the strengths of the *M.S.S.* judgment.

The question of the quality of the asylum determination proceedings is logically different from the question of the appropriateness of the outcome which is reached in a specific case. Legally the two questions need not be related to each other. Putting this point in an even stronger way, whether an applicant's asylum claim is eventually granted or rejected should have no bearing whatsoever on the question of determining whether the procedure followed for reaching this positive or negative outcome has been characterised by sufficient rigour. It is possible for an asylum claim to be granted at the end of a procedure which is defective. In such a case, the asylum seeker-turned-recognised-protected person is unlikely to complain about the quality of the procedure, even though, from the perspective of the rule of law, this situation is highly problematic. Article 13 complaints are at least as important as Article 3 complaints. One could say that from a legal perspective (rather than the perspective of the individual applicant), they are even more important given that they are likely to have a greater influence upon domestic procedures and thus an effect upon the conduct of future cases. This is worth bearing in mind in a context where the possibility of successfully claiming asylum has been made increasingly more difficult over the last 30 years.

The absolute nature of the prohibition on return to Article 3-proscribed treatment could be expected to go hand in hand with a resolve on the part of the European Court of Human Rights to uphold legitimate complaints related to deficient domestic asylum procedures, using Article 13 to the full (given the poisonous authority of *Maaouia v. France* which deems Article 6 inapplicable to any immigration issue).[113] In return cases, the Strasbourg Court has indeed occasionally found breaches of Article 13 of the Convention—*M.S.S* is of course an example. However, the case law in this area has taken a long time to develop and remains weak.

A HUDOC search conducted up to the date of the *M.S.S.* judgment for relevant judgments on Article 13 generates 31 results.[114] The same search, extended to decisions of admissibility (including by the Commission), produces dozens of

[113] *Maaouia v. France*, appl. 39652/98, GC Judgment (ECtHR), 5 Oct. 2000.

[114] The search for judgments up to 6 October 2011 related to 'Article 13' and containing the word 'expulsion' generated 51 results but with quite a number to be considered false positives for our purposes (such as *Young, James and Webster* v. *the United Kingdom; Sheffield and Horsham* v. *the United Kingdom; Anguelova v. Bulgaria*). The same search to which was added the word 'alien' generated 23 results which missed eight relevant decisions from the wider search: *Vilvarajah and Others v. the United Kingdom*, appls 13163/87, 13165/87, 13447/87, 13448/87, Judgment (ECtHR), 30 Oct. 1991; *Jabari v. Turkey*, appl. 40035/98, Judgment (ECtHR), 11 July 2000; *Bensaid v. the United Kingdom*, appl. 44599/98, Judgment (ECtHR), 6 Feb. 2001; *Soldatenko v. Ukraine*, appl. 2440/07, Judgment (ECtHR), 28 Oct. 2008; *Baysakov and Others v. Ukraine*, appl. 54131/08, Judgment (ECtHR), 18 Feb. 2010; *Tehrani and Others v. Turkey*, appls 32940/08, 41626/08, 43616/08, Judgment (ECtHR), 13 Apr. 2010; *Abdulazhon Isakov v. Russia*, appl. 14049/08, Judgment (ECtHR), 8 July 2010; *Dbouba v. Turkey*, appl. 15916/09, Judgment (ECtHR), 13 July 2010.

results[115] indicating that applicants have tried to put Article 13 claims but that these have generally been rejected at admissibility stage.

The HUDOC results indicate that Turkey is by far the most common violator of Article 13 taken in conjunction with Article 3 in return cases. This trend started with the *Jabari* case in which the Court stated that a contracting state had the obligation to conduct a 'rigorous scrutiny' of an individual's claim that removal would expose her to treatment prohibited by Article 3 in absolute terms—which the Ankara Administrative Court had failed to do, having checked 'the formal legality of the applicant's deportation' without examining 'the more compelling question of the substance of her fears'.[116] Russia comes second and Ukraine third in this inverted league table. One country repeatedly found in violation of Article 13 in return cases but in conjunction with Article 8 (not Article 3) is Bulgaria.

Western European countries only occasionally appear in the list.[117] In this group the UK is most often the respondent state, but is found in violation of the Convention only once (in *Chahal*);[118] Belgium is found in violation of the Convention both times it appears (*Čonka*[119] and *M.S.S.*); France the one time it appears (*Gebremedhin*);[120] and the Netherlands never, despite two appearances (*Salah Sheekh*[121] and *A.*[122]).

This relative dearth of case law is puzzling, given the multiple problems reported by legal representatives working in the field of asylum. While the exact details vary across jurisdictions and over time, problems encountered by prospective asylum seekers relate to limited access to legal representation and interpreting services, short periods allowed to lodge claims and appeals against negative decisions, rendering the collection of personal or background evidence and the presentation of cogent arguments difficult, as well as the non-suspensive character of many remedies (whereby an appeal against a rejection of an asylum claim does not automatically suspend the enforced expulsion of the asylum seeker). It is therefore useful to review the case law, which will be done here with a focus on Western European states. This is because these countries consider themselves, and benefit from a perception of being, bastions of the rule of law. The argument put forward

[115] Including both the words 'expulsion' and 'alien', the HUDOC search (conducted on 6 October 2011) for decisions and judgments produced 118 results, which must have ignored relevant cases as explained in the previous footnote.

[116] *Jabari* judgment, para 39. For a recent verdict of violation of Article 13 in a return case involving Turkey, see e.g. *Abdolkhani and Kariminia v. Turkey*, appl. 30471/08, Judgment (ECtHR), 22 Sept. 2009.

[117] There is, in addition, a mushrooming case law concerning the extradition process of presumed 'fugitives' in countries which are not traditionally regarded as democratic bastions. For judgments concluding a violation of Article 13 in the extraditing country, see: *Shamayev and Others v. Georgia and Russia*, appl. 36378/02, Judgment (ECtHR), 12 Apr. 2005; *Soldatenko v. Ukraine*, appl. 2440/07, Judgment (ECtHR), 23 Oct. 2008; *Muminov v. Russia*, appl. 42502/06, Judgment (ECtHR), 11 Dec. 2008; *Baysakov and Others v. Ukraine*, appl. 54131/08, Judgment (ECtHR), 18 Feb. 2010; *Abdulazhon Isakov v. Russia*, appl. 14049/08, Judgment (ECtHR), 8 July 2010.

[118] *Chahal v. the United Kingdom*, appl. 22414/93, GC Judgment (ECtHR), 15 Nov. 1996.

[119] *Čonka v. Belgium*, appl. 51564/99, Judgment (ECtHR), 5 Feb. 2002.

[120] *Gebremedhin [Gaberamadhien] v. France*, appl. 25389/05, Judgment (ECtHR), 26 Apr. 2007.

[121] *Salah Sheekh v. the Netherlands*, appl. 1948/04, Judgment (ECtHR), 11 Jan. 2007.

[122] *A. v. the Netherlands*, appl. 4900/06, Judgment (ECtHR), 20 July 2010.

is that this is a controversial claim in the asylum area, although not one which the Strasbourg Court has been keen to denounce.

Chahal v. the United Kingdom need not retain too much of our attention for the purposes of the present discussion, as the Court found a violation of Article 13 (taken in conjunction with Article 3) because the British advisory panel and courts tasked with reviewing the deportation decision were required under British law to examine whether the Home Secretary had *balanced* the risk to the applicants against the danger to national security (rather than focusing exclusively on whether the deportation put applicants at risk of ill-treatment contrary to Article 3). In a string of other cases, British judicial review proceedings are accepted by the Court to offer sufficient guarantees under the Convention.

Čonka v. Belgium, decided in 2002, is important in that it is the first time that the Court finds a Western European state in violation of Article 13 for a procedural reason in an asylum case. The ruling nonetheless leaves the deficiencies of the domestic asylum procedures largely unchallenged. The applicants were a family of Slovakian nationals of Romany origin who had sought asylum in Belgium. Along with other Slovakian families, they had received a note requesting them to attend the police station on a certain day in order to enable the files concerning their applications for asylum to be completed. This was a ruse to get them to the police station: once there, all the families were served with a fresh order to leave the territory, detained, and, one week later, put on a plane to Slovakia. The Belgian government argued before the Court that two domestic remedies had been open to the applicants: one before the Commissioner-General for Refugees and Stateless Persons and the other before the Conseil d'Etat. The applicants complained that the former remedy was unsatisfactory because '[f]irstly, the alien concerned had no guarantee of being heard since, although that was the practice, it did not constitute a right [and secondly because] he had no access to his case file, could not consult the record of notes taken at the hearing or demand that his observations be put on record'.[123] In respect to the latter remedy, the applicants stressed that it had no automatic suspensive effect and noted that the success rate of applications under the so-called 'extremely urgent procedure' before the Conseil d'Etat was a mere 1.36 per cent.[124] By a tight majority of four votes to three, the Court found a violation of Article 13 in conjunction with Article 4 of Protocol no. 4 prohibiting the collective expulsion of aliens (which was separately found to have been violated in its own right, for the first time in the history of the Court).[125] The Court focused on the non-suspensive character of the remedy without mentioning the problem of the claimants not being able to present as strong a case as possible. This was hardly an indictment of Belgian asylum/protection procedures which signalled that something was fundamentally wrong with the way asylum is processed in Belgium or in Europe more generally.

[123] *Čonka* judgment, para 65. [124] *Čonka*, paras 65 and 66.

[125] In this case, the Strasbourg Court also found a violation of Article 5 regulating detention (unanimously).

The next case to be considered is *Gebremedhin [or Gaberamadhien] v. France*, which deserves a more detailed review. The applicant said he had arrived at Paris Charles de Gaulle Airport on 29 June 2005 and had vainly sought to register his claim for asylum at each change of shift at the airport's police station—about eight times—until he eventually found a police officer willing to do so on 1 July 2005. (The French government contested this would have been possible.[126]) At that point, the applicant was detained in the waiting zone of the airport while the authorities ascertained whether or not his asylum claim was manifestly unfounded. Under French law, were the claim to be manifestly unfounded, the authorities were entitled to try to organise his removal; were the claim not manifestly unfounded, the authorities were required to admit him on the French territory as an asylum seeker. Mr Gebremedhin was interviewed for the first time on 3 July. He says that his explanation that he was a journalist of Eritrean nationality who had been detained and tortured in Eritrea on account of his reporting activities had persuaded the French Office for the Protection of Refugees and Stateless Persons (OFPRA) official conducting the interview to recommend granting him leave to enter the country as an asylum seeker—a crucial step given that aliens must be on French soil in order to lodge an asylum application with OFPRA. (The government denied that such a recommendation was made.)

A second interview took place two days later, with the superior of the first interviewer. The superior found the applicant's account to contain 'a large number of inaccuracies and erroneous references which cast doubt on the truth of his statements'. He recommended that leave to enter be refused, which the Ministry of Interior did on 6 July. The next day, French police officers took the applicant to the Eritrean Embassy. According to the applicant, the ambassador—made aware of the circumstances of his application for asylum by the police officers—refused to recognise him as a national of Eritrea and to issue him with a *laissez-passer*. (Part of this account is contested by the French government.) The same day, the applicant made an urgent application to the relevant administrative court (Cergy-Pontoise) to be granted leave to enter France in order to lodge an application for asylum. In support of this application, he submitted a statement from the NGO Reporters without Borders to the effect that Mr Mihretab—an Eritrean journalist living in exile in the United States who had received a 'Special Award for Human Rights Journalism under Threat' from Amnesty International—had confirmed that Mr Gebremedhin worked as a press photographer, that he had been held at the same time as him (Mr Mihretab) in Zara Prison, one of the harshest prisons in Somalia, and that Mr Mihretab had recognised him (Mr Gebremedhin) on the basis of a photograph which had been sent. On 8 July, the administrative court rejected Mr Gebremedhin's application without holding a hearing. On 14 July, he lodged an application with the European Court of Human Rights, which proceeded to request that France not remove the applicant to Eritrea until

[126] The government said that it had checked the flights to Charles de Gaulle Airport of 29 June 2005 and that there was no passenger with the name of the applicant. The Court did not ask the government to provide the details of the flight on 1 July in which his name would have appeared.

it had examined the case. This Rule 39 indication resulted in the applicant being granted leave to enter France by the French Ministry of the Interior on 20 July. The applicant immediately applied for asylum. He was granted refugee status the following November.

The Strasbourg Court accepted that the applicant had only been able to enter France and to lodge an asylum application because the Eritrean Embassy had refused him a *laissez-passer* and because it itself had granted a Rule 39 interim measure. Thus, without these two intervening circumstances, the applicant might well have been returned to his country of origin without his asylum claim having been properly examined. The Court noted that the applicant had always had an arguable complaint under Article 3 (as demonstrated by the fact that he was later granted the status of refugee), triggering the application of Article 13. The Court refused the French government's submission that the granting of the refugee status in November 2005 meant that the applicant could no longer claim the status of victim under the Convention after that date.[127] Implicitly adopting an *ex tunc* reasoning,[128] the Court noted that by that time, the facts underlying the applicant's Article 13 complaint had already occurred.[129] The Court unanimously found a violation of Article 13 in conjunction with Article 3 because of the lack of access to a remedy with automatic suspensive effect which the applicant had suffered during his time in the 'waiting zone'.[130]

The other arguments of the applicant were not examined by the Court. One was that the purported effective remedies in place in the French system were in practice inaccessible to migrants like him. The French system provided that an asylum seeker could only be refused leave to enter at the border if their asylum application was 'manifestly unfounded'—for example, because they wanted to enter France for work or family reasons. In 2004, 92.3 per cent of asylum claims lodged at border points had been declared manifestly unfounded, with 89 per cent dealt with in four days or less.[131] The applicant argued that 'the very structure of the system [was] ineffective and fail[ed] to guarantee fundamental rights'.[132] The French government replied by relying on the fact that ANAFE, the French NGO which specialises in assisting aliens at the borders and which was intervening in the *Gebremedhin* case, had found that only six unfavourable recommendations made at the border had subsequently been overturned over a six-year period—with 2,278 such negative recommendations adopted in 2005 alone.[133] The Court seemed to accept France's complete confidence in its asylum system.

The applicant had also argued that avenues of appeal were not really open to asylum seekers as '[it was] unrealistic to imagine that a foreigner being held in a waiting zone pending his or her removal in accordance with an enforceable decision which could be enforced at any time, who did not necessarily speak French and did not have access to legal aid, would be in a position to make an

[127] *Gebremedhin* judgment, para 55. [128] See Section VII of Chapter 7.
[129] *Gebremedhin* judgment, para 56. [130] *Gebremedhin*, para 67.
[131] *Gebremedhin*, para 41. [132] *Gebremedhin*, para 41.
[133] *Gebremedhin*, para 48.

application . . . to the administrative court, submit four copies of it by registered letter or by depositing it with the registry, and manage such a technically complex procedure'.[134] The Court did not specifically comment on this argument.

This is the more disturbing since many institutions within the Council of Europe had already highlighted their awareness of problems in this area, as the section entitled 'Overview of Council of Europe' in the judgment indicates.[135] Mentioned in this section are: one recommendation of the Parliamentary Assembly of 12 April 1994 on the right of asylum; one recommendation of the Committee of Ministers of 18 September 1998 on the right of rejected asylum seekers to an effective remedy against decisions on expulsion; a recommendation of the Commissioner for Human Rights of 19 September 2001 concerning the enforcement of expulsion orders; and the Committee of Ministers' adoption of 'twenty guidelines on forced return' of 4 May 2005. All these documents contained provisions directly pertinent to the issue at hand. They signalled how widespread concerns had grown in Europe (not only in France) about domestic procedures facilitating the expulsion of failed asylum seekers. Had the Court been so inclined, it could have relied on these documents in the *Gebremedhin* case, which emerged only due to the determined and relentless efforts of ANAFE and the applicant's legal representative, to affirm the importance of fair asylum determination procedures. Instead of this, the Court ignored the arguments put before it except for the assuredly crucial but nonetheless limited issue of the non-suspensive character of the available remedies.

In order to execute the *Gebremedhin* judgment, France only had to make the remedy before the administrative court suspensive. Further efforts, deployed in difficult conditions of access to detained migrants, therefore had to be made by associations and legal representatives. In 2008, undeterred, Mr Gebremedhin's lawyer, Jean-Eric Malabre, was back at Strasbourg with another case concerning asylum claims made at the French border.[136] This time, the applicant was a journalist from Sierra Leone. The Court refused to examine the complaint under Article 13 because, from April 2009, the country had been reported as moving towards stability. As a result, the Court found in its decision of December 2009 the complaints under Articles 2 and 3 ill-founded. Leaving aside the wisdom or otherwise of relying on a possibly temporary improvement to reject the Article 3 complaint, already alluded to in Chapter 7, it would surely have made more sense for the Court to observe that the Article 3 claim had originally been arguable so that the complaint under Article 13 could be and needed to be examined (*ex tunc*). Instead, the case was declared inadmissible, by unanimity. More positively *I.M. v. France* was declared admissible in December 2010, and led to verdicts of

134 *Gebremedhin*, para 42.

135 *Gebremedhin*, paras 36–38.

136 *Se v. France*, appl. 10085/08, Decision (ECtHR), 15 Dec. 2009, in French only. Mr Malabre also brought to Strasbourg: *Fofana v. France*, appl. 22193/93, Decision (EComHR), 29 June 1994, in French only, alleging that an expulsion to Guinea would breach Articles 3, 6, 8, 9, 10, 11, and 13 ECHR; *MA v. France*, appl. 4920/08, Decision (ECtHR), 16 June 2009, in French only, concerning a Tamil, was struck out when he reported having lost contact with his client (who had apparently joined his brother in the UK).

violation of Article 13 in February 2012.[137] *I.M.* concerned the lack of access to asylum determination procedures for migrants detained in immigration centres.

The Dutch case law sheds further light on the Court's reluctance to find violations of Article 13 in migrant cases. Dana Baldinger, commenting on *Salah Sheekh v. the Netherlands* and the earlier judgment of *Said v. the Netherlands*, observes that '[t]here were clear signs that the ECtHR was dissatisfied with the level of judicial scrutiny offered at national level in the Netherlands'.[138] An anecdote circulating in the Netherlands supports her comment. The evening before *Salah Sheekh* was to be delivered at Strasbourg in January 2007, Judge Myjer, the Dutch judge then sitting at Strasbourg, took the chance—so the anecdote goes—of meeting the Dutch Minister of Justice to hand him the envelope containing the judgment, with instruction to open it the next day. Shaking the envelope, Judge Myjer is understood to have said: 'I'll say only one thing: full and *ex nunc*', i.e. the very formulation used in Dutch law to characterise the standard of review of asylum determinations expected of domestic courts.

Adopted by the Third Section of the Court, *Salah Sheek* signalled a shift in Convention law in that the Court ceased to insist that an applicant who had demonstrated the foreseeability of treatment in breach of Article 3 in the case of return would in addition have to prove the existence of further special features distinguishing them from other segments of the population facing a similar situation.[139] It is clear from the facts as reviewed in the judgment that the Rule 39 measure granted by the Strasbourg Court was instrumental in persuading the Dutch authorities not to proceed with the applicant's expulsion.[140] Even so, the Court found no violation of Article 13. It reasoned that the applicant, who had lodged a non-suspensive objection to the decision to expel him, had then been able to apply to the Regional Court for a stay of the expulsion, pending a decision on his objection. The fact that he had lost before the Regional Court was considered irrelevant by the Strasbourg Court which considered that the applicant had been provided with an effective remedy as 'the word "remedy" within the meaning of Article 13 does not mean a remedy bound to succeed... and the compatibility of the planned removal with Article 3 was examined'.[141]

Salah Sheekh was executed in a way which indicates that national procedures were reviewed in order to avoid producing further violations of Article 3 in the

[137] *I.M. v. France*, appl. 9152/09, Judgment (ECtHR), 2 Feb. 2012, in French only. The UNHCR had intervened and a hearing had taken place in May 2011.

[138] Dana Baldinger, *Rigorous Scrutiny versus Marginal Review: Standards on Judicial Scrutiny and Evidence in International and European Asylum Law* (2013 doctoral dissertation submitted to Radboud University Nijmegen and printed by Wolf Legal Publishers) vii.

[139] *Salah Sheekh* judgment, para 148. This new perspective was confirmed in *NA. v. the United Kingdom*, appl. 25904/07, Judgment (ECtHR), 17 July 2008 adopted, also unanimously, by the Fourth Section on 17 July 2008 in a case brought by a Tamil applicant.

[140] *Salah Sheekh* judgment, para 38.

[141] *Salah Sheekh*, para 154. See also *A. v. the Netherlands*, appl. 4900/06, Judgment (ECtHR), 20 July 2010.

future: the State Secretary of Justice explained in a letter transmitted to the Committee of Ministers of the Council of Europe that general circumstances in the country of origin (e.g. being from a minority group) would now have to be taken into account when assessing whether an individual was at risk of being singled out for persecution.[142] This does not mean that a ruling on Article 13 in *Salah Sheekh* was not needed. Arguably, it would not have been if one knew that asylum procedures were designed throughout Europe to make it possible for genuine refugees to be successful in their asylum application. This, however, is far from the case.

Even the Court's two rulings on Article 13 in the 'fantastic *M.S.S.*' are restrained. Regarding Greece, multiple shortcomings were identified, which is good, given that the case demonstrates that there was no asylum procedure worthy of that description operating in the country. These findings nonetheless came late. The violation found with regard to Belgium was phrased in rather restricted terms. To give an example, the Court noted the physical impossibility of the applicant's lawyer attending a judicial hearing almost 100 kilometres away with only one hour's notice. This is part of what justifies the verdict of violation. What if the hearing had been scheduled in the afternoon? It is regrettable that the Court shies away from making pronouncements of principle. It could have stated, for example, that the issue of asylum is of such vital importance to the applicant that it must be a requirement of the domestic procedure under Article 13 that it is devised in such a way that it leaves sufficient time for an applicant's legal representative to prepare the case fully and in a professional manner. Of course, the Court could go even further and recognise the applicability of Article 6 to asylum procedures, thus reversing *Maaouia*.

It must be the fears either of a backlash by dissatisfied states or of potential 'hordes' of refugees entering Europe which leads the Court to refrain from saying this. Returns to torture or inhuman and degrading treatment occur on a regular basis, as recorded in reports on asylum procedures by organisations concerned by the bias these procedures demonstrate against applicants.[143] Whether the European Court of Human Rights would have been able, through vigorous verdicts of violations of Article 13, to stem the continuous deterioration in domestic asylum procedures throughout European states is difficult to say. What is clear is that it has made little effort to do this and that even when it has tried to do so, such as in *Hirsi Jamaa*, it has not done so in unequivocal terms.[144] It avoids subjecting domestic asylum and/or protection procedures to close scrutiny, despite its repeated declarations that it attaches great importance to Article 3 in view of the 'irreversible nature of the damage which may result if the risk of torture or ill-treatment materialises'.[145]

[142] Resolution CM/ResDH (2010)10 regarding the execution of the *Salah Sheekh* judgment.

[143] See e.g. UNHCR report 'Beyond Proof: Credibility Assessment in EU Asylum Systems', May 2013, <http://www.unhcr.org/51a8a08a9.html>, accessed 22 May 2014.

[144] See the discussion of *Hirsi Jamaa and Others v. Italy*, appl. 27765/09, GC Judgment (ECtHR), 23 Feb. 2012, in Chapter 10.

[145] *Gebremedhin* judgment, paras 58 and 66.

X. Paying the Price for a Lack of Scrutiny: The Rise and Fall of Rule 39 Requests

The Court's lack of engagement with Article 13 claims in return cases has had the effect of generating another type of case law for the Court, namely, that relating to interim measure requests. As we have seen, in cases such as *Gebremedhin* and *Salah Sheekh*, the granting of an interim measure by the European Court of Human Rights was the decisive element which made the seeking of asylum or the shelving of an expulsion order possible. At the beginning of my research, I felt Rule 39 of the Rules of the Court was the perfect illustration of the way migrants were (at times) considered first as human beings at Strasbourg. The President or Acting President of a Section would be called upon to make an immediate decision on whether to grant a Rule 39 request which had just reached Strasbourg. At that time, the most important issue appeared to be the fate of this applicant. As I experienced during interviews, all other matters were put on hold. Consideration for the human being came first.

As my research developed, my views changed. On the one hand, the granting of a Rule 39 request was no more than a bandage which did nothing to counteract the complicity of the Strasbourg machinery in barring refugees from accessing protection in Europe—through timid judgments on Articles 3 and 13 and the refusal to apply Article 6. On the other hand, a number of problems became apparent such that different Sections of the Court did not use the mechanism available to them to extend interim measures under Rule 39 consistently and that the Court would endorse the 'friendly settlements' that states were keen to reach once an applicant had been granted an interim measure, thus preventing the underlying issue from being properly examined by the Court and leading to structural change.[146] Last but not least, legal representatives repeatedly told me that requesting a Rule 39 measure was often the sole tool they had at their disposal for trying to stop the removal of a client whom they believed fitted the legal criteria for international protection, but they were no longer welcome at Strasbourg.

Admittedly the Court was worried and possibly even desperate at the increasing number of interim measures it was receiving as I was doing my field work. During this period, Judge Tulkens was exceptional in expressing the view that, since the Court well knew that such requests were going to arrive, the best way forward was to organise the Court in such a way that it was equipped to respond to them immediately and effectively, including at 5 p.m. on Fridays, when many such requests arrived due to the fact that expelling governments typically chartered flights at weekends. The Court did this to some extent. For example, it instituted in 2010 a unit within the Registry specifically devoted to the examination of Rule 39 requests directed against the UK, the country against which by far the most requests were directed.

[146] See, for a wealth of information on Rule 39: PACE Doc. 11978.

But in August 2011, the Court issued a troubling public statement.[147] It observed that there had been an increase of 4,000 per cent in requests for interim measures between 2006 (112 requests) and 2010 (4,786 requests) and that the increase did not seem to be slowing: 2,500 requests had been received between October 2010 and January 2011.[148] In the face of this 'alarming' situation, the Court stressed that it was not an immigration appeals tribunal and that it 'should only be required to intervene in truly exceptional cases'. Part of the Court's response was to urge governments to 'provide national remedies with suspensive effect which operate effectively and fairly' and to suspend removals to a particular country of origin where a lead case concerning that country was pending. As for applicants and their representatives, they were told that 'requests for interim measures should be individuated, fully reasoned, be sent with all relevant documentation including the decisions of the national authorities and courts, and be sent in good time before the expected date of removal'. This is probably exactly what most legal representatives would have wished to achieve. It is unlikely that it is a lack of diligence on their part which leads them to send incomplete papers at the last minute. The Court might have taken greater account of the state of asylum determination procedures in Europe. It could have said, for example, that it would automatically grant a Rule 39 request when the applicant's legal representative had not been informed of their client's flight details at least 72 hours prior to the flight taking off. Instead it put the onus on the legal representative to submit to the Court a fully reasoned document in good time.

To the relief of the Court, the high level of Rule 39 requests it had seen in 2010 to 2011 have now decreased considerably. This is the consequence of an active strategy pursued by the Court of ensuring that the requests be 'handled in a centralised and coherent manner consistent with the Court's case law',[149] and consisting of a unique decision body composed of three Vice-Presidents of Sections as well as of a central Rule 39 Unit within the Registry of the Court. A member of the Registry explained to me that if I consulted the statistics available on the Court's website, I would see that the strategy had started to produce results.[150] Indeed it has. A total of 1,443 (out of 3,775) requests had been granted in 2010; this had fallen to 108 (out of 1,588), in

[147] This followed most alarmed observations by the Court's President in the speech he had given for the opening of the judicial year, reproduced in the Court's 'Annual Report 2011', available at <http://www.echr.coe.int/Documents/Annual_report_2011_ENG.pdf>, accessed 4 June 2014, 33–46 at 39–40.

[148] 'Statement issued by the President of the European Court of Human Rights concerning Requests for Interim Measures (Rule 39 of the Rules of Court)'. Information added in parentheses in this quotation comes from a release from the Court dated August 2011. At the Second Colloquium on the protection of refugees, asylum seekers, and displaced persons held by the Council of Europe in 2000, Judge Lorenzen had provided the following figures: there had been between 40 and 70 yearly interim relief requests before the Commission between 1992 and 1997, of which 20 to 30 were granted each year; the new Court had received 232 such requests during the first 18 months of its existence (from 1 November 1998) and granted 34: Lorenzen, p. 35, note 26.

[149] As per an email communication by a member of the Registry in response to a query I had made, dated 5 June 2014.

[150] Email referred to in previous note.

Table 12.1 Granted Rule 39 Requests Originating from Selected Countries, 2010 and 2013

Originating Countries	2010	2013
Netherlands	156	25
France	123	21
Finland	81	4
United Kingdom	127	3
Belgium	101	2
Turkey	7	1
Norway	9	1
Italy	19	1
Greece	24	1
Denmark	29	1
Sweden	642	1
Georgia	15	0
Austria	23	0
Cyprus	44	0

Source: Document entitled 'Rule 39 requests granted and refused in 2010, 2011, 2012 and 2013 by responding state', available at <http://www.echr.coe.int/Documents/Stats_art_39_2010_2013_ENG.pdf>, accessed 4 June 2014.

2013.[151] Table 12.1 shows the number of Rule 39 requests granted in 2010 and 2013, respectively, presented by selected country in order of increasing discrepancy between the 2010 and the 2013 figures.

What price this coherent jurisprudence? Asylum seekers have not suddenly ceased to encounter difficulties in accessing the legal system in Europe and the world still counts a number of places which produce high levels of displacement—with Syria currently topping this list and Afghanistan remaining not far behind. It appears that Strasbourg resolved its problem of a heavy Rule 39 caseload by dissuading legal representatives from making such requests. Aware of their poor prospects of success at Strasbourg, I am told some are now taking their cases to the UN Committee Against Torture.

XI. After *M.S.S.*: Afghan Refugees in the Strasbourg Case Law

So what happens to the refugees who have reached Europe? [152] *M.S.S.* should not be understood to indicate that the European Court is sympathetic to their plight.

[151] The 108 figure of successful requests in 2013 included 21 successful requests related to the Russian Federation, up from 17 in 2010. The other figures which showed an increase relate to Ukraine (8 in 2010/9 in 2013), Croatia (0/1), Latvia (0/1), Malta (0/1), Serbia (0/1), Azerbaijan (0/2), Spain (0/3), and Switzerland (0/8).

[152] Relatively few refugees make it into Europe. For example, most Afghan refugees are in Iran, most Syrian refugees in the countries directly neighbouring Syria.

It will suffice here to provide two illustrations from early 2013 confirming the Court's strict stance even towards Afghan nationals.

The Court did not find the removal of a man who had survived serious injuries in a rocket launch in Afghanistan contrary to Article 3.[153] The 'circumstances of the case' recalled in the *S.H.H. v. the United Kingdom* judgment include the fact that 'there were an estimated 800,000 mobility impaired persons in Afghanistan of whom 40,000 were limb amputees'.[154] This seems to have been inserted in order to indicate that disabled persons are not all dead in Afghanistan and thus can survive there. The same section of the judgment observes that '[t]he applicant has shown the resolve and ability to travel to the United Kingdom via various methods of transport', a remark apparently inserted in order to stress that 'he had not shown that there was *no* viable relocation option open to him in Afghanistan'.[155] The Court ruled: 'Whilst full account must be taken of the significant hardship facing persons with disabilities in Afghanistan, including discrimination, a lack of employment opportunities and a scarcity of services [as detailed in various cited reports], it is of some relevance that the present applicant has family members who continue to live in Afghanistan'.[156] There was no evidence that his two sisters 'would *not* provide him with some level of support or assistance'.[157] The Court obviously did not expect the respondent state to bring some positive proof that the sisters were willing or able to support him. In addition, the Court's description of the adult and married sisters as 'family members' cannot but jar, as one knows that they would be given no consideration if they were residing in the UK and the applicant's complaint was that his expulsion would entail separation from his family. The inconsistency between *S.H.H.* and the Article 8 removal case law is indeed one of the points made by the three dissenting judges (in a Chamber of seven).[158]

In *H. and B. v. the United Kingdom*,[159] the first applicant had been a driver for the UN in Kabul and the second applicant an interpreter for the US forces. They both said that they had received threats from the Taliban because of these activities. One explained that his cousin had been kidnapped as a reprisal. The Court accepted that 'the evidence paints a disturbing picture of the attacks carried out by the Taliban and other armed anti-government groups to target civilians with links to the international community'.[160] However, it referred to a report which

[153] *S.H.H. v. the United Kingdom*, appl. 60367/10, Judgment (ECtHR), 29 Jan. 2013, in English only.

[154] *S.H.H.*, para 15.

[155] *S.H.H.*, para 15, emphasis added in order to highlight the negative proof implicitly required of the applicant.

[156] *S.H.H.*, para 93.

[157] *S.H.H.*, para 93, emphasis added in order to highlight the negative proof implicitly required of the applicant.

[158] Joint dissenting opinion of Judges Ziemele, David Thór Björgvinsson and De Gaetano in *S.H.H.*, para 2.

[159] *H. and B. v. the United Kingdom*, appls 70073/10, 44539/11, Judgment (ECtHR), 9 Apr. 2013, in English only.

[160] *H. and B.*, para 96.

stated that 'those who no longer collaborate with the international forces are a low priority for the Taliban, who devote their limited assets in the cities to high profile targets, from serving government officials upwards'.[161] By six votes to one, the Court ruled that the removal of either of the applicants to Afghanistan would not breach Article 3 of the Convention.

Judge Kalaydjieva was the dissenting judge. She concluded her dissenting opinion by stating that she was 'unconvinced that the foreseeable consequences of sending the applicants back to Afghanistan were sufficiently taken into account with regard to the current situation in that country and the way it is likely to develop'. In her view, the absence of updated UNHCR official reports could not be determinative. This was the more so since the UNHCR had publicly stated that its 'worst mistake' had been to organise the mass returns of Afghans. For Judge Kalaydjieva, current available information had failed to establish the ability of the Afghan government to protect the applicants upon their return.

XII. When will the Court Intervene: A Matter of Documentation

In *M.S.S.*, the applicant benefited from a long process of evidence gathering by numerous organisations which had been comprehensively and repeatedly documenting the appalling conditions which existed in Greece. No less than 23 reports emanating from most reputable organisations were put before the Court detailing these conditions.[162] While this was of tremendous help to the applicant, most applicants are not in a position to put before the Court such a level of documentation. The question arises as to the level of proof required before the Court considers a general situation established (as opposed to circumstances personal to the applicant, where the difficulty for the applicant is often to persuade the Court of his credibility). The case law does not explain the standards which the Court follows. The Court is either persuaded or it is not. In *M.S.S.*, it was; in *Mohamed Hussein*, it was not. One suspects that some Sections of the Court have raised the bar higher than others in this respect.

Sufi and Elmi v. the United Kingdom was a lead case adopted by the Fourth Section in June 2011, when this Section was still presided over by Judge Bratza. In this case, the Court undertook a painstaking review of the situation in Somalia, based on 'relevant country information' which consisted of reports from the UK, United States, and Norwegian governments, United Nations reports, as well as successive reports from Amnesty International, Human Rights Watch, the International Displacement Monitoring Centre, the World Food Programme, and Médecins Sans Frontières.[163] The 77-page judgment contemplates all kinds

[161] *H. and B.*, para 98.

[162] *M.S.S.* judgment, para 160.

[163] *Sufi and Elmi v. the United Kingdom*, appls 8319/07, 11449/07, Judgment (ECtHR), 28 June 2011, paras 80–195.

of scenarios one after the other, presented in a very logical way, to arrive at a number of conclusions regarding different parts of the country, including the fact that 'the situation of general violence in Mogadishu is sufficiently intense to enable [the Court] to conclude that any returnee would be at real risk of Article 3 ill-treatment solely on account of his presence there, unless it could be demonstrated that he was sufficiently well connected to powerful actors in the city to enable him to obtain protection'.[164] Examining the origin and situation of each of the two applicants in turn, the Court found unanimously that their removal to Somalia (following criminal conviction in the UK) would violate Article 3 ECHR. While the Court's analysis is intellectually pleasing, it begs the question of how many migrants benefit from such star legal representation that they could submit to the Court the level of documentation which was provided in *Sufi and Elmi*.

Contrast this with one of the last judgments of the Second Section when it still included Judge Tulkens, *Singh and Others v. Belgium*, adopted in October 2012. In this case, the Court assessed the situation of asylum seekers from Afghanistan by reference to two documents issued by the UNHCR in 2010 and 2011, with the latter document itself relying on reports from various sources (going as far back as 1993).[165] For the Court, this was enough to establish that the Afghani applicants, belonging to the Sikh minority, had an arguable claim under Article 3 which needed to be properly examined by the Belgian authorities. The fact that this had not been done led the Court to find that Article 13 had been violated.

States are obviously in a much better position than an individual applicant to collect information about the conditions which exist in a particular country. Given this, the Court could require the applicant to submit some information, but then reverse the burden of proof onto the state to establish that the conditions are not as alleged to exist by the applicant. Such an approach would have allowed the Fourth Section in *Sufi and Elmi* to adopt a relatively short judgment where it stated that the situation in Somalia was such that, barring clear evidence brought by the respondent state that the particular situation of the applicants meant that they would not face ill-treatment in Somalia, a violation of Article 3 had to be found. Similarly, in *Singh* it would have been useful if the Second Section not only found that the domestic authorities should have examined the applicants' claim but also explicitly reversed the burden of proof onto the state, given that the applicants had relied on UNHCR reports. The Court could have said that it was persuaded by these reports in the absence of reliable evidence adduced by the

[164] *Sufi and Elmi*, para 293. The Court commented with realism that: 'It is not possible for the Court to assess the level of general violence in every part of southern and central Somalia and, even if it were to undertake such an exercise, it is likely that its conclusions would become outdated very quickly'. There are many examples, however, where the Court is ready to accept signs that things are getting better in order not to find a violation of the Convention. *H. and B.* is a case in point. In Chapter 7 (p. 221), there is already criticism of the Court for its acceptance of reports which suggest an improvement in a situation which is by nature volatile.

[165] *Singh and Others v. Belgium*, appl. 33210/11, Judgment (ECtHR), 2 Jan. 2013, in French only, paras 44–48.

respondent state to the contrary. In a sense, this is what *M.S.S.* did by explaining that it lent more weight to the version of facts presented by the applicant; implicitly, this must mean that the Court adopted this perspective in the absence of a more credible version having been presented by the state. However, a clearer reasoning in this respect would have been welcome and would have opened up avenues for the development of the Article 13 case law.

XIII. Conclusion

M.S.S. arose because the asylum situation in Greece could hardly have been more abysmal—virtually no one could become a refugee in Greece when the judgment was adopted. Faced with such a situation, the Court woke up. It showed its ability to adopt a strong judgment in an extremely sensitive area. One suspects that this was not easy and that the role of the two national judges was instrumental in producing this result. Strikingly, the Court found violation after violation—not only in respect of Greece but also, and perhaps even more so, in respect of Belgium which had decided to transfer the applicant to Greece under the 'Dublin II' EU regulation. 'Dublin' was inflicted a severe blow.[166] Along with a judgment of the European Court of Justice later in 2011,[167] *M.S.S.* provoked the negotiation of 'Dublin III', which was adopted in June 2013 and came into force on 1 January 2014, providing a number of guarantees which had not existed under Dublin II.[168]

The significance of the Strasbourg Court's judgment in M.S.S. goes beyond this, however, in that it opened promising avenues of jurisprudence at both normative and procedural levels. To give only two procedural examples here, 'the Strasbourg reversal' was nowhere to be seen and the Court was ready to believe the allegations made by the applicant, as these rang true with what was known about the general situation in Greece.

On a less positive note, however, the Court has not been persuaded to repeat a verdict of violation for the transfer of an asylum seeker within the European Union in the three years which followed *M.S.S.*[169] This restraint can be linked to the high threshold it imposes before it finds Article 3 to be engaged, as discussed further in Chapter 13. Another consideration is its long practice of not explicitly stating that domestic asylum determination procedures must be robust—robust in the sense that they allow individuals a fair opportunity to demonstrate that

[166] Francesca Ippolito, 'The Contribution of the European Courts to the Common European Asylum System and its Ongoing Recast Process' (2013) *Maastricht Journal of European and Comparative Law* 20, 261–281.

[167] *N.S. v. Secretary of State for the Home Department* and *M.E. and Others v. Refugee Applications Commissioner and Minister for Justice, Equality and Law Reform* Case C-411/10 and Case C- 493/10, Judgment (Court of Justice of the European Union), 21 Dec. 2011.

[168] Regulation (EU) no 604/2013 of the European Parliament and the Council of Europe of 26 June 2013 establishing the criteria and mechanisms for determining the Member State responsible for examining an application for international protection lodged in one of the Member States by a third-country national or a stateless person.

[169] This changed with the recent *Tarakhel* judgment, on which see note 104.

they would be at real risk of inhuman treatment if returned and thus to avoid removal. In other words, the problem is an underdeveloped Article 13 case law, not to mention the implacable *Maaouia* Article 6 jurisprudence.

It goes without saying that instituting procedures which are not too burdensome upon refugees would inevitably lead to a much greater number of persons having to be granted permission to remain in Europe. This book is ready to argue that we have no option but to open our borders far more than we do presently if we want to be able to claim that we are serious in our commitment to human rights. In case the reasons for this remain unclear, the next chapter presents a series of decisions which demonstrate that the logic of closure at the heart of the Strasbourg migrant case law produces effects which are simply unacceptable from a human rights perspective.

13

The Darkest Case Law: Condoning Rightlessness

(*Bonger et alia*)

In September 2005, the European Court of Human Rights declared inadmissible the case of an applicant who had been refused a residence permit for almost ten years despite being de facto stateless. Not a well-known decision, *Bonger v. the Netherlands*[1] captures the indifference with which the Court has tackled the problem of lack of secure legal status which affects millions of 'irregular' migrants in Europe.[2] The facts in *Bonger* were very specific to the Netherlands. The ruling, however, is at the heart of European human rights law. Although it would be an exaggeration to say that it sums up the Strasbourg migrant case law, it constitutes its logical outcome. Since 2011, *Bonger* has been repeated in another three cases, again all involving the Netherlands.[3]

The key problem which the applicant brought to Strasbourg in *Bonger* was that, whilst there was no plan to expel him, there was also no willingness on the part of the authorities to give him the means to live legally. In concrete terms, the applicant had been refused a residence permit, without which he could neither work nor draw social security benefits from the state. How was he supposed to live? His legal representative submitted that the situation—which had gone on for almost a decade—entailed a violation of his dignity and thus human rights. The Court declared the issue of the denial of a residence permit to fall outside the ambit of Article 3 or any other provision of the European Convention.

[1] *Teshome Goraga Bonger v. the Netherlands*, appl. 10154/04, Decision (ECtHR), 15 Sept. 2005, in English only.

[2] In 2009, the population of irregular migrants in the European Union alone was conservatively estimated at between two million and four million: House of Lords, European Union Committee, 'The EU's Global Approach to Migration and Mobility', HL Paper 91, published 18 December 2012, available at <http://www.publications.parliament.uk/pa/ld201213/ldselect/ldeucom/91/91.pdf>, accessed 14 April 2014.

[3] *I. v. the Netherlands*, appl. 24147/11, Partial Decision (ECtHR), 18 Oct. 2011 and Final Decision (ECtHR), 10 July 2012; *K. v. the Netherlands*, appl. 33403/11, Partial Decision (ECtHR) 18 Oct. 2011 and Final Decision (ECtHR), 25 Sept. 2012; *Mohammad Rafiq Naibzay v. the Netherlands*, appl. 68564/12, Committee Decision (ECtHR), 22 Oct. 2012.

The first case which confirmed the stance adopted in *Bonger* was *I. v. the Netherlands*.[4] *I.* was lodged three months after the Grand Chamber rendered its judgment in *M.S.S. v. Belgium and Greece*. As we have seen in Chapter 12, *M.S.S.* had found, for the first time in the history of the European Convention, a violation of Article 3 due to a state of destitution attributable to the respondent states. *M.S.S.* made no difference to the outcome which the Third Section reached in *I.* Like *Bonger*, *I.*—which the Court specifically distinguished from *M.S.S.*—was unanimously declared inadmissible. This outcome was then repeated in *K.* and *Naibzay*. The slightly different ending in two other cases that also involved the Netherlands, *G.R.* and *H.*,[5] was not fundamentally more satisfactory, as we shall see.

In the wake of World War II, Hannah Arendt produced a masterpiece on *The Origins of Totalitarianism*.[6] In this work, she identified 'the right to have rights' as being central to the protection of the human being in a world of states. She also warned that it was entirely possible for governments to deny individuals this ground right by simply leaving or purposely putting them in a situation of 'rightlessness'. This term is apposite to describe the circumstances of the *Bonger* applicants (by which I mean not only the applicant in *Bonger* but also the applicants in similar cases to *Bonger*).[7]

To use informal terminology which has gained currency, *Bonger* applicants live in 'limbo'. In Catholic doctrine, limbo refers to 'a region on the border of Hell, the abode of the just who died before Christ's coming, and of unbaptized infants'.[8] The expression 'to be in limbo' has passed into the English language to denote a situation where someone is stuck in between impossible options, thus lingering in an unsatisfactory state. In activist circles, the expression is typically used to refer to a migrant who is neither returnable to her country of origin nor possesses the right to stay where she happens to find herself.

In concrete terms, this is often associated with the lack of a residence permit, which prevents the ability to work legally and renders access to decent housing,

[4] The European Court had already condoned a situation similar to *Bonger* in its third violation verdict in an Article 3 removal case. In *Ahmed v. Austria*, appl. 25964/94, Judgment (ECtHR), 17 Dec. 1996, the Court ruled that the removal of the applicant would entail a risk of inhuman and degrading treatment contrary to Article 3. Although the applicant was not removed, he was left without a residence permit, which is widely believed to have led him to take his life.

[5] *G.R. v. the Netherlands*, appl. 22251/07, Judgment (ECtHR), 10 Jan. 2012; *H. v. the Netherlands*, appl. 37833/10, Committee Decision (ECtHR), 19 June 2012.

[6] Hannah Arendt, *The Origins of Totalitarianism* (Cleveland: The World Publishing Company, 1951).

[7] Alison Kesby, *The Right to Have Rights. Citizenship, Humanity, and International Law* (Oxford: Oxford University Press, 2012); Monica Krause, 'Stateless People and Undocumented Migrants: An Arendtian Perspective', in Caroline Sawyer and Brad K. Blitz (eds) *Statelessness in the European Union: Displaced, Undocumented, Unwanted* (Cambridge: Cambridge University Press, 2011) 22–40; Jacqueline Bhabha, 'Arendt's Children: Do Today's Migrant Children Have a Right to Have Rights' (2009) *Human Rights Quarterly* 31, 410–451; Anna Blus, 'Beyond the Walls of Paper. Undocumented Migrants, the Border and Human Rights' (2013) *European Journal of Migration and Law* 15, 413–446.

[8] C.T. Onions (ed.) *The Shorter English Oxford Dictionary on Historical Principles* (Oxford: Clarendon Press, 1973) Vol. I, 1215.

healthcare, and education (including of any children) either difficult or impossible. A series of mundane activities, such as opening a bank account, holding a driver's licence, or leasing a mobile phone, are often out of reach.[9] Needless to say, the accumulation of the deprivation of rights creates an enormous physical and emotional toll for the persons concerned. The lack of legitimate status coupled with the loss of state protection induce extreme vulnerability and an acute sense of hopelessness, not to mention destitution.[10]

Many migrants who are informally described as being in limbo are de facto stateless. The Equal Rights Trust, an organisation which has done much to put the plight of the stateless on the European social map, uses this expression to refer to those who do not have an effective nationality: although in theory they may have one, in practice they do not benefit from the protection of any state.[11] De facto statelessness affects 'failed asylum seekers' who, once their claim to asylum has definitely been rejected, cannot be returned to their country of origin. This can be for a multitude of reasons: perhaps the state which rejected the asylum claim accepts that the individual concerned would be at risk of treatment prohibited by Article 3 ECHR if she was returned; perhaps it is not clear where she comes from at all; perhaps her alleged state of nationality does not recognise her as one of its nationals because she does not have the necessary documentation to prove her nationality status.

To give a sense of the scale of the problem, in the UK it is estimated that 90 per cent of asylum seekers whose claims for refugee status are refused end up remaining in the country.[12] Migrants who have never made a formal asylum claim can also meet the fate of having no prospect of seeing their stay being authorised whilst not being returnable anywhere else. De facto statelessness is on the rise in Europe as it is in the rest of the world,[13] reflecting the characteristics of an era where not only people travel far more than in the past but also state authorities are increasingly intent on controlling their borders and cracking down on those they deem to be 'illegal'.

The European Court of Human Rights has had little to say about the negation of 'the right to have rights' which besets human beings who have the label 'illegal' informally if not formally attached to them.[14] On the one hand, this appears paradoxical given that rightlessness stands directly opposed to the idea of inalienable rights for all human beings. On the other, it appears entirely logical, as the straightforward application of principles which have long been established in the

[9] Brad K. Blitz and Miguel Otero-Iglesias, 'Stateless By Any Other Name: Refused Asylum-Seekers in the United Kingdom' (2011) *Journal of Ethnic and Migration Studies* 37, 657–673 at 664.

[10] Blitz and Otero-Iglesias 'Stateless'.

[11] The Equal Rights Trust, *Unravelling Anomaly: Detention, Discrimination and the Protection Needs of Stateless Persons* (London, 2010) 1.

[12] Blitz and Otero-Iglesias 'Stateless' 661.

[13] Statelessness is conservatively estimated to affect 12 million people worldwide: Equal Rights Trust 3.

[14] One legal scholar who has seen this is Caroline Sawyer: Sawyer, 'Stateless in Europe: Legal Aspects of *De Jure* and *De Facto* Statelessness in the European Union', in Sawyer and Blitz (eds) *Statelessness* 69–107 at 95.

Strasbourg jurisprudence. In this sense, the entirely (internally) consistent *Bonger* case law is perhaps the most serious indictment of what is wrong with the way in which the European Court of Human Rights has long approached, and continues to approach, migrant cases.

This chapter starts by reviewing the *Bonger* case law, describing the Kafkaesque nature of the situation in which the applicants are left, and arguing that the decisions reached are a logical extension of the general Strasbourg migration case law. The *Bonger* case law is then presented as being part of the Article 3 destitution case law (which includes *M.S.S.*, its great exception). It is then observed that it can also be approached as one strand in the residence permit Strasbourg case law. Indeed, the rest of the chapter focuses on the latter case law, which is increasingly abundant and complex. The residence permit case law is introduced by reference to the Article 8 expulsion case law, with which it shares a lottery-like nature. Most complaints regarding residence permit refusals are rejected as inadmissible. Three cases nonetheless escaped this fate and gave rise in 2005-2006 to verdicts of violation. These emerged in very different social contexts. One was the situation of persons of Russian origin living in Latvia without secure status. However, the verdict of violation in this case was overturned by the Grand Chamber, bringing to an end the Latvian strand of the residence permit case law.[15] A second strand is made of cases brought by irregular migrants who have established family life in the state where they reside. It has not stopped growing and shows the Court divided, but overall inclined to refuse to allow what it calls the *fait accompli* of having children induce an obligation for the respondent state to grant the irregular parent a residence permit. A third strand in the residence permit case law is the *Bonger* case law.

The chapter tries to understand the approach followed by the Court by discussing every verdict of violation reached after 2006 because of a residence permit refusal. A first section discusses a parallel to *Bonger*. Consisting of two cases where applicants were not returnable to their country of origin and could not live with their spouse in Switzerland because the spouses were assigned to different cantons, these findings of violation of Article 8 bring into stark relief the anomaly of the *Bonger* case law. The next three sections analyse the following cases: two Russian cases with reasoning—on family life and the need to justify exclusion—which could usefully be adopted across the whole migration case law; one verdict which partly relies on the presence of adult children in the respondent state to find a violation of Article 8; one international child abduction case where the fact that the mother was forced into living illegally in order to resume contact with her child becomes part of the Court's motivation to find a violation of Article 8. These violation verdicts should not detract from the general principle established by the Court that neither Article 3 nor Article 8 can be construed as guaranteeing, as such, the right to a residence permit. The chapter stresses that this and other principles lead the Court to find that statelessness or rightlessness lies outside the

[15] *Sisojeva and Others v. Latvia*, appl. 60654/00, GC Judgment (ECtHR), 15 Jan 2007.

ambit of the Convention. It argues that this is wrong. Being denied 'the right to have rights' runs counter to the very idea of human rights. Such a denial should be seen to breach Articles 3, 6, and 14 ECHR. Why Article 14? Because leaving people without a legal status is the ultimate discrimination which a human being may face within a legal order.

I. Rightlessness under the Convention: The *Bonger* Case Law

The applicant in *Bonger* was an Ethiopian national who had applied for asylum in the Netherlands in 1995. In support of his asylum claim, he had explained that he had been a pilot in the Ethiopian air force, which had led him to carry out military operations, including bombings, during the regime of President Mengistu Haile Mariam; due to this involvement, he said, returning him to post-Mengistu Ethiopia would put him at risk of treatment contrary to Article 3 ECHR. His account was found credible by the Dutch authorities. According to them, it also made him ineligible for refugee status, because of Article 1F of the 1951Convention Relating to the Status of Refugees, which provides that this UN Convention 'shall not apply to any person with respect to whom there are serious reasons for considering that... he has committed... a crime against humanity'. '1F' was applied to Mr Bonger. As a result, he could neither be expelled to Ethiopia, as the authorities accepted that such a removal would entail a violation of Article 3 ECHR; nor could he be admitted to remain in the Netherlands, as the only ground upon which he could have been entitled to a residence permit was asylum—a status refused to him under 1F.

Mr Bonger submitted at Strasbourg that denying him a residence permit, aside from the fact that it rested on the untested presumption that he had committed crimes against humanity (which he denied), made it 'impossible for him to become a full member of the Netherlands society'.[16] He complained that this constituted in itself a violation of human rights and dignity, contrary to Article 3 ECHR.[17] The Court rejected this complaint 'for being incompatible [with the Convention] *ratione materiae* as neither Article 3 nor any other provision of the Convention and its Protocols guarantees, as such, a right to a residence permit'.[18] His application was found inadmissible in a Chamber presided over by Judge Zupančič.

Bonger is not a one-off ruling. A number of similar applications, all directed against the Netherlands,[19] appear on HUDOC. (Additional applications may have been summarily declared inadmissible.) The first case to have generated another ruling is *I.* which was lodged in April 2011, i.e. three months after the

[16] *Bonger* decision, p. 13. [17] *Bonger*, p. 13. [18] *Bonger*, p. 14.

[19] For the policy of the Dutch government, as explained by the State Secretary of Justice to the national Parliament in November 1997 after questions were asked (at the time) about this recent practice, see: Peter J. van Krieken (ed.) *Refugee Law in Context: The Exclusion Clause* (The Hague: Hasser, 1999) Chapter 5.3.

ground breaking Grand Chamber judgment in *M.S.S.*[20] In *I.*, it was accepted that the applicant had been part of the Afghan intelligence service under the communist regime from 1981 to 1997 and in the Junbish-e-Milli militia, which fought the Taliban under General Massoud, from 1992 to 1997. I. explained that, while his wife and four children (the youngest born in the Netherlands) had been granted first refugee status and then Dutch citizenship, because Article 1F of the Refugee Convention was applied to him, he could not gain lawful residence in the Netherlands. As a consequence, he was not allowed to work and earn a living.[21] He was not entitled to benefits in kind, facilities nor social security benefits.[22] In addition, he stated, because his wife was considered to be harbouring an illegal alien, she too was denied various fiscal facilities and benefits.[23] In October 2011, nine months after the delivery of *M.S.S.*, I.'s Article 3 complaint about the 'permanent stalemate'[24] in which he found himself was declared inadmissible.[25] One year later, so was his Article 8 complaint. The very similar *K.* and *Naibzay* cases were also declared inadmissible.

In addition to this case law, *H.* was struck out in June 2012 after the applicant was imprisoned immediately upon his 'self-elected' return to his home country in February that year and his legal representative did not communicate his new contact details to the Court. Yet another application, *G.R.*, ended on a violation verdict of Article 13 in 2012, as we shall see later. HUDOC does not appear to contain anymore similar cases to *Bonger*. It cannot be ruled out that an application similar to *Bonger* would have been summarily refused at Strasbourg. (This was the fate of more than 80,000 applications in 2013.[26]) It is also possible that an understanding has developed in the Dutch legal community that there is no point in making such a complaint.

[20] *M.S.S. v. Belgium and Greece*, appl. 30696/09, GC Judgment (ECtHR), 21 Jan. 2011.

[21] *I.* final decision (2012), para 48.

[22] With limited exceptions such as essential medical care in life-threatening situations or situations which would jeopardise public health: *I.* (2012), para 29.

[23] Allowances to meet the costs for medical insurance, rent, and child care: *I.* (2012), para 40; *I.* partial decision (2011), para 33.

[24] *I.* (2011), para 33.

[25] This was done by the same Third Section of the Court which had decided *Bonger*, but in a bench constituted differently—with the sole exception of the Dutch national judge, who remained Judge Myjer.

[26] There are currently 37 single judges, meaning that on average, in 2013, every single judge rejected over 40 applications per week (when this is calculated over 52 weeks). One wonders what level of scrutiny the single judge applies to the files prepared by the Registry. Summary rejections are hard on an applicant who has previously exhausted national remedies and gone all the way to the highest domestic court, as noted in: <http://strasbourgobservers.com/2014/05/28/stensholt-v-norway-why-single-judge-decisions-undermine-the-courts-legitimacy-2/>,accessed 30 May 2014. See also: Janneke Gerards, 'Inadmissibility Decisions of the European Court of Human Rights: A Critique of the Lack of Reasoning' (2014) *Human Rights Law Review* 14, 148–158; for my remarks on the 'indecency of the Strasbourg procedures', see: Marie-Bénédicte Dembour, *Who Believes in Human Rights? Reflections on the European Convention* (Cambridge: Cambridge University Press, 2006) 127–130.

II. At Issue in the *Bonger* Case Law: A Kafkaesque Stalemate

The summary of the decisions of the facts and complaints of the applicants in the *Bonger* case law suggest a Kafkaesque situation in more than one respect. This section highlights five such aspects—which the Court seems to approach as facts of life rather than elements produced by state action.

The first Kafkaesque dimension of the cases relates to the way in which the applicants are given no opportunity to have the presumption of culpability for the acts at the origin of their problems tested. The presumption of innocence is rightly held to be at the heart of a healthy democratic society governed by the rule of law. Here, it is difficult not to conclude that a presumption of culpability for crimes committed as members of the army or intelligence service of their country's former regime[27] has been applied in order to deny the applicants access to refugee status. In turn, the absence of refugee status has triggered the denial of a residence permit, and thus the rights to work and/or have access to social benefits. What can the applicants do? No route is open to them to have this presumption of culpability tested—and possibly reversed—in a court of law: they have not been tried and there is no intention to try them in the future. Despite the enormity of this scenario in a society which proclaims the presumption of innocence to be a central tenet of its law, the European Court of Human Rights generally does not engage with this point. Specifically challenged on it in *Naibzay*, however, the Court, sitting as a Committee of three judges, replied that the complaint was incompatible *ratione materiae* with the Convention since it related to Article 6 and this does not extend to proceedings and decisions concerning the entry, stay, and removal of aliens, as per *Maaouia v. France*.[28]

The second Kafkaesque dimension of the case law stems from what could be called the *ex futurum* nature of the Court's jurisprudence. The respondent government and the Court both accept that the applicants cannot be removed to their country of origin without a risk that they might be subjected to treatment contrary to Article 3 ECHR. As it is not disputed that such a removal would be against human rights law, removal is not presented as an option. Nonetheless, it seems that much emphasis is placed on the fact that this applies '*in the current circumstances*'.[29] In *I.*, the Court appears to endorse the argument, advanced by the Dutch Deputy Minister, that 'it had not been established that there were no prospects of change in the situation where Article 3 opposed the applicant's removal to Afghanistan, which country was undergoing a period of transition, comprising a complex reconciliation process which had the active support of the international community'.[30] This statement, formally correct rather than practically convincing,

[27] The applicants in *K.* and *Naibzay* were part of the intelligence service of the former communist regime in Afghanistan: *K.* decision, para 4; *Naibzay* decision, para 6.

[28] *Naibzay*, para 25. On *Maaouia v. France*, appl. 39652/98, GC Judgment (ECtHR), 5 Oct. 2000, see Chapter 7 (pp. 234–224).

[29] See e.g. *I.* partial decision (2011), para 11.

[30] *I.* final decision (2012), para 12.

is triply problematic. First, it calls for the applicant to provide proof of a negative fact (the absence of positive prospects). As has been highlighted in Chapter 7, such proof is by its very nature virtually impossible to provide. Second, as we know with hindsight, subsequent events in Afghanistan have arguably shown the unduly optimistic nature of the positive elements identified in the quoted passage. Third, the statement implicitly suggests that because the situation is expected to resolve itself *in the future*, there is no violation of the Convention *today*. Far from tearing this logic apart, the Court chooses not to rule upon the case *ex nunc*, let alone *ex tunc*,[31] but following a method which could be qualified as *ex futurum*, thus dispensing with the need to examine the situation as it exists *now*.

The adoption of an *ex futurum* perspective is especially inappropriate in the *Bonger* case law given the enduring character of the situation of rightlessness complained of. This brings us to a third Kafkaesque feature, namely, the way in which the domestic authorities and the Strasbourg Court do not consider the duration—and likely continuation—of the stalemate. By the time *Bonger* was decided at Strasbourg, the stalemate suffered by the applicant had lasted almost a decade. In *I.*, the Court's 2011 decision refers to a judgment of the domestic Regional Court of the previous year which already noted that 'more than ten years had elapsed'. The domestic court seemed to imply that the applicant had failed to lodge the appropriate proceedings 'if [he] wished to obtain an examination of the proportionality of the *continued* withholding of a residence title', rather than a review of the original decision.[32] The Strasbourg Court did not comment upon the administrative maze which seems to have left the applicant unsure of what to do to get his situation examined as a whole.

G.R. was lodged in 2007 and decided in 2012. Rather than requesting a residence permit directly for himself, the 1F applicant in this case tried to get a residence permit through family reunion with his wife—who had arrived in the Netherlands from Afghanistan the same year as him and had since become a Dutch national. He applied for an exemption from the €830 standard administrative fee. The exemption was refused on the ground that he had not provided additional documents as proof that his family was receiving social assistance. The Court reproached the authorities for their 'extremely formalistic attitude'.[33] (This is an expression which seems to signal that the Court feels the Dutch authorities have overstepped the bounds of acceptability in their treatment of migrants.) It explained: 'The Court fails to understand what the additional documents demanded by the Minister would have added to the social assistance pay slip' given that 'social assistance is not vouchsafed to anyone who has not satisfied the Mayor and Aldermen of his or her inability to meet necessary living expenses'.[34] A violation of Article 13 was found,[35] presumably because the Strasbourg judges felt uncomfortable with the applicant's stalemate whilst they simultaneously did not wish to give a ruling on Article 8, as requested by the applicant. Could not the

[31] On the meaning of these expressions, see Section VII of Chapter 7.
[32] *I.* partial decision (2011), para 12, emphasis added.
[33] *G.R.*, para 55.
[34] *G.R.*, para 54.
[35] *G.R.*, para 55.

phrasing of the Strasbourg verdict itself be regarded as 'formalistic'—a subterfuge which minimises the problems faced by an individual to whom Article 1F of the Refugee Convention is applied? *G.R.* does not provide any direct route for accessing the problematic denial of legal status, which is at the heart of the matter brought by the applicant to Strasbourg. Of course one could object that the judgment precisely opened an indirect route producing the same effect. But what do you do if you are not married to someone who can apply for family reunion? Or if you have not picked up that 'the *G.R.* route'[36] now exists?

A fourth Kafkaesque element arises from the apparent expectation that applicants should demonstrate that no third country is willing to accept them before being considered for a residence permit. In the words of the Regional Court, the appellant's claim 'that not a single country is willing to admit [him] does not, without more, have to be accepted by the Deputy Minister'.[37] Without reflecting upon the conundrum which having to prove a negative fact places on the applicant, in *I.* the European Court reproduces the statement of the Deputy Minister without querying it. One might have thought that the respondent state was in a better position than an individual to find a willing host state for him. The European Court does not indicate that it expects the state to make any intervention in this regard.[38]

A final Kafkaesque element concerns the repercussions of the lack of an authorised status for the conduct of family life. I., for example, stated in his application to Strasbourg that his family had been 'reproached for housing an illegal alien'.[39] Were his wife and children expected to cut all contact with him?[40] If so, why not the rest of society too? One would like to assume that this would not be possible. But can we be so certain?[41]

[36] French trekkers: no pun intended. [37] *I.* partial decision (2011), para 11.

[38] In *Naibzay*, it was not contested that, by the time the Strasbourg Court adopted its ruling in June 2013, 'the applicant ha[d] recently been granted a Belgian residence permit for the purposes of staying with his daughter in Belgium': para 30. Let us note in passing that this was a 'positive' rather than 'negative' fact, as such easy to establish. From it, the Court deduced that 'it has not appeared that it would be impossible for the applicant's spouse and their other children—all of whom are holding Netherlands citizenship—to join [them] in Belgium'. The Article 8 complaint was found manifestly ill-founded. The Court did not discuss the situation of the applicant from his entry into the Netherlands in 1990 until the possibility of joining his daughter in Belgium materialised.

[39] *I.* partial decision (2011), para 33.

[40] The Court ignores the toll the situation must have taken on the family, including the children, of the individuals concerned. In *I.* it reproduces a passage from the Dutch Regional Court, as follows: 'When the impugned decision was taken, his oldest child had come of age, whereas no special relationship of dependency between the applicant and this child has appeared. At that time, the other three children were, respectively, seventeen, thirteen and seven years old. It has not appeared that, if need be, these children could not appeal to their mother and the oldest child for aid and assistance': *I.* final decision (2012), para 13. In what can only be described as callous silence, the Court simply rejects I.'s Article 8 complaint as manifestly ill-founded in a short reasoning which does not mention the applicant's children. Compare with *Hasanbasic v. Switzerland*, appl. 52166/09, Judgment (ECtHR), 11 June 2013, in French only, para 60, reviewed later.

[41] The French have (in)famously invented what is commonly referred to as the *délit de solidarité*, whereby it is a criminal offence to help irregular migrants. The ECtHR condoned this in *Mallah v. France*, appl. 29681/08, Judgment (ECtHR), 10 Nov. 2011. Will the day come when even offering a glass of water to a supposedly 'illegal' migrant will be deemed a criminal offence?

Kafkaesque does not seem too strong a term to describe the circumstances of the applicants in the *Bonger* case law. The Strasbourg Court seems intent on not confronting the situation for what it is. Of course, it may be tempting to assume that 1F applicants are not the kind of characters that a nation would wish to welcome in its midst. However, it bears repeating that applicants in cases similar to *Bonger* have never been tried for a crime. Moreover, human rights defenders, including the Strasbourg Court, surely remain in agreement that human rights are for everyone, including crime suspects. This may not be a popular position, but does this mean that one needs to argue and demonstrate that it is the only tenable human rights position?

III. How We Came to *Bonger, I.*, and *K.*: Long Established Principles and Ways of Reasoning

The Strasbourg failure to find any fault with a situation whereby human beings are denied the rights which would enable them to pursue a life in dignity, on the ground that this situation falls outside the Convention's ambit, is disturbing. This makes the *Bonger* decisions of inadmissibility surprising. In another sense, however, these decisions are merely the logical outcome of well-established strands in the Strasbourg case law. Indeed, the reasoning in *Bonger, I.*, and *K.* is made up of a string of pronouncements which come from past decisions, duly referred to. The logic thus appears implacable and, if one is convinced by it, unassailable.

As we have seen in the previous chapters, the Strasbourg migrant case law has long taken it for granted that non-nationals have no right to live where they would like to, no right not to be separated from their families (barring some exceptional circumstances), and no right to rely on social protection systems which have been devised with people other than themselves in mind—except if they are legally settled migrants who have been formally accepted within the community. To simplify, and going back to rulings discussed at length in previous chapters, *Bonger, I.*, and *K.* are the outcome of *ABC, Üner*, and *Bah*, the judgments reviewed in Chapters 4, 6, and 8 respectively, which asserted that migrants cannot choose where they wish to live,[42] can be separated from their families,[43] and can be denied access to social services.[44] These rulings were themselves the product of long-forgotten decisions of the erstwhile Commission, as the historical approach to the analysis of the case law presented in Parts I and II of the book show.

Summarising the Strasbourg migrant case law in a most general way, one could say that virtually all the decisions it has produced are dependent on the overarching principles according to which, first, it is the state's privilege to control the entry and residence of aliens and, second, domestic rules governing the granting

[42] *Abdulaziz, Cabales and Balkandali v. the United Kingdom*, appls 9214/80, 9473/81, 9474/81, PC Judgment (ECtHR), 28 May 1985.

[43] *Üner v. the Netherlands*, appl. 46410/99, GC Judgment (ECtHR), 18 Oct. 2006.

[44] *Bah v. the United Kingdom*, appl. 56328/07, Judgment (ECtHR), 27 Sept. 2011.

of nationality need not and indeed should not come under the scrutiny of the European Court. These principles do not go without saying, however, as Bas Schotel has demonstrated in respect of the former,[45] and the experience of the Inter-American Court suggests in respect of the latter.[46]

If the European Court had recognised that immigration control and the granting of nationality were not the fields of near-absolute state sovereignty which it has largely taken them to be, it could have deemed it incumbent upon the state *to justify* why it was denying migrants the right to live where they wish, the right to be with their family, or the right to access social protection (to remain in line with the examples given earlier). This perspective would have insisted that the state provides a sound justification for curtailing any of these rights, which one could argue would have meant, amongst other requirements, that the particular case of the migrant(s) concerned needed to be addressed. This scheme would not have presumed that curtailing migrants' rights is in all cases illegitimate, but it would have required that the state justifies why it is curtailing these rights when it does.

What has happened instead is that the European Court has rarely demanded that the state justifies what it is doing. In short, the Court has granted the state too much power. The bias from which the state has thus benefited presents both substantive and procedural aspects. Substantively, at its most general, it has taken the form of naturalising the right of the state to exclude aliens—as well as the prior right conceptually to define its nationals and thus, by implication, 'its aliens'. Procedurally the bias has translated into a tendency to give credit to state allegations, whilst dismissing those of the applicant. Applied repeatedly, these substantive and procedural trends have become general principles which have not been kept in check. The result is an internal logic which, at times, transforms into an unstoppable machine which produces Kafkaesque results, as in the *Bonger* case law. Expressions of dissent by some judges who resolutely declare that the results are ethically unacceptable, even when this means going against the authority of the Grand Chamber,[47] may then be powerless against this judicial machine.

IV. On Destitution and the Inapplicability of Article 3: Back to *Müslim* as if *M.S.S.* had Never Happened

The outcomes in the *Bonger* case law can be explained by reference to the general legacy outlined earlier. However, they can also be traced to two specific strands of Strasbourg jurisprudence which have not yet been reviewed in detail. The first concerns the long and continuing history of declaring inadmissible Article 3

[45] Bas Schotel, *On the Right of Exclusion: Law, Ethics and Immigration Policy* (Abingdon: Routledge, 2012).

[46] See Chapter 5.

[47] See e.g. the dissenting opinion of Judge Power-Forde in *Josef v. Belgium*, appl. 70055/10, Judgment (ECtHR), 27 Feb. 2014, in French only—a case concerning the deportation of a terminally ill mother of three young children.

complaints relating to destitution (notwithstanding *M.S.S.*); the second, the superficially more promising but ultimately disappointing case law on Articles 3 and/or 8 complaints regarding residence permit refusals. These two strands will be reviewed in turn.

A good starting point for a review of the destitution case law is *Van Volsem v. Belgium*, a case which was lodged not by a migrant but by a national. The applicant was a mother who was living in social housing provided by the state with her children, two of them minors, and her daughter's baby.[48] The heating was electric only, and thus costly to run. The applicant predictably became unable to pay her electricity bill. Her power supply was then cut off, leaving the family without heating, lighting, and cooking facilities. A committee of three members of the Commission declared her application inadmissible in 1990. Frédéric Sudre asked at the time: 'Would it not have been possible, in this particular case, to accept that the State was under a positive obligation to adopt positive measures (acceptable housing, regular electricity supply, minimal income) so as to ensure the effectiveness of the right to human treatment and the right to normal family life, as the exercise of these rights is put under threat by poverty'?[49]

This call fell on deaf ears, and for many years it was thought that the Court would resist finding any right to shelter or subsistence provided for under the Convention, whatever the state of destitution in which the applicant found herself. In 2002, however, a potential opening arose as the Court stated in *Larioshina v. Russia* that 'a complaint about a wholly insufficient amount of pension and the other social benefits may, in principle, raise an issue under Article 3 of the Convention'.[50] Although *Larioshina* was declared inadmissible, the pronouncement appeared to raise the prospect of an interpretation possibly more generous to destitute applicants.

This did not happen immediately. In *Müslim v. Turkey*,[51] decided in April 2005, the applicant was an Iraqi national whose claim to asylum had been rejected by the Turkish authorities. His complaint that his removal to Iraq would entail a real risk to his life due to his previous opposition to the Ba'ath Party was found by the Court to have become 'without any object' following the fall of the regime of Saddam Hussein.[52] His second complaint concerned his exclusion from any kind of economic, social, and medical assistance in Turkey, which he alleged entailed a violation of Article 3 and/or Article 8.[53] The Court cited previous case law from the Commission to the effect that, on the one hand, Article 8 does not go as far as imposing on states a general obligation to assist refugees in order to ensure them a certain standard of living and that, on the other hand, there is no right to work

[48] *Van Volsem v. Belgium*, appl. 1464/89, Decision (EComHR), 9 May 1990, not available on HUDOC but reproduced, with a case note by Frédéric Sudre, in (1990) *Revue universelle des droits de l'homme* 349–353. This 'first' (Sudre 349) thus happens to be a Belgian case again.

[49] Sudre 351, my translation.

[50] *Larioshina v. Russia*, appl. 56869/00, Decision (ECtHR), 23 Apr. 2002.

[51] *Müslim v. Turkey*, appl. 53566/99, Judgment (ECtHR), 26 Apr. 2005, in French only.

[52] *Müslim*, para 54.

[53] *Müslim*, paras 55 and 83.

provided in the Convention.[54] The Court found no violation of the Convention. For the unanimous bench presided over by Judge Bratza, the applicant had '*himself chosen*' the standard of living in which he found himself by electing to become a refugee in Turkey.[55] The state of necessity he was enduring, the Court added, was obviously not such that he was forced to leave Turkey, as he was still living there.[56] *Bonger* was decided five months later.

The decision of (in)admissibility in the Slovenian 'Erased' case,[57] introduced in Chapter 5, is also worth noting here. When this case eventually came before the Grand Chamber, Judge Vučinić observed that it concerned 'something extraordinary',[58] namely, the deprivation of the legal status of the applicants through 'erasure' from the Slovenian Register of Permanent Residents. This had had, amongst other consequences, 'the destruction of identity documents, loss of job opportunities, loss of health insurance, the impossibility of renewing identity documents or driving licences, and difficulties in regulating pension rights'.[59] As we have already seen, the Court found the applicants' Article 3 complaint inadmissible in 2007.

It would take the case of *M.S.S. v. Belgium and Greece* for the Court to accept in 2011, for the first and so far only time, that a situation of extreme poverty had entailed a breach of Article 3.[60] This was because of the utmost gravity of the character of the situation in which the applicant—an asylum seeker from Afghanistan—found himself in Greece after being sent back by Belgium under the so-called Dublin Convention. In this case, a sympathetic Court explained:

> 'The applicant' allegedly spent months living in a state of the most extreme poverty, unable to cater for his most basic needs: food, hygiene and a place to live. Added to this was

[54] *Müslim*, para 85. For an approach which encourages the Court to develop labour rights, see: Virginia Mantouvalou, 'Labour Rights in the European Convention on Human Rights: An Intellectual Justification for an Integrated Approach to Interpretation' (2013) *Human Rights Law Review* 13, 529–555.

[55] *Müslim*, para 86, emphasis added in order to stress the conceptualisation of the applicant as a liberal subject free to lead his life as he wishes outside structural external constraints.

[56] *Müslim*, para 86.

[57] *Milan Makuc and Others v. Slovenia*, appl. 26828/06, Decision (ECtHR), 31 May 2007.

[58] Partly concurring, partly dissenting opinion of Judge Vučinićin *Kurić and Others v. Slovenia*, appl. 26828/06, GC Judgment (ECtHR), 13 July 2010.

[59] Vučinić.

[60] *M.S.S.* GC judgment, para 252. Domestic courts can of course be more generous in their interpretation of the Convention than the Strasbourg Court. In the case of *Adam, R (on the application of) v. Secretary of State for the Home Department* [2005] UKHL 66 (3 November 2005), commonly referred to as *Limbuela*, the UK House of Lords ruled that 'It might be possible to endure rooflessness for some time without degradation if one had enough to eat and somewhere to wash oneself and one's clothing. It might be possible to endure cashlessness for some time if one had a roof and basic meals and hygiene facilities provided. But to have to endure the indefinite prospect of both... is in today's society both inhuman and degrading. We have to judge matters by the standards of our own society in the modern world, not by the standards of a third world society or a bygone age' (*Limbuela*, para [78]).This case, which related to a challenge to the then government policy of denying not only the right to work, but also social and financial support to asylum seekers who had failed to claim asylum 'as soon as reasonably practicable' (para [1])], actually turned more on the question of whether or not such a policy could be regarded as 'treatment' for the purposes of Article 3, and whether the UK government could be held responsible for it in the context of cases where the authorities were not themselves directly administering violence or punishment. The Lords unanimously agreed that it could.

the ever-present fear of being attacked and robbed and the total lack of any likelihood of his situation improving. It was to escape from that situation of insecurity and of material and psychological want that he tried several times to leave Greece.[61]

The term 'allegedly' at the beginning of this passage is significant: it signals that the applicant was unable to substantiate his allegations and produce concrete evidence of his experience. What could have been construed as an insuperable weakness leading to the rejection of the applicant's complaint by a judicial regime which generally puts the onus of proof on the applicant, was not an obstacle in this case. In view of reports from various credible sources which made clear that 'the situation described by the applicant exists on a large scale and is the everyday lot of a large number of asylum seekers', the Court saw 'no reason to question the truth of the applicant's allegations'.[62]

Judge Sajó disagreed with the Article 3 violation verdict. In his separate opinion, he remarked that the Court had taken 'into consideration the lack of accommodation . . . and the failure to provide for the applicant's essential needs'.[63] He asked: 'Is this to mean that when it comes to particularly vulnerable people, failure by the State to provide material services that satisfy essential needs amounts to a violation of Article 3?' His response was that: 'The current position seems to be that with regard to vulnerable groups in an undignified material situation, the State is responsible under Article 3 if it is passive over a lengthy period of time'. He continued: 'There seems to be only a small step between the Court's present position and that of a general and unconditional positive obligation of the State to provide shelter and other material services to satisfy the basic needs of the "vulnerable"'. Judge Sajó declared himself attracted, 'on a personal level', to 'the position that humanitarian considerations . . . must guide the actions of the State', but stressed that 'human rights as defined by the Convention differ from humanitarian concerns'.

Judging from the case law which has arisen in the three years following *M.S.S.*, Judge Sajó need not have been so concerned about the *M.S.S.* unprecedented extension of the Convention becoming a trend. Since *M.S.S.* the Court has shown itself inclined to distinguish the abominable conditions in Greece so vigorously denounced in its Grand Chamber judgment from those pertaining in other European countries. At the time of writing, another verdict of a violation of Article 3 due to the destitution in which asylum seekers, irregular migrants, or other persons applying on this basis, has yet to be reproduced. *I.* is one amongst other rulings where one could say that *M.S.S.* has been clawed back. In order to justify its decision in *I.*, the Court repeated *Bonger* and concluded that I.'s Article 3 complaint was incompatible with the Convention *ratione materiae*.[64] The judges were obviously aware that this conclusion might appear to contradict the recent

[61] *M.S.S.*, para 254. [62] *M.S.S.*, para 255.

[63] Partly concurring and partly dissenting opinion of Judge Sajó in *M.S.S.*, no para given.

[64] *I.* partial decision (2011), para 39. In 2011, the Court adjourned his Article 8 complaint regarding the way in which the lack of a residence permit violated his right to respect for family life. In 2012, this complaint was found inadmissible too (by the same bench that had declared the Article 3 complaint inadmissible).

and more authoritative *M.S.S.* They simply distinguished I.'s fate from that met by M.S.S. To quote:

> [The Court finds] no indication in the case file that the applicant's living conditions in the Netherlands would be comparable to the living conditions in Greece of the applicant in the case of *M.S.S.*... or that the applicant's current living conditions in the Netherlands and/or future prospects, either from a material, physical or psychological perspective, would be of such harrowing hardship that the applicant's situation must be regarded as having attained a minimum level of severity required for treatment to fall within the scope of Article 3 of the Convention.[65]

The inadmissibility outcome was then reproduced in *K.* and *Naibzay*, without the Court continuing to feel the need explicitly to distinguish these cases from *M.S.S.* What this chapter calls the *Bonger* line of jurisprudence seems firmly established.[66] It has been applied in non-1F cases, most shockingly, in the Slovenian 'Erased' case.[67]

V. The Residence Permit Case Law in Three Paragraphs

The second strand of case law which needs to be reviewed in order to understand the *Bonger* case law relates to complaints regarding residence permit refusals. No doubt, reflecting the accrued difficulty for migrants to be regularised and the increased impact of this situation on their lives, complaints related to lack of or insecure residence status have become frequent in the last 15 years. Ten years ago, the Court reached three verdicts of violation one after the other, as we shall see. One of them, however, was overturned on referral to the Grand Chamber. It can therefore be said that the general rule is and firmly remains that there is no right to a residence permit under the Convention. There are now occasional exceptions to this rule. These, however, cannot be said to transform the general rule.

The residence permit case law shares striking similarities with the Article 8 expulsion case law reviewed in Chapter 6, which concerned the impact of a forced removal (often after criminal conviction) on the private and family rights of the applicant. This is perhaps not surprising as the one type of case sometimes morphs into the other, such as when the applicant complains of a residence permit refusal but the Court solely addresses the expulsion issue.[68] The first

[65] *I.* (2011), para 41.

[66] It was asserted under the presidencies of Judges Zupančič (*Bonger*), Casadevall (*I.*, and *K.*), and Gyulumyan (*Naibzay*).

[67] See also e.g. *Samsonnikov v. Estonia*, appl. 52179/10, Judgment (ECtHR), 3 July 2012, in English only. The applicant was an HIV-positive migrant born in the respondent state who was refused a residence permit after being convicted of drug offences in Sweden. His Article 3 complaint regarding his lack of access to social aid for subsistence and medical expenses was declared inadmissible. His wider Article 8 complaint regarding the residence permit refusal was found by the majority not to violate the Convention, but not without attracting a strong dissenting opinion by Judges Lazarova, Trajkovska, and Hajiyev.

[68] See e.g. *Udeh v. Switzerland*, appl. 12020/09, Judgment (ECtHR), 16 Apr. 2013.

similarity between the two bodies of case law is that the interests of the individual and those of the state (whether phrased in terms of public order, public good, community, or any other term found in paragraph 2 of Article 8) are at odds, with no real reconciliation between them possible. This is regrettable. It should be possible to see that these interests can overlap, even coincide. For example, avoiding the negative consequences of children growing up with the trauma of being separated from a removed/'illegal' parent could be seen to serve both the individual and the communal interests.[69] As it is, the most commonly applied perspective assumes that the interests at stake are in conflict with each other.

A second similarity is that 'each side' is entirely convinced that they are right and the other side wrong. A third similarity is that the Strasbourg Court seems divided in its support of these two sides. A fourth is that this results in an incoherent case law, which gives the impression of being quite random, like a lottery. Fifth, one could say that this 'lottery' is played with dice which are weighted: there are more chances for the state to win than for the applicant. And with this, we are back to where we started in the introduction to this section, and this is the general rule, which is also the Strasbourg baseline: there is no right to a residence permit under the Convention.

VI. The Implacable Logic of Inadmissibility: The Examples of *Solomon* and *Dremlyuga*

Given the surge of complaints about residence permit refusals shortly before 2000, *Solomon v. the Netherlands*, lodged in 1998, is a good place to start a detailed review of the case law.[70] The applicant in this case was a failed asylum seeker from Nigeria who had a daughter with a Dutch national. For the European Court, his residence in the Netherlands had always been precarious and it had lost what little foundation it might have had when asylum was denied. The Court was 'of the opinion that in these circumstances the applicant could not at any time reasonably [have expected] to be able to continue this family life in the Netherlands'.[71] As an aside, it may be worth noting that the domestic court had considered that the applicant had failed to prove that he was *not* already married, which the Strasbourg Court repeated, without commenting on the near impossibility of bringing decisive evidence to prove such a point. The Strasbourg Court also reported that the Dutch authorities had doubted the applicant's identity,[72] even though (he observed) the examination of his passport by Dutch officials had

[69] In a similar perspective, Sandra Fredman writes: 'State responsibility for ensuring all reach a minimum capability threshold should be viewed as a contribution to the community as a whole, not simply to particular individuals': Fredman, *Human Rights Transformed: Positive Rights and Positive Duties* (Oxford: Oxford University Press, 2008) 232.

[70] *Tunde Solomon v. the Netherlands*, appl. 44328/98, Decision (ECtHR), 5 Sept. 2000, in English only.

[71] *Solomon* decision, p. 6 of 7. [72] *Solomon*, p. 2.

given rise to no criminal prosecution for forgery.[73] *Solomon* was declared inadmissible for being manifestly ill-founded in 2000.

The review of cases conducted in previous chapters did not especially draw attention to residence permit issues. However, they suggest a sea of inadmissibility issues regarding residence permit or security of status. For example, *Mehemi v. France (No. 2)*, decided in 2003 and discussed in Chapter 6, pointed to the refusal by the Court to make it an obligation that a non-national who cannot be expelled on Article 8 grounds be granted a status enabling full integration in their place of residence.[74] Another example, from Chapter 8, is the *Ponomaryovi v. Bulgaria* decision of 2009 which declared inadmissible the part of the applicants' (two brothers) complaint relating to the fact that they had been unable to obtain a residence permit on reaching the age of majority.[75]

To introduce yet another case, the *Dremlyuga* application was found inadmissible two weeks after *Mehemi (No. 2)*.[76] The applicant had argued that the lack of secure status from which he suffered breached a number of Convention provisions, as follows:

- Article 8, due to his inability to conduct his social and professional life normally;
- Article 2 (right to life), due to the socio-economic consequences of this situation upon his life;
- Article 2 of Protocol no. 4 (freedom of movement), due to the restrictions the situation entailed on his ability to circulate;
- Articles 6 and 13, due to the length of the proceedings which he had instituted to try to rectify the situation;
- Article 17, concerning abuse of right (here, by a contracting state).[77]

To reject the Article 8 complaint, the Court started by citing the 'well-established principle of international law' with which we have become familiar.[78] It continued by recalling, with reference to an admissibility decision of 2002,[79] that 'Article 8 of the Convention does not go so far as to guarantee a right to a particular residence permit (permanent, temporary or other), as long as the solution proposed by the authorities allow the individual concerned to exercise freely the

[73] *Solomon*, p. 5. The Strasbourg Court reports this without querying the implications of this fact.

[74] *Mehemi v. France (No. 2)*, appl. 53470/99, Judgment (ECtHR), 10 Apr. 2003.

[75] *Ponomaryov and Others v. Bulgaria*, appl. 5335/05, Final Decision (ECtHR), 10 Feb. 2009.

[76] *Dremlyuga v. Latvia*, appl. 66729/01, Decision (ECtHR), 29 Apr. 2003, in French only.

[77] Article 17 ECHR is very rarely used and, when it is, it is to say the applicant—not the state—has abused the rights provided by the Convention. By contrast, in the Inter-American system, the Court regularly relies on its equivalent, Article 29 ACHR, and this is done in order to further open up its case law: Laurence Burgorgue-Larsen, 'Les méthodes d'interprétation de la Cour interaméricaine des droits de l'homme: Justice in context' (2014) *Revue trimestrielle des droits de l'homme* 97, 23–71 at 27.

[78] *Dremlyuga* decision, at p. 9.

[79] *Sisojeva v. Latvia*, appl. 60654/00. This decision remained unpublished on HUDOC at the time of writing (May 2014).

right to respect for his or her private and family life'. Applying this principle to the facts of the case over three paragraphs, the Article 8 complaint was found inadmissible. Almost inevitably after this first step, the other complaints were also rejected.

VII. The Case Law Evolves: The *Sisojeva, Mendizabal,* and *Da Silva*'s Chambers' Verdicts of Violation

For reasons which are not entirely clear, the applicants in three cases lodged between July 1999 and August 2000 succeeded in not having their complaints declared inadmissible. These three cases went on to attract verdicts of violation at Chamber level in 2005 to 2006. To cite them in chronological order of the Chamber verdicts to which they gave rise, they are: *Sisojeva and Others v. Latvia*,[80] *Aristimuño Mendizabal v. France* (*Mendizabal*),[81] and *Rodrigues Da Silva and Hoogmaker v. the Netherlands* (*Da Silva*).[82]

The period during which these three cases were processed did not see the flow of residence permit complaints declared inadmissible completely interrupted. For example, *Dremlyuga* was lodged in December 2000, thus after *Da Silva, Mendizabal,* and *Sisojeva* had been lodged.[83] *Dremlyuga* was found inadmissible—albeit by majority only—in April 2003. This was two months after *Sisojeva* was declared admissible and one month after a partial decision on admissibility was reached in *Da Silva*. Needless to say, the violation verdicts stood out in the case law and achieved high visibility by comparison to the non-violation verdicts (as well as possible untraceable inadmissibility decisions). This was the more so since each case arose from a rather different political and social context.

Sisojeva and Others v. Latvia related to the dissolution of the Soviet Union and the regaining of independence of a former Russian 'satellite' whose population at the time of its independence comprised 30–40 per cent Russian nationals or stateless persons of Russian origin. *Mendizabal* involved the non-application of EU law, presumably for fear of terrorism, to the applicant, a Spanish citizen residing in France and married to a leader of the Basque separatist group ETA incarcerated in Spain; Ms Mendizabal was repeatedly given short-term residence permits rather than the longer permit to which she was entitled under EU law. *Da Silva* concerned a form of irregular migration more directly in line with the situation of irregularity denounced as problematic by a range of migrants' NGOs. Ms Da Silva was a Brazilian national who had been living in the Netherlands since 1994, having (one assumes) overstayed her tourist visa. A daughter, the second applicant, was born in 1996 from her relationship with a Dutch national. The question

[80] *Sisojeva and Others v. Latvia*, appl. 60654/00, Judgment (ECtHR), 16 June 2005.

[81] *Aristimuño Mendizabal v. France*, appl. 51431/99, Judgment (ECtHR), 17 Jan. 2006, in French only.

[82] *Rodrigues Da Silva and Hoogmaker v. the Netherlands*, appl. 50435/99, Judgment (ECtHR), 31 Jan. 2006.

[83] On 9 July 1999, 23 September 1999, and 29 August 2000, respectively.

for the Court was whether the first applicant could be left without a residence permit, and thus be put at risk of deportation which would separate mother and child, given that the father had made clear that he would oppose the departure of his daughter to Brazil.

It is not immediately clear why *Sisojeva v. Latvia* escaped the fate of numerous previous applications lodged against Latvia by Russian nationals and stateless persons of Russian origin living in Latvia, and found inadmissible, such as *Dremlyuga*.[84] It might be a question of facts as the personal, family, professional, social, and migrant histories of the applicants is not the same from one case to the next. It may also be due to the way a particular bench happens to be constituted. Whatever the reason, it remains that in *Sisojeva* the applicants were a married couple and they had an adult daughter. (The restricted conception of family life adopted by the Court in immigration cases led to the case of another daughter being declared inadmissible.[85]) They had all been residing in Latvia for over 30 years.[86] They complained that they were denied the possibility of obtaining permanent residence permits. They could have obtained temporary permits, but they deemed this offer 'wholly inadequate and humiliating'.[87]

In January 2005, a Chamber drawn from the First Section of the Court found a violation of Article 8 ECHR, by five votes to two. It chose to reiterate 'at the outset' the 'well-established' principle of state immigration control,[88] demonstrating, if need be, that the Strasbourg reversal may lead to verdicts of violation (in the same way that a reasoning which starts with the relevant human rights provision does not necessarily produce a verdict of violation). The Chamber departed from another principle which had previously been established in the Strasbourg case law. In this case, it ruled that it was not sufficient that the applicants had not been issued with any formal deportation order to conclude that they were able to exercise their rights under Article 8.[89] In the opinion of the five majority judges, 'only reasons of a particularly serious nature'—such as the fact that the applicants would have 'acted in a particularly dangerous manner', which they had not—could have justified the obstacles they encountered as they tried to get their position in Latvia regularised.[90]

One year later, in January 2006, a chamber drawn from another section of the Court followed suit and adopted a verdict of violation in *Mendizabal*. In this case, the applicant was not an irregular migrant but a Spanish citizen

[84] A search conducted in the French version of the old HUDOC system on 21 December 2011 for decisions (not judgments) against Latvia containing the words '*titre de séjour*' and 'Russie' produced 24 results. In this list, the earliest application dated from 1999, the latest from 2004; the first decision was adopted in 2000, the latest in 2010. The same search for judgments rather than decisions produced 12 results, with the first dated 28 November 2002 and the latest 31 May 2011.

[85] For a critique, see: Lourdes Peroni, 'Challenging Culturally Dominant Conceptions in Human Rights Law: The Cases of Property and Family' (2010) *Human Rights and International Legal Discourse* 4, 241–264 at 256.

[86] *Sisojeva* judgment, para 58.

[87] *Sisojeva and Others*, appl. 60654/00, GC judgment (ECtHR), 15 Jan. 2007, para 73.

[88] *Sisojeva* GC judgment, para 99. [89] *Sisojeva* GC, para 104.

[90] *Sisojeva* GC, para 108.

who should have enjoyed freedom of movement within the European Union. Probably because she was the wife of a leader of ETA, the local authorities had resisted granting her the long-term residence permit to which she was entitled under EU law. They had repeatedly given her temporary residence permits lasting for between a fortnight and three months. This had happened 69 times over a period of 14 years![91] Ms Mendizabal contended that the arbitrary refusal of the long-term residence permit had caused her enormous difficulties and had led her to live in poverty. Without a long-term residence permit, she had been unable to apply for good, stable jobs and was forced to take unskilled casual work. In an attempt to escape this pattern, she had trained as a beautician, but she found herself facing insuperable obstacles again at the end of this training: difficulties in registering herself with the *Chambre des métiers*, the impossibility of accessing grants supporting enterprise creation; and failure to persuade any landlord to rent her somewhere in which she could practise her profession.[92] Her situation had also prevented her from making plans in her personal life.[93]

The Second Section was allocated the case. By the time it decided on the admissibility of *Mendizabal*, the First Section had already established—in Latvian case law which preceded the *Sisojeva*'s decision of admissibility, including *Dremlyuga*—that Article 8 does not go as far as guaranteeing an individual a particular type of residence permit. The Second Section approvingly cited this principle in *Mendizabal*.[94] However, it also found that a different approach was required in this case due to the European Community nationality of the applicant.[95] Interestingly, the granting of a ten-year residence permit—four years after she had lodged her application and three months after the Chamber's partial decision on admissibility—did not sway the Strasbourg Court to find that the applicant had lost her status as a victim (other applicants have not been so lucky). The Court concluded on a breach of Article 8 of the Convention, with one judge dissenting.[96]

Mendizabal is probably best considered as a one-off case given that EU citizens can generally be expected to escape the dire treatment which the applicant had encountered. Even though it arose from an exceptional EU-related situation, the verdict could nonetheless have helped to introduce the idea that failing to be granted a particular type of a residence permit may violate the Convention in some circumstances. Certainly, the facts of the case vividly illustrated the problems which the lack of a long-term residence permit may create. However, the Court did not think the case was particularly significant: it was not even translated into English.

Da Silva is our third case, the merits of which were decided on 31 January 2006, i.e. a fortnight after the delivery of the *Mendizabal* judgment. The bench of judges was drawn from what was then called 'the former Second Section'

[91] *Mendizabal* judgment, para 76. [92] *Mendizabal*, para 60.
[93] *Mendizabal*, para 61. [94] *Mendizabal*, para 66. [95] *Mendizabal*, para 67.
[96] Judge Mularoni thought the domestic remedies had not been exhausted.

(following a reshuffle between the Sections of the Court).[97] In their submissions, the applicants had stressed that Rachael Hoogmaker, the daughter of Ms Da Silva and the second applicant in the case, was an independent party to the proceedings who 'had her own, individual, interests which also required consideration: it could not and should not be held against her that she had been conceived while her mother was not lawfully resident'.[98] Avoiding the Strasbourg reversal, the first thing the Court said was that there was family life within the meaning of Article 8 ECHR between the two applicants. Even though it was irrelevant to any assessment of the family link which existed between the two applicants, the Court immediately added: 'Rachael was born from a genuine relationship, in which her parents cohabited as if they were married'.[99] Further down, the Court noted that the first applicant's stay in the Netherlands had 'at no time been lawful'[100] and it 'reiterate[d] that persons who, without complying with the regulations in force, confront the authorities of a Contracting State with their presence in the country as a *fait accompli* do not, in general, have any entitlement to expect that a right of residence will be conferred upon them'.[101] However, 'the Government [had] indicated that lawful residence in the Netherlands would have been possible on the basis of the fact that the first applicant and Mr Hoogmaker had [had] a lasting relationship between June 1994 and January 1997'.[102]

The real if missed opportunity for an authorised stay—what could be termed, the applicant's 'quasi-regular status'—may have been the crucial factor which saved the *Da Silva* applicants by providing a distinguishing factor from previous case law, such as *Solomon*, which the Court indeed cited.[103] This would also explain the reference to the parents' 'genuine relationship' at the start of the Court's reasoning.

However, it is difficult to second-guess what motivates a particular outcome. In *Da Silva*, there may also have been another factor, at least for some judges. The Court concluded, in a most gendered fashion:

> In view of the far-reaching consequences which an expulsion would have on the responsibilities which the first applicant has *as a mother*... and taking into account that it is clearly in Rachael's best interests for the first applicant to stay in the Netherlands, the Court considers that in the particular circumstances of the case the economic well-being of the country does not outweigh the applicants' rights under Article 8, despite the fact that the first applicant was residing illegally in the Netherlands at the time of Rachael's birth. Indeed, by attaching such paramount importance to this latter element, the authorities may be considered to have indulged in excessive formalism.[104]

[97] Three judges participated in the benches which decided both *Mendizabal* and *Da Silva*: Judge Costa (a President of Section since 2000 and soon-to-be President of the Court), Judges Jungwiert and Mularoni.

[98] *Da Silva* judgment, para 31.

[99] *Da Silva*, para 37.

[100] *Da Silva*, para 38.

[101] *Da Silva*, para 43. The Court refers here to: *Chandra and Others v. the Netherlands*, appl. 53102/99, Decision (ECtHR), 13 May 2003.

[102] *Da Silva*, para 43.

[103] *Da Silva*, para 43.

[104] *Da Silva*, para 44, emphasis added.

Note the last two words, already highlighted above. The verdict of violation was unanimous.

XIII. Back to the Non-Violation Mainstream: The *Sisojeva* Grand Chamber Judgment

If some had hoped that the three verdicts reviewed in the previous section would mark a decisive evolution in the Strasbourg jurisprudence, subsequent rulings indicated that this was not exactly so. In *Sisojeva*, two judges had dissented with the verdict of violation at Chamber level. Relying on previous case law by both the Court and the Commission, Judges Vajić and Briede had stated that 'Article 8 of the Convention cannot be construed as guaranteeing as such the right to a particular type of residence permit'[105] and that 'when aliens or stateless persons complain of their deportation or in a more general sense of their irregular status in the country, the issuing of a residence permit constitutes in principle an adequate and sufficient remedy'.[106] Applying these principles to the facts of the case, the two dissenting judges were persuaded that 'the regularisation procedures proposed by the Government would allow the applicants to remain without hindrance within Latvian territory, to lead a normal social life there and to enjoy the rights enshrined in Article 8 of the Convention'.[107] On appeal from Latvia, the Grand Chamber agreed with this dissent and reproduced the above-quoted statements almost word for word.[108] It accepted that the matter had been resolved by the offer of five-year temporary permits made by the Latvian government.[109] *Sisejevo* was struck out by Grand Chamber judgment of January 2007.[110] This seems to have happened with extensive deliberation by the judges,[111] however, and Judge Zupančič dissented.[112] This did not bode well for the ability of the Court to speak with one voice on residence permit issues.

This brought to an abrupt end the Latvian residence permit case law. Over 350,000 people are reported to be stateless in Latvia.[113] One presumes that many of them live with the 'inconveniences' of temporary residence permits.

[105] Joint dissenting opinion of Judges Vajić and Briede in *Sisojev*a Chamber judgment, point 1, citing *Mehemi v. France (No. 2)*.

[106] Vajić and Briede, point 2 (b), citing two Court's decisions dated 1999 and 2002 and two Commissions decisions dated 1994 and 1997.

[107] *Vajić and Briede*, point 2 (c).

[108] *Sisojeva* GC judgment, paras 91–102.

[109] *Sisojeva* GC, para 99.

[110] *Sisojeva* GC, paras 103–103. The First Section reached verdicts of violation in two further similar cases, which Latvia had also appealed. Expectedly these were struck out in due course too: *Shevanova v. Latvia*, appl. 58822/00, GC Judgment (ECtHR), 7 Dec. 2007; *Kaftailova v. Latvia*, appl. 59643/00, GC Judgment (ECtHR), 7 Dec. 2007.

[111] *Sisojeva* was twice deliberated at Grand Chamber level: on 23 May and 11 October 2006.

[112] Although *Shevanova* and *Kaftailova* formally appear to have been adopted by unanimity, Judge Zupančič warned in *Sisojeva* that he would have to follow the precedent established in *Sisojeva* in other cases.

[113] UNHCR estimate for 2008 cited in: Blitz and Sawyer 'Introduction' 5.

IX. The Best Interests of the Child versus a *Fait Accompli*: An Inherent Tension, a Divided Court, a Lottery

The residence permit case law is made up of different strands. The geopolitical context of the Latvian case law, where the now stateless are perceived to be yesterday's oppressor,[114] is very different, for example, from that of a migrant from 'the South'—for example, a former colony—who reaches Europe either on a temporary visa or illegally, starts a family there, and present the authorities with this '*fait accompli*'. It is worth noting that speaking of a child as a *fait accompli* neglects the fact that women become pregnant for a variety of reasons and in a variety of circumstances, which the Court overlooks. Despite this, I shall myself refer to the '*fait accompli* case law' for convenience. The label is not ideal, however: not only does it disregard the fact that women often *fall* pregnant unintentionally, but it also fails to reflect the unpredictability of the Court's reasoning and verdicts.

Da Silva was the first verdict of violation in the *fait accompli* case law. There have been another two verdicts of violation. In *Nunez v. Norway*, decided in a Chamber presided over by Judge Bratza in 2011, the children's best interests were understood to militate against the expulsion of the mother to the Dominican Republic. Because of this, their interests 'upset the fair balance under Article 8'.[115] This choice of words is interesting as it leaves one to assume that, if not upset, the 'fair balance' leans towards expulsion. The verdict was not unanimous. Judges Mijović and De Gaetano, dissenting, warned that it sent 'the wrong signal, namely that persons who are illegally in a country can somehow contrive to have their residence "legitimised" through the expedient of marriage and of having children'.[116]

Another verdict of violation, this time unanimous, was reached in *Butt v. Norway* in 2013. In this case, the Court stressed the 'exceptional' circumstances of the case.[117] It reassured states that it saw 'no reason for disagreeing with the [approach of the domestic court, according to which] strong immigration policy considerations would in principle militate in favour of identifying children with the conduct of their parents, failing which there would be a great risk that parents [might exploit] the situation of their children in order to secure a residence permit for themselves and for the children'.[118] In this case, however, there was 'no such risk of exploitation'[119] as the children in question had become adults and their mother had died. The applicants, who had spent over a year in a church

[114] Although this context transpires in the facts recalled in the case law, it is left unaddressed in the reasoning of the Court. The one exception is the dissenting opinion of Judge Ziemele in *Andrejeva v. Latvia*, appl. 55707/00, GC Judgment (ECtHR), 18 Feb. 2009. For a critique of this decontextualisation, see also: Joint dissenting opinion of Judges Sajó, Vučinić and Kuris in *Biao v. Denmark*, appl. 38590/10, Judgment (ECtHR), 25 Mar. 2014, para 7.

[115] *Nunez v. Norway*, appl. 55597/09, Judgment (ECtHR), 28 June 2011, in English with a Russian translation, para 78.

[116] Joint dissenting opinion of Judges Mijović and De Gaetano in *Nunez*, para 1.

[117] *Butt v. Norway*, appl. 47017/09, Judgment (ECtHR), 4 Dec. 2012, in English only, para 90.

[118] *Butt*, para 79. [119] *Butt*, para 80.

asylum and over a month in detention,[120] were awarded €3,000 for non-pecuniary damages.[121]

Verdicts of non-violation far outnumber verdicts of violation in this strand of the case law, however. Suffice it here just to cite three counter-examples to *Da Silva, Nunez*, and *Butt*.[122]

In *Useinovv. the Netherlands*, the applicant was a rejected asylum seeker from the Former Yugoslav Republic of Macedonia who had come to the Netherlands in 1992, age 27, and who, as the asylum proceedings were still pending, had started a relationship with his next-door neighbour; a daughter was born in 1995. The Third Section declared his case inadmissible by a majority in 2006.[123]

In *Priya v. Denmark*, the applicant was an Indian national who had visited Denmark on a three-month tourist visa in 1999, married an Indian national who had acquired a permanent resident permit due to his previous (and then dissolved) marriage with a Danish national, had returned to India, given birth to their first child, re-entered Denmark, been refused a residence permit, remained there illegally, and gave birth to the couple's second child.[124] The First Section declared her case inadmissible also by a majority and also in 2006.

In *Omoregie v. Norway*, the applicant was a Nigerian national who had entered Norway illegally, applied for asylum, and married a Norwegian national with whom he had a child. A verdict of non-violation was reached by five votes to two in 2008. For President Rozakis and four other judges, the child was born at a time when the applicants were not 'entitled to expect that any right of residence would be conferred'.[125] The two dissenters, Judges Malinverni and Kovler, observed that the applicant had had his marriage celebrated by officials in Norway and had committed no criminal offence. In their view, in such a case, the balance of the various interests should have been tipped in favour of letting family life continue in Norway. The majority, however, was not ready to allow a migrant who had not been admitted to the territory of a state confront the authorities with the *fait accompli* of his marriage and parenthood.[126]

In sum, the creation or pursuit of family life 'at a time when the persons involved were [or should have been] aware that the immigration status of one of them was such that the persistence of that family life within the host State would

[120] *Butt*, para 93.

[121] *Butt*, para 94. It is worth researching what happens after a verdict of violation. In the *fait accompli* case law, the Committee of Ministers closed the *Da Silva* case, the applicant having been granted a 'residence permit with retroactive effect': *Da Silva v. the Netherlands*, appl. 50435/99, Resolution (CM), 3 June 2010. In *Nunez*, the applicant was granted a three-year renewable residence permit: *Nunez v. Norway*, appl. 55597/09, Resolution (CM), 11 June 2013. No resolution related to the *Butt* case appeared on HUDOC on 15 June 2014.

[122] There are others. *Solomon* has already been cited. See also e.g. *Antwi and Others v. Norway*, appl. 26940/10, Judgment (ECtHR), 14 Feb. 2012, and references cited note 128.

[123] *Kasim Useinov v. the Netherlands*, appl. 61292/00, Decision (ECtHR), 11 Apr. 2006, in English only.

[124] *Priya v. Denmark*, appl. 13594/03, Decision (ECtHR), 6 July 2006, in English only.

[125] *Darren Omoregie and Others v. Norway*, appl. 265/07, Judgment (ECtHR), 31 July 2008, in English only, para 64.

[126] *Omoregie*, para 64. See also: *Useinov* decision, p. 9; *Priya* decision, p. 9.

from the outset be precarious'[127] becomes the paramount consideration in some cases. Occasionally it is the interests of the applicants—and often, their young children—which prevails.[128] Why the applicant/children sometimes manage to win is difficult to say. What can be said is that, although the Court is divided on this issue,[129] identifying where the Strasbourg mainstream and undercurrents are is not particularly difficult.[130]

X. A Successful Parallel to *Bonger*: The Swiss Canton Case Law

Beside the Latvian and *fait accompli* case law, the *Bonger* reasoning could be regarded as a third strand in the residence permit case law. Its main characteristic

[127] *Omoregie*, para 57. The quoted passage also appears in other decisions and judgments, as a HUDOC search indicates. See e.g., in a non-comprehensive list, *Konstatinov v. the Netherlands*, appl. 16351/03, Judgment (ECtHR), 26 Apr. 2007 (involving Roma applicants, and with the Court disregarding what family means for Romas, as discussed by Peroni 'Challenging' 256–258); *Esmail Narenji Haghighi v. the Netherlands*, appl. 38165/07, Decision (ECtHR), 14 Apr. 2009; *Arvelo Ponte v. the Netherlands*, appl. 28770/05, Judgment (ECtHR), 3 Nov. 2011; *Mehmet Olgun v. the Netherlands*, appl. 1859/03, Decision (ECtHR), 10 May 2012.

[128] See also, on a slightly different line involving potential exploitation and abuse, *Osman v. Denmark*, appl.38058/09, Judgment (ECtHR), 14 June 2011, in English only (involving a young Somali woman who lived in Denmark from age seven to 15, at which stage her parents sent her back to Somalia to take care of her grandmother, as a result of which she lost her entitlement to the residence permit to which she would otherwise have been entitled).

[129] Commentators are also divided. See e.g. Daniel Thym, 'Respect for Private and Family Life under Article 8 ECHR in Immigration Cases: A Human Right to Regularize Illegal Stay?' (2008) *International and Comparative Law Quarterly* 57, 87–112, regretting the 'renewed activism' shown by the Court in the three verdicts of violation of 2005 to 2006 (at 102) and approving the *Sisojeva* Grand Chamber judgment which underlines the need for the Court to 'strike a careful balance between the requirements of effective human rights protection and the preservation of the Contracting Parties' margin of appreciation and the corresponding respect for the normative structure of national immigration law' (at 112). Compare e.g. with Alan Desmond, 'Regularization in the EU and the US: The Frequent Use of an Exceptional Measure', in Diego Acosta and Anja Wiesbrock (eds) *Global Migration Issues: Myths and Realities* (New York: Praeger International, forthcoming) section entitled 'Regularization as a Result of Judgments of the ECtHR'.

[130] *Jeunesse v. the Netherlands*, appl. 12738/10, GC Judgment (ECtHR), 3 Oct. 2014, was decided as this book was reaching the final stages of its production. The Court stated that 'Where confronted with a *fait accompli*, the removal of the non-national family member would be incompatible with Article 8 only in exceptional circumstances' (para 114). However, various such exceptional circumstances were found by the majority of 14 judges to exist in *Jeunesse*, including that the applicant had held Netherlands nationality at birth and had lost it, not by her own choice, but following Surinam's independence (para 115). There was a strongly worded dissenting opinion by Judges Villiger, Mahoney and Silvis. They bemoaned the recognition of particular circumstances which 'seems to override most of the previously followed jurisprudential principles' (para 1 of their dissenting opinion). In their view, '[t]he overriding consideration in [the relevant case law is that the applicants] are foreign nationals, that is to say members of a category in respect of whom the States enjoy, under international law...a virtually absolute right of control over entry into their territory and discretionary power in the matter of admission and residence' (para 4). The remarks castigating the Court for performing 'a balancing exercise of its own' as regards the merits of the applicant's circumstances (para 7) and the virtual annihilation of the state's margin of appreciation (para 8) suggest that the three dissenting judges would have wanted a non-violation verdict which was principled and absolute. Their dissenting opinion concluded that 'the Court is drifting away from the subsidiary role assigned to it by the Convention, perhaps being guided more by what is humane, rather than by what is right' (para 10). These words are most interesting given the way I myself conclude on page 512 of this book.

would be that the applicants cannot be returned elsewhere; they are stranded. The Swiss canton case law could then be regarded as a subset of this. Interestingly, however, instead of producing inadmissibility decisions, the two cases making up the canton case law produced two verdicts of violation.[131]

They were lodged by the same legal representative at a six-month interval. Largely clones of each other, they were decided on the same day, in July 2010. In each case the applicant was a rejected asylum seeker originally from Ethiopia who could not be returned there because at the time Ethiopia refused to take back its own nationals. Each had been granted a residence permit in Switzerland. The problem arose because each married, whilst in Switzerland, an Ethiopian national resident in Switzerland whose residence permit was linked to a canton different from the one to which their spouse had been assigned. The applicant in *Mengesha Kimfe* nonetheless elected to live with her husband. As a result of not residing in her assigned canton, she was denied access to social assistance and medical care. On one occasion the police returned her, handcuffed, to her canton. She also explained that she had had two abortions because the couple could not have sustained a child on social assistance meant for a single adult (€263 per month at the relevant time).[132] The applicant in *Agraw* had a child with her husband but she and the child lived separately from him. The Court found a violation of Article 8 in both cases and awarded each applicant €5,000.

The parallel between the Swiss canton and the *Bonger* case law is at least threefold: (a) the applicants could not be returned to their country of origin; (b) they were unable to lead their family/private life legally; and (c) this situation persisted for years. How do we reconcile the Swiss verdicts of violation—which came with substantial non-pecuniary damages—with the *Bonger* decisions? The major distinction between the two bodies of case law appears to be that the 'Swiss' applicants were not '1F' non-refugees. If this is the crucial point, however, as already observed, this is highly problematic from a human rights perspective, given that the '*Bonger*' applicants should really have benefited from the presumption of innocence. The 1F/non-1F factor nonetheless appears to have been determinant since other differences would suggest that the *Bonger* applicants were actually in a more difficult situation than the Swiss canton applicants.

Three differences can be identified. First, the 'Swiss' applicants were not considered 'illegals' throughout the whole of the Swiss Federation; at least they enjoyed legal status somewhere. By contrast, the *Bonger* applicants were illegal throughout the Netherlands. Second, the plight of the applicants in the Swiss case law lasted for 'only' five years—a period which the Court nonetheless qualified as 'a considerable amount of years'.[133] The *Bonger* applicants had been enduring a situation of rightlessness for over a decade by the time of the Strasbourg ruling—and it could be expected to last much longer given the outcome of the Strasbourg litigation.

[131] *Menghesha Kimfe v. Switzerland*, appl. 24404/05, Judgment (ECtHR), 29 July 2010, in French only; *Agraw v. Switzerland*, appl. 3295/06, Judgment (ECtHR), 29 July 2010, in French only.
[132] *Mengesha Kimfe* judgment, para 52.
[133] *Menghesha Kimfe*, para 71, *Agraw* judgment, paras 31 and 54.

Third, the complaint in the Swiss case law concerned family life as opposed to private life (understood as the whole of social life) in the *Bonger* case law. If one limb were to be understood as more encompassing than the other, it would probably be private life—although in my view one type of violation is no more or less serious than the other. It remains that the *Bonger* violations—if only they had been declared—would have seemed stronger than the Swiss ones.

The Court was clearly sympathetic to the applicants in the Swiss case law. It refused to strike out their cases after they were granted the permit which allowed them to live in the same canton as their spouse. By contrast, in *Naibzay*, after the 1F applicant was granted a residence permit for the purpose of staying in Belgium with his oldest daughter, the Court found his Article 8 complaint manifestly ill-founded.[134] (In an implacable logic, this finding then persuaded the Court to reject the Article 13 complaint too: it was deemed to be related to an Article 8 claim which, as it was inadmissible, was not 'arguable'.[135])

The question arises: why do the Netherlands repeatedly get away with denying any legal status to a string of non-returnable migrants, whilst Switzerland is found in violation of the Convention for a seemingly less serious interference, despite the applicants having been granted a residence permit which resolved their situation? Admittedly the two bodies of case law have evolved in isolation. One cannot imagine that the short, one-off, inadmissible *Bonger* decision of 2005 could have been on the minds of the judges who decided the Swiss canton case law five years later. As for the other *Bonger* case law, it was then either pending (*G.R.* and *H.*) or not yet lodged (*I.*, *K.*, and *Naibzay*). This is to say that the Court would not have been preoccupied with achieving consistency between the two bodies of case law.

It is nonetheless interesting to try to understand, with the benefit of hindsight, the reasons for their hybrid development. An irritation seems to emerge in the Swiss case law at the fact that it was mere administrative inflexibility which had prevented the applicants from living with their spouse. The Court's view seems to have been that there was no good reason for the applicants' plight: their situation was not their fault and it could have been remedied relatively easily. In contrast to the Swiss authorities, the Dutch authorities were clearly motivated by principle. To quote, for example, from 'The facts' of *I.*, 'the Deputy Minister pointed out that the Netherlands State attached great importance to the premise that the Netherlands does not become a safe haven for persons in respect of whom there are strong suspicions that they have committed crimes referred to in Article 1F of the 1951 Refugee Convention'.[136]

Administrative inflexibility against 'innocent' applicants whose stay the state has specifically authorised versus principled motivation against suspected criminals whose stay has explicitly not been authorised appears to be the crucial distinguishing factor between the *Bonger* and the Swiss canton case law. However one looks at it, the *Bonger* case law is problematic. It is not right that the Court refuses to examine whether the state's exercise of sovereignty regarding admission/

[134] *Naibzay* decision, para 30. [135] *Naibzay*, paras 31–34.
[136] *I.* final decision (2012), para 12.

non-authorisation might not have been arbitrary. As can readily be seen, this restraint on the part of the Court shows that the more ideologically entrenched the prejudice against the (presumed criminal) alien, the least likely it is to be defeated by human rights law. Whether the interferences with the rights of non-returnable aliens arise from an almost whimsical lack of accommodation on the part of the authorities or from a principled plan, all the applicants deserve to have their situation examined and, if apposite, remedied.

Let us ask one last time why the Court did not find any violation of the Convention in the *Bonger* case law (with *G.R.* not a particularly significant exception). To tackle the question from a different angle, let us return to the idea that it is the logic of its previous case law which allows the Court to deem the issues brought by the applicants to fall outside the ambit of the Convention. This logic led the Court, in 2011, to declare I.'s Article 3 complaint inadmissible by distinguishing *I.* from *M.S.S.*, as reviewed above. I.'s Article 8 complaint was then declared manifestly ill-founded in 2012, following a reasoning which simply recalled that:

- Article 8 does not entail a general obligation for a state to authorise family reunion;[137]
- the applicant was in no current risk of expulsion to Afghanistan so that there were no realistic prospects of the family being separated through his removal;[138]
- neither Article 8 nor another Convention provision guarantees a right to work;[139]
- To the extent that Article 8 could be engaged in this case, the Court could not find that the Netherlands authorities had struck an unfair balance between the [individual and State's] competing interests at issue.[140]

The *Bonger* outcomes, which are so unpalatable from a human rights perspective as they condone the applicants' rightlessness, suggest that the foundations of much of the Strasbourg case law are problematic. What is needed is a new logic which would enable more humane results to be reached.[141]

XI. Russian Case Law Paves the Way: *Liu (No. 2)* and *Alim*

Some judgments in the Strasbourg residence permit case law contain highly promising pronouncements. For example, this section reviews two verdicts of violation reached in 2011 which display a strong family-law reasoning. They do so in a very simple way: *Liu v. Russia (No. 2)* stresses the reality of the

[137] *I.* (2012), para 44. [138] *I.* (2012), para 45. [139] *I.* (2012), para 48.

[140] *I.* (2012), para 49.

[141] This sentence was written before the diametrically opposed conclusion of Judges Villiger, Mahoney and Silvis in *Jeunesse*, quoted above note 131, came out.

applicants' family ties;[142] whilst *Alim v. Russia* makes it clear that the state must justify the need to exclude a person who has long been on its territory.[143] This simplicity is nonetheless deceptive in that the kind of reasoning displayed is far from always present in the case law. Why does it appear here, then? This question will be discussed. Whatever its answer, the result is jurisprudential features which could usefully be adopted across the whole of the Strasbourg migrant case law.

Liu (No. 2) directly followed from *Liu v. Russia*, decided in 2007.[144] The applicants were a family comprising a husband and wife and their two children. The father had arrived in Russia in 1994 on the basis of a valid visa and married a Russian national. He was refused a residence permit in 2004 and ordered to go back to China in 2005, allegedly because of national security concerns, the nature of which were not disclosed to the applicants, the domestic courts, or even the Strasbourg Court. In the first *Liu* case, the interference with the applicants' family life (identified by the Court as the expulsion rather than the residence permit refusal as per the applicant's complaint)[145] was found to be based on legal provisions falling foul of the Convention requirements for 'quality law', so that there had been a violation of Article 8.[146] Following this verdict, the Russian authorities annulled the deportation order and reviewed the classified documents which had motivated the expulsion. The conclusion they reached in early 2009 was that the refusal of a residence permit to the first applicant had been lawful.[147] Administrative removal proceedings ensued. Mr Liu was ordered to pay a fine for the continuous offence of living in Russia without a valid residence permit, detained, and finally ordered to be expelled to China in November 2009, which is what gave rise to *Liu (No. 2)*.

The reasoning in this latter judgment started with a 'Strasbourg reversal'.[148] The majority of the Court, however, was obviously unconvinced by the state's reasons for expelling the applicant.[149] The Court balanced the competing interests supposedly at stake in a manner different from how it generally proceeds. On the one hand, it minimised the seriousness of the offence committed by the first applicant:

> The Court notes at the outset that the offence for which the first applicant was expelled consisted in unlawfully residing in Russia without a valid visa or residence permit. This offence is punishable under the Code of Administrative Offences by a fine of RUB 2,000

[142] *Liu v. Russia (No. 2)*, appl. 29157/09, Judgment (ECtHR), 26 July 2011, in English only.

[143] *Alim v. Russia*, appl. 39417/07, Judgment (ECtHR), 27 Sept. 2011, in English only.

[144] *Liu v. Russia*, appl. 42086/05, Judgment (ECtHR), 6 Dec. 2007, in English and with a Ukrainian translation.

[145] A similar quid pro quo, whereby the applicant complains of the lack of residence permit but the Court finds that the applicant's deportation (not his lack of papers) would violate Article 8, has already been noted previously (p. 456).

[146] *Liu* judgment, para 69.

[147] *Liu(No. 2)* judgment, para 28.

[148] *Liu (No. 2)* judgment, para 77.

[149] Except for Judge Kovler, who dissented in *Liu (No. 2)* because he assessed the review of the national security concerns undertaken by the domestic courts after the first *Liu* case to have been satisfactory.

to 5,000 (about EUR 50 to 125). The Court considers that the offence was not a particularly serious one.[150]

On the other hand, it assessed the strength of the first applicant's family ties to Russia as follows:

> The Court attaches considerable weight to the solidity of the first applicant's family ties to Russia and the difficulties that his family would face were they to relocate to China. The Court is mindful of the fact that the second, third and fourth applicants are Russian nationals who were born in Russia and have lived there all their lives. They have never lived in China and have no ties with that country. Even though the case file does not contain any information about whether they speak any Chinese, there is little doubt that in any case it would be difficult for them to re-adjust to life in China if they were to follow the first applicant there. Their resettlement would mean a radical upheaval for them, especially for the third and fourth applicants who are not of an adaptable age and who are attending school in Russia. The first applicant's family can, of course, continue to contact him by letter or telephone, and they may also visit him in China from time to time, but the disruption to their family life should not be underestimated.[151]

The minimisation of the offence in the first quotation is interesting. The Court does not spell out whether it is due to the level of the fine set in the Russian code or because the very concept of the offence as a serious one would be objectionable. However, as we have seen in Chapter 11, the Strasbourg Court cannot be said to have fiercely resisted the phenomenon of crimmigration. In *Nunez*, it accepted the 'serious' qualification given to immigration offences by the respondent state.[152] Turning to the second quotation, the Court's assessment of the applicants' family ties can be unreservedly commended. However, the factors mentioned in *Liu (No. 2)* are hardly specific to the Liu family. They are generally relevant to the *fait accompli* cases, but are hardly ever dealt with with the same simplicity.

Two distinguishing factors between *Liu (No. 2)* and the verdicts of non-violation reached in the *fait accompli* case law come to mind. First, in this *fait accompli* case law, the applicants are deemed to have had, at best, a precarious status in the respondent state; Mr Liu had entered Russia with a valid visa and seemed to have enjoyed lawful residence for a decade, during which he started his family life. Second, in the *fait accompli* case law reviewed earlier, the Court does not doubt the reality of the interests of the respondent state in expelling the applicant. By contrast, in *Liu (No. 2)*, the respondent state relied on national security reasons whose genuineness the Court doubted.[153] This context explains the reflections the Court added about Article 13 in *Liu (No. 2)*. To quote:

> The Court reiterates that in immigration matters, where there is an arguable claim that expulsion may infringe an alien's right to respect for his or her family life, Article 13 in

[150] *Liu (No. 2)*, para 83. [151] *Liu (No. 2)*, para 94.

[152] *Nunez* judgment, paras 14, 71, and especially 72.

[153] Why the assessment of national security concerns by supposedly Western democracies should be trusted is open to debate, although the Strasbourg Court does not seem to do so very often. In this sense, the opinion expressed by Judge Kovler in *Liu (No. 2)* appears consistent with the general Strasbourg inclination to trust the state.

conjunction with Article 8 of the Convention requires that States must make available to the individual concerned the effective possibility of challenging expulsion or refusal-of-residence orders and of having the relevant issues examined with sufficient procedural safeguards and thoroughness by an appropriate domestic forum offering adequate guarantees of independence and impartiality.[154]

This is a great pronouncement. Although the Court presents it as a 'reiterat[ion]', it does not cite any previous case law in its support. A HUDOC search conducted in May 2014 for the words 'effective possibility of challenging expulsion' produced only two results apart from *Liu (No. 2)*, both of which involved Bulgaria.[155] A broader search using the words 'sufficient procedural safeguards' and 'immigration' was slightly more successful without, however, producing startling results: it added seven cases to the first list, not all relevant, and mostly again involved Bulgaria.[156]

It is tempting to think that this pronouncement addressed authorities which the Court suspects are prone to disrespecting the requirements of the rule of law, rather than being meant as a general principle which the Court will now be ready to insist must be met by all states parties to the Convention. Even in *Liu (No. 2)*, the Court does not pursue its application. It considers it unnecessary to examine the Article 13 complaint given the conclusion it reached on Article 8.[157] Chapters 7 and 12 have already explained why such a shortcut which results in a failure to pursue issues related to procedural safeguards is highly detrimental to the development of human rights law.

This does not detract from the fact that *Liu (No. 2)* followed a reasoning which sounded refreshingly different from other Strasbourg migrant case law. The same can also be said of *Alim v. Russia*, also decided in 2011.[158] The applicant in *Alim* had arrived in Russia from Cameroon in 1995 as a 14-year-old promising footballer. One is led to understand that an injury in his late teens put an end to his football ambitions. Mr Alim remained in Russia and, in his early twenties, started to live with a Russian national with whom he had a child in 2005. He was lawfully resident in Russia at least from 2004. Expelled from university due to lack of attendance, his visa was revoked in September 2006. A second child was born the following month. He did not register his continued presence around that time, as he should have done. Given this, he should have left Russia and re-entered with a visa. He did not do so, in his words, because 'his wife had recently given birth to their second child and he had to take care of their

[154] *Liu (No. 2)* judgment, para 99.

[155] *C.G. v. Bulgaria*, appl. 1365/07, Judgment (ECtHR), 24 Apr. 2008; *Kaushal and Others v. Bulgaria*, appl. 1537/08, Judgment (ECtHR), 2 Sept. 2010, in English only.

[156] The list included *McCann and Others v. the United Kingdom*, appl. 18984/91, GC Judgment (ECtHR), 27 Sept. 1995, which is unrelated to the concerns of this book, and *Chahal v. the United Kingdom*, appl. 22414/93, GC Judgment (ECtHR), 15 Nov. 1996, reviewed previously.

[157] *Liu (No. 2)* judgment, para 100.

[158] The Chamber in *Alim* counted five judges who had also sat on the bench which decided *Liu(No. 2)*. These judges were: Judges Vajić, Kovler, Steiner, Laffranque, and Sicilianos. The additional judges were Judges Nicolaou and Lazarova Trajkovska in *Liu (No. 2)* and Judges Lorenzen and Hajiyev in *Alim*.

first child'.[159] Subjected to an identity check and unable to produce valid documentation, he was fined, detained, and ordered to be removed, but without the authorities being ready to pay for his travel back to Cameroon. He was released from detention in 2007. His release did not mark the end of his worries however. As he stated 'he had to be discreet because he did not want to be arrested and because the order of administrative removal against him remained enforceable; he could no longer regularise his stay in Russia; he could not work or initiate any administrative procedures concerning marriage or paternity'.[160]

The Court did not question his statements. Despite operating 'the Strasbourg reversal'[161] and noting that 'the applicant's behaviour [was] not entirely beyond reproach', the Court found that 'the attitude of the national authorities [raised] serious questions in terms of Article 8 of the Convention'.[162] It nonetheless recognised the state's (supposed) interests:

> In the Court's view, the possibility for the authorities to react with expulsion may constitute an important means of general deference against gross or repeated violations of immigration regulations. A scheme of implementation of national immigration law which, as here, is based on administrative sanctions in the form of expulsion does not as such raise an issue of failure to comply with Article 8 of the Convention.[163]

The problem was that where 'the interference with the applicant's rights under Article 8 was meant to pursue, as a legitimate aim, the protection of public safety or order', the national authorities should have 'evaluated the extent to which the applicant endangered public safety or order'.[164] They had not done this, so that there was a violation of the Convention. The applicant was awarded €9,000 non-pecuniary damages.[165]

The Court's reasoning in *Alim* is both apposite and powerful in that what it finds defective is the lack of precise justification by the authorities for the interference with the applicant's family and private life.[166] The Russian authorities are reproached for invoking the protection of public safety or order without specifying how the applicant is threatening these. Requiring precise, pointed justifications for curtailing the right of a migrant person is exactly what this book advocates is needed.

This requirement should apply to all states, including Western democracies which invoke the economic well-being of their country to keep migrants excluded. What would therefore be most welcome is to see the *Alim* reasoning extended across the whole of the Strasbourg migrant case law, thus abandoning the implicit understanding that some states need not justify their wish to keep a certain type of migrants out of their territories, because the Court assumes that it goes without saying that it is their privilege to exercise such exclusion.

[159] *Alim* judgment, para 11. [160] *Alim*, para 22. [161] *Alim*, para 77.
[162] *Alim*, para 92. [163] *Alim*, para 93. [164] *Alim*, para 96.
[165] *Alim*, para 108. In *Liu (No. 2)*, the applicant was awarded €1,800, having claimed €3 million: *Liu (No. 2)* judgment, paras 105 and 103.
[166] A notion which the Court recalled encompassed the 'totality of social ties' existing between a settled migrant and the community in which he lives (without addressing the question of how this definition applies to a migrant who is not 'settled'): *Alim*, para 68.

XII. Why did Adult Children Suddenly Count in *Hasanbasic*?

I have identified no more than 14 cases where the European Court concluded a violation of Article 8 due to a residence permit refusal between January 2007—when *Sisojeva* was overturned by the Grand Chamber—and March 2014. Six violation verdicts were reviewed earlier: *Nunez* and *Butt* (*fait accompli* case law), *Menghesha Kimfe* and *Agraw* (Swiss canton case law), and *Liu (No.2)* and *Alim* (Russian case law).[167] Another six violation verdicts arose because the refusal followed the claim, left unsubstantiated by the domestic—mostly Bulgarian—authorities, that the applicant had posed a threat to national security.[168] One, *Osman v. Denmark*, was briefly mentioned in footnote 128 on page 466. The last verdict is called *Hasanbasic v. Switzerland*.[169] It can only be viewed as bizarre.

The first applicant in this case was originally from Bosnia-Herzegovina. He had been legally settled in Switzerland for close to 20 years; his wife, the second applicant, also from the former Yugoslavia, had been settled for over 40 years. The husband decided to return to his country of origin, where the couple had had a house built for their retirement. He informed the Swiss authorities of his decision to leave Switzerland. Four months after his departure, he suffered a heart attack. He now sought to return to Switzerland, where his wife was still based—she had been awaiting her retirement in order to join him in Bosnia-Herzegovina without losing her pension rights—and where he would be able to draw a pension as an invalid. His request for a residence permit was refused on the grounds that he was not financially self-sufficient and had a criminal record. Unanimously, the Court found the refusal of the Swiss authorities to re-admit him in breach of Article 8.

Admittedly some of the respondent government's arguments appeared flimsy, including the reliance on the first applicant's criminal record for road traffic offences. However, the reasoning of the Court is baffling. The applicant had decided to leave Switzerland. The Court does not consider that this fact—in a world of 'managed migration'—is determinant (if unfortunate), leaving the respondent state free either to re-admit him or not. In its assessment of the Article 8 complaint, the Court mentions and takes into consideration, even while saying that it is not doing so as this goes against its own case law, the applicant's adult and financially independent children based in

[167] For a third Russian case in this area, see: *Kiyutin v. Russia*, appl. 2700/10, Judgment (ECtHR), 10 Mar. 2011 (finding a violation of Article 14 in conjunction with Article 8 for refusing a residence permit solely based on the HIV-positive status of the applicant).

[168] *Musa and Others v. Bulgaria*, appl. 61259/00, Judgment (ECtHR), 11 Jan. 2007, in French only; *Bashir and Others v. Bulgaria*, appl. 65028/01, Judgment (ECtHR), 14 June 2007, in French only; *Hasan v. Bulgaria*, appl. 54323/00, Judgment (ECtHR), 14 June 2007, in French only; *Guile v. Lithuania*, appl. 10425/03, Judgment (ECtHR), 16 Dec. 2008, in English only; *M. and Others v. Bulgaria*, appl. 41416/08, Judgment (ECtHR), 26 July 2011, in English only; *Baltaji v. Bulgaria*, appl. 12919/04, Judgment (ECtHR), 12 July 2011, in French only.

[169] *Hasanbasic v. Switzerland*, appl. 52166/09, Judgment (ECtHR), 11 June 2013, in French only.

Switzerland—[170] even though he also had one adult child from a previous marriage living in Bosnia-Herzegovina.[171]

I do not wish to suggest that considering that family relationships continue to exist between adult children and their parents is not a good idea. It actually corresponds to many people's experience of what family relations are, as Judge Spielmann has noted on more than one occasion.[172] But what is disturbing and thus requires an explanation is that this way of proceeding goes against Strasbourg's settled immigration case law. To cite one striking example, *Berisha v. Switzerland*[173] was decided one month after *Hasanbasic*. It concerned the refusal to grant a residence permit to the children of a couple of Kosovo origin who had been living in Switzerland since 1997 and 2007 respectively. The father had had a residence permit since 2005. His wife was allowed to join him on family reunion grounds in 2007. She requested her husband's children to join them three months after her arrival. When one daughter fell seriously ill in Pristina in 2008, and no relative was able to take care of her in Kosovo except her elderly grandmother, she urged the Migration Office to decide the matter promptly. The office refused the children residence permits in April 2009, on the ground that the couple had concealed their existence. (The children were mentioned in tax declarations and other official documents; the woman also explained that it was her lack of knowledge of French which had led her not to mention the children on the form she had completed on arrival.) The children entered Switzerland clandestinely in August 2009, aged 15, 14, and seven. Another request for a residence permit was introduced and rejected in 2010. The matter went through the domestic courts. Although the children were not expelled, they did not have legal status. When the case was finally decided at Strasbourg in June 2013, the Court stated as part of its reasoning: '[W]ith regard to the alleged financial dependence of R. on the applicants, the Court cannot see why he, as well as his sister, could not be supported at a distance, especially when it is considered that they are now 19 and 17 years old respectively. Lastly, with particular regard to the youngest of the three children, B., the Court notes that the applicants are not prevented from travelling—or even staying—with her in Kosovo in order to ensure that she is provided with the necessary care and education so that her best interests as a child are safeguarded'.[174]

Exactly the same judges decided *Berisha* and *Hasanbasic*. The violation of Article 8 was adopted by unanimity in *Hasanbasic*. No violation was found

[170] 'Certes, dans la mesure où les requérants n'ont pas démontré devant la Cour qu'il existe entre eux et leurs enfants des éléments supplémentaires de dépendance, autres que les liens affectifs normaux [references omitted], ils ne peuvent pas invoquer ces rapports familiaux au regard de l'article 8, eu égard à l'âge adulte des enfants. La Cour estime néanmoins qu'ils ne sont pas complètement dépourvus de pertinence pour l'appréciation de la situation familiale des requérants': *Hasanbasic* judgment, para 60. The essence of this quotation is that the Court states it does not take, or cannot take, into consideration the adult children, but then it does.

[171] *Hasanbasic*, para 8.

[172] See e.g. Partly concurring opinion of Judge Spielmann, joined by Judge Kovler, in *Kaftailova v. Latvia*, appl. 59643/00, Judgment (ECtHR), 22 June 2006.

[173] *Berisha v. Switzerland*, appl. 948/12, Judgment (ECtHR), 30 July 2013.

[174] *Berisha*, para 60. See also *I.* final decision (2012), para 13.

in *Berisha* by Judges Raimondi, Lorenzen, Vučinić, and Keller (against the dissenting votes of Judges Jočienė, Karakaş, and, to some extent, Sajó). How can one reconcile these two verdicts? One wonders whether some judges could more easily connect to the possible devastation brought about by an unanticipated health problem which makes one regret having just elected to go and spend one's retirement abroad, than to what it means to have to face the choice of *either* leaving one's children in another state *or* having to relocate there. The only acceptable explanation I can suggest is that in *Hasanbasic*, the Court would have taken into account the situation of the second applicant who enjoyed leave to remain (*permis d'établissement*), as opposed to just a residence permit (*une simple autorisation de séjour*).[175] This, however, would not make sense of the whole case law, as the review of yet another case suggests.

XIII. Illegal Status Aggravates a Violation by the State: *Polidario*

In *Polidario v. Switzerland*,[176] decided like *Berisha* on 30 July 2013 (and with five judges being the same), the reasoning took a most refreshing turn away from immigration control considerations. This was an international child abduction case where the Court referred to the applicant's illegal migrant status not to bemoan her behaviour but in order to stress how the authorities had engendered a precarious situation, given that the only thing they needed to do to regularise her status was to grant her a residence permit—which they did, eventually but belatedly.[177] The Court obviously felt for the mother who had been left without physical contact with her child for many years.

The applicant was a Philippine national who had had a child with a Lebanese man in Switzerland in 2001. When the relationship broke down, she was awarded custody of the child. Due to her illegal status, she was ordered to leave the country, which she did with the child. In 2004, she agreed that her ex-husband could take the child on holiday to Switzerland. He failed to return the child to the Philippines in March 2005 as per their agreement. From 2006, the applicant tried to have the child returned to her or to obtain the necessary documentation which would enable her to visit him in Switzerland. Having been granted a one-week visa in order to attend a judicial hearing in Switzerland in October 2010 regarding the child's custody, she did not have the heart to leave the country when her visa expired. She remained there illegally, which enabled her to resume contact with the child.

She lodged an application at Strasbourg in June 2010. This was communicated to the government in September 2012 and, the following month, she received the

[175] *Hasanbasic* judgment, para 57.

[176] *Polidario v. Switzerland*, appl. 33169/10, Judgment (ECtHR), 30 July 2013, in French only.

[177] *Polidario* judgment, para 75.

residence permit she had long coveted.[178] As in *Mendizabal* and the Swiss canton case law, the European Court refused to strike out the case as requested by the government. It proceeded to find a violation of Article 8 by unanimity, having taken into consideration the four-year absence of any contact except for phone conversations[179] and the two-year period during which she was forced to live 'illegally', therefore 'preventing her from having effective and secure relations with her child', due to the 'lack of legal status' which put her in 'a precarious situation'.[180]

The first paragraph of Article 8 is the focus of the reasoning (without paragraph 2 being discussed at all). The Court starts by noting that it encompasses positive obligations.[181] It then recalls that the Convention is meant to protect concrete and effective rights.[182] This, it says, implies the establishment of an adequate and sufficient judicial arsenal, including for parent and child's reunion.[183] It finally observes that this is an area where measures must be adopted rapidly if separation between parent and child is not to have irredeemably negative consequences.[184] A dozen paragraphs follow which examine the circumstances of the applicant from the angle of the measures which the state took—or, rather, failed to take—in order to facilitate the applicant's reunion with her child.[185] Not only does the Court find a violation of Article 8 of the Convention, it also allocates the applicant the whole sum she requested as pecuniary damage: CHF20,000(€16,223).[186]

I salute the fact that the Court accepted at face value the applicant's explanation to the effect that 'she could not resign herself to going back to the Philippines alone following the few contacts she had had with her son from the time of the January 2010 judicial hearing' so that she had had 'to exercise her right of visit by clandestinely and illegally residing in Switzerland, and thus without being granted a legal status'.[187] Of course I also would not wish to object to the absence of criticism which the Court expressed towards the applicant for having taken such a course. I wonder, however, what would have happened if the case had presented itself rather differently to the Court.

What if the applicant had been subjected to police control and ordered to leave the country, and had then tried to argue that her removal breached Article 8, by separating her from the child she had just started to see again? What would the Court have decided in such a case? Having noted earlier the lottery-like nature of the *fait accompli* case law, I would not venture to predict the outcome. I would expect, however, that the reasoning, tone, and words used in such a case would be rather different from those found in the *Polidario* judgment which has just been reviewed.

Perhaps the judges find it easier to identify with the plight of a mother separated from her child following the father's inobservance of the legally agreed terms

[178] *Polidario*, para 76. [179] *Polidario*, para 73. [180] *Polidario*, para 75.
[181] *Polidario*, para 63. [182] *Polidario*, para 64. [183] *Polidario*, para 65.
[184] *Polidario*, para 66. [185] *Polidario*, paras 68–77.
[186] This is twice the amount allocated seven years earlier to the mother whose baby was taken away: *Moser v. Austria*, appl. 12643/02, Judgment (ECtHR), 21 Sept. 2006, as reviewed in Section X of Chapter 8.
[187] *Polidario* judgment, para 75.

of custody than with, say, a failed asylum seeker who starts a relationship with his neighbour as in *Useinov*. Whatever the response, the residence permit case law is harsh.

XIV. No Right to a Particular Type of Residence Permit

For the people who are at the receiving end of the residence permit case law—because, unlike others, they do not enjoy secure status—the consequences of not having their residence permit complaints heard by the Court can be enormous. Providing the reader is willing to use her imagination, two examples may illustrate this point.

In March 2009, the Court struck out the case of *Said Botan v. the Netherlands* after the authorities granted the applicant a residence permit for the purpose of asylum.[188] In fact, the applicant's complaint had been that she could not access a residence permit for the purpose of family reunion. The permit she had now received (despite a final decision rejecting asylum status in 1997)[189] was liable to be withdrawn as soon as the conditions in Somalia, her country of origin, were deemed to have sufficiently improved.[190] She argued that the permit granted provided 'insufficient protection'. The Court was not moved by this argument and proceeded to strike out the case. This meant that her main complaint was left unexamined. This was that, as per domestic law, she could only apply for a permit for family reunion purposes after having received a provisional residence visa from abroad.[191] Given that there was no representation of the Netherlands in Somalia and that she could not obtain a travel document as there was no functioning Somali government, she could not manage this.[192] (She did not add that, had this been possible, the travel involved would have required setting up care arrangements for her three young children born in the Netherlands.)

To justify the law and their decision in this case, the Dutch authorities had stated: 'If an alien, who had entered the Netherlands without a visa but with the intention of settling there, could be exempted from the visa requirement simply by asserting that it was impossible to return, this would have serious negative repercussions on the policy' of trying to avoid being confronted with the *fait accompli* of having started a family.[193] Further arguments were that family life had started when

[188] *Said Botan v. the Netherlands*, appl. 1869/04, Judgment (ECtHR), 10 Mar. 2009. See also its clone *Ibrahim Mohamed v. the Netherlands*, appl. 1872/04, Judgment (ECtHR), 10 Mar. 2009, as well as *Alem Biraga and Others v. Sweden*, appl. 1722/10, Decision (ECtHR), 3 Apr. 2012, declared inadmissible by a majority.

[189] *Said Botan*, para 7.

[190] *Said Botan*, para 19.

[191] *Said Botan*, para 3. A similar issue is due to be examined by the Grand Chamber in *M.E. v. Sweden*, appl. 71398/12, which was decided at chamber level on 26 June 2014, shortly after the manuscript of this book was sent to the press. *M.E.* involves a homosexual applicant, who married another man in Sweden in September 2011. Sweden insists he needs to go back to Libya to apply for family reunion from there. Judge Power-Forde dissenting, the Chamber found that this did not entail a violation of Article 3, despite the fact that homosexuality is illegal in Libya. The person the applicant married is now a woman.

[192] *Said Botan*, para 10.

[193] *Said Botan*, para 12.

the applicant was not residing lawfully in the country (her husband, by contrast, also from Somalia, had obtained Dutch nationality in 1998), that 'the impugned decision did not constitute a definite refusal of family life being exercised in the Netherlands, but merely an enforcement of legal requirements', and that 'it had not appeared that there were any objective impediments to family life being developed abroad'.[194] Having reaffirmed that 'Article 8 cannot be construed as guaranteeing, as such, the right to a particular type of residence permit', the Court found the applicant's complaint under Article 8 'adequately and sufficiently remedied'—arguably a missed opportunity to use the 'extremely formalistic' expression.

It was not the first case of its kind to have been lodged at Strasbourg. *Ahmed Ali v. the Netherlands and Greece*, which raised similar complaints to *M.S.S.*, was actually lodged one month before *M.S.S.* was lodged.[195] After the *M.S.S.* ruling, the respondent governments assured the Court that the applicant in *Ahmed Ali* would not be transferred to Greece. In their view, this meant that her application was now without substance.[196] In contrast, the applicant explained that she would have been eligible for an indefinite residence permit in 2012, had her original asylum application been examined on its merits timeously.[197] Citing *Bonger*, the Court asserted: 'the protection offered by Article 3 cannot be construed as guaranteeing, as such, the right to a residence permit,... let alone the right to a particular residence permit'.[198] Referring to *Sisojeva*, it continued that it was 'not empowered to rule on whether the individual concerned should be granted one particular legal status rather than another, that choice being a matter for the domestic authorities alone'.[199]

XV. Rightlessness: The Ultimate Discrimination

Ahmed Ali showed the Court unwilling to consider it as part of its remit to check that individuals are given the means to leave behind their precarious status. Even more problematic than this type of decision is the *Bonger* case law. This is a case law which arguably stands opposed to the values enshrined in both Article 3 (prohibition of inhuman treatment) and Article 14 (prohibition of discrimination). As for Article 3, it is difficult to contemplate how leaving someone in a situation of rightlessness, thus denying him a legal status, is not considered a violation of this provision. As for Article 14, such treatment—which denies legal recognition—is surely the ultimate discrimination which the law could conceive against a human being. The *Bonger* case law is also wrong in regard to Article 6 (fair trial guarantees), as already noted. How the Court could rely on the *Maaouia* jurisprudence to brush aside the presumption of innocence is barely conceivable. On any of these three grounds—Articles 3, 14, and 6—the *Bonger* case law is

194 *Said Botan*, para 12.
195 *Hayaati Ahmed Ali v. the Netherlands*, appl. 26494/09, Decision (ECtHR), 24 Jan. 2012.
196 *Ahmed Ali*, para 11. 197 *Ahmed Ali*, para 19.
198 *Ahmed Ali*, para 19. Note the reference here to Article 3, rather than Article 8 as in *Said Botan*.
199 *Ahmed Ali*, para 19.

indefensible. One can only conclude that something is seriously wrong with the Strasbourg case law.

XVI. Conclusion

This has no doubt been the darkest chapter of this book. What it has argued is that the Strasbourg Court has no qualms about rejecting complaints which are about 'the right to have rights'. This, from a human rights perspective, has to be wrong.

On the face of it, there is no reason why the Court should not extend its *Bonger* jurisprudence to stateless applicants stranded in Europe. The story of one of them was recently recounted in a British newspaper committed to raising awareness of the plight of migrants, under the title 'Meet Steven, a man who can't work because he doesn't exist'.[200] Steven (not his real name) is 32 years old and believes he was born either in Zimbabwe or Mozambique. He does not have a record of his birth, so there is nothing to state who he is and from where he is. He arrived in London on a fake passport, having fled a crackdown on opponents to Robert Mugabe's regime in Zimbabwe. His asylum application was rejected. While he was awaiting to hear its outcome, he committed the *fait accompli* scorned at Strasbourg. This is how the journalist put it: '[H]e settled in Cardiff, where he worked at the city's rugby stadium and in warehouses. No one ever asked for identification. He fell in love with a Ugandan student and they set up home and had a baby'. Steven is then quoted as reminiscing with nostalgia: 'It was a normal life like anyone would dream of. Wake up, go to work, come back, play with my daughter. It was perfect'. His girlfriend could not stay in the country at the end of her studies and returned to Uganda with the child given that he could not offer her any security in Britain. Around that time, a law came into force in the UK making it a legal duty for employers to check the documentation of their workers. Steven lost his job, became homeless, and saw his friends turning their backs on him when they learnt he was an illegal migrant. A lawyer informed him that his legal situation was 'bleak, very bleak'.

One could imagine Steven's difficulties becoming a Strasbourg case. Would it be successful? There is little in the rulings reviewed in this chapter which allows one to be optimistic. Approaching the matter from a strictly legal perspective, one understands how principles established at Strasbourg over more than half a century have produced the situation whereby de facto rightlessness does not appear problematic under the European Convention. However, one needs to go beyond a purely legal perspective. The European Court of Human Rights was created in order to ensure that the rise of a dictatorial or arbitrary regime could be nipped in the bud. Its essential role is to protect the inalienable rights of all human beings.

For things to be turned over, and a proper Strasbourg statelessness case law to be developed, it will be necessary for the Court to *see* that it is inhumane to accept that people can be denied more and more rights simply because of their

[200] *The Independent*, Monday 2 June 1014, report by Emma Batha.

immigration status. As already noted, such denials can only be construed as involving an arbitrary discrimination between those deemed to be deserving and those deemed to be undeserving. Of course this discrimination is generally not seen. Naturalising it as the product of a perfectly acceptable technique of sound governmental management makes it invisible in political and social discourse.

Thanks to the awareness-raising work of NGOs, some governments are nonetheless actually beginning to give people means of getting out of the permanent stalemate in which they would otherwise remain. For example, it has become possible to apply for leave in the United Kingdom on the basis of statelessness since 2013.[201] This is a welcome development which hopefully represents a first step towards rejecting the idea of letting people be in a permanent stalemate out of legality.

Returning to the story in the newspaper, Steven is quoted as saying: 'What I'd like most is an ID with my picture on it. I've never had one before. I would work hard and go and find my daughter'. Having identification documents is a comfort and a security which the majority of people take for granted. That this is out of reach for millions in a world where virtually all movements require identification and documentation has to be seen as a breach of human rights of serious magnitude.

This should go without saying at Strasbourg. As *M.S.S.* overturned *K.R.S.*, it is difficult to believe that a case lodged by one of the many Stevens living in Europe will not one day manage to get the *Bonger* case law overturned. The question will then be: is it a true reversal?

[201] See: Alison Harvey, 'The UK's New Statelessness Determination Procedure in Context' (2013) *Journal of Immigration, Asylum and Nationality Law* 27, 294–314. 'Steven' is reported in *The Independent* article to have applied to this procedure.

14

On the Road to Substantive Equality: Due Process and Non-discrimination at San José

(*Nadege Dorzema* and *Pacheco Tineo*)

*Lourdes Peroni**

This chapter reviews the most recent Inter-American migration case law. Reflecting the salience of migration issues today, this case law is expanding rapidly. The Court decided two contentious cases in 2012 and 2013 and delivered an advisory opinion on migrant children as this book was in press.[1] This chapter does not engage in a comparison with the Strasbourg case law. Instead it takes the opportunity to discuss the judgments of *Nadege Dorzema et al. v. Dominican Republic*[2] and *Pacheco Tineo*

* Lourdes Peroni (LLM, Harvard Law School 2004 and Doctor in Law, Ghent University 2014) is a postdoctoral researcher at the Human Rights Centre at Ghent University. I would like to thank Marie-Bénédicte Dembour for inviting me to write this chapter and for commenting so generously and eloquently on its earlier versions.

[1] The Court deliberated the request for this advisory opinion in its 103rd period of ordinary sessions. See IACtHR, Press Release, 9 May 2014, available only in Spanish, <http://www.corteidh.or.cr/docs/comunicados/cp_06_14_esp.pdf>, accessed 29 May 2014. Also, as the manuscript of this book was already with the press, the Inter-American Court decided the case originally known as *Benito Tide Méndez and Others v. Dominican Republic*, a case briefly alluded to in Chapter 10. The hearing in *Benito Tide Méndez* was held in Mexico in October 2013. The case concerns allegations of arbitrary detention and summary expulsion of 27 people, including Dominican nationals and children, from the Dominican Republic to Haiti. The Commission filed the case before the Court in July 2012 because it considered that the Dominican state had not complied with the recommendations of its Merits Report No. 64/12 of 29 March 2012. The Commission has requested the Court to find violations of the rights to juridical personality, humane treatment, personal liberty, fair trial, protection of the family, rights of the child, nationality, property, freedom of movement and residence, equality and non-discrimination, and judicial protection. See the Application of 12 July 2012 filed by the Commission to the Court in Case No. 12.271 *Benito Tide Méndez et al. v. Dominican Republic*.

[2] *Nadege Dorzema et al. v. Dominican Republic*, Merits, Reparations and Costs, Judgment (IACtHR), 24 Oct. 2012. The case has sparked ample legal commentary, including a special issue of *Revue Québécoise de Droit International* (Hors-série, November 2013). See also, Karlos A. Castilla Juárez, 'Migración Irregular y Políticas Migratorias bajo el Análisis de la Corte Interamericana de

v. Bolivia[3] so as to examine where the Inter-American Court is heading in its migration case law. In particular, it focuses on the roads that the Court is navigating in order to ensure that migrants are treated equally and that they benefit from due process guarantees.

The chapter starts by discussing *Nadege Dorzema*, which concerned the killing and injuring of a group of Haitian nationals and the collective expulsion of the survivors by members of the Dominican armed forces. Its facts can only be described as horrific. It therefore came as no surprise that the Court found a number of human rights violations. In line with the Inter-American Court's 'strong appetite for wide-ranging rulings',[4] no less than eight major sets of violations were unanimously found, including violations of the right to life, the right to personal integrity, the right to personal liberty, the right to judicial guarantees, freedom of movement, and non-discrimination in the enjoyment of all these rights. The question, which the discussion offered in this chapter examines, is the extent to which the Court was ready to push the equality/non-discrimination issues in the case. The response is that the Court did address these issues but not without hesitation. This hesitation was compensated for by the Court's willingness to highlight the discriminatory context within which other human rights violations took place. Whether one assesses this compensation as entirely sufficient or disappointingly modest depends on one's perspective.

The chapter continues with an analysis of *Pacheco Tineo*, a case dealing with the expulsion of a family of asylum seekers (parents and three minor children) to the country they were fleeing from: Peru. Again, the facts of the case were such that violation verdicts were bound to arise. The victims had not been given the chance to explain why they thought they should be granted refugee status in Bolivia. Moreover, there had been no time, let alone legal assistance, for them to challenge their expulsion. The Court unanimously found three sets of violations regarding: (a) the right to seek and be granted asylum and the principle of *non-refoulement*, as well as the right to a fair trial and the right to judicial protection; (b) the right to respect for one's mental and moral integrity; and (c) the rights of the child and of the family in relation to the right to seek and be granted asylum, the principle of *non-refoulement*, the right to a fair trial, and the right to judicial protection. For this book, the crucial point is to reflect on the extent to which the Court proved willing to impose procedural guarantees in an area—asylum—which in the Strasbourg system does not even attract the applicability of the fair trial provision. The Inter-American Court, faithful to its firm tradition of paying attention to due process, did not hesitate to identify procedural duties for the states in this area.

Derechos Humanos: El Caso Nadege Dorzema y Otros' (2013) *Revista Vasca de Administración Pública* 95, 125–147.

3 *Family Pacheco Tineo v. Plurinational State of Bolivia*, Preliminary Objections, Merits, Reparations and Costs, Judgment (IACtHR), 25 Nov. 2013, in Spanish only at the time of writing.

4 See Chapter 9, p. 306.

Taking into account *Pacheco Tineo* and other relevant developments, the chapter closes by exploring the road that the Inter-American Court might have been expected to take in what was, at the time of writing this chapter, its forthcoming advisory opinion on migrant children.

I. *Nadege Dorzema*: Continuing on the Road to Equality, Albeit Hesitantly

The events in *Nadege Dorzema* took place in June 2000, after a truck driving about 30 Haitian nationals failed to stop at a checkpoint.[5] Soldiers belonging to the Border Forces Operations Post pursued the truck for several kilometres and opened fire indiscriminately, killing four people.[6] Another person lost his life when the truck turned over and two more while running for their lives as a result of shooting by the border soldiers.[7] Six Haitian nationals and one Dominican national died and at least ten others were injured.[8] The victims were unarmed and attempted no violent reaction against the soldiers.[9] Eleven people were detained and taken to the Dejabón military barracks, where soldiers gave them two options: to work in the fields or to pay them to be returned to Haiti.[10] The detainees collected money, gave it to the soldiers, and were transferred to Haiti.[11] The expulsion of the *Nadege Dorzema* victims may be viewed as one more instance amongst many of collective expulsion of Haitian migrants from the Dominican Republic.[12] Mass deportations were conducted in the 1990s, sparking wide criticism from international organisations and the Inter-American Commission on Human Rights.[13] Among the Court's most notable findings were an excessive use of force by state agents, arbitrary deprivations of life, extrajudicial executions, lack of medical assistance for the injured, demeaning treatment of the bodies of the deceased, collective expulsion of the survivors, and discrimination in the enjoyment of various Convention rights.

Joining the equality road

The *Nadege Dorzema* ruling against discrimination follows the discrimination findings that the Court had reached in the other two contentious migration cases decided previously. In *Yean and Bosico*, as examined in Chapter 10, the Court

[5] *Nadege Dorzema* judgment, para 83. [6] *Nadege Dorzema*, para 83.
[7] *Nadege Dorzema*, para 83. [8] *Nadege Dorzema*, para 83.
[9] *Nadege Dorzema*, para 83. [10] *Nadege Dorzema*, para 130.
[11] *Nadege Dorzema*, para 130.
[12] For example, in the *Benito Tide Méndez* case, the Commission concluded in its Merits Report that 'the summary expulsions occurred in a tense context of collective and mass expulsions of individuals, affecting both Dominicans and foreigners and both documented and undocumented persons who had their permanent residence in the country'. Application filed by the Commission to the Court, 1. In this regard, the Commission noted that skin colour was a decisive factor in the detention of the alleged victims and their subsequent expulsion. Application filed by the Commission to the Court, 1.
[13] For more background information on this phenomenon, see Chapter 10, p. 318.

ruled that the Dominican state had violated the right to equal protection of the children by denying them nationality in a discriminatory manner.[14] In *Vélez Loor*, as discussed in Chapter 11, the Court held that the state of Panama had failed to guarantee Mr Vélez Loor's right of access to justice without discrimination.[15] In condemning the states in these two cases, the Court took different legal routes.[16] In *Yean and Bosico*, the Court primarily applied Article 24 ACHR, which protects the right to equal treatment before the law.[17] In *Vélez Loor*, it applied Article 1(1), which is a general norm imposing an obligation on the state to respect and guarantee the enjoyment of the rights of the American Convention without discrimination.[18]

In finding the violations noted above, the Court addressed different sources of inequality. In *Yean and Bosico*, the discrimination at issue arose from the state's unjustified differential treatment of the children within a wider context of discrimination against Haitians.[19] In *Vélez Loor*, the discrimination in question originated in the state's failure to attend to the particular characteristics of Mr Vélez Loor's situation—i.e. the vulnerability linked to his status as an irregular migrant deprived of liberty—and to adopt measures capable of remedying this situation and ensuring equal access to justice.[20] The forms of equality that the Court upheld in these cases broadly overlap with what Sandra Fredman calls 'recognition' and 'transformative' dimensions of substantive equality. The recognition facet, Fredman explains, aims to 'promote respect for dignity and worth, thereby redressing stigma, stereotyping, humiliation and violence because of membership of an identity group'.[21] The transformative dimension seeks to accommodate 'difference'—be it different identities or different needs—by removing the detriment attached to it.[22]

One may therefore view the equality road that the Court is currently navigating in its migration case law as a two-lane road.[23] One lane leads to recognition by

[14] *The Girls Yean and Bosico v. Dominican Republic*, Preliminary Objections, Merits, Reparations and Costs, Judgment (IACtHR), 8 Sept. 2005, para 174. The Court found this violation in relation to Articles 19 and 1(1) ACHR.

[15] *Vélez Loor v. Panama*, Preliminary Objections, Merits, Reparations and Costs, Judgment (IACtHR), 23 Nov. 2010, para 254.

[16] These routes are described by the Court as follows: '[I]f the State discriminates in relation to respect for or guarantee of a conventional right, the facts must be analyzed in accordance with Article 1(1) and the substantial right in question. If, on the contrary, the alleged discrimination refers to unequal protection by domestic law, the facts must be analyzed in light of Article 24 therein'. *Vélez Loor*, para 253.

[17] *Yean and Bosico* judgment, para 260(2).

[18] *Vélez Loor* judgment, para 253.

[19] *Yean and Bosico* judgment, paras 166, 168, 169, and 170.

[20] *Vélez Loor* judgment, para 254. Another distinction flowing from the Court's reasoning in these cases is that, while the Dominican state should have mostly *abstained from acting* in a discriminatory manner, the Panamanian state *should have acted* so as to compensate for the conditions that in reality hampered equality. *Yean and Bosico* therefore contains mostly a negative obligation and *Vélez Loor* a positive one.

[21] Sandra Fredman, *Discrimination Law* (Oxford: Oxford University Press, 2011) 25 and 28–30.

[22] Fredman 30.

[23] This does not mean that the two lanes may not merge. The recognition and transformation aspects of equality may overlap and reinforce one another.

attending to the social prejudices and racism that subordinate migrants. As exemplified in *Yean and Bosico*, the Court frames the discriminatory treatment of the victims within the broader context of discrimination against Haitian children and racism towards Haitians in the Dominican Republic.[24] The other lane leads to transformative equality by attending to the 'different' needs of some migrants in order to ensure that they are able to exercise their rights equally. In *Vélez Loor*, in particular, the Court attends to the specific needs of irregular migrants deprived of liberty.

With *Nadege Dorzema*, the Court joins the equality road via the recognition lane, albeit with some hesitations. Following the Article 1(1) route, the Court condemns the Dominican state for de facto discrimination against the victims due to their status as migrants in the enjoyment of a series of Convention rights: right to life, right to respect for personal integrity, right to personal liberty, right to a fair trial, freedom of movement, and right to judicial protection.[25] Despite the discrimination verdict, three hesitations can be identified in the Court's reasoning: (a) the Court remains reluctant to pronounce on the structural character of the discrimination; (b) the Court frames part of its reasoning in a 'Strasbourg-like' way; and (c) the Court is silent on any state duty to investigate whether discriminatory motives triggered the violence suffered by the victims.

Wandering off the equality road

The first sign of hesitation can be found in the Court's reluctance to pronounce on the wider context of discrimination in the case. This approach echoes, to some extent, its earlier reluctance in *Vélez Loor*.[26] In *Nadege Dorzema*, the Commission and the victims' representatives had argued that the events had taken place within a structural context of racism and discrimination against Haitians and Dominicans of Haitian origin in the Dominican Republic.[27] The representatives, in particular, had alleged that the *only* reason for the state's conduct was discrimination and xenophobia towards Haitians.[28] Yet the Court announced, without elaborating, that 'it is not necessary to make a ruling on the alleged context of structural discrimination'.[29] There is even less reasoning for the refusal to consider the argument than in *Vélez Loor*.[30] By leaving out the context, the Court risks treating the case as an isolated event of discrimination. The event may thus appear to be the 'fault' of certain individuals rather than the product of broader and

[24] *Yean and Bosico* judgment, paras 168–170.

[25] *Nadege Dorzema* judgment, para 238.

[26] See Chapter 11, Section XIV, 'Vulnerability rather than Equality: Where the Inter-American Court refused to go in *Vélez Loor*'. In *Nadege Dorzema*, the Court also refused to examine the alleged violation of Article 3 ACHR ('Right to Juridical Personality'): *Nadege Dorzema*, para 227. For an analysis of this refusal, see Christopher Campbell-Duruflé, 'The Right to Juridical Personality of Arbitrarily Detained and Unidentified Migrants after the Case of the Guayubín Massacre' (2013) *Revue Québécoise de Droit International* (Hors-série) 429–447.

[27] *Nadege Dorzema*, paras 219 and 220.

[28] *Nadege Dorzema*, para 221.

[29] *Nadege Dorzema*, paras 40 and 228.

[30] *Vélez Loor* judgment, paras 250 and 251.

entrenched social conditions of discrimination.[31] Admittedly, the Court adds that it will examine whether there had been discrimination due to the victims' condition as migrants.[32] However, this is not quite the same as examining the (context of) racial discrimination alleged by the victims.[33]

True, the Court later acknowledges the context of discrimination against Haitian migrants in the Dominican Republic. This acknowledgement is however indirect: the Court simply reports what others have said about 'historical practices of discrimination in the Dominican Republic... demonstrated by the treatment of Haitian migrants'.[34] This approach contrasts with the more straightforward acknowledgement made in *Yean and Bosico*. Indeed, after finding that the state's differential treatment of the Yean and Bosico children was discriminatory, the Court had not hesitated to further situate this treatment 'within the context of the vulnerable situation of the Haitian population and Dominicans of Haitian origin in the Dominican Republic'.[35]

A second sign of hesitation can be found in the way the San José Court operates a Strasbourg-like reversal when framing some of the principles it deals with. When the Court outlines the principles governing permissible differentiations on the basis of migration status and/or nationality, it puts the powers of the state first and the human rights of migrants second.[36] Indeed, the Court starts by recalling that states may treat differently documented migrants from undocumented ones as well as migrants from nationals.[37] Only then does the Court recall that this difference in treatment should be 'reasonable, objective and proportionate and [not harmful of] human rights'.[38] So states may set up entry and exit control mechanisms of migrants as long as these mechanisms respect 'due process and human dignity', irrespective of migration status.[39]

[31] This is how Alan Freeman has famously described the perpetrator and victim perspectives characterising formal and substantive equality, respectively, in the context of US anti-discrimination law. Alan David Freeman, 'Legitimizing Racial Discrimination through Antidiscrimination Law: A Critical Review of Supreme Court Doctrine' (1978) *Minnesota Law Review* 62, 1049–1119 at 1052–1057.

[32] *Nadege Dorzema* judgment, para 228.

[33] The *Benito Tide Méndez* case provided the Court with another chance to address the alleged context of structural racial discrimination against Haitians and Dominicans of Haitian descent in the Dominican Republic. The Commission has argued before the Court that the expulsion of the alleged victims did not follow the procedures in force at the time but 'were de facto expulsions without any legal support or subsequent administrative or judicial review, based on racial prejudices.' Application filed by the Commission to the Court, 7. Moreover, the Commission has proposed expert testimony on 'racial, structural, and institutional discrimination regarding a specific group in the territory of a State.' Application filed by the Commission to the Court, 8.

[34] *Nadege Dorzema*, para 232 and further references in footnote 289. The Court refers to materials by the United Nations Special Rapporteur on Discrimination and its Independent Expert on Minorities, the Inter-American Commission on Human Rights, Human Rights Watch and International Human Rights Law Clinic, Boalt Hall School of Law, University of California at Berkeley.

[35] *Yean and Bosico* judgment, para 168.; see also paras 169 and 170.

[36] *Nadege Dorzema* judgment, para 233.

[37] *Nadege Dorzema*, para 233.

[38] *Nadege Dorzema*, para 233.

[39] *Nadege Dorzema*, para 233.

This reversal is all the more puzzling given the original source of these pronouncements, namely paragraph 119 of Advisory opinion 18/03 'Juridical Condition and Rights of Undocumented Migrants'.[40] What the Court does in *Nadege Dorzema* is to drop the introductory statement of paragraph 119, which says: 'States may not discriminate or tolerate discriminatory situations that prejudice migrants'.[41] The non-discrimination reasoning is the only place where the Court operates a Strasbourg-like reversal in *Nadege Dorzema*. The examination of the other alleged violations proceeds in a 'normal' manner. For instance, in examining whether the expulsion of the Haitian migrants had been conducted following due process guarantees under the freedom of movement and due process provisions, the Court's point of departure is the vulnerability of migrants and the ensuing special obligations for states.[42]

The reversal in the *Nadege Dorzema* non-discrimination reasoning is however accompanied by strong non-discrimination principles concerning the shift of the burden of proof, indirect discrimination, and positive state duties. Thus, aware of the difficulty of proving racial prejudice, the Inter-American Court accepts that in certain cases the burden of proof falls on the state, 'which controls the means to clarify incidents that took place on its territory'.[43] Moreover, the Court recalls that international human rights law does not just prohibit norms and practices that are deliberately discriminatory but also norms and practices that may have a discriminatory impact on certain categories of people.[44] Likewise, the Court emphasises not only the duty to abstain from actions that may directly or indirectly create de facto or de jure discrimination, but also the duty to take positive action to remedy existing discriminatory situations in society.[45] Yet how exactly these principles play out in the case at hand remains obscure in the Court's reasoning. There is no effort to tie these principles in with the particular circumstances of the case. As a result, the overall non-discrimination reasoning remains abstract. The indirect discrimination principles, for example, appear *obiter dicta*, because the Court ultimately treats the case as one of direct discrimination.[46]

The Court's conclusions arise without much elaboration and without any explicit links to the general principles enunciated. Moreover, these conclusions do not mention the word 'discrimination', although one may say that they implicitly point out a pattern of discrimination. The Court holds:

> ...the situation of special vulnerability of the Haitian migrants was due, *inter alia*, to: (i) the absence of preventive measures to adequately address situations relating to

[40] *Juridical Condition and Rights of Undocumented Migrants*. Advisory opinion OC-18/03 (IACtHR), 17 Sept. 2003, para 119. This advisory opinion is reviewed in Chapter 9.

[41] A/O 18/03, para 119.

[42] *Nadege Dorzema* judgment, paras 152–154.

[43] *Nadege Dorzema*, para 229.

[44] *Nadege Dorzema*, paras 234 and 235. One of the Court's references is *D.H. and Others v. the Czech Republic*, appl. 57325/00, GC Judgment (ECtHR), 13 Nov. 2007. In this case, the European Court of Human Rights famously condemned the indirect discrimination of Roma children in schools.

[45] *Nadege Dorzema*, para 236.

[46] Bernard Duhaime and Catherine Lafontaine, 'Human Rights and Migrations in the Americas: Revisiting the *Dorzema et al. vs. Dominican Republic* Case' (2013) *Revue Québécoise de Droit International* (Hors-série) 449–482 at 480.

migratory control on the land border with Haiti and based on their situation of vulnerability; (ii) the violence deployed by the illegal and disproportionate use of force against unarmed migrants; (iii) the failure to investigate the said violence, the absence of testimony by and the participation of the victims in the criminal proceedings, and the impunity of the events; (iv) the detentions and collective expulsion without the due guarantees; (v) the lack of adequate medical attention and treatment to the injured victims, and (vi) the demeaning treatment of the corpses and the failure to return them to the next of kin.[47]

In what may appear as a third hesitation, the Court remains silent on whether the state had failed to investigate whether discrimination might have motivated the agents involved in the incidents. This is so despite the apparently express invitation from the victims' representatives for the Court to examine this point.[48] As a result of this silence in the discussion of the merits, the Court logically says nothing about this issue when it deals with the reparations. Had the Court condemned the Dominican Republic for its failure to comply with this procedural duty, it could have ordered the state to investigate the motives that had triggered the violence. The silence reveals that the Court has yet to develop more specific principles and standards of investigation of violence committed against migrants in general and/or Haitians in the Dominican Republic in particular.[49]

Remaining nonetheless on the equality road

It is important, however, to acknowledge that the *Nadege Dorzema* judgment also contains assertive findings and pronouncements that are useful in the fight against discrimination. Several of the findings under Article 5 ACHR (the right to humane treatment) clearly point to ways in which the victims were treated unfavourably. Thus, the Court notes that the bodies were 'laid haphazardly on the floor of a room in the morgue, with their clothing torn and in positions that could facilitate their rapid decomposition'.[50] In addition, the Court observes that the corpses were buried in a mass grave, with only the Dominican victim escaping this fate.[51] Moreover, when examining the treatment of the survivors, still under Article 5, the Court adopts a strong non-discrimination reasoning in respect of access to health care. It is worth reproducing the enunciated principle fully:

The Court notes that emergency medical care must be provided at all times for irregular migrants; accordingly, the States must provide comprehensive health care taking into account the needs of vulnerable groups. Thus, the State must ensure that goods and services related to health care are accessible to all, particularly the most vulnerable and

[47] *Nadege Dorzema* judgment, para 237.

[48] Duhaime and Lafontaine 'Human Rights and Migrations' 476–478.

[49] Ariel E. Dulitzky, 'El Principio de Igualdad y No Discriminación. Claroscuros de la Jurisprudencia Interamericana' (2007) *Anuario de Derechos Humanos* 13 Universidad de Chile 15–32 at 31 (making this point by reference to the Inter-American Court's wider case law). Dulitzky argues that violence against members of vulnerable groups cannot be investigated using the same standards and criteria applied to other kinds of violence.

[50] *Nadege Dorzema* judgment, para 112.

[51] *Nadege Dorzema*, para 113.

marginalized sectors of the population, without discrimination based on the prohibited conditions set out in Article 1(1) of the Convention.[52]

The Court also compensates, to some extent, for its refusal to determine whether the case fits broader patterns of discrimination against Haitians in the Dominican Republic by sometimes looking at the wider context of discrimination against (Haitian) migrants in other parts of the judgment. For example, in condemning the state for the disproportionate use of force, the Court observes: 'in the context of discrimination against migrants, the use of excessive force in the case revealed the failure to implement reasonable and appropriate measures to deal with this situation to the detriment of this group of Haitians'.[53] Likewise, in examining whether the state acted with due diligence in the investigation of the use of lethal force, the Court holds: 'the State should have investigated the events, taking into account the context of violence and discrimination against this type of victim'.[54] Similarly, in concluding that the expulsion of the victims did not meet the existing legal requirements, in violation of Article 22(9) ACHR prohibiting collective expulsion, the Court acknowledges the context within which the violations took place:

> This action corroborates the conclusion of the Special Rapporteur on contemporary forms of racism, racial discrimination, xenophobia and related intolerance, and the Independent Expert on minority issues concerning the existence of expulsions that are unjustified and violate the rights of Haitian migrants considered illegal by State officials.[55]

Perhaps most notably, the Court addresses the structural character of the discrimination in the reparations. Among the wide-ranging reparations,[56] the Court orders measures aimed at changing some of the conditions at the root of the discriminatory treatment of migrants. The Court, for example, holds:

> Since it has been proved that the State was responsible for a pattern of discrimination against migrants in Dominican Republic, the Court finds it relevant that the State organize a media campaign on the rights of regular and irregular migrants on Dominican territory.[57]

To prevent repetition, the Court also mandates, even more specifically, the training of state agents, including border control agents and those responsible for migration procedures, on 'the principle of equality and non-discrimination applied, in particular, to migrants'.[58]

II. *Pacheco Tineo*: Enlarging the Due Process Road

Pacheco Tineo involved a Peruvian family consisting of a couple and their three minor children (the youngest one of whom possessed Chilean nationality). This

[52] *Nadege Dorzema*, para 108.
[53] *Nadege Dorzema*, para 91.
[54] *Nadege Dorzema*, para 103.
[55] *Nadege Dorzema*, para177.
[56] The judgment includes ten reparation orders, including the obligations to reopen investigations; to determine the whereabouts of the bodies of the deceased, repatriate them, and return them to their next of kin; to provide medical and psychological treatment to the victims; and to pay compensation for pecuniary and non-pecuniary damage. *Nadege Dorzema* judgment, pp. 78–79.
[57] *Nadege Dorzema*, para 272.
[58] *Nadege Dorzema*, para 270.

was not just any family: the parents had been part of the *Castro-Castro v. Peru* case decided by the Inter-American Court in 2006.[59] Back in the 1990s, the parents had been granted asylum in Bolivia but, following a declaration of voluntary repatriation, they had left that country.[60] Instead of repatriating to Peru, they had gone to Chile, where they had obtained asylum.[61] In 2001, the family returned to Bolivia irregularly through the Peru–Bolivia border.[62] They later filed a new asylum request in Bolivia, but the asylum authorities decided not to consider that request on the ground that the earlier declaration of voluntary return indicated that they had implicitly renounced any asylum status.[63] The family was expelled to Peru by the Bolivian migration authorities for violating migration laws, notwithstanding a request from Chile that they be returned to Chile.[64]

Specific procedural standards in migration proceedings: following the well-paved road of due process

In its *Pacheco Tineo* judgment, the Court continues to develop jurisprudential lines established in previous case law in order to reaffirm specific due process guarantees in migration proceedings and to identify yet more specific safeguards in asylum proceedings. The Court achieves this by relying on and combining various provisions of the American Convention on Human Rights, namely Article 8 (the right to a fair trial) and Article 25 (the right to judicial protection) in connection with Article 22 (freedom of movement and residence), more particularly its paragraphs (7) (the right to seek and be granted asylum) and (8) (*non-refoulement*).

In a way that strongly resonates with Advisory opinion 18/03 on undocumented migrants,[65] the Court starts off its examination of due process guarantees in migration proceedings by putting migrants first. Indeed, the Court's point of departure is an emphasis on the need for special duties to attend to the vulnerability of migrants.[66] This does not mean, the Court recalls only afterwards, that states cannot initiate actions against migrants who do not comply with national laws.[67] The Court makes clear, however, that in taking such actions states must respect their human rights without discrimination.[68] Following part of the *Nadege Dorzema* judgment (which was not reviewed in detail in the first section of this chapter), the Court then states the principle that proceedings potentially leading to the expulsion or deportation of a non-national must be individualised, non-discriminatory, and respectful of a minimum set of guarantees.[69]

[59] *Miguel Castro-Castro Prison v. Peru*, Merits, Reparations and Costs, Judgment (IACtHR), 25 Nov. 2006. *Pacheco Tineo* judgment, para 66.

[60] *Pacheco Tineo* judgment, paras 67–69.

[61] *Pacheco Tineo*, para 72.

[62] *Pacheco Tineo*, para 74.

[63] *Pacheco Tineo*, para 86.

[64] *Pacheco Tineo*, paras 93–106.

[65] The Court refers to Advisory opinion 18/03, paras 112, 117, 118, and 119. *Pacheco Tineo* judgment, paras 128–129.

[66] *Pacheco Tineo* judgment, para 128.

[67] *Pacheco Tineo*, para 129.

[68] *Pacheco Tineo*, para 129.

[69] *Pacheco Tineo*, para 133 and *Nadege Dorzema* judgment, para 175.

In fact, it is *Nadege Dorzema* that provides the list of due process guarantees in migration proceedings cited in *Pacheco Tineo*.[70] The Court states that any proceedings potentially resulting in an expulsion or a deportation must observe the following minimum guarantees:[71] (a) to be informed of the charges and of the reasons for the expulsion or deportation—which in turn must include the possibility of stating one's case and contesting charges as well as the possibility of requesting and receiving consular, legal assistance and, if appropriate, translation or interpretation; (b) to be entitled to have the decision reviewed by a competent authority and to appear before that authority for such purpose; and (c) a reasoned and duly notified decision.[72] In an illustration of the 'integrated'[73] character of the Inter-American Court's approach to international human rights law, this list was drawn from several international sources, including the United Nations Human Rights Committee, the African Commission on Human and Peoples' Rights, and the International Law Commission.[74]

The *Pacheco Tineo* contribution: adding an asylum lane onto the due process road

Pacheco Tineo also identifies minimum due process guarantees in the specific context of asylum proceedings. Relying yet again on an extensive array of international sources,[75] the Court embarks on setting up the principles and establishing the ensuing guarantees. It sets out obligations not just for the asylum-granting state, but also for other states into whose territories refugees enter—such as Bolivia in the *Pacheco Tineo* case. Thus, the Court affirms that these states must take into account the refugee status granted by another state when adopting migration measures concerning refugees and therefore show 'special caution' in verifying such status.[76] In other

[70] *Nadege Dorzema*, para 175 and *Pacheco Tineo*, para 133.

[71] *Pacheco Tineo*, para 133. Note that the procedural safeguards reaffirmed in *Pacheco Tineo* are wider in number and scope than the ones recognised in the European system. First of all, Article 6 ECHR does not apply to expulsion proceedings of non-nationals (see discussion of *Maaouia v. France* in Chapter 7, p. 224. True, Article 1(1) of Protocol no. 7 to the European Convention establishes some safeguards against the expulsion of lawfully resident aliens (e.g. submission of reasons against expulsion, revision of case, and legal representation). However, these guarantees are fewer than the ones recognised by the Inter-American Court and their application is seriously limited by the following statement: 'An alien may be expelled before the exercise of his rights under paragraph 1.a, b and c of this Article, when such expulsion is necessary in the interests of public order or is grounded on reasons of national security'. This is of course leaving aside the fact that Protocol no. 7 is binding only on those states that have ratified it.

[72] *Nadege Dorzema*, para 175 and *Pacheco Tineo*, para 133.

[73] For an overview of the integrated view to human rights protection, see: the Human Rights Integration project, 'The Global Challenge of Human Rights Integration: Towards a Users' Perspective' undertaken by various universities in Belgium and the Netherlands <http://hrintegration.be>, accessed 29 May 2014. See also Eva Brems, 'Toward an Integrated View on Multilayered Human Rights' (forthcoming 2014) *European Journal of Human Rights*.

[74] *Nadege Dorzema* judgment, paras 160–163.

[75] *Pacheco Tineo* judgment, para 143. The Court draws significantly from refugee law as well as from UNHCR guidelines, criteria, and authoritative pronouncements.

[76] *Pacheco Tineo*, para 150. In the Spanish version of the judgment, the duty is framed as 'deber de precaución especial'.

words, refugee status must protect the person beyond the borders of the refugee status-granting state.[77] Moreover, the Court recalls that refugees and asylum seekers are protected by the principle of *non-refoulement*.[78] It views this principle as a specific modality of Article 22(8) ACHR, regardless of migration status, and as an integral part of refugee protection under international law.[79] As a result, the Court notes, states cannot return asylum seekers without an individualised and adequate assessment of their applications by means of effective and fair asylum proceedings.[80] One fundamental implication flowing from these principles is that, in asylum-seeking proceedings and in proceedings that may result in the expulsion or deportation of an asylum seeker or a refugee, the state's duties to respect the right to seek asylum and the principle of *non-refoulement* must be examined in connection with the guarantees of fair trial and judicial protection.[81]

The Court develops a detailed catalogue of interrelated procedural safeguards specifically tailored to the situation and needs of asylum seekers.[82] According to the Court, states must provide interpretation services as well as access to legal counsel and representation in the submission of an asylum request.[83] The Court further establishes that the asylum seeker must receive guidance ('*orientación*') on the proceedings to be followed in a language and manner he understands.[84] It adds that the asylum seeker must be given the opportunity to get in touch with the UNHCR.[85] The Court continues the list by stating that the asylum request must be examined objectively by a competent authority and by means of a personal interview, within the framework of proceedings established for that purpose.[86] Moreover, the Court states that the decision must be duly and expressly motivated,[87] and that information about the asylum seeker and the request must be treated confidentially.[88] If asylum is denied, the Court mandates that the person must be provided with information on how to appeal the decision and granted a reasonable time to prepare the appeal.[89] The appeal must have suspensive effects and the person must be allowed to stay in the country while the decision is pending, unless the request is manifestly ill-founded.[90] Regardless of the possibility of appealing, there might be ('*pueden existir*') judicial proceedings within the framework of the right to judicial protection (Article 25) enabling the person effectively and speedily to challenge the possible violations of Articles 22(7) and 22(8) of the American Convention.[91]

[77] *Pacheco Tineo*, para 150.
[78] *Pacheco Tineo*, para 152.
[79] *Pacheco Tineo*, para 152.
[80] *Pacheco Tineo*, para 153.
[81] *Pacheco Tineo*, para 155.
[82] The Court delineates these guarantees in accordance with Articles 8, 22(7), 22(8), and 25 ACHR and taking into account UNHCR criteria and guidelines. *Pacheco Tineo*, para 159.
[83] *Pacheco Tineo*, para 159(a).
[84] *Pacheco Tineo*, para 159(a). I use 'he', following the author's convention of using the masculine form in even-numbered chapters of the book when referring to non-specified applicants.
[85] *Pacheco Tineo*, para 159(a).
[86] *Pacheco Tineo*, para 159(b).
[87] *Pacheco Tineo*, para 159(c).
[88] *Pacheco Tineo*, para 159(d).
[89] *Pacheco Tineo*, para 159(e).
[90] *Pacheco Tineo*, para 159(f).
[91] *Pacheco Tineo*, para 160.

Applying the principles to the case: the absence of procedural guarantees

The application of the principles reviewed above to the case required an examination of the way in which the Pacheco Tineo family's asylum request had been dealt with, on the one hand, and of the way in which they had been expelled, on the other. Since both proceedings had occurred summarily, they both exhibited similar procedural shortcomings.

In examining the way in which the state handled the asylum request, the Court found that the National Commission of Refugees had denied the family asylum without hearing them, without receiving any evidence, without assessing the circumstances in which they found themselves at the time of their request, and without motivation.[92] Moreover, the Court found no evidence that the asylum applicants had been notified of the decision.[93] This lack of notification, the Court added, prevented the asylum seekers from requesting reconsideration of the decision refusing asylum or from seeking judicial remedies against possible violations of due process, their right to seek and be granted asylum, or the *non-refoulement* principle.[94]

More precisely, the Court found that asylum seekers had not been granted the opportunity to state their reasons for entering Bolivia irregularly, for signing a declaration of voluntary repatriation back in 1998, or for filing a new asylum request.[95] As a result, they were unable to indicate whether new reasons motivated this request or whether the old ones subsisted.[96] The Court reasoned that, in this way, the National Commission of Refugees did not even contemplate the possibility that the circumstances may have changed or that new risks may have arisen since the applicants' repatriation.[97] Nor did this Commission evaluate any potential risks they could face.[98] For the Court, what the domestic authorities should have done instead was to have offered guidance on the proceedings to be followed, in accordance with the particular difficulties or specific needs of the Pacheco Tineo applicants.[99] Moreover, according to the Court, the state had a special duty of diligence and caution in handling the asylum application, all the more if it knew that the applicants already enjoyed refugee status in another country.[100] The Court found that the applicants had not had the opportunity to explain the protection they enjoyed in Chile as refugees.[101]

In examining the way in which the state handled the expulsion of the family, the Court noted that the migration authorities had ordered and executed the expulsion summarily.[102] Just like in the handling of the asylum request, the victims were not heard and were not notified of the decision.[103] As a result, they were unable to know the reasons for their expulsion and to introduce any judicial/

[92] *Pacheco Tineo*, para 174.
[93] *Pacheco Tineo*, para 174.
[94] *Pacheco Tineo*, para 174.
[95] *Pacheco Tineo*, para 173.
[96] *Pacheco Tineo*, para 173.
[97] *Pacheco Tineo*, para 173.
[98] *Pacheco Tineo*, para 173.
[99] *Pacheco Tineo*, para 168.
[100] *Pacheco Tineo*, para 179.
[101] *Pacheco Tineo*, para 179.
[102] *Pacheco Tineo*, para 187.
[103] *Pacheco Tineo*, para 187.

administrative remedies against it.[104] In fact, there was no evaluation of the potential risks they could face in the country to which they were to be expelled.[105] Moreover, the Court found that the remedies available to complain against any due process violations during the expulsion proceedings were in practice illusory.[106] The family, the Court noted in this regard, was expelled the day after their expulsion was ordered.[107] Practically speaking, therefore, it was impossible for them to make use of any of the theoretically available remedies.[108]

The *Pacheco Tineo* analysis under Articles 8, 22, and 25 concludes with a significant list of interrelated human rights violations. First, on the denial of asylum, the Court found that Bolivia violated the right to procedural guarantees (Article 8), the right to seek and be granted asylum (Article 22.7), the principle of *non-refoulement* (Article 22.8), and the right to judicial protection (Article 25).[109] Next, the Court found that the expulsion of the family to their country of origin without minimum due process guarantees and aware of the fact that they could have been protected as refugees in another country was also a violation of the right to seek and be granted asylum (Article 22.7) and the principle of *non-refoulement* (Article 22.8).[110] Lastly, the Court found the state responsible for violating the due process guarantees in the administrative proceedings that resulted in the expulsion of the family (Article 8.1) and for violating their right to judicial protection (Article 25).[111]

Passerelle to the equality road?

The Inter-American Court has long been developing specific standards of human rights protection for certain groups in the migration context. Advisory opinion 18/03 addressed the needs of undocumented migrants.[112] *Vélez Loor* attended to the situation of detained migrants.[113] In fact, these developments fit broader developments in the Court's case law. This case law has established enhanced positive state duties towards certain vulnerable groups so that they can exercise their rights on equal terms.[114] The Court has recognised the need for special protection of particularly vulnerable groups, such as indigenous peoples[115] and women (in respect of violence).[116]

104 *Pacheco Tineo*, para 187. 105 *Pacheco Tineo*, para 187.
106 *Pacheco Tineo*, paras 192 and 194. 107 *Pacheco Tineo*, para 192.
108 *Pacheco Tineo*, paras 192 and 194. 109 *Pacheco Tineo*, para 198.
110 *Pacheco Tineo*, para 199. 111 *Pacheco Tineo* para 199.
112 Advisory opinion 18/03. 113 *Vélez Loor* judgment.

114 See Victor Abramovich, 'From Massive Violations to Structural Patterns: New Approaches and Classic Tensions in the Inter-American Human Rights System' (2012) *Aportes DPLf* 16, 24–29 at 26–27. For a brief overview of the protection of vulnerable groups in the Inter-American Court's case law more broadly, see Human Rights Center of the University of Chile, 'Boletín de Jurisprudencia de la Corte Interamericana de Derechos Humanos' 1/2010.

115 See e.g. *The Yakye Axa Indigenous Community v. Paraguay*, Merits, Reparations and Costs, Judgment (IACtHR), 17 June 2005, para 63 and *The Xákmok Kásek Indigenous Community v. Paraguay*, Merits, Reparations and Costs, Judgment (IACtHR), 24 Aug. 2010, paras 270–274.

116 See e.g. *González et al. ('Cotton Field') v. Mexico*, Preliminary Objection, Merits, Reparations, and Costs, Judgment (IACtHR), 16 Nov. 2009, para 258. On the reinforced nature of the due

By recognising that 'certain sectors of the population face legal or *de facto* obstacles to exercising their rights and that special measures are therefore required to achieve parity', the Court moves towards a substantive idea of equality.[117] Indeed, substantive equality does not confine itself to a duty to refrain from discrimination; it requires the state to take a proactive role and to adopt positive steps to promote equality.[118] Moreover, 'instead of aiming to treat everyone alike, regardless of status, substantive equality focuses on the group which has suffered disadvantage'.[119] One way in which this asymmetry inherent in substantive equality manifests itself is in the special or enhanced character of the positive duties towards the most vulnerable: 'states are obliged to provide a level of protection that is more responsive or tailored to their particular needs and concerns'.[120]

Though the Inter-American Court does not explicitly address discrimination issues in *Pacheco Tineo*,[121] it implicitly upholds a substantive idea of equality. In particular, it uses the 'transformation' lane discussed earlier by developing *specific* procedural guarantees capable of addressing the 'different' needs of another group: asylum seekers and refugees. Thus, in requiring states to offer guarantees as specific as guidance on the proceedings to be followed, the opportunity to contact the UNHCR, and confidentiality, the Court ensures that asylum seekers have a *real* and *equal* possibility of enjoying their due process rights when requesting asylum or being expelled.[122] In turn, the effective exercise of their *procedural* rights may ultimately lead to their *substantive* rights being respected. This is all to say that the application of the migration/asylum procedural principles set forth by the Inter-American Court could lead to more substantive equality. To continue with

diligence duties flowing from the *Cotton Field* reasoning, see: Víctor Abramovich, 'Responsabilidad Estatal por Violencia de Género: Comentarios sobre el Caso "Campo Algodonero" en la Corte Interamericana de Derechos Humanos', *Anuario de Derechos Humanos* 2010, Universidad de Chile, 167–182.

117 Abramovich 'From Massive Violations' 27. See also, Lourdes Peroni and Alexandra Timmer, 'Vulnerable Groups: The Promise of an Emerging Concept in European Human Rights Convention Law' (2013) *International Journal of Constitutional Law* 11, 1056–1085 at 1076–1079.

118 See generally Sandra Fredman, *Human Rights Transformed: Positive Rights and Positive Duties* (Oxford and New York: Oxford University Press, 2008) 175–180.

119 Fredman *Discrimination Law* 26.

120 Peroni and Timmer, 'Vulnerable Groups' 1076 (making this argument in the context of the European Convention). This aspect of substantive equality is reflected in the Inter-American Court's principle that special positive obligations are determined based on the vulnerable position of migrants. See *Vélez Loor* judgment, para 98, *Nadege Dorzema* judgment, para 152, and *Pacheco Tineo* judgment, para 128.

121 Unlike in *Vélez Loor*, the Court does not look at whether the *Pacheco Tineo* victims were discriminated against in their access to justice or in the exercise of their due process rights in the light of Article 1(1) ACHR.

122 This approach is in line with the principle the Court has set in *The Right to Information on Consular Assistance in the Framework of the Guarantees of the Due Process of Law*. Advisory opinion OC-16/99 (IACtHR), 1 Oct. 1999, para 119: 'To accomplish its objectives, the judicial process must recognize and correct any real disadvantages that those brought before the bar might have, thus observing the principle of equality before the law and the courts and the corollary principle prohibiting discrimination. The presence of real disadvantages necessitates countervailing measures that help to reduce or eliminate the obstacles and deficiencies that impair or diminish an effective defense of one's interests'.

the metaphor used in this chapter, the 'due process road', when adapted to the needs of particularly vulnerable groups, holds the promise of serving the function of *passerelle* (path) to the equality road.

III. Migrant Children: In Search of Yet More Specific Standards for Another Sub-Group

There is one aspect of the *Pacheco Tineo* case which has not yet been alluded to but which requires attention. The *Pacheco Tineo* reasoning also includes an attempt to adapt the due process road to the more specific needs of yet another sub-group: migrant children. Grounded in Article 19 of the American Convention[123] and interpreting this provision in the light of the UN Convention on the Rights of the Child,[124] the Court specifically develops various principles concerning the participation of children in asylum and expulsion proceedings. The general principle is that children have the right to participate and express their opinions in both sets of proceedings.[125] With respect to asylum proceedings more specifically, the Court establishes that, where asylum seekers are children themselves, they must enjoy specific procedural guarantees to ensure that they get fair decisions.[126] This involves developing procedures that are adequate, safe, and capable of gaining the child's confidence.[127] In regard to proceedings that may result in sanctions for violations of migration laws, the Court holds that children's participation has particular relevance because these proceedings may result in the separation of the family and affect the children's welfare.[128]

Applying these principles, the Court found that the *Pacheco Tineo* children were heard neither in the asylum-seeking proceedings requested by their parents nor in the expulsion proceedings against the family. In the words of the Court, 'the State treated the children as objects conditioned and limited to the rights of their parents, in contradiction with their status as subjects of rights'.[129] In a clear sign that *Pacheco Tineo* ultimately seeks to secure *special* protection of migrant children, the Court holds: 'the [Pacheco Tineo] children had the right to be protected in a *special* manner in the exercise of their due process guarantees... during the administrative proceedings that resulted in their and their parents' expulsion'.[130]

The *Pacheco Tineo* standards of protection of migrant and asylum-seeking children may well be the first pages of another chapter currently being written in San José at the time of writing: an advisory opinion on the protection of migrant children.

[123] Article 19 'Rights of the Child' provides: 'Every minor child has the right to the measures of protection required by his condition as a minor on the part of his family, society, and the state'.

[124] *Pacheco Tineo* judgment, para 219. The Court refers specifically to Articles 12 and 22 of the UN Convention on the Rights of the Child.

[125] *Pacheco Tineo*, paras 223 and 227.

[126] *Pacheco Tineo*, para 224.

[127] *Pacheco Tineo*, para 224.

[128] *Pacheco Tineo*, para 227.

[129] *Pacheco Tineo*, para 228, author's translation. The Court condemns Bolivia for violating Articles 19 and 17 in relation to Articles 8(1), 22(7), 22(8), 25, and 1(1) ACHR to the detriment of the Pacheco Tineo children.

[130] *Pacheco Tineo*, para 228, author's translation. Emphasis added.

This advisory opinion was requested on 7 July 2011 by the then four members of MERCOSUR—Argentina, Brazil, Paraguay, and Uruguay.[131] For the first time, the Court is asked by a number of states acting jointly for an advisory opinion. In essence, the request asks the Court to determine a state's obligations in relation to measures concerning children, their migration status, or the status of their parents.[132] This is with reference to provisions of the American Convention related to the right to life, the right to humane treatment, the right to personal liberty, the right to a fair trial, the right to judicial protection, the rights of the child, the rights of the family, the right to seek and be granted asylum, and the principle of *non-refoulement*.[133]

Following its traditional encouragement of wide participation in its proceedings,[134] the Court made a call for submission of written comments. The call attracted a large number of submissions from a broad spectrum of participants.[135] Comments came from member states such as Costa Rica and Mexico; from bodies of the OAS such as the Inter-American Commission on Human Rights; from international organisations such as UNICEF and the UNHCR; and from state institutions, NGOs, academic institutions, and even individuals. A public hearing was held on 9–10 October 2013 in Mexico (at an extramural Court session) with, again, remarkable participation.[136] Representatives of each of the four requesting states presented their observations. So did the representatives of other states such as Costa Rica, the Dominican Republic, and Panama as well as the MERCOSUR representative, Víctor Abramovich, former member of the Inter-American Commission on Human Rights and known to have been the main author of the request.[137] The Inter-American Commission on Human Rights, the UNHCR, and UNICEF also took part in the hearing.

The request asks the Court's opinion on nine issues, as follows:

1. What are the procedures that should be adopted in order to identify the different risks for the rights of migrant children, to determine the needs for international protection and to adopt, if applicable, special protective measures?[138]
2. What are the due process guarantees that should govern migration proceedings involving migrant children?[139]

[131] Request for Advisory Opinion on Migrant Children before the Inter-American Court of Human Rights of 6 April 2011, <http://www.corteidh.or.cr/solicitudoc/solicitud_eng.pdf>, accessed 29 May 2014 ('AO Request'). For detailed background information on the request, see: Victor E. Abramovich and Laura Saldivia, 'El MERCOSUR como Espacio de Coordinación de Políticas en Derechos Humanos: Antecedentes de la Solicitud de Opinión Consultiva ante la Corte Interamericana de Derechos Humanos sobre Derechos de la Niñez Migrante', in Martín Lettieri (ed.) *Protección Internacional de Refugiados en el Sur de Sudamérica* (Buenos Aires: Universidad Nacional de Lanús, 2012) 255–271.

[132] AO Request, 12. [133] AO Request, 12.

[134] See analysis in Chapter 9, pp. 307–308.

[135] A full list of the written submissions is available at <http://www.corteidh.or.cr/index.php/observaciones>, accessed 29 May 2014.

[136] Parts I and II of the hearing are available in Spanish at <http://vimeopro.com/corteidh/audiencia-publica-opinion-consultiva-sobre-ninez-migrante/video/76568701> and <http://www.corteidh.or.cr/index.php/en/court-today/galeria-multimedia>, accessed 29 May 2014.

[137] Moreover, Abramovich was the head of a leading Argentinean NGO: *Centro de Estudios Legales y Sociales* (CELS).

[138] AO Request, 18. [139] AO Request, 21.

3. How should the principle of detention as a precautionary measure of last resort be interpreted in the framework of migration proceedings involving children accompanied by or unaccompanied by/separated from their parents?[140]
4. What characteristics should alternative measures for the protection of the rights of the child have in order to avoid any kind of restriction of liberty? Which due process guarantees should be offered in the decision-making processes concerning alternative measures to detention?[141]
5. What are the basic conditions that accommodation facilities for migrant children must satisfy and what are the state's main obligations towards children under custody for immigration reasons?[142]
6. If custodial measures are applied to children in migration proceedings, what are the due process guarantees that should govern migration proceedings involving children?[143]
7. What is the content and scope of the principle of *non-refoulement* when a measure that may entail returning a child to a certain country is applied?[144]
8. What are the characteristics that the procedures used to identify a potential request for asylum or recognition of refugee status of a migrant child should have?[145]
9. What is the scope that must be given to the protection of the right of the child not to be separated from her/his parents in cases where deportation is ordered against one or both parents as a result of their migration status?[146]

The nine issues seem to boil down to a request for assistance in providing special protection for migrant children given their vulnerable situation. Indeed, at the heart of the request lies a concern with the incapacity of migration policies to attend to the particularly vulnerable situation of migrant children due to their age and migration status.[147] Moreover, the four states explicitly ask the Court to take into account not only general human rights law principles such as the *pro-homine* and non-discrimination principles.[148] These states also call for the application of the principle of 'special protection', which alludes to the idea that states have special duties towards children due to their special conditions.[149] In short, the fundamental claim seems to be that states should develop policies that are expressly geared towards migrant children.[150]

[140] AO Request, 24–25. [141] AO Request, 26. [142] AO Request, 29–30.
[143] AO Request, 32. [144] AO Request, 33. [145] AO Request, 35.
[146] AO Request, 37. [147] AO Request, 4–5. [148] AO Request, 13.
[149] AO Request, 13. The requesting states here draw from *Juridical Condition and Human Rights of the Child*, Advisory opinion OC-17/02 (IACtHR), 28 Aug. 2002, para 54 and, more specifically, from the Concurring opinion of Judge Sergio García Ramírez, para 27: 'all international instruments pertaining to the rights of the child or minor recognize without a doubt the "difference" between them and adults and the relevance, therefore, of adopting "special" measures with respect to children'.
[150] See e.g. AO Request, 25.

Predicting the answers the Court will provide is of course a risky venture. The groundwork is already in place in San José, including the case law on procedural guarantees in the contexts of asylum and migration. One might surmise that *Nadege Dorzema* and *Pacheco Tineo* could offer a basis for an answer to question 2. *Vélez Loor* could do the same for question 3. In essence, one hopes that the Court will take full advantage of the existing bases in order to make robust pronouncements, adapting already existing principles and standards to the specific situation of migrant children. The Court should not find this task especially challenging given its proven capacity for developing specific standards of protection for other sub-groups of migrants. As we have just seen, *Pacheco Tineo* has already revealed the Court's willingness to address the particular situation of children in asylum and migration proceedings. Moreover, as we have seen in Chapter 11, even *Vélez Loor*, which did not involve child victims, already contained a comment on the need to pay specific attention to families.

In this advisory opinion as elsewhere, one can expect that the Court would want to integrate the views of other specific human rights instruments and materials, including of course the UN Convention on the Rights of the Child, in order to develop more specific principles and standards to protect migrant children. The combination of these international instruments with Article 19 of the American Convention[151]—not forgetting the existing Inter-American jurisprudence on children,[152] including an advisory opinion on children[153]—holds out great promise. But again, whether the Court will use this promising mixture to develop jurisprudence strongly in favour of the human rights of migrant children remains to be seen.

IV. Conclusion

Nadege Dorzema and *Pacheco Tineo* may serve to illustrate how the Inter-American Court is advancing at different speeds in its migration case law depending on the road taken. While *Nadege Dorzema* suggests that the Court may still be travelling the road *to* non-discrimination, *Pacheco Tineo* confirms that the Court continues to travel the road *of* due process. Interestingly, it appears that the due process road includes a lane to substantive equality: the Court firmly follows the 'transformation'

[151] See *The 'Street Children' (Villagran-Morales et al.) v. Guatemala*, Merits, Judgment (IACtHR), 9 Nov. 1999, para 194: 'Both the American Convention and the Convention on the Rights of the Child form part of a very comprehensive international *corpus juris* for the protection of the child that should help this Court establish the content and scope of the general provision established in Article 19 of the American Convention'.

[152] See e.g. 'Street Children' judgment, *The 'Juvenile Reeducation Institute' v. Paraguay*, Preliminary Objections, Merits, Reparations and Costs, Judgment (IACtHR), 2 Sept. 2004 and *The Gómez-Paquiyauri Brothers v. Peru*, Merits, Reparations and Costs, Judgment (IACtHR), 8 July 2004. For an overview of the Inter-American Court's jurisprudence on the rights of the child, see: Juana María Ibáñez Rivas, 'El Rol de la Corte Interamericana de Derechos Humanos en la Protección de los Derechos de los Niños, Niñas y Adolescentes desde su Jurisprudencia', in *Diálogo entre la Iniciativa Niñ@Sur y los Sistemas Universal e Interamericano de Protección de Derechos Humanos* (Buenos Aires: Ministerio de Justicia y Derechos Humanos de la Nación—Secretaría de Derechos Humanos, 2011) 87–109.

[153] A/O 17/02.

lane every time it develops specific guarantees aimed at ensuring that some groups of migrants effectively and equally enjoy their fair trial and judicial protection rights. The Court's travelling of the 'recognition' lane of equality, on the other hand, remains hesitant, as the mixed signals sent by *Nadege Dorzema* indicate. It appears too early to tell whether the Court will eventually navigate this lane of equality more comfortably. What is clear is that opting for the less travelled lane would make 'all the difference'[154] in a region that sometimes appears to be in denial of racism.[155]

V. Postscript

On 19 August 2014, the Inter-American Court unanimously adopted its advisory opinion 21/14 'Rights and Guarantees of Children in the Context of Migration and/or in Need of International Protection.' This opinion establishes an ample catalogue of state obligations, including the following: 1) to identify non-national children who require international protection within their jurisdictions; 2) to guarantee that the migration proceedings involving children are adapted to their needs and offer due process guarantees; 3) to resort to less harmful alternatives than deprivation of liberty of children as a precautionary measure; 4) to incorporate into their domestic law non-custodial measures to be implemented while migration proceedings are being held; 5) to respect the principle of separation and the right to family unity in places used for accommodating children; 6) when personal liberty is restricted in such a way that it may constitute or result in a deprivation of liberty, to respect the specific guarantees operational in this context; 7) to abstain from returning a child to a state where their life, security and/or liberty is at risk or where the child is at risk of being subjected to torture or other cruel, inhuman or degrading treatment; 8) to include the specific guarantees developed for protecting children when establishing procedures aimed at identifying potential asylum applicants and determining refugee status; and 9) to conduct a weighing analysis that prioritises the best interest of the child when deciding on the separation of family members, due to expulsion based on their parents' migration status.

On the whole, and despite the initial reversal *à la* Strasbourg,[156] this is a strong advisory opinion. The Court develops in notable depth and breadth each of the above-mentioned state obligations, drawing from a vast *corpus iuris* on the rights of children, migrants, asylum seekers, and refugees. The opinion is grounded in general state obligations established in the American Convention.[157] They include the obligation to respect the human rights of 'all persons' subject to

[154] This quote is taken from a poem by Robert Frost, 'The Road Not Taken': 'I shall be telling this with a sigh. Somewhere ages and ages hence: Two roads diverged in a wood, and I took the one less traveled by. And that has made all the difference'.

[155] See Ariel E. Dulitzky, 'A Region in Denial: Racial Discrimination and Racism in Latin America' in Anani Dzidzienyo and Suzanne Oboler (eds) *Neither Enemies nor Friends: Latinos, Blacks and Afro-Latinos* (New York: Palgrave Macmillan, 2005) 39–59.

[156] *Rights and Guarantees of Children in the Context of Migration and/or in Need of International Protection,* Advisory Opinion OC-21/14 (IACtHR), 19 Aug. 2014, para 39.

[157] A/O 21/14 paras 61-67.

its jurisdiction – regardless of their reason for being in the state's territory and regardless of their regular or irregular entry[158] – and the obligation to adopt special measures of protection for children.[159] The advisory opinion sends the clear message that the protection of the child 'should have priority over any consideration of nationality or migratory status.'[160]

On 28 August 2014, the Inter-American Court also decided the case originally known as *Benito Tide Méndez et al. v. the Dominican Republic*. The Court renamed the case *Expelled Dominicans and Haitians v. the Dominican Republic*.[161] Numerous violations were found, including violations of the right to juridical personality, the right to nationality, the right to a name, the right to personal liberty, the prohibition of collective expulsion of non-nationals, the right to a fair trial, the right to judicial protection and the rights of the family. This judgment offers, overall, robust protection for migrants. The Court continues to re-affirm the rights of migrants by vigorously insisting on both substance and due process.

[158] A/O 21/14 paras 61 and 62.

[159] A/O 21/14 para 66.

[160] A/O 21/14 para 68.

[161] *Expelled Dominicans and Haitians v. the Dominican Republic*, Preliminary Objections, Merits, Reparations and Costs, Judgment (IACtHR), 28 Aug. 2014, in Spanish only at the time this postscript is written.

15

Conclusion: The Way Forward

This book has documented the characteristics of the Inter-American and European migrant jurisprudence. In short, when compared, one seems ambitious, the other tamed. This goes hand in hand with different ways of applying the law, which appear more or less in tune with the human applicant who has brought the case that requires judicial determination.

Now, Louis Wolcher has argued that the law's fundamental task is to distinguish between suffering which is, and suffering which is not, deemed legitimate.[1] There is no reason why what is true of law in general, should not be true of human rights law in particular. Indeed, this book has shown that, although there is much suffering by migrants that the European Court says must be stopped, there is even more such suffering that it leaves untouched, implying that it is none of its concern.

The idea that there is a tipping point in law between suffering which is considered legitimate and suffering which is considered illegitimate may not be too controversial. By contrast locating where exactly this tipping point should be is a highly debatable matter. One way to summarise this book is to say that, in the view of its author, the European Court does not locate this point early enough, whilst the example of the Inter-American Court shows that it is not beyond international human rights law to do this better, even in as sensitive an area as migration.

I. The Problem with the Strasbourg Case Law

Strasbourg shortcomings—if they are accepted as such—are not peculiar to the European Court. It is at the heart of the socially prevalent logic which, in our era of 'managed migration', allows people enjoying what is deemed to be adequate cultural and economic capital to move whilst attempting to lock others in place. This system rests on the idea that it is perfectly normal for the entry and stay of non-nationals to be authorised or unauthorised by states.

In contrast to the idea that states can exercise almost unfettered sovereignty in this area, this book posits that different treatment on the basis of nationality is a new form of institutionalised racism or at least discrimination. Admittedly, to

[1] Louis Wolcher, *Law's Task: The Tragic Circle of Law, Justice and Human Suffering* (Aldershot: Ashgate, 2008).

this day, such discrimination is largely accepted as ethically unproblematic.[2] This explains why the operation of the Strasbourg reversal, for example, rarely receives objections. For most people it does not appear objectionable that the European Court approaches the migrant, first as an alien (if she is one) who is subject to the control of the state, even though this means that human rights strangely take second place to the sovereignty principle.[3]

Arguably the Strasbourg reversal in immigration matters is the symptom of a deeper problem. Whilst the human rights ethos recognises the equal worth of all human beings, human beings seem to be driven to experience a deep-seated and almost unconscious distrust of the unknown. This translates into a reluctance to treat the foreigner as our equal, where 'we' are implicitly defined as citizens.[4] We therefore need to learn to regard 'the other' as one of our own, i.e. to enlarge our implicit conception of 'our group' until, ideally, everyone is included in our imagination. Striving towards an open and inclusive attitude is a political and ethical value, the defence of which should arguably be an institutional imperative.

Yet, far from resolutely adopting such a perspective, the European Court implicitly shares in a discourse which conceives of migrants as threatening others. This makes it unwilling or unable to put itself in the shoes of migrant applicants. Rather than imagining and understanding what is at stake for an applicant in a given case, the Court often minimises the problems she faces, thus failing to take into account the individual and social measure of the complaints which are brought before it. Related to this, the Court tends to regard migrant applicants as solely responsible for the problematic situation they are in. For example, they should not have had children when their status was insecure; they should have accessed nationality status when the opportunity was there; they should not have assumed that they would be able to settle and work outside their country of origin; etc. Approaching migrants as the masters of their own lives, the Court fails to see that they are evolving within a structure of inequality which limits their options.[5]

[2] Those who attempt to denounce this discrimination, e.g. through the 'no border network', are not highly visible. They are nonetheless increasing in number. See: Imogen Tyler and Katarzyna Marciniak (eds) *Protesting Citizenship: Migrant Activisms* (London: Routledge, 2014); Vicki Squire (ed.) *The Contested Politics of Mobility: Borderzones and Irregularity* (London: Routledge, 2011).

[3] Some may ask, why *strangely*? After all, state sovereignty has been at the heart of the international political order since at least the mid-nineteenth century, if not the Treaty of Westphalia of 1648. However, human rights law was specifically created in order to limit state sovereignty. Obviously the tension between state sovereignty and human rights will not be easily put at rest—how to navigate it is the whole point of human rights law. That the protection of state sovereignty is the starting point of the Strasbourg reasoning is nonetheless, *from a human rights perspective*, unexpected. When the Inter-American Court examines an immigration case, it starts its reasoning with the relevant human rights provisions. That the European Court fails to do the same is puzzling. It does not fail to do this in areas outside immigration. E.g. when it examines a criminal justice case, its reasoning starts with Article 6 ECHR, rather than the duty of the state to protect society from criminals.

[4] The insider/outsider classifications can be drawn in smaller or bigger circles. It may be, e.g., that the legally settled migrant who is conceived as integrated or at least non-threatening is unconsciously assimilated to the citizen who is a national.

[5] See e.g. the discussion of *Moser v. Austria*, appl. 12643/02, Judgment (ECtHR), 21 Sept. 2006 and *Bah v. the United Kingdom*, appl. 56328/07, Judgment (ECtHR), 27 Sept. 2011, included in Chapter 8.

This takes place in a context where the case law generally conceives the interests of the individual migrant as standing in opposition to the interests of the community. In this scheme, the state is taken to act in defence of the community—itself conceived as 'the national community'. As mentioned earlier, the Strasbourg case law obscures the migrant reality. Now, the flip-side of this process is that the experience of the state—as recounted by the state itself—tends to be accepted wholesale by the Court and given prominence in its reasoning.[6] In short, overall the Strasbourg Court supports the state rather than the applicant. This is problematic when the values propounded by the state are themselves problematic.[7]

Putting together the various features of the Strasbourg migrant case law highlighted in this section, one could say that the Court's failure to appreciate the position of the migrant and the bias it exhibits in favour of the state are the visible manifestations of the problem of discrimination on the grounds of nationality which lies at the core of the Strasbourg migrant case law. If this institutional 'racism'[8] were to be understood as a 'coin', it could be said to manifest itself through the neglect of the human person and state bias. These two manifestations would be the visible sides of the coin, with the very essence of the coin (its inherent 'racism'[9]) remaining rather invisible.

II. The Substantive Contours of a Strong Strasbourg Jurisprudence: Articles 3, 6, and 14 ECHR

A different jurisprudential approach is needed at Strasbourg if the migrant applicant is to be given her due place in the high ethical framework which human rights law is expected to provide. Only a multi-pronged approach can hope to address the multiple problems which affect the case law. Of particular usefulness in this regard would be to harness the potential which lies dormant within Articles 3, 6, and 14 ECHR.

Article 3 prohibits inhuman and degrading treatment. Applicants often feel they have been treated inhumanely and thus complain of a violation of this

[6] See e.g. *Vilvarajah and Others v. the United Kingdom,* appls 13163/87, 13164/87, 13165/87, 13447/87, 13448/87, Judgment (ECtHR), 30 Oct. 1991 and *Sivanathan v. the United Kingdom,* appl. 38108/07, Decision (ECtHR), 3 Feb. 2009, reviewed in Chapter 7.

[7] This book does not contest the essential (and difficult) role that the state must play in governing society, but the way it conceives of its role in immigration matters. We need strong and enlightened states, and a Strasbourg Court which helps them to achieve their essential role.

[8] I am using the word 'racism' as a short cut for 'discrimination on grounds of nationality'. This is not ideal. On the one hand, the concept of 'racism' is complex and has come to cover a variety of situations, as noted in: Marie-Bénédicte Dembour, 'Postcolonial Denial: Why the European Court of Human Rights Finds it so Difficult to Acknowledge Racism', in Kamari Clarke and Mark Goodale (eds) *Mirrors of Justice: Law and Power in the Post-Cold War Era* (New York: Cambridge University Press, 2010) 45–66. On the other hand, to imply that discrimination on grounds of nationality is a manifestation of racism is flattening what I am trying to capture. One way out might have been to create a new word, such as 'nationalitism'. However, speaking of 'nationalitism' in my main text would have created its own problems.

[9] Strictly speaking, one should speak of 'nationalitism', as explained in the previous note.

provision. However, the Court requires a high threshold of severity in the treatment inflicted before accepting that Article 3 is engaged. It is submitted here that with more imagination and compassion for what the applicants experience, the Court would naturally be drawn to use Article 3 more often. In situations which do not meet the Article 3 threshold, it could rely on Article 8 in order to denounce less serious difficulties experienced by migrants.

The case law on Article 6 is another area which cries out to be transformed. The *Maaouia*[10] pronouncement should be reversed. It is unacceptable that fair trial guarantees do not apply to procedures which have decisive consequences on the status—and thus rights—of migrant persons. In addition, opportunities should be taken to rely on Article 13 in order to require that domestic remedies are effectively in place and accessible whenever migrants have an arguable case that their rights under the Convention are being breached.

Last but not least, Article 14 prohibits discrimination. The current world order is founded on an implicit classification of human beings with 'good', 'not so good', and 'positively suspicious' nationalities. If the Court could see that this classification is in opposition to the idea that all human beings are equal, it would treat complaints about differences of treatment based on nationality more sympathetically. It would stress the 'very weighty reasons' proviso and emphasise the point that in the absence of such very weighty reasons, differences of treatment breach the Convention. It would commonly (although not always) find these reasons lacking, and thus repeatedly declare violations of Article 14.

Linking this section to the previous one, Article 3 would be a good tool to address the problematic neglect of the human person in the Strasbourg case law; Article 6, the problem of the state bias; and Article 14, the very coin of discrimination.

III. Thinking about Process: Expecting the Court to Act with Equanimity

Law is never just about norms, it is also about process. The substantive transformations identified above are unlikely to happen unless the Court changes the way it processes cases. A reflection on the procedural steps which impede or, on the contrary, facilitate human rights proceedings therefore needs to accompany any debate on substance.

Migrants typically face enormous difficulties in mounting legal challenges. This is especially so if they do not enjoy regular status, and even more so if they are detained or have been removed and thus are no longer present in the country where the challenge takes place. The more precarious their status, the less means they have to organise and form a cohesive social collective.[11] They tend to

[10] *Maaouia v. France*, appl. 39652/98, GC Judgment (ECtHR), 5 Oct. 2000.

[11] There may be exceptions to this trend, such as when a number of 'irregular' migrants take refuge in a church.

be individuals with disparate trajectories who do not physically interconnect for long. For their rights to be advanced under the Convention, legal representatives acting in the defence of both their collective and individual interests will seek to take individual cases to Strasbourg. When such a case comes to Strasbourg, the Court should be attuned to the enormous groundwork which is likely to have been laid by NGOs and others to get it there. It is crucial that the Court recognises the importance of these cases and adapts its procedures accordingly, as befits the situation and as the Convention system permits.

It is not enough for the Court to say that it is aware of the difficulties migrants face in mounting legal challenges. This awareness must translate into special sensitivity in the way it deals with admissibility, friendly settlements, and the burden of proof. To be more specific, migrant cases should not be declared inadmissible lightly, for example out of a syllogistic application of past principles and decisions which lead to an ethically indefensible solution.[12] Friendly settlements which do not confirm that a violation of human rights standards has taken place should be avoided. In the examination of the merits, the applicant should not be landed with an evidentiary burden which she is unlikely to be able to bear, either because the documentation required is non-existent (or barely accessible) or because the facts she is asked to prove are of a negative nature (as such proof is rarely possible to acquire). The Court should be wary of simply accepting state allegations. It should require the respondent state to prove any disputed fact which the state is in a relatively good position to prove. It should insist that the state explains not only what its legal framework provides in theory but also how it actually works in practice.

The Court should strive to find an equilibrium between the interests of the applicant and those of the state. To do this it must insist that the state explains what its interests are rather than assuming that these can be taken for granted. Inevitably, this would lead states to have to justify their immigration decisions. Such insistence must be welcomed as the right way to proceed:[13] acting without justification is an open door to arbitrariness, the opposite of what one seeks to achieve within the democratic paradigm of the rule of law.[14]

Too often, the Court seems to demonstrate a fear of upsetting states. This notably translates into tightly circumscribed rulings, which are valid only for the instant case when they find a violation of the Convention.[15] (By contrast, closures have the tendency to operate implacably.[16]) It is of course important for any court to develop its jurisprudence gradually and prudently. This, however, should not

[12] The perfect example of this is the *Bonger* case law, reviewed in Chapter 13.

[13] Leaving aside the fact that having to provide justification may reveal that the communal and individual interests actually overlap, as discussed above (e.g. p. 457).

[14] Bas Schotel, *On the Right of Exclusion: Law, Ethics and Immigration Policy* (Abingdon: Routledge, 2012).

[15] The children's immigration detention, reviewed in Chapter 11, comes to mind here.

[16] See *Maaouia* but also *N. v. the United Kingdom*, appl. 26565/05, GC Judgment (ECtHR), 27 May 2008 (expulsion of a terminally ill person), not to mention *Abdulaziz, Cabales and Balkandali*, appls 9214/80, 9473/81, 9474/81, PC Judgment (ECtHR), 28 May 1985 (no right to family reunion under the Convention).

prevent the Court from sometimes also being categorical in its affirmation of principles which firmly and proudly stand, so that they apply to a range of circumstances and give a clear message to states as to what is and what is not permitted under human rights law. By thinking bigger, the Court will be bigger.

This is especially important at a time when the Court is under attack by states (of course this is not happening only in relation to migration issues). In response, the Court has seemed willing to retract from earlier pronouncements which had appeared to be an *acquis* of Strasbourg human rights law.[17] It is crucial that it develops and maintains the ability to process cases with equanimity.[18] Otherwise there is a danger that it could lose its soul and *raison d'être*—which is to nip in the bud arbitrariness and a descent into totalitarianism and exclusivism.

IV. The Inter-American Experience

The way rights are conceptualised and realised is always contingent upon social and political circumstances as they exist 'on the ground'. Obviously, Latin America is not Europe. This book has therefore refrained from suggesting that a direct comparison between the Strasbourg and San José case law could be established. It has nonetheless sought to derive insights from reviewing the Inter-American experience as a counterpoint to the Strasbourg system.[19]

To simplify the history of the Inter-American system of human rights protection, one might wish to divide it into three phases: first, the system dealt with mass and gross violations of human rights; second, it examined the requirements of the democratic process; and, third, it started to attend to issues of inequality and exclusion.[20] The first phase was pursued most actively by the Commission from the inception of the system until the 1980s. It famously gave rise to the forced disappearance Honduran case law at the Court. The second phase emerged from the necessity to confront the legacy of a dictatorial past. It led the Court to make pronouncements on a variety of issues such as impunity, freedom of

[17] The most striking example in this respect is probably *Austin and Others v. the United Kingdom*, appls 39692/09 et al., GC Judgment (ECtHR), 15 Mar. 2012, but other cases are disappointing too. See e.g. *National Union of Rail, Maritime and Transport Workers v. the United Kingdom*, appl. 31045/10, Judgment (ECtHR), 8 Apr. 2014.

[18] Equanimity is important for the Court to be in a position to deliver procedural justice, i.e. to convey to the parties that they have been *heard* and treated with *respect* by a *neutral* and *trustworthy* institution. I borrow this understanding of procedural justice from: Eva Brems and Laurens Lavrysen, 'Procedural Justice in Human Rights Adjudication: The European Court of Human Rights' (2013) *Human Rights Quarterly* 35, 176–200.

[19] This type of exercise is perhaps the most needed since the European Convention and the Strasbourg Court are repeatedly acknowledged as constituting the most advanced and effective system of human rights protection in the world. Instead of giving a long list of references, suffice it to refer to the last source I have cited: Brems and Lavrysen 177.

[20] Claudio Grossman, 'The Inter-American System and Its Evolution' (2009) *Inter-American and European Human Rights Journal* 2, 49–65. See also: Victor Abramovich, 'From Massive Violations to Structural Patterns: New Approaches and Classic Tensions in the Inter-American Human Rights System' (2009) *Sur: International Journal on Human Rights* 6, 7–39.

expression, and due process. The third phase started in earnest with the new millennium. It saw the Court developing a case law concerning vulnerable groups, such as indigenous people, women, minorities, children, and of course migrants, in order to try to ensure that they too would be in a position fully to enjoy human rights.

These phases, which are intersecting and overlapping rather than consecutive, can be made to resonate with the image of the coin developed earlier in relation to the Strasbourg case law. In the first phase, the Inter-American Court could be said to focus on dignity and to emphasise that some situations are beyond the pale—they cannot be done to human beings. On this front, the Court's remarkable *pro-homine* approach puts it in excellent stead to denounce inhumane treatment, whoever this treatment affects, including the most vulnerable. The second phase is concerned with procedural requirements. Here, the Court's relentless identification of due process guarantees which must be followed, whatever the cost to the state, is—from a human rights perspective—extremely useful. It provides individuals, whatever their apparent level of powerlessness, with the means to fight for the recognition of their substantive rights. The third phase attends to problems of inequality. Here, one is forced to observe that migrant rulings have refrained from adopting an express equality and/or non-discrimination position after the advisory opinion on migrant workers of 2003. In other words, the Court has yet to take the jump to push the equality agenda, as Latin American legal representatives are inviting it to do.

Does it matter? Let us return to the image of the coin. Its two visible sides seem to be reasonably well taken care of by the Inter-American Court: the human being and her needs are recognised; the state is requested to act diligently. Will these twin approaches enable the core problem of discrimination to disappear of its own accord and be replaced with its positive alternative—equality? This appears to be wishful thinking. Admittedly, indirect attacks on the core problem are possibly the best that we can hope for in the current social and political framework. Something, however, is missing, when one cannot see discrimination for what it is: discrimination. My expectation is that future generations will look back in disbelief at how resistant we were to discerning discriminatory patterns in the world's obviously discriminatory nationality arrangements.

V. What Does the Future Hold?

The current restraint exhibited even by the more activist Inter-American Court on the discrimination question can only suggest that routine violation verdicts of Article 14 are far from around the corner in the Strasbourg system. As for the *Maaouia* reversal predicted by some, only the future will tell if the time has indeed become ripe for the Court to effect it. What about increased findings of violations of Article 3? It is difficult to say. What is sure is that for the Strasbourg Court to follow the substantive road map and to adopt the procedural attitude outlined previously would require the presence on its benches of a number of 'indefatigable defenders of migrants' human rights', to use the words I once applied to Judge Tulkens.[21] The emanation of a state structure, the Strasbourg Court is unlikely to count many activist figures. This is not to deny that progressive judges have always fought unfortunate legacies established in the case law and that they do so with some success.[22] It is nonetheless to acknowledge that a fundamental change in the overall orientation of the Strasbourg case law does not realistically appear to be on the horizon.

In other words, a marked convergence between the two regional courts described in this book is unlikely to arise through the embrace by the Strasbourg Court of a *pro-homine* reasoning more characteristic of its San José sister institution. Could such a convergence result from the San José Court becoming more restrained and state-orientated? This is not unimaginable. The OAS states could start to elect judges to the Inter-American Court who are entirely receptive to the margin of appreciation doctrine and inclined to allow the states greater leeway than at present. In such a scenario the long-settled Inter-American case law should act as a safeguard against the rapid abandonment of principles which appear today to be well established. It cannot be ruled out, however, that the Inter-American Court would be transformed beyond recognition through a steady erosion of its past case law. One must hope that there will be sufficient progressive forces in Latin America to stem such a development, just as there was when the OAS embarked on a process for 'strengthening' (read: weakening) the Inter-American Commission in 2011.

VI. Equality, Open Borders and the Right to Act Humanely

For all the talk about the equal worth of all human beings, we are still very far from equipping ourselves with the tools which would make this motto a reality. In the last analysis, the celebrated 'leaps' in the recent European discrimination case law have not been as great as one would have hoped,[23] and the Inter-American Court remains to take up Latin American activists' call for a stronger stance on

[21] See my tribute to Judge Tulkens on the Strasbourg Observers blog, dated 28 August 2012, available at <http://strasbourgobservers.com/2012/08/28/francoise-tulkens-indefatigable-defender-of-migrants-human-rights/>, accessed 25 April 2014. For 14 years from 1998 to 2012, Judge Tulkens managed time and time again to rally her colleagues around unanimous or near-unanimous verdicts of violation.

[22] Particularly striking in this respect are the verdicts of violation in *M.S.S. v. Belgium and Greece*, appl. 30696/09, GC Judgment (ECtHR), 21 Jan. 2011 and *Hirsi Jamaa and Others v. Italy*, appl. 27765/09, GC Judgment (ECtHR), 23 Feb. 2012, as well as the abandonment of any reference to the 'well-established' principle of state sovereignty in controlling the residence of aliens in many judgments.

[23] Mathias Möschel and Ruth Rubio-Marin, 'Genocide or Nothing: Racial Violence and Evolving Equality Law under the European Convention on Human Rights' (manuscript under submission); Marie-Bénédicte Dembour, 'In the Name of the Rule of Law: The European Court of Human Rights' Silencing of Racism', in Gurminder K. Bhambra and Robbie Shilliams (eds) *Silencing Human Rights: Critical Engagements with a Contested Project* (Basingstoke: Palgrave Macmillan, 2008) 184–202; Dembour 'Postcolonial Denial'.

discrimination and equality, now that the legacy of dictatorial governance need no longer be its near-exclusive focus.

A consistent application of the principle of human equality would obviously have tremendous consequences. Many amongst the more educated and affluent citizenry might fear that it would destabilise the political and economic privileges which they enjoy. The less prosperous may also believe that these privileges, which they had hoped to attain, will escape them forever or that their lives will become ever-more difficult as migrants come and 'steal' their jobs. Given these common if unwarranted perceptions,[24] it is not entirely surprising that human equality is a moral principle which appears too threatening to be allowed to govern human rights law. Ultimately, who are the people who want this principle to be applied across the board, as widely as possible?

Still, the European Court prides itself on being the conscience of Europe.[25] Such a claim cannot but invite the Strasbourg record to be examined, and the Court to be taken to task, on the highest ethical grounds. As this book has demonstrated, time and time again, in the migrant case law, the Court appears comfortable with disregarding the demands of human rights ethics—so much so that it even condones rightlessness—the very antithesis to human rights.[26]

Admittedly, the application of the human rights logic which this book advocates would inescapably turn into a slippery slope towards open borders. This, however, is where the logic of believing in the equality of all human beings leads. As an aside, it is not clear that it would necessarily be to the disadvantage of any citizen. If proclaiming and seeking to practise the values of human rights entails redistributive practices, and thus immediate sacrifices in the form of loss of material advantages for some, the most enlightened political projects speak of developing a selfless and sustainable society, where fulfilment is not measured in capital accumulation, and instead humane values are sought.[27]

Those with the greatest political and economic power do not see this. They wish neither to take this course nor to 'sell it to the masses' as a feasible democratic project which is the most civilised and promising way forward. Meanwhile, the post-World War II project of social democracy is being dismantled. It is not only migrants who are left or placed in a state of precariousness, but an ever greater proportion of the population.[28] Some seem to welcome these developments.[29] I do not.

[24] Social scientists have repeatedly shown these fears to be unfounded. See e.g. Bridget Anderson, *Us and Them: The Dangerous Politics of Immigration Control* (Oxford: Oxford University Press, 2013) Introduction and Chapter 4.

[25] European Court of Human Rights, *The Conscience of Europe: 50 Years of the European Court of Human Rights* (Council of Europe, 2010).

[26] See Chapter 13.

[27] See e.g. Sue Gerhardt, *The Selfish Society: How We All Forgot to Love One Another and Made Money Instead* (London: Simon & Schuster, 2010).

[28] Guy Standing, *The Precariat: The New Dangerous Class* (London: Bloomsbury, 2011). Migrants are but just one class of people who have been demonised: Anderson *Us and Them*.

[29] One newly elected Member of the European Parliament, leader of the 'New Right' Polish party, is reported to favour a 'Dickensian-era style of capitalism in which there would be no labour

In the neo-liberal world which is already ours, it is difficult to be confident that the Strasbourg Court is taking us resolutely on the path of ever better respect for human rights. We should not allow ourselves to sleepwalk, quietly confident that human rights are safe in the hands of a legal, judicial, and political *acquis*. We do need to support movements which appear to best reflect the values of equality and freedom, which human rights law is supposed to embody. We cannot take it for granted that others are already doing this for us. We must also strongly encourage the Court to act upon its claim of acting as the conscience of Europe.

As a final note, I invite the reader to return to a note tucked in Chapter 13 on the *Mallah* case.[30] This concerned the French so-called *délit de solidarité*. A man had been criminally convicted for allowing his son-in-law, who was an irregular migrant, to stay at his house.[31] The European Court found that there was no violation of the Convention. One expects that it will become increasingly important, and not only in respect of migration, to assert that human rights law should never be an obstacle to acting humanely. Acts of kindness, whether by state officials or individuals, should not be a criminal offence. They should be allowed to happen. This is a tall order, but it is an ethical imperative of the universal mind. I leave you with the thought that the right to act humanely should top any human rights list.

laws and market forces could operate unhindered': Remi Adekoya et al., 'Meet the new faces ready to sweep into the European Parliament', *The Guardian*, 26 May 2014.

30 *Mallah v. France*, appl. 29681/08, Judgment (ECtHR), 10 Nov. 2011, adopted by six votes to one, with a dissenting opinion by Judge Power-Forde, discussed above p. 450, note 41.

31 This was after a neighbour had reported him to the police.

Index

Please see under individual main entries for further references relating to ECtHR and IACtHR

The manufacturer's authorised representative in the EU for product safety is Oxford University Press España S.A. of el Parque Empresarial San Fernando de Henares, Avenida de Castilla, 2 – 28830 Madrid (www.oup.es/en or product.safety@oup.com). OUP España S.A. also acts as importer into Spain of products made by the manufacturer.

www.ingramcontent.com/pod-product-compliance
Lightning Source LLC
LaVergne TN
LVHW011857200926
848484LV00002B/465

* 9 7 8 0 1 9 9 6 6 7 8 3 3 *